Archaeology as a Process

Archaeology as a Process

Processualism and Its Progeny

MICHAEL J. O'BRIEN,

R. LEE LYMAN,

and

MICHAEL BRIAN SCHIFFER

 THE UNIVERSITY OF UTAH PRESS
Salt Lake City

10 09 08 07 06 05   5 4 3 2 1

 The Defiance House Man colophon is a registered trademark
of the University of Utah Press. It is based upon a four-foot-tall,
Ancient Puebloan pictograph (late PIII) near Glen Canyon, Utah.

LIBRARY OF CONGRESS CATALOGING-IN-PUBLICATION DATA

O'Brien, Michael J. (Michael John), 1950-
Archaeology as a process : processualism and its progeny / Michael J. O'Brien,
R. Lee Lyman, and Michael Brian Schiffer.
p. cm.
Includes bibliographical references and index.
ISBN 0-87480-817-0 (cloth : alk. paper)
1. Processual archaeology. I. Lyman, R. Lee. II. Schiffer, Michael B. III. Title.
CC75.7.02725 2005
930.1—DC22   2004020485

The University of Utah Press is committed to preserving
ancient forests and natural resources. We elected to print
Archaeology as a Process on 50% post consumer recycled
paper, processed chlorine free. As a result, for this printing,
we have saved:

8 trees (40' tall and 6-8" diameter)
3,410 gallons of water
1,372 kilowatt hours of electricity
376 pounds of solid waste
738 pounds of greenhouse gases

The University of Utah Press made this paper choice because
our printer, Thomson-Shore, Inc., is a member of Green
Press Initiative, a nonprofit program dedicated to supporting
authors, publishers, and suppliers in their efforts to reduce
their use of fiber obtained from endangered forests.

For more information, visit www.greenpressinitiative.org

To Beverly, Barbara, and Annette

Contents

Preface

When we hatched the idea for this book during the 2003 Society for American Archaeology meeting, we wondered how three people so set in their ways personally and intellectually might put aside their differences and work collaboratively. As it turned out, the year we spent writing this book was not only free of conflict but highly stimulating and immensely rewarding. The differences made us compromise in spots, but more than that they forced us to view the field of American archaeology more broadly than we would have otherwise. In addition, our differences acted as checks and balances to ensure that our text was as inclusive as possible and did not promote one intellectual position over another. Of course, in other venues we have been highly partisan, even criticizing each other's work, but we wanted this book to be special. *Archaeology as a Process* is our take on the history of American archaeology from the early 1960s on—a narrative informed by our involvement throughout much of this period in debates on archaeological method and theory. Despite our differing personal histories and intellectual positions, we discovered that our assessments of many events surrounding the development of the new archaeology and its progeny were similar.

We have written this book for a wide audience, hoping that it will appeal to professional archaeologists, graduate students, and even a lay public interested in intellectual history. Perhaps *Archaeology as a Process* will also appeal to philosophers, sociologists, and historians of science. In the decades ahead we expect that other historically minded archaeologists will delve into the post-1960 period in order to dispute our conclusions, clarify issues we have left unresolved, and raise new questions that require research on archival materials. Thus, this volume is merely a starting point for deep historical inquiry into a fascinating, tumultuous period characterized by far-reaching changes in archaeological method and theory.

No book of this coverage can be written without the assistance of a large number of people. Jeff Grathwohl, director of the University of Utah Press, took a personal interest in the book and, as in the past, provided unflagging support throughout the project. Dan Glover, of the University of Missouri, drew the maps, scanned the photographs and cleaned them up where needed, and indexed the book. Alexis Mills edited the manuscript and greatly improved the flow of our discussion. Steve Nash, Robert Preucel, Jeff Reid, Bruce Trigger, Richard Gould, Beverly O'Brien, and Bill Longacre read the entire manuscript and made numerous corrections and suggestions for improvement.

Other colleagues helped us along the way by providing photographs, manuscripts, and advice. For these sundry contributions, we thank Jerice Barrios, Lewis Binford, Richard Boyd,

Anne-Marie Cantwell, Matt Cartmill, Hester Davis, Chris Descantes, Irven DeVore, Nancy DeVore and Anthro-Photo, Richard Diehl, Gary Feinman, Kent Flannery, Mike Fowler, Richard Gould, George Gumerman, Deborah Guzman and Fermilab, Ian Hodder, John House, David Hull, Carl Kuttruff, Carl Lipo, Bill Longacre, Susan Luebbermann, Joyce Marcus, Bob McGimsey, Betty Meggers, Jon Muller, Steve Nash, Jim Neely, Deborah Nichols, Jim O'Connell, George Odell, Tim Pauketat, William Peace, Lori Pendleton, Steve Plog, David Price, Bennett Rogers, Jim Sackett, Julia Sanchez, Merrilee Salmon, Stephen Shennan, Stan South, Janet Spector, Dave Thomas, Bruce Trigger, Todd and Chris VanPool, Leslie Walker, Patty Jo Watson, B. M. Welch, Clyde Wilson, Bill Woodcock, Charlene Woodcock, and Alison Wylie.

Finally, we thank the following organizations for allowing us to use various photographs: Academic Press; American Association for the Advancement of Science; American Museum of Natural History; Arizona State Museum; Arkansas Archeological Survey; Bentley Historical Library (University of Michigan); Cambridge University Press; Fermilab Archives and Visual Media Center; Field Museum of Natural History; Minnesota Historical Society; Museum of Anthropology, University of Michigan; National Anthropological Archives; National Museum of Art; Peabody Museum, Harvard University; Southern Illinois University Photo Service; *St. Louis Post-Dispatch;* and Washington University.

Introduction

Anyone having a passing familiarity with the philosophy of science will recognize that the title of this book is not original. Rather, we borrowed it from David Hull's (1988b) *Science as a Process,* which in our opinion is one of the most insightful books ever written on the conduct of science. Hull was dissatisfied with how the scientific process typically was portrayed by philosophers, and he set out to write an account of how scientists come to know what they think they know about the natural world. Instead of writing a broad, general review of science, Hull narrowed his scope and focused on the history of three intellectual schools that grew up around biological systematics, the science of grouping organisms so that like goes with like. The success of the book is due in part to the detailed treatment Hull gives the subject matter, but systematics per se, no matter how well it is discussed, cannot capture someone's attention the way Hull's book does. Why, after reading 522 pages on the history of systematics, are we disappointed that Hull didn't write a couple hundred more?

The answer lies in how he approached the subject. Hull wrote not only one of the best books on how science is conducted but also perhaps the best book on how scientists conduct themselves. He makes a convincing argument that one cannot hope to understand the history of a science without understanding the people involved. To that end he interweaves theories with personalities, methods with alliances, and results with jealousies. He demonstrates why certain scientific approaches gain approval whereas others do not, and why certain scientists get credited with key ideas whereas other, perhaps more innovative scientists are relegated to footnotes. Above all, he dispels the myth that science is an orderly enterprise, run by men and women imbued with a Platonic idealism that truth wins out in the end and that theories and hypotheses are built one upon another in seamless fashion as our knowledge of the world accumulates.

Much to the contrary, science is done by people who have a lot at stake in terms of time and status, who fight to get their ideas heard and read, and who aren't above conniving and double dealing in order to ensure that those things happen. In other words, science is done by the same kinds of people we meet in everyday life. For an account of how science supposedly operates at the macrolevel, read Thomas Kuhn's *The Structure of Scientific Revolutions* (1962b). However, if you want to know how science *really* works—down at the everyday, human level—read Hull's *Science as a Process.* As someone with a long professional involvement with systematics, Hull has an inside view of the social and conceptual development of the discipline, which he uses to full advantage.

No book on the history of archaeology mirrors Hull's volume. This is not a criticism; rather, it means that extant books take different tacks in examining our field's past. Some focus primarily on methodological issues—survey, excavation, and the like—whereas others tend more toward theory. Some attempt to cover archaeology generally; others are regional in focus. It is fair to say that few regions of the world lack works that deal to some extent with the history of archaeological method and theory. This is especially true of Great Britain, where three excellent books immediately come to mind, all by the late Glyn Daniel: *A Hundred and Fifty Years of Archaeology* (1976), *A Short History of Archaeology* (1981a), and his edited book, *Towards a History of Archaeology* (1981b). The continent likewise is well represented, including Eastern Europe (Malina Jaroslav and Zdenek Vasicek's [1990] *Archaeology Yesterday and Today: The Development of Archaeology in the Sciences and Humanities* is an excellent introduction). More and more, the archaeological history of developing nations is being presented, either in book-length form, such as Dilip Chakrabarti's (1999) *India: An Archaeological History,* or in collections of essays, such as Peter Ucko's (1995) *Theory in Archaeology: A World Perspective.*

Archaeologists of our generation will remember when the only histories of North American archaeology were James Fitting's (1973) edited volume, *The Development of North American Archaeology: Essays in the History of Regional Traditions,* and Gordon Willey and Jeremy Sabloff's (1974) *A History of American Archaeology.* Fitting's book contains eight chapters (plus introductory and concluding chapters) by as many authors, each dealing with a large region comprising one or more of the traditional culture areas—the Southwest, the Southeast, and so on. The book lacks illustrations other than maps showing the general locations of significant sites, and it tends only to chronicle who did what, and when and where they did it. Willey and Sabloff's book, which currently is in its third edition (1993), set the standard against which succeeding histories are often judged. It traces the intellectual growth of American archaeology from the eighteenth century to the late twentieth century and chronicles theoretical and methodological advances made along the way. After reading *A History of American Archaeology,* one has an excellent overview of how intellectual interests have changed over time and how innovative methods and concepts developed by archaeologists working in one geographic area—say, the Southwest—have been adopted by archaeologists working elsewhere.

Other histories of American archaeology have appeared since the publication of those two books, including David Meltzer, Don Fowler, and Jerry Sabloff's (1986) *American Archaeology, Past and Future;* a special fiftieth-anniversary issue of *American Antiquity* published in 1985 under the editorship of Patty Jo Watson; Thomas Patterson's (1995) *Toward a Social History of Archaeology in the United States;* and Alice Kehoe's (1998) *The Land of Prehistory: A Critical History of American Archaeology.* We can add to this list Bruce Trigger's (1989a) *A History of Archaeological Thought,* although it covers a wide geographic range, moving well outside North America depending on the issue under discussion. The organization is topical rather than strictly chronological, and thus Trigger can go into more detail on selected topics than could Willey and Sabloff. The book well lives up to the blurb on its back cover that describes it as "at once stimulating and even-handed" in its treatment of various archaeological schools of thought that prevailed up to about 1985. The new edition will be out in 2006.

Meltzer, Fowler, and Sabloff's (1986) volume emanated from a symposium held at the fiftieth annual meeting of the Society for American Archaeology in Denver in 1985. Participants discussed what they saw as some of the key issues that had concerned archaeologists over the previous 50 years and where they saw the discipline headed. Watson was similarly interested in historical benchmarks that could be used to measure the development of American archaeology out of its nineteenth-century antiquarian roots, where the interest was on artifacts as ends in themselves, to the multidimensional discipline it had become toward the close of the twentieth century. Both her anniversary issue of *American Antiquity* and the volume by Meltzer, Fowler, and Sabloff deserve to be read in their entirety by anyone with an interest in the history of American archaeology.

Patterson (1995) covers American archaeology from roughly the early nineteenth century onward. Each chapter begins with a brief overview of events in American society during a specific period and concludes with an examination of the role played by "the cultural environment"—our shorthand for the social, political, and economic contexts of archaeological practice. Patterson's book is edgier than Trigger's (1989a). Both authors write from a materialist perspective, but Patterson's analysis is much more pointed. He finds that the course of American archaeology has been intricately tied to the ebb and flow of two powerful groups: the older Eastern Establishment (think Andrew Carnegie and John D. Rockefeller Jr.) and the younger Core Culture (think Henry Ford and other non–Eastern Seaboard industrialists). We do not agree with many of his conclusions, but we applaud his style and approach.

Kehoe's (1998) book covers a considerable amount of ground, and like Patterson she interweaves archaeology with the cultural environment in which archaeologists operate. Unlike Trigger and Patterson, Kehoe writes in a highly editorial and personal tone (Fowler 1999; Trigger 2000). Her no-holds-barred treatment of archaeological history makes for an interesting read. The last time we checked the Amazon.com Web site, *The Land of Prehistory* was ranked higher than other histories of archaeology, and that includes one that two of us had a hand in writing, *The Rise and Fall of Culture History* (Lyman, O'Brien, and Dunnell 1997). This tells us that archaeologists are no different than systematists or, we suspect, art historians and sociologists. They want to know about the history of their discipline, but they also want to read something interesting. If the piece is controversial, so much the better. Kehoe

certainly provides the reader an early clue to her intentions when she writes in the acknowledgments, "and to you [white, male] bastards who are too important to engage with someone lacking a prestigious position, I thank you, too, for illuminating the social structure of American archaeology. Without you, I couldn't have written this book" (Kehoe 1998:ix). Being controversial is one thing; being offensive or confrontational is another. This kind of confrontational style might have a (small) place in archaeological discourse, but if used in a book, the narrative loses credibility as history.

Given the choice of several existing books on the history of American archaeology, why write another one, especially if it covers only four decades? The answer to the first part of the question is, we have long had an interest in the history of American archaeology and wanted to share our take on it. We do not consider ourselves historians of archaeology but rather archaeologists who are interested in the history of our discipline, especially that part of it typically termed "method and theory." We are curious about where particular methods were first developed, who contributed which pieces to archaeological theory, and why particular theories and methods were replaced. We appreciate what other archaeologists have written about method and theory, but researching these topics for ourselves not only has given us a better appreciation for the complexity of the subject, but also has allowed us to follow historical connections wherever they might lead. Assembling the results of our inquiry into a publishable form has forced us to create a coherent discussion of the many connections and patterns that together make up American archaeology.

The answer to the second part of the question—Why focus primarily on the post-1960 period?—derives in part from the fact that the period has seen little detailed coverage in relation to the amount of change that occurred. Willey and Sabloff were aware of this, recounting in the preface to their third edition (1993) the mental gymnastics they went through in trying to decide how much space to devote to recent decades. They finally decided that the three chapters into which they divided the period in the second edition was too long in relation to the other periods, so they collapsed their discussion into a single, relatively short chapter. We pick up on many of the threads Willey and Sabloff of necessity left hanging, and follow them to see where they might lead in an intellectual sense.

There is another reason for writing a book on the post-1960 period, and for us it is an important one: it is "our" period. We started college in the mid- to late 1960s, just as processual, or "new," archaeology was gaining traction, and we worked on some reasonably well-known projects in the 1970s. Along the way we were taught by and worked alongside some of the most respected, and sometimes most controversial, archaeologists in the business. Having lived during a particular period does not automatically make you an authority; some would even say it does not give you sufficient detachment to report events evenhandedly. We are not too concerned about these potential shortcomings, realizing that our story is simply one of many that could be told about the recent development of method and theory in American archaeology. The problem, of course, is that every living archaeologist received training in this period or lived through most of it. Thus, there can be no totally disinterested reporters: we all have opinions and prejudices, likes and dislikes. The alternative is to forsake the project of writing the history of this era, leaving it to scholars in some unspecified future—a move that seems both cowardly and shortsighted.

We are not particularly concerned about how tightly or loosely one defines the terms *method* and *theory*. We would expect little debate among archaeologists over the definition of method—normally thought of as a set of techniques for getting a job done—but we would expect considerable debate over the definition of theory. Even the three of us have engaged in more than a little quibbling. Using a narrow definition would make our job easier because we could ignore large sections of the literature, but the result would be a history that other archaeologists would view as unacceptably limited and biased. Thus we adopted a more expansive definition of theory, one that most archaeologists could accept. We reasoned that archaeologists can agree that, at a minimum, theory consists of generalizations employed to answer why-type as well as how-type questions (Schiffer 1988, 2000b). Adopting this definition allows us to bring in such diverse aspects of archaeology as social theory, formation-process theory, and "middle-range" theory or research (Binford 1977b; Goodyear, Raab, and Klinger 1978).

A couple of caveats are perhaps in order. First, we neither provide an exhaustive list of references to archaeological method and theory nor craft a book of epic proportions that, like Sherwin-Williams, covers the methodological and theoretical world. Rather, our goal is to produce a useful, interesting guide to 40 years of intellectual trends in American archaeology. Decisions on what to include were based in part on the importance we attached to a particular contribution, but also on our own interests, especially when they were piqued by unanticipated intellectual connections between seemingly disparate pieces of information that made us examine the connections further.

Second, our coverage is uneven in terms of the time spent on particular periods. By design, the period from roughly 1960 to 1980 is discussed at greater length than the following years. In our opinion (not universally shared [e.g., Trigger 1989a]), the processual movement, which began in the early 1960s and gained momentum throughout that decade, was a critical turning point in American archaeology. We are not claiming that processualism did not build on what came before, nor are we saying that someone other than Lewis Binford, regarded as the architect of processualism, couldn't have said some of the same things. But we *are* claiming that the realignment of archaeology that began in the 1960s was so thorough that its effects are still being felt. Thus in order to understand postprocessualism, evolutionism, neo-Marxism, radicalism, and all the other "isms" that have made their way into and out of archaeology over the past four decades or so, we need to understand what it was they were adding to, railing against, or seeking to replace. We also need to understand which factors of the cultural environment affected their formulation and acceptance.

Thinking in terms of labels—"isms"—can be useful, but it also masks intellectual and behavioral variation. We agree with Patterson (1986:21) that all archaeologists "participate in an interpretive community," but that participation can vary in terms of degree and even kind. In our experience most archaeologists do not place themselves in neat little piles. When pushed, they might say that they have more in common intellectually with a Marxist approach than with a processualist approach, but they wouldn't run around loudly proclaiming their allegiance to Karl Marx. Self-identification as to school—processualism, Marxism, evolutionism, and the like—is a fairly recent phenomenon, as far as we can tell dating back no further than the 1960s and the dawn of processualism. The assignment of others to a particular school of thought has a similar history. A. V. Kidder, for example, never referred to himself (as far as we know) as a culture historian. He and other archaeologists of his generation occasionally stated that they did culture history, but the appellation "culture historian" came at the hands of a later generation.

Judging by the attendance at various symposia on the history of the discipline that have been sponsored by the Society for American Archaeology, those of us interested in the ideas and activities of our intellectual forebears are not a minority. What people find interesting, of course, varies by individual, as we found time and again during our collaboration on this volume, but there is no denying that for most of us, historical interest transcends names, places, and dates. We're interested in who influenced whom, who did not get along with whom and why, and all the myriad interconnections of people's ideas and activities with the cultural environment—the things that Hull showed were so valuable for understanding the growth

of biological systematics. We're interested in what various individuals were trying to accomplish when they wrote a particular article or book, and why something was done the way it was or why something turned out the way it did. Archaeologists are products of both their intellectual and cultural environments—just like historians, biologists, and artists. Any history of archaeology that ignores either paints an incomplete picture.

With respect to the cultural environment, how might we integrate it into a history of American archaeology? Several strategies come to mind. We can use the New Deal era as an example. The federal relief projects of the 1930s and 1940s, established as part of Franklin Roosevelt's attempts to jump-start the economy, pumped considerable amounts of money into archaeological fieldwork connected with the construction of large public works such as dams and reservoirs. The first benchmark of the program was creation of the Tennessee Valley Authority in 1933. Various relief agencies provided the manpower necessary to excavate sites in several reservoirs in Tennessee, Alabama, and Kentucky. It is difficult to overestimate the importance of those excavations in terms of how they changed the prevailing perceptions of the prehistoric past and added a much-needed infusion of precision to fieldwork. Many excavations might have been "criminally inept," as Jesse Jennings (1986:56) so baldly put it, but we agree with James B. Griffin (1985:269) that overall "the benefits far outweighed the deficiencies." We also agree with Kit Wesler (1997:154) that "New Deal–era archaeology shaped today's southeastern archaeology in more ways than most modern practitioners realize."

In writing about New Deal archaeology, we might examine the logistics of the various relief programs that fueled the archaeological fieldwork. Our history would cover who ran which projects, which sites were excavated, and how the findings rewrote the prehistory of the southeastern United States. Edwin Lyon (1996) does exactly this in *A New Deal for Southeastern Archaeology*. He is aware of the cultural processes at work in the nation during the New Deal era, and he uses his knowledge as a backdrop for discussions of the archaeology. Another way of looking at New Deal archaeology would be to treat it as an active social and political process that mirrors what was going on in other areas of contemporary American life. Tom Patterson (1986, 1995) takes this approach, using the cultural environment of federal relief projects not as a backdrop but as the warp threads around which to weave a discussion of archaeology. Both approaches have their merits. Our approach lies somewhere between those of Lyon and Patterson—what in Wesler's (1997) words is a synthetic treatment that emphasizes the interplay of personality and territory, central figures and feuding factions that, given enough time, become separate schools of thought and training.

What about someone's intellectual genealogy? In some cases we want to know a person's intellectual parents, grandparents, brothers, and sisters, as well as the person's own intellectual progeny. Sometimes the individual who has the most intellectual influence on budding professionals is an adviser, but other times it might be someone they worked with in the field. More likely, it will be different people at different times. Disciplinary histories often tend either to treat intellectual genealogies in passing or to ignore them altogether. We view them as essential for figuring out why a discipline took one particular path over another. The attention Hull pays to intellectual genealogy is what makes *Science as a Process* (1988b) such a valuable historical work. He takes pains to identify intellectual lineages and to illustrate how, at a more-inclusive scale, related lineages form intellectual clades: groups of people related to each other through common intellectual ancestors. In spatial terms, these intellectual clades, or schools, often can be traced to a few centers—what we can think of as breeding grounds. In biological systematics competing schools of thought and practice arose at the University of Kansas Museum of Natural History and the American Museum of Natural History, both of which competed with places such

as the Museum of Comparative Zoology at Harvard. Competing intellectual breeding grounds exist in archaeology, and recognizing them contributes greatly to understanding the history of the discipline.

After identifying major features of the cultural environment and assessing their influence, and after completing the genealogies, are we in a position to answer why something turned out the way that it did? It is much easier to answer how-type questions than why-type questions. Answers to how-type questions often can be found by patiently digging through the literature, perhaps conducting personal interviews to obtain more leads and insights. Our compelling interest, however, is explanations—to craft answers to the "whys?" Those can be formulated only by linking observations with some theory about the way disciplines evolve. In our view the world is a competitive stage, and organisms, humans included, strive to perform competently, and in some cases better than other members of their species (or discipline). In their attempts to do better than other members, organisms sometimes adopt short-term strategies and, at other times, longer-term strategies. The catch is, no one can predict with certainty which, if any, strategy will be effective in a given situation. In some cases those two kinds of strategies mesh well, but in others they clash. How well the strategies work at a given time is what determines which individuals (and schools) outcompete other individuals (and schools) for available resources such as jobs, grants, journal pages, honors, good press, and graduate students.

Archaeology, then, is a process—the comings and goings of people, activities, and ideas—like any other in the natural world. It is driven by the same mechanisms—transmission, selection, and so on—that drive any other evolutionary process. The process works the same irrespective of whether archaeology is a science—or whether we *think* it is or is not a science. Ironically, disagreements in the discipline over whether archaeology is a science, a humanity, or something else entirely actually fuel the archaeology-as-process engine perhaps more than in less-reflective disciplines. Not only do archaeologists get to argue about the scientific merits of, say, behavioral archaeology versus evolutionary archaeology, they also get to argue about whether archaeology is/could/should be a science.

This debate has profound theoretical implications that dramatically shape the ontological and epistemological course of archaeology. There is ample room for disagreement, and archaeologists have never been shy about disagreeing. Competition is rampant and appears to be getting more intense, perhaps because there are more archaeologists competing for the same or, in some cases, declining resources. This competition exists despite occasional efforts aimed at getting archaeologists to play nicely together. Such efforts are well intentioned, but they don't always serve the best interests of the discipline. Archaeology—a cultural and material process—necessarily involves divergent and competing interests. Our history of recent decades of American archaeology highlights some of these features.

I

The "Old" Archaeology

So little work has been done in American archaeology on the explanatory level that it is difficult to find a name for it. The term "functional interpretation"...has gained a certain amount of currency in American studies...but it is not entirely satisfactory, since it implies that the functional is the only explanatory principle involved. We have substituted here the broader "processual interpretation," which might conceivably cover any explanatory principle that might be invoked.... Practically speaking, it implies an attempt to discover regularities in the relationships given by the methods of culture-historical integration. Whatever we choose to call it, the important consideration is that... we are no longer asking merely what but also how and even why.

—GORDON WILLEY AND PHILIP PHILLIPS, *Method and Theory in American Archaeology*

When Gordon Willey and Philip Phillips published *Method and Theory in American Archaeology* in 1958, they could not have known that their remarks, as well as their term "processual interpretation," anticipated the birth of what would become the dominant approach in American archaeology—one that its chief architect, Lewis Binford (Figure 1.1), would label "processual archaeology" (Binford 1968a). It, too, would "attempt to discover reg-

ularities" in cultural processes as evidenced by the archaeological record, and to answer questions of "how and even why." Proponents of that approach would begin to refer to it as the "new archaeology" because to them it represented a break with traditional archaeology, or what became widely known in the 1960s as "culture history."

By the mid-1960s the term *culture history* was being employed derisively to bolster some processualists' belief that earlier archaeologists had little interest in anything other than the most basic questions of what, where, and when (Binford 1968a; Flannery 1967; Martin 1971). This was, in many respects, a straw man. Culture historians *did* routinely furnish explanations for variation and change in the archaeological record—explanations informed, if only implicitly, by the theories coming out of the American historical-ethnology school of cultural anthropology (Harris 1968b). These explanations invoked as mechanisms "diffusion," "migration," "independent invention," and other culture-historical processes visible ethnographically. Binford (1963, 1965, 1968a) railed against the underlying theory, which he said modeled culture as a stream of ideas or norms that significantly influence what people do. He referred to the theory as the "aquatic view" of culture. Binford argued that accounts stemming from this perspective were not "scientific" explanations and that culture history would have to be replaced.

Culture history was never replaced. Processualists rejected some of the basic explanatory mechanisms of traditional culture history—diffusion, migration, and the like—together with its allegedly descriptive and inductive epistemology, but they did not cease to build cultural chronologies or to do the things archaeologists had always done. What, where, and when—converted into form, space, and time (Spaulding 1960b; Willey 1953a)—are foundational to archaeology, regardless of the brand. It is inconceivable it could ever be otherwise, else archaeology would become so metaphysical and esoteric that no one would pay much attention to it. Processualism represented a change in how the archaeological record was viewed, as well as the purported causes of cultural variation, but it did not replace culture history.

To understand the role played in American archaeology not only by processual archaeology but by other approaches that either grew out of it or were a reaction to it, we need to understand something of the pre-1960 period. Such understanding will, as Paul Bohannan and Mark Glazer (1988:xv) put it, "save [us] a good deal of unnecessary originality." This dictum was ignored by more than a few processualists in the 1960s and '70s, who either forgot or never knew that their forebears also had an interest in cultural processes. That interest was not expressed by culture historians at the same level of intensity as processualists eventually would, and not in the same philosophical terms, but it was there. Nevertheless, it took second seat to the more pressing business at hand: the construction of cultural chronologies.

By the time Willey and Phillips were writing, the archaeological record of the Western Hemisphere was reasonably well known, much

FIGURE 1.1. Lewis Binford, Kirksville, Missouri, 2003. (Photograph by Amber Johnson, courtesy Lewis Binford.)

of it admittedly in outline form, and several syntheses of large pieces of that record had recently appeared (e.g., Griffin 1952; Martin, Quimby, and Collier 1947). Willey and Phillips were writing at the dawn of radiocarbon dating, an event often heralded as the beginning of the chronological revolution in archaeology. Radiocarbon was a boon to establishing chronological control, but despite what some archaeologists claimed (e.g., Johnson 1967), it did not signal a revolution in American archaeology (Lyman 2000) (though perhaps it did for post-Neolithic Europe [Renfrew 1973a]). After Willard Libby and his students at the University of Chicago's Institute for Nuclear Studies showed the archaeological usefulness of an unstable carbon isotope in 1947 (Taylor 1985, 2000), it was used more to refine existing New World chronologies than to create new ones.

The real chronological revolution in American archaeology occurred several decades earlier, when prehistorians working in the Southwest concluded that human occupation of North America was more ancient than previously thought. During the first two decades of the twentieth century it was commonly (although not universally) believed that the tenure of humans in North America did not exceed a couple thousand years and that during that short time little significant cultural change had, or could have, taken place. But then archaeologists were confronted with evidence that did not conform to a shallow past and began to change their minds. The revolution started in the prehistoric pueblos of north-central New Mexico around 1914 (Kidder 1915; Nelson 1913, 1916; Wissler 1915) and ended in a bison-bone bed in northeastern New Mexico just over a decade later (Figgins 1927).

Knowing that humans' tenure in North America extends back some 11,000 years or more is important, but without the ability to produce a temporal ordering of artifacts and the deposits in which they occur, archaeology is reduced to a jumble of materials that might as well date to a single point in time. This is why Berthold Laufer (1913:577), an expert on Chinese art and artifacts at the Field Museum in Chicago (Bronson 2003), considered chronology "the nerve electrifying the dead body of history." Maya prehistorian Alfred Tozzer (1926:283) put it only slightly differently: "[A]rchaeological data have an inert quality, a certain spinelessness when unaccompanied by a more or less definite chronological background." Chronological ordering requires the construction of units that measure the passage of time; in archaeology these units typically are artifact types.

One complaint from the processualists (e.g., Plog 1973a, 1973b, 1974) was that the units created by culture historians were less than ideal for studying culture change, although many processualists continued to use them. For several reasons, then, it is important to look back, if briefly, at those units to examine how and why they came into existence and why they've stayed around so long. Answers to questions of how and why suggest some of the reasons why a different kind of archaeology began to emerge in the 1950s and why it became influential in the 1960s. Examining those questions allows us to explore one of the central tenets of this book: that the intellectual position of any archaeologist is at least partially a result of those who came before, whether they advised and instructed the individual in question or merely did the fieldwork on which someone's knowledge of a portion of the past rests.

In this chapter we first outline how culture history originated by emphasizing that of the three dimensions of variation expressed by the archaeological record—time, space, and form—time is invisible. But if one is to write a pre*history* of human artifacts, then the age of those artifacts must somehow be made visible; that is, inferred. Archaeologists working in the first half of the twentieth century took that as their top priority. Second, we show how

and why the goals of archaeological research began in the 1950s to shift away from chronology and history and toward something else. That "something else" was processualism.

MEASURING TIME WITH ARTIFACTS

There has long been a tendency in American archaeology to state that a "stratigraphic revolution" occurred during the second decade of the twentieth century (e.g., Browman and Givens 1996; Strong 1952; Willey and Sabloff 1993). Recent research, however, has shown that many archaeologists prior to 1910 were both excavating in a manner that is readily considered stratigraphic and segregating artifact assemblages by stratum (Browman 2002; Lyman and O'Brien 1999). Still, it was difficult to determine how much time was represented in a given stratigraphic section. Some archaeologists, principally those aligned with Harvard's Frederic Ward Putnam (Figure 1.2), thought considerable time was represented in the archaeological record of North America (Meltzer 1983, 1985), similar to what had been found in Europe (Grayson 1983). Others, principally those aligned with the Bureau of Amer-

FIGURE 1.2. Frederic Ward Putnam, second curator of the Peabody Museum of American Archaeology and Ethnology at Harvard, 1909. (Courtesy Peabody Museum, Harvard University.)

FIGURE 1.3. William Henry Holmes, second director (he changed the title to "chief") of the Bureau of American Ethnology, ca. 1905. (Courtesy National Anthropological Archives, Smithsonian Institution.)

ican Ethnology's William Henry Holmes (Figure 1.3), did not. The issue that received the most attention in print was the putative occupation of the continent during the last glacial age, which was estimated on the basis of European varve analysis to have ended roughly 10,000 years ago. Putnam and his allies (e.g., Haynes 1893; Putnam 1897; Wright 1892) said there was considerable evidence that humans had been present in North America that long ago; Holmes and his followers (e.g., Holmes 1892, 1893, 1897) denied that such evidence existed.

In reality, the argument was more complex than that. The Holmes group refused to believe that the tenure of humans in North America could be more than a few thousand years at most, let alone extend into the last glacial period. In their view, the Bureau of American Ethnology's Cyrus Thomas had proved that fact in the 1880s when he debunked the myth that an extinct race of moundbuilders had erected the thousands of earthen structures so evident

across the eastern United States (Thomas 1884, 1891, 1894). Instead, the builders of the mounds were the ancestors of Native American peoples whom early European explorers and settlers had found residing in the region. To Thomas, Holmes, and others, the archaeological record did not produce the kinds of differences in tools that were thought to signify great time depth. Thus Franz Boas (Figure 1.4) could announce at the turn of the century that "it seems probable that the remains found in most of the archaeological sites of America were left by a people similar in culture to the present Indians" (Boas 1902:1).

For Boas, "similar in culture" meant more or less similar in time. One of Boas's students, Alfred Kroeber (1909), used this reasoning in commenting on Max Uhle's (1907) stratigraphic sequence of tools from shell middens along San Francisco Bay. Kroeber did not discount the value of Uhle's method of stratigraphic excavation; rather, he questioned the significance of the chronological indications of cultural change Uhle documented. Kroeber noted that not only had Uhle found few artifacts but also the few he had recovered showed no marked cultural changes through the sequence. This meant no new "types" of artifacts had been introduced. Kroeber, like most other Americanists, was searching for differences in culture traits of a magnitude that would suggest major qualitative differences among cultures on an order similar to that represented by

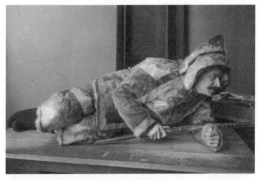

FIGURE 1.4. Franz Boas demonstrating the use of an Eskimo harpoon, ca. 1900. (Photograph by R. Weber [negative no. 3220], courtesy Department of Library Services, American Museum of Natural History.)

FIGURE 1.5. *Left to right:* Nels Nelson, Abbé Henri Breuil, Hugo Obermaier, Paul Wernert, and Pierre Teilhard de Chardin at Castillo Cave, Spain, 1913. (Photograph by M. C. Burkitt [negative no. 124770], courtesy Department of Library Services, American Museum of Natural History.)

Europe's Paleolithic–Neolithic–Bronze Age–Iron Age sequence. Thus the relatively minor change Uhle documented was merely "a passing change of fashion in manufacture or in manipulation of the same process" and not "to be compared even for a moment with a transition as fundamental as that from palaeolithic to neolithic" (Kroeber 1909:16).

Americanists would begin to reconsider how time, and hence culture change, could be measured, thanks in part to Clark Wissler, curator of anthropology at the American Museum of Natural History in New York and a former student of Boas's at Columbia. Wissler sent Nels Nelson (Figure 1.5) to the Rio Grande River valley of north-central New Mexico in 1912 specifically to construct a chronology of Puebloan cultural development and to determine how much time depth that chronology represented. Nelson had trained under Kroeber at the University of California and had tried his own hand at stratigraphically excavating shell middens along San Francisco Bay (Nelson 1906, 1910). In New Mexico, he immediately suspected that evidence of considerable time depth might be found along the Rio Grande and its tributaries: there were far too many sites to have all been occupied simultaneously. Also, the physical environment was too harsh to have

supported the number of people indicated by all those sites. Therefore, they must have been occupied at different times, but how was he going to demonstrate this?

Nelson (1913, 1916) excavated several sites, including San Cristobal (Figure 1.6), the one for which he is best known. After collecting pottery sherds from arbitrarily defined vertical proveniences (Lyman, O'Brien, and Dunnell 1997; Lyman and O'Brien 1999; O'Brien 2003), he created types based on painted pottery designs and examined how the absolute frequencies of the types varied across proveniences. Nelson found that the frequencies fluctuated smoothly and gradually over time, displaying basically unimodal distributions. This provided him with a chronological ordering of pottery types. Then, by means of typological cross matching, Nelson determined the relative ages of other sites in the region. Leslie Spier, a colleague of Nelson's at the American

FIGURE 1.6. Stratigraphic cut made by Nels Nelson through the midden deposit at San Cristobal, New Mexico. (From Nelson 1916, courtesy American Museum of Natural History.)

Museum, stated that Nelson's use of changes in type frequencies was "the first exposition of a refined method for determining exactly the time sequence of archaeological materials in a primitive area" (Spier 1931:275). Nelson's work signaled the beginning of the chronological revolution in American archaeology, as later archaeologists would characterize it.

Harvard-trained archaeologist Alfred Kidder was another Southwesternist who detected temporal change in artifacts, and in 1915 he began to address questions of chronology by excavating at Pecos Pueblo, just to the north and east of where Nelson was working (Kidder 1916). Kidder, like Nelson, saw change in how the pottery was decorated. He sorted the painted designs into five types and put them in order—a seriation—based on his ideas of how the designs had evolved (Kidder 1917). This technique, termed "phyletic seriation" (Lyman, O'Brien, and Dunnell 1997), had been used in Great Britain to order gold coins (Evans 1850) and in Egypt to order predynastic graves (Petrie 1899, 1901). Kidder was aware of these studies. He confirmed by means of stratigraphic excavation that his ordering was chronological.

While working at Pecos Pueblo, Kidder and his wife, Madeleine, mimicked Nelson's technique—later referred to as "ceramic stratigraphy" or "percentage stratigraphy" (Lyman, Wolverton, and O'Brien 1998)—but used natural rather than arbitrary vertical units, and relative rather than absolute frequencies of pottery types (Kidder and Kidder 1917). The Kidders found that their ceramic types, like Nelson's, tended to display unimodal frequency distributions over stratigraphically defined time. They reasoned that the types were good temporal markers because they occupied different positions in the temporal continuum.

While on leave from the University of California in 1915 to conduct ethnographic fieldwork for the American Museum, Kroeber visited Zuni Pueblo, New Mexico, to the west of where Nelson and Kidder were working. During his walks across the countryside he noticed great differences in the designs on pottery scattered on prehistoric sites as well as on sites that, based on the condition of houses and other architectural features, the Zuni had abandoned during more recent times. Kroeber also observed that some decorations showed up only on pottery from prehistoric sites, whereas other designs occurred on pottery from what he suspected were more recent ruins. Were the kinds of pottery really of different ages? Like Nelson and Kidder, Kroeber had identified a chronological problem, and to solve it he invented the technique known as frequency seriation (Kroeber 1916). He created several pottery types and used them to order his surface collections to reflect the continuous and gradual passage of time, as if one type slowly faded away while a younger type gradually increased in frequency (Lyman and Harpole 2002). To Kroeber, this image of time characterized how culture change usually operated—as a slow, continuous phenomenon. This is how he had described what Max Uhle had found in the California shell middens, and how for several more years he would view the entire North American archaeological record (e.g., Kroeber 1923).

Kroeber concluded that the temporal implications of the arrangement of his surface-collected assemblages could be confirmed through excavation. At Wissler's direction, Spier (1917) continued Kroeber's archaeological work near Zuni the next year. He seriated surface-collected assemblages based on the relative frequencies of pottery types and used percentage stratigraphy to test the chronological significance of his and Kroeber's seriations. He also inferred that the spatial distributions of various pottery types reflected the movement of peoples across the landscape.

The notion that time was a continuum may have grown imperceptibly out of what became known as the "direct historical approach" (Steward 1942), the method Cyrus Thomas had used so successfully to debunk the mound-builder myth in the 1880s (O'Brien and Lyman 1999b). It later was used by Duncan Strong (1935) and Waldo Wedel (1938) on the Great Plains, not only as a means of tracking the passage of time but also for identifying the ethnicity of the people responsible for artifact assemblages (Lyman and O'Brien 2001a). The analytical protocol of the direct historical approach was simple: to construct a relative chronology of artifacts, one began with the most recent, or historically known, end of the chronological continuum and then simply worked backward in time, using similarity in artifact form or function as the basis for putting assemblages closer together or farther apart in time. The direct historical approach worked well in some cases for connecting the artifacts of ethnographical groups with those of late prehistory, but it broke down with increasing age.

It is not surprising that American archaeologists turned to the ethnographic record for help, trained as they were (and still are) in anthropology departments. During the first several decades of the twentieth century, few archaeologists were, in fact, specialists, but many anthropologists happened to do some archaeology. Kroeber is a prime example; Clark Wissler, Clyde Kluckhohn, and Julian Steward are others. More importantly, the training these individuals received meant that they were steeped in the ethnological theories of the moment. At that time there was a particular approach to doing anthropological, including archaeological, research. Anthropologists held to the notion that culture was transmitted over time and across space, and they came to refer to the unit of transmission as a culture trait or culture element (Lyman and O'Brien 2003a). This notion—we hesitate to refer to it as a theory—allowed Boas (1896) to reject the universal cultural evolutionism of Herbert Spencer, Edward B. Tylor, Lewis Henry Morgan, and others because he could show that different histories of migration, diffusion, and invention could produce the same constellation of culture traits that made up a particular evolutionary stage. This "induced investigators to trace the distribution and history of customs and beliefs with care so as to ascertain empirically whether they are spontaneous creations or whether they are borrowed and adapted" (Boas 1904:522).

The research program Boas initiated was originally known as "historical ethnology" (Goldenweiser 1925) and later as "historical particularism" (Harris 1968b). With few exceptions, Boas's students and other advocates of historical ethnology took on virtually any competitor, as Robert Lowie (1912, 1918) did against the vestiges of universal cultural evolutionism and Alexander Goldenweiser (1916) did against diffusionism. It didn't take long before problems with the basic method of historical ethnology were recognized (Radin 1933), though many anthropologists continued their attempts to work out the history of the particular culture(s) they studied and to improve various analytical techniques (e.g., Clements, Schenck, and Brown 1926; Steward 1929). It was within historical ethnology that the triumvirate of explanatory mechanisms—diffusion, migration, and invention (not to ignore other mechanisms such as trade)—became deeply ingrained in ethnologists as well as archaeologists. One tracked the spatiotemporal distributions of culture traits, whether behaviors or artifacts, to get at the history of a culture, which itself was little more than a constellation of traits. This was the conceptual baggage bequeathed to archaeologists: they were to write culture history and explain that history in terms of the movement of traits underpinned by ideas in the minds of the culture bearers (Lyman and O'Brien 2004b). The popularity principle stated by Nelson and adopted by culture historians was merely an explicit statement of the notion that culture was a stream of ideas transmitted over time and across space—what Binford (1965) would later call the "aquatic view" of culture change.

To return to archaeology, the true analytical revolution early in the twentieth century resided in the recognition that time could be measured using artifacts *if* those items were classified in particular ways, such as Nelson, Kidder, and Kroeber had done when they built pottery types based on changes in decoration. Stratigraphy played an important role in chronology building, but initially for confirmation rather than discovery. The principle of superposition as represented by stratified archaeological deposits was assumed to provide a valid chronometer that could be used to check whether traits such as pottery decorations displayed unimodal frequency distributions across superposed strata. Inferences that these distributions measured the passage of time could be tested and empirically confirmed or refuted—actions later said by processualists to characterize a science. But stratigraphy did not long remain the test medium for chronology. When stratigraphy shifted to a medium of discovering time based on the principle of superposition, other aspects of archaeological epistemology shifted as well.

MEASURING TIME WITH UNITS OF DEPOSITION

With stratigraphic confirmation of Kidder's, Nelson's, and Kroeber's seriated pottery sequences in hand, Clark Wissler (1917) proclaimed that a "new archaeology" had emerged—a term that would be used on more than one occasion over the next fifty years. It is unclear whether by *new archaeology* Wissler meant that time now could be measured continuously by means of changing artifact frequencies, or that superposed strata could be used as the basis for measuring the passage of time. We think he meant the latter, even though the use of superposition was anything but "new" in 1917. Despite the inventiveness of his own colleagues at the American Museum, Wissler himself never shook the view that distinct strata denoted discontinuous occupations by multiple successive cultures. Maybe the differences from one stratum to the next weren't on an epochal scale similar to the cultural stages evident in Europe, but they were still distinct enough to signal that different cultures were represented.

Even Nels Nelson may have succumbed to the temptation of this view. Years after he worked in New Mexico, Nelson (1932:105) stated that the uninterrupted flow of the stream of culture could be monitored by observing "a few cross-sections of the flow taken at strategic points." Note the words "strategic points." Where were these? Were they so obvious— grand disjunctions, perhaps—that there could be no doubt where to monitor the flow, or were

they selected by the archaeologist to best fit analytical needs? We think Nelson might have meant the latter, but we're not sure. The reason for the uncertainty is that by the mid-1920s almost all archaeologists were coming to view those cross sections not as arbitrary boundary markers of the chronological continuum but as boundaries of real cultural units, often thought of as "occupations."

The roots of this kind of thinking can be seen in the work of Manuel Gamio (1913) in the Valley of Mexico. Boas (1913) had Gamio excavate stratigraphically in order to test a suspected chronology of cultures as reflected in pottery (Figure 1.7). Gamio identified what amounted to "index markers": pottery types diagnostic of particular cultures, each of which occupied a discrete stratigraphic position. Armed with marker types, one didn't need to calculate relative percentages of artifact types to measure the flow of time. Now time could be carved up into separate periods, each defined by its own types. (This was very much in the tradition of French Paleolithic archaeology, which grew out of paleontology rather than anthropology [Chazan 1995; Sackett 1981; van Riper 1993].)

The next step was obvious: If marker types could be used as chronological indicators, couldn't they also be used as cultural indicators? The answer, it seemed, was yes, and by the early 1930s the use of index markers, pottery or otherwise, as cultural identifiers was widespread in American archaeology. One of the methodological leaders in this effort was George Vaillant, whose work in the Valley of Mexico on Gamio's "cultures" was sponsored by the American Museum (e.g., Vaillant 1935, 1937).

Regional syntheses, such as those provided for the Southwest by Alfred Kidder (1924, 1927) and Harold Colton (1939), focused on precisely this kind of dual unit that simultaneously allowed the measurement of time and the identification of distinct cultural units. This was problematic. On the one hand, that artifact types could mark the passage of time was testable initially with stratigraphic data and,

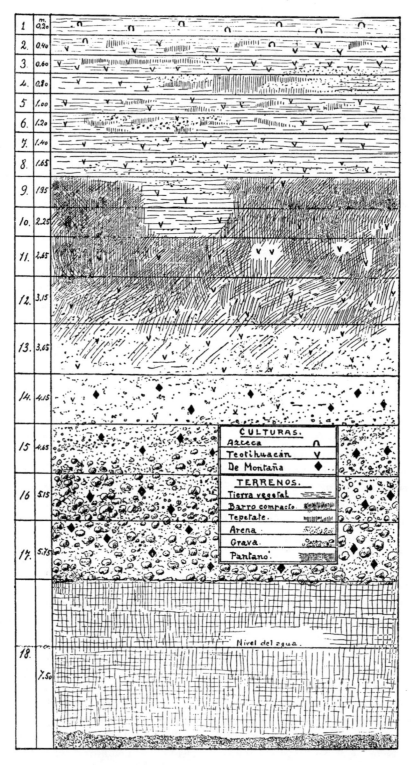

FIGURE 1.7. Manuel Gamio's stratigraphic profile at Atzcapotzalco in Mexico City. Note the varied thicknesses of the arbitrary levels and the vertical distribution of different artifact forms (index markers), which Gamio assigned to one of three cultures (inverted *U*, *V*, and diamond symbols). (After Gamio 1913.)

shortly thereafter (in the Southwest), with dendrochronological data (Nash 1999). That artifact types might measure some sort of ethnicity, on the other hand, was not testable except in the present or very near-term past (e.g., Collins 1927). Why would archaeologists, who ostensibly wanted to test their ideas with empirical data, abandon their one criterion of science—testability? The answer to this question involves artifacts and how they are classified.

THE ARTIFACT CLASSIFICATION PROBLEM

Nobody would question that tools are made according to some conception of the final product, however vague and incomplete the concept in the artisan's mind. If this were not the case, shapeless blobs of matter would result from human efforts to make tools. This holds true whether we are talking about inexpensive mass-produced shovels today or projectile points manufactured 5,000 years ago. The question that many archaeologists ask is, can we figure out what someone was thinking when he or she made a tool? Whether we can answer that question has long been debated in American archaeology, and we will come back to it at various points throughout the book. Here our interest is in how the question was handled in the pre-1960 period.

Early on, several archaeologists, including James Ford (1936) and Irving Rouse (1939), suggested that it might be possible to understand something of the mind of a prehistoric toolmaker, but they did not pursue the matter in any rigorous fashion, nor did anyone else. For starters, no one was sure how to test such a possibility. Ford (1954b) expanded on his contemporaries' view of the unclear relationship between an artifact and the underlying conception of that artifact in the artisan's mind by noting that even the artisan was not too clear about the relationship. Therefore, identifying prehistoric "mental templates," as they came to be known thanks to James Deetz (1967), seemed less important to culture historians than other tasks, such as building cultural chronologies.

The possibility that mental templates underpinned artifact types, however, created a marked confusion over whether artifact types were analytical (etic) units or were somehow ethnologically real (emic) units (Dunnell 1980, 1986). The confusion is apparent in Alex Krieger's (1944) discussion of typology. Krieger, like virtually all his contemporaries, was circumspect about how closely an archaeologist's artifact types matched the artisan's conceptions or cultural norms. His major contribution was to argue that a good type must pass the historical-significance test—it must have a continuous distribution in time and space. Nelson's, Kidder's, and Kroeber's decoration-based types from New Mexico had that feature. To Krieger and other culture historians, spatiotemporal contiguity denoted the flow of ideas between and among people who were in contact with each other.

The critical issue for archaeologists was how prehistoric cultures were to be recognized. In general, these were defined as recurrent assemblages of types thought to represent culture traits (Colton 1939; Ford 1938; Gladwin and Gladwin 1930; McKern 1939). The fact that they were recurrent reinforced the notion that a set of shared ideas comprised a distinctive culture despite the fact that similarity was at least in part a result of how items were classified. The implication of recurrence was nonetheless a profound theoretical notion that again reflected the aquatic view. It locked prehistorians into a particular set of limited explanations (diffusion, migration, invention), and it suggested how artifacts were to be sorted and studied in order to explain the composition and distribution of cultures (Colton and Hargrave 1937; Ford and Griffin 1938; Gladwin and Gladwin 1934; McKern 1937).

One means of recognizing prehistoric cultures was by stratigraphic positioning, but remains were not always stratified. Index markers—artifacts that existed for only a brief time—were another means. They could be used across wide areas to identify artifact assemblages that belonged to the same culture. Index markers that closely resembled each other must represent contiguity of the ideas that underlay their manufacture, such as when two flowing cultural streams of ideas had intersected. Similar types represented some sort of common ancestry, or homologous similarity. Or did they? Kroeber (1931) had noted the importance to paleontologists of distinguishing between homologous and analogous similarity, the latter denoting functional convergence rather than common ancestry. Archaeologists, however, failed to develop analytical means of testing empirical instances of this critically important distinction (Binford 1968a), despite a few efforts by ethnologists to do so (Lyman 2001).

Failure to develop a means to distinguish between analogous and homologous similarity resided in the lack of an explicit, well-developed theory of how cultures evolve that was applicable to archaeological materials. Early attempts to derive such evolutionary histories from the archaeological record used wording such as "one artifact type descended from another," but any notion of relatedness in a genetic-like sense was largely metaphorical. When the wording became more literal and less metaphorical—as it did under the guidance of Harold Colton (1939; Colton and Hargrave 1937) and Harold Gladwin (e.g., Gladwin and Gladwin 1930, 1934), neither of whom had anthropological training—the reaction within the discipline was decidedly negative.

Gladwin used terms for his cultural units—roots, stems, branches—that implied a phylogenetic tree, but in the face of criticism he quickly abandoned many of the evolutionary connotations of such wording (Gladwin 1936). J. O. Brew (1946) published the death notice for such unabashedly evolutionary notions with his pithy insight that inanimate objects do not breed. Brew pointedly suggested restricting the term *evolution* to the transmission of genetic material. The result was a continued reliance on the notion that culture was best viewed as a braided, constantly flowing stream of ideas in which various cultural rivulets come together, break apart, and converge again in an endless, open cycle, thus demanding that mechanisms of culture change concern diffusion, migration, invention, and the like.

CONTINUING STRUGGLES

Whether time and space figured into archaeological classification was an issue separate from how classificatory units were actually used. With few exceptions—primarily the work in New Mexico by Nelson, Kidder, and Kroeber—almost all archaeological units, no matter the purpose for which they were created, were used as cultural identifiers of one sort or another. This was the tradition that went back to Gamio's work in the Valley of Mexico and continued up through the classifications in the Southwest by Kidder (1936) and Colton (1939) and in the Southeast by Ford (1936, 1938). Ford was somewhat of an enigma when it came to cultural identification. Although he used artifacts (pottery in particular) as cultural identifiers, he typically stressed the arbitrariness of both the artifact types and the "cultures" archaeologists identified. This set him against other leading archaeologists, including James Griffin and Philip Phillips (O'Brien and Lyman 1998). Ford's reasoning was simple: If the artifact types were artificial, and most archaeologists believed they were, then how could the "cultures" be anything but artificial?

Not everyone agreed that artifact types *were* artificial. Albert Spaulding (1953b), for one, suggested that statistical techniques could be used to discover types. Note that Spaulding did not say to "create" types but to "discover" them. In Spaulding's view, if artifact types were discoverable, they must have had some reality in the minds of the prehistoric artisans. If so, then perhaps one could identify prehistoric societies. Further, because it was equivalent to a mental template, a type's unimodal frequency distribution over time was readily (and in a way, theoretically) explained by the popularity principle. We suspect that Spaulding held the view that artifact types were more or less equivalent to culture traits, and culture traits reflected concepts in the minds of the culture bearer (Lyman and O'Brien 2003a)—an explicit statement of normative theory as later described by Binford (1965).

Ford responded that this was nonsense (Ford 1954a), Spaulding (1954b) replied in kind, and Ford (1954c) produced a final statement on building types. Unfortunately, this statement conflated properties of types as real in an emic sense and properties of types as analytical constructs. Spaulding's clear, concise statistical method found more favor than Ford's among culture historians, particularly among processual archaeologists of the 1960s and '70s. The latter is not surprising because Spaulding was one of Binford's mentors at the University of Michigan (Chapters 2 and 3). Ford had no explanatory theory to undergird his position, and his discussions were often muddled. Also, his types for measuring time were built by trial and error. Spaulding couldn't abide by such haphazard procedures and preferred statistical objectivity that could be warranted through reference to the fact that distinct cultures and ethnicities, however defined, were ethnographically visible (O'Brien and Lyman 1998). If they were ethnographically visible, then perhaps they were archaeologically visible as well. This caught the attention of anthropologically oriented archaeologists and contributed to what became known as "ceramic sociology" (Chapter 3).

One hallmark of the 1950s was the creation of a systematic means of classifying the archaeological record on a large scale. The prime architects of the system were Philip Phillips and Gordon Willey (1953). The basic elements of the classification were two units—components and phases—that had been around in various guises since the mid-1930s (Lyman and O'Brien 2003b). *Components* were stratigraphically delimited aggregates of artifacts that were more or less equivalent to occupations, or communities. *Phases* were sets of virtually identical components and thus were the archaeological equivalents of societies. Operationally, the definitive attributes of components and phases were derived empirically from archaeological materials, not imposed on them on the basis of some theoretical model. As a result, the defin-

itive criteria could be modified in light of new evidence. Given the empirical derivation of their definitive criteria, it is not surprising that phases not only were "remarkably stable" (Phillips and Willey 1953:622) but were also viewed as real units in the sense of an ethnographer's "cultures."

Because Phillips and Willey were concerned explicitly with culture history, they employed the by then typically used axiom that "typological similarity [denotes] cultural relatedness [which in turn] carries with it implications of a common or similar history" (Willey 1953a:363–364). They also discussed in depth two units that had been around informally for a long time and that Willey (1945) had defined formally. Each unit had clear implications for the flow of cultural ideas across time and space. *Horizons* were archaeological manifestations that had extensive distributions in space but limited distributions in time. *Traditions* were manifestations that had extensive distributions in time but limited distributions in space. Together they were the integrative units of choice that would provide the warp and weft to the tapestry of culture history, to use Rouse's (1954) terms. Horizons suggested diffusion across space, and traditions indicated either cultural stability and persistence, or diffusion through time.

Willey and Phillips did not address how or why artifact styles should diffuse across space or through time, but no one else at the time did either. Incongruously, given their interests in what they called the "historical relatedness" of cultural phenomena, most archaeologists either did not believe or did not discuss the fact that theories of cultural transmission—the process that produces homologous similarity between artifacts and human behaviors through descent with modification—had much to offer. They ignored explicit statements by ethnologists regarding the influence of cultural transmission on culture change (e.g., Bruner 1956). Instead, the aquatic view served as a sort of commonsensical explanation for what were seen as formal similarities among archaeological materials.

FIGURE 1.8. Leslie White, Ann Arbor, Michigan, ca. 1968. (Courtesy Bentley Historical Library, University of Michigan.)

THE EVOLUTION OF CULTURE (AND OF CULTURES)

By the 1950s an alternative emerged, and it was not constrained by the need for theories of cultural transmission. This was cultural evolutionism, with two brands from which to choose: Leslie White's (1943, 1959) and Julian Steward's (1955). The choice depended on whether one was interested in the evolution of culture in general or that of specific cultures. If the former, White's brand was better; if the latter, Steward's brand was the obvious choice. Similarities between the two approaches were more apparent than real (Sahlins and Service 1960), although many anthropologists and archaeologists tended to misunderstand this key point. The works of both men would be highly influential in setting the agendas of the new archaeology of the 1960s, and thus we give them more than casual treatment.

White's evolutionism was, and still is, the more difficult of the two to comprehend. For one thing, White was not a clear writer. For another, he was interested in several things at once, and in people's minds these interests tended to blur. Thus White (Figure 1.8) often is remembered strictly as an evolutionist even though most of his theoretical writings had little to do with evolution. They had to do with culture and how to study it—what White (1949, 1959) labeled "culturology." White first coined this term in 1947 and defined it as "the scientific study of the distinctive feature of man known as culture" (White 1947:210). Robert Carneiro (1981), Richard Barrett (1989), and others have argued persuasively that there is a disconnect between White's cultural theory—captured best in his comment that "culture must be explained in terms of culture" (White 1949:141)—and his materialist-based evolutionary theory. It appears as if two different people were writing: one a culturologist interested only in the inner workings of culture, and the other an evolutionist interested only in culture as a progressive process. Recent examination of White's ethnographic monographs and his field notes indicates an overlap between his ethnographies and his theory, but it was minimal (Whiteley 2003).

White's followers tended to view his evolutionism as a new and radical way of explaining change in culture (with a big C), not changes in specific cultures (with a little c). White, however, did not see his evolutionism as anything particularly new. He always claimed that it did not "differ one whit in principle from that expressed in [Edward B.] Tylor's *Anthropology* in 1881" (White 1959:ix). White could have easily included Lewis Henry Morgan (1877) and Herbert Spencer (1851, 1876). White was interested in cultural evolution as a progressive process, the key to which lay in how humans captured and used energy. To White, culture evolves as people harness more energy per capita per unit of time, or as they increase the efficiency of how the energy is put to work (White 1943). White (1949:390–391) called this his "basic law of evolution," and he used it to explain every aspect of culture: "Culture thus becomes primarily a mechanism for harnessing energy and of putting it to work in the service of man, and, secondarily, of channelling and regulating his behavior not directly concerned with subsistence and offense and defense. Social systems are therefore determined by technological systems, and philosophies and the arts express experience as it is defined by technology and refracted by social systems."

White's "basic law of evolution" appeared to explain why the archaeological record looked the way it did—or so some archaeologists thought (e.g., Meggers 1960; see below). Quite a number who thought so were White's first-generation intellectual progeny at the University of Michigan. James Ford, a case in point, had been imbued with the cultural-evolutionary spirit after taking graduate courses from White in the 1930s. Although Ford never really understood what White was advocating (O'Brien and Lyman 1998), he continually cited him when needing to define culture or explain why culture changed. As we shall see shortly, Ford would come under some heavy criticism for his Whitean notions.

Ford might have been impressed with White's evolutionism, but Julian Steward certainly was not. Steward (Figure 1.9) did his graduate work under the guidance of Alfred Kroeber and Robert Lowie at Berkeley, and it is likely that Kroeber, who focused in part on the relationship between natural environmental zones and cultural types (e.g., Kroeber 1939), reinforced Steward's interest in the ecology of cultures (Clemmer and Myers 1999; Kerns 2003; Murphy 1970). Exposure to Kroeber and Lowie also would have reinforced any latent notions Steward had regarding the importance of particularistic history. (We review Steward's cultural ecology more fully in Chapter 3.)

Ignoring the point that White's evolutionism would have fit comfortably with that of Tylor, Morgan, and Spencer (whom Steward labeled "unilinear" evolutionists), Steward assigned the label "universal" evolutionism to White's work. This was Steward's way of keeping it both distinct and distant from his own brand of evolutionism, which he labeled "multilinear." Steward (1955:19) defined *multilinear evolutionism* as being interested "in particular cultures, but

FIGURE 1.9. *Right,* Julian Steward with unidentified Native American man (probably Louis Billy Prince, chief of the Stuart Lake Carrier Indians), Fort St. James, British Columbia, 1940. (Negative no. 56197, courtesy National Anthropological Archives, Smithsonian Institution.)

instead of finding local variations and diversity troublesome facts which force the frame of reference from the particular to the general, it deals only with those limited parallels of form, function, and sequence which have empirical validity." For Steward, the "local variations and diversity" were what mattered in evolution. Identifying them was the evolutionist's first step, followed closely by matching them to the physical environment in which they occurred.

Steward expected to find concordances between such things as technology and environment, irrespective of geographic region, but he also expected to find nonconcordances. These he viewed as multiple, more or less distinct solutions to similar adaptive problems—hence the term "multilinear evolution." It was the differences that needed explaining, and in Steward's view such explanations were beyond White's evolutionism. Steward (1960) was particularly clear about this in his review of White's (1959) *The Evolution of Culture.* Steward (1937:101) was not shy about admitting that many of his own ideas rested on notions of "economic determinism" and thus that history mattered tremendously. But he also sought what he called "cultural regularities," or laws, and spelled out three requirements for identifying regularities (Steward 1949:3): "(1) There must be a typology of cultures, patterns, and institutions.... (2) Causal interrelationships of types must be established in sequential or synchronic terms, or both.... [and] (3) The formulation of the independent recurrence of synchronic and/or sequential interrelationships of cultural phenomena is a scientific statement of cause and effect, regularities, or laws."

In Steward's view, laws of cultural processes, or simply cultural regularities, were detectable, but echoing his teachers, he said they should be built inductively. To illustrate what he meant, Steward (1949) offered a "trial formulation" of the development of civilizations in different areas of the world. To underscore that his formulation was based on multilinear evolutionism, he identified what he called "eras" and stated that these units "are not 'stages,' which in a world evolutionary scheme would apply equally to [all environments]. In these other kinds of areas, the functional interrelationship of subsistence patterns, population, settlements, social structure, cooperative work, warfare, and religion had distinctive forms and requires special formulations" (Steward 1949:23). Thus, his "eras" were decidedly different than Whitean cultural stages, at least in Steward's view. Eras were rank-ordered units that represented the process of cultural change and allowed cross-cultural comparison. In our view Steward's eras were *not* much different than White's stages.

Not surprisingly, given his emphasis on technology and the physical environment, Steward developed a strong following among archaeologists (e.g., Willey 1961; see Chapter 3). Unlike White, Steward spoke the archaeologist's language. His articles and monographs—especially *Basin-Plateau Aboriginal Sociopolitical Groups* (Steward 1938), which he finished while working for the Bureau of American Ethnology—were well known in archaeological circles before Steward moved to Columbia University in 1946 (Murphy 1977). Knowing more than a little about archaeology, Steward would have been sympathetic to the archaeologist's inferential needs, such as having relatively easy empirical access to technological and ecological aspects of culture (e.g., MacWhite 1956). Linking technology via ecology with society and ideology allowed one to climb up the inferential ladder (Chang 1967a) with some security—from technology, the most straightforward and closely tied to the material record; to subsistence and economy; to social and political organization; and finally to ideology, the most tenuous and farthest removed from the empirical record. By the time Steward moved to the University of Illinois in 1952, his name was synonymous with the Shoshoni and Northern Paiute Indians—a synonymy that in the succeeding decade would make Steward a significant figure in American archaeology. Toward the end of his career Steward began to have serious doubts about multilinear evolutionary theory with respect to its "analytic or explanatory value" (Manners 1973:886).

Cultural evolutionism was on a lot of people's minds in the 1950s (Carneiro 2003). Steward published *Theory of Cultural Change: The Methodology of Multilinear Evolution* in 1955, and White published *The Evolution of Culture: The Development of Civilization to the Fall of Rome* in 1959. Further, Marshall Sahlins and Elman Service edited *Evolution and Culture* (1960), which was geared toward reconciling the views of Steward and White, who were their mentors. Finally, the centennial celebration of Darwin's (1859) *On the Origin of Species* was an event marked by anthropologists as well as biologists. That celebration yielded two works that had significant impacts on anthropology: *Evolution and Anthropology: A Centennial Appraisal*, edited by Betty Meggers and published by the Anthropological Society of Washington (Meggers 1959), and the three-volume *Evolution after Darwin*, edited by Sol Tax and published by the University of Chicago Press (Tax 1960).

The Tax volumes contain papers from across the disciplinary spectrum—biology, anthropology, sociology, and history. Not only do the papers form a historical statement of where evolutionism was a century after Darwin, they also are a reminder of the pluralistic nature of the term "evolution" (Carneiro 2003). Biologists have their meanings, anthropologists have their own, and so on. With one exception, the Meggers volume is limited to contributions by anthropologists. She assembled specialists from all four traditional subdisciplines, together with Ernst Mayr, an architect of the "modern synthesis" in biology that united paleontologists, geneticists, and naturalists under the Darwinian banner (Huxley 1942). The chapters in the Meggers volume reveal a surprising diversity of views on evolution. They show that despite the fact that anthropologists of all persuasions were interested in applying evolutionary principles in their work, there was a distinct lack of consensus as to what those principles were and how they could be applied. Equally clear is that anthropologists still embraced a clear separation between organic evolution and cultural evolution, just as they had in the post-Boasian era.

In the lone article by an archaeologist in the Meggers volume, William Haag took a conservative approach to evolutionism, noting that "it is only reasonable to assume that the field in anthropology that can most profitably use evolutionism to arrive at [a] new height is archeology" (Haag 1959:105; see also Haag 1961). Haag had received his Ph.D. in ethnozoology at the University of Michigan, where he was greatly influenced by White. When Haag said that archaeology could profitably use evolutionism, he was referring to White's brand. Throughout the chapter Haag defended White against "errors" made by Steward in his criticism of Whitean evolution, pointing out that, in his opinion, Steward was more of a unilinear evolutionist than was any nineteenth-century evolutionist. Haag (1959:98) noted that Steward's brand of evolution was "quite adequate in its limited application and should be encouraged by emulation." There is nothing quite like damning with faint praise to make a point.

Another chapter in the Meggers volume is by Harvard ethnologist Clyde Kluckhohn. Based on the bulk of his writings, he is not usually considered an evolutionist, but it turns out that Kluckhohn had plenty to say about evolutionism. In fact, he was downright exuberant about its potential for advancing the goals of anthropology. He strongly advocated banning the "false biologic analogy," as Kroeber (1958:34) had put it, and "pressing parallels between different spheres" of inquiry (Kluckhohn 1959:154). He said that if there is "a certain orderliness in nature, it should not be surprising if some principles are found to prevail across the conventional boundaries of, say, biology, psychology, and culture. Indeed there is empirical evidence of still wider sweep. The same basic equation represents significant and similar relationships ranging from physics to economics...to linguistics...to biology...to culture" (Kluckhohn 1959:154).

It might appear as if Kluckhohn was suggesting that Darwinism is as appropriate a vehicle for examining language and culture as it is to examine the organic world. But that's not exactly what he was saying. The key words in the above quote are "similar relationships"; he did not say "identical relationships." A few paragraphs later, he states that "we should, on occasion, banish conceptual timidity and explore likenesses in process without regard for the traditional separation of disciplines" (Kluckhohn 1959:155). In using the terms "similar relationships" and "likenesses in process," Kluckhohn was saying that he viewed biological evolution and cultural evolution as *parallel* processes, not aspects of the same process. Cultural evolutionism was not much different in 1959 than it had been in the late nineteenth century.

This did not stop a few archaeologists from attempting to integrate one form or another of evolutionism into their analysis. Here we are not referring to instances of archaeologists paying lip service to evolutionism, but rather real efforts to use it as an explanatory framework. Betty Meggers (Figure 1.10) was one who throughout the 1950s and early '60s showed a continuing interest in applying White's evolutionism (Meggers 1954, 1960, 1961). Her main interest was in trying to discover correlations between subsistence practice, especially

FIGURE 1.10. Betty Meggers in her office at the National Museum of Natural History, 1972. (Courtesy Betty Meggers.)

agriculture, and social organization. In a volume honoring her former professor at Michigan, Meggers's essay called on White's law that energy capture (technology) exerts a strong influence on culture: "If agriculture is a significant culture-building force and environment is an important determinant of agricultural productivity, then it should be possible to find some correlation between the level of development that a particular culture has reached and the agricultural potential of the environment that it occupies" (Meggers 1960:306).

Cornell University ethnologist Morris Opler, in an article published in the *Southwestern Journal of Anthropology*, found Meggers's effort strained because it "assumed that every series of variations has evolutionary significance" (Opler 1961:7). But then Opler found anything vaguely resembling evolutionism strained, especially if it was derived from the work of Leslie White. Meggers was not a unique target for Opler, who made it his business to comment on various uses of evolutionism by misguided anthropologists. In 1962 James Ford produced a short training manual aimed at South American archaeologists, and in it he expounded his

view of culture. Ford asserted that anthropologists study culture, not people. Cultural forms, he continued, are not created by individuals; new forms—whether of social customs, religion, or pottery—can come only from preceding forms (Ford 1962). This statement, which obviously followed White's (1949) views, echoed one Ford had made more than a decade earlier in the published version of his dissertation: "It is understood that individuals do not 'create' ideas. The concept of 'free will' seems to have no place in science. Individuals receive ideas from other humans, sometimes combine them, less frequently discover them in the natural world about them, and almost always pass them along to others" (Ford 1949:38).

Opler (1963:902) characterized Ford's position as holding that "man has developed his enormous and intricate brain, his powers to remember and record the past, his abilities to probe the minute and the remote, his capacity for invention, communication, and planning, in order to remain a supermoron fit only to fetch and carry for Mother [Cultural] Evolution." That was an interesting turn of words: Mother Evolution—that sounds similar to what Russians call their homeland, which is exactly the effect Opler wanted. Opler was, to coin a word, a Marxaphobe. He saw the materialist hand of Karl Marx in everything White and his followers did.

In the same article in which Opler found Meggers's use of White's law strained, Opler tossed a hostile and vicious remark at her. As background, Meggers had defended White against Steward's (1953:318) assertion that "White's law of energy levels…can tell us nothing about the development of the characteristics of individual cultures." Of course it can't, replied Meggers, as White himself had noted: "the evolutionist's formulas…are not applicable to the culture history of tribes and *were not intended for this purpose*" (White 1945:346; emphasis added). Anthropologists and archaeologists to this day still fail to realize, as did Steward, that White *knew* his brand of evolutionism had nothing to do with the "culture history of tribes," as he put it. He was interested *only* in the evolution of culture, not specific cultures. As Eric Wolf (1960:150) put it when reviewing White's 1949 book *The Science of Culture*, "in White's terms, the study of the process of [natural] selection [working on individual cultures] would be history; the evolutionist would concern himself only with the construction of a *genealogy of forms*."

Recognizing, as she phrased it, the "unanimity" of opinion between Steward and White over what White's evolutionism could not do (and was not intended to do), Meggers (1960:302) had made the apparently innocent remark that "the effect of such unanimity has been to remove evolutionary theory from the practical tool kit of the field anthropologist to the high plane of philosophical discussion." Here, we think, Meggers was concerned that Steward's brand of evolutionism was eclipsing White's brand for the very reason White had stated: his evolutionism had absolutely nothing to do with the "culture history of tribes." This gave it an ethereal feel, whereas Steward's multilinear evolutionism was something anyone could get their arms around and use. The purpose of Meggers's paper was to rescue "evolutionary theory" (she meant White's brand) from the high plane and to show how it could "be used as a guide in understanding the dynamics of individual cultures" (Meggers 1960:302). This was clever phrasing on Meggers's part, as she was attempting to show that White's evolutionism had real-world, on-the-ground applications. Steward's evolutionism, if we read between Meggers's lines, was not a theory. White's evolutionism, however, *was* a theory, and it could in fact be used to explain individual cases.

In commenting on her use of White's law, Opler (1961:13) stated that "apparently the 'practical tool kit' Dr. Meggers urges upon the field of anthropologists is not quite so new as she represents, and its main contents seem to be a somewhat shopworn hammer and sickle" (Opler 1961:13). This was a particularly insensitive, even stupid remark to make, especially given the general mood in America at the time. Opler, however, had waited a long time

to get back at Meggers for what he felt was a deliberate slight on her part fifteen years earlier when she failed to cite some of his work (Meggers 1946; see also Opler 1946 and especially Peace and Price 2003). Opler now saw a chance to put the knife in Meggers and White simultaneously.

Not even a decade earlier, much of the nation's attention had been centered on the hunt for suspected Communists, first by the House Un-American Activities Committee, then by Joseph McCarthy's Senate Permanent Subcommittee on Investigations. Anthropologists were not immune from the witch hunt (Nader 1997), and when Opler penned his remark in 1961, the wounds in anthropology were still raw from the outcome of the hearings. A number of anthropologists had come under fire for their alleged connections to the Communist Party, and several were fired by their home institutions as a result, including Morris Swadesh from City College of New York and Gene Weltfish from Columbia. Some of the rawness of the wounds was created by the fact that while this was going on, the American Anthropological Association sat on its hands and did nothing to support its members who were under suspicion (Price 1997).

Aside from the inappropriateness of the remark, Opler knew that it didn't apply to what White, much less Meggers, was advocating. In the article baiting Meggers, Opler went on at length to show that in tracing their evolutionary genealogy to Tylor and Morgan, White and his followers conveniently skipped over several generations of Marxist thinkers, including Marx and Engels. Tellingly, on Opler's list of Marxist thinkers were Vladimir Lenin and Joseph Stalin, two of the most feared individuals of the twentieth century. It did not trouble Opler that this made no sense intellectually. The "tenor" of White's theory might have been Marxist (Layton 1997), and he might have been a member of the Socialist Labor Party (Peace and Price 2001; Shankman and Dino 2001), but White wasn't a Marxist. There actually was very little of Karl Marx in anything White ever wrote. White talked about the three tiers of technology, society, and ideology, but he never discussed, at least in any incisive manner, the control of labor, unequal access to resources, or a dialectic between environment and the three tiers of culture. And if there was no dialectical materialism, then how could it legitimately be called Marxist? Opler, who had been a student of White's at the University of Buffalo in the late 1920s, was, as Marvin Harris (1968b:637) put it, "one of the relatively few figures in anthropology who may be reckoned as well-acquainted with Marxist theory." Opler thus knew that there was not a trace of dialectical materialism in White's work. He was simply red-baiting.

As long as one lumped White in with Lenin and Stalin, why not go further and add Nikolai Bukharin to the mix? Opler did. But putting Bukharin on the same list with Marx, Engels, and Lenin made about as much sense as putting White on it. Bukharin was a man whom Lenin (in his December 1922 bedside "testament") called an important theorist, but someone who never fully understood the dialectic. Opler undoubtedly knew of Lenin's remark, so why would he list Bukharin? Either Opler disagreed with Lenin, which we doubt, or he wanted to hang yet another red ornament on Leslie White's genealogical tree, with no regard for whether it actually belonged there.

Opler's remarks were met with outrage by some, and Meggers received numerous supportive comments from her colleagues, several of whom also wrote Leslie Spier, the editor of the *Southwestern Journal of Anthropology,* to register their complaint about the article's tone (Peace and Price 2003). Meggers responded to Opler, but she took the high road, again pointing out that the sole reason for writing the article was "because it seemed to me that too much attention is paid to talking about theory, defining terms, and tracing the history of ideas, and too little is devoted to seeing if or how theories work" (Meggers 1961:353). This more or less ended the Opler-Meggers affair, although Opler continued his jabs at White (e.g., Opler 1962), even labeling him as anti-Semitic (Peace and Price 2003). Meggers

emerged from the affair unblemished. She would go on to more controversies, but these would be over strictly archaeological matters, such as the hypothesized movement of prehistoric people and pottery from Japan to Ecuador (Meggers and Evans 1962; Meggers, Evans, and Estrada 1965). Professionally, White fared well, too. The generally favorable reception that his ideas on culture and cultural evolution received during the 1950s presaged their reception in archaeology during the 1960s and '70s.

There is a footnote to the White-Meggers-Opler affair. The first issue of the *American Anthropologist* for 1962 listed as "president-elect" of the American Anthropological Association "Morris E. Opler, Cornell University, Ithaca, N.Y." We wondered if perhaps Opler's 1961 article had come out after members had voted on officers, or at least during the voting period, but it didn't happen that way. The article came out in the first issue of the year, being in fact the lead article in that issue. Balloting for society officers took place later in the year, just prior to the November meeting. By that time members would have read or heard about the controversy. Our guess is that many of them undoubtedly supported Opler, at least in private, or they didn't care one way or the other.

But that's only half the footnote. In the first issue of the *American Anthropologist* for 1963, in the line directly beneath the one listing Opler as president of the AAA, was the name of the new president-elect: "Leslie A. White, University of Michigan, Ann Arbor, Mich." In retrospect, it seems ironic that the leading anthropological society in the United States would be led, in back-to-back years, by one of the most right-leaning anthropologists in the country and then by one of the most left-leaning. Or maybe this was not as ironic as it seems. Perhaps it was just a classic example, albeit on a tiny scale, of the dialectic that so fascinated Marx and Engels. Regardless, the tug of war between right and left being felt in the AAA would, in a few years, extend to almost every corner of American culture.

Two people who did not join the movement toward evolutionism in anthropology during the 1950s were Gordon Willey and Philip Phillips, who made no mention of Leslie White in *Method and Theory in American Archaeology*. They did mention Julian Steward but focused strictly on the classification scheme he had developed a decade earlier for Middle America and the Andes (Steward 1948). Steward defined six "periods," which Willey and Phillips correctly pointed out were better thought of as "developmental stages," despite Steward's (1949) protestations to the contrary. They then worked out a similar classification for the entire Western Hemisphere, naming their "stages" Early Lithic, Archaic, Formative, Classic, and Postclassic. Willey and Phillips stated that theirs was not an effort to explain the archaeological record but rather an attempt to structure what was known about it. They also were careful to point out that their classification was in no sense an evolutionary one, although they could see where the reader might think it mirrored Steward's multilinear evolutionism.

Evolution, whether biological or cultural, entails change, and to measure it one needs very specific kinds of units. Willey and Phillips knew this, and they also knew that Americanists had not done a particularly good job of creating units of change, although it wasn't for lack of trying. Their own system provided a means of classifying archaeological phenomena, but it did not enable the measurement of culture change in any way other than the traditional one of stacking up in columns and arranging in rows prehistoric cultures called "phases." This procedure created units that were internally homogeneous, thus implying cultural stasis within the spatiotemporal coordinates of the units, and forcing virtually all change into the borders defining the units (Plog 1973a, 1973b, 1974). Change was no longer continuous, as Jim Ford had envisioned it; rather, it was discontinuous and occurred only between periods of stasis of varying duration.

This concept sounded like what Kroeber and others had espoused so many decades earlier. In sum, the cultural units archaeologists created may have reflected actual periods of stasis and events of change, but given how they were created, it was virtually impossible to test if that was the case or if change had been more or less continuous. Whatever the case, it was the construction of spatiotemporal frameworks—what processualists would later somewhat inaccurately refer to as "descriptive" models—more than attempting to understand why those frameworks looked the way they did that occupied the energies of culture historians. Many of them were content with such work, but virtually from the beginning some were not.

THE SEEDS OF DISCONTENT

Units that allowed the segregation of formal variation in artifacts across the spatiotemporal dimensions had been designed and used by culture historians since the second decade of the twentieth century. Willey and Phillips wrote *Method and Theory in American Archaeology* to reduce the number of units and to specify the analytical utility of the few that remained. But the overarching reason was to nudge archaeologists out of their singular focus on time, space, and form and into an emphasis on the processes that produced the archaeological record. The cultural processes Willey and Phillips had in mind were none other than the "diffusion-migration-invention" ones of their predecessors. But they also wanted more: they wanted archaeologists to consider the "cultural and social aspects" of the archaeological record (Willey and Phillips 1958:6). Thus, for Willey and Phillips, it was time to move beyond the description of artifact forms and distributions and to try to discern their anthropological implications.

Was this nudging on the part of Willey and Phillips something new? Hardly. Although the bulk of archaeological effort was directed toward answering the what, where, and when questions, the literature makes it clear that these were only the most basic goals held by many archaeologists working between 1915 and 1950. American archaeologists fully subscribed to ethnologist Roland B. Dixon's dictum that "archeology is but prehistoric ethnology and ethnography" (Dixon 1913:558), but their efforts often fell short. Julian Steward and Frank

Setzler (1938) noted the general failure of archaeologists to interpret their data in terms of problems that were broad enough to be useful to the student of culture. Not surprisingly, given Steward's interests in human interaction with the physical environment, they hoped for more discussion of subsistence and the relationship of the archaeologically represented culture to the physical environment. They also hoped for interpretations of artifacts in terms of their functional roles in the configuration of human behavior and activity, arguing that "surely we can shed some light not only on chronological and spatial arrangements and associations of [cultural] elements, but on conditions underlying their origin, development, diffusion, acceptance and interaction with one another. These are problems of cultural process" (Steward and Setzler 1938:7).

Similar pleas were made a few years later by John Bennett, who started out professionally as an archaeologist but switched to ethnology. Bennett (1943) believed, incorrectly we think, that efforts to reconstruct cultural dynamics from artifacts were not favorably received by many archaeologists. He believed that if archaeologists would pay as much attention to an artifact's function as they did to its date of manufacture, they would be aligning their discipline more closely with ethnology. A few years later, Bennett suggested that one reason archaeologists avoided making inferences about cultural dynamics was that archaeology, "of all 'sciences,' must guard against speculative theory and imaginative hypotheses, since archaeology is the most profoundly 'historical' science of all, the discipline in which conclusion is most closely bound to the actual perceptible, touchable, countable evidence" (Bennett 1946:198). This, we think, is a more accurate statement than what Bennett had expressed a few years earlier. Archaeologists were *hesitant* to make inferences about cultural dynamics, not hostile to the idea. A similar sentiment was present in paleontology, a sister discipline of archaeology that is also—in Bennett's terms—a "profoundly historical science" (Jepsen, Mayr, and Simpson 1949). Why should these two historical disciplines allegedly be so hesitant to write theory and test hypotheses?

Bennett (1946) blamed the reticence on an empirical tendency in archaeology, which he attributed to the interest in trait lists and trait-element studies of Kroeber and his associates at the University of California, Berkeley. Archaeology had been firmly entrenched in empiricism long before Kroeber and his students and colleagues began producing the culture-element distribution lists (e.g., Klimek 1935; Kroeber 1936). Further, archaeologists of the 1930s and 1940s *were* fascinated with trait lists, the construction of which was central to anthropological methods of historical ethnology (Lyman and O'Brien 2003a). Bennett suggested that any theory of historical continuity subscribed to, if only implicitly, by archaeologists using those methods was in no sense proved but was simply a good working hypothesis that allowed inferences about the past to be made. Similarly, any theory of culture involving the differences between folk and urban societies (e.g., Redfield 1947) "permits inferences about the meaning of archaeological remains because it assumes that culture objects have some structural relation to the culture and society producing them" (Bennett 1946:200). The gist of Bennett's remarks would be echoed a few years later by Willey and Phillips, and slightly later by Binford and the processualists.

Bennett was not the only critic of archaeologists' seeming preoccupation with trait lists and the like. Writing a few years before Bennett, Clyde Kluckhohn, another archaeologist-turned-anthropologist, similarly noted the reluctance of archaeologists to translate their data into something an ethnologist could appreciate. Kluckhohn (1939, 1940) suggested two reasons for this hesitancy. First, archaeologists feared that they would be shown to be wrong, and second, such conjectures were antithetical to the inductive historical approach that most archaeologists (and paleontologists) followed. This was, strictly speaking, an accurate assessment; archaeologists—like all historians and scientists—do work inductively at least some of the time (Chapter 4).

FIGURE 1.11. Walter Taylor, Carbondale, Illinois, 1971. (Courtesy Southern Illinois University Photo Service and Jon Muller.)

During much of the first half of the twentieth century, culture historians were laboring to write culture history and construct cultural chronologies, and here they worked both inductively and deductively as they tested, corrected, and refined the spatiotemporal distributions of their cultural units. But Kluckhohn leaped to the incorrect conclusion that ethnological conjectures were antithetical to archaeologists. To the contrary, they had long been interested in ethnological issues. They were, after all, anthropologists first and archaeologists second, but most of them chose not to focus primarily on ethnological issues unless they were historical in nature. At the time, history was still seen more as an idiographic discipline rather than a nomothetic one. One could speak of history as a science of individual things characterized by a uniqueness in space and time, and increasingly historians were seeking historical synthesis and generalization. But the problem was that "causality in history is infinitely complex, and it is this fact which explains why history had such difficulty in constituting itself as a science" (Berr and Febvre 1932:361).

It seems to us that culture historians bought into this distinction because their anthropologist teachers had bought into it (Lyman and O'Brien 2004a).

Kluckhohn's comments had minimal impact on American archaeology, but the same cannot be said of a lengthy critique made by one of his Harvard doctoral students, Walter Taylor (Figure 1.11). Taylor's pointed remarks formed a large part of his dissertation, which appeared in 1943 and was later published jointly by the Society for American Archaeology and the American Anthropological Association as *A Study of Archeology* (Taylor 1948). Taylor urged his colleagues to be more anthropological, but he departed from Kluckhohn in how he delivered his argument. Whereas Kluckhohn merely patronized archaeologists, Taylor lambasted them—at least some of them, including some of the most prominent. In so doing he did not make the logical error Kluckhohn had by asserting that archaeologists were not interested in ethnological issues. Rather, Taylor said that understanding culture was an important goal of archaeology—or so one would gather from what archaeologists said. Taylor concluded, however, that what archaeologists said and what they actually did were entirely different.

It was one thing for Taylor to take on his peers in print, but it was another to take on the likes of Alfred Kidder, who at the time probably was the most respected figure in American archaeology, and James Griffin (Figure 1.12), who had developed an outstanding reputation in eastern United States archaeology. Taylor wrote this about Griffin's work:

[O]n a number of occasions [Griffin] has either stated or implied that the ultimate aim of archeological investigation is to reconstruct the life of the past. But it is difficult to credit him with anything more than lip service to these ideals. Time and time again he has failed to make use of the data at hand, to synthesize into any sort of picture the information gathered from a site or area, to abstract from the material objects their meaning for the life of their former possessors, to

FIGURE I.12. James Griffin, Phoenix, Arizona, 1988. (Photograph by Thomas Holland.)

Despite such remarks by establishment archaeologists, the few who bothered to respond to Taylor (1948) (e.g., Burgh 1950) dismissed his arguments altogether. As Richard Woodbury (1954:293) put it in one of the few published reviews of *A Study of Archeology*, "it hardly seems a justifiable procedure to condemn a scholar, in archaeology or in any other field, because his accomplishments fall short of his ambition." And Taylor had certainly condemned Kidder, Griffin, Emil Haury, and several other prominent prehistorians. Those archaeologists who entered graduate school after World War II did not feel the sting of Taylor's critique as had their mentors, and it seems that more than a few of the younger generation found Taylor to be inspirational. Lew Binford (1972b:2) referred to the used copy of Taylor's book that he bought and that "still sits on my book shelf—full of stratified marginal notes, reflecting something of the changes in my thinking since 1955."

interpret in terms of broad categories such as subsistence and social groupings the information from archeological materials. He has consistently failed to follow up leads which might have led him to some significant information concerning the life of the people and has been content merely to investigate factors of taxonomic, i.e., comparative, significance. (Taylor 1948:81)

These were bold accusations coming from someone just out of graduate school, and as one can imagine, Taylor's comments were not received warmly. Despite the valid parts of his critique, many archaeologists chose not to acknowledge them, at least in print. Perhaps most ironically, when published in 1948, Taylor's remarks came at a time when some archaeologists were thinking about questions other than what, where, and when. Gordon Willey, for example, had earlier noted that once chronological matters had been dealt with, one should attempt to "give [them] flesh and body in the form of a full and 'functional' culture description" (Willey and Woodbury 1942:236).

But *A Study of Archeology* was more than critique: it was Taylor's (1948:93–94) introduction of the "conjunctive approach" as a means of turning archaeology into prehistoric ethnology, defining the method as "the elucidation of cultural conjunctives, the associations and relationships, the 'affinities,' *within* the manifestation under study. It aims at drawing the completest possible picture of past life in terms of its human and geographical environment. It is chiefly interested in the relation of item to item, trait to trait, complex to complex...*within* the culture-unit represented and only subsequently in the taxonomic relation of these phenomena to similar ones outside of it." In other words, the conjunctive approach looked primarily at the inner workings of a culture unit and only secondarily at how it might relate to other culture units in a taxonomic framework. It was an attempt to transfer the still-trendy British functionalism into archaeological practice, but Taylor offered little guidance, much less any concrete methods, for how to carry out the conjunctive approach.

Binford (1965) would later point out that Taylor's approach rested on the aquatic theory of culture. In our view, Taylor gave that theory a much clearer expression than anyone else writing between 1920 and 1960. The important point is that the conjunctive approach rested on an ontology no different than traditional culture-historical archaeology. Perhaps for this reason, Woodbury and others made the obvious gambit of requesting a concrete example of how Taylor's proposed panacea would allow archaeology to attain the loftier goal of understanding the operation of extinct cultural systems. Taylor never produced one, although he intended to use his decade-long study of sites in northern Mexico as an example. Taylor's failure to produce a case study was, in our view, hardly a reason to ignore his suggestions, many of which anticipated those of the processualists (Chapter 2).

As a footnote, the backlash to Taylor's scathing and unmerciful critique of American archaeology (and archaeologists) did not preclude his obtaining a job. He was hired by Southern Illinois University at Carbondale in 1958 to develop a department of anthropology (Euler 1997). He had very few doctoral students over the years—five is the number we've heard—and in that respect he did not have much of an impact on archaeology. But he didn't need it. No one else in the history of American archaeology has had, or likely will ever have, as big an impact with a single publication. In terms of the intellectual strategies we mentioned in the introduction, what Taylor did certainly worked, but it came at a pretty hefty price in terms of bitter feelings between Taylor and many of his colleagues.

Bitter memories sometimes die hard. In 1985, at the fiftieth annual meeting of the Society for American Archaeology in Denver, a panel of distinguished archaeologists reminisced in front of a packed house about how the discipline had changed over the years. Jerry Sabloff, the moderator, innocently asked if any panel members cared to comment on the furor that Taylor's monograph had created forty years earlier. Several panelists made critical remarks, and Griffin, whom Taylor had berated so pointedly, snapped, "Harvard never should have given him a degree." A few seconds later, Walter Taylor got up from his seat, which was toward the front of the ballroom, walked down the aisle, and left the room. He never again attended an SAA meeting. Taylor was seventy-two at the time, and Griffin, eighty.

Griffin undoubtedly would not have subscribed to Patty Jo Watson's (1983:x) suggestion that Taylor's motive in writing *A Study of Archeology* was "not to generate ill will but rather to stimulate examination...of aims, goals and purposes by American archaeologists." Nor, we suspect, would Griffin have taken Taylor at his word when he stated in the foreword to the fourth printing of his book that he still believed that the critique was "of archeological theory and practice, not of men" and was as "fair as I could make it" (Taylor 1968:2).

Regardless of Taylor's motive, which we will never really know, his message was beginning to resonate. *A Study of Archeology* captured more attention than it might have otherwise because of its confrontational tone, but Taylor's invitation to make archaeology more anthropological was not original. Nor would the invitation end with him. In one of the more quoted phrases from the preprocessual days, Philip Phillips, paraphrasing Roland Dixon's (1913) earlier comment, remarked in 1955 that "New World archaeology is anthropology or it is nothing" (Phillips 1955:246–247). Willey and Phillips (1958:2) repeated that sentence in their book, and Binford (1962a) used it in the opening sentence of his seminal paper, "Archaeology as Anthropology." This statement more than any other fuels our sense that by the early 1950s there existed a general restlessness in American archaeology. By that time extensive surveys had located thousands of sites, untold numbers of sites had been sampled, millions of artifacts had been placed into types, and numerous cultural chronologies had been built. Archaeologists, trained as anthropologists, were tired of the same old ends and saw anthropology as providing an avenue to something new.

To make archaeology anthropological, one *had* to study culture and its processes. Joseph Caldwell, of the Illinois State Museum, underscored that point in a *Science* paper, "The New American Archaeology," published a year after Willey and Phillips's book. Caldwell (1959:304) noted that the new archaeology was "tending to be more concerned with culture process and less concerned with the descriptive content of prehistoric cultures," which he labeled "dull and uninteresting." Caldwell's message wasn't news to most archaeologists. They had long believed that culture processes were important, but they typically used the traditional diffusionist sorts of cultural processes while erecting a basic time-space framework of cultural forms (e.g., Meggers 1955). At the time, these processes were still largely the ones many ethnologists discussed (e.g., Murdock 1956; Spindler and Spindler 1959). What, then, made Caldwell's "new archaeology" so new?

ON THE EVE OF PROCESSUAL ARCHAEOLOGY

The 1950s witnessed an increasing number of efforts to understand the social systems represented by extinct cultures. Some of these were commonsensical, such as Albert Spaulding's (1952:262) suggestion that the elaborately constructed Adena burial mounds in the Ohio Valley contained the remains of individuals of "great prestige," whereas other individuals were simply cremated and buried in place. William Sears (1954, 1958), an expert on the southeastern United States, was more explicit about the potential social, ceremonial, and ritualistic meanings of the covariant associations of artifacts, elements of tomb construction, and earthen mounds at sites along the Gulf Coast. Other scholars sought different sorts of social information from the archaeological record. Paul Martin and John Rinaldo (1950) studied community-pattern data in the Southwest and drew up a developmental history of possible social structures based on change in such characteristics as room size, settlement size, and distributions of functional classes of artifacts.

Gordon Willey (Figure 1.13) himself had recently produced what can be considered the first systematic study of settlement patterns, noting that the Virú Valley, Peru, project involved "the study of human adaptation to the valley environment over a long period of time" (Willey 1953b:xvii). In a masterful stroke, Willey (1953b:1) made legitimate the study of how human settlements were distributed across the landscape when he argued that "settlement patterns are, to a large extent, directly shaped by widely held cultural needs, [and so] offer a strategic starting point for the functional interpretation of archeological cultures."

A few years later, K. C. Chang (1958:298) sought to "work out an outline of objective procedure which will allow the archeological skeleton to regain its ethnological flesh and blood." He advocated "world-wide cross-cultural survey" rather than simplistic ethnographic analogies, and was inspired by Willey's settlement-pattern work to seek "some correlation between the settlement pattern of a dwelling site and the social grouping of its occupants" (Chang 1958:298). His goal was to identify prehistoric social units such as households and communities, and he urged that archaeologists do this "rather than identify archeological regions and areas by time-spacing material traits, since cultural traits are mean-

FIGURE 1.13. Gordon Willey, Virú Valley, Peru, 1946. (Courtesy Gordon Willey.)

ingless unless described in their social context" (Chang 1958:324).

In an article on social and religious systems, Sears (1961) made several points that anticipated nearly verbatim many statements that would appear later in the 1960s. First, he argued that different categories of evidence were required for different sorts of information on prehistoric social organization, and that collecting the various information would require different field techniques. Second, he noted that inferences and reconstructions derived from one class of data must be verified and correlated with those from other classes. In more modern terms, multiple lines of evidence and patterned covariation of variables would help confirm a hypothesis. Third, fieldwork should be guided by a problem so that the artifacts and contextual information collected are appropriate to the questions at hand. A feature such as a burial mound, for example, should be excavated and analyzed "as a fossilized ceremony rather than as a repository for pots, sherds, and bones" (Sears 1961:227). Finally, Sears stated that he believed the study of processes of change was archaeology's most important goal. Similar statements would echo this rallying cry of processual archaeology.

Commentators on Sears's article, as is often the case for articles given the unique treatment that *Current Anthropology* affords, were equally divided in the sense of favoring or finding fault with his arguments. Some suggested that to accomplish what Sears advocated required the use of what became known as ethnoarchaeology (Chapters 5 and 7)—using modern ethnographic analogues to interpret the past. Several commentators noted that there appeared to be two goals of archaeological research. One, the historical goal, was readily identifiable; the other, the processual goal, was not so distinct. Sears was advocating the second goal, but he was simultaneously not advocating abandoning the first. This was a point with which all commentators seemed to agree, regardless of whether they thought the second goal was attainable. Sears again displayed remarkable prescience in his response to the commentators. His last sentence reads, in part, "there is no substitute for the use of the scientific method, applied through the theories and bodies of information which have been developed by cultural anthropology and through the techniques which are part of the stock in trade of a trained archaeologist" (Sears 1961:245).

Another sign that something new was afoot in American archaeology during the late 1950s was that Robert Ehrich found it necessary not only to inform his European colleagues, in a European journal (Ehrich 1961), of the uniquely American relationship between anthropology and archaeology but also to publish very similar remarks in a leading American journal (Ehrich 1963). In those two papers, Ehrich mirrors the comments of others who indicated that American archaeology minimally had two goals. The first was a historical one aimed at reconstructing the "actual history of cultural development both in general and in particular instances and to gain an understanding of the laws and processes which may be involved." The second goal was a nonhistorical one aimed at studying the "actual functioning of individual cultures [and] the interrelationships of their parts" (Ehrich 1961:623, 1963:16). He referred to the latter as "paleoethnography" and suggested that one might compare sequences of historical development and paleoethnographies "to derive principles of culture change"—what he referred to as "paleoethnology" (Ehrich 1961:624, 1963:18). Paleoethnography and paleoethnology were done by means of ethnographic analogy. Ehrich cautioned against making too simplistic an analogy because, if anything, ethnographic data suggested there were no clear-cut, immutable correlations between, say, aspects of social organization and subsistence base.

Julian Steward had also advocated a cautious position when he discussed cultural variation, pointing out that sometimes there were concordances between cultures—distinct cultures arriving at similar solutions to similar ecological or adaptive problems—but other times there weren't. Had Ehrich pointed to a potential problem with Whitean cultural evolutionism? Maybe, but certainly not to White, who consistently maintained that he was interested in the evolution of culture, not in the evolution of cultures. Cultural variation from a historical perspective held no interest for White. Cultural variation of a functional sort, however, *was* of considerable interest to White and would become one of the phenomena many processualists would seek to study and understand (Chapter 2).

These cases are not just a few selected ones favored by a few individuals. The discipline as a whole seemed to be restless, as evidenced by the fact that the Society for American Archaeology sponsored, with substantial financial assistance from the Carnegie Corporation of New York, a series of seminars in 1955 on various topics such as culture contact, culture stability, and types of community patterning. As Robert Wauchope (1956:v) noted in the preface to the volume resulting from the seminars, "I sometimes wonder whether the Corporation actually had confidence in the intellectual curiosity of archaeologists or whether they just wanted to see how stupid we really were, for over the past twenty years or so the stereotype of the American archaeologist has somehow come to be a pretty dull sort of clod, with most of his gray matter under his fingernails." One reviewer of the volume, highly respected anthropologist Edmund Spicer (1957:186), noted that it reflected "the growing effort to utilize archaeological data in the general understanding of cultural processes." Another remarked that all of the "participants have attempted to probe the limits of archeological inference, as it can contribute to or extend culture theory, derived largely from ethnological sources" (Siegel 1957:925). To us, if not to some of Wauchope's contemporaries, it appears that archaeologists in the 1950s also had gray matter between their ears.

Between about 1915 and 1950, most Americanists spent their time documenting formal, temporal, and spatial variation in the archaeological record. Although critics such as Walter Taylor argued that archaeologists had divorced themselves from anthropology, this was not entirely true. Archaeologists never surrendered the belief that their discipline was a special form of ethnology and thus could contribute to general anthropological theory. They wanted to be more than simply the tail on "an ethnological kite" (Steward 1942:341), but they were unsure of how to do that. Knowing that they had access to the entire time span of human cultures, they also appreciated that the materials they collected varied tremendously in age. Thus the first order of business was to gain control of the temporal dimension, after which they could attend to other issues such as social and political organization. Interest in such issues is evident in the early settlement-pattern studies strongly influenced by Gordon Willey's work in Peru (Chapter 3).

Not surprisingly, many early attempts at "paleoethnography" (Ehrich 1961, 1963) were problematic. Some efforts rested on ethnographic analogy, which as a basic method in the archaeologist's tool kit underwent some evolution and diversification itself (Lyman and O'Brien 2001c). The direct historical approach had been underpinned by what were termed "specific historical analogs"; cultures that were viewed as evolutionary descendants of the archaeological culture under scrutiny were used as the source of interpretive analogues. That practice changed in the 1950s when archaeologists added "general comparative analogues" to their tool kit (Chapters 5 and 7). These could be any ethnographically documented culture that occupied a similar environment and had a similar level of technology to the archaeological culture under study. Not by coincidence, Julian Steward's multilinear evolutionism became a popular approach, and his study of the Shoshoni and Northern Paiute (Steward 1938) became the source of a widely used, general comparative analogue (Chapter 3). This loosening of the restrictions on the acceptability of interpretive sources produced not only a "new analogy" (Ascher 1961a) but also a growing interest in experimental archaeology (Chapter

5). Both sources of interpretive models would come to play critical roles in the 1960s as processual archaeology arrived on the scene.

By 1960 the number of universities producing anthropologists specializing in archaeology was growing, up from the handful that had produced most of the Ph.D.s up to that point. It is difficult to say whether this contributed in any direct way to the growing pluralism in archaeology, but if nothing else that growth expanded the job market. This, in turn, meant more professors in the classroom, which meant archaeologists came into contact with more students. This meant there were more minds to shape and more potential acolytes for anyone charismatic enough to take advantage of the situation. One such person was Lew Binford, who had some concrete ideas about how to save archaeology from itself. As we will see in Chapter 2, he would pick up plenty of help along the way.

2

A New Perspective in Arch(a)eology

Indeed, there is so much wonderful new research going on in the Southwest that it is difficult to keep up with it all. I am so encouraged and excited by all these new directions. Whatever the impact of the small beginnings that we started in the New Archaeology so many years ago, I am overjoyed to have been able to witness the astounding growth in Southwestern archaeology over these forty years.

—WILLIAM A. LONGACRE, "Exploring Prehistoric Social and Political Organization in the American Southwest"

Bill Longacre (Figure 2.1) was too modest when he referred to the "small beginnings" that he and other "new archaeologists" started in the Southwest back in the 1960s. No other region saw more sustained activity by processualists than the Southwest, and no processualist had a greater impact on Southwestern archaeology than Longacre. There was nothing about Arizona or New Mexico that held a special attraction for Longacre and his processualist colleagues; they worked there because the region offered fieldwork and employment opportunities. For Longacre, his so-called small beginnings can be traced to his graduate years at the University of Chicago, which by all accounts (e.g., Longacre 1998) had an aura of intellectual excitement in the late 1950s and early '60s. Having studied social anthropology as an

undergraduate at the University of Illinois, Longacre was perhaps more receptive than most to the new archaeology's mission to make the discipline more anthropological.

The list of archaeology graduate students at Chicago during that period is impressive. As Longacre (2000) tells it, in his cohort were James Brown, Kent Flannery, Leslie Freeman, James Hill, Stuart Struever, and Robert Whallon. And, of course, Sally Schanfield—who would become Sally Binford (Figure 2.2)—was there, researching the Middle Paleolithic with Clark Howell. A younger cohort included Margaret Hardin, John Fritz, and Fred Plog, and an older one included Patty Jo Watson (Figure 2.3) and Frank Hole (Figure 2.4) For all practical purposes we can add Lewis Binford to the older cohort. Binford joined the anthropology faculty at Chicago in 1961, three years before receiving his Ph.D. from the University of Michigan. He was only a year or two older than Hole and Watson, and they all had had roughly the same amount of field training. This was a group of smart people, four of whom—Binford, Flannery, Hole, and Watson—were later elected to the National Academy of Sciences, arguably the most prestigious scientific body in the world.[1] This collective of Chicago graduate students would be the first to take up the label "new archaeologists," or simply "processualists."

FIGURE 2.1. William Longacre at Chodistaas Pueblo, Arizona, 1978. (Negative no. 55606, courtesy Arizona State Museum.)

The stated goal of the new archaeology was to study cultural processes and to contribute to anthropological theory. As detailed in Chapter 1, this was not a new idea, although few processualists pointed that out. Like their predecessors, they understood that cultural processes, which are dynamic phenomena, are represented by a static archaeological record. New archaeologists argued that getting at those processes required two things. First, the basic notion of culture had to be retooled from a normative, idea-based concept to one that was behavioral, systemic, and materialist. Second, archaeology had to be conducted scientifically, which to some processualists meant working deductively rather than inductively, and using ethnographic analogy in a rigorous manner.

The inductive approach came to be equated, wrongly, with an archaeology that began and ended with rote descriptions of artifacts and assemblages (Chapter 4). These mundane exercises that created the "facts" of the archaeological record were taken to typify "traditional archaeology"—the archaeology that Joseph Caldwell in his "New American Archaeology" paper in *Science* (1959:304) had labeled "dull and uninteresting" (Chapter 1). Inductive

archaeology often was slow and tedious because, according to the processualists (e.g., Binford 1968a; Deetz 1970; Longacre 1970a, 1970b, 2000), traditionalists had to await the accumulation of sufficient data for the facts to speak for themselves. But as the impatient processualists pointed out, no accumulation of facts, no matter how large, could speak unless the archaeologist asked processual questions and designed deductively structured research to answer them.

In pushing the agenda for quicker results written in anthropological terms, the processualists were both loud and demanding, heaping scorn on the traditionalists for their views on culture and the scientific method. The traditionalists responded (e.g., Bayard 1969; Kushner 1970), but the "young turks," as Flannery (1973a) referred to his cohort of processualists a decade later, kept up the pressure. And it *was* pressure as opposed to polite discourse, often coupled with an "I'm-better-than-you-are" attitude.

We remember attending national meetings in the 1970s and witnessing the swagger of the processualists—the "Mafia," as Binford

FIGURE 2.2. Lewis and Sally Binford at a UCLA Halloween party, 1966. (Courtesy Lewis Binford.)

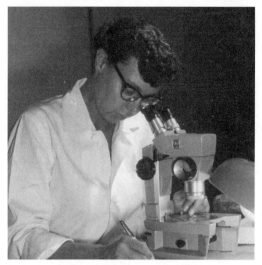

FIGURE 2.3. Patty Jo Watson in the basement of the Oriental Institute, University of Chicago, 1967. (Courtesy Patty Jo Watson.)

work to dress them up, are not particularly relevant to discussions of poverty, segregation, or war in Southeast Asia. The nation was in the mood for change, and in some instances people didn't much care where it came from. Increasingly, novelty was something to be prized, and last year's model was quickly replaced by this year's.

This push for novelty went for people, too. The catch phrase of the '60s came from Berkeley activist Mario Savio, who said, "You can't trust anyone over thirty." This was nothing more than one man's view of the well-publicized generation gap in American society. Savio was the same person who said the following to demonstrators before they entered the University of California's Sproul Hall to begin their sit-in in December 1964: "There is a time when

(1972b:13) reported they were called—as they made their way along, encumbered by students and other acolytes vying for their attention. When Binford recalled that even in the early days of processual archaeology graduate students would constantly stop him outside a meeting room with, "'Dr. Binford, Dr. Binford, I'm working on _____, and I wonder if you have any suggestions as to how I might analyze that kind of data'" (Binford 1972b:13), he wasn't exaggerating. We remember standing on the sidelines and imagining Elvis backstage, silently hoping that one day we, too, would have groupies. Of course, that kind of thinking undermines the notion that intellectual change should be for the betterment of humankind and not for personal gain, and so perhaps we were in a minority.

The changes that were going on in American archaeology were a microcosm of greater changes in the United States. By the early 1960s, students on the nation's campuses were beginning to call for radical change in everything, including university curricula. Classroom learning was now supposed to be "relevant" to everyday life. In archaeology, the diffusionist explanations of earlier years rang hollow. Chronological orderings, no matter how you

FIGURE 2.4. Frank Hole alongside ground stone artifacts from excavations on the Deh Luran Plain, Khuzistan, Iran, ca. 1968. (Photograph by James Neely.)

the operation of the machine becomes so odious, makes you so sick at heart, that you can't take part; you can't even passively take part, and you've got to put your bodies upon the gears, and upon the wheels, upon the levers, upon all the apparatus, and you've got to make it stop. And you've got to indicate to the people who run it, to the people who own it, that unless you're free, the machine will be prevented from working at all."[2]

We won't credit (or blame) Savio and the Free Speech Movement for jamming the apparatus of Americanist culture history, but we will say that it is not especially surprising that some of its wheels ground to a halt when and where they did. The temptation to replace the old apparatus with something new was just too strong to ignore in the early '60s, especially when several of the most well respected, older members in the discipline—Gordon Willey and Philip Phillips, for example—had provided clues as to how to go about creating a replacement. And if you were going to create a replacement, you might even change its name, if ever so slightly—or so the story went.

A curious belief arose that one could identify at a glance the writings of the new archaeologists because of how they spelled *archeology*—without the second *a*, the way it had been done for decades in *American Anthropologist* and for close to a century by the federal government. The Government Printing Office's explanation for substituting *e* for the ligature *æ* around 1890 (Rowe 1975) was to reduce costs, but the processualists supposedly preferred the short version to distinguish their kind of archaeology from culture history. Two important books, *New Perspectives in Archeology* (Binford and Binford 1968a) and *Anthropological Archeology in the Americas* (Meggers 1968), seemingly gave substance to the belief. Nonetheless, the spelling of *archaeology* turned out to be a poor guide to an author's views on new and old. After all, journals and many book publishers have rigid house styles. Binford's classic papers in *American Antiquity,* for example, all have the *ae*.

In the rush to promote their approach, the more radical processualists swept out the earlier literature—"redlined" it, to use Schiffer's (2000b) colorful phrasing—labeling most of it as little more than descriptive lists of artifacts, all arranged in nice spatial rows and chronological columns, most of it irrelevant to achieving archaeology's anthropological goals. Binford himself often was uncharitable to his predecessors' efforts, but he tended to phrase his objections less belligerently than Walter Taylor. But the products of cultural historical research—the site reports, survey reports, and syntheses—could not be redlined if one were going to work in a particular area. New archaeologists had to immerse themselves in the minutiae of culture history—the pottery types and their chronological ordering—even if they believed that the types measured nothing interesting about the past except, imperfectly, time and history. Moreover, almost everyone still used the culture-historical units—phases, stages, periods, and the like—to talk about their pieces of the archaeological record. Otherwise, communication, even among processualists, would have ceased. Thus, the archaeological literature has had, and continues to have, a large hand in reproducing, in generation after generation, the products of culture history—at least artifact types, chronologies, and culture units. As Fred Plog (1973a) observed, all archaeologists are culture historians to one degree or another.

THE ARCHITECT OF PROCESSUAL ARCHAEOLOGY

No one did more during the 1960s and '70s to make archaeology anthropological than Lew Binford, and no one else had stirred up more controversy along the way. Binford, it seemed, had opinions on everything, and he published them at a prodigious pace. Table 2.1 is a list of Binford's papers that appeared during a thirty-year span (1962–1991). It is a selective list, containing only articles in major journals and excluding books, book chapters, book reviews, and other sundry pieces. Few archaeologists can claim that they published an average

Table 2.1. Article-Length Publications by Lewis Binford, 1962–1991

N	Publication
8	*American Antiquity*
1	*Ethnohistory*
7	*Anthropological Papers, Museum of Anthropology, University of Michigan*
9	*Southwestern Journal of Anthropology/Journal of Anthropological Research*
2	*American Anthropologist*
5	*Current Anthropology*
1	*Scientific American*
5	*Journal of Anthropological Archaeology*
1	*Antiquity*
1	*Man*
1	*Yearbook of Physical Anthropology*

of 1.3 articles per year in the top journals in anthropology *and* sustained that effort over three decades. Moreover, it's one thing to write articles and books but another to have readers become engaged with your ideas. We suspect that Binford is the most read and cited American archaeologist of the last forty years, producing a large share of the "scientific capital" that exists in the archaeological marketplace (Wylie 1983). Certainly a quick perusal of the ISI Social Sciences Citation Index bears out the impact his publications have had, and continue to have, on archaeology both in the United States and abroad.

Binford is widely recognized as the chief architect of the new archaeology—a role that he has acknowledged on more than one occasion. His first major article, "Archaeology as Anthropology," published in *American Antiquity* in 1962, typically is regarded as processualism's birth announcement. It was the last of twelve articles in the issue in which it appeared, suggesting to us that the editor at the time, Tom Campbell of the University of Texas, had no reason to suspect that it was anything out of the ordinary. No one would have. Binford followed that seminal contribution with several articles during the 1960s (e.g., Binford 1963, 1964a, 1965, 1967, 1968d) that helped set both the agenda and tone for the new archaeology.

In terms of what it did for the processual movement, nothing matched the book that Binford coedited with his then-wife, Sally— *New Perspectives in Archeology* (Binford and Binford 1968a). Charles Redman, a second-generation processualist, later referred to its publication as marking "the crossing of a threshold" (Redman 1991:296). The book grew out of a symposium that the Binfords had put together for the American Anthropological Association meeting in Denver in November 1965.[3] (Incidentally, that symposium was so well attended that James Sackett, an Old World specialist who had received his Ph.D. from Harvard in 1965, purportedly leaned over and whispered the famous line, "My God, Lew, they're standing up in the rear" [Binford 1972b: 12]. Whether that story is true or simply part of the processualist lore, by 1965 there was growing interest in what Binford and his Chicago friends were up to.)

One means of broadening interest in the new archaeology was to take the processual message to anthropologists. Perhaps expecting to secure ringing endorsements for archaeology's renewed commitment to anthropology, the Binfords asked several prominent anthropologists to comment on the papers presented at the Denver meeting. Not surprisingly, the comments, for the most part, were laudatory. Two sym-

FIGURE 2.5. Richard Lee interviewing !Kung San (now Jul'hoansi) in northwestern Botswana, ca. 1967. (Photograph by Irven DeVore, courtesy Nancy DeVore and Anthro-Photo File.)

posium discussants were Harvard anthropologists Richard Lee (Figure 2.5), an ethnologist, and Irven DeVore (Figure 2.6), a primatologist, both of whom were becoming well known for their studies of the !Kung San (now Jul'hoansi) of southwestern Africa's Kalahari Desert. At

the time of their remarks, Lee and DeVore were preparing for the international Man the Hunter Conference that would be held at the University of Chicago the following April. Their comments at the Binfords' symposium (DeVore 1968; Lee 1968), coupled with the articles that came out of the Man the Hunter Conference (Lee and DeVore 1968), would have far-reaching effects in archaeology that even they could not have envisioned.

Lee and DeVore's message to archaeologists at the Denver meeting was to use the ethnographic record as a source of information helpful in understanding the archaeological record. To that end, Lee offered a proposal: the creation of a graduate course in which each archaeology student would be required to spend three to six months doing an ethnographic field project in order to develop insights helpful in assessing the prehistoric record. He suggested calling such a program "interpretive archaeology." The light bulb must have gone on for several in attendance that day because within a decade ethnoarchaeology would become a popular approach for acquiring ethnographic information

FIGURE 2.6. Irven DeVore studying activities of !Kung San (now Jul'hoansi) in northwestern Botswana, 1965. (Photograph by Stan Washburn, courtesy Nancy DeVore and Anthro-Photo File.)

FIGURE 2.7. *Right,* Paul Martin and *left,* Fred Plog in front of the main house at the Vernon, Arizona, field station, 1973. (Courtesy Steve Plog.)

where he served as a program director in the early 1960s after leaving the University of Michigan.

Martin (Figure 2.7) also commanded considerable respect as both a researcher and a teacher. A specialist in ceramic typology, he spent his entire career working on Field Museum–sponsored projects in the Southwest (Herold 2003; Nash 2001, 2003), beginning with Lowry Ruin, a twelfth-century pueblo in southwestern Colorado, in the 1930s. In 1956 Martin moved the headquarters of the Southwest Archaeological Expedition from the Pine Lawn–Reserve region of western New Mexico to Vernon, Arizona (Figure 2.8). Martin was, in Longacre's (2000:293) recollection, someone who "during his whole long career…was anxious to get at the behavior of past peoples and explore their ways of organizing themselves." Within a few years he would get his wish, as the Vernon field station and nearby sites became the major proving ground for processual archaeology (Chapter 3).

Over the years, Martin provided resources that were used by generations of Chicago and Arizona graduate students to apply their new ideas in his NSF–supported field projects (Figures 2.9 and 2.10). By the time of the AAA symposium in Denver several Chicago graduate students, including Longacre and James Hill (Figure 2.11), had produced processualist products based on work conducted with Paul Martin's encouragement and financial support. In inviting him to be part of the symposium in Denver, the Binfords were recognizing his contributions to furthering the careers of Longacre, Hill, and others, and thereby giving some traction to the new archaeology.

Martin did not provide an article for *New Perspectives,* but Spaulding did—one he had presented at the annual meeting of the American Association for the Advancement of Science in 1965. In part because of his well-publicized "debates" with Jim Ford in the early 1950s (Chapter 1), Spaulding had developed a reputation for his use of statistics or, more properly, for his advocacy of their use in pattern discovery. But it wasn't statistics that he took up in

that could be used to interpret the archaeological record. Ethnoarchaeology had deep roots in the discipline: the term *ethnoarchaeologist* dates to the early twentieth century (Fewkes 1900), but with few exceptions (e.g., Ascher 1962; Gould 1966, 1968a, 1968b; Thompson 1958) it was not widely pursued until the 1970s (David and Kramer 2001; Schiffer 1978a). Then, processualists began heading off to Africa, Australia, Alaska, and other distant locations to see how the natives did things (Chapters 5 and 7).

The Binfords chose as their symposium chairmen two "senior men in the field who have consistently encouraged and inspired many of us and have aided greatly the development and acceptance of new ideas" (Binford and Binford 1968b:vii): Albert Spaulding of the University of Oregon and Paul Martin of the Field Museum of Natural History in Chicago. Binford had taken courses with Spaulding at Michigan and had considerable respect for him (Binford 1972b), as did many in the discipline, especially in light of his efforts to increase the level of funding for anthropology in the budget of the National Science Foundation (NSF),

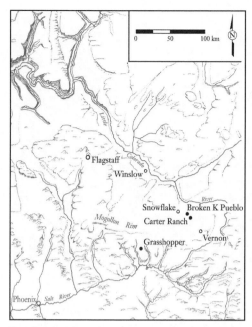

FIGURE 2.8. Map of northeastern Arizona showing significant archaeological sites in and around Vernon.

his article (Spaulding 1968): it was the philosophy of science. All three references in Spaulding's article were to works by philosophers. In reading his remarks, one might wonder where Spaulding had been hiding his philosophical interests all the time he was battling Ford over pottery types and the like. We suspect that he acquired them later, during his stint at NSF, where for the first few years he served as the director of the History and Philosophy of Science Program before taking the helm at the Anthropology Program. Spaulding was too detail oriented simply to have served as a titular head. Rather, he would have become familiar with the latest developments in the history and philosophy of science, which at the time included the work of Carl Hempel, a logical empiricist who in the 1970s would become a household name in processual archaeology (Chapter 4).

Spaulding was clear about his vision for archaeology's future: to make archaeology a science. For Spaulding, being scientific meant

FIGURE 2.9. Personnel of the Southwest Archaeological Expedition in front of the field camp connected with the excavation of Carter Ranch Pueblo, Arizona, 1965. *Front row, left to right:* James Van Arsdell, Jeff Brown, Charles Peters, Jim Hill, Marcus Winter, John Zilen, John Fritz, Kubet Luchterhand, and Mark Leone. *Back row, left to right:* Paul Martin, Fred Bloom, William Englebrecht, George Zarins, Norman Yoffee, Scott Ryerson, Martha Perry, and Bill Longacre. (Negative no. A103029, courtesy Field Museum of Natural History.)

FIGURE 2.10. Personnel of the Southwest Archaeological Expedition in front of the field camp connected with the excavation of Carter Ranch Pueblo, Arizona, 1968. *Kneeling, left to right:* Steve Plog, Paul Martin, and Tom Zanic. *Seated, left to right:* Judith Conner, Nancy Wilmsen, Mary McCutcheon, Joe Traugott, Rosalind Duncan, Walter Gargan, Charles Vanasse, Mike Schiffer, Bonnie Laird, John Zilen, Mrs. Thomas Kuhn (guest), and Margaret Sticklan. *Standing, left to right:* Lawrence Straus, David Burkenroad, Paul Smith, Chris White, Jim Hill (guest), Aron Winchester, Craig Morris, Thomas Kuhn (guest), Fred Plog, Mark Leone, Ezra Zubrow, and Marsha Zubrow. (Negative no. A101493, courtesy Field Museum of Natural History.)

that research designs and analytical protocols should be geared toward producing explanations. Spaulding (1968) asked rhetorically if there were not two kinds of explanations for the way the world works: historical and scientific. We say "rhetorical" because Spaulding (1968:34) recognized really only one kind of "serious" explanation, "the nomological or covering-law explanation [of Hempel]. All serious explanations relate the circumstance to be explained to relevant general laws or at least to empirical generalizations. Explanations may be deductive, in which case the covering law admits of no exceptions, or they may be probabilistic-statistical (or inductive, if you prefer), in which case the covering law has the form of a frequency distribution."

Spaulding's discussion was taken directly out of Hempel's (1962) paper "Deductive-Nomological vs. Statistical Explanation." Spaulding might have been attracted to this work because Hempel did not write off humans or other organisms as falling outside the scientific umbrella. Most of his work on laws and explanation dealt with the physical sciences,

but biological phenomena could also fit comfortably within his approach. Spaulding knew that despite best efforts, anthropology—and, by extension, archaeology—might fall short of "the deductive elegance of physics" (Spaulding

FIGURE 2.11. *Left to right:* Jim Hill, Bill Longacre, and John Fritz at the Vernon, Arizona, field camp, 1965. (Negative no. 103027, courtesy Arizona State Museum.)

1968:34). "Clearly," Spaulding (1968:36) continued, "anthropological explanations are characteristically probabilistic-statistical rather than deductive, and they are partial rather than complete.... Anthropologists are not forbidden, however, to struggle toward covering generalizations with greater powers of prediction and retrodiction. They can strive to sharpen statements of the frequency distributions underlying probabilistic explanations, to make explanations more complete." Finally, Spaulding (1968:37) acknowledged that anthropology differs in some respects from physics, but it is nonetheless a science because it seeks to discover relationships in its data that can be accounted for by covering-law explanations. By *covering law*, Hempel meant a generalized law that "covers" (explains) specific empirical phenomena.

Spaulding's comments sowed the seeds for what would become in the early 1970s *the* most important aspect of the new archaeology: Where do laws come from, and what role do they play in explanation? We don't want to preempt the detailed discussion of these issues in Chapter 4, but we need to at least foreshadow it. Spaulding made what we view as a fundamental error by referencing Hempel's distinction between probabilistic-statistical and deductive-nomological explanations, and then saying that archaeology might fall short of "the deductive elegance of physics" (Spaulding 1968:34). Although he was not alone, Spaulding misunderstood the relationship between stochasticism and determinism. It is not an all-or-nothing proposition, with probabilistic sciences on one side and deterministic sciences on the other. Albert Einstein knew this, hence his famous statement that God doesn't roll the dice with the universe, meaning simply that things being treated as probabilistic need more investigation before we can understand the underlying principles. Lacking other information, probability theory is a good starting point to justify more investigation, but one should use it as just that, not as the answer to the problem.

Despite Spaulding's enthusiasm for demonstrating that anthropology and archaeology could be scientific, one ingredient missing from his discussion was "theory." For him and the other symposium participants, theory was something that went hand in hand with method. Everyone knew what it was, so there was no need to define it. Spaulding appeared to be saying that theory was synonymous with explanation, and like Hempel, he was talking about how to *structure* explanations (e.g., deductively), not where the generalizations employed in explanations come from. Most scientists today accept that explanations derive in part from theory, in that theories suggest relevant variables and their relationships, and they can lead to the formulation of lower-level generalizations that can serve as covering laws.

For logical empiricists such as Hempel (1962, 1965b) and Ernst Nagel (1961), explanation is a two-tiered affair. Empirical phenomena are explained by lower-level covering laws, including (sometimes) empirical generalizations, and the covering laws in turn are explained by theories. Thus, a "complete" scientific explanation might make reference both to the relevant covering law(s) and to the appropriate theory; however, in the history of science, many covering laws are discovered experimentally and precede the formulation of relevant theory. They can even survive the latter's demise. Spaulding either did not understand the difference between theory and explanation or, more likely, chose to ignore it. So did most others at the time, including Lew Binford, although that would change abruptly in the 1970s. What Spaulding was advocating was the creation of more empirically derived generalizations that could serve as covering laws. But as Binford (1977b:5) himself later noted, "statistical or probabilistic statements as to relationships between things are simply complex empirical facts." A mature science would also need theories to explain those relationships—an issue that we discuss in greater detail in Chapter 4.

Binford contributed both the opening and closing chapters to *New Perspectives*. "Archeological Perspectives" (Binford 1968a) was much more than an introduction to the rest of the book, for it rapidly became a blueprint for what the new archaeology was supposed to look like. Yet in reading it today, one gets the impression that Binford was proposing not so much a different approach as a road map around some of the major obstacles that had impeded American archaeology from the start. Few issues raised in *New Perspectives* were new. Previous generations of archaeologists had talked about, for example, social organization, kinship and marriage, and even methodological issues such as classification, but rarely had there been such unanimity on how to deal with those issues, nor had there been case studies that tackled them with apparent success.

Binford had to demonstrate in his introductory chapter that the book did indeed offer "new perspectives." To do that he introduced three traditional topics of archaeological concern—the reconstruction of culture history, the reconstruction of past lifeways, and the study of culture process—and showed how methodological and theoretical impediments had foiled previous investigations. Regarding the reconstruction of culture history, Binford pointed out that despite an interest in genealogical connections among cultural units, archaeologists had no objective means of distinguishing between analogues and homologues. Binford argued that this "inherent unsolved problem of method and epistemology" required "an overhaul of method and theory" (1968a:10, 11). His suggested "new" analytical protocol, however, was simply the traditional one with the addition of statistical techniques such as those outlined by James Doran and Frank Hodson (1966) to assist one to "measure likenesses" (Binford 1968a:11). This, in Binford's view, would allow one to formulate arguments "about the probability of one [cultural] taxon being the cultural ancestor, descendant, or collateral relative of another taxon (e.g., Doran and Hodson 1966; Hodson, Sneath, and Doran 1966), or whether another unit might be more appropriately considered" (Binford 1968a:11).

The references Binford cited contained descriptions of data-clustering methods that today would be included in numerical taxonomy (Hull 1988b). He was echoing what Spaulding,

his teacher, had taught him: statistically significant clusters of archaeological stuff indicated cultural significance. In Binford's case they were not Spaulding's attribute clusters, representative of cultural norms or mental templates, but rather artifact clusters representative of historically related cultural taxa. Whether they indeed were or not was debatable, just as it was in biology (Lyman and O'Brien 2003b; O'Brien and Lyman 2003a).

In discussing the reconstruction of past lifeways, Binford went into considerable detail about the misuse of cultural analogues, claiming that "so long as we insist that our knowledge of the past is limited by our knowledge of the present, we are painting ourselves into a methodological corner" (Binford 1968a:14). Binford devoted some time in the mid-1960s to considerations of ethnographic analogy and how the ethnographic record could be used to interpret the archaeological record (e.g., Binford 1967, 1968b; see also S. R. Binford 1968). It would occur to Binford and others in the '70s and '80s that the real problem was not methodological but ontological. Inferring the nature of past human processes and activities was being constrained by the indiscriminate use of modern analogues; a view that the past was no different than the present denied the existence of change (Chapter 5).

Binford (1968a) criticized traditional efforts to study cultural processes, suggesting instead a multistage procedure of observation, generalization, testing, reformulation, additional testing, and so on. He was largely silent in "Archeological Perspectives" with respect to the identity of culture processes or how to discern them in the archaeological record. In earlier articles Binford (e.g., 1962a, 1963, 1965) listed the same mechanisms of cultural change as those invoked by culture historians. This should not be surprising given that at the time he was writing, formal discussions of culture change by ethnographers and ethnologists were little more than descriptions of the traditional mechanisms long used by the historical ethnologists (e.g., Murdock 1956; Spindler and Spindler 1959). They continued to be the major mechanisms discussed well into the mid-'70s (Woods 1975).

"Archeological Perspectives" (Binford 1968a) was Binford's first thorough presentation of his views on the use of inductive and deductive research strategies. In it he cited Hempel, but his treatment of the philosophy of science was not as extensive as Spaulding's. Binford (1968a:17) asserted that "our knowledge of the past is more than a projection of our ethnographic understanding [through analogy]. The accuracy of our knowledge of the past can be measured; it is this assertion which most sharply differentiates the new perspective from more traditional approaches. The yardstick of measurement is the degree to which propositions about the past can be confirmed or refuted through hypothesis testing—not by passing personal judgment on the personal qualifications of the person putting forth the propositions."

Where Spaulding saw anthropology as a statistical science, Binford saw a deductive-nomological science built around the discovery of laws of cause and effect. Binford wrote about the difference between an empirical generalization and a hypothesis (a tentative law), and discussed how one went about testing a hypothesis. Spaulding had ignored the distinction between empirical generalizations and hypotheses because to him only empirical (statistical) generalizations were possible in anthropology. Binford introduced words that would soon become commonplace in the processual literature, such as observation, proposition, deduction, prediction, bridging argument, and confirmation. If he was aware of a major difference between his position and Spaulding's on the nature of explanation in anthropology, he declined to comment.

Binford concluded his introduction to *New Perspectives* by reiterating that the kind of archaeology being espoused in the book was indeed new. He also warned that the new archaeology would bring with it a new order, so much so that the "radical" chapters in *New Perspectives* would render obsolete much traditional method and theory, along with familiar archaeological problems. Speaking in visionary terms, Binford (1968a:27) predicted "an expansion of the scope of our question-asking which today would make us giddy to contemplate. Despite a recent statement that one should not speak of a 'new archeology' since this alienates it from the old (Chang 1967a:3), we feel that archeology in the 1960's is at a major point of evolutionary change. Evolution always builds on what went before, but it always involves basic structural changes."

Binford was right: archaeology in the late 1960s was at a major turning point, and the changes were significant enough to warrant being labeled "new." But not everyone agreed. K. C. Chang, a Yale archaeologist who had been trained at Harvard by Hallam Movius and Gordon Willey, was "not impressed by the phrase 'new archaeology' that one sometimes finds in the current literature" (Chang 1967a:3). Why? Because, as he pointed out in the introduction to his book *Rethinking Archaeology,* "what is old today was new in its own time, and what is now new will become old tomorrow. To say an archaeology is new is to alienate it from the old, whereas one could more profitably absorb and reorganize the old. Rethinking is a constant and routine mental process that brings about renewal at every turn" (Chang 1967a:3).

Close reading of Chang's book indicates that he followed his own advice, effectively rewriting archaeological terminology using anthropological and human-behavioral terminology; for example, "a settlement is an archaeological unit of behavioral meaningfulness" (Chang 1967a:15). Here Chang admitted that he was heavily influenced by Clyde Kluckhohn (Ferrie 1995:320). Thus Chang's notions had roots much earlier (e.g., Taylor 1948) and had come to find more consistent expression in the 1950s (e.g., Caldwell 1959; Willey and Phillips 1958).

Is it appropriate to say that Binford "founded" the new archaeology? Some sources think so. The *Britannica Concise Encyclopedia* for 2003 states under the entry "Lewis R(oberts) Binford" that he "initiated what came to be known as the 'New Archaeology.'" *Initiated* is a synonym for *founded* or *started*, so it appears that the *Britannica* assigns Binford the seminal role in the processual movement. In one sense this is correct, but it is also naive. Schools of thought do not emerge from a void: they build on what came before them. Binford, who clearly saw the process of archaeology as an evolutionary one, pointed this out when he said that evolution builds on what comes before. Still, we don't want to minimize Binford's impact. He might not have put archaeology on the road toward processualism (that had happened earlier), but he got it running boldly down that road rather than creeping cautiously along.

Binford sensed a general discomfiture with American archaeology as it was being practiced in the late 1950s, and he played off it when he penned "Archaeology as Anthropology" in 1962. Had he not written that article, someone else would have written one similar to it. Why? Because many, if not most, of the new archaeology's components were already present during the 1950s as intellectual variants. Given the simmering dissatisfaction and the demographic and social changes occurring in American society and the intellectual academy during the early 1960s, others would have stepped forward to create a processual-like program in opposition to culture history. Although there is no denying that Binford was a highly skilled rhetorician, we cannot totally agree with Bruce Trigger's (1989a) claim that it was Binford's rhetoric that made processualism appear so different from what preceded it. New approaches are not invented; rather, they coalesce and are personified.

In Western culture all complex inventions, both conceptual and material, are assigned authorship—an inventor—regardless of the many contributions made by the anointed person's predecessors and contemporaries. The legitimacy of that attribution serves as a focal point for endless discussions regarding the nature and extent of the change that the inventor supposedly wrought (Kuhn 1962a). The bottom line, however, is found in a quote from Francis Darwin (1914:9), who was pointing out the earlier contribution of Francis Galton to Adolph

Weismann's views on germ-cell continuity: "But in science the credit goes to the man who convinces the world, not to the man to whom the idea first occurs. Not the man who finds a grain of new and precious quality but to him who sows it, reaps it, grinds it and feeds the world on it." And Binford was the consummate farmer, miller, and grocer.

Whether the new archaeology represented a major paradigm shift has been disputed since the late 1960s, when archaeologists discovered physicist-turned-historian Thomas Kuhn's book, *The Structure of Scientific Revolutions* (1962b). Did processual archaeology represent a paradigm shift in the way that Kuhn meant, as a wholesale structural replacement of one approach by another? Paul Martin (1971) certainly believed this. In his article "The Revolution in Archaeology" he relates how processualism changed his life. He even hosted Kuhn in the field in 1968 (Figure 2.10). Two young processualists on Martin's staff, Fred Plog (Figure 2.12) and Mark Leone (Figure 2.9), relentlessly fed Kuhn details on recent developments in archaeology, hoping that this great historian of science would pronounce processualism a scientific revolution. But through it all Kuhn remained noncommittal.

Robert McCormick Adams, on the faculty at Chicago and director of the Oriental Institute from 1962 to 1968, also believed a revo-

FIGURE 2.12. Fred Plog investigating a prehistoric granary, Black Canyon, Arizona, 1971. (Courtesy Steve Plog.)

lution had occurred. In a review of archaeological research strategies written for *Science* in 1968, he pointed out that the new archaeology was "less an explosion than a revolution in the sense that it is a broad shift from one paradigm to another not unlike the shifts which Thomas S. Kuhn [1962a, 1962b] has metaphorically outlined for the history of physics" (Adams 1968:1187). As an aside, Adams spoke of the new archaeology with a somewhat tempered approval, pointing out that despite the rhetoric, there had been few processual products.

It might at first seem a bit odd that the director of the Oriental Institute—that staid organization founded by James Henry Breasted and funded by John D. Rockefeller, Jr.—would agree in principle with what the processualists were attempting to do. Adams, however, was only four years older than Binford and had received his Ph.D. from the University of Chicago in 1956, just three years ahead of Patty Jo Watson. Thus, agewise and careerwise, he was not that far removed from the Chicago-bred processualists. Also, whether he realized it or not, Adams was playing a pivotal role in shaping the future of processual archaeology with his work on state formation (e.g., Adams 1960, 1962, 1965, 1966; Adams and Nissen 1972). His work in the Near East, coupled with his knowledge of the archaeology of the New World and the Far East, led to his writing *The Evolution of Urban Society* (1966), which became the foundation for a generation of processual studies of complex society (Chapter 7).

The authors of this book agree that processualism was a "reform movement," to use Guy Gibbon's (1989:1) term, but they disagree as to whether processualism represented a paradigm shift. Schiffer—who studied with the Binfords as an undergraduate at UCLA, spent four summers at Vernon, and did his graduate work at the University of Arizona—believes that the advent of the new archaeology was a scientific revolution in the larger Kuhnian sense ("larger" because there are several senses in which Kuhn used the term). O'Brien and Lyman agree with David Meltzer (1979) that to count as a paradigm shift in the larger Kuhnian sense, as a sci

entific revolution, processualism would have had to break with its predecessor metaphysically, not simply methodologically (see Custer 1981 and Meltzer's [1981b] response).

In Meltzer's view this break did not occur because paradigm replacement entails structural change in a discipline. No structural change, no paradigm shift. Binford probably would agree with Meltzer that a paradigm shift must involve structural change, but he would argue that processual archaeology *did* produce such a change (Binford 1968a:27). Schiffer would add that the structural change had many components, the most far-reaching of which was at the level of explaining cultural/behavioral variability and change. In Schiffer's view this led to the replacement of what Binford (1965) referred to as "normative theory" (the "aquatic view" of culture) by materialist ecological and neoevolutionary theory (Schiffer 1988).

O'Brien and Lyman wouldn't necessarily disagree, but they don't see a clean break between the traditionalists' undeveloped use of normative theory (in which culture is viewed as an abstraction from behavior) and the processualists' use of that theory to underpin their first substantive products (Chapter 3). A bending, yes— and one that affected considerably more than simply method and technique—but not a complete break. The difference initially was an additional explicit definition of culture as humankind's extrasomatic means of adaptation, which meant that the functions of artifacts, not just their styles, became an additional analytical focus. This focus had modest beginnings long before 1962 (Kirch 1980). But speaking of Kuhn, we collectively wonder if Binford would agree with him that scientists have long supported theories not only on epistemological grounds but because of personal predilection and even prejudice and animosity. We come back to this point throughout the volume.

Whether or not a paradigm shift occurred, major changes took place in how archaeologists went about their business. Recognition of those changes was immediate, not something that came through retrospection. When Binford suggested in 1962 that archaeology needed theoretical and methodological overhauling to become more anthropological, he was following a familiar trail blazed by Walter Taylor (1948), Betty Meggers (1955), Philip Phillips (1955), and Joseph Caldwell (1959). But their calls, issued a decade and a half or less before Binford's article, produced little significant change. In Taylor's case, the reaction was a mix of hostility and benign neglect because of the offensive manner in which he framed the call. Binford also challenged people, but his comments tended to be aimed at disciplinary practice in general rather than at individuals (with a few exceptions, discussed later). Binford made positive suggestions on how to make the discipline into an anthropology of the past—an anthropology that he had learned in large part from Leslie White while a graduate student at the University of Michigan.

Binford achieved such rapid and widespread success for several reasons. First, his alternative to traditional archaeology, unlike Taylor's, was a relatively complete program. In less than ten years he put out a package that covered the gamut of archaeological method and theory as it was viewed in the 1960s. Second, he was a charismatic leader whose overpowering lecturing and debating styles inspired confidence in the message. Schiffer recalls that Binford fostered a cultlike following. His lecture style mimicked, perhaps unconsciously, that of a southern Baptist preacher. He did not use lecture notes, yet his lectures were so engaging that few students complained when he ran ten or fifteen minutes past the end of class. His sheer physical presence and the forcefulness of his delivery (Figure 2.13) added nonverbal elements to his lectures that inspired people to believe his every word. And although he counseled against ad hominem arguments in print (e.g., Binford 1968a), in class he would dismiss ideas and arguments he did not like as "nonsense" or "garbage," implying that their advocates were dolts, sort of like Groucho Marx's "Who are you going to believe—me or your eyes?" By discarding the traditional means of evaluating the work of others based on their expertise and credentials (Thompson 1956), Binford "was wip-

FIGURE 2.13. Lewis Binford lecturing at UCLA, 1967. (Photograph by Jerry Morris.)

ing the slate clean, saying in effect that a young person entering archaeology could write on that slate something significant" (Schiffer 1995a:3). As a student, it was exhilarating as well as a strong recruitment incentive to be told you could take on the establishment on a level playing field and also make significant contributions.

Another reason for Binford's success was that at Chicago he was surrounded by smart people who, when they began teaching at other universities, also attracted smart people. But the key factor underlying the Binfordian program's broad influence was the coincident demographic and social changes taking place in American society and universities, which enabled new generations of processualists to find academic positions and reproduce the program. Thus, by the early 1970s processualists were able to dominate theoretical and methodological discourse in American archaeology.

Domination does not signify a replacement, however. After all, the new archaeologists made precious few converts among traditionalists (Paul Martin being the most visible), and as of 1970 the old guard still retained most of the professional positions in American archaeology. And even though processualism was making ever-greater inroads, there was a wide middle ground between the traditional and the new. That is where one would have found most archaeologists, especially those not recently trained. In the mid-1970s David Hurst Thomas took an informal poll of 640 archaeologists, asking if they were "new," "traditional," or something else. Not unexpectedly, the answers were mixed, with one person responding that the survey was a "particularly loathsome example of simplistic reductionism." So much for labels. One interesting result was that even in the mid-1970s, at the height of the processualist movement, fewer than one in five Americanists felt comfortable calling themselves "new archaeologists" (Thomas 1989:58).

So what were Thomas's own feelings about labels and movements, particularly processualism?

> I suggest that the new archaeology is best used to describe a commanding development within the history of Americanist archaeology. I relegate the new archaeology to historical contexts, for it describes a movement within archaeology that began in the early 1960s with the work of Lewis Binford; much of this agenda has been absorbed into mainstream archaeology. Those people who actually called themselves new archaeologists were really affirming that they liked what Lewis Binford said. I like what he said too, but I also liked several things that the "traditionalists" had said decades before and a number of things people have said more recently. (Thomas 1989:60)

Thomas's comments probably reflected the views of most Americanists at the time.

Using Thomas's data as a benchmark, we bring the story up to 1994, when the Society for American Archaeology conducted a survey of its 5,000-plus members. One of the questions on the comprehensive survey form was, "If you were asked to label the type of archaeology that you practice, or the 'school' of archaeology to which you belong, what label would you adopt?" The questionnaire listed eight options, but when she analyzed the data, Melinda Zeder (1997) combined some of the categories. Evolutionary archaeology was included with processual archaeology, and Marx-

ist archaeology, critical theory, and gender studies were included with postprocessual archaeology. The data, by age cohort and gender, are shown in Figure 2.14.

Zeder's intriguing analysis gives us a pretty clear picture of archaeologists' views in the mid-1990s. In brief, archaeologists in the two youngest cohorts (20–29 and 30–39), regardless of gender, identified themselves most often as processualists. Those in the two oldest cohorts (60–69 and 70–79) identified themselves most often as culture historians. Cultural ecology is represented fairly consistently across the cohorts, indicating that any attempts to bury ecology as an archaeological interest are premature (Chapter 3). Postprocessualism was well represented among younger archaeologists, but not among those over forty. One of Zeder's (1997:128) conclusions was that "there is no evidence that processual archaeology (which, along with its founders, is now decidedly middle-aged) is about to be eclipsed by a nascent postprocessual paradigm." We agree. Whatever it was that Binford and the early processualists crafted, three decades later 40–45 percent of the 150 youngest archaeologists filling out the SAA questionnaire didn't mind labeling themselves processualists.

MOTIVES AND RED HERRINGS

What motivated Binford to propose a change in the way Americanists practiced archaeology? Several of his autobiographical sketches offer some insight. In *An Archaeological Perspective*, composed primarily of articles he published while a graduate student at Michigan and an assistant professor at Chicago, Binford talks about the reasons he wrote some of them. "Archaeology as Anthropology" (1962a) grew out of a growing dissatisfaction Binford had with the state of American archaeology in the late 1950s. Succeeding articles—"'Red Ochre' Caches from the Michigan Area: A Possible Case of Cultural Drift" (1963), "A Consideration of Archaeological Research Design" (1964a), "Archaeological Systematics and the Study of Cultural Process" (1965), and "Smudge Pits and Hide Smoking: The Use of

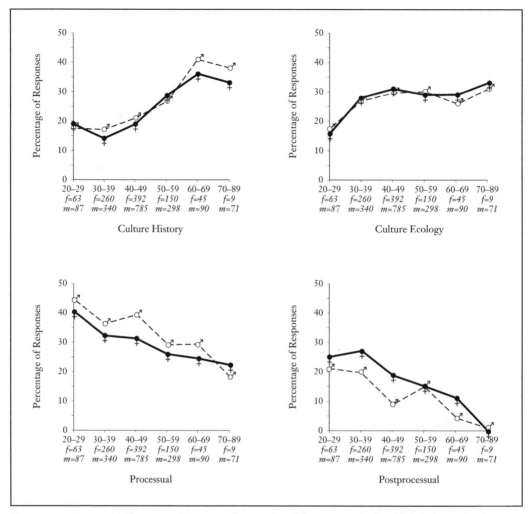

FIGURE 2.14. Percentage of responses in 1994 to the question, "If you were asked to label the type of archaeology that you practice, or the 'school' of archaeology to which you belong, what label would you adopt?" The responses are arranged by age cohort and gender (males are circles with arrows; females are circles with crosses). Percentages total 100 percent when read across the four responses. For example, of the eighty-seven male respondents who fell in the 20–29-year age range, 18 percent identified themselves as culture historians, 17 percent as cultural ecologists, 45 percent as processualists, and 20 percent as postprocessualists. (After Zeder 1997.)

Analogy in Archaeological Reasoning" (1967)—were written to elaborate some point Binford was thinking about or working on at the time. For example, the 1963 article resurrected the anthropological concept of "cultural drift" as a means of explaining nonfunctional variation within artifact assemblages. In several key respects the paper raised the same issues that Robert Dunnell would address fifteen years later—issues surrounding the analytical dichotomy between style and function (Chapter

8). Unlike the other articles, "A Consideration of Archaeological Research Design" is more methodological, the major points being the value of a regional approach in processual archaeology and the need for probability sampling (Chapter 3). The article was written after Binford's first field season in the Carlyle Reservoir of southern Illinois (Binford 1964b). That work eventually included the excavation of Hatchery West (Figure 2.15), which received considerable notice because it was published in the Society for American Archaeology *Memoir* series (Binford et al. 1970).

These papers are important from a historical perspective because of what they tell us about Binford's view of processual archaeology, but our main interest here is in "Post-Pleistocene Adaptations" (Binford 1968c), which is the final chapter of *New Perspectives*. Binford (1972d:341) claimed that not until he published that piece had he "achieved a processual model that was not developed for the explicit accommodation of a specific body of archaeological data. This was a different kind of model; its implications began to reach in the direction of law-like propositions, the goal of science." Here Binford was championing deductive methods. "Post-Pleistocene Adaptations" was a reanalysis of the origin of agriculture in the Near East and its causes, and Binford's conclusions were quite different from those reached by previous investigators.

One might think that the work was a natural outgrowth of earlier work—that by 1965, when he wrote the first draft for the Denver meeting, Binford had realized that simple inductive pattern recognition was not getting him where he wanted to go. Instead, he needed a model that dealt with culture process in a deductive manner. Undoubtedly this is true; otherwise Binford could not have written the paper as he did. But in one of the autobiographical notes in *An Archaeological Perspective,* he tells us that this work had a unique motivation. Whereas his earlier articles were "battles with ideas," "Post-Pleistocene Adaptations" derived from his battles "with men" (Binford 1972d:339). To be exact, it derived from his battles with one man—Robert Braidwood (Figure 2.16), an Old World archaeologist with whom Binford had taught at the University of Chicago.

Binford could not have picked a more impressive opponent. Braidwood had achieved a sterling reputation as a Near Eastern archaeologist, earned through fieldwork conducted under the auspices of the University of Chicago's Oriental Institute. Braidwood's name became synonymous with scientific archaeology

as a result of his excavations at the Neolithic site of Jarmo in the Zagros Mountains of northern Iraq, which he carried out between 1948 and 1955 (Braidwood and Braidwood 1950, 1953). The project was designed to study early village life in the Near East and to recover evidence of early food production (Braidwood 1958, 1960; Braidwood and Howe 1960, 1962). What made it especially innovative was the research team Braidwood assembled, which included not only archaeologists but also specialists in several aspects of the environment, including botany and zoology. At the time, the only similar team had been put together by Grahame Clark for his excavations at Star Carr in North Yorkshire, England (Clark 1954). The next comparable team would be one assembled by Richard MacNeish in the 1960s for work in the Southern Highlands of Mexico (Chapter 3).

According to Binford (1972b), Braidwood, as a member of the anthropology department at Chicago, had recommended against granting him tenure, labeling Binford "incompetent." Braidwood, by Binford's own admission, had hurt him deeply, and Binford wanted to hurt him back. That was why he wrote "Post-Pleistocene Adaptations." After reading it, we're not sure how it was supposed to "hurt" Braidwood. Although critical of Braidwood's ideas on the origins of agriculture and settled life in the Near East, it by no means belittles them (but see Binford and Binford 1966b), nor does Binford launch an ad hominem attack against Braidwood. Instead, he lays out an argument that calls into question Braidwood's nuclear-zone model, which postulated that the change from food procurement to food production took place within "potential nuclear area[s]...where a whole constellation of plants and animals possible of domestication were available" (Braidwood 1963:322). Binford even kept himself in check when remarking on Braidwood's infamous claim (Braidwood and Willey 1962:342) that pre-Neolithic groups had not become involved with food production because their "culture was not ready to achieve it." Binford (1968c:334) pointed out that "it was not that culture was unready, but rather

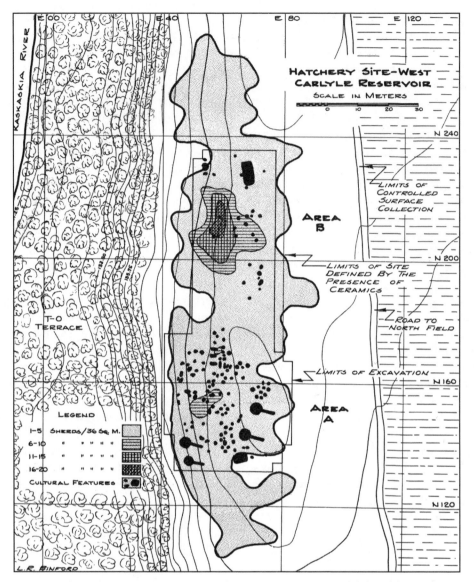

FIGURE 2.15. Map of the Hatchery West site in the Carlyle Reservoir of southern Illinois. Shown are locations of subsurface features (houses, pits, and the like) relative to the distribution of sherds on the surface of the site. Hatchery West became a model project because of the innovative manner in which surface artifacts were compared against subsurface features. (From Binford et al. 1970, courtesy Society for American Archaeology.)

that the selective conditions favoring such changes had not previously existed." For Binford, the new selective conditions occurred at the end of the Pleistocene (about 10,000 years ago), when a worldwide rise in sea level led to the exploitation of seasonal resources such as migratory fowl and anadromous fish. This led to sedentism and "established for the first time

conditions leading to marked heterogeneity in rates of population growth and structure of the ecological niche of immediately adjacent sociocultural systems" (Binford 1968c:334). Local populations grew, which led to pressure on the resource base. To counteract this, groups fissioned, and daughter groups ventured off to the surrounding countryside—"contexts of a much less spectacular character," as Braidwood and Willey (1962:343) referred to them. There, the daughter groups intensified their relations with wild plants, which eventually led to domestication and food production.

"Post-Pleistocene Adaptations," still one of Binford's most-cited papers, would be responsible in part for a wholesale reconsideration both in anthropology and archaeology of the role played by population growth in culture change (e.g., Cohen 1975, 1977; Dumond 1965; Spooner 1972). But not everyone was impressed with Binford's case study in processual archaeology. One detractor was Joseph Caldwell, who reviewed *New Perspectives* for *American Anthropologist* (Caldwell 1971). It was Caldwell who a dozen years earlier had heralded a shifting interest in American archaeology and the emergence of new issues and problems—what he had labeled the "new American archeology" (Caldwell 1959). In his review of *New Perspectives,* Caldwell sniffed that "Post-Pleistocene Adaptations" was a "tedious and extraordinarily formal attempt to show that all who have worked in this range of time in the Old World have been using the wrong assumptions" and did "not offer any impressive improvements" on earlier efforts (Caldwell 1971:412). Caldwell's harsh words seem a bit puzzling until one reads in his "new American archeology" article that part of what he saw as the shift of interest in 1959 "must be ascribed to the outstanding work of V. Gordon Childe and others in the Old World" (Caldwell 1959:303). Binford hadn't thought much of Childe's (1934, 1936, 1944) ideas and had said so in "Post-Pleistocene Adaptations."

Caldwell might have had another reason for dismissing Binford's piece. He had received his Ph.D. from the University of Chicago in 1957,

FIGURE 2.16. Robert Braidwood in the basement of the Oriental Institute, University of Chicago, holding a mortar from Jarmo, Iraq, ca. 1968. (Courtesy Patty Jo Watson.)

having gone back to school long after completing his undergraduate education. Caldwell's most substantial contribution was a modified version of his doctoral dissertation, *Trend and Tradition in the Prehistory of the Eastern United States,* which was published jointly by the American Anthropological Association and the Illinois State Museum in 1958. One of the most important contributions of the monograph was Caldwell's introduction of the concept "primary forest efficiency" to account for the traditional belief in the conservatism of Eastern Woodlands prehistoric groups. One could invoke efficiency, for example, to account for the then-apparent lack of agriculture in the East: "The hunting-gathering pattern was developed to a peak of efficiency and jelled, so to speak, in the very heart of eastern cultures" (Caldwell 1958:327; see also Caldwell 1962).

Caldwell's notion of a primary forest efficiency was the very kind of construct that the processualists would pursue across the landscape in an effort to rid their kingdom of such demons. Yet Binford didn't do this in "Post-Pleistocene Adaptations." To the contrary, he cited Caldwell's monograph with apparent approval. He did it, however, not because of the usefulness of this construct but because Caldwell was presenting evidence that groups can regulate their populations for long periods of time, provided they have a stable food supply. This was evidence Binford wanted for his own argument—that once in a while something happened to upset the balance, causing human groups to cross the critical threshold. That "something" was a growing population.

Caldwell's notion of primary forest efficiency was derived directly from Braidwood's "primary farming efficiency," which Braidwood (1951) saw as the economic basis of civilizations. Braidwood, along with Fred Eggan, had been a mentor to Caldwell while he was in the doctoral program at Chicago, a role for which Caldwell thanked him in the preface to *Trend and Tradition*. Binford had dared to criticize Braidwood, and Caldwell stood up for his former professor when he reviewed *New Perspectives*.

We have no way of judging, at least from the published record, whether Binford was ever successful in convincing Braidwood that he was wrong about Binford's intellect. What we find interesting are the external social factors that, at least in Binford's view, fostered his antipathy toward Braidwood and contributed to the motivation for writing "Post-Pleistocene Adaptations." Consider, for example, Binford's reminiscence about his family's social standing in the South:

> As far back as I can remember I was told what a fine family I had come from; yet we lived during the [D]epression in anything but grand style. The society into which I emerged, where I saw my father humiliated by snobbish, socially pretentious men, left its mark. I was frequently embarrassed by my thick accent. I was made to feel that my family and I had to earn any respect we received on a day-to-day basis. Respect was not something to be expected because of a secure social position. Braidwood's manner, his style of living, and his voice all prompted emotions going back to my childhood. These are the social scars we all carry. (Binford 1972d:340)

All of us encounter people in daily life whom we would prefer to avoid. What makes Binford's story noteworthy is that he cited the social differences between himself and Braidwood as having played a role in his writing of "Post-Pleistocene Adaptations." This story has obvious salience to Binford. Indeed, its elements reappear in an interview Binford did with Colin Renfrew that was published in *Current Anthropology* (Renfrew 1987a) and in one he did with Paula Sabloff, published as *Conversations with Lew Binford: Drafting the New Archaeology* (Sabloff 1998).

Can we make too much of the cultural environment in attempting to contextualize a discipline's development? Yes, for there is the danger that we may focus only on those elements of the environment that make the course conform to our expectations and that further other agendas. To a large extent, in *Land of Prehistory* Alice Kehoe falls into this trap when discussing Binford. As mentioned earlier, Kehoe doesn't shrink from confrontation, but in several places in the book an unspoken agenda—to discredit Binford and, by extension, processualism, at any cost—taints her interpretations. For example, in one place she employs Binford's autobiographical notes not as a means of understanding his actions and motives but to draw a parallel between processual archaeology and, of all things, scientific creationism.

> Much of the New Archaeology of the first postwar generation parallels Scientific Creationism in its obsolescent conceptualization of science, and this is no coincidence because both movements were drawn from the worldview taught in conservative American Protestant congregations. Lewis Binford acknowledges his Southern "hills-south, hard-working" origin (Binford 1972[d], 340), though he hasn't discussed his undergraduate training at Virginia Polytechnic, a school that would soon after his graduation hire Henry Morris, later a founder of the Institute for Creation Research. The hills-south, hard-working society that conditioned young Binford owes a substantial portion of its heritage to the Scots emigration that also gave America the Presbyterian Princeton Seminary, fountainhead of Fundamentalism. Contextualizing intellectual history does uncover some unexpected bedfellows. (Kehoe 1998:xiii–xiv)

Virginia Polytechnic Institute did hire Henry Morris, a hydraulic engineer, and later he did found the Institute for Creation Research. But VPI did *not* hire Morris because he was a creationist. Neither did Rice University before that.

This is tantamount to claiming that the University of Michigan hired Leslie White because he was a socialist. White was hired because Julian Steward's departure in 1930 created an opening for an anthropologist, not for a socialist. When university administrators later learned of White's political leanings, they were not pleased (Carneiro 1981; Peace 1993). One can only wonder what administrators at VPI thought of Morris's creationist creed. What Kehoe does here is use social history to "support" her story of how a "remarkable shift [occurred] in the 1970s from a profession visibly nearly exclusively white, male, Protestant, and American-born, to one that now reflects a far broader range of social positions" (Kehoe 1998:xiv). Kehoe views this shift as the "true revolution" in American archaeology, not the new archaeology of Binford and the other processualists. In an anthropology generally committed to scientific evolution, Kehoe could not have found a better way to denigrate processualism than by linking it, red-herring style, to scientific creationism.

Kehoe (1998:xiv) claims that to understand the shift she is talking about, we need to comprehend not only "the societal revolution instigated by the mid-century G.I. Bill, but also the contributions of professional women omitted from the standard histories of archaeology." The G.I. Bill did make it affordable for many working men to go to college, and certainly the roles of women in the field (and the conditions under which they worked) have been underreported until recently (e.g., Claassen 1994; Conkey and Gero 1997; Cordell 1993; Hays-Gilpin and Whitley 1998; Nelson, Nelson, and Wylie 1994; Sørenson 2000; White, Sullivan, and Marrinan 1999). Kehoe (1998:xiv), however, asserts that the change in the course of American archaeology was because "the old guard lost its power to exclude" as a result of the "influx of men from working-class and 'ethnic' backgrounds into the academy, and the protection given women by the 1964 Civil Rights Act" (see also various chapters in Kehoe and Emmerichs 1999). "Only now," she continues, "in the middle 1990s, are consequences emerging within the intellectual content of the discipline" (Kehoe 1998:xiv). Of course, she is ignoring the changes in intellectual content that took place earlier as a result of processualism. Likewise, she is mute on the still earlier intellectual changes that resulted from the work of the American Museum of Natural History in New Mexico.

No doubt the Civil Rights Act of 1964—specifically Title VII, which prohibits employment discrimination on the basis of race, color, religion, sex, and national origin—had a beneficial effect on the status of women in archaeology, but the act itself was the result of changing perceptions of women in the workplace that had begun decades earlier. Similarly, contrary to Kehoe's claim, the "influx of men from working-class and 'ethnic' backgrounds" into the academy was nothing new in the 1960s. In fact, men from working-class families had long been at the center of American archaeology. Jim Ford grew up in Water Valley and Clinton, Mississippi, the son of an Illinois Central railroad engineer. Jimmy Griffin was born in Atchison, Kansas, to a railroad-equipment supplier. Gordon Willey was born in Chariton, Iowa, to a pharmacist. These men, arguably among the midcentury leaders in archaeology, were decidedly *not* from positions of prestige. Insofar as the distribution of social power is concerned, the institution from which one graduated and where one was employed—the basis for building the "old-boy networks"—were far more important than one's social class.

In another move to link Binford to creationism, Kehoe reached back to a small Pacific island and 1954. Binford had mentioned in his interviews with Colin Renfrew (1987a) and Paula Sabloff (1998) that during the mid-1950s, while an army corporal assigned to occupation forces in Okinawa, he had become interested in archaeology (Figure 2.17). Binford did not, however, bring up an article published in the March 16, 1954, edition of *Pacific Stars and Stripes*. In an interview with an army reporter, Binford opined that the "world flood, mentioned in religion and verified by geologists, was responsible for the mass migration to the

Ryukyus [Islands] and for the high location of the [pithouse] holes" (*Pacific Stars and Stripes* 10[74]:8). We have all said or written things we later wish we could retract, just as we've all changed our views as we gain new knowledge and insight. Binford's early belief in the literalness of a biblical story does not explain his capability less than a decade later to effect significant change in American archaeology. If anything, one can regard the more mature Binford's untempered materialism as signaling rejection of his earlier beliefs.

Kehoe used the *Pacific Stars and Stripes* interview in an effort to embarrass Binford and to reinforce her contrived connection between scientific creationism and the new archaeology:

FIGURE 2.17. Lewis Binford examining artifacts from Okinawa, Ryukyu Islands, 1954. (Courtesy Lewis Binford.)

> Both uphold an obsolete model of science that premises a real world out there awaiting discovery through human reason; a corollary premise is that humans have the capability to comprehend fully this world, if they use proper methods of discovery and interpretation. Scientific Creationists hark back to the concept of a Book of Nature presented by God, alongside the Book of Scripture. Spaulding, Binford, and their disciples left God out of the matter. Scientific Creationists and New Archaeologists are positivists insofar as they assume data exist in a pure state, and it is the task of scientists to recover these uncontaminated and offer unvarnished interpretations hewing closely to the observations. (Kehoe 1998:119)

As we shall see in later chapters, archaeologists have called into question many of processual archaeology's fundamental assumptions without resorting to comparing it to scientific creationism.

Did processualists sometimes overreach in their claims to having acquired knowledge about the past? Yes. Was there unbridled optimism that the past *could* be understood pretty much in its entirety? Yes. Certainly Binford was optimistic, stating in "Archaeology as Anthropology" that the "formal structure of artifact assemblages together with the between element contextual relationships should

and do present a systematic and understandable picture of *the total extinct* cultural system" (Binford 1962a:219). But did processualists believe that data exist in a pure state? No. After all, they argued vociferously for new theoretical and methodological tools for handling data. Were the processualists positivists? Taken as a whole they were ("empiricists" is probably a better word), but a commitment to positivism is not a felony offense in science, despite what Kehoe implies. The main objective of processual archaeology was to do science, and Binford suggested that Hempel's deductive-nomological model of explanation and the hypothetico-deductive method furnished the keys. As several philosophers of science pointed out in later years (see Chapter 4), the construal of positivist scientific methods by some processualists was overly narrow, but this did not prevent them from doing innovative and influential research.

We should also appreciate that although the processualist program was generally positivist, practitioners had different views on how to make archaeology more scientific. Processualism was not nearly as unified as the stereotypes attacked by later critics would imply. For example, not all processualists were Hempelians (Flannery 1973a), nor did everyone find Leslie White's culturology inspiring. Processualism consisted of some widely shared theoretical and methodological commitments, but significant variation—even some dissent—was present. In the 1970s and '80s, a number of these non-conforming positions would develop into major departures from the program.

If one feels compelled to label processualism's epistemological and methodological commitments, we would eschew "positivism," which has come to mean little more than "explicitly science-oriented method in search of general laws and theories," in favor of "pattern recognition." Above all, the new archaeology was a search for pattern in data sets, regardless of their source or nature. The pattern-search approach, tied to the belief that cultural behavior in the past was patterned, was a key methodological commitment. Curiously, it was never appreciated that searching for patterns in data sets was not entirely compatible with a strict hypothesis-testing approach, unless one deduced from a hypothesis nothing more specific than the existence of some pattern (as did the early ceramic sociologists, as we explore in Chapter 3).

Pattern recognition seemed to trump other elements of processualism, as even Binford's methodological and empirical works demonstrated. Binford spent the 1960s trying to put into practice what Albert Spaulding, the quintessential statistical archaeologist, had taught him. Why else did Lew and Sally Binford return to France in 1968 to search for patterns in François Bordes's Mousterian data from the site of Combe Grenal in the Dordogne (Figure 2.18)? Bordes (1961) believed that the patterned differences in artifact layers that he saw in Mousterian sites were best explained by positing the existence of different Neandertal groups. As one group moved out of a rockshelter after leaving behind its distinctive combination of tools, another group moved in and deposited its own tool combination atop the older ones, and so on through time. The Binfords disputed this interpretation, arguing early on (Binford and Binford 1966a) that the differences were functional—the result of different activities—not ethnic and stylistic.

Despite the importance of pattern recognition, it was not the end product of a processualist's analysis. Finding patterns was only a preliminary step, as Binford (1972d:338) pointed out: "It is a common error to feel that something has been explained when a particular form of patterning can be subsumed under a general cognitive category." Explanation, to many processualists in the late 1960s and early '70s, lay in the use of the deductive-nomological model (based on deterministic laws) (e.g., Fritz and Plog 1970; Watson, LeBlanc, and Redman 1971). Ironically, the inductive-statistical model, also discussed by Hempel (1965b) and seemingly more appropriate for the new statistical orientation, for the most part was overlooked until it was introduced to archaeologists by philosophers of science in a more general version known as the "statistical relevance" model (Salmon 1982; Salmon and Salmon 1979). But deterministic laws were not emerging in profusion from processual studies. Nor did the early new archaeologists seem interested in exploring the possible role of theory for explaining patterns discerned in the archaeological record.

As mentioned earlier, the processual literature of the 1960s is strangely silent on the subject of theory. For example, the term is absent from the indices to *New Perspectives* and *An Archaeological Perspective*, whereas "explanation" is prominent in both. It is a mistake to think that processualists had no idea that theory could play a role in archaeological explanation; they did understand that point, but it was more of an implicit understanding. The reason for this is clear, at least as it pertains to the early days of processualism. The processualists did not have to create theory; they merely had to borrow it from ethnology, specifically from Leslie White's culturology and evolutionism, and from Julian Steward's cultural ecology. The filter through which this theory was funneled from ethnology to archaeology was Lew Binford.

BINFORD ON CULTURE
AND CULTURE PROCESS

Shifting the ontological basis of American archaeology in the 1960s meant redefining two concepts: *culture* and *culture process*. As noted in Chapter 1, for many anthropologists and archaeologists of the 1950s, culture processes included the standard ones observed in ethnographic settings: invention or innovation, diffusion, migration, and the like. White had different views. In *The Evolution of Culture*, White (1959:17) implied that culture processes are the "functions" of a cultural system. Earlier he had defined *the* culture process as "a stream of interacting cultural elements.... In this interactive process, each element impinges upon others and is in turn acted upon by them. The process is a competitive one: instruments, customs, and beliefs may become obsolete and eliminated from the stream. New elements are incorporated from time to time. New combinations and syntheses—inventions and discoveries—of culture elements are continually being formed" (White 1950:76). In "Archaeology as Anthropology," Binford (1962a:217) defined *process* as "the operation and structural modification of systems." He was not the only person at the time who was adopting White's views on process. Robert Carneiro, a cultural anthropologist and another of White's students, defined a process as "the interaction through time of the elements of a system as the system changes from one state to another" (Carneiro 1960:145). That change from one state to another was cultural evolution.

Binford (1962a:218) paraphrased White's (1959) definition of culture as "the extrasomatic means of adaptation for the human organism," but his discussion indicates that another reading for the word "means" could have easily and perhaps more accurately been "system." According to this definition, a culture no longer is defined as a set of ideas transmitted from individual to individual, shared by a group, and resulting in similarities and continuities across time and space. Although this normative definition had been widely adopted by archaeologists, Binford viewed it as being

FIGURE 2.18. *Right*, François Bordes at Combe Grenal, France, ca. 1965. (Photograph by Henry Wright, courtesy Lewis Binford.)

inadequate for generating any kind of useful hypotheses of cultural process. It did not allow the measurement of multivariate phenomena, permitting the measurement only of "unspecified 'cultural differences and similarities,' as if these were univariate phenomena" (Binford 1965:203). Changes in trait frequency through time were seen as results of diffusion, drift, or migration, all viewed as being quite natural and regular occurrences.

> Cultural differences and similarities are expressed by the normative school in terms of "cultural relationships" which, if treated rigorously, resolve into one general [interpretive] model. This model is based on the assumption of a "culture center" where, for unspecified reasons, rates of innovation exceed those in surrounding areas. The new culture spreads out from the center and blends with surrounding cultures until it is dissipated at the fringes, leaving marginal cultures. Cultural relationships are viewed as the degree of mutual or unilateral "influence" exerted between culture centers or subcenters. (Binford 1965:204)

Binford was especially critical of the "aquatic view" of culture:

Interpretive literature abounds in phrases such as "cultural stream" and in references to the "flowing" of new cultural elements into a region. Culture is viewed as a vast flowing stream with minor variations in ideational norms concerning appropriate ways of making pots, getting married, treating one's mother-in-law, building houses, temples (or not building them, as the case may be), and even dying. These ideational variations are periodically "crystallized" at different points in time and space, resulting in distinctive and sometimes striking cultural climaxes which allow us to break up the continuum of culture into cultural phases. (Binford 1965:204)

The "cultural phases" to which he referred were the Willey-and-Phillips units: archaeological complexes of shared artifact types that were treated as if they were a historical ethnologist's culture. Binford (1965:205) made the point, which was appreciated at some level by many archaeologists, that these "normative" constructs obscured potentially informative variation: "This emphasis on shared traits in our system of classification results in masking differences and in lumping together phenomena which would be discrete under another taxonomic method.... We should partition our observational fields so that we may emphasize the nature of variability in artifact populations and facilitate the isolation of causally relevant factors." Binford was calling for a new archaeological systematics that placed a priority on discovering and explaining nonnormative variation. Yet, as discussed below, his concept of "pattern" included a normative element. His real target of criticism was the mentalist component of traditional normative theory, for which he wanted to substitute a behavioral component: pattern.

To Binford, a culture was a system of interrelated subsystems and elements that varied in composition and structure depending on its context in time and space and also on situational factors such as a group's demographic composition. Only archaeologists had access to the entire time depth of the existence of cultures, and thus they were the ones who could contribute to an anthropological understanding of how and why cultures changed. Binford (1962a:224) echoed Walter Taylor when he stated that archaeologists had a "responsibility" to further the aims of anthropology and to use their data to solve "problems dealing with cultural evolution or systemic change." Heady stuff, but how were archaeologists to operationalize those ideas? Binford (1962a:219) presented in two sentences a plan for putting these ideas into practice, thereby establishing a basis for the research agenda he would follow for the remainder of his career: "I would consider the study and establishment of correlations between types of social structure classified on the basis of behavioral attributes and structural types of material elements [artifacts] as one of the major areas of anthropological research yet to be developed. Once such correlations are established, archaeologists can attack the problems of evolutionary change in social systems."

Ideas about how cultural systems worked and evolved had to be tested "against ethnographic data" (Binford 1962a:223) because it was only in the ethnographic context that one could actually witness the operation of culture processes ("dynamics"). Ethnographic data would form the basis of explanatory models, or what Binford (1962a) referred to as "frames of reference." As an aside, he used that term fifteen years later (Binford 1987b) and also as part of the title of his most recent book, *Constructing Frames of Reference* (Binford 2001)—a magnum opus that serves as a fitting culmination to a forty-year career of trying to educate archaeologists about how to learn about the past. The volume contains a plethora of useful ethnographic and environmental data that will, as Stephen Shennan (2004:511) put it, be "pillaged by researchers for years to come." Similarly, some of Binford's conclusions will undoubtedly be quoted by students and professionals "like preachers citing scripture" (Lekson 2001:558). Following a precedent he set about twenty-five years earlier (Binford 1977b), Binford does not start with a general, high-level explanatory theory, instead presuming that the data will speak for themselves. Such a patently inductive approach is at odds with his even earlier arguments regarding deduction and hypothesis testing as *the* way to make archaeology a science.

The key to the concept of frames of reference was in using ethnographic information in a new way. Ethnographic analogues had previously served as interpretive devices, as exemplified in Robert Ascher's (1961a, 1961b) work. Ascher (1961a:317) wrote that in a general sense "interpreting by analogy is assaying any belief about nonobserved behavior by referral to observed behavior which is thought to be relevant." Modern nonindustrialized people used tools of a particular form when undertaking a particular task. A prehistoric archaeological example of that same form was interpreted by analogy to have been used for the same task and thus to represent the same behavior. Binford argued that were archaeologists to continue this kind of analogical argument, they would "at best increase [their] understanding of archaeological observations in terms of ethnographically described situations" (Binford 1967:10). This represented a set of potentially limited possibilities and reaffirmed that the past was no different than the present.

To escape this limitation, Binford (1967:10) recommended that one study the covariant relationships between independent classes of phenomena because this would eventually produce "general laws of cultural variability." Ruth Tringham (1978:188) described the protocol a decade later: Binford's (1967) procedure "includes examining (1) spatial correlates, (2) temporal correlates, and (3) formal correlates and associated activities of the hypothesized ethnographic activity... and also observing the presence or absence of the same correlates in the archaeological data." LeRoy Johnson (1972:369) identified the key interpretive aspect of this procedure when he noted that by phrasing the analogy-based inference as a hypothesis, the deduced consequences of the hypothesis (typically referred to as "test implications" by the processualists) are "linked together with other things [via the hypothesis] in a highly insightful way to produce a new understanding." Not everyone comprehended these critical aspects of studying the covariation of multiple variables in order to escape the confines of ethnographic data (compare Munson 1969 with Binford's [1972g] rebuttal).

Binford's point was that human behavior, irrespective of spatial and temporal coordinates of particular behaviors, was patterned. Further, "data relevant to most, if not all, the components of past sociocultural systems *are* preserved in the archaeological record" (Binford 1968a:22). Here again was the optimism Binford had first expressed in "Archaeology as Anthropology" (Binford 1962a). Similarly, several processualists (Deetz 1968a; Hill 1966; Longacre 1968) noted that their operating assumption could be phrased something like this: "Human behavior is patterned, and the patterns detected in the archaeological record reflect those behaviors." More optimism. But to carry out this anthropologically oriented agenda, with its focus on culture processes, the processualists needed data. Those data could come from a number of sources, the primary one being artifacts.

CHANGING VIEWS OF ARTIFACTS

The idea that artifact types had emic meanings had been implicit in American archaeology from the start, but it was made explicit by Albert Spaulding (1953b, 1960a), who advocated the use of statistical procedures to discover clusters of attributes (one cluster per specimen) that occurred more frequently than random chance allowed. In combination with refinements periodically suggested for classifying artifacts (e.g., Kluckhohn 1960; Krieger 1960; Phillips 1958; Rouse 1960; Sears 1960; Smith 1962), more and more archaeologists became explicit in suggesting that artifact types had some sort of "cultural significance," as James Gifford (1960) put it. Gifford advocated the use of the type-variety method of artifact classification first formally described by Joe Ben Wheat, Gifford, and William Wasley (1958).

On one hand, when Wheat, Gifford, and Wasley spoke of an artifact "variety," they had in mind an analytical (etic) unit that measured a small spatiotemporal range. It was a subunit under artifact "type," with types having larger spatial and temporal distributions than varieties. Gifford (1960), on the other hand, while agreeing that types and varieties were useful tools for purposes of culture history, made two further assumptions that he and his coauthors had not made earlier. First, varieties approximate actual material ceramic manifestations of individual and small social-group variation in a society. Second, because types generally include multiple varieties, they are summations of individual and small-group variation. Types both reflect cultural values and are a "ceramic idea or 'esthetic ideal' the boundaries of which were imposed through the value system operative in the society by virtue of individual interaction on a societal level" (Gifford 1960:343).

Gifford argued that most people in a culture conform to the demands of a majority of the norms. To substantiate this claim, he quoted various statements by Alfred Kroeber and Clyde Kluckhohn, both of whom had argued that a culture is patterned over time and space as a result of limitations and constraints on innovation that originate in a culture's values or standards. For Gifford (1960:343), then, artifact types "equate themselves with the crystallization of conscious or unconscious...esthetic images conditioned by values." This basic notion that artifacts were made to some sort of culturally dictated convention was reiterated two years later by Watson Smith (1962:1167), who argued that a fictional female potter was subject to "an alarmingly ramified set of intellectual complexes that act to control her ultimate [ceramic] output. Some of these are restrictive, some are expansive. We call them Tradition and Imagination, Conservatism and Invention," respectively.

This is what Binford (1965) had referred to as the traditional, "normative" view of culture, with its emphasis on innovation, diffusion, and migration. Binford (1983b:6) later referred to this as "the view that history causes history."

This simply would not do in the new, processual archaeology. Redefining culture as a means of adaptation provided a host of explanatory options centered around the notion that culture will change when its environmental context changes, where "environment" is broadly construed to include cultural as well as natural phenomena. Thus a culture changes because of adaptive necessity, reducing, at least for Binford, the circularity in saying that culture (ideas) changes because ideas (culture) change. It could be argued that there also is circularity in saying that culture (adaptation) changes because adaptive necessity changes.

But if artifact types were to have emic connotations and also to reflect their functions in terms of adaptation, they had to exhibit two rather different properties. Binford (1963) recognized this. In effect, he argued that what today would be termed "cultural transmission" unmediated by selection would be operative only "within the individual's cultural idiolect or the shared behavioral aspects of culture"; the cultural system, on the other hand, would be modified "through processes of readaptation or evolutionary change" (Binford 1963:92). This is because formally different elements of culture, such as decorative motifs, can be "functional equivalents" when their formal properties crosscut functional classes, and thus they can change by the vagaries of cultural transmission—what Binford labeled "drift"—without affecting the basic structure of the cultural system.

Cultural drift was "a process of formal modification in culture content, particularly within classes of functional equivalents or in relative frequencies of stylistic attributes which may crosscut functional classes" (Binford 1963:93). Stylistic variability was that which varies "with the social context of manufacture exclusive of the variability related to the use of the item"; "historical continuity and social phylogeny are particularly amenable to analysis through the study of stylistic attributes" (Binford 1965:208). Again, "stylistic attributes are most fruitfully studied when questions of ethnic origin, migration, and interaction between groups is the subject of explication" (Binford 1962a:220).

One curious feature of the Binfords' work with Bordes's Mousterian materials was their use of his types. They indicated that these types were "descriptive" (shape related) rather than strictly stylistic or functional. Thus, Bordes's types were at best a very crude measure of functional variation—assuming general correlations between form and function. It was not that Lew suddenly forgot the style-function distinction that he had made a few years earlier (Binford 1963). We suspect that other reasons led to the use of this typology. First of all, the Binfords had to show that, even using Bordes's types, there was a considerable amount of unexplained interassemblage variation. Second, they had to remain in Bordes's good graces to obtain access to his Mousterian collections. Using his collections to create another typology would have been unthinkable, especially to Sally, who had established good rapport with the sometimes volatile Frenchman. Third, the Bordes typology was the unquestioned gold standard of Mousterian lithic analysis, and Middle Paleolithic archaeologists flouted that convention at the risk of their reputations.

The debate over the meaning of variation in the Mousterian artifact assemblages continued until Bordes's death in 1981 (Binford 1989b). It has not yet been resolved. Early on, James Sackett (1968:73) had made clear how critical it was to classify artifacts such that human activities could be "consistently isolated and interpreted." He stressed that the "question of tool function is especially crucial in view of the emphasis a cultural ecological approach places upon the reconstruction of economic tasks" (Sackett 1968:75). These concerns finally led to what came to be referred to as "use-wear" studies—microscopic examination of wear patterns on tools to determine how they were used (e.g., Frison 1968; Keeley 1974b; Morse and Goodyear 1973; Nance 1971; Semenov 1964; Tringham et al. 1974; Wilmsen 1968a, 1968b). We examine some of these studies in Chapter 5. Lew was aware that use-wear analysis would be required to construct a credible functional

typology for the Mousterian artifacts—he said so in a class at UCLA in 1968, as Schiffer recalls—but that would have been regarded as an undertaking far too ambitious at the time.

Although social and practical reasons led the Binfords to use the Bordes system, even though it was an imperfect measure of artifact function, other processualists had a Spaulding-esque faith in the power of statistics to reveal past behavior. Indeed, some processualists apparently believed that the objectivity of statistical methods would detect patterning among artifacts and variously identify types (statistically significant clusters of attributes) and tool kits (statistically significant clusters of types), and thus the archaeologist didn't need to worry about what the classification actually was measuring. Simply input the attributes or types, and the computer would do the rest. As might be expected, some who commented on statistical and computer-assisted classification efforts (e.g., Benfer 1967) found such methods useful, but others wondered about the appropriateness of various techniques in archaeological settings (e.g., Sackett 1969). Jim Hill (1972), in a detailed processualist treatment of classification, affirmed J. O. Brew's (1971) point that classifications were not rote methods but rather problem-oriented measuring instruments whose construction required great care. Again, Binford (1968a) had argued that numerical taxonomy would solve culture history's problem of how to distinguish between analogues and homologues, but whether it could be used for addressing other problems was unclear.

Alex Krieger (1960:146) identified the most serious problem in using statistical methods to discover artifact types when he noted that "a different set of 'types' would result for each site or run of material treated"; that is, the types would be specific to the set of specimens analyzed. This was disputed by Donald Tugby (1965), who in an early overview of statistical methods argued that they allow one to identify clusters of phenomena at various scales (attributes, discrete objects, sets of discrete objects). He noted that "at the first step in archaeological research—the definition of a basic unit—there is some uncertainty about the criteria to be employed in choosing the relevant attributes" and that, following Julian Steward (1954), one could distinguish among morphological types, historical-index types, functional types, and cultural types (Tugby 1965:4). Tugby failed to indicate, however, how attributes were to be chosen to build any one of these typologies, yet this is where the problem identified by Krieger actually originates. Indeed, by choosing different attributes, one will create different types. The nature of the resultant types, whether generated statistically or by other methods, depends entirely on the attributes chosen. Kluckhohn (1960:136) had emphasized that "one makes certain that the criteria [attributes] chosen are actually relevant to the purpose or purposes at hand," but he admitted the difficulties of executing this dictum and furnished no procedure or guidance for choosing attributes. Spaulding (e.g., 1960a) seems never to have thought of this as a significant problem.

The excitement in American archaeology created by Lewis Binford's early thoughts on such topics as culture, systems, and analogy snowballed throughout the 1960s. Archaeology entered the next decade on a rush of enthusiasm, for seemingly processualism had become, like postwar science in general, an "endless frontier." For diverse reasons—some of them academic, some of them undoubtedly personal—Binford made it his mission to reconfigure archaeology into something an ethnologist would recognize. That Binford's plan all along was to create an anthropological archaeology should not have been too surprising to anyone reading *American Antiquity* in 1962. The title of his first article, after all, was "Archaeology as Anthropology," and its opening sentence was, "It has been aptly stated that 'American archaeology is anthropology or it is nothing' (Willey and Phillips, 1958, p. 2)" (Binford 1962a:217). As we noted earlier, that phrase had been recycled from an earlier statement by Phillips (1955:246–247) that read, "New World archaeology is anthropology or it is nothing." Strengthening the link between

archaeology and anthropology had been on the agenda of the Phillips-and-Willey generation long before Binford's pronouncement.

Binford added a new, and strident, voice expressing the general unrest in American archaeology when he wrote "Archaeology as Anthropology." But his commitment to anthropology went beyond underscoring Phillips's one-liner, for he followed up the 1962 publication with a series of articles that by the end of the decade had sketched out the shape of a "new," anthropological archaeology. Much of Binford's success can be attributed to having landed his first academic job in a prestigious department that attracted very bright and ambitious students. Although ensconced in a conservative department, these students were ready to countenance change. Had he gone to a college or small university, especially one lacking a graduate program in anthropology, his impact might have been far different. Binford found a receptive audience for his ideas, but the give and take that occurred at Chicago was hardly one sided. Others worked out not just details of Binford's program but also key elements and their implications.

Binford was a master at using every tool at his disposal to promote processualism, in the process promoting himself—too much, some would say, including Jimmy Griffin (1976), under whom Binford had worked at Michigan. Binford would have been the perfect front man for most sales promotions; the only difference in archaeology was that he was selling his own product. And it was a product in which he firmly believed. In some of his early publications Binford revealed a quality employed by good salespeople: the ability to be ambiguous or to resort to confusion when pushed for specifics. This works particularly well when you haven't quite figured out everything and are making it up on the fly, or when you say something and later have to make it sound as if that's not exactly what you said. Take this sentence, which James Stoltman (1984) highlighted in his review of Binford's *Working at Archaeology*: "If we recognize that cultural systems are differentially localized in different places and are internally differentiated, then we must expect some of the more visible archaeological patterning to refer to these internal differentiations and their differential disposition in space, not systems change or differences in the identity of systems per se" (Binford 1983c:65).

Binford's sometimes confusing style wasn't limited to the written word, as he demonstrated in an interview with Paula Sabloff in 1982.

Paula Sabloff: You have a reputation as being rough around the edges in language.

Lewis Binford: If I'm trying to say something that I don't think has been said, there's no trite way of saying it. A cliché is usually pretty meaningless and also obvious to anyone who reads it. If you're trying to say something with the same words that everybody else is using, but you think you don't want them to think about it the same way, you have to play with the way you use words. If an editor or person reads my sentence, which I wrote in clear prose, and says, "Yeah, I know what you're saying," then I know that he missed the point; and I take that sentence and make a whole paragraph out of it to make sure that he understands what is different about what I am saying. I write so that people have got to read and reread it so that maybe they have got the meaning.

PS: Why? Why didn't you think the first time worked?

LB: Because they translated it into what they thought I was saying, not what I was say-

ing. In a sense, the clearer writing is, the more ambiguous the terms are.... In other words, the clearest sentence would be the sentence that everybody would give meaning to immediately. But the degree [to which] they all do it the same way is not at all clear.

PS: You mean in scientific writing.

LB: That's right. And if I'm trying to manipulate a reader, I can't do it by making him think he knows what I'm saying. Because if I think I'm saying something that he doesn't know; or I think I'm saying something new, then why should he think it's all so clear and he's thought it all along? (Sabloff 1998:63)

Any serious challenges to Binford were still far off in the 1960s. Discovering cultural processes was still firmly at the top of the agenda, and it was becoming increasingly clear, at least to some processualists, that the path to those processes led through the philosophy of science, deductive methods in particular. Hints in this direction had been dropped by Albert Spaulding (1968), but by 1970 those hints had become full-fledged statements by archaeologists-turned-philosophers—a topic that we examine in Chapter 4. But first, what about products of the new archaeology? One can talk all day about culture and processes, but without salable products, customers will begin to drift away. In the case of processualism, those products were being cranked out even as Binford was penning "Archaeology as Anthropology." We inspect some of those early products in Chapter 3.

3

The First Processualist Case Studies

We may explain changes or differences in certain attributes of artifacts or features in terms of variations in prehistoric economy; such explanations may be largely irrelevant for explaining variations in motor habits as documented in the same artifacts. If we treat both these kinds of variation as undifferentiated measures of cultural difference, we are scarcely getting reliable information about past cultural systems.

—Lewis R. Binford, "Archaeological Perspectives"

Although there had long been an awareness in American archaeology that artifacts have to be classified in different ways to serve different analytical purposes (e.g., Brew 1946; Steward 1954), the traditional practice was simply to rely on classifications constructed to measure time and space, irrespective of the questions being posed. Not surprisingly, with their new analytical questions, processualists developed new classification systems. For a convenient synopsis of what the early and influential case studies that employed these systems looked like, probably the best single source is Sally and Lew Binford's (1968a) *New Perspectives in Archeology*. In his review of the book Mark Leone (1971) pointed out that its chapters represented "innovative breakthroughs" in three areas of anthropological

archaeology: systems theory, cultural ecology, and materialist-oriented evolution. To be sure, elements of each had appeared in the 1950s and early 1960s, Leone noted, but their newness lay in how they were integrated and interrelated under the processualist banner. He argued that a conceptual shift had allowed the ecology of a landscape to be integrated with human technologies and economies. That conceptual shift included Leslie White's (1949, 1959) evolutionary theory and Julian Steward's (1955) cultural ecology, together with attempts to discern their interrelationships.

We agree with Leone that the processualists' conceptual breakthroughs were in the applications of systems theory, cultural ecology, and materialist-oriented evolution. Although coming from different disciplines, systems theory and cultural ecology shared a concern for discerning systems, identifying their components, and seeking among the latter various connections established by flows of matter, energy, and information. These were, and are, valuable conceptual tools, but the key ontological underpinning of the entire processualist approach was materialist-oriented (cultural) evolution. The chapters in *New Perspectives* also disclose another important area in which processualists worked, one that became known as "ceramic sociology" (Binford 1983b; Graves 1998; Longacre 2000; Redman 1991).

CERAMIC SOCIOLOGY

Bill Longacre's (1963, 1970a, 2000) historical statements are helpful in reconstructing some of the efforts geared to developing a sociology based on the analysis of prehistoric pottery (see also Graves 1998). In the late 1950s the Field Museum's Paul Martin, known in the Southwest as "Pottery Paul," hired Constance Cronin (Figure 3.1), a University of Chicago graduate student in social anthropology, to carry out stylistic analyses of some Southwestern pottery types. Cronin (1962) found that specific design elements would occur on pottery from one site but not from another. In Longacre's (2000:294) words, she concluded that "decoration of pottery might reflect the learning frameworks of mothers teaching daughters, who taught their own daughters, and so on." Longacre, Martin, and Jim Hill took this to signify that if one added the spatial distribution of such variation—in terms of the combinations of decorative elements—one might be able to test propositions about postmarital residence behaviors and descent (Longacre 2000). In effect, these learning frameworks would create localized microstyles, a conclusion that on its surface was not in the least revolutionary. Indeed, Longacre (1963), in discussing these expectations, showed their compatibility with the prevailing type-variety system. But their close relationship to culture-historical understandings of ceramic variability did not prevent Cronin's research and, especially, the later efforts by Longacre and Hill from becoming hallmark case studies of the new archaeology.

The fact that some archaeologists were actually attempting to ascend the ladder of inference to learn about past social organization—something K. C. Chang (1967a:13) later referred to as engaging in "the fancy game of socio-cultural reconstruction"—caught the at-

FIGURE 3.1. Constance Cronin, Chicago, ca. 1960. (Courtesy Stephen Nash.)

tention of Chicago's newest archaeologist, Lewis Binford. The ceramic research going on at Chicago under Martin's auspices dovetailed perfectly with Binford's (1968a:23) claim that the limits to our knowledge of the past were set not by the archaeological record but by archaeologists' "methodological naiveté." Longacre (2000:294) reported that Binford "was very supportive of our initial attempts at Ceramic Sociology but added new directions including computer-assisted techniques."

These initial efforts included the dissertations of Longacre and Hill, which were based on multivariate analyses of pottery obtained through fieldwork in east-central Arizona undertaken as part of Martin's expeditions. The efforts apparently validated Spaulding's belief, so vigorously promoted by Binford, that statistics could be used for discovering significant, previously unsuspected archaeological patterns. Ironically, the Achilles heel of these studies would turn out to be the statistics themselves, as well as the many auxiliary assumptions, explicit and implicit, needed in their application and interpretation. Reactions to the Longacre and Hill studies would profoundly influence the directions of archaeology in the 1970s and 1980s.

Longacre's dissertation, on Carter Ranch Pueblo (Figures 2.8 and 3.2), was completed in 1963. It was followed by a host of highly visible publications on the site (Longacre 1964, 1966, 1968) and an updated version of his dissertation (Longacre 1970c). Longacre also published an edited book, *Reconstructing Prehistoric Pueblo Societies* (1970d), whose introductory essay traced an interest in prehistoric social organization to the late nineteenth-century founders of Southwestern archaeology. Analyses of materials from Broken K Pueblo (Figures 2.8 and 3.3) formed the basis of Hill's

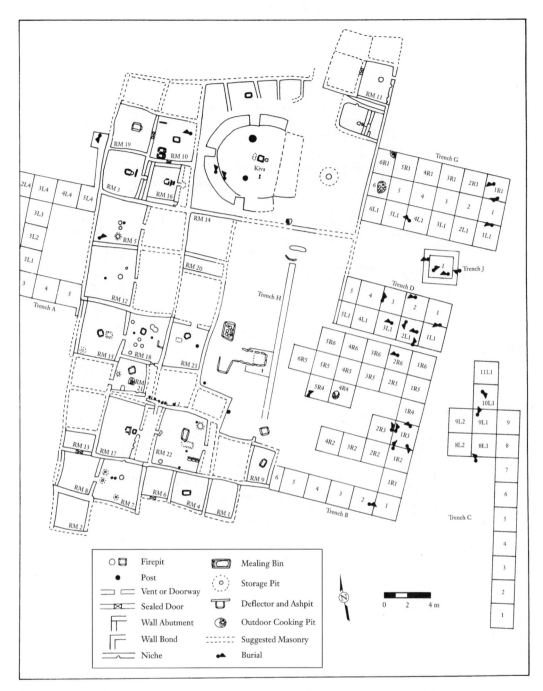

FIGURE 3.2. Ground plan of Carter Ranch Pueblo, a twelfth-century A.D. site in east-central Arizona. (After Longacre 1970c.)

dissertation (Hill 1965) and of subsequent publications (Hill 1966, 1968, 1970b), including the monograph version of his dissertation (Hill 1970a). Hill's chapter in *Reconstructing Prehistoric Pueblo Societies* (Hill 1970b) was a methodological statement on how to reconstruct different aspects of social organization.

Another founding member of the ceramic-sociology school was James Deetz, who graduated from Harvard University in 1960. Deetz's

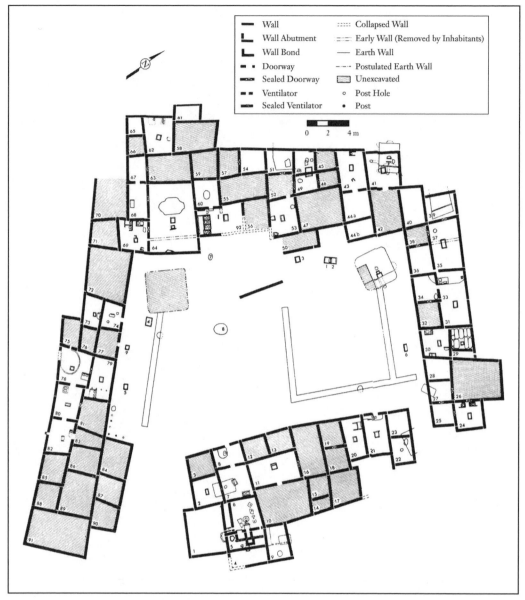

FIGURE 3.3. Ground plan of Broken K Pueblo, a twelfth- and thirteenth-century A.D. site in east-central Arizona. (After Hill 1970a.)

(1960) dissertation on pottery from the Medicine Crow site in South Dakota was later published as *The Dynamics of Stylistic Change in Arikara Ceramics* (Deetz 1965). Like Hill and Longacre, Deetz had a chapter in the Binfords' *New Perspectives* (Deetz 1968a). There, Deetz spelled out the analytical and interpretive algorithm he used on the Medicine Crow sherds. Like Binford and the Chicago processualists,

Deetz placed considerable emphasis on patterning, noting that typologies are made possible because culturally patterned behavior causes covariation among some attributes in a large artifact sample. If cultural patterns change, then patterns of attribute covariation might also change. Thus, "a connection between social structure and ceramics might be seen in the possible changes in design configurations in ceramics as they reflect a change in the residence rule of the culture which produced them" (Deetz 1965:2).

For example, in instances where pottery making is a female craft and matrilocal residence prevails, patterns of ceramic manufacture should be passed down by women from generation to generation (mothers teaching daughters), creating consistent patterning of design attributes. If, however, the matrilocal residence pattern is disrupted by any outside stress, the formerly tight associations among design elements of a matrilineal group's pots would break down; the attributes would therefore be associated more weakly, tending toward randomness. Thus, changes in patterns of social organization might be reflected in changes in ceramic-attribute patterns. Why should it be assumed that pottery making was a female craft? Because ethnographic studies in the Southwest and elsewhere showed that in the vast majority of cases females made and decorated pottery.

Deetz compared proportions of sherds displaying particular design elements across three temporally sequential assemblages. His analysis revealed an apparent decrease in the association of design elements, leading Deetz to conclude that a change away from matrilocality was most likely responsible. To use the terms of Hill and Longacre, the social distance between groups had decreased, and thus cultural transmission between them had increased, leading to less exclusivity in patterns of attribute association. At about the same time, Binford (1965:204) was formulating a generalization about social distance: "Culture is transmitted between generations and across breeding populations in inverse proportion to the degree of social distance maintained between the groups in question." (Deleting the words "degree of" makes what Binford was saying more precise.) This lawlike generalization would underlie most studies of ceramic sociology, including those of the Chicago group.

In his analysis of pottery from Carter Ranch Pueblo, Longacre's theoretical and methodological arguments were virtually identical to those of Deetz, beginning with the most general assumption that "social demography and social organization are reflected in the material system" (Longacre 1970c:28). Longacre (1964:1454) had earlier offered a more specific argument: "If there were a system of localized matrilineal descent groups in the village, then ceramic manufacture and decoration would be learned and passed down within the lineage frame, it being assumed that the potters were female as they are today among the western Pueblos. Nonrandom preference for design attributes would reflect this social pattern." Indeed, "the smaller and more closely tied the social aggregate, the more details of design will be shared.... [D]ifferential relative frequencies of designs may suggest the delimitation of various social aggregates" (Longacre 1970c:28). On the basis of statistical analyses, Longacre found an apparent pattern consistent with localized matrilineal groups: certain design elements were nonrandomly associated with distinct blocks of rooms at Carter Ranch. Longacre also found evidence of what he took to be status differentiation and sexual division of labor.

Like other processualists, Hill assumed that human behavior is patterned and that this creates patterns in the archaeological record. In his analysis of Broken K Pueblo, Hill (1966:12) took as his problem to "find as many clusters or patterns in the data as possible, and then to interpret them as reflecting parts of a village activity structure and social organization." He recognized the importance of controlling for temporal differences among his collections so that the aggregates of artifacts would not comprise what would later be termed "coarse-grained," or "palimpsest," assemblages (Binford 1978, 1980, 1981a), but he ultimately had to assume that all the room blocks were occupied at the same time. In one straightforward analysis, which has withstood later scrutiny, Hill showed with simple statistical analysis (of artifacts, ecofacts, and features inside structures) that there were several room types at Broken K. Drawing on ethnographic data from the Western Pueblos, he interpreted these room types in functional terms: storerooms, habitation rooms, and kivas (ceremonial structures).

Following in Longacre's footsteps, Hill (1966) employed multivariate statistics (factor analysis) on pottery design elements and claimed to have discerned several matrilocal residence units. However, the design element associations were not as strong as those that Longacre found at Carter Ranch. In seeking an explanation for this weaker ceramic patterning, Hill noted that Broken K was a bit younger than Carter Ranch and that the end of Broken K's occupation corresponded with a period of environmental stress. A change in the natural environment, Hill suggested, might have led to a social response. More specifically, he proposed an environmental perturbation that reduced the local carrying capacity (see Zubrow 1971, 1975)—the amount of needed resources (Glassow 1978)—and thus the size of the resident population, prompting a greater level of intravillage integration and reduction in social distance. Here Hill deftly nested his ceramic-sociology study within the materialist-evolutionist theoretical framework that Binford was bringing into prominence. But to reiterate: the assumptions about ceramic style that underpinned these studies owed much to the culture historians. Ceramic sociology needed neither Leslie White nor Julian Steward, only the optimism that clever analyses could produce patterns interpretable as traces of past social organization (Graves 1998; Watson 1977).

Other case studies helped to establish the plausibility of the processualist claim that inferences of social organization were within archaeological grasp. Some of these studies are noteworthy for their ingenuity. Working in east-central Arizona with the support of Paul Martin, Mark Leone, a University of Arizona doctoral student, employed stylistic variation over time in pottery from Hay Hollow Valley to test the materialist hypothesis that at the community level, economic autonomy leads to social autonomy (Leone 1968a, 1968b). His index of social autonomy, based on the degree of community exogamy, was pure ceramic sociology.

Not surprisingly, Leone assumed that women were the potters and that they taught this craft to their daughters. If so, he proposed, then the pottery of exogamous patrilocal communities, where upon marriage women move to their husbands' communities, should exhibit more stylistic variation than the pottery in matrilocal communities. As his index of economic autonomy, Leone charted changes in agriculture dependence. Finding similarities in the shapes of the graphs of agricultural dependence and stylistic variation, Leone concluded that social autonomy was in fact correlated with economic autonomy. This study was explicitly framed as an exercise in hypothesis testing and, like one of Longacre's early papers on Carter Ranch Pueblo, was published in *Science*. The appearance of processual papers in this prestigious journal helped to enhance both the program's visibility and credibility.

Robert Whallon (1968) drew on Deetz's work in his own analysis of design elements on Owasco and Iroquois pottery from New York. He found a trend in younger sites toward increased intrasite homogeneity in designs, from which he inferred decreasing social contact among villages. Whallon found what he took to be solid evidence for less strongly integrated social units early on, with a trend toward matrilocal residence and matrilineages later in time. He suggested the cause of these changes resided in resource intensification in the face of population increase and a trend toward complex social organization.

What were some of the reactions to these ceramic-sociological studies? Spaulding (1966) found Deetz's (1965) study to be "an admirable contribution," if statistically unsophisticated. Although he agreed that Deetz was to "be commended," Wesley Hurt (1966) questioned the validity of Deetz's assumption that residential change was the dominant factor in the degree of variation in design-element styles. This was questionable, Hurt argued, because Deetz's materials dated to the protohistoric period, when indigenous peoples were experiencing many disruptions. Margaret Hardin Friedrich, based on her study of potters and pottery designs in a Tarascan (Mexico) village, found the studies by Deetz, Longacre, and Hill to rest "on a naive view of culture as consisting of sets of objective elements correlated with one another in a limited and mechanical fashion" (Friedrich 1970:332). Her data indicated that not all design variables reflected variation in the intensity of communication among painters. Thus one could not automatically assume that all prehistoric design variables on pottery from an Arikara village or from a pueblo were transmitted in mechanical fashion.

LeRoy Johnson (1972) pointed out that there were no ethnographies that correlated intrasite distribution of tools with postmarital residence. The processualists recognized this, which is why they began to search for laws and later to conduct ethnoarchaeological research (Chapter 7). Their goal was to generate correlations between sociocultural behaviors and archaeological phenomena so that when prehistoric instances of the phenomena were encountered, they could be treated as signatures of the behaviors. Albert Bartovics (1974) evaluated Hill's and Longacre's studies in terms of supposed criteria of experimental science. He listed four "attributes" of experiments, implying they were necessary and sufficient for the distinction of a scientific experiment: (1) objectivity in analysis, (2) manipulative control of key variables, (3) a hypothetical mechanism that causes change, and (4) demonstration of a cause-and-effect relationship. Neither of the processualist studies he examined met all of the criteria, but Bartovics succeeded in identifying ways to strengthen such studies, such as by using modern observations to pinpoint cause-and-effect relationships between cultural processes and archaeological phenomena.

Michael Stanislawski (1973) pointed out that Longacre's study of Carter Ranch rested on normative theory—a statement that applies equally to the work of Deetz, Hill, Leone, and Whallon. Recall that normative theory (artifact types reflect cultural norms and are diffused by means of cultural transmission), a bête noire of processualism, was ascribed by Binford (1963,

1965) to the traditionalists' paradigm of reconstructing culture history. The extent to which that kind of theory actually underpinned culture history is debatable (Lyman and O'Brien 2004b; Leone 1972b), but it is clear that it formed the basis of ceramic sociology (Plog 1983). William Allen and James Richardson (1971:42, 43) put it well in two sentences: First, the studies had to assume that females were "taught by their mothers and other related females to select certain combinations of attributes which were prescribed by lineage norms." Second, when the lines of transmission were broken by a shift to nonmatrilocal residence, "women who once selected certain combinations of attributes which were prescribed by the lineage norms [could now] choose designs with greater freedom (as a result of moving outside of their matrilocal unit), and there resulted a lower degree of patterning [homogeneity] in the finished artifact[s]."

Stanislawski (1973) also noted that Longacre's study was internally contradictory and lacking in multiple working hypotheses. This deficiency would soon be addressed by at least some processualists (Chapter 4). Stanislawski found it ironic that Longacre would claim that he was eschewing historical explanations in favor of processual ones when the basis of his argument for matrilocality was derived from a notation Ruth Bunzel (1929) had made in her monograph *The Pueblo Potter* that her Hopi informants mentioned their mothers as a source of information about pottery production. Wasn't this history, Stanislawski asked? He pointed out that Bunzel had made it clear that Hopi women also learned designs from each other as well as from looking at prehistoric sherds. They also borrowed designs from other communities. In short, there was no rule that limited where a woman's designs could come from.

In addition to reviews that focused on the underlying tenets of the ceramic-sociological studies, there were those that focused on methodological issues. George Cowgill (1968), for example, could not replicate Leslie Freeman and Jim Brown's (1964) findings from Carter

Ranch, and Joseph Lischka (1975) had a difficult time reproducing Hill's results from Broken K. The most extensive criticism was voiced by Don Dumond (1977), who identified several epistemological as well as methodological problems with the work of Deetz, Longacre, and Hill. Dumond pointed out that to identify residence units in the archaeological record, the analyst has to be able to exclude all other possible sources of variation that could be expected to produce similar artifact distribution patterns. In Dumond's estimation each of the three studies fell short in terms of control and/or replicability. His conclusion was that "these studies do not demonstrate a coincidence between patterns in archaeological ceramic elements and residence units, although Deetz's study did raise some possibility of it" (Dumond 1977:345). He added that the very fame of the studies raises questions about archaeology, anthropology, and the effective pursuit of scientific endeavor.

All employ a framework that conceives of systemic relationships of cause and effect. All conceive of archaeological communities as containing potential evidence of complex relationships of variables relating to the adaptation of a people to their social and natural environment. All three studies followed a procedure of introducing hypotheses and generating tests of them against data. Only Deetz, however, before accepting his initial hypothesis considered alternative propositions that might explain the patterning he found. Both Longacre and Hill, on the other hand, apparently sought for patterns and accepted such skewed distributions as they found as confirmation of the initial hypotheses. (Dumond 1977:345)

Dumond, in effect, was saying that Hill and Longacre found exactly what they wanted to find because they hadn't considered other possibilities. One doesn't have to read between the lines of Dumond's article to see that he found such ills to plague much of the new archaeology, especially given that he titled his review "Science in Archaeology: The Saints Go Marching In."

Similar shortcomings in the early ceramic-sociological studies continued to be pointed out well into the 1980s (e.g., Graves 1985; Plog 1980; Schiffer 1989; Skibo, Schiffer, and Kowalski 1989). Regardless, one or more examples entered nearly all introductory textbooks that appeared in the 1970s, such as Frank Hole and Robert Heizer's (1973) *An Introduction to Prehistoric Archeology* and David Hurst Thomas's (1979) *Archaeology*. The case studies were presented as credible, if not entirely successful, attempts to infer social phenomena. They thus transmitted to new generations of aspiring archaeologists a measure of optimism on the potential of the archaeological record to yield anthropological information. Spaulding (1968) had identified the inescapable dependence of archaeology on cultural anthropology for sources of interpretation and explanation. Similarly, various reviewers of the early case studies pointed out that the building of interpretive models would require a great deal more work with modern peoples (Caldwell 1971; Ellis 1972; Leone 1971).

The more critical reviews, especially Stanislawski's (1973), spurred processualists (Longacre, in particular) to conduct ethnoarchaeological studies to better understand relationships between nonmaterial elements of a society and their material correlates. If they were going to postulate such things as postmarital residence rules, then they had better base their inferences on more than a single ethnographic study. There are hints that the processualists knew this even before the reviews started appearing. In their chapters in *New Perspectives*, Bill Longacre and James Ayres (1968) and Bobby Jo Williams (1968) produced examples of what would become known in the 1970s as "ethnoarchaeology," "living archaeology," and "middle-range theory"—topics that we take up in Chapter 7.[1]

Deetz turned elsewhere for generalizations. In his chapter in Betty Meggers's (1968) *Anthropological Archeology in the Americas*, Deetz (1968b:121) indicated that what eventually would be known as historical archaeology could result in "quite sophisticated refinements in the method and theory of modern archeology and anthropology." He demonstrated some of the refinements in a series of innovative studies of headstones with Edwin Dethlefsen (Deetz and Dethlefsen 1965, 1967, 1971; Dethlefsen and Deetz 1966) (Figure 3.4). Deetz and Dethlefsen were interested in evaluating archaeological techniques such as frequency seriation for inferring diffusion and design evolution. In so doing, they performed some unique tests of the popularity principle that underpinned traditional culture history and also showed that one could track the geographic spread of culture traits.

THE STUDY OF SYSTEMS

The idea that a culture could be conceptualized and studied as a system had numerous effects on archaeological research after 1960. Studies that adopted a systems framework reached well beyond questions asked in ceramic sociology about marital residence patterns and the like. A case can be made that a systems perspective—delineating subsystems, specifying their hierarchical and horizontal relationships, and identifying matter-energy interactions among subsystems and between the system and the environment—literally was at the core of processualism. The centrality of systems thinking in the new archaeology was expressed most forcefully by Kent Flannery (Figure 3.5) in his review of Gordon Willey's (1966) first volume of *An Introduction to American Archaeology*, a massive two-volume synthesis of the prehistory of North and South America that grew out of his earlier summaries of Western Hemisphere prehistory (e.g., Willey 1960).

Flannery's (1967) review, "Culture History v. Cultural Process: A Debate in American Archaeology," was a short and pointed comparison of the old and new approaches to archaeology. With respect to systems, Flannery (1967:119) noted that "the process school would like to move crucial decisions...farther from the individual by arguing that systems, once set in motion, are self-regulating to the

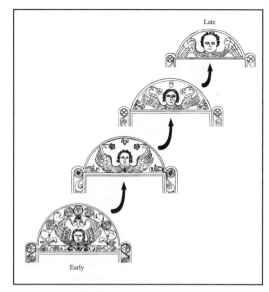

FIGURE 3.4. A phyletic seriation of gravestones from a cemetery in Charlestown, Massachusetts, showing reduction in cherub-head design complexity between 1720 and 1760. The sequence was based on headstones of known date, but it illustrates the technique of arranging groups of specimens based on a proposed evolutionary sequence, here a design sequence. The gravestones came from a single graveyard, thus meeting one of the criteria of the standard seriation model— that what is being measured is variation in time rather than variation in space. James Deetz and Edwin Dethlefsen (1965) explored this important issue relative to New England headstones, pointing out the effect of geographic distance on the appearance and disappearance of various headstone designs. (After Dethlefsen and Deetz 1966.)

FIGURE 3.5. *Right,* Kent Flannery at a Fourth of July party, Oaxaca, Mexico, 1971. (Photograph by Carl Kuttruff.)

point where they do not even necessarily allow rejection or acceptance of new traits by a culture." This was a different way of looking at culture that made the culturological perspective of Leslie White (e.g., 1959), who had also talked about culture as a system, seem moderate by comparison. The views that Flannery articulated so clearly would decades later be a foil for postprocessualists, who insisted that people, as sentient agents, be put back into studies of the past (Chapter 8). Flannery would also moderate his position substantially (Chapter 7).

It was one thing to talk about culture as a system, but it was quite another to structure archaeological research so as to be able to examine not only the system but why the system changed structurally. Although Taylor's "conjunctive approach" acknowledged connections between the parts of a culture—he was, after all, a functionalist—we find little in *A Study of Archeology* that suggests he offered a blueprint for how to get at the causes of structural change. Few archaeologists in the 1940s and 1950s did. The most influential article that tackled this problem was Flannery's (1968a) "Archeological Systems Theory and Early Mesoamerica," which appeared in Meggers's *Anthropological Archeology in the Americas*. It has elements in common with several other pieces he published around the same time (Flannery 1965, 1966), including one he coauthored with Michael Coe (Flannery and Coe 1968) for the Binfords' *New Perspectives*.

Flannery's chapter in the Meggers volume had the most far-reaching influence because it integrated the major theoretical components of processualism in an attempt to solve a long-standing problem: the origin of maize domestication. Flannery began with the Whitean definition of culture, but he took it more literally than most archaeologists and joined it to Julian Steward's ecological approach. As the extra-somatic means of adaptation, a cultural system is coupled by the technologies of its subsistence and settlement subsystems to an environmental context. Thus, the scheduling of subsistence activities by a prehistoric group is tied (adapted) to the seasonal availability of plant and animal

resources (more on that below). A change in the environment prompts a change in these subsystems, which then has ripple effects throughout the cultural system.

Operationalizing what might be thought of as a human-ecology approach required detailed knowledge of prehistoric environments and fostered the development of paleoecological methods and subdisciplines such as paleoethnobotany and zooarchaeology. Flannery himself had considerable experience in the latter, having written his dissertation on faunal remains from sites in the Tehuacán Valley of Mexico (Flannery 1964). The data these fields generated had been discussed in the 1950s (e.g., Braidwood and Braidwood 1950; Meighan et al. 1958a, 1958b; Taylor 1957) but with rare exceptions were not analyzed thoroughly or consistently until the 1960s. Not until the advent of modern cultural resource management studies in the 1970s did funding become available in the United States for supporting the training of full-time specialists in these new fields (Chapter 6).

The only systems theorist Flannery cited in his paper in the Meggers volume was Magoroh Maruyama, a Japanese systems philosopher then at Stanford. Flannery built his argument around Maruyama's influential paper, "The Second Cybernetics: Deviation-Amplifying Mutual Causal Processes" (Maruyama 1963). As a result of Flannery's lead, Maruyama became a household name in archaeology in the late 1970s (e.g., Hill 1977b; Salmon 1978), despite the fact that his article contained not a single example drawn from human behavior. To understand the lure that cybernetics held for archaeology requires that we first understand something about systems theory—a supposedly unifying conceptual framework (it wasn't) that also caught hold in anthropology and other social sciences in the 1960s. The work of German theoretical biologist Ludwig von Bertalanffy (1950a, 1950b) is regarded as seminal in systems theory, although Binford recommended that his students read the work of biologist James Grier Miller, the creator of living-systems theory (e.g., Miller 1965a, 1965b).

To von Bertalanffy, systems—at least those that he referred to as "open systems"—constantly interact with their environments, in the process acquiring new properties. Open systems can obtain and concentrate energy. Because that energy is eventually turned into work and heat, such systems do not conflict with the Second Law of Thermodynamics. As such, systems evolve. Systems theory focuses not only on how the parts of a system are arranged and what their functions are, but also on the kinds of relations that connect the parts into a whole. The axiom underlying systems theory is that no matter how complex the world is, there are always different types of organization that structure that complexity at some scale. This organization can be described in terms of concepts that are independent of the specific corner of complexity into which we might be looking—thus, the claim of generality in *general* systems theory.

In his review of Willey's (1966) synthesis of North American prehistory, Flannery described how a system functioned:

Once a system has moved in a certain direction, it automatically sets up the limited range of possible moves it can make at the next critical turning point. This view is not original with the process-school archeologists—it is borrowed from Ludwig von Bertalanffy's framework for the developing embryo, where systems trigger behavior at critical junctures and, once they have done so, cannot return to their original pattern. The process school argues that there are systems so basic in nature that they can be seen operating in virtually every field—prehistory not excepted. Culture is about as powerless to divert these systems as the individual is to change his culture. (Flannery 1967:119)

This was a pretty bold assertion: systems, like the Energizer Bunny®, just keep going and going, regardless of what culture does. In one respect this was an odd statement to make because with humans the system *is* culture; the two cannot be separated. Flannery undoubtedly realized this because the next year, when

he published "Archeological Systems Theory and Early Mesoamerica" (Flannery 1968a), he bypassed general systems theory in favor of Maruyama's (1963) "second" cybernetics. He also passed over the issue of culture as a system, focusing solely on one subsystem, food procurement.

It is unfortunate that Flannery didn't make clear that his focus was not on general systems theory but on a more ecological model. He later referred to this lack of clarity as "perhaps the biggest mistake I made" (Flannery 1986b:19) with respect to the 1968 paper. It *was* a big mistake, coming on the heels of the review of Willey's book, in which Flannery cited von Bertalanffy with favor. Flannery could have cleared up the confusion in his 1973 "Archeology with a Capital S" paper (Chapter 4), answering James Doran's (1970) criticism and probably warding off Merrilee Salmon's (1978) later criticism, but he didn't.

Cybernetics, known as the science of control, is best viewed as a special case of systems theory, although the two terms often are used synonymously. Cybernetics was the brainchild of MIT mathematician Norbert Wiener (1948, 1950), who adapted it from Claude Shannon's (1948; Shannon and Weaver 1949) information theory. With significant help from William Ross Ashby (1956), Kenneth Boulding (1956a, 1956b), Heinz von Foerster (1949), and others, Wiener moved it into the social sciences from the physical sciences and engineering. With cybernetics, systems are viewed not simply as open entities but as adaptive and self-regulating entities. Key to self-regulation are negative-feedback loops that allow a homeostatic system to monitor the state of a component and to make subtle adjustments that keep the state within a specific range of values, just as a thermostat regulates the temperature inside a house. Maruyama (1963) labeled this model the "deviation-counteracting mutual causal system," or the "first cybernetics." This is the cybernetics of stability, of systems and subsystems that undergo continuous minor adjustments, none of which provoke structural change.

Maruyama was interested instead in what he called the "deviation-amplifying mutual-causal system," or the "second cybernetics" (in the vernacular, these processes were known as "positive feedback"). Deviation-amplifying mutual-causal systems include "all processes of mutual causal relationships that amplify an insignificant or accidental initial kick, build up deviation and diverge from the initial condition" (Maruyama 1963:164). Although negative feedback retards any changes, the second cybernetics deals with systems that do change as a result of cascading effects through positive feedback from the initial "kick." Maruyama's choice of words—first and second cybernetics—was unfortunate because by the mid-1960s these terms had already acquired quite different meanings. "First-order cybernetics" meant the science of systems as observed by the scientist, and "second-order cybernetics" meant the science of observing systems. The latter cybernetics was based on the belief that no system can truly be studied objectively—that the observer is an integral and inseparable part of a system (von Foerster 1981).

Flannery (1968a) used Maruyama's two kinds of cybernetics to examine the evolution of food-procurement systems in the Southern Highlands of Mexico. He characterized the period 5000 B.C.–1500 B.C.—the transition from food collecting to sedentary agriculture—as "one of gradual change in a series of procurement systems, regulated by two mechanisms called seasonality and scheduling" (Flannery 1968a:68). Seasonality is the periodization of the resource base, when plants ripen or deer are at their prime. Scheduling is a cultural activity that resolves conflict between different procurement systems. Flannery (1968a:79) pointed out that "under conditions of fully-achieved and permanently-maintained equilibrium, prehistoric cultures might never have changed. That they did change was due at least in part to the existence of positive feedback or 'deviation-amplifying' processes."

In the Mesoamerican case, the accidental initial kicks to the system that started the

deviation-amplifying processes were genetic changes that had taken place in one or two plant species that had built up mutualistic relationships with humans over the millennia. Under this scenario, "the exploitation of these plants [maize and its genetic relatives] had been a relatively minor procurement system compared with that of maguey, cactus fruits, deer, or tree legumes, but positive feedback following these initial genetic changes caused one minor system to grow all out of proportion to the others, and eventually to change the whole ecosystem of the Southern Mexican Highlands" (Flannery 1968a:79).

Flannery (1968a:85) summarized the advantages of a cybernetics model for explaining culture change: "For one thing, it does not attribute cultural evolution to 'discoveries,' 'inventions,' 'experiments,' or 'genius,' but instead enables us to treat prehistoric cultures as systems." Further,

we no longer think of the preceramic plant-collectors as a ragged and scruffy band of nomads; instead, they appear as a practiced and ingenious team of lay botanists who know how to wring the most out of a superficially bleak environment. Nor do we still picture the Formative peoples as a happy group of little brown farmers dancing around their cornfields and thatched huts; we see them, rather, as a very complex series of competitive ethnic groups with internal social ranking and great preoccupation with status, iconography, water control, and the accumulation of luxury goods. (Flannery 1968a:67)

Feedback models offered a way around linear cause-and-effect models, a point brought to general attention when Frank Hole and Robert Heizer published the third edition of their textbook, *An Introduction to Prehistoric Archeology* (1973). In it they discussed systems theory in great detail and provided examples of how feedback models worked.

Despite its allure, systems theory had a weakness: it had little to say about change, except to point out that systems either changed in response to external environmental perturbations or they died out. That systems theory was derived from studying systems that did not evolve does not inspire confidence in its ability to deal with change in cultural systems. Anthropologists and archaeologists are interested in more cultural-system-specific principles that actually get at the mechanisms and processes of change. By the mid- to late 1970s, archaeologists (e.g., Athens 1977; Plog 1975) and philosophers of archaeology (e.g., Salmon 1978) began to see the limitations of systems theory, and it assumed less and less of a role in American archaeology. Viewed strictly in these terms, systems theory was yet another dead end for archaeologists searching for a source of explanation. It had to be a dead end because it could offer no causal explanation for anything. But looked at differently, systems theory can be considered a higher-level abstraction of cultural-ecological principles. This is why systems thinking and cultural ecology (see below) so thoroughly interpenetrated, as in Flannery's work.

Schiffer points out that it is doubtful that his own early formulations of cultural formation processes (Chapter 7) would have taken the shape they did without the stimulus of some systems theory. Our colleague Jeff Reid put his finger on it when he once said that a dose of systems theory was really good when one was a first-year graduate student. Systems theory could get one thinking about how superficially unrelated things might be connected; how systems were structured to process flows of matter, energy, and information; and how to ask questions about complex behavioral phenomena in the search for environmental/demographic causes of system change, and so on. By the late 1960s and '70s, aspiring new archaeologists were reading systems theory, cultural ecology, and materialist cultural evolution simultaneously. Each person had to forge some sort of synthesis that made sense, and different processualists came up with different mixes and emphases.

CULTURAL ECOLOGY

Flannery's analysis of the rise of food production in the Southern Highlands of Mexico was one of a growing number of studies during the 1960s that fit comfortably under the broad rubric *cultural ecology,* a term that can be traced in anthropology to the work of Julian Steward beginning in the late '30s. Another "human ecology" arose in the social sciences at large and can be traced to earlier work by the University of Chicago school of urban ecology, particularly the writings of Robert Park and Ernest Burgess (e.g., Park, Burgess, and McKenzie 1925). Steward (1955:5) denied any connection between his cultural ecology and the Chicago human ecology, and in strict terms he was right to do so. His method was narrowly focused, in his view serving primarily as a companion to his multilinear evolutionism.

Ecology, regardless of the modifier that preceded it, was not limited to the esoteric writings of social scientists. By 1960 the seeds were being sown in American society for a greater appreciation of the role of the natural environment in everyday life and how it was being degraded through pollution, overuse of natural resources, unrestrained development, and the like. Humans were soiling their own nest at an alarming rate, and their habits were having a spillover effect into other peoples' nests. "Wastefulness has become a part of the American way of life," wrote pop sociologist Vance Packard in his 1960 best-seller *The Waste Makers.* Although Americans listened to what Packard had to say, his message seemed muted compared to Rachel Carson's warning in *The Silent Spring* (1962) that pesticides would "still the song of birds and the leaping of fish in the streams."

Ecology became an important component of college curricula, and by the mid-1960s had been brought wholesale into cultural anthropology through the work of Andrew Vayda (e.g., 1969; Vayda and Rappaport 1968), Anthony Leeds (e.g., Leeds and Vayda 1965), Roy Rappaport (e.g., 1967, 1968), Richard Watson and Patty Jo Watson (1969), and others (see

Butzer 1982 and Hardesty 1977, 1980). This version of cultural ecology was sometimes referred to as the "second" cultural ecology to distinguish it from Julian Steward's "first" cultural ecology, but by the end of the '60s all ecological work involving humans and their social and physical environments usually was referred to as "ecological anthropology."

Not surprisingly, the neofunctional accounts that dominated ecological anthropology were rarely if ever questioned at the time. (Some of the studies were heavily criticized later. Rappaport's [1968] classic *Pigs for the Ancestors: Ritual in the Ecology of a New Guinea People* was one of these, which prompted a greatly expanded later version [Rappaport 2000].) This was not surprising because many Americans, especially academicians, had come to believe that the "civilized" world had crossed an invisible threshold, leaving behind a state of innocence that could never be recaptured. In contrast, there were noncivilized peoples out there who still lived in equilibrium with their environment, who had developed practices and beliefs that functioned to keep them well adapted to their resource base. The ecological anthropologist's goal was to document as many of these groups as possible before they, too, fouled their nests. But for them, environmental degradation— overexploitation of resources and pollution—would be a result of Western contact. This was more than neofunctionalism; it was another reflection of anthropology's chronic, naive idealization of the "other"—Rousseau's noble savage in ecologist's clothes. As Jared Diamond (1992), Thomas Headland (1997), Charles Redman (1999), Shepard Krech (2000) and numerous others have pointed out, there has never been a period when humans lived in perfect harmony with their environment. These criticisms, came later, however, and only after three conceptual shifts. First, the notion of pristine environments died. Second, hunters and gatherers no longer were viewed as superior ecologists. The third shift, involving modern technology, was more profound, and its ramifications are still being felt.

As revolutionary changes took place in genetics and molecular biology in the latter part of the twentieth century, with the specter of "genetic engineering" looming ahead, the biological research community enjoyed enormous growth. This was true in the academy, in federal institutes, and in the private sector, not only in numbers but also in resources, social power, and prestige. Social scientists began to pay attention to the new biological findings, which had high visibility in scientific journals, in the media, and in popular culture such as science fiction. Even some anthropologists, a minority opinion at first, adopted the heretical view that humans were not that different biologically or behaviorally from other organisms and that much of their behavior was genetically determined. At the very least, it was argued, anthropologists could draw on some of the analytical methods and conceptual tools used in various branches of biology and adapt them to the study of human behavior. Such efforts remain important today in anthropology and archaeology (Chapter 8).

For several reasons, then, by the 1970s ecological anthropology had moved well away from Julian Steward's cultural ecology. The fundamentals of Steward's approach, however, were well entrenched in archaeology, especially in the western United States. This was because so many of Steward's insights and data came from Great Basin societies and, to a lesser extent, those of the southern Columbia Plateau. His ecological notions—especially as they related to sociopolitical organization and economy vis-à-vis the physical environment—fueled discussion among Great Basin archaeologists (e.g., Thomas 1973, 1974, 1983) long after multilinear evolution had run its course as an explanatory tool. In addition, his findings were widely used as analogues in studies of hunter-gatherers outside the Great Basin. We pick up this point again in Chapter 5.

Steward's interest in human-environment interactions began in his teenage years, part of which were spent in the Great Basin (Kerns 1999, 2003). This interest was fostered through an undergraduate major in biology and geology at Cornell University. Marvin Harris (1968b) stated that Steward's exposure in graduate school at the University of California to geographer Carl Sauer surely contributed to his interest, but Steward denied it (Kerns 1999). Despite his use of the term "ecological" in an early article ("Ecological Aspects of Southwestern Society" [Steward 1937]), it probably was much later when Steward formulated the basic framework of what would become known as the cultural-ecological method (Clemmer 1999).

Not until 1955 and the publication of *Theory of Cultural Change: The Methodology of Multilinear Evolution* did Steward explain what cultural ecology entailed: "a method for recognizing the ways in which culture change is induced by adaptation to environment" (Steward 1955:5). Later, in an entry for the *International Encyclopedia of the Social Sciences*, Steward (1968) presented his most readable account of cultural ecology, which he defined as "the study of the processes by which a society adapts to its environment. Its principal problem is to determine whether these adaptations initiate internal social transformations or evolutionary change. It analyzes these adaptations, however, in conjunction with other processes of change. Its method requires examination of the interaction of societies and social institutions with one another and with the natural environment" (Steward 1968:337).

Cultural ecology, then, viewed culture as a system, but its main focus was not culture in the abstract sense but on-the-ground cultures, or "societies," as Steward had started calling them. It focused on the process of how societies adapt to their physical environments. Steward made an important distinction between "internal social transformations" and "evolutionary change," but he did not follow it up. This was unfortunate because he was pointing out the difference between change and evolution. Whereas evolution involves change—evolution *is* change—the reverse is not true: Not all changes in a society are of an evolutionary sort.

When a chameleon alters its skin color, this is change but not evolution. When three-toed hipparionine horses became one-toed equines, that was evolution. Unlike Steward, most anthropologists, including White, tended to use the terms *change* and *evolution* interchangeably.

Despite efforts by others to unify aspects of his and White's versions of evolutionism (e.g., Sahlins and Service 1960), Steward continued to peddle his own brand. In the 1968 encyclopedia entry, he referred to the "cultural ecological method of analyzing culture change or evolution," pointing out that it

> differs from that based on the superorganic or culturological concept. The latter assumes that only phenomena of a cultural level are relevant and admissible, and it repudiates "reductionism," that is, a consideration of processes induced by factors of a psychological, biological, or environmental level. The evolutionary hypotheses based upon this method deal with culture in a generic or global sense rather than with individual cultures in a substantive sense, and they postulate universal processes. Cultural ecology, on the other hand, recognizes the substantive dissimilarities of cultures that are caused by the particular adaptive processes by which any society interacts with its environment. (Steward 1968:337–338)

Here Steward was pointing out the difference between his position and that of White. To Steward, the "method of cultural ecology" was part one of a two-part operation for understanding the development of cultures. Multilinear evolutionism was the second part.

We agree with Marvin Harris (1968b) that the link between Steward's cultural ecology and cultural materialism has been obscured by a misplaced focus on evolutionism. The beauty of what Steward proposed lay in its search for a science of history and its ability to generate potentially falsifiable statements about relationships between humans and their social and physical environments. That was the cultural ecology side, not the multilinear evolutionism side, which was still as grounded in the cultural evolutionism of the nineteenth century as White's universal evolution, despite Steward's best efforts to distinguish his own brand.

For Steward, there were three important phenomena: culture, society, and environment. A culture could be defined by the traits it did (or did not) possess. Traits were (supposedly) empirical units, meaning they could be observed and, importantly, counted. As one would expect in a materialist approach, the most important traits were those related to economy and food acquisition. Steward (1955) referred to these as a culture's "core." The core was not necessarily restricted to purely technological traits. Depending on the circumstance, it could include "such social, political, and religious patterns as are empirically determined to be closely connected" with the core (Steward 1955:37). Radiating out from the core were other "secondary features" that are "determined to a greater extent by purely cultural-historical factors—by random innovations or by diffusion— and they give the appearance of outward distinctiveness to cultures with similar cores" (Steward 1955:37).

With the benefit of hindsight, we can appreciate that secondary features might have been helpful in deciding if two or more cultures were somehow related—another way to frame the homology/analogy problem. But for Steward and his processualist followers in archaeology, secondary features were treated as a distraction that interfered with the real job: comparing cultural cores to understand why cultures took the evolutionary pathways they did. Why, for example, did many of the same features (traits) occur among, say, a patrilineal hunting-and-gathering group in West Africa and a patrilineal hunting-and-gathering group in the Great Basin of the United States? These two groups were not phylogenetically related, so the similarities had to be a result of something else. The environments are totally different in terms of terrain, vegetation, and rainfall, so it makes no sense to say that the groups were similarly adapted to similar environments.

For Steward, the answer resided in the cultural cores of the groups: similar solutions not to similar environments but to similar environmental *problems*. Those problems transcended the actual kind of environment in which a group lived. Thus a hunter-gatherer in West Africa and one in the Great Basin might well face exactly the same economic problems and develop the same kind of kinship system, technology, and social hierarchy (similar solutions to similar problems) despite exploiting entirely different plant and animal resources. If this were the case, then why not use one or both societies as general analogues, regardless of geographical location? Further, didn't the existence of such parallelisms or convergences reflect the operation of cultural laws—what Steward (1949) referred to as "regularities"? Processualists were quick to answer yes, which helped to fuel their search for nomothetic (lawlike) regularities (Chapter 4).

Steward's anthropological legacy was the recognition that the physical environment was more than a simple stage on which human activities took place (Rhode 1999). His ideas on culture and the environment, the basics of which he had worked out by 1937, ran counter to the prevailing notion of the first half of the twentieth century that culture was either environmentally determined (e.g., Huntington 1915, 1919; Mason 1896; Wissler 1926) or limited in terms of its expression—what became known as environmental "possibilism" (Forde 1934). In Steward's view, human activities were carried out as part of an ecological relationship with the physical environment: biota, temperature, rainfall, landforms, and so on. The kind of relationship that Steward was talking about became more of an archaeological focus throughout the late 1940s and into the '50s. As indicated in Chapter 1, at least part of the reason for this stemmed from K.C. Chang's (1967a) ladder of inference, which asserts that archaeologists have the most direct access to technological and economic aspects of past cultures, less direct (if any) access to sociological aspects, and finally, even less direct access to ideological aspects.

When Robert McCormick Adams reviewed Steward's *Theory of Culture Change,* his remarks were by and large laudatory. Adams (1956:195) wrote that Steward's approach

> represents a considerable departure from such "theory" as is implicit in traditional archaeology, with its greater emphasis on the description of discrete cultural phases than on the reconstruction of connective links and trends cementing successive phases together into intelligible developmental sequences. With the increasing preponderance of studies of cultural change in archaeology as well as anthropology this volume assumes as much importance for the prehistorian as for the student of contemporary societies, even though only a few of the papers are directly concerned with the interpretation of archaeological data."

Adams perceptively noted that Steward's multilinear evolution had as its goal the detection of regularities that would be the basis for cultural laws. He also noted that these cultural laws were, in Steward's view, "strictly cause-and-effect relationships, with the independent operation of identical causality in parallel cases as a crucial methodological feature" (Adams 1956:195). In other words, after observing in multiple independent cases of what seem on other grounds to be instances of cause and effect—whether synchronic ecological relationships or deviation-amplifying feedback relationships that produce change over time—it would be possible from those multiple evolutionary cases to derive laws of culture process. Although Adams (1956:196) questioned whether this approach would provide "a convincing picture of cultural change as process...or whether we will only have acquired a more suggestive taxonomy of change," he concluded by noting that Steward's approach was "among the most powerful analytic tools available for the interpretive reconstruction of cultural change out of the midden record." In the years to come, archaeologists would come to agree with Adams.

FIGURE 3.6. *Center,* William Sanders with workmen at Santa Clara Coatitlán, Mexico, 1977. (Courtesy Deborah Nichols.)

THE STUDY OF SETTLEMENT

By the time Kent Flannery began using cybernetics to examine the rise of food production in the Southern Highlands of Mexico, the ecological approach had become well integrated into archaeology. One person who had a leading role in this integration is William Sanders (Figure 3.6), who received his Ph.D. from Harvard in 1957 and has spent his entire professional career at Pennsylvania State University. Not only did Sanders lay the groundwork in the 1950s for the settlement-pattern studies of Highland Mexico for which Penn State and the University of Michigan became well known (e.g., Blanton 1972; Blanton et al. 1982; Hirth 1980; Kowalewski et al. 1989; Nichols 1996, 2004; Parsons 1971; Parsons et al. 1982; Sanders 1965, 1967, 1971; Sanders, Parsons, and Santley 1979), he also showed that patterns of settlement were visible manifestations of human ecological relationships. His book *Mesoamerica: The Evolution of a Civilization,* coauthored by Barbara Price (Sanders and Price 1968), underscored the importance of an ecological approach in archaeology in the same way that Rappaport's *Pigs for the Ancestors* underscored it for cultural anthropology.

One of Sanders's earliest articles was on what he labeled the "Central Mexican Symbiotic Region," one of several geographical regions in Mexico that contained economically

FIGURE 3.7. *Center,* Richard MacNeish with *left,* Angel García Cook and *right,* Melvin (Mike) Fowler at Coxcatlán Cave, Tehuacán Valley, Mexico, 1962. (Photograph by Frederick Peterson, courtesy Mike Fowler.)

interrelated groups. Sanders (1956:115) was interested in how this interrelatedness expressed itself across the landscape: "Settlement pattern is, in effect, human ecology, since it is concerned with the distribution of population over the landscape and an investigation of the reasons behind that distribution." Sanders's article appeared in a volume edited by his dissertation adviser, Gordon Willey, titled *Prehistoric Settlement Patterns in the New World* (Willey 1956). Contributors pointed out what had been done in terms of settlement-pattern analysis and where future work should be concentrated. Even though most of the chapters contained few results, the book was one of those rare volumes that achieve landmark status almost immediately after publication. As Jeff Parsons (1972) put it, the book broadcast the analytical potential of settlement study to a wide audience.

Anyone reading Parson's statement today might well wonder why an early book on settlement patterns could enjoy such success, given that the chapters did not contain especially impressive results. The answer is that up to that time, settlement-pattern studies were anything but commonplace. We suggested in Chapter 1 that the first true settlement-pattern study was undertaken by Willey in the Virú Valley of Peru for his dissertation at Columbia. He didn't set out to undertake such a study, for he was quite content to dig test pits up and down the valley and develop a cultural chronology. Julian Stew-

ard, for whom Willey had worked at the Bureau of American Ethnology, had other ideas: "Why didn't I concentrate on overall settlement patterns in the valley, with particular reference to when and how these patterns changed through time and what the changes implied?" Willey (1988:236–237) recalled. "He [Steward] reminded me of his 1937 article on 'Ecological Aspects of Southwestern Society' and how he had done this in the Southwest. No one, he complained, had ever followed up on this sort of thing. We (the archaeologists) were all too busy running around classifying potsherds.... He went on to tell me that the aforesaid 1937 article—which he then referred to, half in jest, as his 'most famous theoretical paper'—had been rejected by the *American Anthropologist* for publication before *Anthropos* accepted it. I followed Julian's advice." By doing so, Willey's name would become synonymous with settlement-pattern studies (Vogt and Leventhal 1983).

Another contributor to Willey's volume was Richard MacNeish (Figure 3.7), who had received his Ph.D. from the University of Chicago in 1949. At the time he wrote the chapter for Willey's volume, MacNeish was alternating between field projects in Canada and northern Mexico. He had become interested in the transition from mobile hunting and gathering to sedentary agriculture, and had excavated a series of rockshelters in the Mexican state of Tamaulipas (MacNeish 1958, 1992). The excavations pushed the origins of maize agriculture back to the third millennium B.C., but MacNeish and the botanists on his team believed that the corncobs they examined were too well developed to have represented the earliest maize. The conclusion seemed obvious: The domestication of maize had taken place much earlier and probably not in Tamaulipas. MacNeish focused his search first in Honduras, then in Guatemala, and finally in southern

FIGURE 3.8. Excavation units in Coxcatlán Cave, Tehuacán Valley, Mexico, 1962. (Courtesy Mike Fowler.)

Mexico, examining rockshelter after rockshelter to find the right conditions for the preservation of 6,000-plus-year-old corncobs—if they were present. Early in 1961 he finally found what he was looking for in a series of rockshelters in the Tehuacán Valley in the state of Puebla (Figure 3.8). MacNeish spent the next four years there, during which he undertook a comprehensive survey of the valley (MacNeish et al. 1972). Subsequent work showed that numerous sites were missed, but this could be said of almost all surveys.

MacNeish understood the importance of regional settlement patterns, and he was an avowed disciple of Julian Steward's. This dated back to his days at Chicago, where, as Flannery and Joyce Marcus (2001:5–6) point out in their biographical memoir of "Scotty" MacNeish, "he wrote a class term paper for Robert Redfield on Julian Steward's recently published *Basin-Plateau Aboriginal Socio-political Groups* (1938). Steward's monograph so impressed Scotty that, for the rest of his career,

his syntheses made virtually every region he investigated sound like the Great Basin. He often used a model, inspired by Steward's description of the Paiute, in which foragers broke up into microbands in lean seasons and came together to form macrobands during times of plenty." One part of the seven-stage model MacNeish (1964) proposed for the settlement pattern of the Tehuacán Valley is shown in Figure 3.9. Notice that as Flannery and Marcus point out, the annual round of the Tehuacaneros included the amalgamation of related microbands during the wet season and the breakup of these macrobands during the dry season.

The lasting contribution of the Tehuacán Valley survey is not in the results but in how, together with Bill Sanders's work in the Valley of Mexico, it brought the analysis of settlement patterns to the forefront of American archaeology—something begun by Willey and helped along by Braidwood, Adams, and others at the Oriental Institute (see Wilkinson 2000). One feature that MacNeish's and Sanders's projects

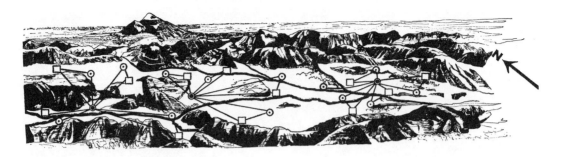

FIGURE 3.9. Richard MacNeish's stage 2 (6800–5000 B.C.) of the settlement-subsistence pattern he proposed for the Tehuacán Valley, Mexico. Shown are three bands, each occupying distinct regions of the valley. Groups live in microbands during the fall (squares) and the dry season (circles with small dots). In the spring, related microbands coalesce to form macrobands (circles with large dots). (From MacNeish 1964, courtesy American Association for the Advancement of Science.)

had in common was their decidedly materialist-deterministic slant, to borrow a term from Willey and Sabloff (1993:237). In his pioneering work in the Virú Valley, Willey (1953b:1) defined settlement pattern as "the way in which man disposed himself over the landscape on which he lived." This came to be interpreted as, "how physical features of the landscape influenced that disposition." That settlement-pattern studies had a materialist-deterministic perspective was unquestioned in the 1960s, but Sanders would come under heavy attack for it several decades later. Ironically, one of the most vocal critics would be Flannery, who would argue that settlement systems are complex amalgams and to understand them may require more than a purely materialist model that ties settlement location to such things as specific landforms or soil types (Chapter 7). In fairness, Sanders never insisted that human settlement decisions are dictated exclusively by physical-environmental factors. Rather, he said that subtle systemic interrelationships between many significant factors—including natural resources *and* social institutions—condition settlement (Sanders 1971). Even so, he assumed that factors apart from the physical environment were secondary (Sanders 1967). Sanders was attempting "to isolate the primary factor and only incidentally discuss other determinants of settlement patterns" (Sanders 1967:53).

Irving Rouse (1972:96) had perhaps a broader view of settlement pattern, defining it as the "manner in which a people's cultural activities and social institutions are distributed over the landscape." Bruce Trigger, whose early work (e.g., Trigger 1965, 1968a, 1968b) was seminal to the growth of settlement-pattern studies, went even further, defining the goal of settlement archaeology as understanding the "functioning systems of economic, political and effective relationships" within social groupings of people (Trigger 1967:151). This definition paralleled Gordon Willey's (1953b) earlier definition. Settlement archaeology, Trigger advised, should direct its inquiries toward both the synchronic and diachronic aspects of the social relationships of past human populations. As Jerry Sabloff and Wendy Ashmore (2001:18) noted in a retrospective of settlement-pattern analysis, these concerns "clearly meshed well with the systems and evolutionary interests of the 1960s 'new archaeology.'"

In an early overview of settlement-pattern studies, Jeff Parsons (1972) stated that one of the more significant contributions was the "settlement-system" concept, a refinement of K. C. Chang's (1962) "annual subsistence region." Parsons speculated that Howard Winters may have been the first American archaeologist to use the term *settlement system* formally, in a study of prehistoric settlement in the central Wabash River valley of Indiana

(Winters 1963). In a later publication, Winters (1969) distinguished between settlement pattern and settlement system. He defined *settlement pattern* as "the geographic and physiographic relationships of a contemporaneous group of sites within a single culture," and *settlement system* as "the functional relationships among the sites contained within the settlement pattern...the functional relationship among a contemporaneous group of sites within a single culture" (Winters 1969:110). To Winters, the limits of a culture were defined by the distribution of distinctive stylistic traits.

Winters was another University of Chicago Ph.D. who had a chapter in the Binfords' *New Perspectives*, this one a piece on Late Archaic–period trade and value systems in the Midwest. By the time the book appeared, Winters was just about to publish *The Riverton Culture: A Second Millennium Occupation in the Central Wabash Valley* (1969), the study in which he distinguished between settlement patterns and settlement systems. That monograph, together with several articles by fellow Chicago graduate Stuart Struever, reoriented Midwestern archaeology and ushered in a long period of settlement-system analysis and a coordinated approach to the archaeological record similar to MacNeish's work in the Tehuacán Valley. Struever also had a chapter in *New Perspectives*. In it he discussed the importance of long-term interdisciplinary research in understanding subsistence systems and settlement patterns (Struever 1968a). The chapter was an outgrowth of an earlier article (Struever 1965) on settlement dynamics south of the western Great Lakes and paralleled his chapter (Struever 1968b) in *Anthropological Archeology in the Americas* (Meggers 1968).

All three of Struever's papers were concerned with seamlessly interdigitating settlement systems, cultural ecology, and systems thinking under a materialist banner, and in showing their worth for conducting long-term, large-scale research projects. His geographic focus was the lower Illinois River valley—an area that had long received archaeological attention because of its large burial mounds, elaborately decorated pottery, and exotic goods such as obsidian, copper, and grizzly-bear canines. In *New Perspectives*, Struever (1968a) examined the change in subsistence-settlement systems from the Early Woodland period (450–200 B.C.) to the Late Woodland period (200 B.C.–A.D. 400). Like others working in the lower Illinois River valley, Struever pinpointed three major changes: (1) rapid and marked population increase; (2) development of complex ceremonial-mortuary activity that reflected increased status differentiation; and (3) extension and intensification of interaction between groups scattered over much of the eastern United States. The precise nature of human interactions in the lower Illinois River valley has been debated ever since Struever's path-breaking work appeared (e.g., Braun 1985, 1987; Braun and Plog 1982; Neiman 1995; O'Brien 1987), but most of the corrections and refinements have emerged directly from the kinds of ambitious multidisciplinary projects that he so articulately advocated.

Struever's contributions to American archaeology would go well beyond his early processual work in Illinois. He had a vision for archaeology (e.g., Brown and Struever 1973) that was based on the development of research programs supported financially by corporations and individuals—literally hundreds or thousands of individuals—as opposed to government grants alone. Struever appreciated early on that the minuscule budget of the Anthropology Program in the National Science Foundation could furnish only token funds toward the kinds of long-term, large-scale interdisciplinary research projects that processual archaeology demanded. Although NSF did sometimes support processual projects in the fieldwork stage, it was unable to fund specialists for the many years of analysis and report writing that large assemblages of artifacts and ecofacts entailed.

To demonstrate that private funding could do the whole job, from fieldwork to publication, Struever needed a base of operations, and in 1964 he founded the Center for American Archeology in Kampsville, Illinois, as a research component of Northwestern University. The

Kampsville operation provided archaeologists, students, and members of the public with a hands-on tutorial in how big-time archaeology was conducted within an interdisciplinary framework, similar to what Braidwood had done in the Near East. Struever's involvement with Kampsville came to an end in the early 1980s, and in 1983 he moved his affiliation to the Crow Canyon Archaeological Center in Cortez, Colorado. A great many processualists were trained at Kampsville and Crow Canyon, some of whom began their involvement while in high school.

Struever raised hundreds of thousands of dollars by making personal pitches to civic groups (Figure 3.10), business leaders, and otherwise wealthy individuals. No processualist was better at translating the new archaeology into terms a literate layperson could understand. Clearly, Struever's personal qualities as a charming and gifted public speaker were what made him an effective fundraiser. Most archaeologists lacked his talent and scaled back their ambitions, making do with tiny NSF grants, volunteer student labor, and/or field school funding. The funding situation would begin to change in the mid- to late 1970s with the advent of modern cultural resource management, which was another indirect impact of the environmental movement on archaeology (Chapter 6).

Lew Binford's blueprint for processual archaeology evolved over several years, and numerous archaeologists, including his students, contributed to it. Nowhere is this better illustrated than in the development of ceramic sociology. In fact, some of the processual studies were underway before Binford arrived at Chicago in 1961. Jim Deetz, another key contributor to ceramic sociology, was a Harvard doctoral student, not a Chicago student, and he had completed his dissertation on Arikara pottery in 1960; it was not a product of Binford's influence. Binford (1983b:17) pointed out in a retrospective that he "never advocated a 'ceramic sociology.'" To him, Longacre, Hill, and the others were using pottery to go beyond

FIGURE 3.10. Stuart Struever speaking to the National Accelerator Laboratory Women's Organization, Batavia, Illinois, 1970. (Courtesy Fermilab Archives and Visual Media Services.)

what culture historians had done and to demonstrate that properties of the archaeological record were referable to properties of past cultural systems that most archaeologists considered not generally accessible. Longacre (2000:294) reported that Binford "was very supportive of our initial attempts at Ceramic Sociology," but by the time Binford came along, they had already begun their analyses. The man with whom Hill and Longacre were working, Paul Martin, gets a healthy share of the credit for ceramic sociology, although with typical modesty he downplayed his own role (Martin 1971). Martin supported the efforts not only of Hill and Longacre but of later processualists such as Leone, Schiffer, Zubrow, and Fred Plog, whose collective work led to claims of "Southwestern chauvinism"—a derisive term when used by non-Southwesternists but a term of pride when used by those working in the Southwest (Longacre 1973).

The high point of the emerging processualist movement was the Binfords' symposium at the 1965 American Anthropological Association meeting in Denver, which brought together various younger archaeologists for the purpose of test marketing the new products. On the basis of this symposium, no one could have doubted that the breeding ground for processualism was then at the University of Chicago. Many of the contributors—Kent Flannery, Frank Hole, Bob Whallon, Bill Longacre, Jim Hill, Stuart Struever—were or had been graduate students at Chicago when Lew Binford arrived in 1961. But change happened quickly. By the time the proceedings of the 1965 symposium were published as *New Perspectives in Archeology* in 1968, Chicago had been all but abandoned as the center of processualism. Only a few more students—such as Fred Plog, John Fritz (Figure 2.9), and Geoff Clark—would finish their Ph.D.s and become influential new archaeologists. The Binfords had moved west: first to the University of California, Santa Barbara, in 1965; then UCLA in 1966; then the University of New Mexico in 1968.

Although the Binfords' stay there was brief, UCLA became a center of processualism with the arrival of Plog, Jim Hill, Jim Sackett, and Bobby Jo Williams (technically a physical anthropologist but with archaeological interests). Sackett had received his Ph.D. at Harvard, and Williams his at Michigan. Hill and Plog were both Chicago Ph.D.s. Plog had Near Eastern specialist Robert McCormick Adams as his dissertation adviser, but carried out his fieldwork in Arizona under Paul Martin's auspices. All but Plog had contributed chapters to *New Perspectives*. By 1968 the University of Michigan was beginning to rival UCLA as a processualist breeding ground through the addition of Flannery and Whallon to its anthropology faculty. Longacre had moved to the University of Arizona, which was quickly becoming another processualist center.

The late '60s was a Golden Age for processualists. This was more than simply having a new "ism" with which to identify. Young processualists fed on the ferment of new ideas, enjoyed the fellowship of kindred spirits also taking part in the grand mission, and reveled in

the opportunity to help shape a self-proclaimed scientific revolution. Processualism had its detractors, but the movement was not going to be held back by critics and their carping. New movements in science thrive on controversy (Barber 1961). Without it they can easily escape notice, no matter how "good" their science is. Perhaps if Alfred Wegener had had a large core of combative young followers like Binford had, plate tectonics wouldn't have required a half century to be taken seriously. Advocates of a new approach, especially vocal advocates, subscribe to the old Hollywood chestnut attributed to Tallulah Bankhead: "It doesn't matter what they say about you, as long as they spell your name right." And Binford was an easy name to spell.

Binford also had the qualities of an excellent salesman. Along with other young processualists, he understood that to sell any new product, from perfume to fertilizer, one needs to advertise, advertise, advertise. In the process, one educates the consumer on specific, user-relevant advantages of the new product over the old. From an evolutionary standpoint it might be claimed that if advertised correctly, a new scientific approach is as likely to enhance one's attractiveness to potential mates as a new perfume, but more relevant would be its advantage in attracting new graduate students and other followers (not that, on occasion, the roles of graduate student and potential mate don't become mixed). There are numerous ways to advertise, including getting one's name in as many meeting programs as possible. Although contributed articles count, it's much more prestigious to be an invited speaker. Colleagues at other universities are helpful here.

Another way to advertise is to become part of what R. P. Chaney (1972) referred to as "quoting bees": circles of intellectually compatible researchers who quote each other's work extensively. This is especially useful for reminding younger members of the discipline who the major players are. Quoting bees are also useful in cases where tenure committees rely on citation indices as a measure of a candidate's value. There is also self-citation, which gives one the opportunity to present his or her entire publication list, or at least selected segments thereof (not that we would ever be guilty of this). But beware: One should not depend on this strategy for tenure because some citation indices do not count self-citations.

With respect to promotional strategies, there are also certain things that one should *not* do. The most important one is never to criticize (at least publicly) your close associates, for others may generalize such critiques to the entire movement and all its members. Processualists thoroughly understood this bit of common sense. When they assessed the work of other processualists, their comments were favorable, often excessively so. In his review of *Anthropological Archeology in the Americas* (Meggers 1968), which contained chapters by Flannery, Deetz, and Struever, Hill (1970c:392) remarked that the goal of the volume was to present a sample of current trends in anthropological archaeology, and in Hill's view "this goal has been achieved remarkably well," with most of the chapters being "so well written that they will be found useful for teaching both graduate and undergraduate courses."

Mark Leone, in his review of *New Perspectives* (Binford and Binford 1968a), claimed that despite criticism that the authors were following narrow programmatic statements or were engaged in "doily weaving," the chapters "represent the first serious innovations in archaeology since the 1920's" (Leone 1971:222). When reviewing Longacre's (1970d) edited volume on reconstructing prehistoric social organization, Binford found the contributions by his own students to indicate that "something is happening in archeology representing a new orientation in method and theory" (Binford 1971:1225).

Lost in the excitement of identifying cultural processes and thus returning archaeology to its rightful place as an anthropological endeavor was one lone voice of caution—not the voice of a wizened culture historian who hated any kind of change, but that of a well-respected ethnologist, Marvin Harris. In a way, it's ironic that Harris, an archmaterialist and thus someone who might have been expected to embrace

processualism in its entirety, would urge Binford and his associates to tread cautiously when entering the conceptual territory of ethnology. Lew and Sally had asked Harris to comment on the work presented at the American Anthropological Association meeting in 1965, and his remarks were published in *New Perspectives* (Harris 1968a).

Unlike most of the other commentators, Harris, using very gentle language, issued what he termed an exhortation: "Archeologists, shrive yourselves of the notion that the units which you seek to reconstruct must match the units in social organization which contemporary ethnographers have attempted to tell you exist" (Harris 1968a:359–360). Harris saw nothing to be gained from turning archaeology into the anthropology of the past:

As archeologists, you have a number of observational procedures consisting of measuring instruments and the techniques through which you push these measuring instruments. Out of these operations you are capable of defining entities whose reality, I assure you, is every bit as well grounded as the entities which are now being discussed at great length by ethnographers dealing with contemporary sociopolitical systems. To set yourselves free, you have only to reflect upon the prodigious research effort now being expended by your colleagues in cultural anthropology upon the attempt to state the cognitive rules by which sociocultural systems are allegedly governed. (Harris 1968a:360)

Harris urged processualists to abandon the attempt to reconstruct descent systems—something that Binford (1983b) could later claim (rightfully) he really hadn't advocated. In fact, to this point Harris's comments didn't apply to Binford's own work except tangentially, but he followed up with a remark that would one day impinge directly on Binford's work:

You have knowledge of the material remains of populations, and thus you can develop techniques for measuring variations in the demographic and behavioral characteristics of such populations over long periods of time in relationship to specific complexes of biological, natural, and cultural features of their ecosystems....

Ultimately, what we seek I presume in common, is the explanation of the differences and similarities in sociocultural phenomena. You are in a better position to provide such explanations because of your greater time span and because you can be relatively free from the mystifications which arise from the emic approach. You therefore ought not to permit your activities to be compressed into the narrow compass of attempting to link up with ethnographic data. (Harris 1968a:360)

It was just such data, however, that Binford would use in the 1970s to structure his investigation of prehistoric hunter-gatherers.

It is not at all clear that Harris, at least in the 1960s, would have criticized such an approach. Rather, his remarks were intended to underscore the potential of the archaeological record itself to furnish evidence on processes of cultural change. He did not want to see an ethnography of the past framed in terms of cultural-anthropological constructs that were emically contaminated. But Harris would have applauded attempts to do ethnography more behaviorally, in the service of generating principles that could be used to infer past behavior. How various processualists, including Binford, dealt with Harris's warning is a story we take up in Chapter 7. Our immediate interest is the issue that many who came into archaeology during the early 1970s remember most of all—perhaps the defining issue for the times and the topic of seemingly endless discussions: how to make archaeology scientific.

Making Archaeology Explicitly Scientific

[S]cientific research seeks to account for empirical phenomena by means of laws and theories which are objective in the sense that their empirical implications and their evidential support are independent of what particular individuals happen to test or to apply them; and the explanations, as well as the predictions, based upon such laws and theories are meant to be objective in an analogous sense.

—CARL G. HEMPEL, "Aspects of Scientific Explanation"

Philosopher Carl Hempel could not have more accurately described the main goal of processual archaeology as it began hitting its stride in the late 1960s: to move archaeology beyond description and toward the production of scientific explanations. As Hempel phrased it, scientific explanations do not depend on the individuals proposing them. They depend instead on laws that describe the behavior of the phenomena under investigation and on establishing the relevant initial conditions for the case at hand. In archaeology the observable phenomena are the materials that were made, used, and discarded by humans. According to the processualists, if those materials were analyzed properly, they could be used as proxy measures for their makers' behaviors and social organization, and thus form the basis for discovering the laws behind why humans do the things they do.

During the 1970s, many processualists affirmed that the search for laws was their primary goal. This view was perhaps given its most strident expression by John Fritz and Fred Plog, whose article "The Nature of Archaeological Explanation" (1970) became a lightning rod both for archaeologists, hostile and friendly, and for philosophers of science interested in what archaeologists were up to. Despite the early optimism of Fritz and Plog and some of their colleagues, formulating and testing laws was not as easy—intellectually or logistically—as these processualists might have first thought. Logistically, the scientific approach was a hard sell within archaeology because it implied that earlier archaeology had been unscientific, and even within processualism there was considerable disagreement over what constituted adequate scientific explanation. Intellectually, archaeologists who turned to philosophy for guidance came away with different, often conflicting, advice.

Before examining some of these forays into philosophy and their effects on attempts to characterize archaeological explanation, it is worthwhile to pause and take stock of where processualism was on the threshold of its tenth birthday—not so much in terms of products per se (discussed in Chapter 3) but in terms of what various archaeologists thought of the approach. Even if we cast a wide net in defining the term, processualists made up only a fraction of the practicing Americanists in the early 1970s.

What did the nonprocessual majority think of the new archaeology? In some ways this is a rhetorical question because most processualists were not concerned with what nonprocessualists thought. For its most ardent proponents, processualism was supplying the discipline with much-needed rigor and direction; nonprocessualists were viewed at best as users of processualist products and at worst as obstructionists who would throw up any roadblock to halt the infusion of scientific objectivity into archaeology. But ignoring the traditionalists for a moment, what did the processualists themselves think about the new archaeology on the verge of its milestone anniversary? As it turns out, some of them didn't view it too kindly.

REACTING AND TAKING STOCK

How did the person most associated in the pre-Binfordian days with calling for an overhaul of American archaeology react to the new archaeology? We're speaking of Walter Taylor, who got the opportunity to voice his opinion in a review in *Science* of the Binfords' *New Perspectives in Archeology*. Taylor (1969:382) characterized the volume as provocative, stimulating, and significant, and he identified four areas that set the contributions apart from the traditional approach. First, the authors used a much larger range of detailed empirical data and "cultural conjunctives," and they were willing to make broad cultural inferences based on those conjunctions. Second, many of the inferences concerned nonmaterial aspects of culture, though limited primarily to those dealing with social organization. Third, the inferences were based on ethnographic data. Fourth, the use of statistical analyses was, Taylor thought, quite significant.

What did Taylor think of processual archaeology in general? Overall, he found nothing wrong with its basic principles, and he provided a better summary of them than perhaps Binford had: (1) that archaeological objects reflect the cultural systems of which they were a constituent part; (2) that archaeological objects can be expected to inform the archaeologist about those systems, even their nonmaterial aspects;

(3) that the ultimate goal of archaeology, which is the formulation of laws of cultural process, can best be attained through explicating and explaining cultural similarities and differences; and (4) that the accuracy of knowledge about the past can be validated and measured not simply by using ethnographic analogy but by formulating and testing hypotheses.

Taylor didn't dispute these principles because he didn't believe they were new. Rather,

a full discussion of a very similar overall approach to our discipline [has] been in print since 1948 [Taylor's *A Study of Archeology*].... The systemic view of culture has been a basic premise of American anthropology, including archeology, certainly since Malinowski, if not since Boas, and as for Binford's other tenets, I can point to passages in *A Study of Archeology* covering each of them, even that of testing hypotheses.... What the Binfords have produced in this book is not an exposition of the theory and practice of a new perspective but an explicit restatement of an old one, with some new and modern additions, together with some very pertinent, cogent, stimulating examples of current archeological research resulting from it. What they have provided has been sorely lacking in American archeological literature, and their contribution is to be honored in substance and as long overdue. But if, as Lewis Binford says, "archeology in the 1960's is at a major point of evolutionary change," it is because at long last action is catching up with idea, performance with old perspective. (Taylor 1969:383–384)

If we are to believe Taylor, then, it was he, not Binford, who really started the processual movement. Taylor felt compelled to make this point again three years later in an article with the provocative title "Old Wine and New Skins: A Contemporary Parable" (Taylor 1972). This was a considerable stretch on Taylor's part—less a case of old wine than sour grapes. But such behavior, disputes over precedence, is typical of science (e.g., Merton 1969; Reif 1961). Because of this and other not-so-pleasant aspects of the sociology of science, some have wondered if teaching the history of science might be ill advised (e.g., Brush 1974; Conant 1960). We think just the opposite. With respect to Taylor's views, we agree with Gordon Willey and Jerry Sabloff (1993) that although there are elements of the new archaeology program in Taylor's *A Study of Archeology,* there are also major differences. Binford's program featured a materialist cultural-evolutionary point of view and a systemic model of culture incorporating that evolutionary point of view. Taylor's did not.

Willey and Sabloff (1993) make an excellent point with respect to the kind of model of culture and culture change that a functionalist position such as Taylor's engenders. It is either a clocklike model, which has no internal sources of change, or a model in which all the feedback is negative. The feedback the model receives damps change, thus reinforcing the status quo and precluding change. What are needed, according to Willey and Sabloff, are models that contain both positive and negative feedback and that are both intelligent and self-correcting (adaptive). This is a model of a living system, the point Kent Flannery (1968a) made in his paper on early food production in Mesoamerica (Chapter 3).

The book in which Taylor's "old wine" article appeared was edited by Mark Leone (1972a), who had completed his Ph.D. at the University of Arizona in 1968 and was teaching at Princeton. Designed for teaching, this book was a milestone in processual archaeology, testifying to the program's already strong presence in the discipline. In addition to Taylor's chapter, Leone's book contains reprints of Binford's seminal statements as well as several relatively new articles outlining programs to operationalize the new archaeology. A year earlier, in his review of *New Perspectives,* Leone remarked that the revolution in archaeology appeared to be over and that "suddenly the new archeology is everybody's archeology. The rhetorical scene is quiet" (Leone 1971:222).

It might have seemed quiet to Leone, but other archaeologists would have disagreed. Several detailed, article-length critiques of processual archaeology appeared about that time (e.g., Bayard 1969; Kushner 1970), and others would soon appear (e.g., Dragoo 1975; Dumont 1975; Johnson 1972). A catalyst for some of these critiques was *New Perspectives,* and another was Binford's first volume of "greatest hits"—*An Archaeological Perspective* (1972a; see also Binford 1983a, 1989a)—and the stories it contained about his childhood, his educational background, and the birth of processualism (Chapter 2). B. Robert Butler (1974:646) bitingly suggested that a more appropriate title would have been "The Collected Writings of an Archaeological Positivist, 1962–1972, Complete with Commentary."

Some of the criticism was directed at specific tenets of processualism, but there was also a thinly disguised frustration on the part of nonprocessualists who had been talked down to, preached to, and told just how unscientific, historical, and misguided they were. Pointing out the pluses of one's approach and the minuses of someone else's can be a useful strategy as long as the arguments are couched in appropriate terms. But when they become vitriolic and ad hominem—extremes that didn't always make it into the literature but were part of the processualist rhetoric of the time (Schiffer 1995a)—one risks alienating a large segment of the target population. As Don Dragoo (1975) pointed out, the antagonistic attitude of some processualists toward the traditionalists undoubtedly retarded the acceptance of the processual approach. A more effective strategy, sometimes, is to heap praise on one's opponent for what he or she has done, then point out some shortcomings in the work, then add a little more praise, then do some more dissecting, and so on. If done delicately, there is no backlash, and even one's opponent feels good about the operation. That does not mean the opponent will give in, only that animosity will be avoided.

Although few processualists had that genteel capability—Pat Watson and Bill Longacre were (and still are) conspicuous exceptions—pinning the blame on individual personalities does not suffice. That sort of explanation implies that processualism just happened to attract nasty people. In fact, as the responses to Taylor indicate, mean-spirited debate had taken place long before the new archaeology came along. Thus, we doubt that an influx of nasty processualists can account for this eruption of incivility in archaeological discourse. Rather, we should seek to identify the intellectual, social, and demographic factors that might have been at work. As Thomas Kuhn pointed out, when the holders of a new paradigm challenge the old, a predictable social and often generational schism develops in which even ad hominem arguments can flourish; communication becomes more difficult, passions flare, and feelings get bruised. This is the price that all sciences pay during major paradigm clashes. (The point holds, regardless of whether or not one views the advent of processualism as a paradigm shift.)

We should also point out that although Watson and Longacre are exceedingly nice people, gentility did not insulate their works from sometimes withering, occasionally harsh critiques. As we discuss below, a book that Watson coauthored with Steven LeBlanc and Charles Redman received flak from many quarters. Likewise, as noted in Chapter 3, Longacre's Carter Ranch study (e.g., 1970c) suffered a host of less-than-gentle critiques (e.g., Dumond 1977; Stanislawski 1973).

Criticism of processualism came from varied quarters, including from those outside the country. British archaeologist Cecil Hogarth (1972), writing in the journal *Antiquity*, labeled the new archaeology "newspeak archaeology" because of the prolific use of nontraditional terms in processualist writings, almost as if the terms and concepts gave what was being said more of a scientific air. Writing from New Zealand, Donn Bayard (1969) pointed this out as well in a critique in *American Antiquity*. Bayard was so irritated by the "newspeak" that a few years later he and his students at Otago University circulated a lampoon of processualism (Figure 4.1) that carried the title "New Analytical Archaeological Perspectives" and the

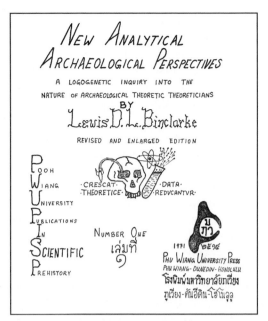

FIGURE 4.1. Cover of a 1971 "article" lampooning processualism that was created by Donn Bayard and his students at Otago University, New Zealand.

byline "Lewis D. L. Binclarke"—an obvious hybrid of the name "Lewis Binford" and that of British archaeologist "David L. Clarke," considered by many to be Binford's intellectual twin. This was a misnomer; Clarke was not a processualist. Any attempt to view his greatest work—*Analytical Archaeology* (Clarke 1968)—as a piece of processualist writing is misguided at best. He was, however, tolerant of processualists, on one occasion even providing a venue (Clarke 1972b) in which several of them, including Jim Hill, published.

There is a certain injustice, if not hypocrisy, in charging the processualists with jargon mongering. In the first place, as Binford pointed out in the interview with Paula Sabloff (1998), new concepts and new ways of thinking about phenomena require new terms. New terms force listeners and readers to learn the new concepts and facilitate precise, unambiguous communication. Thus, all mature sciences have no end of subject-specific jargons, as a glance at any issue of *Nature* or *Science* will demonstrate. Second, traditionalists themselves, as scientists, also had proliferated countless new terms in archaeology, from the 600-plus named pottery types of the American Southwest to the innumerable labels invented for culture units in every region. Unless one learned the culture-historical "newspeak"—which would have been unintelligible, for example, to nineteenth-century archaeologists—it was impossible to make sense of the archaeological literature.

The criticism was not limited to major journals such as *Antiquity* and *American Antiquity.* Iain Walker, writing in a nonrefereed but well-read publication, the *Conference on Historic Site Archaeology Papers,* railed against the processualists' verbiage and tone, but his criticism was leveled more specifically at Binford and his disparaging views on the place of history in archaeology. As we shall see below, a recurrent theme in the early 1970s was the question of whether archaeology is a science or history. More importantly, can it be both? The catalyst for Walker's (1972) scathing remarks was Binford's (1972e) response to criticism that Lee Hanson (1971) had directed toward the pipestem-dating formula that Binford (1962b) had used to bracket the occupation of Fort Michilimackinac, Michigan. The use of pipestems as chronological tools traces its ancestry to J. C. Harrington (1954), who in the early 1950s was looking for a means of dating clay smoking pipes, which were ubiquitous on some historical-period sites in the eastern United States. He found such a tool in the diameter of the stem bore, which consistently narrowed from about 1620 to 1800. Binford (1962b) thought Harrington's methods of computing occupational dates were "clumsy," and he used Harrington's data (or so it appeared [see Walker's discussion]) to calculate a regression formula in which he plotted calendar years against bore diameter.

The formula appeared to work well for materials from Virginia and North Carolina, but it fell apart at Fort Michilimackinac. Binford (1962b) explained the variance as the result of the reappearance of particular "early" pipe styles in addition to the advent of new styles. Hanson (1971) criticized Binford's approach, saying that Binford understood nothing about

the manufacture of pipes or their commercial history. Binford (1972e) shot back that Hanson had no idea how science operated and was behaving like a historian, regardless of whether he was one by training. Walker (1972) responded that this was the problem with the processualists, Binford in particular: in their quest for universal laws they looked with disdain on specific events and on the historians who tried to understand them. To carry out that quest, Walker continued, processualists apparently didn't need to know much about artifacts or their history. Walker ended his long retort with a patronizing proposition for Binford: Read some history. To that end, he presented a list of sixteen books, even arranging them in the order that Binford should read them. Until he had read the books, Walker (1972:193) concluded, "while it would be unrealistic to ask Binford to return to his [undergraduate] field of forestry and wildlife conservation he might at least have the good grace to stay out of historical archaeology—a field about which he has amply demonstrated he knows nothing—until such time as he has demonstrated some ability to comprehend historical evidence." We don't know if Binford worked his way through Walker's reading list, but we suspect not.

In addition to losing potential recruits through his intellectual positions and strident style of argument, Binford had even exasperated some supporters, especially processualists at the University of Michigan, when he published *An Archaeological Perspective* (1972a). He not only detailed the reasons for his dislike of Robert Braidwood (Chapter 2) but also drew an unflattering picture of Jimmy Griffin, director of the Museum of Anthropology at the University of Michigan and the first chairman of Binford's doctoral committee. (Griffin later resigned from the committee because of his animosity toward Binford, and Richard Beardsley took his place.) Griffin had many supporters—there were few archaeologists whom he did not know or had not helped with one problem or another—and was a commanding presence in the field. Binford was not on a par with Griffin at the time. Binford, though, *wanted* that kind of standing, and one means of attaining it was to take on someone of higher standing. That person was Griffin. Binford used that same strategy, or so he believed, with Braidwood and again with François Bordes over the interpretation of Mousterian assemblage variation.

Binford (1972f) related, obviously with great delight, the events surrounding that December day in 1965 in Bordes's laboratory in Bordeaux when at last he had his shot at the title: "With each 'round' Bordes was finding out about me and I was finding out about him; we both liked what we found. All of a sudden Bordes jumped up and came around face to face. I stood up almost automatically. He put his hand on my shoulder, looked me directly in the eyes, and said, 'Binford, you are a heavyweight; so am I.' I put my hand on François' shoulder; he turned: 'Let's go drink some good wine.'" Thus at age thirty-four Lew Binford was declared a heavyweight contender by the preeminent French Paleolithic scholar. And at age forty-one he told the world about it. In his mind he hadn't knocked out any of the champions, but he had stood up to their hardest shots and even delivered some of his own. Griffin (1976) would relate his views on the Binford-Griffin match a few years later.

The processualist rank and file took a less pugilistic approach, but even here there was lack of unanimity on not only methodological issues but also epistemological ones. There were slight but growing tensions in the processualist camp, and nowhere did they appear more clearly than in chapters of Charles Redman's edited volume, *Research and Theory in Current Archeology* (1973a), an outgrowth of a symposium at the 1971 American Anthropological Association annual meeting. This book is invaluable for what it tells us about the state of processualism at the start of its second decade and what some of its proponents saw as its pros and cons. Authors of the twenty-two chapters varied from processualists to those with more traditional leanings, such as Braidwood, one of the editor's mentors at Chicago. Binford was not among the contributors.

History or Science?

Several papers in the Redman volume commented on the divisiveness that the processual movement had brought to American archaeology, especially the gulf it had created between those who viewed archaeology as history (or at least history done scientifically) and those who viewed it as science. Bill Longacre (1973:333) pointed out that "both sides in the theoretical and methodological debate that has caused such ferment in our discipline must exhibit more tolerance and respect for each other's interests and work. This is not to discourage constructive criticism, [which is] not only useful but critical to our continued growth." Longacre's conciliatory appeal to end the hostility and ad hominem arguments that had typified the past several years would fall mainly on deaf ears over the next decade.

Pat Watson (1973b) similarly noted the divide between those who viewed archaeology as history and those who viewed it as science, and she rebutted arguments made by several archaeology-as-history proponents, including Jacquetta Hawkes (1968) and Donn Bayard (1969). For Hawkes, archaeology is history, and any attempt to make it scientific is specious. Bayard likewise viewed archaeology as historical in nature, arguing that because archaeology is a discipline, it can never be a science. He later tried to backpedal from this view (Bayard 1978), perhaps because even he realized the weakness of his argument. Whether something is scientific does not depend on its tenets, methods, and so on forming a coherent discipline. Bayard (1969:382) also wondered "if archaeology really requires a set of specifically archaeological theory, other than the accepted principles of inference and interpretation and a hopefully augmented emphasis on methods of field work and data collection, plus the general framework of anthropological theory. I have the impression that much archaeological theorizing results from a defensive attempt to establish the discipline as a 'real science.'"

Watson (1973b) stressed that archaeology is indeed a science, but it is not, as she put it in a similar chapter she did for Colin Renfrew's (1973c) *The Explanation of Culture Change,* "delimited by the use of computers, test tubes, Pearson's r, calipers, or lab coats" (Watson 1973a:48). It is, rather, a science centered on building laws of cultural processes. One strategy for selling that point of view at the expense of the opposing viewpoint was to misrepresent history as mere particularistic chronicle. Watson, however, staked out a more accommodating middle ground, suggesting that although archaeology is a science, there is room for opposing viewpoints, and that upon close inspection those viewpoints might not be so opposed after all.

Watson was correct on the merits of the middle ground but overly optimistic on the willingness of archaeologists to find, much less appreciate, it. The discussion over whether archaeology is science or history has roots deep in the earlier part of the twentieth century. Like a locust, it would emerge from time to time, make a loud noise, then head back underground to await its next opportunity. The issue first emerged in mid–twentieth-century anthropology with two exchanges, one between Franz Boas and Alfred Kroeber, and the other between Kroeber and Leslie White (Lyman and O'Brien 2004a). Walter Taylor (1948) was one of the first American archaeologists to distinguish between history and science when he wrote that historical disciplines are nonexperimental and deal with actual, nonrepeating, unique events. Taylor indicated that historians follow four analytical steps: (1) defining a problem; (2) collecting, analyzing, and criticizing data; (3) placing the data in chronological sequence; and (4) integrating and synthesizing the data so as to establish interrelations among the phenomena in the temporal series. Taylor urged that archaeology shift from being a discipline concerned with descriptive, idiographic (particularizing) history to being a nomothetic (generalizing) science.

Gordon Willey and Philip Phillips's (1958) description of what they termed "processual interpretation" was the attempt to find regularities in the relationships given by the methods of culture-historical integration. Another step in the direction of nomothetic science was their claim that such interpretations, when based on discovered regularities, were causal explanations. They were followed shortly thereafter by Joseph Caldwell (1959), who pointed out that archaeology was becoming more concerned with culture process and less concerned with the descriptive content of prehistoric cultures. As a result, Caldwell saw two kinds of problems, one historical and the other general. The former was concerned with the identification of specific cultures, the latter with the identification of cultural processes. Unlike some of the 1960s new archaeologists, Caldwell apparently saw room in archaeology for addressing both kinds of problems.

Providing the source of the model for making archaeology a science were the established sciences such as chemistry and physics. Betty Meggers (1955) examined the "hard" sciences to determine if archaeology fell into that category. She noted that sciences have laws—both universal and probabilistic—and she saw, correctly, that the anthropology and archaeology of the time used interpretive principles such as environmental determinism and diffusion to explain cultural phenomena. These principles had been based on generalizations derived from observed patterns, just as in the model sciences. Thus, Meggers argued, the suggestion was false that humans were too individualistic in their behaviors and/or that social behavior was too complex to be subsumed under lawlike principles. Without using the words, Meggers summarized the then-perceived differences between nomothetic science and idiographic history, arguing that archaeology was the former.

Meggers made her argument (1955) in a volume she and her husband, Clifford Evans, edited: *New Interpretations of Aboriginal American Culture History* (Meggers and Evans 1955). Based on the last two words of that title, we suspect Meggers and many, if not all, of the contributors to the volume believed that culture history was scientific. In fact, American archaeologists had long thought that what they did was scientific (Lyman, O'Brien, and

Dunnell 1997), and until about 1950 it largely involved constructing, testing, and refining cultural chronologies on the basis of empirical evidence.

Archaeologists also were constructing inferences in a scientific manner about technology, subsistence, and other behavioral phenomena believed to be accessible from archaeological remains. Beginning in the late 1940s, successively more archaeologists tried to explain changes in the behavioral phenomena ordered by various chronologies (Lyman and O'Brien 2001a)—Caldwell's (1959) sec-

FIGURE 4.2. Bruce Trigger on the Nile River, 1992. (Photograph by Barbara Welch, courtesy Bruce Trigger.)

ond recognizable goal of archaeological research. Nevertheless, virtually no processual archaeologist agreed with the idea that archaeology conducted prior to 1962 was scientific. That was the year that Lew Binford (1962a) emphasized what was later characterized as the "need for developing a 'scientific' (usually as opposed to a 'historical') archaeology" (Bayard 1969:376). It was precisely the charge that traditionalists were not scientists that rankled nonprocessualists the most—and for good reason.

The most accommodating contributor to Redman's volume was Bruce Trigger (Figure 4.2), who saw archaeology as being both science and history. More specifically, Trigger regarded history as being integral to a scientific archaeology: "I wish to demonstrate that both idiographic, or particularizing (i.e., historical), and nomothetic, or generalizing, disciplines are vital components of a scientific study of human behavior" (Trigger 1973:95). This was in line with a slightly earlier statement Trigger (1970) had made about how to incorporate scientific and historical goals into archaeology. Accompanying that statement, however, was criticism directed at processualists for duplicating work already done in the social sciences. Apparently, Trigger believed that archaeologists could obtain from other disciplines all the laws and theories they needed to do scientific history, a position that Schiffer (1975b) roundly criti-

cized. Nonetheless, Trigger saw room in archaeology for a nomothetic component, but it was entirely secondary to the idiographic (historical) component.

In Watson's (1973b) view, Trigger had the roles reversed. To her, the contribution of the idiographic approach was in its ability to deliver the particulars that both helped create the laws and provided the phenomena that the laws explained. To Trigger, the goals of historical research are as explanatory as the goals of the nomothetic social sciences. He recognized the value of theory to scientific explanation but pointed out that historians are more interested in the unique features of recurrent types of events than in the features shared by those events. In Trigger's view, idiographic history is important because the complexity of the variables involved in sociocultural relationships explains the uniqueness of historical events; nomothetic explanation emphasizes the features that classes of events have in common.

As already noted, the arguments over history and science that took place in the 1970s had deep roots. Anthropologists throughout the twentieth century felt compelled to argue that the discipline is a science when it focuses on historical questions (Lyman and O'Brien 2004a). Few provided explicit definitions of science, history, or historical science, although authors occasionally listed some of the characteristics of each. More frequently, they simply applied the descriptors *nomothetic* to science and *idiographic* to history. One noteworthy exception to these general patterns is a more recent statement by David Aberle:

> The historical sciences are historical because they deal with entities and groups of entities that have traceable continuity over time, but that also change. They are scientific because they have methods for choosing among competing hypotheses about the nature and order of changes in the phenomena under study and methods as well for choosing among competing hypotheses that attempt to explain those changes. The first of these analyses is the process of historical reconstruction. In this approach there is no antithesis between history and science, or between history and evolution. The methods and goals of historical science are scientific; its products range from particular histories to tests of general propositions. (Aberle 1987:556)

We agree with Robert Carneiro's (2000:216) recent observation: "Nothing inherent in the totality of events constituting history renders them unsuitable to serve as raw material for a science of culture. After all, the phenomena of every science come to us not only as particular and unique, but also as intricately bound up with each other. Yet all the factors at work are carefully sorted out and categorized by the scientist, and laws are derived for their individual behaviors." Carneiro (2000:218) identified a critical stumbling block to scientific history when he noted that to a "traditional historian, an event is always concrete and particular; it happened once and will never recur. As such, it is to be described and explained in terms of the unique constellation of circumstances that preceded and surrounded it, that gave it its distinctiveness and individuality." The key, he pointed out, is to dissolve individual, singular events "in the universal solvent of general types and classes" (Carneiro 2000:219). We agree, but add the qualification that unit construction, testing, and revision must take place simulta-

neously with building, testing, and revising explanatory theory. We find the distinction between history and science to be false unless history is defined narrowly as simple chronology—what came before what. Although there are epistemological differences between the two, science is not inherently superior to history (Cleland 2002). One feature that tends to set the historical sciences off from nonhistorical sciences such as chemistry and physics is the long-term causal connections between historical phenomena (Ereshefsky 1992; Frodeman 1995; Gould 1986).

In the final analysis, because archaeology draws from such an intellectually and temperamentally diverse group of people, it may be that there will always be some people who prefer to dote on the particulars of a unique case and ask particularistic, historical questions, and other people who are fascinated by the general and ask their questions accordingly. Maybe, in this case, it really comes down to a continuum of individual tastes and preferences whose extremes seem wholly incompatible. What is important is that by the early 1970s at least some processualists were not completely denying a role for history in archaeological explanation. In some cases the allowance undoubtedly was viewed as a means of placating the older generation, but in other cases it was genuine. History was, to be sure, afforded only a small role, but it was a role nonetheless.

Others, however, claimed there was absolutely no room for a special sort of historical explanation in science. In his chapter in Chuck Redman's book, Albert Spaulding took issue with any kind of historical explanation, including "how possibly" explanations and genetic explanations. Such "claims for explanations free from the covering law requirement have a striking feature in common—they are all false" (Spaulding 1973:340). Biologists and paleobiologists would have been surprised to hear this, given the roles of both "how possibly" and genetic explanations in historical sciences. Would Spaulding have claimed that historical science is not science? We don't know the answer, because neither Spaulding nor any other processualist raised it at the time. It would be raised forcefully, however, in the 1980s by archaeologists with an evolutionistic bent (Chapter 8).

Spaulding never claimed that archaeologists could not or should not explain historical events. He merely denied that such explanations could be formulated without the use of laws that, in most historical explanations, remain implicit. The most important implication of Spaulding's seemingly radical position—one that Binford, Schiffer, and a few others adopted—was that to make historical explanations scientific, one had to render transparent the lawlike generalizations that gave them plausibility. Watson's middle ground, as well as Trigger's later position, demonstrated why the term "scientific history" was not an oxymoron to some processualists: to them, historical explanation involves accounting for particular events by employing documented contextual factors and explicit generalizations about human behavior. Culture historians, most of whom believed that they had been doing science long before processualism arrived, would have supported this claim by pointing to their use of the scientific method and scientific research tools. On the other hand, whether there is a uniquely historical mode of explanation that requires no laws remains an unresolved issue in modern archaeology (and probably in philosophy as well).

Law and Order versus Systems Theory

Spaulding saw a split developing within the processualist camp with respect to archaeological explanation, but he saw it as being "much less important" than the one between historians and scientists—the latter being a "kind of division that will be resolved by research and theory construction" (Spaulding 1973:348). The former rift was between what he termed the "general systems people" and "other scientific archaeologists." Spaulding's comments could have come only as a result of his having read a draft of Kent Flannery's submission to the Redman volume, amusingly titled "Arche-

ology with a Capital S" (1973a). An early draft of this article began circulating widely in late 1971 and built Flannery's reputation as someone who could inject humor—with a bite—into archaeological writing. It also was the first in a series of articles and books in which he barely disguised the identities of those being ridiculed. Flannery was not particularly happy with the direction in which he saw processualism heading: "I feel somewhat like the male black widow spider who, having broken down the female black widow's resistance with great struggle and persuasion, suddenly realizes that his first date is not going to be all it was cracked up to be" (Flannery 1973a:48).

Flannery commented on five "interesting phenomena" that had occurred since his review of Gordon Willey's (1966) first volume of *An Introduction to American Archaeology* (Chapter 2). Phenomena 1 and 4 were obvious to everyone: Processualism was popular, and not everyone agreed with it. Phenomenon 3 was obvious to many people: Some bad archaeology had been done in the name of processualism. Phenomenon 2 was also fairly obvious: Certain processualists, once they "had achieved some degree of national prominence (or tenure), forgot they had ever espoused processual studies and hastened to join the old guard on the pretext of 'bridging the generation gap'" (Flannery 1973a:49). These "cop-outs," as Flannery referred to them, formed one part of the major backlash to processualism, the other part being the "young fogeys": "a large group of young archaeologists, many still in their twenties, who are harshly critical of process studies and militantly committed to purely inductive analyses of 'real' data from traditionally conducted excavations" (1973a:49). We have no idea what percentage of American archaeologists this might have represented, but we suspect it was small. There was still a huge silent majority whose members went about their business without thinking twice about whether they agreed with or objected to the new archaeology.

Flannery's fifth phenomenon—the least mentioned, but in his terms perhaps the most theoretically significant—was a schism that had developed within processualism. Flannery pointed out that it was present almost from the start. In his opinion the schism was more over a difference in method than in goals, but this is debatable. He went on to state that during the previous decade two different approaches had arisen in processualism, and we can easily agree with that. But those approaches had their roots in epistemology *and* method, not in method alone. These roots were visible in Spaulding's (1968) earliest discussion of laws in archaeology and how those laws might be discovered. Were the "laws" actually laws in the sense that they were invariant, or were they more "regularities"?

Flannery divided the processualists into two groups. One group was the "law-and-order" processualists, who "believe that Carl Hempel rose from the dead on the third day and ascended to heaven—where he sits at the right hand of Binford—[and], to use their own words, 'have made the formulation and testing of laws (their) goal'" (Flannery 1973a:50). Flannery referred to the other category of processualists as "'Serutan' ['Natures' spelled backward, as the mid-century laxative commercial put it] (or 'Ex-Lax')" archaeologists, who "pursue a systems-theory framework and derive their nickname from an inordinate interest in the 'natural regulation' of systems" (Flannery 1973a:51). Given his work with applying cybernetics to archaeology (Chapter 3), Flannery was easily identifiable as a member of the Serutan school. This dichotomous grouping of processualists was similar to one Flannery (1967) had made earlier between "process theorists" and "law-seeking theorists."

Flannery poked fun at the law-and-order crowd, noting that the Hempelian approach

> has produced some of the worst archeology on record. In some cases, the statistics used have been so much more powerful than the raw data deserved, that one feels he is watching a grenade launcher being turned on a field mouse. In other cases, it seems that in order to discover a "natural law" in the

allotted six weeks of his field season, the investigator was forced to attack a problem of the utmost trivia; this has produced a series of low-level generalizations that some critics have called "Mickey Mouse laws."[1] These laws have even emerged from the lips of colleagues whom I regard as sane, serious, and competent men. For example, at a genuinely exciting seminar on the Bushmen I learned that "the size of a Bushman site is directly proportional to the number of houses on it." From a Southwestern colleague, I learned last year that "as the population of a site increases, the number of storage pits will go up." I am afraid that these "laws" will always elicit from me the response, "Leapin' lizards, Mr. Science!" (Or as my colleague, Robert Whallon, once said after reading one of these undeniable truths, "If this is the 'new archeology,' show me how to get back to the Renaissance.") (Flannery 1973a:51)

Cleverly phrased, but neither of Flannery's examples met the formal definition of a law. They were instead particularistic empirical generalizations that did not deal with dynamic processes at all. No competent processualist ever would have called such statements "laws." More than that, Flannery had exaggerated the prevalence of law-and-order archaeology among processualists. Indeed, few processualists actually set out to formulate or test laws; mostly they practiced, as Fred Plog later put it (Schiffer 1995a), a sophisticated culture history. It is true, however, that whether in the service of nomothetic or idiographic goals, many processualists adopted a formulaic hypothesis-testing format that sometimes produced poor work.

Flannery's critique of law-and-order processualism included other elements. "Serutan" archaeologists, according to Flannery, had serious doubts that cultural "laws" could be adequately tested by statistical procedures. He asked whether some of the correlations that processualists saw in their data might be the result of contingent or accidental relations—a point that Watson, LeBlanc, and Redman had recently raised in their book, *Explanation in Archeology: An Explicitly Scientific Approach* (1971). A high correlation might not say anything about causality, but if it did, how would we know? The odds are that complex systems contain a high percentage of coincident correlations that are not the result of a cause-and-effect relationship. In summarizing the systems position, Flannery noted:

> "Serutan" archeologists are not for chaos and against law. They recognize the existence of universal or nearly universal principles that govern a system's operation (principles such as positive and negative feedback, and the increase of information-processing institutions with systems of a higher order of complexity). But these archeologists are skeptical about the existence of an undiscovered set of "covering laws" that are specific to human behavior. Hence they are less concerned with a search for "laws of human behavior" than with a search for the ways human populations (in their own way) do the things that other living systems do. They tend to avoid "if *A*, then *B*" assertions because their systems orientation makes them skeptical of linear causality; they prefer feedback models in which causality is multivariate and mutual. (Flannery 1973a:52)

Flannery's distinction between law-and-order and Serutan archaeologists was sharply drawn, but such a dichotomy did not necessarily reflect the actual beliefs and research practices of most processualists, who saw no incompatibility between a commitment to systems theory (or at least a systems perspective) and seeking laws. Binford, after all, had ardently supported the search for laws while at the same time advocating the use of systems theory. As we saw in Chapter 3, systems theory had run its course more or less by the mid-1970s, a few years after Flannery wrote his chapter for Redman's book. One might, therefore, be tempted to think that the split in processual archaeology—between the systems theorists and the law-and-order archaeolo-

gists—would have closed with the declining importance of systems theory. This is not true; rather, even as Redman's book was coming on the market, the Michigan brand of processualism was morphing into what, for lack of a better term, we refer to as "anthropological archaeology," with an increased emphasis on ecology and a newfound emphasis on social and political organization and cross-cultural comparison.

The risk we run in using that term is that it makes it sound as if everything that came before it was not influenced by ethnology. We are not implying this, as our discussions up to this point should have made clear. American archaeology from the beginning was strongly influenced by ethnological goals and interests, and this certainly was the case with processualism. Binford went to great pains to show how archaeology, by concentrating on culture as a system, could become a retooled ethnology of the past. By the early 1970s this emphasis was beginning to shift in some quarters away from culture per se and toward topics such as the evolution of complex societies. The major difference between pure systems archaeology and anthropological archaeology was a decided emphasis in the former on external catalysts for change. Not surprisingly, given his interests in systems theory and his training under Robert Braidwood at Chicago, Flannery, together with some of his colleagues at Michigan—Henry Wright and Jeff Parsons, for example—would train generations of archaeologists who cut their teeth on the ethnological writings of Morton Fried, Elman Service, and others.

We leave that discussion until Chapter 8. Our focus now is on the last major gasp of systems-theory advocacy in archaeology, which found expression in an important book that resulted from a seminar held at the School of American Research in Santa Fe, New Mexico, in 1970. The seminar was organized by Jim Hill of UCLA, who edited the volume that appeared seven years later, *Explanation of Prehistoric Change* (1977a). As Hill (1977b:x) put it in the preface, "the purpose of the seminar was to learn and communicate as much as we could about methods and theories for explaining change in human sociocultural systems—with emphasis on data from prehistoric systems." The first three chapters—two by Hill and one by Fred Plog, who at the time was at Arizona State University—are devoted to describing systems theory. The participants were trying to learn exactly what it was and how it might help them in their efforts to explain stability and change within sociocultural systems. Remember, although the book did not appear until 1977, the seminar was held in 1970, while systems theory was still of considerable interest to archaeologists. Five chapters—by Arthur Saxe (Ohio University), Richard Ford (University of Michigan), Michael Glassow (University of California, Santa Barbara), Henry Wright (University of Michigan), and Bill Sanders (Pennsylvania State University)—presented applications of systems theory to particular prehistoric cases. Plog wrote another chapter after the seminar to demonstrate the utility of simulation models.

The importance of *Explanation of Prehistoric Change* lies in what it tells us about the state of processualism almost a decade after its birth. Perhaps most noticeable is that although many of the chapters revolve around systems theory (e.g., Hill 1977c), science and laws are the real current that ties them together. This supports our interpretation that what Flannery identified was perhaps not the most accurate characterization of what processualists were thinking and doing. Seminar participants were attempting to understand systems theory and to link it to the construction of laws—to work both sides of Flannery's street at once. The approach to science that underlay the search for laws was Carl Hempel's deductive-nomological model of explanation, which we discuss in the following section.

Melvin Perlman, a sociologist from Brock University in Ontario, Canada, was the seminar discussant. In both his chapter (Perlman 1977) and in the published account of the discussions that took place, Perlman questioned the utility of Hempelian models of science for the social sciences, particularly the parts dealing with building laws. As Jim Judge (1978) observed in his review of Hill's book, Perlman's views were refreshing, but given the responses he received from the other seminar participants during discussion, they were the views of a voice in the wilderness. Challenging Hempel on the eve of his peak popularity in archaeology was, as Judge put it, an act of courage. The question is, was Perlman correct that Hempelian models of explanation might not work in the social sciences? Before striving to answer that question (on which we three disagree, and probably always will), we need to see exactly what the processualists were bringing back from their forays into the philosophical literature.

PROCESSUALISM AND THE PHILOSOPHY OF SCIENCE

If the new archaeology was designed to replace traditional archaeology, one strategy to hurry its replacement was to argue that the traditional approach, culture history, was underpinned by a faulty theory of culture—"normative theory" (Binford 1963, 1965). But as we discussed in Chapter 3, the characterization of that theory rested more on how it was used by the processualists themselves than on any products generated by culture historians (Lyman and O'Brien 2004b). For whatever reason, by the late 1960s little mention of culture history's supposedly "normative approach" was being made (but see Cordell and Plog 1979). By that time the processualists had found a better way of showing the inadequacy of the traditional approach: define archaeology as a science and label what they were doing (or wanted to do) as scientific. By default, pretty much everything else was history, not science. Why? Because it was unconnected to the formulation of generalizing laws, and without laws, one could not operate scientifically.

To this point we've provided only the simplest sketch of what laws are and how they fit into processual archaeology. Here we furnish a more complete picture of the "nomothetic enterprise," which in hindsight was no small operation for a discipline whose practitioners, or

FIGURE 4.3. Carl Hempel at the University of Pittsburgh, 1983. (Courtesy Merrilee Salmon.)

ical empiricism (which technically has deeper roots than the Vienna Circle [Parrini, Salmon, and Salmon 2003; Stadler 2003]).

When members of the circle (many of whom, like Hempel, were Jews) began leaving Europe in the face of the Nazi juggernaut, one country to which they immigrated was the United States, and one place that absorbed many of them was the University of Chicago. Hempel, who had received his doctorate from the University of Berlin in 1934, was among those; he later taught at, among other places, Queens College, Princeton, and the University of Pittsburgh. Hempel's approach to scientific explanation was laid out in a series of articles and books, the most important of his early publications being "Studies in the Logic of Explanation," which he coauthored with fellow emigré Paul Oppenheim (Hempel and Oppenheim 1948). Important later publications include two books, *Aspects of Scientific Explanation and Other Essays in the Philosophy of Science* (1965b) and *Philosophy of Natural Science* (1966). The first book is a collection of reprinted articles, with the exception of the last entry, "Aspects of Scientific Explanation" (Hempel 1965a). It was that chapter in particular that attracted the attention of archaeologists.

at least most of them, had received no formal training in science, much less scientific methods. To convert historical thinking into scientific thinking required models of science, and one place from which to borrow them was philosophy, where numerous models of archetypal sciences such as physics and chemistry were available. Following the lead of Binford and Spaulding, several processualists fastened onto the deductive-nomological model of Carl Hempel and, to a lesser extent, his inductive-statistical (statistical-nomological) model as *the* paradigms of scientific explanation.

Who was Hempel, and why did some processualists favor his model of scientific explanation over others? In the simplest of terms, he (Figure 4.3) was a second-generation member of what was known as the Vienna Circle, a group of philosophers, mathematicians, and scientists living in pre-Nazi Europe. The philosophical bent of the Vienna Circle was decidedly anti-metaphysical and pro-verification; what was important was what could be verified empirically. There was no sense studying a bunch of "what if's" when there were "what are's" to be explained. The key was to identify the "what are's" and construct a logical framework with which to explain them. The terms used to categorize the Vienna Circle's philosophical outlook are *logical positivism* or *log-*

Hempel's views on the scientific process underlay Binford's first explicit application of the philosophy of science to an archaeological problem. In "Some Comments on Historical versus Processual Archaeology" (1968d), which appeared in the *Southwestern Journal of Anthropology* (now the *Journal of Anthropological Research*), Binford criticized a traditional, culture-historical explanation for the collapse of Maya civilization put forth by Jerry Sabloff and Gordon Willey (1967). Paraphrasing the "distinguished philosopher of science, Carl Hempel," Binford (1968d:268) noted that "an explanation consists of two parts: First, the events believed to be relevant which temporally precede the event to be explained are set forth; second, a set of general laws is formulated which connects the 'causes' with their 'effects' in such a way that if we know that the earlier events have taken place, we would be able to predict the event we wish to explain."

In Binford's view, Sabloff and Willey had documented a temporal sequence of events, but their argument that an earlier event caused a later one failed to meet the requirements of a scientific explanation because it lacked laws relating the kinds of events making up the so-called explanation. General laws regarding cultural dynamics had to be written in order for archaeology to explain events scientifically. Because such laws were absent, Binford said, it was impossible to evaluate the Maya case in scientific terms. The collapse of the 1,100-year-old Maya civilization as a result of an invasion by some unidentified people, as Sabloff and Willey claimed, was not a *scientific* explanation, in Binford's opinion, because there were at least two alternative, yet unconsidered, possibilities. First, an invasion didn't necessarily precipitate a collapse of an indigenous society, and second, a collapse, if it had occurred, might have resulted from something other than an invasion.

Binford could have stopped there, but he continued his attack on standard historical explanations. Citing Spaulding (1968), he noted that there is no such thing as historical explanation but only the (lawful, Schiffer would say; theoretical, O'Brien and Lyman would say) explanation of historical events. Both Binford and Spaulding were unfamiliar with the works of philosophers who had analyzed the biological and paleontological literatures, and both were using only Hempel's model of "hard" science as a guide while bypassing models of historical sciences. History did not figure prominently in Hempelian models, and as noted in Chapter 3, philosophers debated the existence and role of laws in historical sciences.

Binford also argued that Sabloff and Willey had built an inductive argument—reasoning from facts or events to a conclusion or cause.

What they should have done, in his opinion, was to argue in the opposite direction, or deductively. It is clear, however, in the following Binford quote, that the reference to "proceed dialectically" indicates that Binford understood that the scientific method involves *both* induction and deduction. What seemed important to him was that the deductive step—that of testing hypotheses—actually be carried out: "Explanation begins for the archaeologist when observations made on the archaeological record are linked through laws of cultural or behavioral functioning to past conditions or events. Successful explanation and the understanding of process are synonymous, and both proceed dialectically—by the formulation of hypotheses (potential laws on the relationships between two or more variables) and the testing of their validity against empirical data. Hypotheses about cause and effect must be explicitly formulated and then tested" (Binford 1968d:270). This protocol was the only sound scientific method, according to Binford, who was, remember, paraphrasing Hempel.

Given their supposedly inductive predilections, culture historians allegedly tended to hold that the archaeological facts would speak for themselves (Binford 1968a). As Jim Hill (1972:67–68) put it, if the culture historians believed that "data can be collected prior to and separate from problem or hypothesis formulation, it is also reasonable that field work can be adequately carried out by a man who has no interest in theory, problems and so forth." Under this view, Hill noted, it is our own perceptions of artifacts and so forth that give them meaning. This sounds very much like what the postprocessualists would argue a decade or so later (Chapter 8).

Some of the more traditionally inclined archaeologists seemed to understand the lack of objectivity in such a view (e.g., Chenhall 1971), but certainly not everyone did (Swartz 1967). The final nail in what the processualists saw as the coffin containing traditional (inductive) methods was the realization that if Hempel's suggested procedure was not adopted, then archaeologists would be forced to accept Raymond Thompson's (1956) position that the only means of assessing an interpretation is to evaluate the competence and expertise of the individual who made it. This clearly was unacceptable to processualists, especially Binford, who believed that in science no interpretation should be accepted exclusively on the basis of authority. But here is a key point: seemingly lost in the rhetoric about models of the scientific process was the fact that Hempel never claimed that induction played no role in scientific explanation. In fact, it played a significant role, as we will see shortly. Binford seems to have been one of the few who understood this.

"Some Comments on Historical versus Processual Archaeology" (Binford 1968d) hit a nerve within the processualist movement and led to a flurry of publications on how to do scientific (read "Hempelian") archaeology. The stream of articles began with a short piece by John Fritz and Fred Plog (1970), "The Nature of Archaeological Explanation," which grew out of papers they presented at the Society for American Archaeology meeting in 1968. Fritz and Plog contrasted the Hempelian "logical positivist school" with the "narrow inductivist or empiricist school" allegedly followed by culture historians. This was, to our knowledge, the first time that archaeologists had contrasted those two kinds of scientific method, and the contrast was grossly misleading. For one thing, Hempel was an empiricist. For another, induction played a significant role in Hempel's view of how science worked. Thus, in contrasting "logical positivism" with the "inductivist or empirical school," Fritz and Plog were contrasting Hempel with Hempel.

Fritz and Plog cited with approval two of Hempel's publications: his 1966 book *Philosophy of Natural Science* and "Studies in the Logic of Explanation" (Hempel and Oppenheim 1948). As an example of "narrow inductivist or empiricist" reasoning, Fritz and Plog chose B. K. Swartz's (1967) "A Logical Sequence of Archaeological Objectives." Swartz did not refer to his suggested protocol as inductive method, but it was. It ran through the

following sequence of steps: (1) preparation, (2) data acquisition, (3) analysis, (4) interpretation, (5) integration and comparison, and (6) abstraction. Hempel (1966) characterized the inductive method as incorporating the following steps:

(1) Observe and record all the facts;

(2) Classify and analyze all the facts; and

(3) Derive generalizations from the facts.

 An optional step is

(4) Test the generalizations with additional facts.

Despite the similarity in terms, inductive and deductive processes of science are only distantly related to inductive and deductive logic. For some reason, standard textbooks—and not only those in archaeology—often mangle the discussion of induction and deduction as forms of argument. Jane Kelley and Marsha Hanen, whose *Archaeology and the Methodology of Science* (1988) is a very readable account of archaeology and the philosophy of science, put it this way: "the standard textbook characterization of deduction as proceeding from general to particular and induction as proceeding from particular to general is incorrect, for the difference has nothing to do with generality or particularity. It is rather that, in a correct deduction, the truth of the premises guarantees the truth of the conclusion; in acceptable inductive inference, all the premises may be true and the conclusion yet be false" (Kelley and Hanen 1988:174).

Inductive arguments have more information in their conclusions than in their premises. They are what philosophers of science refer to as "ampliative" arguments. An example of the form of an inductive argument by enumeration would be:

(1) Paleoindian projectile point 1 is fluted;

(2) Paleoindian projectile point 2 is fluted;

(3) Paleoindian projectile point 3 is fluted...

(4) Paleoindian projectile point N is fluted.

Therefore, the conclusion is either (1) that Paleoindian projectile point N + 1 will be fluted or (2) that all Paleoindian projectile points are fluted. The potential weakness of such inductive arguments should be apparent.

This leads to further questions when inductive methods are employed in archaeology. Which "facts" should be recorded when one is acquiring information? Surely there is an infinite number of facts that one might record, or observations that one might make, regarding an archaeological site or an assemblage of artifacts. What kinds of analytical manipulations should one put the facts through? Should they be added, multiplied, and divided by three; sorted into red ones, blue ones, and striped ones; counted, weighed, or heated to 100 degrees Celsius? Inductive procedures provide no analytical guidelines for answering these questions. Even so, inductive *arguments* are still essential to the archaeological process. Indeed, we have no choice but to generalize about the characteristics of populations on the basis of our samples.

Fritz and Plog's logic was unassailable with respect to the necessity of identifying problems, formulating working hypotheses (when possible), and specifying analytical protocols prior to analysis. They erred, however, in characterizing all of culture history as exemplifying the narrow inductivist strategy. First, culture historians often began fieldwork with a specific research problem and sometimes also had explicit—and testable—hypotheses that were evaluated in the course of research, making use of accepted analytical methods. Second, they failed to note that essential inferences, whether made by traditionalists or processualists, require important inductive steps. Take, for example, chronology. Time (as in when artifacts were made and used) is invisible in the archaeological record in that it must be inferred from contemporary evidence using techniques such as stratigraphic excavation, seriation, cross dating, and radiocarbon dating. Because the archaeologist can seldom predict exactly what chronological evidence will turn up in a given excavation, much less the dates such evidence

will yield upon analysis, the inference of time demands, as does all scientific research, *inductive* procedures, as Hempel (e.g., 1965b) consistently noted.

It is clear that in characterizing culture historians as "narrow inductivists," Fritz and Plog created a caricature. Certainly some traditional projects had been poorly designed, with implicit problems, and failed to furnish justifiable inferences; yet others produced stunningly sound knowledge about the past that remains rock-solid to this day. Not only did Fritz and Plog overlook the testability of some of the culture-history hypotheses, they also overlooked the important role played by induction in the Hempelian version of the scientific process. Of course, if one seeks to replace one approach with another, then an obvious strategy—not always fair or effective—is to show (or allege) that the old approach is fatally flawed, leaving the favored replacement as the better candidate. In our view, the accusation that culture historians weren't doing good science, or even science at all, created much more hostility toward processualism than its ideas about the nature of culture.

In addition to advocating a deductivist approach (and only a deductivist approach), Fritz and Plog were lobbying for law formulation as a consequence of accepting Hempel's deductive-nomological model of explanation. Indeed, they noted that "all archaeologists employ laws in their research…whenever inferences about the past are used in interpreting data excavated in the present" (Fritz and Plog 1970:405). The problem is, how do we know whether any given statement is really a law as opposed to an empirical generalization or an unverified processual hypothesis? Without being able to make such distinctions, archaeologists can only *hope* that the generalizations they're using are laws. Binford's (1968d) argument, and one with which all processualists could agree, was that archaeology needed laws that had been validated in the context of the epistemology of science.

An obvious way to distinguish laws from other kinds of nomothetic (generalizing) statements is to apply a widely acceptable definition. Fritz and Plog defined a law as a statement of relation between two or more variables that is true for all times and places. Hempel referred to such statements as invariant laws: they "assert general and unexceptional connections between specified characteristics of events" (Hempel 1966:55). This definition may be useful in screening out empirical generalizations that apply only to a given time and place; however, Fritz and Plog's definition is so restrictive that it also eliminates many other kinds of useful laws. As behavioralists would point out later, many scientific laws have boundary conditions, which means that they fall far short of universality. Such laws may predominate when it comes to cultural behavior (e.g., laws that pertain only to mobile hunter-gatherer societies or large cities). Others describe relationships probabilistically, not deterministically. Although Fritz and Plog recognized probabilistic (often referred to as "statistical") laws, they noted that the logic behind them, induction, was quite different than that behind the model they were promoting: Hempel's deductive-nomological model.

Fritz and Plog allowed no role for a law that might apply to only 95 percent of cases. They wanted universal, deterministic laws that applied to all cases at all times and in all places. Not surprisingly, given their interpretation of the kind of laws archaeology needed, it was Fritz and Plog whom Flannery (1973a:50) mainly had in mind when he discussed law-and-order processualists, quoting, without attribution, their line, "those of us who are interested in processual analysis have made the formulation and testing of laws our goal" (Fritz and Plog 1970:405). (Curiously, Flannery [1973a: 51] also called Plog's [1968] settlement-pattern analysis an "elegant" result of the Hempelian approach. Ironically, that research, which involved the statistical analysis of site distributions to test the hypothesis that water was the principal determinant of site location in the American Southwest, produced no laws of any kind.)

A common confusion in the early processualist literature was the conflation of law and hypothesis. As usually employed in science, a hypothesis is merely an assertion: it can be a tentative explanation, a tentative theory, a tentative law, or even a tentative empirical generalization. Fritz and Plog defined hypothesis as a testable statement of relation between two or more variables that is plausible but not confirmed. Clearly, they defined hypothesis as an unconfirmed law (a lawlike statement)—an uncommonly narrow definition. Perhaps this unfortunate equation of tentative law and hypothesis led to the erroneous conclusion that because many processualists were claiming to test hypotheses, they were thereby attempting to establish laws. Most processualist hypotheses, however, turn out to be tentative explanations or empirical generalizations, not so different from those offered by culture historians.

How does a lawlike hypothesis become a law? To Fritz and Plog (1970:405), the answer seemed self-evident: "A law is confirmed when the researcher demonstrates that a relationship between variables in a hypothesis is true." Using the hypothetico-deductive method, one gathers and evaluates relevant evidence for or against the hypothetical law. In this deceptively simple claim, Fritz and Plog glossed over the social dimension of confirmation: a supposedly confirmed hypothesis does not become a law until it is accepted as such by the members of the relevant scientific community. In making such judgments, community members usually assess the alleged law's fit with prevailing theories and, in what was anathema to Binford, take into account the reputation of the person reporting the new law.

There was another problem in the way that processualists, often influenced by Fritz and Plog's article (and its critics), construed the scientific process: a tendency to blur or conflate the two models they had presented (Hempel's deductive-nomological model of explanation and the hypothetico-deductive model for testing hypotheses). Moreover, many processualists failed to appreciate that neither model could be used for *generating* hypotheses, and that of these two models only the hypothetico-deductive model was appropriate for *testing* hypotheses (confirmation in the narrow, non-social sense). The result was a series of confusing discussions and arguments by archaeologists interested in establishing laws of cultural dynamics.

Michael Levin, a philosopher, was one person who realized that processualists such as Fritz and Plog were confusing discovery with justification (Levin 1973). Simplistically, discovery involves the generation of hypotheses for testing, whereas justification involves the testing procedure itself. Hempel was interested more in the latter than in the former (Kelley and Hanen 1988). Thus, Levin (1973:393) pointed out, in a devastating (but see Plog 1982), point-by-point critique of Fritz and Plog's article, that the deductive-nomological model "is entirely irrelevant to the problem of determining where laws—or laws worth testing—come from and how they are to be discovered. Equally irrelevant is the problem of corroborating a law-candidate once it has been proposed.... [This] is the activity of which the hypothetico-deductive model gives an account. The hypothetico-deductive model of corroboration has as little to do with the *formation* of hypotheses as does Hempel's model of explanation." Levin's quote makes clear that science, as apparently construed by processualists, involves three distinct activities: (1) the formulation of hypotheses, (2) the use of laws for explaining empirical phenomena, and (3) the testing of hypotheses. Processualists, however, were trying to accommodate all three activities with just two models.

The rest of our discussion will be simplified if we first examine the structure of the Hempelian hypothesis-testing process, which entails five steps:

(1) Explicitly state a specific problem;

(2) Suggest a series of possible solutions. These are the (multiple working) hypotheses to be tested;

(3) Deduce test implications from the hypotheses. The test implications spec-

ify the data (or "facts") that one should expect to encounter in the field and during analysis if a hypothesis is correct;

(4) Go to the field or laboratory and generate data relevant to the hypotheses under study;

(5) Compare the data with the hypotheses and choose the hypothesis that best fits the data based on the number of kinds of data and their independence of each other.

Note the differences between the five-step Hempelian hypothesis formation/testing model and the Hempelian deductive-nomological model of explanation. In the deductive-nomological model one begins with one or more general laws (L_N) and antecedent conditions (C_N) and proceeds to a description of the category of empirical phenomena (E) to be explained. The model looks like this:

$$L_1, L_2, L_3, \ldots L_N$$

$$C_1, C_2, C_3, \ldots C_N$$

$$\overline{}$$

$$E$$

A particular empirical phenomenon is said to be explained by the general law(s) when it matches conditions and characteristics of all *E* within the model. This is because *E* is a deductive consequence of the specified laws and antecedent conditions. Again, the explanation says nothing about hypothesis formation and testing. This does not mean that those activities are unimportant, only that they are separate issues.

Ideally, the end result of the Hempelian hypothesis-testing process is rejection or confirmation of the hypothesis. Because hypotheses are (usually) formed inductively, a premium is placed on the criteria used to select among the large number of available hypotheses. Here is a significant difference between Hempel and another philosopher of science, Karl Popper. Whereas the Hempelian approach allows rejection or confirmation, the Popperian ap-

FIGURE 4.4. *Left to right:* Patty Jo Watson, Steven LeBlanc, and Charles Redman at Caÿönü, Turkey, 1970. (Courtesy Columbia University Press and Patty Jo Watson.)

One archaeologist who read the manuscript was Frank Hole, who passed it along to his students at Rice University. O'Brien was one of them and remembers having the impression that it was going to be an important book, but at the time he was more interested in excavating shell middens along the Texas coast than reading about scientific explanation. Lyman was enrolled in a seminar in archaeological method and theory at Washington State in 1974. What he remembers most about the volume was thinking that $5.75 was an awful lot to spend on a 200-page textbook. Others were more impressed with the detailed treatment Watson and her coauthors gave the thorny issue of scientific explanation. Of course, there were critics (see below), but then they had never published a book-length treatment on science.

Right, wrong, or somewhere in the middle, Watson, LeBlanc, and Redman laid their cards on the table with respect to laws. The book is a lengthy, in-depth discussion of the thesis that "a basic goal of scientific archeology is...to establish general laws concerning cultural process...that enable explanation of cultural differences and similarities" (Watson, LeBlanc, and Redman 1971:23). This was nothing new. Not only had some culture historians embraced it, becoming scientific had been processualism's goal from the beginning, as Binford and numerous others continually pointed out. The authors advocated adopting the Hempelian deductive-nomological model of explanation as the means by which archaeology could become scientific. Again, this was nothing new; advocacy of the deductive-nomological model could be traced to Spaulding's (1968) comments in *New Perspectives*.

The authors' discussion of explanation was derived from *Aspects of Scientific Explanation and Other Essays in the Philosophy of Science* (Hempel 1965b). They did not reference Hempel's (1962) "Deductive-Nomological vs. Statistical Explanation," which had been the basis of Spaulding's (1968) programmatic state-

proach (Popper 1959, 1968) allows only rejection. A hypothesis might receive temporary support—meaning it has not as yet been rejected—but it can never be verified using Popperian logic. Both approaches, however, employ deduction in the testing phase, which means that the hypothesis serves as the assumption or premise, and the predictions as conclusions.

A Textbook for Science in Arch(a)eology

To clear up some of these problems and to put archaeology on a sound scientific footing, Patty Jo Watson, Steven LeBlanc, and Charles Redman (Figure 4.4) wrote *Explanation in Archeology* (1971). All three authors trace their intellectual roots to the University of Chicago. Watson and Redman received their doctorates from Chicago—Redman the year the book was published—and LeBlanc was one of Watson's doctoral students at Washington University in St. Louis. There was considerable anticipation in the archaeological community for the book's release. Because the authors had asked several colleagues to read a draft of the manuscript and offer comments, it was no secret what the book would say.

ments. Watson, LeBlanc, and Redman (1971:5) stated that "a scientist explains a particular event by subsuming its description under the appropriate confirmed general law, that is, by finding a general law that covers the particular event by describing the general circumstances, objects, and behavior of which the particular case is an example." This definition is faithful to how Hempel and Oppenheim (1948) defined explanation but without the encumbrance of philosophical terminology.

Watson and her colleagues also did an excellent job of summarizing another feature of the Hempel-Oppenheim model, that of prediction.

An explanation is not considered adequate unless the general laws and the statements describing the circumstances pertaining in the particular case in question logically could have enabled the observer to *predict* the particular case. This is sometimes referred to as the parity of explanation and prediction, which means that statements of explanation are *logically* equivalent to statements of prediction in any given case....

A particular event is predicted before it occurs by referring to the general law of which this particular event and its circumstances are an instance, just as the particular event is explained after it has occurred by referring to the general law of which this is an event and its circumstances are an instance. (Watson, LeBlanc, and Redman 1971:5; emphases added)

Although there is no *logical* distinction between explanation and prediction, Watson, LeBlanc, and Redman pointed out that there is a *practical* distinction, which

arises empirically because we can know and understand things and events only in a temporal context. Although there is an equivalence of logical structure between explanation and prediction, practically speaking, we can predict an event only if we know the general law and the circumstances for the particular event before the occurrence of that

event. If the event has already occurred, we can explain it only by reference to the general law and the particular circumstances. We can also in this way "postdict" the occurrence of past events, and then look for evidence in the archeological record to test such "predictions about the past." A most important result of the logical equivalence is the fact that confirmed explanations are just what allow us to make reliable predictions about the future. (Watson, LeBlanc, and Redman 1971:5–6)

Note the clause "we can predict an event only if we know the general law *and the circumstances for the particular event before the occurrence of that event.*" This created a wrinkle because it added more to the explanatory algorithm than simply laws: it added time and space. Laws were still deterministic, but the phenomena to be explained had temporal and spatial coordinates. This kind of discussion got close to arguments in which biologists and paleontologists had been involved for more than a decade (O'Brien and Lyman 2000a).

Watson, LeBlanc, and Redman (1971:7) talked about statistical laws in the following terms: "Statistical or 'probabilistic' laws are especially characteristic of the social sciences and these, too, are deterministic. Nonstatistical laws determine particulars; statistical laws determine *groups* of particulars." The first part of that last statement contains a flaw: a deterministic law, by definition, determines one group containing *all* particulars. We think what the authors meant was that *inductive* laws that are not statistical determine particulars. We base this conclusion on their use of the following quotation from Richard Rudner's *Philosophy of Social Science*: "generalizations in social science are usually probabilistic in character. Such generalizations claim only what is compatible with the observation of individual exceptions. Indeed, such assertions refer to no individual cases, but only to classes or sets of individual cases" (Rudner 1966:67).

Watson, LeBlanc, and Redman (1971:7) drew on an analogy from the physical sciences to amplify Rudner's remarks: "A nuclear physicist can predict with great accuracy the half life, or rate of disintegration, of a radioactive element, even though he does not determine precisely when any individual atom of that element will decay. Similarly, a social scientist utilizing statistical or probabilistic laws about cultural processes can predict the results of such processes, even though he does not determine precisely the seemingly random events or decisions on the individual level." Note that Watson, LeBlanc, and Redman stated that, like invariant laws, statistical (probabilistic) laws are also deterministic (nomological).

This reasoning followed that of Hempel (1965b:302), who had gone to great lengths to show that explanations using either kind of law are nomological: "either of them accounts for a given phenomenon by 'subsuming it under laws,' i.e., by showing that its occurrence could have been inferred—either deductively or with a high probability—by applying certain laws of universal or of statistical form to specified antecedent circumstances. Thus, a nomological explanation shows that we might in fact have *predicted* the phenomenon at hand, either deductively or with a high probability, if, at an earlier time, we had taken cognizance of the facts stated in the explanans." (The *explanans* encompasses laws and antecedent conditions.) Hempel said "either deductively *or* with a high probability" because explanation through the use of statistical laws almost always is inductive, not deductive, although it is possible for statistical-nomological laws to be deductive.

What did archaeologists think of the prescribed Hempelian remedy to the discipline's ills as summarized by Watson, LeBlanc, and Redman? British archaeologist Colin Renfrew (1973b:1928, 1929) agreed with them that *the* criterion of science is testability, but he took the adoption of Hempel's "restrictive notion of science" as embodied in the use of general laws to be wrong, "and its advocacy in so central a position in a book such as this to be harmful." He expressed concern that an archaeologist might become unnecessarily focused on the

form rather than the content of explanations. He also suggested that writing laws of culture is an impossible goal that may confuse rather than clarify what constitutes a valid and scientific explanation in archaeology. These remarks were from someone who was, in general, strongly in accord with the goals of processualism.

David Clarke (1972a) suggested that Watson, LeBlanc, and Redman were advocating the wrong model of how to do science. David Tuggle (1972), who was trained by Bill Longacre at Arizona, found the book's coverage of the philosophy of science to be limited in scope and too one-sided. Robert Schuyler (1973) also thought that the authors' coverage of alternate and conflicting views within the philosophy of science was too narrow, which dated the book. His point was that the logical empiricism being advocated by Watson and her colleagues was in fact falling out of favor among philosophers of science just as it was being advocated by processual archaeologists.

Renfrew, Schuyler, and Tuggle all questioned whether certain examples of cultural laws that Watson and her colleagues cited were, in fact, laws. Schuyler (1973:372) noted that the book left him feeling like he was "floating in a theoretical vacuum" that the authors "attempt to fill with general systems theory and ecology." He concluded, unfairly, that the authors and many of their processualist colleagues displayed a poor grounding in anthropological theory. Tuggle (1972; see also Tuggle, Townsend, and Riley 1972) also did not pull his punches when he noted that Watson and her colleagues failed to provide a clear discussion of the nature of laws and also failed to explore the nature of explanation. A few archaeologists who were aware that Hempel's deductive-nomological model of explanation was becoming outmoded among philosophers ceased citing Hempel and invoking the deductive-nomological model. Instead, they simply referred to laws, lawlike statements, experimental laws (after Nagel 1961), nomothetic statements, or more vaguely, "principles" (Reid, Schiffer, and Rathje 1975).

Which examples failed to convince Schuyler, Renfrew, and others that it was possible to construct laws? Based on analyses of archaeological materials performed by others, Watson, LeBlanc, and Redman (1971:39) suggested the following "hypothetical general law": "If the *formal* characteristics of Broken K Pueblo rooms are the same or closely similar to those in contemporary pueblos, the *functional* characteristics are also the same or closely similar." They stated that, when so worded, the law is of limited scope because of the specificity of the circumstances. Renfrew and Schuyler were skeptical that the statement was even a law, and so are we. Indeed, this statement was merely an analogy of the sort typically used in American archaeology (Wolverton and Lyman 2000). As Robert Ascher (1961a:317) put it, "in its most general sense interpreting by analogy is assaying any belief about nonobserved behavior by referral to observed behavior which is thought to be relevant." Flannery (1973a) just might have had the pueblo room case in mind when he immortalized the phrase "Mickey Mouse laws."

The supposed law of pueblo room function does not literally concern cultural processes, the alleged subject of interest. Cultural processes were originally defined by Binford as the dynamic causes and effects operating among the components of a cultural system or between systematic components of a culture and the environment in which the culture resides. If there is a law embedded here somewhere, then it must be more general and must pertain to dynamics. An example might be that "the spatial distribution of human behaviors and activities (causes) results in artifacts with different functions being differentially distributed across space (effects)."

Processualists did sometimes propose or actually employ possible laws of culture change. One oft-cited example comes from early ceramic-sociological studies (Chapter 3). This law, of which there are many published versions, can be stated approximately as follows: "As a society's cultural-transmission networks are disrupted by the infiltration of individuals enculturated in another society, nonfunctional (stylistic) phenomena will become more heterogeneous, change more rapidly, or both" (e.g., Binford 1963; Deetz 1965). That this is a lawlike statement—it pertains to dynamics and seems testable, at least in principle—is indisputable. However, where some processualists erred was in assuming that any such lawlike statement could be tested using evidence from the archaeological record. In fact, the archaeological testing of such a lawlike statement would require a very complex network of inferences, each of which has some degree of uncertainty (Chapter 5). The cumulative result would doubtless be a very weak test. In appreciating these limitations, many processualists, including Binford and Longacre, eventually turned to ethnoarchaeology, which provides a much more appropriate "laboratory" for testing many kinds of laws about cultural dynamics (Chapter 7). Other kinds of laws are more appropriately tested on archaeological evidence, which, after all, furnishes the only record of long-term cultural change available to social scientists (e.g., Plog 1974; Schiffer 1975b).

Perhaps spying an opportunity to shoot fish in a barrel for easy ink, additional philosophers were drawn into the debates over the applicability of various models of science to archaeology, focusing especially on points raised by Watson, LeBlanc, and Redman. One opportunist was Charles Morgan (1973, 1974), who pointed out once again that the deductive-nomological model was no panacea. It had problems, such as offering a poor characterization of laws, but Morgan offered no clarifications. Further, laws were construed as universal rather than probabilistic (statistical). Curiously, Morgan (1973) wondered if explanation, instead of being *the* goal of science, was in reality merely a byproduct of the scientific enterprise, which in his view was an effort to gain knowledge about the world and how it works. We are not sure what the difference is. Watson, LeBlanc, and Redman (1974) defended their position, noting that to explain something is to say that it is of a certain general kind. They

FIGURE 4.5. Richard and Patty Jo Watson on their way to work at Washington University, St. Louis, 1990. (Courtesy *Washington University Magazine* and Patty Jo Watson.)

competitors. Part of the reason, too, for Hempel's influence was the apparent simplicity of his ideas. He could be abstruse at times, but his models were clear enough. Another reason had to do with the fact that when Albert Spaulding formally introduced archaeologists to the scientific approach in his comments in *New Perspectives* (Spaulding 1968), it was to Hempel's brand, not someone else's. Binford was simply following his mentor's lead when he adopted Hempel as a guide. Fritz and Plog were students at Chicago during the mid- to late 1960s, so it is easy to see why they read Hempel. In 1969 Pat Watson and her husband, Richard Watson (Figure 4.5), a philosopher of geological science, coauthored *Man and Nature: An Anthropological Essay in Human Ecology* (Watson and Watson 1969). On the first page of the first chapter they argued that anthropology can be a science because man is part of nature, and they defined science as "a search for laws pertaining to the characteristics and behavior of all natural objects" (Watson and Watson 1969:3). The only philosopher cited in the references (other than Watson [1966]), is Hempel (1965b). At the time, Richard Watson (e.g., 1969a) was clearly a Hempelian, advocating a deterministic, deductive-nomological model of scientific explanation.

The processualists' devotion to strict Hempelian deduction began to fade as they came to realize that research is rarely if ever entirely inductive or deductive (Hill 1972; Kelley and Hanen 1988; Smith 1977). Rather, it combines both. This realization was helped along by another philosopher of science, Merrilee Salmon (Figure 4.6), who with her husband, Wesley Salmon (Figure 4.7), taught at the University of Arizona during the 1970s. Wesley Salmon had started out working in the logical-empiricist tradition of Hempel but had moved away from it in the 1960s and toward causality (e.g., Salmon 1967, 1971). It was to the Salmons that processualists and behavioralists at Arizona and elsewhere turned during the mid- to late '70s if they were interested in what philosophers of science had to say

argued that if archaeology was to be a science, it had to adopt the methods of science, and the deductive-nomological model and the hypothetico-deductive method were surely scientific.

Virtually every philosopher who had something negative to say about the models of science being touted in archaeology indicated that there was considerably more diversity in the philosophy of science than the ideas of Carl Hempel. For example, biologists were seriously considering Karl Popper's (e.g., 1959) work as a source of models. Archaeologists also could have looked to their sister disciplines of geology (e.g., Kitts 1963a, 1963b) or paleontology (e.g., Simpson 1963, 1970), where individuals were examining the logic and philosophical structure of these patently historical disciplines.

So why did processualists choose Hempel? There undoubtedly are several answers to this question, some of which we may never know. One simple explanation is that at the height of processualism Hempelian philosophy had few

(Salmon 1975, 1976, 1978; Salmon and Salmon 1979).

Unlike Levin, Morgan, and other philosophers who had no real familiarity with or long-term commitment to archaeology, Merrilee Salmon—trained at Michigan in the philosophy of mathematics—became a philosopher of archaeology (among other things). She and her husband visited field projects, including Grasshopper—then the site of the University of Arizona's field school (Figure 2.8)—and she sat in on courses taught by Longacre and Schiffer. In one contribution (Salmon 1976), she elegantly clarified the important roles of induction and deduction in the scientific process. In others she addressed the limitations of the deductive-nomological model of explanation, advocating an appreciation for the role of causal explanations employing probabilistic models and laws. With Wesley Salmon (Salmon and Salmon 1979), she introduced as an alternative the "statistical-relevance model," which became a cornerstone of behavioral archaeology.

The statistical-relevance model was intended to remedy a serious defect in Hempelian models of statistical explanation: seemingly, they al-

FIGURE 4.6. Merrilee Salmon, ca. 1973. (Courtesy Merrilee Salmon.)

lowed only for the explanation of events with a high probability of occurrence. The statistical-relevance model argued that even events with a very low probability could be explained so long as the investigator was able to assemble, in the explanans (laws and antecedent conditions), all statistically relevant variables along with the relevant statistical law(s). This was explicitly a causal model of explanation, but it was not deterministic. Determinism was simply the special case where the probability of occurrence was 1.0.

For Arizona archaeologists the statistical-relevance model was a liberating formulation because it gave guidance for handling the rare events that archaeologists commonly attempted to explain. It also affirmed that laws—albeit statistical ones—were necessary for explanation, a point that Salmon underscored in her 1982 book. Merrilee Salmon's engagement with archaeology and archaeologists at Arizona demonstrated that philosophers could make positive contributions to the discipline not only by clearing up misunderstandings but also by introducing archaeologically appropriate models. Alison Wylie (Figure 4.8), who briefly studied with the Salmons at Arizona and received her Ph.D. from the State University of New York at Binghamton in 1982, would continue that tradition (Chapter 8).

We agree with Willey and Sabloff (1993: 231) that the appearance of Watson, LeBlanc, and Redman's *Explanation in Archeology* "marked the end of the first phase of the New Archaeology when its basic tenets were presented and detailed and the beginning of the second or operational phase...which emerged in the early 1970s with the growing concern about the pragmatic and uniquely archaeological problem of finding the most secure ways of linking past behaviors with material remains." We also agree with them that intellec-

FIGURE 4.7. Wesley Salmon, ca. 1985. (Courtesy Merrilee Salmon.)

FIGURE 4.8. Alison Wylie, Fort Walsh National Historic Site, Canada, 1973. (Courtesy Alison Wylie.)

tual developments during the 1970s and '80s suggest that the volume had more impact in the area of its subtitle, *An Explicitly Scientific Approach*, than in the area of its main title.

Archaeology came out of the exercise with a better appreciation for the exactitudes of science, not to mention an appreciation for the shifting sands of philosophy. Even archaeologists who had not entered the fray undoubtedly took a fresh look at how they structured their arguments and justified their interpretations. Perhaps most importantly, there was an awareness of the difficulties involved in deriving scientific explanations. And somewhere along the way, the term *theory* made an appearance. The word had always been used in archaeology—systems theory, normative theory, and the like—but here we are referring to a clear recognition that theory is explanation at a higher level. It is surprising how infrequently the term appeared, for example, in the early archaeological discussions of the philosophy of science. Similarly, when it appeared in the archaeological literature of, say, the pre-1980 period, the term was used in almost every conceivable sense except as the kind of construct that serves in science to explain empirical regularities.

Steve LeBlanc made that point in an article he coauthored with UCLA mathematician-turned-archaeologist Dwight Read, titled "De-

scriptive Statements, Covering Laws, and Theories in Archaeology" (Read and LeBlanc 1978). Their main argument was that, in the late '70s, there was still a basic lack of explanatory theory in archaeology. LeBlanc wasn't changing his mind from what he, Watson, and Redman had advocated—the formation and testing of hypotheses—but he was saying that it was not enough. Importantly, Read and LeBlanc, quoting philosopher of science Ernst Nagel (1961), specified that a formal theory is more than confirmed hypotheses. It must be made up of what we would term units or categories of phenomena, and statements about the interrelationships and interactions of the empirical phenomena placed in those units. They also argued, correctly in our view, that a theory is not tested for correctness with empirical data, but rather if the theory does not apply to a real-world situation, then either its units, its statements of interrelationships, or both have to be reworded or reconstructed. In this Read and LeBlanc were echoing what Binford had long preached—the need for "reality-based" theories.

For many new archaeologists, however, the largest problem facing the discipline was epistemological: that of developing more sophisticated approaches to inferring past behavioral and organizational phenomena. John Fritz (1972), in a thoughtful contribution to Mark Leone's (1972a) reader, cogitated on this problem, framing it is as one of inventing reliable measuring instruments. Schiffer (1972b) took a different tack, arguing that inferring past behavior required the use of cultural laws. In illustrating this argument with an attempt to reconstruct the quantitative dependence on maize at Shabik-eschee village, a Basketmaker III site in Chaco Canyon, New Mexico, he pointed out the many cultural laws that would be needed to establish this kind of inference. In his synthetic model of inference, he dissected the marital-residence inferences of his mentors, Hill and Longacre, showing that implicit laws abounded. Schiffer later expounded this theme further (Schiffer 1975b), contending that cultural laws—whether implicit or explicit—permeated the practice of archaeology (Chapter 7).

In his chapter in Chuck Redman's book, Albert Spaulding (1973:348) argued that "the new archaeologists are surely right in arguing that we will never know what we can learn about past human behavior in the absence of a vigorous program of hypothesis formulation, careful research in the light of the hypothesis formulated, and so on in the endless scientific spiral of interaction between theory and observation." A great many archaeologists, processualist or not, would have agreed with that statement—so many that one might wonder why there was any rancorous debate over archaeology's goals. But we're quoting selectively here; what we're not quoting is Spaulding's call for law formulation. Here is where the processualists parted company from the traditionalists, and where even some of the processualists began to differ among themselves. Processualism by the early '70s was not a monolithic approach or paradigm growing slowly under the guiding direction of Lew Binford. Whatever processualism was—and it was different things to different people—it was taking on a life of its own, sending out shoots in different directions to colonize new ground. That new ground included systems theory, law formulation, and hypothesis testing.

Binford played no significant part in the debates over the kind of science archaeology should become, nor did he ever explicitly use systems theory. The processualists who had connections with him at Chicago, as well as their students and Binford's students at UCLA and New Mexico, were the ones carrying the torch. This would not be unexpected in science: Someone begins a movement, trains a cadre of replacements, then eases out of the picture and lets them take over. This is the way it seemed with Binford, whom we left recounting his head-to-head encounter with François Bordes in 1965. The capstone to that encounter was the article by Sally and Lew in *Scientific American* (Binford and Binford 1969) in which they claimed to have identified more than a dozen distinct, recurring groups of Mousterian tools. They took the existence of this statistical pattern as evidence that the tool groups had behavioral significance—an example of processualism's pattern-recognition approach. Using the definition that culture is humankind's extrasomatic means of adaptation, the Binfords proposed that a shift in climate caused alterations in the distributions of resources, which in turn precipitated a series of adaptive readjustments among the users of Mousterian tools. To fully understand those shifts in adaptations, Lew would pursue ethnoarchaeological research in general and zooarchaeological research in particular (Chapter 7).

One gauge of how well an approach is doing relative to its competitors is the amount of criticism it draws. We view critical reactions as being more important to the success of an approach than noncritical reactions because criticism draws people's interest; they want to see what all the commotion is about. A natural reaction is to think, "If processualism is getting this kind of attention, then it must be pretty important." And by the 1970s processualism was the focus of considerable critical attention. We've already seen some of it as it applied to specific articles and books, and we saw what Walter Taylor thought of the new archaeology generally. What about other perceptions?

Gilbert Kushner (1970), an Arizona-trained cultural anthropologist, objected strongly to what he saw as an almost exclusive focus by processualists on the physical environment at the expense of the social environment. In his view a processualist explanation was that if the environment changed, then culture changed. Kushner viewed processualist causes as extracultural, with no possibility of intracultural causation. He also argued that simply noting that a culture adapts to changing environments is not only *not* an explanation but requires that the analyst determine why the culture adapted the way that it did and not in some other way. He argued that this requirement demands historical data, something that in his view the processualists didn't seem to acknowledge. Finally, anticipating the postprocessualist arguments that would appear in the 1980s, Kushner (1970) noted that the processualists tended to ignore the individual human being, and in his opinion this was not good. Although he accurately identified a decided processual emphasis on the physical environment—a legacy of Julian Steward's that was passed down through Gordon Willey, Robert Braidwood, Bill Sanders, and others—Kushner made it sound as if the processualists never acknowledged the importance of the social environment in effecting culture change. This was a gross mischaracterization.

Criticisms originated not only from outside the fold of processualists but from inside as well. Mark Leone (1972b), in a chapter of his edited volume *Contemporary Archaeology,* argued that of the three goals of archaeology— the writing of culture history, the reconstruction of past lifeways, and the study of culture process—the first was basically complete; the second could not be achieved by applying scientific techniques, no matter how well or poorly science itself was understood; and the third had yet to be either operationalized or realized. Leone saw many new methods in processualism but little in the way of explanatory theory other than what had been borrowed from anthropology. That included cultural ecology and cultural materialism, which in Leone's view together produced an evolutionism under which the history of cultures was rendered as a sequence of developmental stages with little if any consideration of how and why one stage changed to another. Further, the methods didn't really help in attaining the third goal.

Leone (1972b:20) observed that the "strident claim made by many new archaeologists [of] greater sophistication in the use of scientific method [was] one of the most annoying." This was because (1) what passed for sophistication in the philosophy of science was really rhetoric; (2) efforts to follow the protocol dic-

tated by the philosophy of science constituted the area of archaeology in which more mistakes were made and less justice done; and (3) new methods and techniques don't change worldviews or ultimately produce better science. Kushner (1973) agreed with Leone, which caused Schiffer (1975c) to point out that it seemed incongruous that Leone would claim that the reconstruction of past lifeways was impossible, given that such reconstruction was a necessary foundation for explaining cultural change, regardless of the nature and origin of one's explanatory models and theory.

Jerry Sabloff, Thomas Beale, and Anthony Kurland (1973) liked the fact that processual archaeology had moved the discipline in a direction focusing on problems, and they agreed that the hypothetico-deductive model was a good one to use for problem solving. They also appreciated that processualists were forcing archaeologists in general to be more explicit about what they were doing and why they were doing it. But they also had a decided distaste for the deductive-nomological model, largely because they believed that it was impossible to create laws of cultural dynamics and processes. Without citing him, they echoed Leone's (1972b) comments with statements such as the "new archaeology's stress on a positivist approach to explanation and its championing of Hempel's model of deductive reasoning in archaeology have been brought forward with more argumentative polemic and greater emphasis than any other aspect of the new archaeological paradigm" (Sabloff et al. 1973:108); despite the processualists' reliance on the hypothetico-deductive method, "their substantive case studies have tended to rely on simple versions of [that] method for the organization of their arguments" (110); "it is apparently impossible to construct a hypothetico-deductive structure that does not ultimately rest on inductive confirmation and—in archaeological analogy—on a major premise in the form of an empirical generalization" (111); and "theoretical discussion of the Hempelian strategy has proceeded on an inexplicably naive level" (112). Sabloff and his colleagues argued that it was impossible to test cause-and-effect relations in archaeological settings because the dynamics had to be inferred. They anticipated Richard Gould's (1978c, 1980) misgivings about analogical reasoning when they pointed out that interpreting anomalies requires recourse to still other ethnographic analogies that actually provide parallels (Chapter 5).

To Sabloff, Beale, and Kurland, history is not subject to experimentation. It is an open and changing system full of dissimilar events. Thus, universal laws do not apply to history. They found it disturbing that the processualists assumed that because it was difficult to see the individual in prehistory, he or she could be ignored. This view anticipated later comments by archaeologists interested in agency theory (Chapter 8). Remember, it was Willey and Sabloff's (1967) article on the collapse of Maya civilization that Binford (1968d) used as one of his whipping boys. How much of the sting still remained when Sabloff and his colleagues (1973) put pen to paper is unclear. In any event, some years later, when Sabloff joined Binford at New Mexico, all would be forgiven.

Ezra Zubrow (1972), a Longacre student who had worked at Vernon under Paul Martin's general direction, aligned himself with Leone (1972a) and argued that there had been no real revolution as yet in archaeology, contrary to Martin's (1971) claim. Zubrow pro-vided data that seemingly backed up his claim: 2,092 references to articles and books written by eighty well-known scholars and published since 1969. In short, there was no indication that there were "classic" pieces of processualist literature, and the most-cited reference was not to a "theoretical statement of the new potential paradigm" (Zubrow 1972:204). This was a myopic statement, given that scientific revolutions do not necessarily happen in the same short span of time in which political revolutions usually occur.

Finally, Don Dumond (1977) spelled out how in his view the processualists were misinterpreting Hempel by noting that whereas the processualists believed that confirmation of hypotheses resulted in laws, Hempel (1966:8) had clearly indicated that even if "a test implication inferred from a hypothesis is found to be true, [this] does not prove the hypothesis to be true. Even if many implications of a hypothesis have been borne out by careful tests, the hypothesis may still be false." Hempel's statement refers in part to the fact that *confirmation* requires induction (Hill and Evans 1972; Smith 1977). These and other such cautions and critiques offered by rank-and-file processualists as well as by nonbelievers no doubt was a catalyst for some rethinking of the processualist paradigm. But other changes were afoot as well, as we shall see in Chapter 5.

5

Science or History?

*Before I go on with this short history let
me make a general observation—the test of
a first rate intelligence is the ability to hold
two opposed ideas in the mind at the same
time, and still retain the ability to function.*

—F. SCOTT FITZGERALD, "The Crack-Up"

The chapter epigraph, from F. Scott Fitzgerald's autobiographical essay "The Crack-Up," is useful not because it's a touchstone for any particular topic discussed in this chapter, but as a reminder of how difficult it is simultaneously to illustrate how archaeology works as a process and to paint a useful synopsis of American archaeology in the second half of the twentieth century. The two objectives overlap to a degree, but in several respects they are, as Fitzgerald put it, "opposed ideas in the mind."

This dialectic would have been of interest to the processualists of the early 1970s, who found themselves engaged in discussions with archaeologists who viewed the discipline strictly as history as opposed to science (Chapter 4). Some processualists, such as Albert Spaulding (1973), regarded archaeology *only* as a science. Others, such as Pat Watson (1973b), took a softer stance and left the door open to the possibility that archaeology could be both science and history. Our opinion, as will become clearer as we reference some of our own work in succeeding chapters, is that archaeology *is* science, although it has a distinctly historical component. But our definition of history is different

than most—a difference based on our view that history can furnish explanations. This doesn't mean that it always *will* provide explanations, only that it has the capability to provide some explanations some of the time.

Our definition of history follows from a discussion by biologist Robert O'Hara in which he separates history from "chronicle":

> [G]enerally speaking a *chronicle* is a description of a series of events, arranged in chronological order but *not* accompanied by any causal statements, explanations, or interpretations. A chronicle says simply that A happened, and then B happened, and then C happened. A *history*, in contrast to a chronicle, contains statements about causal connections, explanations, or interpretations. It does not say simply that A happened before B and that B happened before C, but rather that B happened *because* of A, and C happened *because* of B. . . . history, as distinct from chronicle, contains a class of statements called *narrative sentences*, and narrative sentences, which are essential to historical writing, will never appear in [chronicles]. A narrative sentence describes *an event*, taking place at a particular time, with reference to *another event* taking place at a *later* time. (O'Hara 1988:144)

Part of what we hope to accomplish in this book is to chronicle four decades of American archaeology—who wrote what, when it appeared, and what it said. But that is secondary to presenting our take on archaeology as a process: how and why American archaeology took the course it did and is continuing to take. This entails writing what O'Hara calls "narrative sentences," which we then use to explain the process. Up to this point we've been fairly successful in going back and forth between chronicle and history, but from here on things get a little rough. For a variety of reasons American archaeology expanded rapidly in the mid-1970s in terms of the number of directions in which it headed. This places a significant burden on anyone attempting to write a useful chronicle of the period. It means that we have to be highly selective in what we include, in the process skipping over a lot of original and interesting work.

One measure of the discipline's growth during the late 1960s and early '70s, and especially of its influence in higher education, is the number of students who took archaeology courses on college and university campuses. If we extrapolate from enrollments in anthropology courses generally, we find that that number skyrocketed. Note the data for total credit hours in the anthropology department at the University of Arizona for the period 1964–1978 (Figure 5.1). The department's credit-hour production jumped from fewer than 800 in 1964 to 3,000 in 1971. It fell in 1973 to about 2,500 before climbing again. Beginning in 1976 it began dropping every year, in 1978 reaching the same level as in 1965.

Data from the Institute of Medicine's 1985 report *Personnel Needs and Training for Biomedical and Behavioral Research* (Table 5.1) show a similar trend nationwide. The number of undergraduate and graduate students enrolled in anthropology courses increased markedly from 1960 to 1973–1974, with a parallel trend in the number of B.A. degrees in anthropology awarded during that period. In 1960 slightly more than 5,000 undergraduate students were enrolled in anthropology courses nationwide; in 1974 more than 6,000 undergraduate students were awarded *degrees* in anthropology. Based on personal experience,

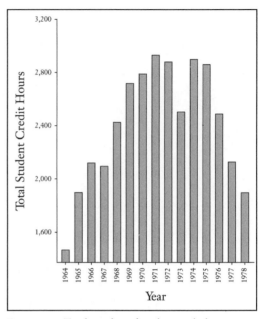

FIGURE 5.1. Total number of student credit hours produced by the University of Arizona Department of Anthropology for the years 1964–1978. (Data compiled by J. Jefferson Reid; after Schiffer 1979b.)

archaeology not only shared in these enrollment gains but often led them.

Are these figures representative of a shift in students away from other fields and toward anthropology, or do they simply reflect an overall increase in the number of students in colleges and universities generally? Undoubtedly more students were on the nation's campuses in 1973–1974 than in 1960—a result of the postwar population bulge known as the "baby boom"—but the right-hand column in Table 5.1, which lists the ratio of undergraduate anthropology degrees to all B.A. degrees, shows a steady increase from 1961, the first year for which data are available, to 1974. This is a clear indication that anthropology majors as a percentage of all majors were increasing.

Anthropology was truly a hot major in the 1960s and early 1970s. Why? One reason might have been because it offered a safe haven for those not inclined to major in anything that required more in the way of mathematical skill than high school algebra. But this was as true after 1974 as it was before. We suspect there are better reasons. For one,

TABLE 5.1. Anthropology Enrollments in Colleges and Universities, B.A. Degrees Awarded in Anthropology, and Ratio of Anthropology B.A.s to Total B.A.s, 1960–1984

Year	Total Enrollment	Undergraduate Enrollment	Graduate Enrollment	B.A. Degrees Awarded	Anthro B.A.s/Total B.A.s
1960	5,887	5,025	862	413	n/a
1961	7,437	6,431	1,006	484	0.0013
1962	9,120	7,983	1,137	577	0.0015
1963	11,399	10,061	1,338	746	0.0018
1964	14,278	12,726	1,552	964	0.0021
1965	15,679	13,808	1,871	1,203	0.0024
1966	19,123	16,800	2,323	1,503	0.0029
1967	23,284	20,600	2,684	1,825	0.0032
1968	28,331	25,282	3,049	2,261	0.0036
1969	34,288	30,610	3,678	2,990	0.0041
1970	40,691	36,774	3,917	3,711	0.0046
1971	45,318	40,627	4,691	4,386	0.0052
1972	48,476	43,475	5,001	5,156	0.0058
1973	47,477	42,243	5,234	5,625	0.0060
1974	45,472	39,902	5,570	6,002	0.0063
1975	45,481	39,713	5,768	5,624	0.0060
1976	44,124	38,062	6,062	5,188	0.0056
1977	41,625	35,681	5,944	4,844	0.0052
1978	39,215	32,487	6,728	4,300	0.0046
1979	36,366	29,830	6,536	3,998	0.0043
1980	34,108	27,765	6,343	3,606	0.0038
1981	32,637	26,315	6,322	3,342	0.0035
1982	n/a	n/a	6,118	3,077	0.0032
1983	n/a	n/a	5,948	n/a	0.0029 (est.)
1984	n/a	n/a	5,693	n/a	n/a

colleges and universities in the 1960s were the recipients of increased federal funding in the social sciences and humanities through Title VI of the National Defense Education Act of 1958. The act was the result of the Cold War, although the precipitating factor was the launch of the Soviet satellite Sputnik on October 4, 1957. Sputnik weighed less than 200 pounds and was only about the size of a basketball, but the fact that it was up there, orbiting the Earth as the only artificial satellite, was a clear signal that America had fallen behind the Soviet Union not only technologically but in its efforts to enhance its prestige abroad. Something had to be done to shift the balance back in favor of the United States.

Title VI was intended to provide the means necessary to train students specifically in area studies and languages. Its origins can be traced to a report issued by the Social Science Research Council that proposed a series of steps to safeguard national interests against the growing threat of communism. The primary steps included increasing the relevance of the humanities, particularly foreign languages, and linking the humanities to the social sciences (Katzenstein 2001). The number of area-study and language programs on campuses increased after 1948, but the rate of increase grew dramatically after Title VI was enacted.

Title VI funding was not difficult to obtain, and universities and colleges across the country put together proposals that requested money for new faculty positions. They also beefed up the staffing of their admissions and financial aid offices to meet the demands imposed by the annual increase in students, many of whom obtained money for tuition under a separate pro-

vision of the NDEA. State-supported schools, especially, could not turn away qualified students, so they created more courses for them. They also expanded their curricula by establishing new majors, using new faculty brought in under Title VI. Some institutions began teaching anthropology for the first time, whereas others added graduate programs. Still others reached the threshold where hybrid departments of anthropology and sociology or some other discipline(s) could be split, with each discipline placed in its own unit.

Figure 5.2 shows the distribution of archaeologists and nonarchaeologists in full-time positions in American and Canadian departments between 1950 and 1977, arranged by the year in which the Ph.D. was granted. The data were compiled from the 1978–1979 American Anthropological Association's *Guide*. For example, more than 150 nonarchaeologists who received their Ph.D.s in 1974 found full-time

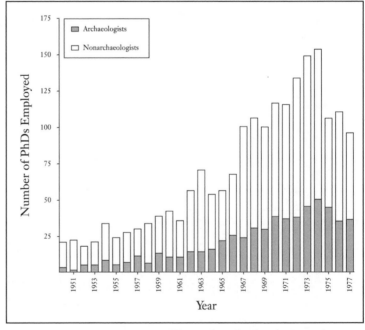

FIGURE 5.2. The number of archaeologists and nonarchaeological anthropologists, by year of Ph.D., employed full-time in American and Canadian universities in 1977. (Data compiled from the 1978–1979 *Guide to Departments of Anthropology*, published by the American Anthropological Association; after Schiffer 1979b.)

employment, as did 50 archaeologists. Compare those numbers to the minuscule numbers for the 1950s. Also notice where the two curves, especially that for nonarchaeologists, begins to shift upward dramatically.

As important as curricular expansion was to increasing the number of anthropology students, we suspect many students were attracted to anthropology because they viewed it as being more relevant to modern issues than other fields were. And social relevance was a key issue on college campuses in the late '60s and early '70s. Events in society at large had dramatic impacts on a student's decisions about which courses to take. Longer-range implications had to do with a student's choice of major and the decision whether (and where) to go to graduate school. Social factors have always played a role in such decisions, but they were particularly salient between, say, 1964 and 1974.

One catalyst for some of the social concerns of that period was the change in student housing. The lack of preparedness on the part of colleges and universities to house the bulge of new students in the 1960s forced more and more students to live off campus. Student housing being what it is, white, middle-class kids oftentimes found themselves living in neighborhoods that were less affluent than those in which they had been raised. They saw—many of them for the first time—the face of poverty and despair, especially on the part of African Americans, and they were upset by it. Why wasn't the government taking care of poor people? And what about impoverished people in Vietnam, Cambodia, and Laos who were being bombed by the U.S. military? Why had decisions about the future of poor people around the world been taken out of their hands and placed in the hands of powerful, rich white men whose personal agendas did not include the welfare of those people? Who was going to speak for these voiceless groups?

The litany is familiar to anyone who grew up in the '60s—the great hopes and excitement, as well as the fears, that grew out of the Kennedy administration but that slowly morphed into a black cloud of pessimism under

Lyndon Johnson, reaching a head in 1968. Things couldn't get much worse, many people told themselves as they sat back on New Year's Eve of that year and recalled the events of the past twelve months: the massive Tet Offensive in Vietnam that reshaped the war and ultimately resulted in Johnson's decision not to seek re-election; the student riots at Columbia University in New York; the assassinations of Martin Luther King in Memphis and Robert F. Kennedy in Los Angeles; and the riots between police and Abbie Hoffman's Yippies in the streets outside the Democratic Convention in Chicago. It was a bleak period in American history, and anthropology enrollments soared.

As did faculty in other disciplines, many anthropologists took part in the campus demonstrations and other activities that characterized those unique times, and they created or modified lectures to reflect feelings and events. They also took part in teach-ins—after-hours (or in many cases during-hours) assemblies of faculty and students who met to discuss any number of important topics, from the war in Southeast Asia, to the civil rights movement in the South, to the optimum indoor lighting conditions for home-grown recreational plants. Because they are trained and housed in anthropology departments, archaeologists usually mirror in most respects their colleagues in the other subfields. Thus we agree to an extent with Tom Patterson, who in his book *Toward a Social History of Archaeology in the United States* comments that the new archaeologists "attempted to redefine the field and redirect inquiry to problems that they saw as relevant not only to anthropology but also to society as a whole" (Patterson 1995:113). Archaeologists may tend to be less socially conscious and less activist than cultural anthropologists, but we think the general point is still valid: the social concerns of the 1960s did get mirrored in archaeology.

Patterson, however, claims that to redefine the field, the processualists had to forge alliances both within anthropology and with specialists outside it, such as geologists, soil scientists, and botanists. He further claims that the results of these alliances were reductionistic and deterministic. We totally disagree: processualists neither *had* to forge alliances with anthropologists and nonanthropologists, nor were the products of those alliances reductionistic and deterministic. As discussed below, some collaborations in which archaeologists were involved in the 1970s yielded results as significant as any the discipline had produced.

Some processualists were interested in the social relevance of what they were doing. John Fritz's (1973) "Relevance, Archaeology and Subsistence Theory" is a case in point (see also Fritz and Plog 1970; Martin and Plog 1973; Rathje 1974; Rathje and Murphy 1992; Reid, Schiffer, and Rathje 1975). Others were not, or more precisely, if they had such an interest, the literature does not reflect it. Without question, those of us educated in the '60s and '70s were exposed regularly to discussions about global issues such as war, overpopulation, racism, pollution, and resource depletion—discussions that made us think about the issues and, in some cases, to worry about them. What archaeologist in his or her right mind *wouldn't* worry if told of impending global doom, especially if the person doing the telling sounded authoritative—someone like Stanford biologist Paul Ehrlich, who in his book *The Population Bomb* (1968) predicted that at a minimum ten million people, most of them children, would starve to death worldwide during *each* year of the 1970s? But if there was one thing our processualist upbringing taught us, it was to question everything. So after catching our breath and thinking about what Ehrlich was proclaiming—and he was not alone in making this kind of dire prediction—we began wondering if overpopulation had ever been a problem for, say, Neolithic farmers. And we went out and researched the problem, finally reaching the conclusion that Ehrlich had as little chance of being right about the number of people dying during the 1970s as he did about another of his predictions—that England would not be around in the year 2000.

Learning how to separate good science from bad was not the only thing we learned in school. We also came to the realization that, in choosing research interests, archaeologists are apt to seize upon the topic of the moment, whether it's population increase, climatic change, human destruction of the tropics, or sudden catastrophes such as volcanic eruptions and earthquakes. These were headline topics at the time, and they became part of archaeology. Were they socially relevant? Yes, but this isn't necessarily why they became incorporated into archaeology. They became part of archaeology because they were interesting and because they were hot.

By definition something is "hot" because a lot of people are paying attention to it. If so, and you're among the first to integrate whatever it is into your research agenda, there's a good chance you might grab some attention (and some research funding), fleeting as it might be. And with all the topics available in the 1970s, processualists were like kids in a candy store. They could figure out that students of the day were interested in certain topics more than others, and these topics flowed smoothly out of the processualist agenda of the '60s, with its interests in cultural ecology and the environment. Processualism did not have to be retooled in order to attract more customers.

Regardless of the social relevance of the anthropological/archaeological curriculum, the bubble burst in the mid-1970s, when there was a dramatic decline both in undergraduate enrollment in anthropology courses and the number of degrees awarded. This was true in the behavioral sciences generally (Institute of Medicine 1985). By 1981 anthropology had lost 40 percent of its undergraduate enrollment from its all-time high in 1972, when more than 43,000 students were enrolled in anthropology courses. Similarly, it lost a staggering 45 percent of its degree recipients from its all-time high in 1974. Clearly, anthropology was losing its appeal among the baby boomers, at least at the undergraduate level.

The reasons for this downturn are varied, but an important one was the realization that a degree in anthropology or psychology didn't offer the same level of marketability that other degrees did. Moreover, the job market had reached a saturation point in terms of the number of anthropologists it could handle. The late '70s were a time when students would ask with all earnestness, "What can I do with a degree in anthropology?" O'Brien remembers when a father and daughter showed up in his office in 1980, his first year teaching at Missouri. The father asked if O'Brien could please talk his daughter out of anthropology and into a field that would help ensure her acceptance to the Delta Airlines flight attendant school. Anyone in academia at that time has similar anecdotes. It was tough to push a liberal arts major. And if the truth be told, professors themselves were discouraging undergraduates from majoring in anthropology, given the dismal outlook for jobs.

It was a different matter at the graduate level, where enrollments continued to climb into the late 1970s before they started falling (Table 5.1). Some of the difference undoubtedly results from the amount of time it takes to earn a graduate degree, meaning that those graduating in the late '70s were undergraduates in the early '70s. The decline in graduate enrollments that began in 1979 was a reflection of the decline in undergraduates that had begun in 1973. But there was something else at work in keeping the number of graduate students elevated: a windfall that anthropology, specifically archaeology, received from the federal government. If we could break down the graduate student statistics in Table 5.1 by subdiscipline, we undoubtedly would see a much higher percentage of archaeologists in the later years compared to, say, the late '60s or early '70s. This was because there were jobs for archaeologists, whereas the market for cultural and biological anthropologists had all but dried up. As it turned out there were *lots* of jobs for archaeologists—for a while. We cover this topic in Chapter 6 and only touch on it below.

As far back as the 1930s the federal government had funded archaeological work in advance of construction projects undertaken on public lands. For example, dozens of sites had

been excavated prior to completion of the large Tennessee Valley Authority reservoirs in Alabama and Tennessee (Haag 1985; Lyon 1996), and dozens more had been excavated in advance of the Corps of Engineers reservoirs on the Missouri River in North and South Dakota (Jennings 1985, 1986). But the total amount of money spent on all federal projects combined prior to 1970 was trivial compared to government spending in the following decade alone. As had always been the case, archaeologists not only were the ones doing the work, they were the ones writing the regulations and overseeing the quality of the work. Processualists who could not find employment in academia found employment in federal agencies. They wrote the scopes of work for proposed projects, and they selected the contractors.

Competition in contract archaeology was fierce, and to set oneself and his or her institution—at first museums and anthropology departments, later private companies—apart from the others required an innovative research proposal. What better way to distinguish yourself from competitors than to adopt a systems-analysis approach for the study of the such-and-such river valley? Or to propose to test a battery of alternative hypotheses for explaining the settlement-subsistence regime of a prehistoric population? Of course, every other proposal probably said pretty much the same thing. Indeed, the proposals might be so similar that the choice by agency archaeologists might come down to the methods and techniques being proposed (although we don't want to overlook vestiges of age-old networks and other kinds of sweetheart arrangements). Thus you might want to point out that you were going to implement a high-powered survey design built around a 20 percent stratified systematic unaligned sample. As a final touch, you might want to throw in something about nearest-neighbor analysis or Thiessen polygons. Anyone doing archaeology in the 1970s remembers that the failure to incorporate one or more of those methods into a research design could be fatal. Such methods were becoming common in archaeology, and they were straight out of ssual school. At one level, the '70s can nbered as the decade of methods, esas they were related to spatial sampling. We discuss some of these later in the chapter.

Methodological issues certainly were foremost on reporter Allen Hammond's mind when he reviewed the new archaeology for *Science* in 1971: "The trend [of the new archeology] toward a modern social science is most clearly evident in the methodologies of the new movement—including careful research design, randomized data sampling, statistical analysis, and modeling techniques—which while common in a field like sociology are radically new for archeology" (Hammond 1971:1119). It is interesting that Hammond focused on methodological issues as opposed to ontological, epistemological, or theoretical matters, but that was because the methodological ones were so visible, especially to a layperson. It is also interesting that Hammond compared archaeology to sociology. He made no comments about what sociologists thought about their own discipline at the time, although it is clear from the literature (e.g., Willer and Willer 1973) that there was by no means universal agreement over the direction that sociology should take. It is also clear that the disagreement in sociology, as in archaeology, was over much more than method.

One issue that loomed large in archaeology was the use and misuse of analogy, especially ethnographic analogy. Some processualists believed that if the potential of the new archaeology was to be fully realized—if laws of culture process were to be written—then archaeologists had to become ethnographers in order to infer which human behaviors created which kinds of archaeological signatures. Those debates became rancorous in the 1980s as archaeologists tried to build what Lew Binford (1977b) referred to as "middle-range theory," the purpose of which is to provide a bridge between the static archaeological record and the dynamics of past human behaviors that created that record. We set the stage for the later discussion of middle-range theory (Chapter 7)

by examining here the roots of efforts to build the kind of bridges that Binford had in mind.

THE USE OF ANALOGY

Analogy is the act of making a comparison in order to argue that two or more phenomena are similar in some respect. Sometimes analogical arguments go further by specifying that the similarities are the result of a particular kind of relationship between A and B. This is the difference between argument from example and argument from analogy. Unfortunately, terms often have multiple meanings, and *analogy* is one of them. In fact, its multiple meanings can be in conflict. In biology, analogy rests on a very specific kind of relationship that two or more phenomena share. That relationship is based on function. This serves to separate analogy from homology, which itself rests on a very specific kind of relationship, a genealogical (historical) one. Two genealogically related phenomena can, and often do, exhibit traits that serve the same function, but that similarity is historically based. Paleontologist George Gaylord Simpson (1961) made an important observation with respect to monozygotic twins. Two persons are monozygotic twins not because they are similar. Rather, they are similar *because* they are monozygotic twins. Conversely, two genealogically unrelated organisms can also exhibit traits that serve the same function, and maybe the traits even look similar, but that similarity is based solely on the fact that the organisms "found" common solutions to common adaptive problems. Their similarity is said to be "analogous," whereas the similarity between the related phenomena is said to be "homologous." Outside of biology, the term "analogy" is used as a general term to denote suspected relationships, regardless of origin.

As important as analogy was to the new archaeology—ceramic sociology, for example, rested in part on analogical inference—it was not something that Binford or any other processualist proposed anew. Archaeologists (e.g., Kroeber 1931) had long commented on the difference between analogues and homologues, as they had on the use of analogical arguments generally (e.g., Anderson 1969; Brumfiel 1976). One of the clearest statements on analogical reasoning was by Robert Ascher (1962), whose definitions were soon incorporated into processualist studies. For him, an analogical argument was one that inferred that if two phenomena shared, say, five visible properties, then they would also share additional properties. Although not the first to do so, Ascher (1961a) distinguished between two kinds of analogical argument as used by archaeologists: specific, or direct historical, analogies, and general comparative analogies. The first grew out of the direct historical approach (Strong 1935; Wedel 1938) and demanded that the source analogue be from a direct evolutionary descendant of the prehistoric (unknown) subject phenomenon. Given such an evolutionary connection—akin to the biologist's homology—the inference would be strengthened by the fact that the similarities were the result of a genetic-like connection as opposed to only functional similarity.

Because many prehistoric phenomena had no apparent evolutionary descendants, and many ethnographically documented phenomena had no obvious archaeological ancestors, archaeologists by the 1950s were beginning to search for general comparative analogues rather than relying on specific historical analogues (Lyman and O'Brien 2001c). Ascher (1961a) spelled out the procedure for choosing a general comparative analogue: The source phenomena was to be from a culture that occupied the same kind of environment and had the same level of technological sophistication as the archaeological subject. The implicit notion seems to have been that these restrictions would strengthen the inference because the similarities between source and subject would be constrained—a result of functional convergence. Think back to the discussion in Chapter 1 of Julian Steward's multilinear evolutionism, which was built on the premise that functional convergence is not an uncommon occurrence.

Binford (1967) argued that simple listing of similarities between source and subject, even given the restrictions of general comparative analogy, would not allow inferences in which the past was different than the present. Thus he reasoned that one must search for covariation of multiple independent variables in order to have several lines of evidence, all hopefully pointing to the same conclusion. Many archaeologists did not pay heed to this but pursued patterned relationships between human behaviors and the archaeologically visible residues created by those behaviors. The perceived necessity of finding correlations between particular human behaviors and particular archaeological signatures prompted numerous studies (e.g., Brain 1967; Gould 1968a, 1968b; South 1977a, 1977b, 1978; White 1967) and culminated in two edited volumes in the late '70s, one by Richard Gould (1978a) and one by Carol Kramer (1979a). In between, there were numerous papers on the relationship between archaeology and ethnography (Binford 1968c; Chang 1967b; J. D. Clark 1968; Freeman 1968; Klejn 1973; Orme 1973, 1974), monographs of commentary and case studies (e.g., Donnan and Clewlow 1974; Spriggs 1977; Watson 1979b), and an issue of *World Archaeology* (1971) devoted to exploring the relationship.

One of the most important ethnoarchaeological monographs of the '70s was John Yellen's (1977) *Archaeological Approaches to the Present: Models for Reconstructing the Past*. This study of !Kung San (Jul'hoansi) camps in southwestern Africa was part of the long-term Harvard University project in the Kalahari directed by Richard Lee and Irven DeVore (Chapter 2). Yellen (Figure 5.3) found a number of patterned relationships between activities and their archaeological signatures. Focused on the regularities of specific processes, from butchering large game to camp maintenance, Yellen's generalizations were widely applied by archaeologists to mobile hunter-gatherers in other parts of the world. His findings underscored the claim of processualists and behavioralists (Chapter 7) that process-specific lawlike statements, of broad applicability, could arise from ethnoarchaeology if the right kinds of questions were asked.

FIGURE 5.3. *Left,* John Yellen interviewing !Kung San (now Jul'hoansi) in northwestern Botswana, ca. 1967. (Photograph by Irven DeVore, courtesy Nancy DeVore and Anthro-Photo File.)

Ethnographic information provided a basis for analogical reasoning in archaeology, but it was not the only basis. Some archaeologists turned to experimental work as a means of interpreting archaeological phenomena. There was considerable overlap between approaches, but it is easier to treat each of them separately, which we do below, beginning with experimental archaeology. It's important to remember, however, that both experimental archaeology and ethnoarchaeology rest on the notion of uniformitarianism, which forms a third entry below. We are focusing here only on the early stages of ethnoarchaeology, up to about 1977. We pick up the topic again in Chapter 7.

Experimental Archaeology

We like Ascher's (1961b:793) definition of experimental archaeology: "imitative experiments" that are aimed at "testing beliefs about past cultural behavior." By "imitative" Ascher meant experiments that simulate past conditions. Such experiments entail "operations in which matter is shaped, or matter is shaped and used" (Ascher 1961b:793). Ascher suggested

that in designing an imitative experiment, the experimenter should follow five steps:

(1) State the probable working hypothesis in testable form.

(2) Select the materials to be used in the experiment, with a greater chance of success probable if materials that were available in "an aboriginal setting" are chosen.

(3) Perform the experiment with the materials; that is, apply the hypothesized behaviors to the materials and do so multiple times using alternative behaviors.

(4) Observe the results and record the appearance of the affected materials.

(5) Infer a relationship among the behaviors, the materials, and the results of applying the behaviors to the materials.

Several archaeologists were already more or less following Ascher's suggested protocol (e.g., Pond 1930; Witthoft 1955), and others began experimenting with a wide range of materials in the '60s and '70s (e.g., Crabtree 1972; Saraydar and Shimada 1971, 1973; Swanson 1975). Enough articles had appeared by the mid-'70s that a compendium of case studies appeared (Ingersoll, Yellen, and MacDonald 1977). Two of the editors of the book indicated that they liked Ascher's (1961b) definition of experimental archaeology, but they preferred to expand it to include not only replicative studies but also those that "tested the methods and techniques of experimental archaeology; those that concerned site formation and deterioration; and those concerned with the relationship between material and nonmaterial culture in societies functioning at present"

FIGURE 5.4. Participants in the 1975 Advanced Seminar in Ethnoarchaeology held at the School of American Research, Santa Fe, New Mexico. Back row, left to right: Rhys Jones, Diane Gifford-Gonzalez, Mike Schiffer, Patrick Kirch, Michael Stanislawski. Front row, left to right: William Rathje, Ruth Tringham, Frank Hole, Richard Gould. (Courtesy School of America Research.)

(Ingersoll and MacDonald 1977:xii). That last category of studies was what became known as "ethnoarchaeology." To Ingersoll and MacDonald, the strength of experimental archaeology was in its ability to narrow the range of possible explanations of phenomena by eliminating improbable and unlikely explanations.

In one of their first publications, Jeff Reid, Mike Schiffer, and Bill Rathje (1975) argued that experimental archaeology and ethnoarchaeology together comprised one of the nomothetic strategies of a behavioral archaeology (Chapter 7). By studying modern behavior— either that of the archaeologist in creating an experimental system or that of living peoples observed by the ethnoarchaeologist—experimental and ethnoarchaeological research would generate the lawlike principles needed for archaeological inference. The units of such study would be specific processes, from biface reduction to urbanization.

In experimental archaeology, variables such as the raw materials and the human behaviors that influence those materials can be manipulated (controlled) by the anthropologist, whereas in ethnoarchaeological work the behaviors and their outcomes are simply ob-

served. According to Ruth Tringham's (Figure 5.4) definitions, ethnoarchaeology is "the structure for a series of observations on behavioral patterns of living societies which are designed to answer archaeologically oriented questions. 'Experimental archaeology'—that is, experiments as part of archaeological investigations— on the other hand, comprises a series of observations on behavior that is artificially induced. Both may involve more or less rigorously controlled conditions and recorded results" (Tringham 1978:170).

Tringham argued that although it was not the first such study, the publication in English of Russian archaeologist Sergei Semenov's *Prehistoric Technology: An Experimental Study of the Oldest Tools and Artefacts from Traces of Manufacture and Wear* in 1964 served as a major catalyst for experimental archaeology (Tringham et al. 1974). We agree. The original 1957 Russian edition of Semenov's book was cited by J. Sonnenfeld (1962) in an article in which he described and illustrated the edge wear experimentally generated on stone tools. Specifically, Sonnenfeld (1962:56) wanted to see "if there was a relationship between form and function which could yield to form a determining role as a criterion of function." But rather than study gross morphology, Sonnenfeld examined use wear. Here was a clearly illustrated and relatively straightforward means of inferring whether an item identified as a knife actually had been used to cut, or a scraper had been used to scrape: Did the items in question display modifications that matched in form the use wear created on experimental replicates?

Damage to edges of stone tools quickly became important data for inferring artifact function. Morphological attributes such as edge *angles* (Wilmsen 1968a) were one thing; edge *damage* was a more direct reflection of the actual application of force to an edge. The former were rather easily measured using, say, a goniometer (e.g., Hester, Gilbow, and Albee 1973), whereas the latter required microscopes and, if you wanted to illustrate what you had seen, a method of photographing the damaged edges of stone flakes (e.g., MacDonald and Sanger 1968). Even with this new technology in hand, a potential problem remained. Although damage was a more accurate reflection of tool use than were ethnographic analogues based on an object's general form (Nance 1971), the problem was that not all damage was necessarily the result of use. Some might be caused by manufacturing activities (Keeley 1974a, 1974b) and some by postdepositional trampling, agricultural tillage, or other processes—a fact known for more than a century (Grayson 1986). Thus, experimental work was chosen to be the way to identify features of use-related damage that were distinct from other sorts of damage (e.g., Sheets 1973). The literature grew rapidly in the 1970s (Olausson 1980) and culminated in two influential books—one edited (Hayden 1979) and the other a single-authored book advocating a particular approach (Keeley 1980).

The goals of use-wear studies were not limited to determining the function of a tool but included such things as reconstructing the economic activities of prehistoric groups (Keeley 1974b). This required knowledge of artifact function as well as representative samples of all kinds of use-wear manifestations in an assemblage. Experiments by Tringham and her colleagues (1974) provided landmark descriptions of edge damage, but they could distinguish only between wear that had been generated by working "hard" materials such as bone, antler, and wood, and wear that had been generated by working "soft" materials such as meat, hides, and nonwoody plants. They were, however, able to distinguish gross modes of use such as scraping, whittling, cutting, and sawing.

After undertaking an enormous series of experiments that used stone tools in realistic tasks, and employing magnification of 100–400X (much higher than those used by Tringham's group), Lawrence Keeley (1977) stated that he could identify six broad categories of polish, each resulting from working a different kind of material: wood, bone, hide, meat, antler, and nonwoody plants. Blind tests (Keeley and Newcomer 1977) seemed to confirm the validity of what Keeley had found experimentally. George Odell (1975:230) echoed the position of Tringham—his Harvard adviser—on recording not just the kind of edge damage but also its location and distribution on a tool, the form of the tool, edge angles, and any other attributes that "might bring us closer to a realistic and multivariate appraisal" of tool function.

There was considerable discussion of the proper protocol for doing experiments with replicated stone tools (Keeley 1974b; Odell 1975). One advantage of making and using replicates is that individual variables can be held constant while others vary. For example, raw material can be held constant while activities vary. One area of disagreement was in the power of magnification necessary to produce reliable (replicable) and valid identifications of different kinds of use wear. In Keeley's (1977, 1980) method—which became known as the "high-power approach"—the entire tool was scanned at 100X, and the identification of function of particular areas was done at 200X and occasionally at 400X. Only at these high powers did the diagnostic polishes he used to identify worked materials become visibly distinct.

Tringham and her colleagues (e.g., Odell and

Odell-Vereecken 1980) used a "low-power approach" involving 40–100X magnification. Different costs and benefits attend both, but it was clear by the time the debate was in full swing that different approaches were better suited for different research questions (Hayden 1979). Further, and most significant in the context of this discussion, one commentator observed that even after more than a decade of study of use wear on stone tools, "there [are] as yet no generally agreed upon minimum standards of experimental design" (Kamminga 1980:59). This lack no doubt contributed to the debates over the validity of conclusions offered by different researchers. Use-wear analysis continues to expand as more archaeologists take the time to learn the various analytical protocols (e.g., Grace 1996; Hardy and Garufi 1998; Odell 2001; Shea 1992).

Early Ethnoarchaeology

Archaeologists might have to design and implement their own experiments for determining such things as artifact function, but do they have to do their own ethnographic research? Can't they instead rely on ethnographers to do it for them? The answer might once have been that archaeologists could borrow the findings of their ethnographer colleagues, but by the 1960s this was no longer the case. Archaeologists came to realize that, as Daniel Stiles (1977) put it, ethnographers typically are not concerned with the same problems as archaeologists, so they do not record many of the things that are (or might be) relevant in an archaeological study.

Maxine Kleindienst and Pat Watson (1956) had noted this problem two decades earlier in a short, excellent article, "Action Archaeology: The Archaeological Inventory of a Living Community," that was published in a student journal little read outside of the University of Chicago. "Action archaeology" was a colorful term for what eventually became known as "ethnoarchaeology," which Stiles (1977:88) defined as "the use of ethnographic methods and information to aid in the interpretation and explanation of archaeological data" (Stiles

1977:88). Carol Kramer (1979b:1) subsequently defined it as the investigation of "aspects of contemporary sociocultural behavior from an archaeological perspective [in an effort to] systematically define relationships between behavior and material culture not often explored by ethnologists, and to ascertain how certain features of observable behavior may be reflected in remains which archaeologists may find." (For more definitions of ethnoarchaeology, and for the most comprehensive overview of dozens of ethnoarchaeological studies, see Nicholas David and Carol Kramer's text, *Ethnoarchaeology in Action* [2001]).

Analogy in general and ethnographic analogy in particular were important components of processualism from the start, but ethnoarchaeology was not. This was Bill Longacre's (1974) point when he discussed the ceramic-sociology research that he, Jim Deetz, and Jim Hill had carried out (Chapter 3). That research was based on two assumptions: that "the materials in an archaeological site are highly structured and patterned," and that "the patterns are the direct result of the behavior of the people who made, used, and discarded or abandoned the materials" (Longacre 1974:54–55). These were too general to be useful in interpretive endeavors, so they had to be supplemented with other assumptions: that females made and decorated pottery, and in turn taught their daughters how to make and decorate pottery. Longacre (1974:61) reasoned that the "preliminary results" he, Deetz, and Hill had found "support our belief in the validity of these primary assumptions. Indeed, we can continue to attempt to assess their validity by treating them as law-like generalizations and deducing testable hypotheses about aspects of behavior and organization of extinct communities." But recall that Lew Binford (1962a) had argued that the validity of such assumptions, lawlike generalizations, or whatever they might be called, could not be done using archaeological data when the variables of interest had to be assumed or inferred. One had to do the testing where the variables of interest were directly observable, and the only place where aspects of behavior and community social organization were observable together was in the ethnographic record.

Longacre (1974) suggested that archaeologists adopt an approach that was logically and empirically valid with respect to establishing lawlike generalizations. He identified the approach as "undertaking field work in a situation where both the patterns of material culture and the behavior and organization of a society were observable; it would mean doing field work in a living society" (Longacre 1974:61). In other words, it meant doing ethnoarchaeology, or as Richard Gould (1968b) had termed it, "living archaeology." (Gould early on distinguished between ethnoarchaeology, which he defined as "a much broader general framework for comparing ethnographic and archaeological patterning," and living archaeology, which he defined as "the actual effort made by an archaeologist or ethnographer to do fieldwork in living human societies, with special reference to the 'archaeological' patterning of the behavior in those societies" [Gould 1974:29].)

Gould's work exemplifies much of the ethnoarchaeological program as it existed in the early 1970s. Gould (Figure 5.4) started his graduate career at Chicago and was in one of Binford's seminars. After a year he transferred to Berkeley. While there, he carried out ethnoarchaeological fieldwork among the Tolowa Indians of California, the results of which he used to help interpret the archaeological situation at the Point St. George site in Del Norte County (Gould 1966). Gould's ethnoarchaeological research did not receive much attention outside California until he began work in Australia, studying highly mobile peoples in the Western Desert (Figure 5.5). Gould (1968a) argued that research among living peoples provided new possibilities for interpreting the lithic remains of prehistoric hunting-and-gathering peoples. He suggested that perhaps one would eventually be able to write "rules" of behavior, akin to rules of grammar, by which

FIGURE 5.5. Richard Gould and two Ngatatjara Aborigine workmen at Puntutjarpa Rockshelter, Western Australia, 1967. Gould calls this his Anthropology 101 class, only here he isn't doing the teaching. (Courtesy Richard Gould.)

archaeological materials were patterned (Gould 1968b).

Gould later remarked that "for the archaeologist, the ethnographic assemblage is a kind of baseline against which to compare earlier assemblages and tool types in other parts of the world" (Gould, Koster, and Sontz 1971:149). In particular, he believed that formal similarities between ethnographic and archaeological tools would suggest similarities in tool function. But that same year he began to question this notion when he noted that ethnographic analogy was not the best way to interpret the archaeological record "on the grounds that the application of such analogies may cause the archaeologist to risk assuming the very thing he should be trying to find out" (Gould 1971:143). Reliance on ethnographic analogy might blind the archaeologist to alternative interpretations. A few years later Gould (1974) may have been nodding toward Binford's (1967) suggested search for covariation of independent variables when he indicated that the ethnoarchaeologist should use patterned material remains to build a model that is of use in inferring the behavior of ancient people. He alluded to slowly piecing together the model using multiple kinds of information: stone tools and debitage, structures, hearths, faunal remains, and sherds.

After more than a decade of studying living peoples from an archaeological perspective, Gould (1978b:816) argued that ethnoarchaeology was "a new kind of anthropology—the anthropology of human residues." This anthropology was focused on the behavior of discard. Karl Heider (1967) had made this perspective clear when he remarked that archaeological emphasis should be on function and disposal rather than on artifact manufacture—how houses and ceramic vessels are used and what happens to them afterward. Africanist Glynn Isaac (1967) did one of the first modern systematic experiments on what happens "afterward," and Michael Stanislawski (Figure 5.4) discussed recycling and discard of pottery among the Hopi (Stanislawski 1969a, 1969b). As Gould (1978b:816) observed, the "easy assumption" that potsherds were usually discarded in a garbage heap or midden and thus "go to heaven" was quickly shown by ethnoarchaeological observation to be false.

Gould (1978b:825) characterized ethnoarchaeology as having an "unabashed materialist bias" given its focus on the various ways in which items are made, used, and discarded, as well as its lack of concern for human cognition. For him, the goal of ethnoarchaeology is to produce hypothetical lawlike propositions that can be tested against other present and past cases. In Gould's view, this avoids the necessity of assuming precisely what it is that an archaeologist is trying to find out about the past—the "fallacy of affirming the consequent" (Gould 1978b:832; see Hempel 1966:8 for formal definition). The perception that a particular case could be subsumed under a law was a powerful magnet, although Gould would shortly come to reject this position.

So far, then, analogues derived from ethnographic observations were viewed as being hypothetical and requiring testing to ensure their validity. Why such a protocol? Because in Pat Watson's (1979a) view, archaeologists assume there is an isomorphism between relationships that are observable now—relationships between present behavior and the material result of present behavior—and relationships inferred

for the past; any science, historical or not, must subscribe to the tenets of "uniformitarianism." In terms typically found in introductory textbooks, uniformitarianism is a doctrine based on the premise that "the present is the key to the past." As Watson would be the first to point out, however, the principle of uniformitarianism is much more complex and contentious than her statement indicates.

Uniformitarianism and Human Behavior

Ruth Tringham argued that experimental archaeology is only as valuable as "the boundaries of appropriateness" of individual experiments (Tringham 1978:172). By this we believe she meant to underscore the degree of influence of the historically contingent context (Simpson 1963, 1970) of the experiment on its results. Indirect evidence of this intention is found in her discussion of what she termed experiments focused on the "nature and properties of materials with a view to understanding their potential for human exploitation" (Tringham 1978:182). These were, in her view, "basic-level materials tests" whereas "behavioral experimentation" was "upper level" (Tringham 1978: 183). The latter involved testing the relationship between humans and the materials they manipulate, between the influence of social variables on results, and so on.

That such "upper level" relationships were in fact historically contingent (more on that below) is clear from Tringham's notation that the skill level, age, and strength of the manipulator would also influence the result. This prompted her to conclude that "because of the complexities of the human variable...the inferences which can be made from behavioral experiments are inevitably more dubious than the conclusions drawn from lower-level [materials] testing" (Tringham 1978:184). Tringham here voiced a concern that would eventually be echoed by other archaeologists, though sometimes for other reasons. The problem reduces to whether an unquestioning and unqualified subscription to a simplistic view of uniformitarianism—the present is the key to the past—is warranted.

At the same time that Tringham's remarks were circulating, Warren DeBoer and Donald Lathrap (1979:103) described the extreme form of her observation without referencing her when they noted that if one could not assume

> that a relatively obvious isomorphism exists between behavior and its derived archaeological representation, then the archaeologist is left in either of two peculiar situations. Either he becomes a practitioner of an over-extended uniformitarianism in which past cultural behavior is 'read' from our knowledge of present cultural behavior, or he must eschew his commitment to understanding behavior altogether and engage in a kind of 'artifact physics' in which the form and distribution of behavioral by-products are measured in a behavioral vacuum. This is the familiar quandary of choosing between a significant pursuit based on faulty method or one which is methodologically sound but trivial in purpose.

Thus, between Tringham on the one hand and DeBoer and Lathrap on the other, the archaeologist could either be unsure of the validity of behavioral inferences based on ethnoarchaeology or experimental archaeology, or be confident in inferences that concerned mere mechanical properties of artifacts.

George Gaylord Simpson (1963, 1970) distinguished between these two possibilities by identifying what we would call two distinct ontologies: "The unchanging properties of matter and energy and the likewise unchanging processes and principles arising therefrom are *immanent* in the material universe. They are nonhistorical, even though they occur and act in the course of history. The actual state of the universe or any part of it at a given time, its configuration, is not immanent and is constantly changing. It is *contingent...or configurational....* History may be defined as configurational change through time, i.e., a sequence of real, individual, but interrelated events" (Simpson 1963:24–25).

What Simpson was getting at is this: various chemical and physical processes are immanent and thus produce predictable outcomes, but the particular spatiotemporal and geological contexts in which they are active produce unique, unpredictable configurations. The critical adjectives here are *particular* and *unique,* with *configuration* defined as the unique expression of particular combinations of immanent processes in operation in more or less unique sequences at particular intensities (Wolverton and Lyman 2000). Biologically speaking, each organism is the result of immanent processes such as genetic transmission and ontogenetic development of the phenotype, but it is also the result of its lineage's genetic history—the configurational sequence by which the organism arose—and the environment in which the organism developed (Simpson 1963). Genetic mutation *will* occur—it is immanent—but which gene will mutate is unpredictable, as is the form the mutation will take and whether the selective environment in which it occurs favors it or not. These are all configurational properties.

Richard Watson (1966:173) labeled Simpson's argument a "false thesis." He believed that the root of the problem resided in Simpson's confusion of a particular historical event such as *a* chemical reaction or *an* erosional event with a "type" of event such as a kind of chemical reaction or the process of erosion: "types are abstractions and as such [are] part of our conceptual equipment, but as types [they are] not part of the actual world of events.... [P]*articular* events have specific coordinates in time and space, and as such are part of the actual world.... Types of events obviously neither occur nor recur, and particular events as such obviously cannot recur" (Watson 1966: 175).

Watson was correct on this point: there is a world of difference between kinds, which are "ideational" units (Dunnell 1986; Lyman and O'Brien 2002; O'Brien and Lyman 2002a), and the individual things placed in them. Those "things," regardless of whether they are objects or events, are "empirical" units. Thus erosion is an ideational unit, and a *particular* erosional event is an empirical unit. David Hull (1974: 47–48) made the same distinction using the terms "individuals" and "classes": "A unique event is one that happens to be one of a kind. A necessarily unique event is defined in terms that preclude any other instance of this event. The usual way of defining an event so that it is necessarily unique is by specifying particular spatiotemporal coordinates for it. No two objects can occupy the same place at the same time.... [S]cientific laws cannot refer to specific individuals, only to classes of individuals."

Watson (1966:177) argued that sciences are amenable to laboratory experimentation and "concern subject matters ideally adjusted to investigation by man." This possibility exists because sciences such as chemistry use general types. In contrast, history employs very specific types. Here laws can be written, but only if the specifics of a particular event are included in the law. For Watson, uniformitarianism implies only that the basic laws remain the same, leaving open the possibility that given different values for the variables in those laws, things can change. Thus, laws with the values of their included variables unspecified underpin science, whereas laws with their values tightly specified underpin history. Therefore, Simpson's distinction between immanence and configuration and the distinction between history and science are unnecessary and false.

Simpson (1970) disagreed with Watson's view. History was important to Simpson, and to ignore its particularities was inconceivable. Simpson argued that Watson had erred because he failed to realize that laws concern immanence, whereas history concerns configuration. Watson had argued that the evolution of *Homo sapiens* was a unique historical event only if we deny that a similar evolution was possible at another time or place. Surely, Watson contended, there are laws that, if written in specific terms, would allow us to predict such an evolutionary event. Simpson responded that certainly there *are* laws that govern such things as mutation, selection, and the evolution of species, but it is obvious that those laws don't explain the actual appearance and structure of particular species. What are needed are historical (configurational) rather than immanent explanations.

Watson received his B.A., M.A., and Ph.D. degrees, all in philosophy, from the University of Iowa. He also earned an M.S. in geology from the University of Minnesota, where his adviser was Herbert Wright (Figure 5.6), a Quaternary geologist and paleoecologist (e.g., Watson and Wright 1980) with interests in archaeological problems (e.g., Martin and Wright 1967; Wright 1968). Watson held to the tenets of uniformitarianism no doubt in part because of his training in geology, and he often responded to those who commented on those tenets (e.g., Watson 1966, 1969a, 1969b, 1970). For Watson, "causal processes in nature operate in regular ways in given circumstances to form all natural features and events"; this principle "is, when assumed as the foundation of scientific inquiry, an expression of our faith that the world is regular, lawful, and thus intelligible" (Watson 1969b:219).

In a piece read by many archaeologists, Watson indicated that

archaeologists who propose laws of cultural evolution [and] of human behavior assume—as do other scientists—that the past was like the present, and although combinations and rates may have been different then from what they are now, the basic behavioral characteristics of men and material were not different then from what they are now. This may in fact be wrong. But if human nature and the environment were radically different in the past from what they are now, we assume that there has been lawlike change from the past to the present that can be derived and understood from its physical remains. This general uniformitarianism is the primary procedural or methodological assumption of archaeology, as it is of all other sciences. (Watson 1976:621)

A few years earlier Watson (1972:212) had characterized the new archaeology as consisting of "an acceptance of the covering-law model of scientific explanation, with an emphasis on

FIGURE 5.6. *Back row, right,* Herbert Wright, *back row, left,* Dick Wright, *back row, center,* Richard Watson, and villagers from near Harsin, Kermanshah, Iran. (Courtesy Patty Jo Watson.)

the hypothetico-deductive method for the testing of conclusions derived from archeological data." This model rested directly on the principle of uniformitarianism (Salmon 1953). Where did that principle come from?

Without using the term, James Hutton (quoted in Scharnberger, Bushman, and Shea 1983:312) stated the principle of uniformitarianism in 1795: "There are operations proper to the surface of this globe by which the form of the habitable earth may be affected; operations of which we understand both the causes and effects, and, therefore, of which we may form principles for judging of the past." The principle was used with great success as a guiding scientific concept in the writings of Charles Lyell (Gould 1979, 1982a; Haneberg 1983; Hooykaas 1970; Wilson 1972). It received its name in an 1832 review by William Whewell of the first volume of Lyell's (1830) *Principles of Geology* (Mayr 1982). Today, uniformitarianism typically is used to denote what Stephen Jay Gould (1965:223) labeled "methodological uniformitarianism," defined as "a procedural principle asserting spatial and temporal invariance of natural laws." It is equivalent to what some historical scientists (e.g., Hooykaas 1970; Simpson 1970) refer to as "actualism."

The Punch Line

The failure of archaeologists to explore the extensive literature on uniformitarianism and actualism caused those advocating ethnoarchaeology and experimental archaeology to spend considerable time rediscovering some of the strengths and weaknesses of the protocol. Notice we said *some* of the strengths and weaknesses. Further, what one archaeologist saw as a weakness was not necessarily identified as such by other archaeologists. Thus, Pat Watson (1977) strongly advocated continuing ethnoarchaeological studies such as Longacre's (1974) on the influence of social interaction on the history of ceramic design elements. She noted that the first generation of processualist studies—those by Cronin, Deetz, Hill, and Longacre—had been criticized but, by the mid-1970s, had spawned a new round of research on the topic (e.g., Bennett 1974; Plog 1976a, 1976b). This second generation of researchers tested and evaluated the results of the '60s with much more sophisticated statistical analyses (e.g., Plog 1976b, 1978), and they borrowed models of social interaction from geography (e.g., Plog 1976a).

The first generation had assumed that variation among ceramic designs was simple when in fact it was extremely complex. Much more ethnoarchaeological research was necessary if any understanding was to be gained. Given the notions of her husband, Richard Watson, perhaps it is not surprising that Pat Watson subscribed without qualification to the application of uniformitarian principles to archaeological interpretation. This would lead her into a debate with another ethnoarchaeologist, Richard Gould, who as we noted earlier had begun to see problems in applying the principle of uniformitarianism archaeologically. We save that debate for Chapter 7, noting here only that Gould (1978c:254) pointed out that although not without value, ethnographic analogies "suffer from an inherent limitation—they cannot inform us about prehistoric behavior patterns that have no modern counterpart or analog."

In the place of ethnographic analogy Gould suggested archaeologists use what he called the "contrastive method," which sought to avoid assumptions about the relevance of uniformitarian laws to human behavior. The contrastive method, according to Gould, supplements explanations based on analogies because it causes archaeologists to contrast the differences between ethnographically observed residues of human behaviors and the portion of the archaeological record under study. Those patterns observed in the archaeological record for which no modern analogue can be found are the contrasts in need of explanation, and in Gould's view they underscore the fallacy of uniformitarianism-based thinking. Those unmatched patterns represent uniquely prehistoric behaviors. The punch line, then, is that the present is the key to the past, but only in qualified ways.

STATISTICS AND ARCHAEOLOGY

Like ethnographic analogy, statistics has a long history of use in anthropology, dating back at least to the work of Samuel G. Morton, a Philadelphia physician and anatomist who devised a cranial index that supposedly could be used to distinguish between various human races (Morton 1839). Morton was a polygenist, meaning that he saw races as having separate origins, with the skulls of each race evolving independently; there was little overlap in shape between, say, the "average" skull of a European and that of an American Indian. Morton decided that skulls with large brain cases were from more-intelligent races, whereas those with smaller brain cases were from less-intelligent races. It just so happened that European skulls had the largest brain cases, at least by his measurements, and those from Africans and Australian aborigines had the smallest. Of course, the basis of Morton's work (polygeny) was later thoroughly discredited, as was his key working assumption (cranial capacity equals intelligence). We also know that he cooked his data to "prove" the correlation between cranial capacity and "race" (Gould 1981).

If one were feeling waggish, one might say that the use of statistics in anthropology hasn't changed much since Morton published his study. In the late 1970s David Hurst Thomas (1978:231) saw something in archaeology that caused him to comment that the discipline "is experiencing growing pains and the increasing abuse of statistical methods is perhaps the most severe of all." Thomas was referring to abuses committed by processualists who were simply following Albert Spaulding's (1953a, 1960a, 1968) advice to make their work more quantitative. Writing a few years after Thomas, Sheldon Scheps (1982) referred to the problem as "statistical blight."

Abuses or not, it would be difficult to envision doing anthropology today without statistics, regardless of subdiscipline. Before he published his statistics text, *Figuring Anthropology* (1976), Thomas (Figure 5.7) surveyed anthropology graduate programs in the United States to learn what kind of statistical requirements they set for their students. He found that more than half the programs either required or strongly suggested competency in statistics. Today that figure probably would be much higher. Thomas was convinced that anyone wanting to understand anthropological data in the form in which they were increasingly being reported had to have a working knowledge of

FIGURE 5.7. David Hurst Thomas working on his book *Figuring Anthropology*, Gatecliff Shelter, Nevada, 1975. (Photograph by Susan L. Bierwirth, courtesy American Museum of Natural History and Lori Pendleton.)

statistical inference, defined as using principles of probability theory to derive defensible conclusions about a population based on a sample of that population.

Thomas backed up his conclusion by analyzing the anthropological literature to see how the use of statistical inference had changed through the years. Using articles in four major journals—*American Anthropologist, American Journal of Physical Anthropology, American Antiquity,* and *Language*—as a sample, he calculated the percentage by year of those that employed statistical inference. (The percentages by subdiscipline are shown in Figure 5.8.) Around 1950 the percentage of ethnological articles containing statistical inference increased markedly, at least as reflected in *American Anthropologist.* We think much of the increase was a result of the availability and early popularity of the Human Relations Area Files, which were used for cross-cultural studies (Murdock 1940). The files were reminiscent of the culture trait lists for which Alfred Kroeber and the University of California, Berkeley, became famous in the 1930s (Driver 1938; Dri-

ver and Kroeber 1932; Klimek 1935; Kroeber 1936). But despite this trend in ethnological uses of statistics, in anthropology generally in the 1950s and '60s there seems to have been little perceived necessity for learning statistical techniques (Driver 1953, 1965). Although graduate departments were beginning to emphasize statistical knowledge, only 2 percent of the articles published in 1970 in *American Antiquity* included statistical inference.

Statistics in archaeology dates at least to Leslie Spier's work in the early twentieth century using normal frequency distributions (1916) and a form of simple least-squares regression (1917) to determine if the frequencies of pottery types in collections he had seriated fluctuated monotonically. A later and perhaps better known use of statistical techniques was the development of what came to be known as the Brainerd-Robinson coefficient. Archaeologist George Brainerd (1951b) had advocated the use of "statistical manipulations" as a way to aid archaeological systematics. He had participated in the analysis of materials collected by the Rainbow Bridge–Monument Valley expedition in northeastern Arizona and southeastern Utah, sponsored by the Ford Motor Company. In this study, statistical methods were used to calculate a standard deviation for the frequencies of sherds of pottery types relative to a complete sample (Beals, Brainerd, and Smith 1945). Brainerd (1951a) presented to statistician W. S. Robinson the problem of ordering collections of artifacts based on the relative frequencies of the constituent types. Robinson (1951) calculated what he called an "agreement coefficient," which was a measure of the similarity of two collections, and arranged a set of the coefficients in a matrix with the largest values on the diagonal and the coefficients decreasing toward the opposite corners.

Donald Lehmer (1951) protested that the Brainerd-Robinson coefficient failed to take into account varying sample sizes, and he advocated the use of the mean standard error of the abundance of each type in two samples. Robinson and Brainerd (1952:60) responded by saying that "Lehmer has confused two very

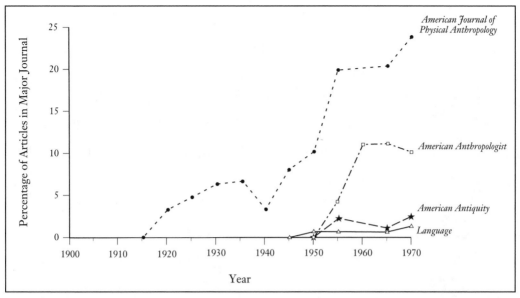

FIGURE 5.8. Graph showing annual fluctuations in percentage of articles in four major journals—*American Anthropologist, American Journal of Physical Anthropology, American Antiquity,* and *Language*—that employed statistical inference. (After Thomas 1976.)

different statistical problems, *viz.*, the problem of estimating a population parameter and the problem of testing the statistical significance of an observed result." They concluded their response with the testy yet accurate quip that "our first knowledge of Lehmer's critique was its appearance in print, and we regret that this fact has forced us to expound in an archaeological journal upon matters which ought to be relegated to a course in elementary statistics" (Robinson and Brainerd 1952:61). Lehmer, to our knowledge, never again raised a statistics-related issue.

Efforts such as Spier's, Brainerd's, and Robinson's were seldom acknowledged in the archaeological literature or emulated prior to 1960. Most archaeologists did not really understand what statistics entailed. During the course of research on Southeastern archaeologist James Ford, O'Brien and Lyman (1998) interviewed several of Ford's contemporaries who flinched at the mention of his "seriations" (they usually were not true seriations) and stated that they simply did not comprehend the "statistics" behind those seriations. They misunderstood that Ford never used statistics—one aspect of

his work that so irritated Albert Spaulding (1953a, 1954a, 1954b). But because Ford used numbers and his graphs looked, well, graphish (Figure 5.9), many of his colleagues figured his seriations fell into the mysterious category of statistics. Most of them didn't trust Ford's numbers anyway (Phil Phillips and Jimmy Griffin were particularly frank about it [Phillips, Ford, and Griffin 1951])—and if the truth be told, they didn't trust any numbers more complex than percentages.

Things began to change, albeit slowly, by the late 1950s. We agree with Dave Thomas (1978) that this statistical awakening was the result of a realization that one needed to understand at least what a mean and standard deviation were if radiocarbon dates were to be used correctly (Driver 1953). Participants in a specially convened symposium held in July 1959 on quantitative methods in archaeology made several recommendations that went beyond these simple measures. One was that archaeologists should familiarize themselves with the basic principles of sampling theory, and another was that some agreement should be reached on standard descriptive statistical methods (Heizer

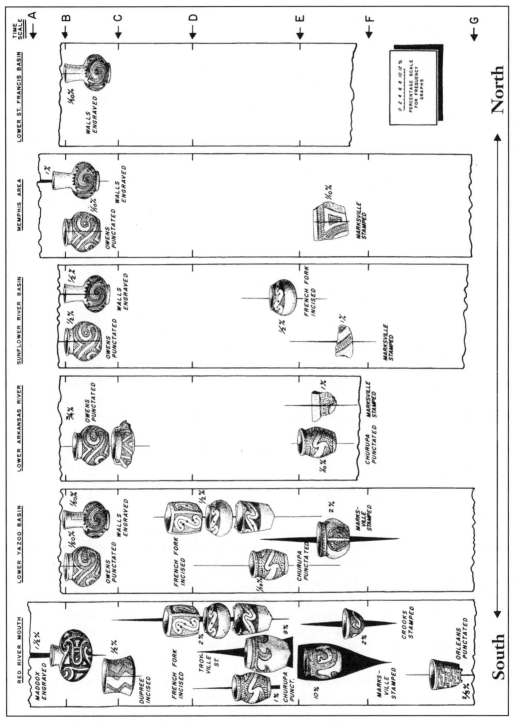

FIGURE 5.9. South-to-north profile from the mouth of the Red River in eastern Louisiana to the lower St. Francis River basin in eastern Arkansas showing James Ford's reconstruction of the history of pottery decorations featuring contrasting roughened and smoothed vessel surfaces. (After Ford 1952.)

and Cook 1960). In less than a decade, both recommendations were beginning to be followed as archaeologists searched for patterning in their data sets.

Classification and Pattern Recognition

A notable advantage that archaeologists working in the 1960s had over their predecessors was access to electronic computers (e.g., Brown and Freeman 1964) and, especially later in the decade, statistical packages. These technological changes enabled much more detailed, intensive, and extensive artifact analyses than were previously possible. Statistical packages could be used in black-box fashion, meaning that they could be employed even when, as was often the case, archaeologists did not understand the assumptions and limitations of the statistics they were using. Lew Binford (1972f) documented how he had spent many hours with a hand-crank calculator in the late 1950s. That would change in the early 1960s with the commercialization of computers that could do complex statistical manipulations of huge masses of data in a veritable blink of an eye. Having worked with the old keypunch computers in our student days, and then later with desktop and laptop computers, we have a feel for what it must have been like to shift from slide rules and hand-crank calculators to those first electronic monsters.

The impact of computers on archaeology was twofold. First, archaeologists could create large, searchable databases—something that was impractical in the pre-computer days. Second, they became more familiar not only with statistical methods generally but with probability and sampling theory specifically (e.g., Binford 1964a; Cowgill 1964; Rootenberg 1964; Vescelius 1960). Among the earliest computer-assisted statistics were factor analysis and principal components analysis, both of which are nearly impossible to apply to large data sets without a computer.

A classic application of factor analysis is found in Lew and Sally Binford's study of Mousterian artifact assemblages (Binford and Binford 1966a, 1969). After using factor analysis to identify mutually covariant sets of artifacts, those sets in turn were inferred to represent particular human behaviors. These inferences were based on the assumptions that archaeological patterns reflect human behavioral patterns; that maintenance behaviors can be distinguished from extractive behaviors; and that extractive tasks were performed by work groups at resource extraction loci, whereas maintenance activities were undertaken by a larger fraction of the social group at a residence location. The mass of data the Binfords mustered, the analyses they performed, and the graphs they created to display all of the variability were virtually unprecedented. Similar studies (e.g., Freeman 1966; Sackett 1966) paralleled the Binfords' Mousterian work, which no doubt convinced other archaeologists that computer-based multivariate analyses had utility. This was desirable in principle, but as we'll see below, it did not always turn out so well in practice.

Early computer-assisted work also focused on artifact classification, expanding the earlier analyses of Spaulding (e.g., 1960a) and others. Bob Whallon (1972) pointed out that the basis of much of the classificatory work was numerical taxonomy, the purpose of which was to identify nonrandom clusters of attributes that were then used to define artifact types. Basically, these sorts of approaches assume that clusters are ethnographically real. Mario Borillo (1974) characterized such underpinning assumptions as transcendental and therefore beyond scientific investigation. He also pointed out that Whallon's statistically sophisticated confirmation of the alleged validity of the traditional pottery types depended on his intimate knowledge of those types, which he (Whallon) could then replicate. In Borillo's (1974:373) view, Whallon's (1972) effort exemplified at least part of "the delusion of the 'new archaeology'—that the rigor of the mathematical apparatus *implies* the rigor of the archaeological result."

Dave Thomas (1972a) also advocated the use of numerical-taxonomic methods to build "natural" artifact classes. He argued that there was no theoretical conflict between this relatively new, objective procedure and the more subjective procedure of traditional archaeological systematics. But he acknowledged that the natural classes were only the first step in classification: if one wanted to build historical index types, then the classes produced by numerical taxonomy would likely have to be modified to reflect the passage of time. He also identified the important criterion of any taxonomy, which is the usefulness of the resulting units.

Significantly, Thomas made several critical points, including that numerical taxonomy is not a "panacea for all maladies of typology"; that the systematist should beware of the "diaphanous computer mystique and the fallacy of misplaced concreteness"; and that one had to remember an axiom of data processing— "garbage in, garbage out" (Thomas 1972a:40, 46). Thomas argued that the types resulting from numerical taxonomy are stable, predictable, and objective, which is true. Given the way they are formed, they couldn't be anything else. But the real question is, are the types useful?

Andrew Christenson and Dwight Read (1977) took serious exception to Thomas's advocacy of numerical taxonomy, largely because they agreed with David Hull (1970) that no universal, ultimate, all-purpose classification could be constructed using numerical taxonomy or any other method because such a system did not exist. Rather, using theories about the data and the way in which the world is organized, one selects a small number of classificatory criteria from an infinite number of criteria. Several other archaeologists also made this argument (e.g., Dunnell 1971, 1973a, 1973b; Hill and Evans 1972; Schiffer 1976). Thomas (1978:236) himself later pointed out that "numerical taxonomy has failed because it does not tell us anything useful or new."

Another punch line to Christenson and Read's discussion was that an archaeologist, when strictly following the procedures of numerical taxonomy, in which attributes are not weighted, might fail to detect attribute clusters. Thus they recommended the use of r-mode factor analysis, wherein variables are correlated and variable clusters—the factors—are formed. As might have been anticipated, there was a response to their claims (Aldenderfer and Blashfield 1978; see also Thomas 1978), but of more interest is their rejoinder (Read and Christenson 1978), in which they fell back on the one claim that seemed to underpin any advocacy of the use of statistically based classification—that what was desired was an objective classification procedure. How such an objective procedure can exist is not at all clear, given that the analyst chooses the attributes. The desire for an objective procedure goes back to Spaulding's belief that emically real types can be discovered *if* the correct—here objective in the form of statistical—method is used.

Given their interests in human behavioral variation, processualists also sought methodological rigor in identifying nonrandom clusters of artifacts in space. Here, too, Whallon (1973, 1974a) suggested methods for making such identifications, and Michael Dacey (1973), a geographer, outlined another. Don Dumond (1974) discussed ways to statistically detect clusters of artifact types comprising tool kits. John Speth and Greg Johnson (1976:36) clarified two of the underpinning assumptions to both kinds of analyses when they noted that "archaeologists frequently expect that classes of artifacts belonging to the same [tool] kit will be correlated positively [and that] different tool kits [will be] segregated in spatially discrete activity loci." Tom Riley (1974) pointed out the case-specific nature of the application of statistical procedures, and that some of the techniques developed in geography and ecology demanded samples from all spatial units under investigation. Schiffer (1974) added that these techniques merely identified random and nonrandom clusters among the data sets. What those clusters meant in terms of human behaviors was an entirely separate issue that went unremarked in Whallon's (1973, 1974a) discussions. Whallon (1974b) noted that he was well aware of such difficulties and had merely "wished to share [his] knowledge of the existence of the method[s]."

An underappreciated aspect of Riley's (1974) comment is his implication that statistical techniques geared toward detecting patterning, including randomness, among data sets were inductive. This was antithetical to processualist arguments that archaeologists must operate deductively. Read (1974:4) stated that "statistical analysis is basically a methodology for testing the validity of certain postulated relations between variables, and statistical theory, per se, is not part of the process of developing theory in anthropology." But he went on to add, not surprisingly for someone trained as a mathematician, that rigorous mathematical models of anthropological phenomena furnish a means of formally stating relationships among variables, and so might yield insights into the operation of cultural processes. This perspective would eventually contribute to a proliferation of simulation studies (Hodder 1978). Christenson (1979a) echoed Riley's and Read's concerns but put a different spin on them when he observed that the use of complex statistical techniques seemed to rest on the assumption that human behavior and culture were complex and thus demanded complex analytical methods. Christenson argued that one should assume the subject phenomena are simple and thus begin with simple statistical techniques, working up to more complex ones according to deductively derived expectations.

By the mid- to late '70s archaeologists were routinely incorporating statistical methods into their work, whether it be a chi-square analysis, calculating a z-score or a Pearson's r, or performing a t-test. The minuscule percentage of statistical archaeology articles that Thomas (1976) reported for 1970 rose substantially as processualists realized that science demanded not simply quantification but sound inference (induction). Using statistical inference rather than seat-of-the-pants inference gave processualists a shot at being taken seriously by scientists outside the discipline. And yet when it came to statistical inference, most of the shots archaeologists were taking were at their own feet. Good intentions were one thing, but skillful execution was another. The arguments that

we summarized above—on classification, pattern recognition, and the like—were honest efforts to improve statistical applications in archaeology. By the mid-1970s such improvement was desperately needed.

The year 1976 might be considered a watershed in statistical archaeology for two entirely different reasons. First, Lew Binford invited Albert Spaulding to present the 1976–1977 Harvey Lecture at the University of New Mexico, which Spaulding titled "On Growth and Form in Archaeology: Multivariate Analysis" (Spaulding 1977). The invitation to present this prestigious lecture signified both the growing importance of statistics in archaeology and Spaulding's role in that growth. (There was an irony in Spaulding's topic, but we'll come back to that shortly.) Second, 1976 was the year Dave Thomas published his statistics text, *Figuring Anthropology*. The book unfortunately contained numerous typographical errors, which prompted Thomas (1986b:xi) to quip in the corrected second edition, "I learned one sterling lesson: Never again will I attempt to correct galley proofs around the campfire."

Errors or not, the original book—the first statistics text with purely anthropological examples—was used widely in graduate anthropology courses. In fact, for many years it was the only such book on the market, finally being joined by Stephen Shennan's *Quantifying Archaeology* (1988), Dick Drennan's *Statistics for Archaeologists: A Commonsense Approach* (1996), and Lorena Madrigal's *Statistics for Anthropology* (1998). Why did Thomas feel compelled to write a textbook on statistics, a project that most of us wouldn't touch for any amount of money? He doesn't come right out and say it in the book, but what he said a few years later leads us to suspect that by the time he started writing, he had become irritated by the increasing number of bad statistical applications that were appearing in print. He had a chance to address those concerns in a solicited article that appeared in a special issue of *American Antiquity* (1978),

"Contributions to Archaeological Method and Theory," that Schiffer edited.

Thomas titled his contribution "The Awful Truth about Statistics in Archaeology," and it was a no-holds-barred assault on statistical excesses. The article infuriated some readers, in large part because they disliked both Thomas's tone and his proclivity for tossing in cute quotes from famous people outside archaeology—W. C. Fields, Robert Frost, and so on. But few archaeologists who read the article carefully could disagree with the content. Thomas praised the work of several colleagues—referred to as the "GOOD"—and ripped the work of others—referred to as the "BAD" (the misuse of statistics) and the "UGLY" (the abuse of statistics). The reason he got away with assigning names to instances of misuse and abuse was because he also called his own number several times. People are likely to react less negatively if you point out errors in some of your own work while doing the same with theirs. Thomas noted, for example, that in a study of nearly 9,000 stone tools from New Guinea (White and Thomas 1972), he used principal components analysis to search for patterning. The results showed that 98 percent of the variance in tool shape was contained within three components (variables): general size, width, and edge angle. Very gratifying results, but Thomas made one slip: he interpreted the major components strictly on the basis of high positive values, whereas in any standard correlation analysis both positive *and* negative values are important. Oops. Unfortunately, none of the colleagues to whom Thomas had circulated the study realized the error; only after publication was the mistake pointed out (e.g., Whallon 1974c).

Thomas saved his most strident criticism for probability sampling (which we save for the following section) and multivariate analyses. In his opinion the traditional rationale for using multivariate techniques was often "insidious" and ended up doing archaeology "a grave disservice" (Thomas 1978:241). His remarks on that rationale are too good to "sample":

Although variously phrased, the logic begins with a simple statement like this: "Culture is not a univariate phenomenon…on the contrary, culture is multivariate, and its operation is to be understood in terms of many causally relevant variables which may function independently or in varying combination" (Binford 1965:205). Or, the refrain can begin like this: the subject matter of anthropology is culture; we know that culture is very complex, in fact anthropologists have so much trouble even *defining* culture that Kroeber and Kluckhohn (1952) compiled 161 definitions of what anthropologists think culture is; culture is so complex, involving interactions of so many variables, that culture is multivariate. *Therefore*—and here it comes—because culture is complex and multivariate, the *methods* we use to study phenomena must also be complex and multivariate. What begins as a legitimate observation about the complex nature of culture all too often becomes perverted to a call for more complex analytical methods, particularly multivariate statistical methods, in order to handle culture's inherent complexities. (Thomas 1978:241)

Thomas was correct in his assessment, which is why we noted earlier that the subject of Spaulding's Harvey Lecture at the University of New Mexico in 1976 was ironic. Spaulding was extolling the virtues of multivariate statistics at the same time that those very techniques were becoming increasingly abused. Although Spaulding had an excellent background in statistics, most archaeologists did not. What Spaulding had to say, however, sounded good. Specifically, it sounded scientific. And Spaulding made it seem as though multivariate approaches were not too difficult to master. More than a few archaeologists found that anyone can throw some data in a hopper, search the manual to find where the "on" switch is, and push it. If there is one guarantee in life, it is that one will always get results from a statistical operation. Cluster analysis produces clusters, and factor analysis produces factors.

But what do the results mean? Multivariate-statistical results can be exceedingly difficult to interpret, which is why Thomas (1978:241) referred to multivariate techniques as "archaeology's court of last resort"—to be used only after exhausting simpler techniques.

That was Andy Christenson's (1979a) point: Start simply and work up to more complex techniques *if* the data warrant. Predictably, a few archaeologists (e.g., Matson 1980) took what Thomas had to say as condemnation of the entire multivariate program in archaeology when, in fact, Thomas had gone to great lengths to point out that that was *not* what he was saying. As he put it (Thomas 1978:242), "only the naive will read into this argument an indictment of all multivariate and computer applications" (see also Thomas's [1980] response to Matson). One came away from reading the criticisms with the feeling that Thomas was more correct than even he realized. If the critics couldn't read a fairly straightforward article without completely misinterpreting it, they probably had no business interpreting the results of a complex multivariate analysis.

Probability Sampling

Given that the goals of processualists went well beyond building cultural chronologies, they realized that a few deep test trenches through the middle of the largest site in an area would not produce the data needed to answer questions about the diversity of human behaviors that took place. Archaeologists working in the preprocessual days worried about how representative their samples were, but the typical response was to collect ever larger samples. The thinking was, the larger the sample, the more likely one was to approximate the target population of artifacts. From the beginning Binford (e.g., 1964a) emphasized probability sampling as a guide to the collection of archaeological materials. Not surprisingly, one immediate concern was how large a sample had to be in order to be "representative" (Cowgill 1964). Various researchers worked toward empirically deriving a universal sample size that in some sense was representative or adequate (Mueller 1974

and various chapters in Mueller 1975), but this approach was flawed because it ignored variation in population parameters. The more heterogeneous the population, the greater the sample size needed. It was eventually recognized that accurate estimates of different population parameters often require samples of different sizes (Hole 1980; Plog, Plog, and Wait 1978; Schiffer, Sullivan, and Klinger 1978). Even in a single population a sample that is adequate for estimating one parameter may not be adequate for estimating others.

We say "it was eventually recognized" because, as with multivariate statistics, the uses of sampling in archaeology ran from the good to the ugly. Thomas (1978:236) had some unkind words for those uses: "There is a feeling afoot that if archaeological things are not probability sampled, they haven't been properly dealt with. This seems particularly prevalent among graduate students and contract archaeologists. The reasoning goes something like this: if it is probability sampled, then it's good archaeology; if it's not probability sampled, then it's bad (read "old fashioned," "traditional," "normative") archaeology. Of course this is incorrect. Many situations simply do not require probability sampling, as both statisticians and some archaeologists (e.g., Flannery 1976[b]) are quick to point out."

Thomas was correct that there was a feeling in the late 1970s that if you didn't sample, you could not be a processualist in good standing. Traditionalists argued that archaeology had been conducted for years without an emphasis on sampling; the processualists regarded that as yet one more sin to chalk up against the older generation. In reality, good archaeology *had* been conducted for years with little or no thought given to explicit sampling procedures, but reality was changing. As more and more archaeologists were drawn into cultural resource management, sampling became one of *the* two most important issues (the other being site significance). As we discuss in Chapter 6, the contract archaeology of the '70s, in stark contrast to that of earlier periods, was built around the concept of sampling.

Sampling in archaeology routinely occurs at many levels—from a collection of artifacts, to pits or houses at the site level, to sites themselves at the regional level. Thomas's reference to Flannery in the above quote concerned a discussion of sampling at the regional level (Flannery 1976b). Flannery's point was this: if one has the time and money to survey an entire valley, or whatever the universe might be, then there is no need to worry about sampling. There are numerous examples of so-called total survey coverage: Richard Blanton's survey of the Ixtapalapa Peninsula in the Valley of Mexico (1972) and his survey of the zone around Monte Albán in the Valley of Oaxaca, Mexico (1978), are typical. Most archaeologists, however, do not have the luxury of spending large blocks of time in the field, just as they do not have the time and money to excavate an entire site, which brings us to Flannery's other point: if you can't survey an entire region—"if, for example you can only survey a 20% sample—for heaven's sake, do it in such a way that you have some idea of the reliability of your results" (Flannery 1976b:132). In other words, do it in such a way that you know where sites are *not* located as well as where they *are* located. Also, do it in such a way that you maximize the possibility that the sample (the sites found) is representative of the target population (all sites in the universe).

Flannery's discussion of sampling was built around an imaginary dialogue that he had with two Mesoamerican archaeologists—a traditionalist, referred to as "the Real Mesoamerican Archaeologist," and RMA's young, pain-in-the-ass processualist sidekick, labeled "the Skeptical Graduate Student." The particular topic was sampling at the regional level, but similar conversations on other aspects of sampling occur throughout Flannery's (1976c) *The Early Mesoamerican Village,* which became one of the most widely read and frequently cited archaeology books of the late '70s. (The book is still in print, thirty years after it was published.) Flannery used a decade of work that he and his students had carried out in the Valley of Oaxaca to examine different aspects

of sampling and how to establish different kinds of sampling regimes. By far the most influential chapter in the book, one that was widely circulated for years before the book was published, is Steve Plog's (1976c) "Relative Efficiencies of Sampling Techniques for Archeological Surveys."

It was Plog's work more than anything else that introduced American archaeologists to some of the spatial sampling issues that geographers such as Peter Haggett (e.g., 1965) and Brian Joe Berry (e.g., Berry and Marble 1968) had been working on since the early 1960s (see also Crumley 1979). Plog (Figure 5.10) wanted to determine the effects of different sampling techniques on the estimation of a population parameter. He examined the efficiency of four sampling designs (simple random, stratified random, systematic, and stratified systematic unaligned) and two kinds of sampling units (quadrats—in this case, squares—and transects [actually, long, narrow rectangles instead of lines]). None of the other three sampling designs showed a greater precision in estimating the population parameter than simple random sampling. Further, smaller sampling units provided greater precision than larger ones.

FIGURE 5.10. Steve Plog, Chevelon Valley, Arizona, 1973. (Courtesy Steve Plog.)

Importantly, Plog never said *don't* use one of the sampling designs other than the simple random kind, although some archaeologists read it that way. What he said was, "this study suggests... that, for surveying unknown areas, the simplest sampling designs well may be the most practical" (Plog 1976c:158). There may, however, be excellent reasons to stratify a universe to be sampled—for example, to determine whether site distribution correlates with landforms or vegetation zones, and whether those correlations change through time. One regional sampling program that had those determinations as one of its goals was the Cannon Reservoir Human Ecology Project, a multiyear project centered on the Salt River valley of northeastern Missouri. The Salt Valley is part of the southern Prairie Peninsula, a mosaic of environments that was formed during early postglacial times by a unique set of climatic factors (Transeau 1935). At a macroscale, the two most obvious biomes are the tall-grass prairie and the deciduous forest, which interdigitate to form a dendritic pattern of peninsulas of grassland and timber. At a microscale, the two large biomes break down into an amalgam of complex, patchy biomes, the composition of which undoubtedly conditioned human responses to the region.

To investigate those responses and how they changed over time required knowledge of environmental change in the region and the spatial distribution of biomes. A doubly stratified random sampling scheme was used. The first stratification was by slope position category, or "drainage class." Each drainage class correlated with a discrete set of landform types as well as other important environmental variables (Warren and O'Brien 1981). The five drainage classes together partitioned the study area into a series of ribbonlike zones that roughly paralleled the courses of major streams or capped upland interstream divides (Figure 5.11). Classes contained distinct arrays of topographic features, and tests showed that they significantly reflected patterned variation of dominant biome distributions, forest species compositions, tree diversities and densities, soil

characteristics, and prehistoric and historical-period site locations. The study area was also stratified into five geographic areas, each of which was sampled independently to ensure dispersion of survey units across the study area. To survey the doubly stratified study area, legal quarter-section units (160 acres) were used as sampling quadrats. Eventually 178 units, representing 10 percent of the 441-square mile project area, were surveyed.

The Cannon Reservoir survey and numerous others of its generation continued to build on the exploratory work of Plog (1976c) with respect to sampling-unit construction and survey design, but they also were influenced by Dave Thomas's work in Nevada. Thomas's innovative survey was built around determining the time depth involved in Julian Steward's (1938) ethnographically documented pattern of land use followed by the Great Basin Shoshoni (Figure 5.12). Thomas selected his area (the northern Reese River valley), drew up a sampling design (1969), collected information by survey (Figure 5.13), modeled and ran simulations of the documented land-use pattern (1972b), and compared his archaeological data to the models (1973, 1974). He found that the pattern as manifest archaeologically had a time depth of 4,500 years. Here was empirical demonstration that statistical methods—in this case, probability sampling—could produce the kind of results that processualists were looking for: land-use patterns over time.

The 1970s witnessed considerable scurrying around on the part of processualists as they took the initial successes of the program as inspiration, heeded some of the criticism that it had engendered, and constantly worked at making theoretical and methodological improvements. In an early retrospective, Ezra Zubrow (1980:21) noted that as of the late 1970s, "there has not been a classic theoretical synthesis perhaps because ultimately there has not been a body of cohesive theory. Rather, there appears to be a series of independent theoretical studies and methodological innovations which are approaching theoretical discoveries."

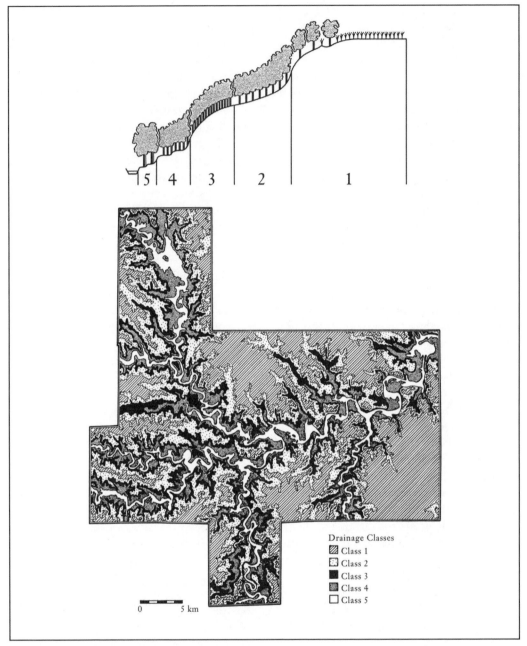

FIGURE 5.11. Topographic position of drainage classes in the Cannon Reservoir Human Ecology Project area, northeastern Missouri. (From Warren and O'Brien 1981.)

We agree, and add that part of the problem was the diversity of analytical goals being sought by archaeologists. Lack of a common goal meant that one could have as many kinds of archaeology as there were archaeologists.

If a single theme can be identified for processualism in the '70s, it was the continued belief that archaeology should be a scientific enterprise. As the decade wore on, one heard less about laws and more about other features of science. In various ethnographic settings processualists began to carry out tests of assumptions about the relationship between the static archaeological record and the dynamic human behaviors that created it. There were disagreements over how best to do this, and as we will see in Chapter 7, that particular research avenue not only continued to be contentious but gradually diverged from mainstream archaeology to become a separate subdiscipline.

Other methods adopted by the processualists in their desire to be scientific included statistics. Of particular interest were multivariate techniques and probability sampling, but as is often the case when individuals are swayed by the apparent sophistication of a new tool, they needlessly buy three without really understanding how they work. Such was the case with statistics. Ironically, the problem was exacerbated by increasingly accessible computer technology and software, but many of the problems were identified, if not solved, by the late 1970s. Archaeologists then turned their attention to building stronger interpretive models. Some of those models found immediate homes in the new contract archaeology—what soon became known throughout the discipline as cultural resource management. Once archaeologists became comfortable with the fact that research and resource management were not by definition mutually exclusive, some processualists began using the latter as a showcase for the former. We examine both in Chapter 6.

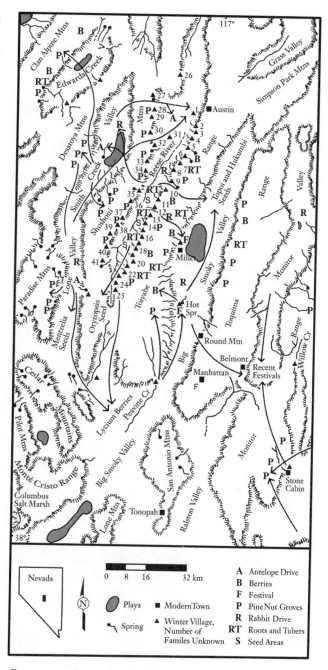

FIGURE 5.12. Seasonal round of the Western Shoshoni and Northern Paiute in the central Great Basin. (After Steward 1938 and Thomas 1979.)

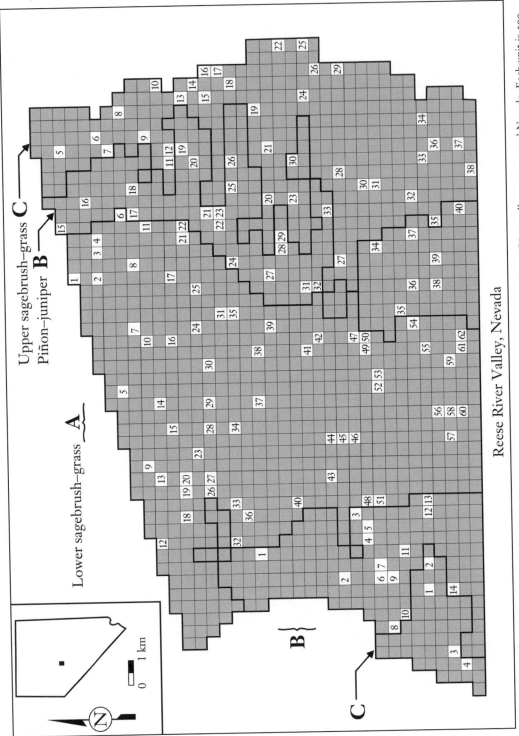

FIGURE 5.13. Distribution of sampling units used by David Hurst Thomas to survey the northern Reese River valley, west-central Nevada. Each unit is 500 meters on a side. The letters A–C represent modern environmental zones that were used to stratify the sampling area. Ten percent of each zone was then sampled (numbered squares). (After Thomas 1973.)

6

Fortunes to Be Made (and Lost)

*Seeking archaeologist to head cultural re-
source management program in department
of anthropology. Opportunity for part-time
teaching. Responsible for developing and ad-
ministering contracts. One-half (or none of)
salary provided by departmental funds,
other half to be secured from contracts and
grants. Non-tenure-track position.*

—L. MARK RAAB, "Cultural Resource
Management in the University"

How many of us who entered the job market in the late 1970s will ever forget such
an ad? Whether Mark Raab was referring to
an actual ad or creating a composite doesn't
change the reality of the situation: tenure-track
positions in archaeology were almost impossible to find, but if you were willing to accept the
challenge of writing proposals for a living, and
perhaps teach the occasional course, then academia might provide a home.

The '70s witnessed the rise of archaeology
as big business, courtesy of a government that
because of recent legislation suddenly found it
could no longer get away with the last-minute
salvaging of bits of information from sites
about to be destroyed by federal construction
projects. The government now needed archaeologists who were part of the planning process;
who were given enough time to make informed
judgments as to whether a site was worth excavating; and who were given the money to do

the job properly. The federal government also
needed its own staff of archaeologists to implement the new regulations, and it needed access to "consultants" whom it could hire to undertake fieldwork. This kind of consultation
was not always cheap, especially as archaeologists began not only to appreciate the costs of
doing archaeology without volunteer labor, but
also to realize that the government had deep
pockets. The nation's universities had never
been shy where federal contracts were concerned, and archaeological contracts were no
exception. Although individual archaeologists
sometimes took the initiative to become involved in this kind of archaeology, universities
strongly urged their archaeologists to become
entrepreneurs—to go "digging for gold," as Bill
MacDonald (1976) put it.

And why *wouldn't* universities do some urging and cajoling? There were fortunes to be
made, apparently with few drawbacks. What
risk is there in giving someone an office and a
phone and telling him or her to go get some
contracts? The risk is only slightly greater if the
person is guaranteed a half-time salary for a
year, especially since the university will recoup
its investment if it hits on just one sizable contract. And suppose it scores several? And suppose they are large? Suppose they are very, very
large? Think of the number of graduate students a department could attract because of
its sudden ability to increase financial support.

Think of the indirect (overhead) funds that a university could rake in—especially if its rate was upwards of 60 percent. And think of the prestige that goes along with being the chairperson of a department—and a *social science* department at that—bringing in over $1 million a year in external support, particularly in 1970s dollars.

With these kinds of potential paybacks, a university could gamble on giving a person a phone, a desk, and half a salary. Lots of universities took that gamble and plunged headlong into what became known as *cultural resource management,* recognized universally by its acronym, CRM. This actually was a misnomer because in the overwhelming majority of cases the term was being used to refer strictly to archaeological resources (Fowler 1982; McGimsey 2003). This is primarily the context in which we use the term here, recognizing that archaeological resources are but one segment of the cultural landscape (Alanen and Melnick 2000; Barton 2001; Hayden 1997; Tyler 1999).

One problem with what universities were doing was that they were ill equipped to "manage" any kind of cultural resource, be it an archaeological site, a historic house, or a collection of antique furniture that came as a bequest. They were, however, equipped to collect and expend money, and if they had to first figure out how to manage cultural resources in order to get the key to the federal coffers, they assumed they could do that. But most couldn't or, better stated, most didn't.

The three of us had extensive experience with CRM early in our careers, and collectively we saw both the good and the bad of how archaeological resources were managed—or sometimes mismanaged. We didn't plan on entering contract archaeology right out of graduate school, but tenure-track positions were

scarce, and competition for them was fierce (just as it is today). We appreciated having jobs, but to be honest, we were not looking forward to spending our entire careers doing CRM. Schiffer spent two years working for the Arkansas Archeological Survey, the first as director of the Cache River Archeological Project (Figure 6.1). He later secured a tenure-track teaching position at the University of Arizona. The Cache Project received national attention because of the wide dissemination of the final report (Schiffer and House 1975) and the subsequent publication of a summary article in *Current Anthropology* (Schiffer and House

FIGURE 6.1. *Right,* Mike Schiffer in the Cache River basin, northeastern Arkansas, 1974. (Courtesy Arkansas Archeological Survey.)

1977a). It didn't hurt that the Arkansas Archeological Survey was widely recognized as a leader in the professional conduct of CRM.

O'Brien spent three years directing the University of Nebraska's Cannon Reservoir Human Ecology Project in northeastern Missouri. In 1977 it was the largest (in terms of money allocated) CRM project in the country. It would soon be dwarfed by programs such as the Chief Joseph Archaeological Project in the state of Washington (Campbell 1985), the Dolores Archaeological Project in southern Colorado (e.g., Breternitz, Robinson, and Gross 1986; Petersen and Orcutt 1987; Petersen et al.

1985), and the FAI-270 Project (e.g., Bareis and Porter 1984) in the American Bottom of western Illinois. Like the Cache Project, the Cannon Project demonstrated that research and management goals were not incompatible and that peer-reviewed outlets were amenable to publishing the results of CRM projects (e.g., O'Brien 1984; O'Brien, Warren, and Lewarch 1982).

In contrast to the positive experiences of his two colleagues, Lyman worked at Oregon State University for four years in a half-and-half position before moving to the University of Missouri. OSU did not have a large ongoing project like Cache or Cannon, so he was expected to cover the "soft" side of his salary through successfully bidding on as many contracts as it took. Lyman wasn't particularly successful, and he saw firsthand the competitive, seamy side of CRM, such as trying to bid against someone whose so-called research design for surveying a national forest tract was such that he could cost it out at two cents an acre. That's not a typo: *two cents an acre*. Far from being an isolated incident, this happened across the country. The free enterprise system is supposed to keep costs down, but at some point the cliché "you get what you pay for" comes into play. The competition between archaeologists bidding on the same contract resulted in low cost to government but often in injustice to the profession and especially to the archaeological record. Archaeologists had to eat, however, and honor and commitment aren't edible.

After witnessing such behavior, some people began to wonder if the archaeology of the 1970s was in some ways beginning to resemble that of the days of the Works Progress Administration or the River Basin Surveys. Any similarities, however, were illusory. More than one archaeologist who lived through all three periods said they had never seen anything like the '70s. In the days of the RBS the bottom line was on getting material out of the ground as quickly as possible, analyzing it, reporting the information, and then moving on to another site. There was little or no competition among institutions involved in salvage operations, be-

cause there were plenty of opportunities for everyone.

Jesse Jennings, who was involved in RBS archaeology, stated his perceptions of the differences between salvage archaeology and CRM:

> CRM and its inventories require a work force of specialists far larger than the salvage operation ever mustered, but the contributions to archaeological knowledge remain scandalously small for funds expended. Even worse and far more serious are the losses the CRM contract archaeologists themselves suffer. Those include reduced self-esteem, loss of autonomy and independence of action, and eroded scientific integrity, as bureaucrats and contracting officers reduce archaeology to numbers and even prescribe the procedures to be used in the field. The salvage model is clearly superior to CRM if the goal is enrichment of knowledge of the American heritage. (Jennings 1985:293)

Those are harsh words, and we would venture to guess that not even Jennings would have applied them to all CRM programs. But there was more than a kernel of truth in what he was saying, both in terms of product and the effect that CRM had on archaeologists.

In assessing the earliest contributions of CRM, Schiffer (1975a:1) pointed out that "it is hardly necessary to document in any detail the dismal research record of contract archaeology. A glance at the bibliography of any compendium of method and theory...will attest to the negligible impact of contract 'research' on modern archaeological thought." The more chilling fact was that at the time he was writing, modern archaeological thought had had little or no impact on contract archaeology. Given the remarkable changes in archaeological method and theory that had occurred in the 1960s, the failure of most contract archaeologists to reference it had to be a result of ignorance or a conscious effort to separate what they did from what the processualists were doing. As we will examine later, archaeologists interested in "pure research" did little to help bridge the gap.

A few years later, Schiffer and George Gumerman (1977b:9) noted that "the dramatic upsurge in contract-supported archaeological activity...has precipitated a second crisis in American archaeology, far different from the initial crisis of a rapidly dwindling resource base.... Even the casual observer of the bulk of

FIGURE 6.2. Charles (Bob) McGimsey in the University of Arkansas law library, Fayetteville, 1971. (Courtesy Bob McGimsey.)

contract reports cannot help but note that there has been a marked indifference to standards of quality research." The belief that substandard work was being performed was not restricted to a few archaeologists trained in major departments. Spurred by its president, Charles (Bob) McGimsey of the University of Arkansas (Figure 6.2), the Society for American Archaeology in 1974 used a $39,750 grant from the National Park Service to sponsor a series of seminars related to contract archaeology. The final report of the seminars, known as *The Airlie House Report* (McGimsey and Davis 1977), was edited by McGimsey and Hester Davis, also of the University of Arkansas.

Of the six major topics addressed in the seminar report, none was more important than the reporting of archaeological investigations, a process captured by seminar participant Stan South as shown in Figure 6.3. Seminar participants identified nine categories of information that should be addressed in an archaeological report—shown on the cow's stomach in Figure 6.3—the most important of which was the theoretical base of the research. A report needed to lay bare the assumptions underlying the archaeological problem and to state explicitly how propositions and testable implications were derived. The *Airlie House Report* also called for peer review of reports. Despite the existence of these guidelines—and their ac-

ceptance by many archaeologists and state historic preservation officers—there was still a belief (e.g., Longacre 1981a; see Hester 1981 for a reply) that many CRM reports contributed little of a substantive nature to archaeology generally.

The seminar series raised the awareness of the archaeological community and perhaps contributed to the improvement of some reports, but its effectiveness was reduced by the long delay in publication. By the time *The Airlie House Report* was published in 1977, the profession had begun to tolerate bad CRM reports or, at best, reports that were unworthy of publication and had very limited distribution (see Brose 1985; Raab et al. 1980). Also in response to the need for quality control in CRM studies, a large segment of the archaeological community formed a new society in 1976, the Society of Professional Archaeologists. The organization was created partly in response to the concern that agencies and firms soliciting archaeological work might soon require archaeologists to be licensed. The thought was that if archaeologists began policing themselves first, it would appear to the agencies (and the public) that archaeologists were finally putting their house in order in terms of developing research standards and a code of ethics. The backlash to this movement was swift, with many archaeologists at the 1976 Society for American Archaeology meeting in Dallas sporting pins that read "Register sites, not archaeologists." SOPA membership grew for a while but was never a dominant force in American archaeology. It now is in a planned "dormant state," according to the Web site of the Register of Professional Archaeologists, to which SOPA voted "to transfer its responsibility, authority, and assets." ROPA is alive and well (Lipe and Stepon-

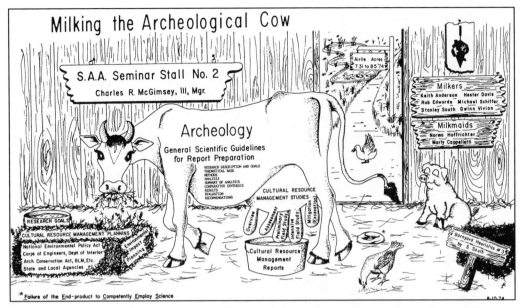

FIGURE 6.3. Stanley South's perspective on the relations among various components of cultural resource management, highlighting the scientific guidelines for archaeological report preparation put forward by participants in one of the Airlie House seminars. (From McGimsey and Davis 1977.)

aitis 1998) and perhaps will attract more participation than SOPA did.

This, then, was the archaeological landscape in the mid-1970s. In this chapter we examine that landscape from several perspectives, one of which is the nature of CRM and how it differed from the federal archaeology programs from which it evolved. Why did it turn out so differently? What were some of the new issues that CRM archaeologists had to face? More importantly, what, if anything, does American archaeology's flirtation with big business tell us about archaeology as a process? As bleak as the archaeological landscape might have looked in the mid-'70s, it did not stay that way for long. By the late '70s things weren't perfect, but clearly some very original and significant CRM work was being done. Many of the improvements were methodological, but by that time theory was also playing an important role. The most innovative work gave something back to the discipline instead of simply taking from it.

MANAGING THE NATION'S ARCHAEOLOGICAL RESOURCES

At about the time that processual archaeology

was born, J. O. Brew (1961) and Frederick Johnson (1966) noted that the increased rate of land modification across the United States was destroying the archaeological record at an unprecedented rate (Figure 6.4). There was plenty of evidence for such a statement. For example, Ray Williams (1967) estimated that land leveling, which consists of using large mechanized scrapers to move soil from one part of a field to another to bring it to grade (Figure 6.5), had affected almost 50,000 acres in southeast-

FIGURE 6.4. Construction of Table Rock Dam on the White River in southwestern Missouri, 1956. (Courtesy American Archaeology Division, University of Missouri.)

FIGURE 6.5. Two major types of equipment used in land alteration in southeastern Missouri: *top,* a land plane and *bottom,* a land leveler. The photographs were taken in Pemiscot County in 1965, but they could have been taken anywhere in the meander-belt region of the Mississippi River valley. The land that is planed or leveled is fairly flat to begin with, but the machines remove all traces of elevational differences, including swales, natural levees, point-bar deposits, and prehistoric mounds. (From Williams 1967.)

phisticated avocationalists, and pothunters continued collecting artifacts for private use or sale (Adams 1971; Nickerson 1962, 1963; Sheets 1972). Pothunting was especially problematic in the Southwest and the Mississippi Valley, where ceramic vessels often were elaborately decorated, bringing princely sums on the antiquities market. Looting was not a recent phenomena in either area, having been well documented in the nineteenth century (e.g., Thomas 1894).

Clearly, the destruction of sites and the looting of artifacts required action if any of the archaeological record, increasingly described as a "finite resource," was to be preserved and protected for the future. This expression of a growing ecological consciousness was another upswing in the conservation ethic that has cycled through the history of the United States. Each upswing had its folk heroes—Henry David Thoreau, Theodore Roosevelt, Aldo Leopold— but what attracted their attention was the isolation of a New England pond, the beauty of the untamed West, or the majesty of a sandhill crane in flight—not the prehistoric pots beneath a cornfield in southeastern Missouri. By the time the plight of the nation's archaeological record became impossible to overlook, archaeologists and bureaucrats had already begun to develop conservation strategies. Although little could be done to slow site destruction on private lands, laws were passed throughout the twentieth century to protect federally owned sites. But did these laws have the teeth to make a difference?

The first law to address archaeological resources dates to 1906, when at the urging of various groups, Congress passed the Antiquities Act (Public Law 34-209) to protect against vandalism of ruins, monuments, and anything else of antiquity on lands owned or controlled

ern Missouri between 1955 and 1965. That was bad enough, but then in 1966 alone, more than 21,000 acres were leveled—the equivalent of roughly 33 square miles of land in one of the richest archaeological zones in the country. Add to that the figures derived for eastern Arkansas (Ford, Rolingson, and Medford 1972), and it was a disaster of epic proportions.

A similar rate of site destruction was occurring across the country, a result not only of farming activities but also of construction projects (Davis 1971, 1972). Sites were also being excavated by an increasing number of well-intentioned but methodologically unso-

by the federal government (Thompson 2000). Passage of the Historic Sites, Buildings, and Antiquities Act of 1935 (PL 74-292) strengthened the provisions of the earlier act and led to the eventual formation, in 1945, of the Inter-Agency Archeological Salvage Program—a cooperative venture of the National Park Service, the Smithsonian Institution, the Bureau of Reclamation, and the Army Corps of Engineers. Its purpose was to locate, assess, and salvage archaeological materials from proposed reservoir areas throughout the United States. The role of the NPS in salvage archaeology was written into law with the passage in 1960 of the Reservoir Salvage Act (PL 86-523), which directed all agencies involved in reservoir construction to notify the Secretary of the Interior when planning projects. This law was intended in part to ensure that funding was available for what had otherwise been a largely underfunded enterprise, but sufficient funds were never appropriated (Reaves 1976).

Thus, on the eve of the birth of processualism, a loosely coordinated salvage component was firmly entrenched in American archaeology. Some processualists—Lew Binford, for example—had considerable experience with salvage archaeology (e.g., Binford 1964b; Binford et al. 1970). With the arrival of processualism in the 1960s, however, the scientific credibility of salvage projects became suspect. Artifacts were being saved, and various kinds of data were being recorded, but to what end other than the fulfillment of a legal mandate? What research questions were guiding these efforts? Did they go beyond the same spatiotemporal systematics that had long driven culture history (King 1971)? This and similar questions spawned at least a low-level debate between processualists (e.g., Longacre and Vivian 1972) and those with more traditional leanings (e.g., Gruhn 1972). The processualists argued that one must have a research question or problem in mind in order to determine appropriate information collection strategies. Traditionalists were not so inclined, arguing that it was more important to salvage as much as possible and worry about research questions

later. This issue, as we discuss later, became one of the benchmark topics in CRM during the 1970s.

Additional archaeology-related legislation was passed in the late 1960s, beginning with the National Historic Preservation Act (PL 89-665) in 1966 (see King 1998 for a history). No one at the time had the slightest idea of the nightmare that this act would impose on archaeology. In concept, the legislation was appealing. It gave the Secretary of the Interior considerable authority and directed him or her to create a National Register of Historic Places, a list of significant archaeological and historical sites. The act also called for establishing an Advisory Council on Historic Preservation, which, through Section 106 of that act, was given a review-and-comment function in instances where National Register properties were to be affected adversely by federally funded activities (see King 2000 for a history of Section 106). The same day that the National Historic Preservation Act was passed, the Department of Transportation Act (PL 89-670) also became law, directing the transportation secretary to protect historic properties.

At the close of the decade came what McGimsey (1976) later called the most important piece of archaeological legislation ever passed: the National Environmental Policy Act of 1969. McGimsey, as we point out below, was in a position to make that statement. The act called for the creation of environmental impact statements *before* any project was undertaken on federal land, or on private land when the project required a federal permit or license. By the time regulations were written and interpreted by the courts, environmental impact statements came to include archaeological, historical, and other cultural resources. As important as this legislation was in requiring forecasts of the adverse impacts that projects would likely have on archaeological sites, it did not require that those adverse impacts be mitigated. That would soon change.

In 1971 President Richard Nixon signed into law Executive Order 11593: Protection and Enhancement of the Cultural Environment, which attempted to pull together diverse pieces of legislation, especially those pertaining to the National Register. One key component of the order was a directive to federal agencies to develop criteria and policies for evaluating properties that might be included on the National Register. Although it had been created under the National Historic Preservation Act of 1966, no formal set of guidelines for site eligibility had been compiled. Executive Order 11593 addressed that deficiency.

It was in this confusing arena of legislative acts and executive orders that archaeologists and government agencies found themselves in the early 1970s. The NPS was still the lead agency relative to archaeological investigations, and by all accounts other federal agencies were willing to have it continue to shoulder the responsibility. But it was becoming increasingly difficult for those other agencies to ignore archaeological properties on their lands. For example, agencies were now required to submit environmental impact statements for each proposed project, a headache that many of them simply did not know how to handle. Previously, if the Corps of Engineers wanted to build a reservoir, they would work through the Inter-Agency Archeological Salvage Program, administered through the NPS, to have the archaeological work done. Now the law required *the corps* to ensure that the work was carried out. It was during the early 1970s that government agencies other than the NPS—for example, the Bureau of Land Management, the Forest Service, the Bureau of Reclamation, and the Corps of Engineers—started hiring large numbers of archaeologists, most of whom were recruited to compile inventories of sites on federal lands and to write environmental impact statements.

In effect, the legislation created unheard-of opportunities for archaeology students, though many of them soon found out that the opportunity came with a price. Some prospered in government positions, becoming accustomed to the regimentation and paperwork, but others did not. Many of the early crop of archaeologists who took government positions either

had their Ph.D.s or were doctoral-level students. They had been brought up on the doctrines of the new archaeology and were interested in things other than the compliance process. Many of them took government positions as a stopgap measure until they could find teaching and research positions at a university. They soon learned, however, that it was extremely difficult to leave government service and return to a university setting. Not only were college and university positions scarce, but there was a glut of new Ph.D.s ready to compete for positions (Chapter 5). Also, government jobs often paid well and offered greater security than academic employment, since obtaining tenure was not a certainty. Faced with these realities, well-trained archaeologists who had been attracted to government positions either had to stay and try to make a difference in how federal archaeology was done, or start looking for positions outside archaeology. What they didn't know was that another option was waiting for them. In fact, no one could have foreseen what was about to happen to American archaeology.

FIGURE 6.6. Carl Chapman in Vernon County, Missouri, ca. 1984. (Courtesy *St. Louis Post-Dispatch*.)

THE MOSS-BENNETT BILL

By the late 1960s archaeologists agreed that the funding available for federal archaeology was too limited to accomplish the kind of work needed. Carl Chapman of the University of Missouri (Figure 6.6) and Bob McGimsey decided to do something about it, and they launched what at first was a two-man campaign in the halls of Congress. McGimsey later pinpointed the start of the lobbying effort:

Our presence in Washington can be traced directly to the three Mississippi Alluvial Valley Conferences, which had been convened by Jimmy Griffin [University of Michigan], Hester Davis [Arkansas Archeological Survey], and me in 1968. From those conferences (attended by over fifty archaeologists who were active in the Valley at the time) came three things: a basic regional research design, the pamphlet "Stewards of the Past," 60,000 copies of which were distributed nationwide [published in 1970 through the Extension Division, University of Missouri], and the conviction that federally sponsored activities other than dam building posed a serious threat to archaeological resources nationwide, and, therefore, that some solution must be developed on a national level. Legislation must be introduced that would authorize any federal agency whose actions adversely affected archaeological resources to expend agency funds to mitigate this adverse effect. At that time agencies were contending, correctly, that their appropriations did not permit such expenditure. Hence Carl's and my trip. (McGimsey 1985:326)

The trip to which McGimsey referred happened in July 1969, when, as he says, "Carl Chapman took me in hand and led me to Washington to talk to members of Congress" (McGimsey 1985:326). That trip was only the first of many that Chapman and McGimsey would make over the next five years. McGimsey noted that during that time he spent more than 200 days in Washington and talked with the legislative staff of every senator and every representative from every state. The task was grueling.

I would normally start a day on the top floor of a particular congressional office building explaining the purpose and appropriateness of the legislation to each congressional staff on that floor, and then work my way down to ground level. Wherever possible, I attempted to identify myself with an archaeologist from that state or territory.... Thanks to the organization in the various archaeological societies and the intense interest of most archaeologists it was almost always possible for me to say that I was speaking for "so and so" who was not able to be present.... After making basically the same presentation dozens of times, I became very appreciative of the signs most members maintained in their offices telling what State I was "in." (McGimsey 1985:328)

The "intense interest" that McGimsey attributed to archaeologists enabled the proposed legislation to be seen as coming from a larger segment of society than two archaeologists. The Society for American Archaeology urged its members to write their representatives and senators and to urge other societies to get behind the proposed legislation. The effort eventually paid off handsomely. The draft bill was jointly sponsored by Senator Frank Moss of Utah and Congressman Charles Bennett of Florida in 1969, but it was not signed into law until 1974. The final legislation was titled the Archaeological and Historic Preservation Act of 1974 (PL 93-291), though few archaeologists ever knew it as anything other than Moss-Bennett. If there is an archaeological hall of fame, the plaques of Moss and Bennett should be placed alongside those of Chapman and McGimsey (Figure 6.7), for it was those four individuals who finally pried open the government coffers and fed a generation of archaeologists. Naturally, some of these ate better than others, because one aspect of the law's effect on the growth of archaeology was the competition that it engendered.

FIGURE 6.7. *Left,* Charles (Bob) McGimsey and *right,* Carl Chapman holding the Distinguished Service Awards they received from the Society for American Archaeology, 1975. They were the first recipients of the award. (Courtesy Bob McGimsey.)

The key element that Moss-Bennett added to previous legislation was guidelines for spending federal money on archaeological mitigation. These guidelines represented innovative legislation, but the end result was not necessarily what archaeologists had hoped for. Because of the important role one of the stipulations played in American archaeology during the 1970s and '80s, we discuss it in some detail. This stipulation, almost a magic word in archaeological circles (and eventually in public ones as well), was what we might call the one-percent solution. To understand the evolution of this term, we again call on Bob McGimsey.

> While the law was being drafted, it was assumed by all involved that the Department of [the] Interior, as the only federal agency with a staff of professional archaeologists, would assume administrative responsibility for conducting essentially all of the research. It was, therefore, appropriate that a provision be made in the legislation for the transfer of funds from other agencies to the National Park Service, and that it administer the conduct of research. During early drafting, it was pointed out to those of us involved that there was no possibility for the passage of legislation that authorized unlimited transfer from one federal agency to

> another.... [W]e were challenged to come up with some percentage that would...be acceptable by the archaeological profession and the federal agencies.... [I]n the final version, 1% became the guideline. The intent was for this to be a limiting guideline only for the funds transferred by another agency to the National Park Service. Shortly after passage, a Corps of Engineers lawyer interpreted the 1% limitation to apply to the total funds expended by the agency for *all* archaeology on a project, not just as a limit on transferred funds as had been intended. (McGimsey 1985:330, emphasis added)

Most archaeologists did not understand that, as written, Moss-Bennett did not exclude agencies from spending more than 1 percent of project costs on archaeological work; it only limited the amount of money that an agency could transfer to the park service (McGimsey 1989). Regardless, most agencies began contracting directly with archaeologists instead of going through the park service, thus reducing the role of that agency in federal projects. In addition, agencies weren't going to pay more than they were forced to, and they all began to see the 1 percent figure as a ceiling on archaeological expenditures. Even if they had understood the nuances, archaeologists wouldn't have complained, given the fact that they had just come into more money than they had ever seen. The only question was, how did one get the machine to start cranking out greenbacks? The answer came immediately: You put in a bid, along with everyone else. Gone were the days when a university worked as a sole-source contractor through an arrangement with the park service or a state highway department. Now, universities had to read the *Commerce Business Daily,* as other government contractors did, to find out about upcoming projects.

Even before Moss-Bennett became law, private archaeological firms began springing up around the country, but the number skyrocketed after 1974. (The earliest true archaeological consulting company of which we are aware is Scientific Resource Surveys, founded by

Roger Desautels of Costa Mesa, California, in the early '60s.) As government agencies began taking over responsibility for projects, they soon found that the capabilities of their in-house archaeologists were being outstripped, and so they were forced to go outside. Agency archaeologists became less archaeologists and more managers, given that it fell to them to write scopes of work, to select contractors, and to ensure that the chosen contractors stayed in compliance and on schedule. The early days under Moss-Bennett were complicated by the fact that few archaeologists, including those in the government, understood the tangle of CRM legislation, especially how the laws dovetailed with one another.

WHAT DOES "SIGNIFICANT" MEAN?

During the 1970s, archaeology was beset with a series of dilemmas. Ever since the signing of Executive Order 11593 in 1971, the National Park Service had been struggling with the development of guidelines for determining which sites were eligible for inclusion on the National Register. These guidelines came to be known as "criteria for determination of significance," or simply, "eligibility criteria." The park service solicited the help of the archaeological community in constructing criteria, but as Schiffer and John House (Figure 6.8) noted in the late

FIGURE 6.8. John House in the Cache River basin, northeastern Arkansas, 1974. (Courtesy John House.)

1970s, "the topic of significance...is by far the most controversial issue" in American archaeology (Schiffer and House 1977a:64).

The National Historic Preservation Act of 1966 listed criteria for evaluating whether a cultural property merited nomination for listing on the National Register. These became known as the significance criteria. One criterion, which stated that a site could be labeled significant if it were likely to yield important information, was problematic in that it was too open-ended. After all, everyone had his or her own notion of what constituted a significant resource. The number of articles that appeared on the subject within a short span of time was staggering (e.g., Barnes, Briggs, and Nielsen 1980; Dixon 1977; Dunnell and Dancey 1978; Glassow 1977; Grady 1977; House and Schiffer 1975b; King 1978, 1983; King and Lyneis 1978; Klinger and Raab 1980; McGimsey and Davis 1977; Moratto and Kelly 1977, 1978; Raab and Klinger 1977, 1979; Schiffer and Gumerman 1977a; Schiffer and House 1977a, 1977b; Scovill, Gordon, and Anderson 1972; Sharrock and Grayson 1978). Some archaeologists argued that sites should be determined significant or not on their perceived ability to produce data relevant to current archaeological problems (e.g., House and Schiffer 1975b; Schiffer and House 1977a). Others (e.g., Lipe 1974) argued that representative portions of the resource base should be preserved intact for future investigation, given that no one can predict future theoretical and methodological directions. The issue is still relevant to American archaeology (e.g., Hardesty and Little 2000).

The *Airlie House Report* (McGimsey and Davis 1977:31) had this to say about "significance": "The fact that archeological sites and the information they contain are our only clues to much of human life in the past makes every site potentially significant. It is generally recognized, however, that defining significance implies some frame of reference, problem orientation, geographic, temporal or other context, against which an archeological phenomenon is to be evaluated. A site is therefore more or less significant relative to some criterion or criteria." This was a reasonable explication of the concept, though it could be difficult to identify the appropriate context in any given case. What, then, were some of the criteria and contexts that were identified?

Mark Raab and Timothy Klinger (1977: 362) suggested that an archaeological resource could be deemed significant "in relation to explicit, problem-oriented research designs" because those designs identify a "specific research question on which the resource in question may be expected to inform." Floyd Sharrock and Donald Grayson (1979) agreed in principle, but they noted that this seemed too narrow and specific to the research problems popular when the significance evaluations had to be made: "'significance' is a dynamic concept varying through space, time, and even perhaps across investigators [making it] extremely difficult to demonstrate that any site lacks the potential of becoming significant" (Sharrock and Grayson 1979:327). Thus they argued that the general National Register criterion of the *potential* for a site "to yield information important in prehistory or history" was key. Raab and Klinger (1979) clarified that they had not meant that a few narrow research problems constituted the only way to operationalize the significance concept. Rather, broad-based questions that encompass much of the variation in the archaeological record were preferable because such questions would result in more archaeological resources being preserved.

Michael Glassow (1977) agreed that research problems could be too narrow a basis for significance assessments, and he identified some variables that one might use in implementing Raab and Klinger's procedure. The variables were variety (consider all the diverse kinds of cultural resources), quantity (consider samples of the full range of frequencies and densities of resources), clarity (consider resources with the full range of horizontal and vertical boundaries, from diffuse to distinct), integrity (consider resources with minimal degrees of disturbance), and environmental context (consider sites in all the diverse environmental settings)—all of which sound like planks

in the processualist platform. In many respects, Glassow's suggestions had been stated several years earlier by William Lipe (1974), who argued for conserving a large sample of the entire range of diversity within the archaeological record without consideration of significance. To operationalize such ideas requires that one already know a great deal about the archaeological record. For this reason, we suspect that Lipe was arguing for the preservation of diverse pieces of landscape rather than a sample of particular cultural resources.

Michael Moratto and Roger Kelly (1977, 1978) listed several types of significance, including historical, ethnic, public, and scientific (research). Bob Dunnell and Bill Dancey (1978) suggested that the significance of cultural resources could be evaluated from either or both of two perspectives. The general public and most laws took a humanistic perspective and found portions of the archaeological record significant for their cultural heritage value, meaning they had historical, political, and/or emotional value to particular human populations or ethnic groups. The humanistic perspective identified by Dunnell and Dancey (1978), then, included the historical, ethnic, and public sorts of significance as previously identified.

The alternative perspective saw the archaeological record as a body of scientific data. It is an empirical record, Dunnell and Dancey (1978:2) argued, that "is unintentional and thereby unbiased by human historical motives, [thus] it is the only source of data that bears directly on the evolution of all kinds of societies and cultures, that allows us to assess success and failure of particular cultural adaptations without recourse to value judgments, and that provides the necessary information to delineate the conditions and circumstances under which particular forms develop, spread, and succeed while others fail." The humanistic perspective seeks to preserve the record in perpetuity, whereas the data-for-research perspective seeks to conserve the record for future use in the form of scientific study.

Discussions of significance continued into the 1980s (e.g., Bobrowsky 1982; Lynott 1980; Madden 1983; Raab 1984). Joseph Tainter and John Lucas (1983) argued that the significance criteria specified in the 1966 National Historic Preservation Act should be rewritten to acknowledge that significance was not a property inherent in selected cultural resources but rather was an extrinsic value assigned to particular resources by individuals. Tom King of the Advisory Council on Historic Preservation agreed but thought that the rewriting would be impractical. He urged the development of a more flexible and less-centralized system for evaluating cultural resources (King 1985). A few years later, Bill Butler of the National Park Service's Interagency Archeological Services protested that many archaeologists simply misunderstood the concept of significance, which contributed to the ever-increasing size of the literature on the subject. He argued that cultural resources that were "important" were significant, and those that were important were those that had something to contribute to "theoretical and substantive knowledge" (Butler 1987:821). But this was unhelpful, for as Schiffer (1975a) and others had pointed out years earlier, *every* site can furnish important information for some research question. Thus, every site is important from the standpoint of research potential.

Regardless of how one approaches the problem of significance and the criteria used to establish it, the National Register was never intended to be a planning document but rather a preservation tool (Grady and Lipe 1976). However, the opinion was often voiced (e.g., Aten 1974), though it lacked any statutory basis, that the federal government should spend money for mitigation only on register-eligible sites. This, unfortunately, became the official opinion of federal agencies: no determination of eligibility, no money. The result was nightmarish. Archaeologists had to complete endless amounts of largely meaningless paperwork in order to obtain register eligibility. At first, forms had to be filled out stating precisely why *each* site was eligible. The archaeologist might have

hundreds of sites with which to contend—for example, in a large reservoir area—but no one wanted to complete hundreds of federal forms. Eventually it became possible to nominate entire archaeological districts, which lessened the bureaucratic burden.

Some of the sites might have received a small amount of excavation to determine depth of deposit, presence of prehistoric features, and the like, but in essence the archaeologist often was being asked to do what was nearly impossible: to make determinations of significance based on very little information. What if the initial excavation units just happened to hit the only prehistoric pits on a site? Or suppose the few initial excavation units happened to miss the dozens of pits that were present? The former site probably would have been declared eligible, whereas the latter would not. One could argue that more work should have been done during the testing phase to learn more about the sites, but when an archaeologist was faced with a large number of sites and not enough time and money, additional work became impossible.

Archaeologists quickly figured out that eligibility meant funding, and so determinations of eligibility became important. This did not necessarily lead to more sites being judged eligible than otherwise would have been the case; sometimes only one or two sites would be forwarded to the Advisory Council, but the forms would read as though the sites were second only to Pompeii in terms of significance. Most archaeologists, however, conscientiously attempted to plow through the regulations and to devise statements of significance that fairly represented the resource base. Others did not. Some recognized that their hands would be tied by their initial selection of sites, and they attempted to cover the bases accordingly by nominating as many sites as possible. What was needed was flexibility during the mitigation stage of a project. If, upon closer examination, a site did not yield the kind of information for which it received its eligibility status, it could be declassified as an eligible site, and work could be moved elsewhere. Eventually, these kinds of trade-offs were built into the memo-randa of agreement that were signed by the Advisory Council, the state historic preservation offices, and the funding agencies, but in the early years of Moss-Bennett no one had worked out such arrangements.

ACADEMIC ARCHAEOLOGY VERSUS CONTRACT ARCHAEOLOGY

It was obvious by the 1970s that there was a widening gap between two populations of archaeologists, each of which made its living in quite different ways (Gumerman 1973; King 1971; McGimsey 2003). One population worked in academia, teaching and doing research nine months of the year while devoting perhaps six to eight weeks each summer to fieldwork funded by a National Science Foundation or Wenner-Gren grant, by a small contract with the National Park Service, or by tuition paid by field school students. Archaeologists in the other population made their living doing contract archaeology, with perhaps four to eight months of the year devoted to fieldwork and the remainder to writing reports and drafting proposals for future work. Academic archaeologists did so-called pure research, whereas contract archaeologists had the stigma of being constrained by the requirements of an agency that oftentimes did not appear to care about the archaeological record.

Some of the wounds caused by the increased alienation that CRM archaeologists felt from the rest of the profession were self-inflicted; in some cases, contract archaeologists deserved their unsavory reputation. But the alienation was partly a result of jealousy on the part of academic archaeologists and nonarchaeologists. The reasons had a lot to do with money. Obtaining federal funds for pure research has always been difficult because there are more qualified proposals than the available funds can support. We can use data from the National Science Foundation as a guide, since it has been the major source of anthropological and non-contract-related archaeological funding since it was founded in 1950.

John Yellen and Mary Greene (1985), both with the NSF Anthropology Program, stated that between 1954 and the close of the government fiscal year 1983, the program (which grew out of the earlier Anthropology and Related Sciences Program) had awarded slightly less than $42 million dollars to archaeological projects (not including dissertation improvement awards) out of the roughly $96 million dollars spent on all anthropology projects combined. Archaeology projects had garnered about 44 percent of the money, with the remaining 56 percent split among the other subfields. The average archaeological grant was about $33,000. Yellen and Greene showed that although the amount of funding to archaeological projects grew over time, the level of support in terms of constant dollars (funding level adjusted for inflation) declined dramatically (Figure 6.9). For example, the 1983 level fell to a point where it was only one-third as high as it had been in 1968.

Equally informative are the locations of funded projects. In the thirty-year period between 1954 and 1983, 40 percent of these projects were carried out in the United States and Canada. But breaking the thirty-year period down into smaller increments shows that the

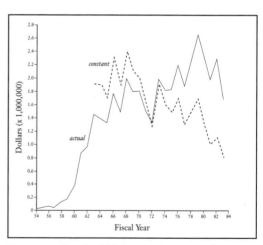

FIGURE 6.9. Levels of National Science Foundation funding for archaeology in actual dollars, 1954–1983, and "constant" dollars (adjusted for inflation), 1963–1983. (After Yellen and Greene 1985.)

level of funding for projects in the United States and Canada fell by 14 percent between 1979 and 1983, whereas levels for Middle America, Europe, Africa, and South America rose 3 to 6 percent. Yellen, Greene, and Louttit (1980) argued in response to Richard Casteel's (1980) criticism of the NSF that the decreased support for research in the United States probably was a result of the rise of CRM archaeology, their logic being that since CRM money was easier to obtain, fewer archaeologists were approaching NSF. Yellen and Greene (1985) later backed off this explanation in light of their data, which showed a relatively continuous decline in funding for U.S. projects since 1962.

If one really wants to understand the source of frustration in the 1970s for archaeologists who were unaccustomed to, or uninterested in, doing contract archaeology, look at the amount of federal money that was spent on contract projects in any given year. Even as early as the mid-'60s, Robert Heizer (1966) estimated that in California $100 of contract funding was available for every dollar of noncontract money. The best, and probably the most accurate, statement regarding the dramatic increase in CRM funding was made by Bob McGimsey (1985:330): "A study I made in 1971 indicated that approximately one million dollars of public money on the state and federal level was spent to recover or preserve archaeological resources. Ten years later that figure had increased to an unknown total, but estimates range from *one hundred to two hundred million dollars*" (emphasis added). Even if we take McGimsey's lower figure, an estimate that is well within the ballpark, more money was spent on contract archaeology in *one* year than the NSF had passed out to *all* anthropology— not only to archaeology—programs since its inception. Given that level of funding, it is little wonder that so many archaeologists became willing to accept not only a battery of regulations and restrictions on the kinds of work they could do, but also the disdain and jealousy of their colleagues.

If money—or more precisely, jealousy over money—played a role in fueling the controversy over the legitimacy of CRM, it shared center stage with basic philosophical arguments over how archaeology should be done. One of the earliest and clearest airings of the controversy regarding the appropriateness of contract archaeology as a legitimate research enterprise was Tom King's (1971) paper "A Conflict of Values in American Archaeology," which was updated as "Resolving a Conflict of Values in American Archaeology" (King 1977b). King exemplifies someone who shifted from a university research position to one with the National Park Service. King's (1977b:87) sense of frustration in trying to do contract archaeology in a university setting—in essence trying to do scientific archaeology for government agencies who didn't want scientific archaeology done—was typical of the time: "In 1969/70, as chief archaeologist at the UCLA Archeological Survey, I was keenly aware of the pragmatic difficulties engendered by this conflict. The Survey was heavily involved in salvage, but the shadow of Louis [sic] Binford, who had left UCLA in 1968, lay long across the minds of graduate students.... We at the Survey felt a need to make our operations scientifically relevant, and this need was often hard to square with our equally serious obligations to the agencies for whom we did free or contract salvage."

King noted that contract archaeology was basically incompatible with a deductivist approach. On one hand, "fieldwork in the context of [the deductive] approach is a tool employed after the archaeologist has recognized and defined a problem, framed hypotheses relevant to the problem, and designed tests of the hypotheses to which fieldwork is found to relate. The kinds of field techniques employed are determined by the test requirements, within limits of feasibility" (King 1977b:89). On the other hand, the inductivist method "is based on the assumption that a valid and worthwhile body of fact will have been attained when enough data have been gathered to permit synthesis and inference.... According to an inductive ethic, every bit of information can be used in synthesis; presumably, *all* information can be and should be gathered" (King 1977b:89).

It should have come as no surprise that government agencies in the 1960s were not particularly impressed with the new archaeology: "To the agency or industry supporting an archaeological project...the outcome and indeed the existence of the research is truly 'incidental'.... Government and business do important things other than archaeology, and the public archaeologist, like it or not, must be a part of their doing" (King 1983:156). The agencies that controlled the purse strings—particularly the park service—had established policies and administrative structures that were used to doling out money on an as-needed basis for archaeology. They also were used to receiving nice, fat descriptive reports that listed all the sites found and the artifacts recovered. They were not used to hearing about sampling design, problem formulation, and hypothetico-deductive approaches.

For their part, archaeologists and their institutions, dedicated as they were to induction,

> could easily handle, and intuitively justify, piecemeal salvage. Such work was justified on the basis of the familiar jigsaw analogy: When we have enough pieces, the picture will become clear. It was not necessary to wonder on what basis we perceived the shape of the pieces, and there was no need to worry about what phenomena we would like to see most clearly pictured when we got through. The central definitive focus of the archaeologist's life, and the measure of one's adequacy in relation to one's professional peers, was fieldwork; the more of it one did, the further one would advance the discipline.... Further, it was entirely proper for students to spend vast amounts of time in the field doing salvage and in the laboratory doing analyses and writing, toward no other goal than the preparation of "descriptive site reports" that proceeded through standard stages to present the collected data for future reference (Swartz 1967)—another piece added to the puzzle! (King 1977b:90–91)

Such an approach was logically inconsistent with the goals of a deductivist archaeology.

Standard site reports, rich with artifact description, were not the product of choice of the deductivists, who might not even be interested in the removal of artifacts from a site. But if one were drawn to contract archaeology, with its inductivist orientation and procedural guidelines, one ran the risk of being "branded...as a mere technician unsuitable to the cloisters of academia" (King 1977b:91). There was a way out of the dilemma, though in retrospect no one could have predicted how quickly a change in attitude would come about. And, happily, the change suited almost everyone, regardless of intellectual predilection. Ironically, especially in light of the above comments about CRM being anathema to the deductivist approach, the change occurred when some of the new archaeologists dropped their preoccupation with polemical statements about deductivist archaeology and started doing CRM.

One such archaeologist was Schiffer, who first at UCLA through Lew Binford and then at the University of Arizona through Bill Longacre had been steeped in the deductive approach and knew the ins and outs of processualism. He also knew how to apply some of the new archaeology to a contract situation, in this case the Cache River Archeological Project, an investigation undertaken by the Arkansas Archeological Survey in northeastern Arkansas. Uncharacteristically, Schiffer did not want to include here more than the briefest mention of the project, believing that to do otherwise would be self-serving. Characteristically, O'Brien and Lyman overruled him.

There are three reasons for discussing the Cache River Project in detail. First, more than any other project in the 1970s, it demonstrated that it was possible to combine research objectives with the dictates of CRM. Second, the project set the standard against which subsequent CRM studies were judged—in terms of both quality and return on cost. The 339-page (single-spaced) report that summarized the findings in the Cache Basin (Schiffer and House 1975) cost the Corps of Engineers a mere $48,000, though Schiffer and House (1977a:63) noted that the actual cost of the project was closer to $80,000–$100,000 if donated services were figured in. That was a bargain even in those days. Third, a lengthy account of the project was published in *Current Anthropology,* accompanied by numerous responses (Schiffer and House 1977a). That forum gives us an excellent vantage point from which to survey the CRM landscape as it appeared in the mid-'70s.

The contract that the Arkansas Archeological Survey signed with the Memphis District of the Corps of Engineers in 1973 called for a survey of the entire Cache River basin. The contract also required an assessment of the significance of any sites that were found, as well as recommendations for mitigating the impact that channeling the river would have on the archaeological record. One important feature of the project was its multistage research design, a concept that had been widely discussed in archaeology (e.g., Redman 1973b; Struever 1971) but rarely applied. Many archaeologists thought it should be avoided "lest one spoil the thrill of discovery" (Schiffer 1979b:8). "Multistage" meant literally what the name implied: fieldwork and analysis were to be structured in a series of stages, each building on the previous one.

Chuck Redman (1973b) identified four stages in this type of research design: general reconnaissance of a region; intensive survey and reconnaissance of (probabilistically) selected areas; controlled surface collections of selected sites; and finally, excavation of various sites chosen on the basis of surface indications. That surface artifacts often indicated good places to excavate had long been recognized, but several key studies in the late 1960s and '70s (Binford et al. 1970; Hanson and Schiffer 1975; Redman and Watson 1970; Roper 1976; Tolstoy and Fish 1973) investigated the precise nature of surface-subsurface relationships. Studies focusing on the surface record increased in number throughout the '70s (e.g., Thomas 1973, 1974), the majority of which took place in CRM contexts (Lewarch and O'Brien 1981; O'Brien and Lewarch 1981).

In large part because of the Cache Project,

the role of a research design in CRM had become clear by the late '70s (Goodyear, Raab, and Klinger 1978). Some projects were simply so large that a guide as to what to do first and what to do second was mandatory. More importantly, it was becoming evident that one simply could not excavate sites haphazardly and collect artifacts piecemeal and expect to have a set of data that allowed any but the most superficial research questions to be answered. If the archaeological record in a proposed reservoir area was to be effectively destroyed, and recovery of some information was the only thing that stood between total loss and something that might inform us about the past, then whatever was recovered damn well better inform us about something. Given that contract archaeology was generating a significant majority of the new data produced every year, those data had to be worthwhile substantively, theoretically, and/or methodologically from the perspective of the discipline *and* the managing agencies for whom the work was being done. Agencies were beginning to scrutinize what they were paying for, and if they didn't like what they saw in terms of getting their money's worth—as well as fulfilling legal mandates—then the contract program and all the money it brought to the discipline might be in jeopardy. Clear and explicit research designs were mandatory to maintaining the professionalism and credibility of the discipline.

One substantive area in which the Cache Project provided innovation was areal survey (House and Schiffer 1975a), although one critic pointed out serious flaws in the sampling design (Hole 1980). The project was not the first to confront the issue of regional sampling, and it certainly would not be the last, but the various topics that Schiffer and House considered in setting up their survey project had rarely been mentioned in the CRM literature. As discussed in Chapter 5, sampling in general was a topic of considerable interest in the late 1960s, especially with respect to techniques that were appropriate for obtaining representative samples of the archaeological record. No longer was it sufficient, for example, to dig a big hole in the center of a large site and plot variant artifact forms against their stratigraphic positions. Neither was it sufficient to walk casually across the landscape and call it surveying.

On the one hand, haphazard sampling procedures had been more or less standard prior to the '60s, when there had been little need to explain why you dug or surveyed the way you did. Processualists, on the other hand, were interested in a diverse array of other sorts of questions, many of which required sophisticated sampling designs (e.g., Plog, Plog, and Wait 1978; Schiffer, Sullivan, and Klinger 1978). As Stuart Struever (1971:14) put it, given the view of culture as an adaptive system, the key phrase is "structural differentiation" in the sense that different activities involving different people produce many and varied "quantitative and spatial relationships between various classes of archaeologically recoverable material remains."

The sampling issue became immediately germane in CRM because archaeologists realized that despite the protestations of federal agencies, reservoirs and other large project areas could not be surveyed completely at a high level of intensity. The agencies, however, were operating under the National Environmental Policy Act and Executive Order 11593, the latter calling for an inventory of *all* sites on federal lands by July 1, 1973. After that date, federal agencies would be out of compliance. Of course, the date was totally unrealistic. *Any* date would have been unrealistic, given that no agency could ever hope to identify every site—every trace of past human activity—on the lands under its jurisdiction.

In light of strict interpretation of the law, the original contract for work in the Cache Basin called for a complete survey of the sixty-five-

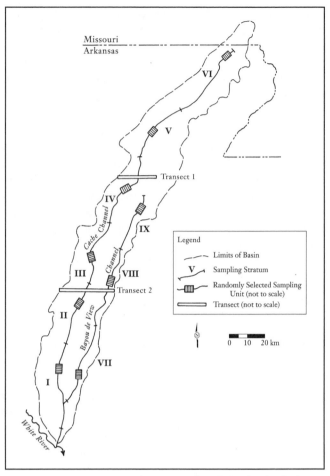

FIGURE 6.10. Survey-sampling design for the Cache River basin, northeastern Arkansas. (From House and Schiffer 1975a, courtesy Arkansas Archeological Survey.)

square-mile direct-impact zone as well as an estimate of resources in the indirect impact zone. Schiffer and House convinced the Corps of Engineers that they had neither the time nor the funding for such a survey and that a sample of sites in the region, if obtained correctly, would yield the needed information. The corps agreed, and an 11 percent survey was conducted in direct-impact and indirect-impact areas through a mix of different-size sampling units (House and Schiffer 1975a) (Figure 6.10). (The sampling design for the Cannon Reservoir Human Ecology Project in northeastern Missouri, mentioned in Chapter 5, was built on the Cache model.)

In producing the thirty-two-chapter final Cache Project report, Schiffer and House demonstrated that contract reports did not have to be dull reading. As Leland Ferguson (1977:289) pointed out in his review, "The report was open within itself to new ideas, as well as to an occasional point of mirth." Dan Morse (1975:113) even referred to Schiffer as a "gadfly." Ferguson (1977:289) pointed out that "here was a project that was fully and consciously open to both criticism and new ideas." This was true; it *was* open to both. The significance of the Cache Project was not simply in the novelty of its sampling or its demonstration that appropriate method and theory could be applied in a CRM situation; rather, it was in demonstrating that appropriate archaeological method and theory could be used as intelligent management tools.

Most archaeologists never doubted that good archaeology could be practiced under the rubric of CRM; what was entirely unclear in the 1970s was how to mesh disparate goals. The Cache Project was one of a number of CRM projects that by the mid-'70s were beginning to demonstrate that the two sets of goals could, at least conceivably, be meshed with a minimum of conflict. The majority of such projects were in the Southwest (e.g., Canouts 1972; Goodyear 1975; Raab 1976a), though another project by the Arkansas Archeological Survey, Pine Mountain (Raab 1976b), deserves consideration.

When Schiffer and House summarized the Cache Project in an article for *Current Anthropology,* the editor sent the piece to fifty people for comment and received responses from seventeen. Those responses were published alongside the article, and four additional responses were included in a subsequent issue. Various individuals quibbled with this point or that, but as a whole the responses to the article were positive. Several responses were from archaeologists in other countries faced with the same problems as their colleagues in the United States: working through bureaucracies in an effort to gather as much archaeological information as possible before sites were destroyed.

At least one respondent marveled at the amount of money that had been spent on the Cache Project compared to what was available in developing countries.

Several common themes emerged from the comments: (1) the Cache Project showed that CRM and anthropological research were compatible; (2) federal contract funds were becoming increasingly important sources of revenue for archaeologists, even though there were constraints on how the money could be spent; (3) the principles and methods of modern (processual) archaeology served both scientific and CRM interests better than traditional principles and methods did; (4) CRM was reactive but needed to become proactive in the sense of being incorporated into the planning phases of land-modification projects; (5) probabilistic sampling was a way around financial and temporal limitations of CRM projects; (6) CRM projects needed to incorporate multistage fieldwork; (7) the hydra of evaluating the significance of a cultural resource plagued all contract archaeology; (8) not all contracting agencies were as flexible as the Memphis office of the Corps of Engineers; (9) many reports resulting from contract archaeology saw limited circulation within the profession, creating what would become known as the "gray literature" (e.g., Brose 1985); and (10) archaeologists doing contract work must be cost efficient in their endeavors and not pad their budgets at the expense of the agency.

THE IMPACT OF CRM ON THE PROFESSION

All the issues raised by those who commented on the Cache Project became increasingly important in American archaeology. By the late 1970s all archaeologists were affected by CRM, regardless of whether they actually worked on contract-related projects. No longer could those who disdained CRM bury their heads in the sand; the ethical, legal, and pragmatic issues surrounding contract archaeology were ubiquitous. One issue that took center stage was communication. How were the numerous reports being generated through CRM to be distributed to researchers requiring the data? Not every project could be summarized in *Current Anthropology* as the Cache Project was. One of the Airlie House seminars in 1974 concerned the "crisis in communication." Participants noted that the "current mechanisms for communication among active participants in archaeology are something less than adequate" and that "a means must be developed whereby information is distributed or otherwise made available to the audience who needs it most" (McGimsey and Davis 1977:81, 83).

As a result of the so-called communication crisis, many university departments doing contract work initiated in-house publication series with titles such as "Reports of Investigations," "Occasional Papers in Archaeology," and "Anthropological Papers of the University of ____." Figure 6.11 shows the number of reports issued by the Arizona State Museum in its *Archaeological Series* from 1970 to 1977. The highest output was in 1975, when thirty reports were made available. But for several years—the period of rapid increase—the ASM had few if any competitors for archaeological contracts. By 1977 the situation had changed dramatically, hence the decline in the number of reports.

Several specialized journals were started as additional outlets of information. One of the more promising was *Contract Abstracts and CRM Archaeology* (later renamed *American Archeology*), first published in 1980. Like so many other start-up journals and monograph series, it was undercapitalized from the beginning and died later in the decade. Although these outlets helped to make data available, or at least publicized their availability, they were not the perfect solution. For one thing, the quality of reports was uneven, a result of the lack of peer review, which was recognized almost immediately (e.g., Longacre 1981a). But as one commentator noted, "[F]ield work is best not done at all unless it is destined to be published" (Hester 1981:494), even if in a nonreviewed series.

In his plenary address to the Society for American Archaeology in 1982, Colin Renfrew made the following comment:

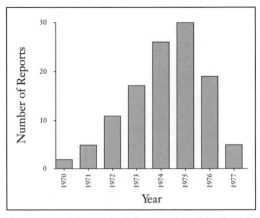

FIGURE 6.11. The number of reports issued by the Arizona State Museum in its *Archaeological Series* from 1970 to 1977. The highest output was in 1975, when thirty reports were made available. (After Schiffer 1979b.)

General Pitt Rivers firmly asserted that in archaeology a discovery dates from the time of its publication. I am criticizing a system, which the profession has allowed to grow up, where a CRM contract can legally be fulfilled by filing a private report with the contracting agency, or at best a limited-circulation report, without the obligation of real publication or of the adequate process of wide peer review which genuine publication automatically offers. By publication I mean the report is printed in an existing journal, or produced in a run of at least one hundred copies that are disseminated to the contracting body, the [state historic preservation office], relevant local and federal agencies, major libraries outside the state [where the work was done], and is publicly available for purchase. (Renfrew 1983:7)

Two years earlier, *American Antiquity* book review editor Ezra Zubrow had made a somewhat different observation.

The result of the numerous [new and old] local or in-house publishing outlets is a greater access to publishing than there has ever been before. Large amounts of archaeological work and data are now being reported. There is probably far less loss of data. Excavated, surveyed, or salvaged sites now are placed into a printed record rather than being simply in storage in some museum warehouse. On the other hand, there are disadvantages. These publications are so scattered and in so many different formats with such very limited distribution that one needs considerable luck and dedication to be able to find even those site reports which are most germane to one's own work. (Zubrow 1981:444)

And, Zubrow added, the *cost* of books was sky-rocketing. He found that the average price of an archaeological book submitted to *American Antiquity* for review had tripled between the 1965–69 period and the 1975–79 period, from a little less than six dollars to almost seventeen dollars.

The difficulty in keeping track of the increasing volume of archaeological literature in a single region prompted Lyman (1985, 1997; see Schmidt 1984) to suggest that the archaeology of the interior Pacific Northwest was "translucent," meaning that whereas one could dimly see a "shape" in the literature, it was impossible to pick out the "color" or "outline." Between 1960 and 1994, the percentage of what legitimately could be called "published" reports decreased from 100 percent to less than 8 percent, with the remaining percentage made up of small-run, in-house reports (15 percent) and unpublished reports (77 percent). One begins to understand the magnitude of the problem when one considers that an estimated 17,500 reports had been generated in Oregon alone by December 2000 (Gilsen 2001). Similar figures could be documented for any region of the United States. (As an important aside, what these statistics miss is the large number of non-CRM projects that were never reported. Academic archaeologists, with severely limited resources for analysis and report writing, had themselves often failed to bring projects to the publication stage.)

Not only did CRM increase the number of reports one had to produce, it dramatically increased the amount of *stuff* one had to contend

with: artifacts, maps, photographs, notes, and all the other documentation that typically accompany a field project of any duration. What was one to do with all these materials? A strategy of "no-collection"—make observations of artifacts in the field and leave them there—was typically, though not always, neither feasible nor scientifically sound (Butler 1979; see Beck and Jones 1994). Museums naturally were viewed as potential repositories for artifacts and records, but there were questions about their curation standards and whether they had adequate space (Christenson 1979b; Marquardt, Montet-White, and Scholtz 1982). Curation, it turns out, was much more than simply putting artifacts and notes in cardboard boxes and stacking them in a storage facility. Artifacts and accompanying documentation were public property and as such needed to be curated in perpetuity—a term that museum and university lawyers hate—and made accessible to interested scholars. Anyone who has done intensive archaeological analysis of collections made by someone else, regardless of whether the collections were generated under the auspices of CRM, will probably have horror stories about missing records and artifacts.

Growing concerns about curation became a key issue in what became known as *conservation archaeology*, a term that sheltered myriad aspects of resource management under its umbrella. Broadly speaking, conservation archaeology was a segment of resource management dealing with the development and implementation of measures to protect resources. The American Society for Conservation Archaeology was founded in 1974 to find ways to stabilize and preserve archaeological properties as opposed to excavating them. For example, instead of excavating a site on the edge of a reservoir, it might be protected by constructing a wing dam to divert waves from the shoreline or by covering the site with riprap. As the notion of conservation evolved, it began to include such things as curation. By the late 1970s, as archaeologists began to realize the ethical responsibilities that went along with CRM—that "management" didn't mean "rip it out of the ground"—conservation archaeology and CRM often were used synonymously (Schiffer and Gumerman 1977a).

The conservation ethic began to show up in journals, and in 1978 the new editor of *American Antiquity*, Jerry Sabloff, initiated a column that was meant to feature the personal opinions of the associate editor for current affairs or guest commentators who would address major issues in conservation archaeology. Sabloff also initiated a new section on CRM. He was succeeded as editor by Dena Dincauze in 1981, and she discontinued the section, suggesting that "it is appropriate to merge contributions which might be published there into the regular ARTICLES and REPORTS sections, in recognition of the integration of 'public archaeology' into the mainstream Americanist practice" (Dincauze 1981:467). She also changed the current affairs section to a "forum" to better reflect the trends and issues considered there.

In 1974 the newly constituted Association for Field Archaeology began to publish a quarterly journal, *Journal of Field Archaeology*, under the guidance of James Wiseman, a classical archaeologist at Boston University. Although its focus was on fieldwork, from the first issue the journal included a section, "The Antiquities Market," which provided "a forum for commentary on the illicit traffic in antiquities" (Wiseman 1974:2). In 1977 the journal added a new section with the long title "Preservation and Rescue: Challenges and Controversies in the Protection of Archaeological Resources." Tom King, the section editor, did not want to publish legislative updates or results of contract-sponsored research. Rather, he viewed the section as "a forum for the discussion of principles, major problems, methods, and, if you will, particular aspects of theory" as well as "peculiarities of preservation or rescue work" (King 1977a:473). He listed five types of material he considered appropriate for inclusion:

1. articles on planning, political, organizational, and technical problems bearing on preservation and rescue, including both articles that deal with such problems in the abstract and case studies;

2. articles dealing with the history of archeology-in-the-public-service, through time and in different places;

3. articles on techniques that are particularly applicable to preservation and rescue work, ranging from an improved method for communicating research results to an improved method for the deployment of bulldozers;

4. articles on method and theory: we need to keep in mind that working with reference to public laws and emergency situations often make us re-think our basic concepts about how archaeology ought to be done; and

5. challenges and controversies: presentations of, and responses to, issues and opinions about preservation and rescue matters. (King 1977a:473)

King's section lasted through the 1982 volume. Our favorite article was a short piece, "The Archeologist as Cowboy: The Consequence of Professional Stereotype," by Ned Woodall (an archaeologist) and Philip Perricone (a sociologist), both of Wake Forest University. Woodall and Perricone (1981:506) argued that archaeology "has created a body of myths, legends, and culture heroes serving to generate a self-image. Essentially, this image shows the rugged individual laboring under hardships others could not or would not accept, wresting a romantic prize from the forces of destruction, be they federal agencies, pot hunters, or the Dim Mists of Antiquity." The lone individual displays resourcefulness, energy, and a certain degree of *machismo* characterized by hard drinking, a beard, cowboy boots, and jeans. More importantly, "archeologists *did* things— more precisely, they dug sites" (Woodall and Perricone 1981:507). In stark contrast, preservationists typically were portrayed in archaeology as wealthy older females, a stereotype out of the late nineteenth and early twentieth centuries. Woodall and Perricone urged archaeologists to dispel the myth of the cowboy and to get down to the business of conservation and preservation.

THE IMPACT OF CRM ON METHOD AND THEORY

We suspect that the impact of CRM on archaeological method and theory is obvious, but maybe it is worth summarizing a few of the more important changes that were ushered in. The first had to do with the scale and intensity of archaeological surveys. Although Executive Order 11593, which mandated the inventory of all cultural resources on federal lands, was manifestly impossible to carry out, several federal landholding agencies, including the National Park Service and the Forest Service, took some important steps toward complying. The resultant surveys were, by the standards of previous academic studies, quite large scale. The National Environmental Policy Act also required a large number of surveys. The combined effect of EO 11593 and NEPA was immediately to highlight some of the shortcomings of method, theory, and techniques for conducting surveys. For example, archaeologists had routinely avoided doing intensive (close-interval) surveys in forests because of the obvious barriers to visibility and accessibility. However, when presented with large tracts of forested lands that under federal law needed to be surveyed, archaeologists began to experiment with new or previously underutilized survey techniques such as shovel testing, coring, and remote sensing (e.g., Alexander 1983; Connolly and Baxter 1983; Krakker, Shott, and Welch 1983; Lightfoot 1986, 1989; Lovis 1976; Lynch 1980; McManamon 1984; Nance 1979; Shott 1985, 1989; Wobst 1983).

Each survey in such an environment was an experiment, and the accumulating totality of the experiments increased our knowledge about the appropriateness of various techniques in specific environmental situations (Ammerman 1981; Kintigh 1988). Large-scale surveys also furnished the opportunity to conduct experiments with various probability-sampling techniques, which disclosed their strengths and limitations, and to employ relatively new techniques of computer-assisted analyses. Together, the vast increase in the number and sizes of surveys and the willingness of archaeologists to try out different techniques and methods furnished the basis for new formulations of survey method and theory (e.g., Banning 2000, 2002; Nance 1983; Nance and Ball 1986; Schiffer, Sullivan, and Klinger 1978; Schiffer and Wells 1982). Indeed, much of what has been said in textbooks (e.g., Dancey 1981; Rathje and Schiffer 1982; Thomas 1989) about the design of large-scale surveys draws upon experience gained in CRM projects.

One of the things that came out of the emphasis placed on surveys by the dictates of CRM was a better appreciation for what had long been an overlooked part of the archaeological record. Archaeologists came to realize that much of the record consisted of small artifact scatters—a class of phenomena that had always held second-class status to sites that were, as Dunnell (1992c:26) put it, "homogeneous artifact mines." These mines were places where chronological orderings could be constructed and typological systems formulated, which meant that as long as those were the goals of archaeology, small sites would be bypassed completely. This changed as archaeologists were forced to manage resources and to determine what made a site significant (e.g., Talmage and Chesler 1977). Many traditional archaeologists, especially those who had experience in earlier salvage archaeology, had a difficult time with these issues, but to the younger processualists they were ripe for exploitation. Two interrelated topics that filled the journals during the 1980s and early '90s were the small survey (e.g., Aldenderfer and Hale-Pierce 1984; Miller 1984) and what came to be known as "siteless survey," or "off-site survey" (e.g., Davis 1975; Dunnell and Dancey 1983; Foley 1981; Lewarch and O'Brien 1981; O'Brien and Lewarch 1981; Thomas 1975; Wandsnider and Camilli 1992).

Because many of the mitigative excavations, carried out in increasingly larger numbers beginning in the mid-1970s, sought to conform to the multidisciplinary emphasis of the new archaeology, they created an insistent demand for analytical specialists. Given the availability of project funds to support such analyses, many students became geoarchaeologists, paleoethnobotanists, zooarchaeologists, and so on. Previously these specialists had been scarce, had been based in other disciplines, and had often donated their services. Increasingly, specialists developed knowledge bases more appropriate for handling archaeological materials and human-affected environments. The overall employment opportunities provided by CRM projects made it possible for the discipline to support, for the first time, large numbers of specialists who succeeded in extracting ever-more behavioral information from ecofacts such as seeds, bones, and sediments. Augmenting a small genre of earlier manuals (e.g., Shepard 1956) was a proliferation of specialized manuals and textbooks for analyzing various kinds of material that comes from the ground (e.g., Hayden 1979). Today, such reference works, which cover both the analysis of materials (e.g., Adovasio 1977; Andrefsky 1998; Bass 1995; Behrensmeyer and Hill 1980; Dibble and Shott 2004; Gilbert 1990; Gilbert, Martin, and Savage 1981; Hurley 1979; Pearsall 2001; Piperno and Pearsall 1998; Reitz and Wing 1999; Rice 1987; Whittaker 1994) as well as the contexts in which they occur (e.g., Albarella 2001; Butzer 1971; Dincauze 2000; Holliday 1993; Stein and Farrand 2001; Waters 1997), number in the dozens.

A final point: because CRM projects forced archaeologists to visit places they might ordinarily have avoided, and to excavate sites they might have preferred to ignore, the complete range of variability in archaeological materials began coming to light in many areas, especially those that had previously been little studied by academic projects. Indeed, the prehistory of many areas, such as the Southwest (e.g., Crown and Judge 1991), was rewritten on the basis of the rich information provided by contract archaeology projects. This greater appreciation for variability in the archaeological record, and in the cultural behavior that created it, is continually redounding in the development of new archaeological theory for explaining variability and change.

After more than a decade of grappling with implementing the intent (if not the letter) of various federal laws, American archaeologists by 1980 had learned a lot about managing archaeological resources—or at least about how the federal government, and in many cases state governments, wanted them managed. It had become clear that to do public archaeology—a term brought into mainstream archaeology by Bob McGimsey (1972; but see McGimsey 1989 and Little 2002)—demanded more than simply the sound application of archaeological methods and explanatory models. It demanded that an archaeologist know more than the length of a 2 x 2-meter unit's diagonal and how to excavate square holes. An archaeologist had to be a little of many things, including an accountant, a lawyer, a politician, a publicist, a business manager, and a social worker. And it was clear, as Tom King (1983) pointed out, that an archaeologist had enormous responsibilities—to the archaeological record (don't mess with it unless absolutely necessary), to colleagues (don't denigrate them as you compete for contract monies [unless, of course, it is done in retaliation]), to the profession (if you collect information, make it publicly available), to contractors and clients (provide them with useful management recommendations), to the law (obey the statutes), and to the public (they deserve to know about their nation's cultural heritage). The latter includes groups whose ancestors created the items that formed the archaeological record. Anyone who has worked in public archaeology knows that efforts to behave ethically toward one of these entities will perhaps result in unethical behavior toward another. It is indeed a fine line one walks in doing public archaeology. And yet what is seldom appreciated even today is that an archaeologist who obtains research funds from the National

Science Foundation or Wenner-Gren has exactly the same ethical obligations as someone who makes a living from contract archaeology.

The complexion of CRM began to change after 1980. The number of large-scale projects declined significantly from the level of the mid- to late '70s. Rising to take their place were literally tens of thousands of smaller contracts that ranged anywhere from road and street repair, to runway-extension projects, to the construction of public housing. There was a similar rise in the number of private firms that actively bid on archaeological contracts. Although we have no hard figures to back up this claim, we guess that the number of private archaeological contracting companies quadrupled from the 1970s to the 1980s. There was still plenty of money to be made, and the scaling back in size of the projects actually made it easier for the smaller firms to survive. They had found their niche, and it was defined by the $10,000 survey project and the $100,000 excavation project.

Many of the larger companies active in the highly competitive archaeology market of the '80s were engineering and environmental-assessment firms that had expanded their staffs in the '70s to include archaeologists. They could withstand some of the heat generated from the fierce competition for archaeological projects and also carry their archaeologists through lean periods. However, many of the firms whose only business was archaeology could not weather the downturns and either folded or at-tached themselves to other private concerns. Many small colleges and universities that had geared up in the '70s for what appeared to be an unending supply of outside funding also were hard hit as a result of the fierce competition, and most of them abandoned their contract archaeology programs in the '80s.

No matter on which side of the contract fence a person stood, the archaeology of the 1970s and '80s was different than that of the '60s. Contract archaeologists and noncontract archaeologists alike recognized the importance of research designs and sampling, although as we saw in Chapter 5, sophistication in such things as probability sampling and multivariate analysis often lagged well behind good intentions. Archaeologists, regardless of stripe, had long depended on analogy, especially ethnographic analogy, for their models. The arguments over the proper use of analogy that took place in the '60s were mere warm-ups for those that took place later. By the late '70s everyone had something to say about analogy, or so it seemed. Similarly, everyone seemed to be talking about behavior, both present and prehistoric. Behavior certainly was not a new topic in archaeology, but it was one that was at best implicit in the formulations of traditionalists and the early processualists. That would change as a handful of processualists fought to make the study of behavior the centerpiece of the new archaeology. It is to these issues that we turn in Chapter 7.

7

Home on the Middle Range

Scientific ideas compete in an open market-place. Each offers the possibility of a plausible solution to what might be a potentially significant problem. In its promise, an idea will attract other scientists—fellow explorers who will articulate, criticize, and ultimately determine the ideas' actuality. While these explorers can breathe life into an idea, their absence or defection leads to its death. Ideas without recruits become like Bishop Berkeley's proverbial unheard falling tree.

—DAVID L. KRANTZ AND LYNDA WIGGINS, "Personal and Impersonal Channels of Recruitment in the Growth of Theory"

This quote, gleaned from David Hull's (1988b) *Science as a Process*, is an excellent summary of the role that ideas play in science. Ideas compete in an open marketplace, and each offers the possibility (often phrased as a promise) of a plausible solution to a scientific problem. And without recruits, ideas die. As good a summary as the quote is, however, something basic is missing—a description of *how* ideas compete. In a make-believe world, scientific ideas would sit side by side like contestants in a beauty pageant, going through their routines, waiting for the judges (scientists) to cast their votes. So many points for poise, so many for answering questions correctly, and so on. Scores are based on individual merit, mean-

ing that nothing one contestant does directly affects another's score.

But in the real world, scientific ideas do not sit idly by. They want to win, and they don't mind taking matters into their own "hands." And they're devious in how they go about trying to win—tripping their opponents, feeding them misinformation, and even making up lies about them if it will help. Of course, scientific ideas have "hands" only in a metaphorical sense. They need assistance in carrying out their mischief—assistance in the form of a vehicle (Dawkins 1982; Hull 1988a) that both nourishes them and transports them from place to place. Those vehicles are scientists. Evolution has shaped individuals of our species to be excellent carriers of ideas.

Over evolutionary time, ideas have co-opted their vehicles, getting people to do their bidding—the tripping, the feeding of misinformation, and so on. To be successful, ideas need their vehicles not only to fight against vehicles carrying opposing ideas but also to recruit third-party vehicles, those not yet involved in the struggle. Vehicles recruit by bringing the ideas they carry into close proximity to a third-party vehicle and attempting to communicate with it. If things work out to an idea's advantage, an exact copy (or, because of some slight communication error, a more-or-less accurate facsimile) becomes embedded in the new vehicle. This kind of transfer characterizes all social learning, not just the learning of science. The newly recruited vehicle then recruits other vehicles, and so on, in an expanding, branching network. Winners and losers among scientific ideas are determined by the number of vehicles (scientists) that wind up carrying one particular idea as opposed to those carrying its competitors.

Lew Binford understood the recruitment process. Early in his career he used personal as well as professional means to attract and inculcate novitiates (Chapter 2). He influenced a generation of young scholars at Chicago, and by the end of the 1960s had recruited other students at Santa Barbara, UCLA, and the University of New Mexico. He was charismatic in the classroom and delighted in attracting students away from the traditional ways of doing archaeology and toward an anthropological archaeology. But as processualism evolved out of its early mold and started moving in directions different than those Binford had in mind, he began to feel like some of the traditionalists must have felt in the early '60s as they were pushed aside by the young processualists. Binford wasn't happy when his acolytes grew up and started their own recruiting efforts. And yet, ironically, if he had trained them well, this was exactly what they were supposed to do.

As discussed in Chapter 4, Binford played almost no role in setting the direction of American archaeology during the early '70s, when processualists were immersed in philosophy and discussions over the structure of science. In our opinion, the period from roughly 1970 to 1977 was the low point of Binford's career. He published few articles (e.g., Binford 1972c, 1973), and the two books that came out were a collection of his published essays (Binford 1972a) and a collection of articles by his students (Binford 1977a). As Binford (1983b) tells it, he withdrew from the Society for American Archaeology in the early '70s after the editor of *American Antiquity* rejected his reply to Patrick Munson's (1969) comment on his smudge-pit article (Binford 1967). Jerry Sabloff persuaded Binford to rejoin the SAA in 1978, by which time he was beginning to emerge from

his self-imposed exile and to reclaim territory he had staked out in the '60s.

Binford found the theoretical landscape to be very different than the one he had left a few years earlier. Competitive approaches had risen to challenge some of the basic processualist tenets Binford had laid out in the '60s. The competitors varied, but they had a common origin in earlier discussions on the proper use of uniformitarianism, ethnoarchaeology, experimental archaeology, and ethnographic analogy (Chapter 5). The discussions became more sophisticated and philosophically informed throughout the '70s and into the '80s, at which point a young philosopher of archaeology, Alison Wylie, joined in. Binford would jump into the discussions in the late '70s by pointing out what he saw as a problem with using ethnographic analogy: shoehorning the archaeological record into the ethnographic present. He would quickly introduce a new concept— middle-range theory (Binford 1977b)—as a means of translating a static archaeological record into a dynamic cultural system. But, more importantly, middle-range theory served as a recruiting tool that co-opted some of his critics.

The proper use of analogy was not the only issue raised by challengers to processualism. Ethnoarchaeological observation and experimental archaeology undertaken during the '60s had led not only to an increased understanding of how the archaeological record is formed but also to a concern that these formation processes were being ignored. The first person to voice the issue in more than an anecdotal sense was Robert Ascher (1968), who observed that the archaeological record is in a continuous process of deterioration and disorganization. Ethnoarchaeological studies published during the '70s were beginning to demonstrate that the archaeological record might not be a direct reflection of cultural processes and human behavior. If true, this would be an obvious threat to Binford's program. He had claimed as early as 1962 in "Archaeology as Anthropology" that the "formal structure of artifact assemblages together with the between element contextual relationships should and do present a systematic and understandable picture of *the total extinct* cultural system" (Binford 1962a:219). His fieldwork in the '70s, for example in Alaska (Figures 7.1 and 7.2), was based on that claim. What would happen if, to borrow a statistical metaphor, the correlation coefficient between the archaeological record and past cultural processes was significantly less than one?

What became known as formation-process studies grew throughout the 1970s, largely in the hands of Schiffer and other archaeologists at the University of Arizona. This eventually led to a debate between Binford and Schiffer regarding the relationship of the archaeological record to past human activities. Schiffer and others argued that without an understanding of formation processes, both natural and cultural, it was improper to assume that the record accurately reflected human behavior. Archaeologists sometimes paid lip service to natural processes, but little or no effort had ever been expended in trying to understand the complex relationships between human activities of interest, cultural formation processes, and specific artifact patterns. "Behavioral archaeology" took the investigation of formation processes and the codification of their regularities (in the form of models, theories, and laws) as one of its first missions. Reconceptualizing the relationship between past behavioral systems and their archaeological records was one of the first real challenges to Binford's program, and he had too much at stake intellectually not to combat an effort to steer archaeology in directions that he himself had not set.

In some ways the period from the mid-1970s to the early '80s was one of the most interesting in American archaeology. By the beginning of that period, processualism had evolved into a mature approach, albeit not a fully unified one. Gone was some of the polemic that had characterized earlier discussions over science and the scientific method, as processualists settled down to the more difficult job of seeking laws as opposed to writing about how to discover them. But any sense that processualism would become more unified as laws were discovered was illusory. By the end of the period—say, 1983—processualism had been fractured into several pieces. It's easy to say it now, given the marvels of hindsight, but such fracturing was predictable because by the mid-1970s American archaeology had become a highly competitive marketplace for ideas.

Processual archaeology itself had grown out of such a marketplace in the early 1960s when Binford did his first serious recruiting. It was predictable that other recruiters would come along and vie for their own recruits. As we will see, two of the most high-profile recruiters of the '70s and '80s were Kent Flannery and Bill Sanders, neither of whom was tied to the tenets of Binfordian processualism, although Flannery came closer than Sanders. Whereas Binford and the behavioralists (Schiffer, in particular) were fighting over one set of recruits, Flannery and Sanders were jousting over another. With one exception, and it was a glaring one, none of the four combatants particularly cared what was going on outside his immediate contest. That exception, as we will see, was Flannery.

THE COMPETITIVE MARKETPLACE OF PROCESSUAL ARCHAEOLOGY

Lew Binford made a strategic error in the early 1970s: he gave back a lot of hard-won ground. He did this because he ignored a maxim that he had followed zealously in the '60s: Those who control the media of intellectual interaction have the best chance of attracting the most recruits. One medium is personal encounters—those made at professional meetings, in the classroom, and so forth. As important as networking might be in some fields, it is overrated in science. We are not implying that it has no value—who hasn't heard of people getting jobs through "the old-boy (or old-girl) network"—but personal encounters are nowhere near as important in science as are print media such as books and journals. But of transcendent importance are works that have undergone peer review prior to publication. In science, and the same is true in the humanities, what matters is not the sheer number of pages one publishes but the number of pages carrying the imprimatur

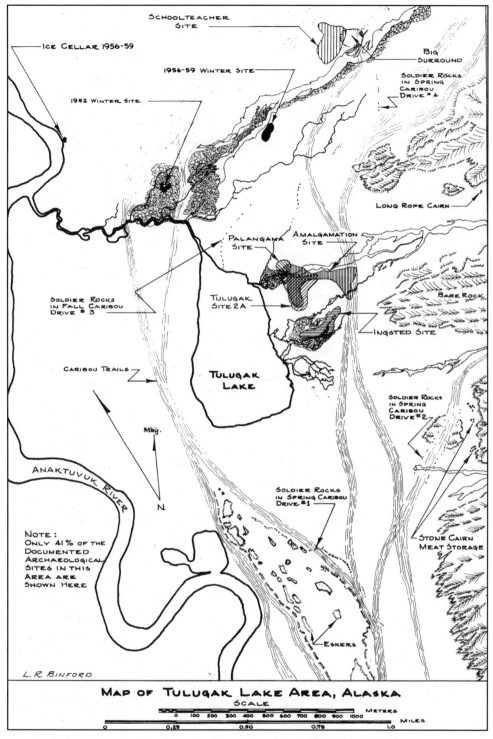

FIGURE 7.1. Map of the Tulugak Lake area, Alaska, made by Lewis Binford, showing some of the sites examined during his ethnoarchaeological fieldwork in the early 1970s. One goal of Binford's project was to investigate how hunters (here, caribou hunters) moved across the landscape in search of food. (From Binford 1983d.)

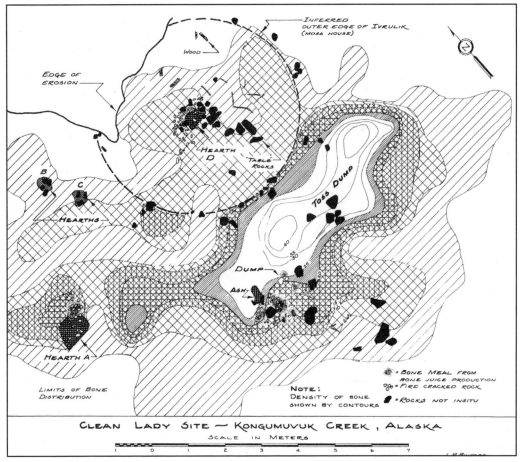

FIGURE 7.2. Plan map of the Clean Lady site, Kongumuvuk Creek, Alaska, made by Lewis Binford, 1971. In addition to investigating how hunters moved across the landscape in search of food, Binford was interested in how those hunters used their "lifespace"—for example, where within an encampment people cooked, ate, and discarded food remains. (From Binford 1983d.)

of one's professional colleagues. And that imprimatur can be gained only through the peer review, or refereeing, process.

No editor could possibly know everything about a field, and so he or she counts heavily on reviewers to help determine the veracity of an author's claims. This practice of farming out submissions to specialists was established in science (then called natural philosophy) by the Royal Society of London at the end of the seventeenth century. Then as now, when an article or book is published in a respected outlet, it means that two, three, or sometimes more reviewers have read the original submission (or a revised version) and found it acceptable. This

carries significant prestige for the author. If other scientists cite the paper, it enhances the author's prestige. Scientists (and their ideas) live on in citations by other scientists. Citations, of course, can mean someone is either acknowledging something of value in a publication or criticizing the work. One might prefer to have the former, but the latter means that at least the work has been noticed. Invisibility in the scientific literature signifies the death of an idea.

Publication means more than prestige. Often it is closely connected with the issue of promotion and remuneration and, especially, tenure, which more or less guarantees a faculty member a lifetime contract, regardless of whether that person ever publishes another article or book. (As our colleague Mike Shott [2004:36] put it, "[T]enure review focuses many minds, but the granting of tenure relaxes some of them.") Thus, achieving tenure becomes the single most important goal in the life of a young academician. Everything that he or she does during the probationary period—typically six years—is, or should be, directed toward that goal. Without tenure, no matter how good one's ideas are, he or she won't be around to pass them on in the academy, where so much recruitment takes place. People denied tenure may get a position somewhere else—Binford, after being denied tenure at Chicago, was hired at Santa Barbara—but this is unusual. Competition is just too fierce to allow many second chances.

The tenure decision rests to a large degree on the number of peer-reviewed publications one has. At major research universities, especially today, non-peer-reviewed publications count for little or nothing, although the rules at some universities were less demanding in the early 1970s. From the standpoint of personal fitness, it is counterproductive to put a lot of time and effort into reports that will have little or no influence on the discipline. A first-rate report that only ten or fifteen people see, let alone read, cannot help one's tenure case. Even if thousands of people read the report, it may not matter unless it was peer reviewed. Conversely, peer review is no guarantee that a journal or book series has a wide distribution—or that a particular article or book will be read by more than a few people. Even so, it carries an inestimable weight in the scientific community *because* it is peer reviewed (Bloom 1999; Maddox 1989).

Now we can begin to see the root of a major problem facing American archaeology in the 1970s—the lack of useful reports on contract-based projects. This was not a new problem; it had been recognized back in the days of the River Basin Surveys (Jennings 1985). Knowing what we now know, shouldn't it have been obvious that there was going to be a problem?

What incentive did someone have to produce a CRM report that met more than minimum contract requirements? We're not arguing that there wasn't an ethical issue involved; an archaeologist took money for a service and was obligated to turn in a report. Most archaeologists did, in fact, turn in reports, if for no reason other than to ensure access to future contracts. In the contract world, contractors who consistently failed to meet their responsibilities were blacklisted and might never receive another contract. But there are reports, and then there are reports. A person could discharge his or her contractual obligations and still produce a report nearly useless from an archaeological standpoint. Some departments and research units, such as the Arkansas Archeological Survey, began sending manuscripts out for peer review in an effort to overcome the stigma attached to non-refereed reports, but without much success.

Despite the importance placed on peer-reviewed publishing, faculty members at research universities are supposed to be good at several other things, such as training graduate students and teaching undergraduates. These activities have some worth from the standpoint of intellectual fitness. Graduate students are especially important in recruitment activities because, given certain enculturation strategies, they have the potential to become one's intellectual clones. Robert Boyd and Peter Richerson (1985) provide an excellent discussion of the kinds of information transmission that can go on between teacher and student. Undergraduate students are potential recruits as well, but on average they are not as sophisticated as graduate students and require more background information. Also, most of them disappear after graduation. But even graduate students require information as well as inculcation. This takes time.

The question becomes, where does one invest his or her time so as to maximize intellectual fitness? Which efforts will potentially yield the most recruits, who themselves will attract recruits? It doesn't do any good to attract recruits if your ideas die with them. They have to go out and spread the ideas for the system to work. Binford might not have had to think too hard about which effort would yield the greatest return, because during the 1960s he was firing on all cylinders—in print, in the classroom, and at meetings—and there were no viable competitors except traditionalists. But for us mere mortals who lack Binford's genius and energy (not to mention his charisma), peer-reviewed publishing is the clear investment choice. This sounds crassly careerist, but we think it is a true picture of immensely productive people whose very identities are bound up with their academic accomplishments.

With respect to publishing, Binford found out in the early 1970s the power that journal editors have. That power is manifest in such things as enlarging or constraining the production of knowledge (Shanks and Tilley 1989). Edwin Wilmsen, who had received his Ph.D. at the University of Arizona under Bill Longacre's tutelage and then joined the faculty at the University of Michigan, assumed the editorship of *American Antiquity* in 1970. He welcomed processual papers, seemingly the more radical the better, which often dismayed traditionalists, but he was also the editor who rejected Binford's response to Pat Munson's (1969) smudge-pit article. When referring to the rejected manuscript, Binford (1983b:19) pointed out that "[t]he new editor had just started a policy of peer review. My article was sent out for review and returned with a rejection notice plus copies of the comments from my 'peers.' One reviewer went on and on about how I was only motivated to prove myself right, concluding that my discussion had no intellectual merit. Another said that 'finally' someone had put me in my place and that I was just trying to wiggle my way out of a 'clear intellectual defeat.' I appealed to the editor but to no avail[.] I thought it clearly unfair to publish an answer to my article but to refuse to publish my reply."

Binford had a good point, but even replies to replies should be vetted in the arena of peer review. Most journals do blind reviewing, which means that an author is not supposed to know who reviewed an article unless the reviewer drops his or her anonymity. The purpose of this system is to allow the reviewer to present an honest opinion without fear of retribution or fear of ruining a friendship, although reviewers sometimes hide behind anonymity to take cheap shots at a rival (see Hammond 1984). This is why reputable journals need tough-minded editors who will overrule reviewers when needed. Oftentimes an author can identify a reviewer, especially when the latter includes a list of references that should be added to the paper under review. The reviewer is almost certainly on that list, perhaps the one whose name appears most often. Conversely, some journals have tried to make the entire process anonymous by removing the author's name from copies sent to reviewers. *American Anthropologist* did this in the 1980s. The author of the article was always easy to spot, using the same reasoning as above: the person with the most citations in the list of references was usually the author.

We were surprised to learn that papers in *American Antiquity* did not undergo formal peer review prior to Wilmsen's tenure as editor, although a later editor, Jeff Reid, had pointed it out in one of his editorials (Reid 1990). Regardless, it has been the leading journal in American archaeology since it was founded in 1935 as the official publication of the Society for American Archaeology. In a way, the fact that four of Binford's early articles were published in *American Antiquity* is all the more remarkable because Binford didn't have the option of suggesting other budding processualists as possible reviewers. But neither did he have to suffer insults at the hands of reviewers. His first three articles were published under the editorship of Tom Campbell (University of Texas) and the fourth under that of Robert Bell (University of Oklahoma). Both editors were traditionalists, and although they may not have agreed with Binford's arguments, they were intellectually generous enough to give him his say.

Prior to the founding of *American Antiquity* in 1935, *American Anthropologist* published the majority of American archaeology papers, and it continued to publish them after *American Antiquity* came along. Leslie Spier started the *Southwestern Journal of Anthropology* at the University of New Mexico in 1945, not as a competitor to *American Anthropologist* but as another outlet to serve the ever-growing number of anthropologists in the United States (the name was changed to the *Journal of Anthropological Research* in 1973). Both *American Anthropologist* and the *Southwestern Journal of Anthropology* carried early processual-archaeology articles by Binford and other Chicago processualists. So did the prestigious journal *Science*.

American Antiquity changed editors at irregular intervals, although by the 1970s the usual term was approximately three years. Potential editors made their interests in the job known to the executive committee of the SAA, which then selected an editor from among the applicants. Frank Hole took over from Wilmsen in 1974. In his first editorial, Hole (1974) pointed out that his policy would be to accept articles that were of general interest, that were theoretically and methodologically sound, and that were well written. Hole also noted that he would be happy to receive comments and suggestions concerning the operation of the journal. One suggestion he received had never been tried: the production of special issues, using guest editors who would be in charge of picking articles and seeing them through the review process. Hole agreed to do this, and two special issues were produced—one edited by Brian Fagan and Barbara Voorhies, "Essays on Archaeological Problems" (1977), in honor of Albert Spaulding; and the other one edited by Schiffer, "Contributions to Archaeological Method and Theory" (1978).

Schiffer had been critical of the direction he saw the journal beginning to take during Hole's editorship, and Hole gave him the chance to right that perceived wrong—almost an unheard of gesture in science generally and certainly in archaeology specifically. Predictably, Schiffer's issue was filled with articles by processualists and those who could fit in that camp without too much trouble, including Robert Dunnell, George Gumerman, Jim Hill, Steve Plog, Colin Renfrew, Stanley South, and Dave Thomas. The issue also carried an article on systems theory by Merrilee Salmon and one on "archaeo-ethnology" by Martin Wobst. In addition, it contained an article by Eugene Sterud, "Changing Aims of Americanist Archaeology: A Citations Analysis of *American Antiquity*—1946–1975." Sterud (1978) claimed that the citation analysis showed the impact that processual archaeology had had on the discipline—at least based on the number of processual articles cited in articles appearing in *American Antiquity*. In a rebuttal to Sterud's claim, Roger Cribb (1980) suggested that perhaps the journal did not simply reflect changing emphases in American archaeology, but rather was leading those changes by providing a forum in which methodological and theoretical issues could be aired. This, of course, is what Schiffer was claiming had *not* happened most recently, hence Frank Hole's turning over the reins to him for an issue.

Not content with this opportunity to nudge the discipline back to where he thought it should be heading, Schiffer that same year initiated an annual volume of papers titled *Advances in Archaeological Method and Theory*, published by Academic Press. The purpose of the series was to help "identify what archaeology is and is not," based on its efforts to serve as a medium for "distilling and disseminating progressive explorations in method and theory" (Schiffer 1978b:xiii). *Advances* morphed into *Archaeological Method and Theory* in 1987 when it moved to the University of Arizona Press, and then into the quarterly *Journal of Archaeological Method and Theory* when it moved to Plenum Publishing in 1994. One reason for the early success of *Advances* was its unique format. Authors were discouraged from submitting articles on narrow topics. Instead, they were encouraged to take a topic—regional survey, for example—and to present a state-of-the-art discussion of it. The series became known as an encyclopedia of current archaeological method and theory—not that the volumes necessarily pleased everyone (e.g., Hole 1979).

Academic Press began publishing two other archaeological journals—*Advances in World Archaeology* and the *Journal of Anthropological Archaeology*—in 1982. *Advances* lasted until only 1987, whereas *JAA* is still being published. In an editorial that appeared in the first issue of *JAA*, Bob Whallon (1982:1) stated that "anthropological archaeology aims primarily to explain the organization, operation, and evolution of human cultural systems" and that the goal of the journal was to "serve as a focus for contributions to theory and methodology in archaeology." It seemed method and theory were on everyone's mind in the 1970s and '80s, and Academic Press took advantage of it. Note that two of the three journals were in the hands of editors—without defined term limits—who had studied under Binford. Advocates of processualism, in several variants, were now in control of major archaeological journals.

Academic Press was not satisfied to publish only journals. Between 1971 and about 1985 the press more or less owned the archaeology market in terms of the books that people were buying, reading, and citing. During that period Academic Press published 132 volumes (Table 7.1), most of them in one of three series dealing with prehistoric archaeology and a fourth dealing with historical archaeology. The peak output occurred in 1982, when 18 volumes were published (Figure 7.3). The first series (under the earlier imprint Seminar Press) was titled "Studies in Archaeological Science." The other three were the "New World Archaeological Record" series, with Jimmy Griffin as consulting editor; "Studies in Archaeology," with Stuart Struever as consulting editor; and "Studies in Historical Archaeology," with Stan South (Figure 7.4) as consulting editor. Impor-

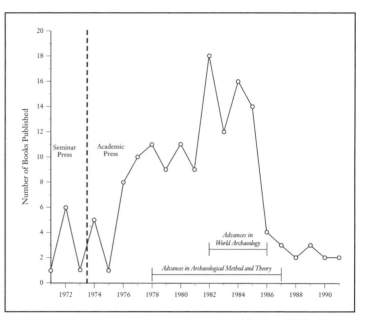

FIGURE 7.3. Annual number of books published by Academic Press for the period 1971–1991. Also shown are the life spans of the Academic Press journals *Advances in World Archaeology* and *Advances in Archaeological Method and Theory*. Academic Press began life as Seminar Press and changed names after 1973.

FIGURE 7.4. Stanley South at the Spanish colonial town of Santa Elena (1566–1587), Parris Island, South Carolina, 1997. (Courtesy Stanley South.)

tantly, Academic Press employed peer review in the selection of volumes to publish.

The willingness of a major commercial publisher to produce volumes on archaeological research, many of which were both data oriented as well as method and theory oriented,

Table 7.1. Volumes on Archaeology Published by Academic Press, 1971–1991

1971 (Seminar Press)
The Study of Animal Bones from Archaeological Sites, by R. E. Chaplin

1972 (Seminar Press)
An Archaeological Perspective, by L. R. Binford
Land Snails In Archaeology, by J. G. Evans
Public Archeology, by C. R. McGimsey III
Methods of Physical Examination in Archaeology, by M. S. Tite
The Aztecs, Maya, and Their Predecessors: Archaeology of Mesoamerica, by M. P. Weaver
Ancient Skins, Parchments and Leathers, by R. Reed

1973 (Seminar Press)
Dating Methods in Archaeology, by J. W. Michels

1974 (Academic Press, subsequently)
The Casper Site: A Hell Gap Bison Kill on the High Plains, edited by G. C. Frison
The Study of Prehistoric Change, by F. T. Plog
The Stone Age Archaeology of Southern Africa, by C. G. Sampson
Archaeology of the Mammoth Cave Area, edited by P. J. Watson
Neolithic Cultures of Western Asia, by P. Singh

1975
Soil Science and Archaeology, by S. Limbrey

1976
Fish Remains in Archaeology and Paleo-environmental Studies, by R. W. Casteel
Cultural Change and Continuity: Essays in Honor of James Bennett Griffin, edited
  by C. E. Cleland
The Early Mesoamerican Village, edited by K. V. Flannery
Hunter–Gatherer Subsistence and Settlement: A Predictive Model, by M. A. Jochim
Behavioral Archeology, by M. B. Schiffer
Prehistory of the Nile Valley, by F. Wendorf and R. Schild
Prehistoric Man and His Environments: A Case Study in the Ozark Highland,
  edited by W. R. Wood and R. B. McMillan
Hillforts: Later Prehistoric Earthworks in Britain and Ireland, edited by D. W. Harding

1977
European Towns: Their Archaeology and Early History, edited by M. W. Barley
*For Theory Building in Archaeology: Essays on Faunal Remains, Aquatic Resources,
  Spatial Analysis, and Systemic Modeling*, edited by L. R. Binford
Exchange Systems in Prehistory, edited by T. K. Earle and J. E. Ericson
The Individual in Prehistory: Studies of Variability in Style in Prehistoric Technology, edit-
  ed by J. N. Hill and J. Gunn
Anthropology in Historic Preservation: Caring for Culture's Clutter, by T. F. King,
  P. P. Hickman, and G. Berg
Conservation Archaeology: A Guide for Cultural Resource Management Studies,
  edited by M. B. Schiffer and G. J. Gumerman

TABLE 7.1. continued

1977 continued

Method and Theory in Historical Archeology, by S. South

Research Strategies in Historical Archeology, edited by S. South

Archaeological Approaches to the Present: Models for Reconstructing the Past, by
J. E. Yellen

Spatial Archaeology, by D. L. Clarke

1978

The Nautical Archaeology of Padre Island: The Spanish Shipwrecks of 1554, by
J. B. Arnold III, and R. Weddle

Nunamiut Ethnoarchaeology, by L. R. Binford

Monte Albán: Settlement Patterns at the Ancient Zapotec Capital, by R. E. Blanton

Prehistoric Hunters of the High Plains, by G. C. Frison

European Prehistory, by S. Milisauskas

Social Archaeology: Beyond Subsistence and Dating, edited by C. L. Redman,
M. M. Berman, E. V. Curtin, W. T. Langhorne, N. M. Versaggi, and J. C. Wanser

Prehistoric Patterns of Human Behavior: A Case Study in the Mississippi Valley, by
B. D. Smith

Mississippian Settlement Patterns, edited by B. D. Smith

Prehistoric Coastal Adaptations: The Economy and Ecology of Maritime Middle America,
edited by B. L. Stark and B. Voorhies

Chronologies in New World Archaeology, by R. E. Taylor and C. W. Meighan

Social Process in Maya Prehistory: Studies in Honor of Sir Eric Thompson, edited by N.
Hammond

1979

*Analytical Archaeologist: Collected Papers of David L. Clarke, Edited and Introduced by
His Colleagues*

Principles of Archaeological Stratigraphy, by E. C. Harris

Lithic Use-Wear Analysis, edited by B. Hayden

The Basin of Mexico: Ecological Processes in the Evolution of a Civilization,
by W. T. Sanders, J. R. Parsons, and R. S. Santley

Reindeer and Caribou Hunters: An Archaeological Study, by A. E. Spiess

Paleonutrition: Method and Theory in Prehistoric Foodways, by E. S. Wing and
A. B. Brown

Transformations: Mathematical Approaches to Culture Change, edited by C. Renfrew and
K. L. Cooke

Volcanic Activity and Human Ecology, edited by P. D. Sheets and D. K. Grayson

Experimental Archaeology, by J. Coles

1980

*The Cherokee Excavations: Holocene Ecology and Human Adaptations in Northwestern
Iowa*, edited by D. C. Anderson and H. A. Semken, Jr.

Animal Diseases in Archaeology, by J. Baker and D. Brothwell

TABLE 7.1. *continued*

1980 continued

Modeling Change in Prehistoric Subsistence Economies, edited by T. K. Earle and A. L. Christenson

Rock Shelters of the Perigord: Geological Stratigraphy and Archaeological Succession, by H. Laville, J.-P. Rigaud, and J. Sackett

Florida Archaeology, by J. T. Milanich and C. H. Fairbanks

Guitarrero Cave: Early Man in the Andes, edited by T. F. Lynch

Prehistoric Hunters of the High Andes, by J. W. Rick

Parmana: Prehistoric Maize and Manioc Subsistence along the Amazon and Orinoco, by A. C. Roosevelt

The Archaeology of New England, by D. R. Snow

Prehistory of the Eastern Sahara, by F. Wendorf and R. Schild

Prehistoric Mining and Allied Industries, by R. Shepherd

1981

Landscape and Society: Prehistoric Central Italy, by G. Barker

Bones: Ancient Men and Modern Myths, by L. R. Binford

A Study of Prehistoric Social Change: The Development of Complex Societies in the Hawaiian Islands, by R. H. Cordy

Modern Material Culture: The Archaeology of Us, edited by R. A. Gould and M. B. Schiffer

Demographic Archaeology, by F. A. Hassan

Strategies for Survival: Cultural Behavior in an Ecological Context, by M. A. Jochim

Prehistoric Foraging in a Temperate Forest: A Linear Programming Model, by A. S. Keene

Foundations of Northeast Archaeology, edited by D. R. Snow

Great Lakes Archaeology, by R. J. Mason

1982

Prehistory of Japan, by C. M. Aikens and T. Higuchi

Contexts for Prehistoric Exchange, edited by J. E. Ericson and T. K. Earle

Maya Subsistence: Studies in Memory of Dennis E. Puleston, edited by K. V. Flannery

The Agate Basin Site: A Record of the Paleoindian Occupation of the Northwestern High Plains, by G. C. Frison and D. J. Stanford

Paleoecology of Beringia, edited by D. M. Hopkins, J. V. Matthews, Jr., C. E. Schweger, and S. B. Young

Village Ethnoarchaeology: Rural Iran in Archaeological Perspective, by C. Kramer

Hohokam and Patayan: Prehistory of Southwestern Arizona, edited by R. H. McGuire and M. B. Schiffer

The Cannon Reservoir Human Ecology Project: An Archaeological Study of Cultural Adaptations in the Southern Prairie Peninsula, edited by M. J. O'Brien, R. E. Warren and D. E. Lewarch

TABLE 7.1. *continued*

1982 continued

Theory and Explanation in Archaeology: The Southampton Conference, edited by
C. Renfrew, M. J. Rowlands, and B. A. Segraves

Philosophy and Archaeology, by M. Salmon

The Cuicatlán Cañada and Monte Albán: A Study of Primary State Formation, by
C. S. Spencer

Polities and Power: An Economic and Political History of the Western Pueblo, by
S. Upham

A Prehistory of Australia, New Guinea, and Sahul, by J. P. White and
J. F. O'Connell

Archaeology of Urban America: The Search for Pattern and Process, edited by
R. S. Dickens, Jr.

Models of Spatial Inequality: Settlement Patterns in Historic Archeology, by
R. Paynter

*The Archaeology of Social Disintegration in Skunk Hollow: A Nineteenth-Century Rural
Black Community*, by J. H. Geismar

Australian Stone Hatchets, by F. P. Dickson

The Inca and Aztec States 1400–1800: Anthropology and History, edited by
G. A. Collier, R. I. Rosaldo, and J. D. Wirth

1983

Indians of the Upper Texas Coast, by L. E. Aten

Working at Archaeology, by L. R. Binford

Coba: A Classic Maya Metropolis, by W. J. Folan, E. R. Kintz, and L. A. Fletcher

Spanish St. Augustine: The Archaeology of a Colonial Creole Community, by
K. Deagan

European Economic Prehistory: A New Approach, by R. Dennell

The Cloud People: Divergent Evolution of the Zapotec and Mixtec Civilizations, edited by
K. V. Flannery and J. Marcus

The Establishment of Human Antiquity, by D. K. Grayson

Archaeological Hammers and Theories, edited by J. A. Moore and A. S. Keene

Archaeology of the Central Mississippi Valley, by D. F. Morse and P. A. Morse

*Quaternary Coastlines and Maritime Archaeology: Towards the Prehistory of Land Bridges
and Continents*, edited by P. M. Masters and N. C. Fleming

Archaic Hunters and Gatherers in the American Midwest, edited by J. L. Phillips
and J. A. Brown

Ceramics, Chronology, and Community Patterns: An Archaeological Study at Moundville,
by V. P. Steponaitis

1984

Prehistory of Oklahoma, edited by R. E. Bell

Faunal Remains from Klasies River Mouth, by L. R. Binford

Prehistoric Europe, by T. Champion, C. Gamble, S. Shennan, and A. Whittle

TABLE 7.1. *continued*

1984 continued

Paleopathology at the Origins of Agriculture, edited by M. N. Cohen and
   G. J. Armelagos

Prehistory of the Southwest, by L. Cordell

Cozumel: Late Maya Settlement Patterns, by D. A. Freidel and J. A. Sabloff

Quantitative Zooarchaeology: Topics in the Analysis of Archaeological Faunas,
   by D. K. Grayson

The Inka Road System, by J. Hyslop

Kingsmill Plantations, 1619–1800: Archaeology of Country Life in Colonial Virginia, by
   W. M. Kelso

The American Frontier: An Archaeological Study of Settlement Pattern and Process, by K.
   E. Lewis

McKeithen Weeden Island: The Culture of Northern Florida, A.D. 200–900,
   by J. T. Milanich, A. S. Cordell, V. J. Knight, Jr., T. A. Kohler, and
   B. J. Sigler-Lavelle

California Archaeology, by M. J. Moratto

Mortuary Variability: An Archaeological Investigation, by J. M. O'Shea

*Cannon's Point Plantation, 1794–1860: Living Conditions and Status Patterns in the Old
   South*, by J. S. Otto

The Origins of Agriculture: An Evolutionary Perspective, by D. Rindos

Past and Present in Hunter Gatherer Studies, edited by C. Schrire

1985

The Analysis of Prehistoric Diets, edited by R. I. Gilbert, Jr., and J. H. Mielke

Prehistoric Hunter-Gatherers: The Emergence of Cultural Complexity, edited by
   T. D. Price and J. A. Brown

Prehistory of the Indo-Malaysian Archipelago, by P. Bellwood

*Shawnee Minisink: A Stratified Paleoindian–Archaic Site in the Upper Delaware Valley of
   Pennsylvania*, edited by C. W. McNett, Jr.

Thermoluminescence Dating, by M. J. Aitken

Domestic Pottery of the Northeastern United States, 1625–1850, edited by
   S. P. Turnbaugh

The Archaeology of Slavery and Plantation Life, edited by T. A. Singleton

The Archaeology of Frontiers and Boundaries, edited by S. W. Green and
   S. M. Perlman

The Upper Paleolithic of the Central Russian Plain, by O. Soffer

The Palynology of Archaeological Sites, by G. W. Dimbleby

*Beyond Domestication in Prehistoric Europe: Investigations in Subsistence Archaeology
   and Social Complexity*, edited by G. Barker and C. Gamble

Prehistory of the Eastern Arctic, by M. S. Maxwell

Paleoanthropology and Paleolithic Archaeology in the People's Republic of China, edited
   by W. Rukang and J. Olsen

TABLE 7.1. continued

1986

Guilá Naquitz: Archaic Foraging and Early Agriculture in Oaxaca, Mexico, edited by K. V. Flannery

Archaeology of the Lower Ohio River Valley, by J. Muller

Navajo Land Use: An Ethnoarchaeological Study, by K. B. Kelley

Qsar es-Seghir: An Archaeological View of Medieval Life, by C. L. Redman

1987

Radiocarbon Dating: An Archaeological Perspective, by R. E. Taylor

Regional Dynamics: Burgundian Landscapes in Historical Perspective, edited by C. L. Crumley and W. H. Marquardt

The Horner Site: The Type Site of the Cody Cultural Complex, edited by G. C. Frison and L. C. Todd

1988

Phytolith Analysis: An Archaeological and Geological Perspective, by D. R. Piperno

Quantifying Archaeology, by S. Shennan

1989

Debating Archaeology, by L. R. Binford

The Flocks of the Wamani: A Study of Llama Herders on the Punas of Ayacucho, Peru, by K. V. Flannery, J. Marcus, and R. G. Reynolds

Paleoethnobotany: A Handbook of Procedures, by D. M. Pearsall

1990

New York City Neighborhoods: The 18th Century, by N. A. Rothschild

The Chacoan Prehistory of the San Juan Basin, by R. G. Vivian

1991

Prehistory of the Oregon Coast, by R. L. Lyman

Moundbuilders of the Amazon, by A. C. Roosevelt

provided a tremendous boost to archaeologists seeking to publish their research results. It also put the results within easy reach of those in the discipline. These were the gravy years for presses because university libraries were still flush with acquisition funds. Even a book with a tiny projected audience could at least break even through library sales. Vast inflation in book prices and shrinking library budgets would soon put an end to this.

Given the emergence of Academic Press as the leading publisher in American archaeology, having a book published there was yet another fitness-enhancing strategy. It signaled to others that you had something important to say, albeit at a cost of $39.95 or more (earlier books were considerably less expensive). But simply because one has something important to say does not mean that he or she will ever have the opportunity to say it. Just as with journal editors, book editors wield tremendous clout. Indeed, consulting editorships are sometimes little more than honorific positions. A press taps someone who has significant standing in the field so that the series carries an important imprimatur. Acquisition editors, in contrast, are the real power at a press, whether commercial or academic. They are the ones who seek out interesting (and hopefully profitable) manuscripts, schmooze with potential authors at meetings, make the case to a consulting editor that a book should be in a particular series, pick the reviewers (or decide to skip the review process entirely), and present the manuscript to their editorial boards.

An important reason for Academic Press's success was Bill Woodcock (Figure 7.5), an engaging and enterprising acquisitions editor who understood the discipline as no archaeology editor before him had. He also knew more archaeologists on a first-name basis than any competitor did, and he went out of his way to solicit manuscripts not only from established archaeologists but from young, relatively unknown ones, including the three of us. No small amount of credit for any success we enjoyed early in our careers must be given to Woodcock, who left Academic Press in 1986 for Princeton University Press and is now retired from publishing. Notice in Figure 7.3 the effect Woodcock's departure had on Academic Press's book production, which fell to two volumes in 1988. Stated more accurately, Woodcock's decision to leave Academic Press was based on management's move to reduce drastically the press's presence in the archaeology arena—a decision that killed *Advances in World Archaeology* and *Advances in Archaeological Method and Theory* (Figure 7.3). Other publishing houses, especially Plenum (now Springer-Verlag), and a few university presses (including the University of Utah Press), gladly rushed to fill the vacuum left by Academic Press's sudden departure from the marketplace.

Other archaeologists undoubtedly would echo our sentiments concerning Bill Woodcock, including Pat Watson, Chuck Redman, Kent Flannery, and Lew Binford, all of whom published books with Academic Press. We can add Jim Hill and Fred Plog, both deceased, to this list. In fact, it's fair to say that Academic Press was the processualists' publisher of choice.

FIGURE 7.5. Bill Woodcock at Palenque, Mexico, 1985. (Photograph by Charlene Woodcock, courtesy Bill Woodcock.)

Books are excellent vehicles in which to air one's views because they can accommodate extended treatments. Whereas journal articles (supposedly) require concise, crisp statements, books are more forgiving. They really become stages from which one can launch into long soliloquies as opposed to abbreviated monologue. Books certainly gave Binford and Flannery stages from which to launch their messages. Between 1972 and 1983 they published a combined eight books with Academic Press.

Here we focus on Flannery, who by the early 1970s had emerged as an important spokesman for cultural evolutionism—something for which the University of Michigan had long been known, though not yet for applications to the archaeological record. We commented previously on Flannery's early work with systems theory (Flannery 1968a) and his critical comments about both traditional archaeology (Flannery 1967) and processualism (Flannery 1973a); here we examine the period during which Flannery not only made his greatest intellectual contributions but also ensured that his views left a lasting mark on the discipline. In terms of the work they did and the intellectual progeny they spawned, Flannery was as important as Binford in shaping American archaeology after the mid-1970s.

MICHIGAN EVOLUTIONISM

Flannery was one of three University of Chicago–trained archaeologists to join Michigan's anthropology department in the mid-1960s, the other two being Henry Wright and Bob Whallon. Writing a few years later, Binford (1972b) considered all three as having processualist leanings. On the surface this appears to be true. Whallon had a chapter in *New Perspectives in Archeology,* as did Flannery, who had drawn a sharp contrast between traditional archaeology and processual archaeology in his review of Gordon Willey's (1966) *An Introduction to American Archaeology* (Chapter 3). Further, he had published articles that most archaeologists, and especially students (such as we three at the time), believed were processual. Indeed, these works were considered models of how the program should be applied (e.g., Flannery 1966, 1968a, 1972). But is it accurate to call Flannery a processualist? Yes, but with a caveat. Flannery, as with Whallon and Wright, is a processualist in the broadest sense of the term, not in the strict Binfordian sense. Note what Flannery (1994:118) saw as the genesis of processualism: "Processual-[ism], in terms of, let's say, how it was seen in the 1960s...comes out of the ecological work...in which people began to use simulation models in conjunction with ecological data." Binford obviously would disagree.

Flannery and Wright trained under Robert Braidwood at Chicago and worked on various Old World projects sponsored by the Oriental Institute. Flannery also took part in Richard MacNeish's project in the Tehuacán Valley of Mexico (Chapter 3). Thus it is not surprising that Flannery's and Wright's interests lay in the direction of cultural evolution, especially the rise of complex societies. Nor is it surprising that both ended up at the University of Michigan, long a bastion of cultural evolutionism.

Willey and Jerry Sabloff make an excellent point as to whether some of the archaeological discussions that took place in the 1970s and '80s were "processual" or not. Beyond processualism's direct influence on Americanist research,

the philosophy of the New Archaeology has caused a profound attitudinal change in the discipline of American archaeology. This change is reflected in a greater concern with problem definition in research planning and in the linking of the goals of the understanding of cultural process with those of understanding cultural history. Most American archaeologists see no conflict in this, and their practices of the past thirty years reveal such partial, covert, or even subconscious accommodations to the tenets of the New Archaeology. In this way, the cultural focus of the New Archaeological revolt of the 1960s soon entered and came to compose the mainstream of American archaeology by the end of the 1970s. (Willey and Sabloff 1993:257–258)

Willey and Sabloff's conclusions seem sound. The legacy of the new archaeology wasn't that it produced clones. Rather, it produced a change in how archaeologists thought about the past and, more importantly, how they approached the study of the past. This is evident in the work not only of Flannery but also of Wright (e.g., 1977, 1981, 1986, 1998; Wright and Johnson 1975) and Whallon (1972, 1973, 1974a; Whallon and Brown 1982). The bottom line is not whether someone was or was not a processualist according to Binfordian standards. Rather, it is whether that person's work had an effect on the discipline. And by the 1970s the University of Michigan, in large part through the presence of Flannery, was identified as a leading center for cultural evolutionism—an approach that has had and will continue to have an important role in archaeological practice (Feinman 2000a; Spencer 1997).

Flannery has the ability to make complex subjects understandable to a large audience. His early articles—"Farming Systems and Political Growth in Ancient Oaxaca, Mexico" (Flannery et al. 1967), "Archeological Systems Theory and Early Mesoamerica" (Flannery 1968a), "The Olmec and the Valley of Oaxaca: A Model for Inter-Regional Interaction in Formative Mesoamerica" (Flannery 1968b), "Origins and Ecological Effects of Early Domestication in Iran and the Near East" (Flannery 1969), "The Cultural Evolution of Civilizations" (Flannery 1972), and "Origins of Agriculture" (Flannery 1973b)—were widely read and cited not only by Mesoamericanists but also by just about any archaeologist trying to apply systems theory. (In *An Archaeological Perspective* Binford [1972h:339] referred to Flannery's [1969] "Origins and Ecological Effects" article as one of the few processual models that had been developed up to that point.)

As noted in Chapter 4, Flannery also has the ability to write in a humorous fashion—something few archaeologists can do because the humor usually comes off as being forced and contrived (and seldom survives peer review). Maybe they can inject a sly comment here or there—as Jimmy Griffin did in his reply (Griffin 1976) to some of Binford's less-than-kind comments about him (Binford 1972a)—but not to the extent that Flannery has. In reviewing *The Early Mesoamerican Village* (1976c), Flannery's first book (published by Academic Press), Robert Wauchope (1977:656) referred to it as "three treats in one package," by which he meant that it was a solid contribution to Mesoamerican archaeology; it was an excellent treatment of various archaeological methods; and it was fun to read. Interspersed among the chapters Flannery and his students wrote about aspects of the archaeological record in the Valley of Oaxaca, Mexico, are snippets of an imaginary, often humorous conversation on method and theory that Flannery held with three individuals. We introduced two of them in Chapter 5—the Real Mesoamerican Archaeologist and the Skeptical Graduate Student. A third is the Great Synthesizer—someone with an uncanny ability to tie together everyone else's work in a neat package. Flannery's three major characters are thinly veiled caricatures of real people—some composites, some not. One has no trouble, for example, in identifying Willey as the Great Synthesizer, who emerges from Flannery's pen as a cross between a brilliant traditionalist and Lewis Carroll's White Rabbit, always running late for important engagements.

We view this as one of the more interesting of all fitness-enhancing strategies: drawing a contrast between you and your competitors in a humorous, and sometimes self-deprecating manner. This makes it essentially impossible for those criticized to reply directly. For example, in the concluding chapter to *The Early Mesoamerican Village*, which Flannery titled "A Prayer for an Endangered Species," he pointed out that the three main characters in his story "reside in all of us. In earlier and more innocent years, I happily committed every sin I have attributed to them. Rolling out of the Jeep every morning to take another biased sample, sticking a phone booth into an unknown site, removing an endless stream of 20-cm levels, bad-mouthing the very professors from whom I had learned the most. And archaeology has never been more fun" (Flannery 1976a:369). By poking fun at himself, Flannery could deflect the charge that he was simply grinding an axe when he turned the spotlight on his colleagues. He used the same strategy, to even greater effect, in "Archeology with a Capital S" (Flannery 1973a), where he put law-seeking archaeologists—his competitors at UCLA and Arizona—on the defensive.

Flannery's early experiments with humor and ridicule were merely warm-up acts for his plenary address to the American Anthropological Association in 1982, titled "The Golden Marshalltown: A Parable for the Archeology of the 1980s." Based on the number of people who have told us they were in the audience in Los Angeles in December 1981 when Flannery gave the address, we estimate that the crowd was equaled in size only by the two million or so in attendance at Yankee Stadium in 1956 when Don Larsen pitched the only World Series perfect game. Word of the address spread rapidly throughout the profession, and everybody wanted to have a personal attachment to it.

In the address, Flannery pointed out that serious ills were afflicting American archaeology. Instead of simply listing them, Flannery created another series of thinly veiled characters in a story about a mystical plane ride that he shared with several colleagues as they returned from a national meeting. One character was cast as a faithful servant to the study of culture, which Flannery viewed as archaeology's true calling. The other two were cast as miscreants of one sort or another. Some archaeologists loved what Flannery had to say, some hated it, a few said they didn't care, but everyone read the piece when it appeared the next year in the *American Anthropologist* (Flannery 1982b).

The unsavory characters—the Born-Again Philosopher and the Child of the Seventies—are described this way:

The [Born-Again Philosopher] came out of graduate school in the late 1960s, and he teaches now at a major department in the western United States. He began as a traditional archeologist.... [but] discovered Philosophy of Science, and was born again.

Suddenly he found the world would beat a path to his door if he criticized everyone else's epistemology. Suddenly he discovered that so long as his research design was superb, he never had to do research.... No more dust, no more heat, no more 5-ft squares. He worked in an office now, generating hypotheses and laws and models which an endless stream of graduate students was sent out to test....

Like so many of his academic generation, the Child of the Seventies had but one outstanding characteristic: blind ambition. He had neither the commitment to culture history of my generation nor the devotion to theory of the generation of the 1960s. His goals were simple: to be famous, to be well paid, to be stroked, and to receive immediate gratification. How he got there did not matter. Who he stepped on along the way

did not matter. Indeed, the data of prehistory did not matter. For him, archeology was only a vehicle—one carefully selected, because he had discovered early that people will put up with almost anything in the guise of archeology. (Flannery 1982b:265–266)

Flannery's two characters teach at universities somewhere "in the desert," and they are interested in cataloging the trash that is being thrown away on the plane as it makes its way east. It doesn't take much imagination to figure out that those universities in the desert are the University of Arizona and Arizona State University, whose anthropology departments have never been particularly friendly with that of Michigan. The roots of animosity extend back well past our collective memories. Conditions became icy in the early 1970s, when a rift occurred between the departments at Michigan and the University of Arizona that was felt across the discipline—this despite the fact that the departments on occasion hired each other's graduates. It may actually have started as a feud between faculty at Michigan and members of Paul Martin's field school at Vernon, Arizona, primarily Mark Leone and Fred Plog, the latter of whom was teaching at Arizona State at the time Flannery wrote his essay.

By 1982 the University of Arizona, which throughout the late 1960s and early '70s was recognized as a center of processualism, had become a breeding ground for behavioral archaeology, which although conceived in Binfordian processualism had moved in a different direction than its parent. This redirection was done largely at the hands of Jeff Reid (Figure 7.6), Bill Rathje (Figure 5.4), and Schiffer (e.g., Reid, Rathje, and Schiffer 1974; Reid, Schiffer, and Rathje 1975; Schiffer 1972a, 1975a, 1976, 1983), who saw what they considered to be explanatory and methodological holes in processual archaeology and moved to fill them.

Filling holes is distinct from replacing one paradigm with another. The behavioralists were brash, and they championed their position, but they did not see what they were doing as rep-

FIGURE 7.6. *Left to right*: Jeff Reid, Bill Longacre, and Julie Lowell at Chodistaas Pueblo, Arizona, 1984. (Negative no. 65435, courtesy Arizona State Museum.)

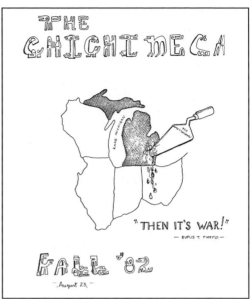

FIGURE 7.7. Cover of the fall 1982 issue of *The Chichimeca*, the anthropology student newsletter at the University of Arizona, showing a Marshalltown trowel plunged into Ann Arbor, the home of the University of Michigan. The newsletter contained a lampoon of Kent Flannery's "The Golden Marshalltown: A Parable for the Archeology of the 1980s" (Flannery 1982), in which he had made several critical remarks about the Arizona faculty (and, by implication, the manner in which they train their students). The quote "Then it's war!" comes from the 1933 movie *Duck Soup*, in which Groucho Marx plays Rufus T. Firefly, the newly appointed dictator of Freedonia.

resenting a complete break with processualism. In a retrospective look at the long-term work conducted at Grasshopper Pueblo by three generations of University of Arizona archaeologists, Reid and Stephanie Whittlesey (2005) point out that in their view there was no "paradigm shift" from the culture-history approach of Ray Thompson, to the processualist approach of Bill Longacre, to the behavioralist approach of Reid. There were, to be sure, differences in problem orientation, but the changes evident over the thirty-year period were gradual, not punctuational.

Schiffer and Reid received their doctorates at Arizona in 1973 and were soon hired as faculty members there. Together with Rathje, a Harvard graduate, they produced a new generation of behavioral archaeologists. Both Rathje and Schiffer were fingered by name in Flannery's essay—Rathje for his Tucson Garbage Project (e.g., Rathje 1974) and Schiffer for his interest in discovering archaeological laws (e.g., Schiffer 1972b, 1975b, 1976, 1978a, 1979a) and for his purported lack of fieldwork skills. Graduate students at Arizona struck back with a short essay, "The Real Story of the

Golden Marshalltown," which appeared in their newsletter, *The Chichimeca* (Figure 7.7). It outdid Flannery's in terms of the number of laughs generated per page, although we're guessing that the circulation of *The Chichimeca* was a bit short of *American Anthropologist*'s.

Flannery has consistently made it clear that he has no interest in discovering or using laws, feeling "uncomfortable at the threshold of philosophy" (Flannery 1986a:511). In fact, he has gone out of his way to ridicule laws and their discovery—in public addresses (Flannery 1982b), in book chapters (Flannery 1973a 1986a), and even in book reviews (Flannery 1977). Rather, he has, as Gary Feinman (2000b:237) put it, "forged a critical intermediate position between noncomparative, highly inductive positions (strict historicism and archempiricism) and the rigid universalizing approaches that search for covering laws, prime movers, and unilinear sequences of change.... [Flannery recognized that] the historical pathways to sedentary farming villages... or to the rise of states are never strictly alike, but certain notable processes can be seen across different temporal and spatial cases." Most orthodox processualists would argue that those "notable processes" can themselves be described by lawlike generalizations, but the important point is that Flannery has consistently emphasized a historical perspective on change. In his mind, this transcends any fixation on the "universalizing approach" that Feinman mentions, but which almost no one actually practices (not even Schiffer).

Flannery has never strayed very far from the Whitean notion of "culturology" as the primary anthropological focus, and with one major exception, he has wavered little from White's version of cultural evolutionism. The one exception is that Flannery, at least the Flannery of the mid-'70s onward, is no technological determinist. We say from the mid-'70s onward because the earlier Flannery stuck pretty much to a hybrid cultural evolutionism derived, probably through Robert Braidwood, from Julian Steward and especially Leslie White. Indeed, Flannery (1968a) began with the Whitean definition of culture and linked it to Steward's ecological approach, thus viewing a cultural system as being coupled to its environmental context by the technologies of its subsistence and settlement subsystems (Chapter 3). A change in the physical environment—for example, a drought—causes changes in the seasonal availability of plant and animal resources. These in turn effect changes in parts of the cultural system—for example, in the scheduling of subsistence activities and so on.

The Flannery of the mid-'70s (the roots are evident even a few years earlier [Flannery 1972]) did not deny that the physical environment played a significant role in cultural evolution, but he began to seek other sources of change. Here is where Flannery made his boldest break—not only from White and Steward but also from Braidwood. But even this state-

ment doesn't do Flannery's position justice. If one reads closely Flannery's substantive articles and books, it becomes clear that his "causes" are multiple and his explanations complicated. This is why Flannery has consistently advocated a systems approach. Even when his discussion of culture as a system is less nuanced than in his earlier work (e.g., Flannery 1968a), he is still treating sociopolitical entities—chiefdoms, states, civilizations—as complex systems.

The systems perspective, which is essentially agnostic with respect to causes (that is, different causal factors can have similar or different effects, depending on the cultural system) is not without implications for the recruitment of protégés. By allowing that anyone's favorite causal factor could be important in some cases, Flannery's systems perspective erects over the discipline a big metatheoretical tent. Thus, virtually any archaeologist could, in the 1980s, feel comfortable identifying with Flannery—except, of course, those whom he ridiculed.

There is another side to Flannery's perspective besides systems that adds to his popularity. That side has to do with how he views humans—not as automatons but as active participants in shaping their own destinies. We are not suggesting that Flannery is unique in this regard—or even close to it (or that he prefigured what became known as "postprocessualism" [Chapter 8]). Most archaeologists, even the arch-empiricists and law-and-order processualists that he has parodied, do not forget that humans have a cognitive side. The comment has often been made that certain aspects of human life do not leave traces in the archaeological record and therefore are beyond our ability to study and understand. Flannery himself has pointed this out. But he has also consistently spoken of prehistoric peoples as if they were real individuals and not simply analytical units. In this he is not far removed from his Ph.D. adviser, who once cautioned not to lose sight of the "Indian behind the artifact" (Braidwood 1959:79).

Flannery's personal feelings about his subject matter—people—are evident in his discussion of the excavation of Guilá Naquitz, a small

FIGURE 7.8. *Right,* Kent Flannery and Mexican workmen below Guilá Naquitz Rockshelter, Oaxaca, Mexico, 1966. (From Flannery 1986c, courtesy Academic Press and Kent Flannery.)

that grew out of the works of Childe and Braidwood: where, when, and why did Near Eastern peoples start settling in villages and begin domesticating plants and animals? At the other end of the complexity spectrum, where, when, and why did the descendants of those same peoples begin living in urban centers?

In simplified form, Childe (1936), drawing on the work of Raphael Pumpelly, an American geologist-archaeologist, suggested that humans, plants, and animals had been drawn to oases during periods of environmental degradation at the end of the Pleistocene. Given their

rockshelter in the Valley of Oaxaca (Flannery 1986c). Flannery spends as much time discussing his Zapotec workmen, "the real excavators of Guilá Naquitz" (Flannery, Moser, and Maranca 1986:67), and the daily activities that went on in the field—the conversations, the camaraderie, the high jinx—as he does discussing the excavation itself (Figure 7.8). The accompanying photos identify not only the various activities being carried out—screening, excavation, and so on—but also each person shown, regardless of whether he or she was a Zapotec worker, a student from the United States, or a student from Mexico (Figure 7.9).

At Chicago, Flannery's first exposure to archaeology was through his participation in Braidwood's Oriental Institute Iranian Prehistoric Project (Flannery 1982a). Another member of that project was Frank Hole, also one of Braidwood's Ph.D. students. In 1963 Hole and Flannery (Figure 7.10), together with James Neely (Figure 7.11), a graduate student at the University of Arizona, excavated two small villages on the Deh Luran Plain of Khuzistan (Hole, Flannery, and Neely 1969). A major goal of the project was to generate a chronological sequence for Deh Luran, but the excavators were also interested in several age-old questions

FIGURE 7.9. Excavation of Guilá Naquitz Rockshelter, Oaxaca, Mexico, 1966. *Top, left,* Eligio Martínez and *right,* Chris Moser sort and package remains. *Bottom,* Silvia Maranca excavates a Postclassic vessel. (Courtesy Academic Press and Kent Flannery.)

FIGURE 7.10. *Left,* Frank Hole and *right,* Kent Flannery at Ali Kosh, Khuzistan, Iran, 1963. (Courtesy James Neely.)

While still a graduate student "specializing in zooarchaeology" at Chicago, Flannery "camped out on [Richard] MacNeish's doorstep for a chance to analyze his fauna" from the Tehuacán Valley rockshelters (Flannery 1997:660). This was Flannery's first experience with Mesoamerican archaeology—slightly later he worked with Michael Coe on the prehistory of coastal Guatemala (Coe and Flannery 1964a, 1964b, 1967; Flannery and Coe 1968)—and the one that would directly influence his decision to initiate the Valley of Oaxaca Human Ecology Project a few years later (Flannery 1986b). Like the Deh Luran and Tehuacán Valley projects, an overarching goal of the Oaxaca work was to understand the origins of village life and domestication as well as the development of cities. Similar issues were at the heart of settlement-pattern studies.

We discussed in Chapter 3 how Bill Sanders's work in the Valley of Mexico during the 1960s brought the analysis of settlement patterns to the forefront of American archaeology. We also pointed out that Sanders's most vocal critic would be Flannery, who would argue that set-

newfound propinquity, all three in essence became "domesticated" together. The plants, which grew in dense stands around the oases, attracted animals. Because the plants were a predictable and reliable food source, the animals tended to stay around the water holes, which in turn attracted people's attention. The animals became used to a human presence and over time became domesticated.

Braidwood didn't buy the oasis hypothesis, proposing instead that the earliest post-Pleistocene settlements were not in the river valleys but on the "hilly flanks" of the Zagros Mountains of western Iran. He envisioned much less post-Pleistocene climatic degradation than Childe did, and instead viewed domestication and village formation as being part and parcel of a general "settling in" by early Neolithic peoples (Braidwood and Reed 1957). During this settling-in period, humans became familiar with storage, milling stones, sickles, and other technological "advances" that ensured people were "ready" for domestication and agriculture (Braidwood and Willey 1962:342). It was in reaction to this view that Binford (1968c) wrote "Post-Pleistocene Adaptations" (see Chapter 2). Flannery never criticized his adviser directly, although it is clear that he disagreed with Braidwood's "settling in" explanation.

FIGURE 7.11. James Neely working with aerial photographs during a survey of the Deh Luran Plain, Khuzistan, Iran, 1969. (Courtesy James Neely.)

tlement patterns, as well as the systems behind them, cannot be understood through purely materialist models that tie settlement decisions to such factors as specific landforms or soil types. Actually, Flannery's criticism went well beyond settlement patterns per se and eventually encompassed Sanders's views on the entire spectrum of sociopolitical development in Highland Mesoamerica. By the 1980s a rift had developed between identifiable groups of investigators studying the origins and development of social complexity. We are oversimplifying, but on one side was the "Penn State group," composed of Sanders and those adhering to the materialist view—for example, Robert Santley and Deborah Nichols. On the other side was the Michigan group, made up of Flannery and others with a decidedly less materialist view—for example, Joyce Marcus, Richard Blanton (Figure 7.12), Elizabeth Brumfiel, Stephen Kowalewski (Figure 7.13), Gary Feinman (Figure 7.13), and Charles Spencer.

FIGURE 7.12. Richard Blanton, Oaxaca, Mexico, 1972. (Photograph by Carl Kuttruff.)

Ironically, many of those in the Michigan group can trace their methodological and theoretical roots at least in part to Sanders. Blanton's intellectual lineage, for example, includes his dissertation adviser at Michigan, Jeffrey Parsons, who, although he also received his Ph.D. at Michigan, had surveyed the Texcoco portion of the Valley of Mexico as part of Sanders's overall project (Parsons 1971). Blanton, in turn, surveyed an adjacent segment of the valley, the Ixtapalapa Peninsula, for his dissertation, publishing it in Sanders's *Occasional Papers in Anthropology* series at Penn State (Blanton 1972). Kowalewski, and later Feinman, became involved with Blanton's surveys of the Valley of Oaxaca (e.g., Blanton 1978; Blanton et al. 1982, 1993, 1999; Kowalewski 1990, 2003; Kowalewski et al. 1989). The survey training they received from Blanton makes them

Sanders's intellectual heirs, but they are also heirs of the Michigan tradition of cultural evolutionism that traces back through Blanton, Flannery, and Leslie White.

It would be inaccurate to claim that the rift between the two traditions was entirely intellectual—it wasn't—but it took a while for the more personal aspects to achieve prominence. Generally speaking, the intellectual disagreement was over the extent to which material factors conditioned cultural evolution. The Penn State group believed that factors related to the physical environment played *the* key role in conditioning culture, and so they could be used to explain instances of culture

FIGURE 7.13. *Left,* Gary Feinman and *right,* Stephen Kowalewski, Oaxaca, Mexico, 1977. (Courtesy Gary Feinman.)

FIGURE 7.14. Main plaza at Monte Albán, Oaxaca, Mexico, looking southwest from the North Platform. (Courtesy Richard Diehl.)

change. A hypothetical explanation might go like this: Because people living in the Valley of Oaxaca during the Late Formative period needed X hectares of arable land to feed a population of size Y, they located their village so that the X hectares were within a two-kilometer radius of the village. As the population grew, the villagers had three options: (1) intensify their production (perhaps through irrigation); (2) bring additional land under cultivation; or (3) move to a new location.

Alternatively, the Michigan group, while not denying the explanatory importance of techno-environmental factors, also considered other causes of culture change, such as those of a political nature. Blanton, for example, reasoned that the placement of Monte Albán on the summit of a hill, 400 meters above the valley floor (Figure 7.14), had nothing to do with irrigable land but everything to do with defense and politics around 200 B.C. He proposed (Blanton 1976a, 1976b, 1978) that Monte Albán was a "disembedded capital" founded by a coalition of chiefs in a neutral, defensible location that was set apart from agricultural activities—a place designed to function primarily as an administrative center.

The rift between the groups intensified when Sanders and Nichols moved out of their neighborhood, the Valley of Mexico, and poked their heads into Michigan's backyard, the Valley of Oaxaca. The source of the tension was an article, "Ecological Theory and Cultural Evolution in the Valley of Oaxaca," in which Sanders and Nichols (1988:52) expressed the opinion that there was "considerable room for skepticism of [the Michigan group's] assertion that there is no relationship between resource availability, population growth and distribution, and political evolution in the valley." Not surprisingly, the Michigan group, many of whom had the opportunity to respond to the article, did not take kindly to what Sanders and Nichols had to say. In fact, rarely has any set of *Current Anthropology* responses contained as many pointed and hostile remarks. Blanton (1988:52) stated that it was "difficult to know where to start a commentary on such a convoluted mess of illogic, misinformation, and epistemological crudity." Feinman and Linda Nichols (1988:55) ventured that the article "violates...scientific canons and offers a distorted view of man-land relations in ancient Oaxaca." Kowalewski and Laura Finsten

(1988:59) considered it "annoying to have to correct for the record the facts [the article] ignores or mangles."

Flannery (1988:58) likewise didn't think much of the Sanders and Nichols article, claiming that "Monte Albán cannot be understood without taking into account its defensive walls, the twenty or more temples in its main plaza, its hieroglyphic records of conquest, and its inscriptions justifying royal power by establishing royal genealogies." But Flannery's response was more than simply about errors, interpretation, and the like. He pointed out that Sanders and Nichols's piece was the eighth in a series of attacks by the Penn State group, especially by Sanders and Santley, against the Michigan group's conclusions vis-à-vis the founding and growth of Monte Albán. He labeled Sanders's approach "vulgar materialism," adding in his inimitable way that Sanders was "probably the only archaeologist left who could survey the Vatican and conclude that it was best explained by access to good farmland" (Flannery 1988:58).

FIGURE 7.15. "Glyph" that adorned the cover of *Debating Oaxaca Archaeology* (Marcus 1990). (Courtesy Museum of Anthropology, University of Michigan, and Joyce Marcus.)

Flannery undoubtedly was still annoyed by several reviews that Santley had done of the Oaxaca Project, including one titled "Obscured by the Clouds" (Santley and Arnold 1984)—an obvious reference to a book edited by Flannery and Marcus (1983), *The Cloud People: Divergent Evolution of the Zapotec and Mixtec Civilizations.* Many of Santley's reviews appeared in the *Journal of Anthropological Research,* which was published by the University of New Mexico's anthropology department, Santley's academic home. One could question an editor asking someone in his department to review books and monographs when he knows that that "someone" will not like the books, but that's a perk that goes with being editor—

sort of like home-field advantage to a football team. The Michigan group made good use of its own home-field advantage in 1990. Joyce Marcus, a Mesoamerican archaeologist and epigrapher (Marcus 1976, 1993) who had as much of a stake in the Monte Albán exchange as anyone, edited a monograph that appeared that year in the *Anthropological Papers* series published by the Museum of Anthropology at Michigan. Marcus (1990a) titled it "Debating Oaxaca Archaeology." The "glyph" that adorned the cover (Figure 7.15) pretty much said it all.

The monograph grew out of a symposium on Oaxaca archaeology that Marcus and Flannery chaired at the 1987 meeting of the Northeast Mesoamericanists Society in Philadelphia. The symposium addressed two topics: the intensely negative reaction by Sanders and his colleagues to the findings of the Oaxaca Project, and the proliferation of supposed factual misinformation. Marcus (1990b:ix) pointed out in the preface that "hardly a month goes by that we do not find ourselves misquoted, or our discoveries misdated or inaccurately described." The monograph was the Oaxaca Project's attempt to set the record straight. If, after the monograph appeared, the record *wasn't* set straight, it wasn't for lack of effort. The Michigan group came out with its guns blazing in an attempt not only to correct published misstatements but also to beat back the deterministic explanations of Sanders and his colleagues for the rise of Monte Albán.

The chapter containing the most invective is by Flannery and Marcus, who in one place show a photograph of a monastery in Greece, the buildings perched precipitously on a rocky pinnacle, 400 meters above the valley floor—an obvious parallel to Monte Albán. The caption reads in part, "Hey, Bill Sanders! Explain to us again how access to good farm land is the most important variable determining settlement location." Ouch. This was not the surest way to remain on someone's holiday gift list. Neither is referring to your colleagues, one by name, as "turkeys." Well, actually they didn't say the person was a turkey; they said that "he gets very nervous every year just before Thanksgiving" (Flannery and Marcus 1990:64). To our knowledge, no archaeologist had ever referred to another one in avian terms, but we might have missed an instance or two. Regardless, the chapter by Flannery and Marcus quickly became well known, and not only among Mesoamericanists. Everyone wanted to see what all the fuss was about and why such a vitriolic statement was needed in the first place.

While focusing their attention on the fireworks in the chapter by Flannery and Marcus, readers might have overlooked Rich Blanton's (1990) short chapter, "Theory and Practice in Mesoamerican Archaeology: A Comparison of Two Modes of Scientific Inquiry." We think Blanton put his finger on the reasons for the severe disagreements between two of the most visible research groups investigating the origin and development of complex societies in the New World. As such, his findings are central to our discussion of how science operates. We disagree with several of Blanton's conclusions, but we applaud the manner in which he came at the problem. To Blanton, the crux of the matter is found in two disparate views of science: the paradigm-replacement model of Thomas Kuhn, which he views the Penn State group as following, and the Michigan group's hypothesis-falsification model of Karl Popper. The two models are different enough to Blanton that, although they can coexist within a community of scientists studying the same issues, conflict is inevitable: "[Sanders] thinks our activities gratuitously undermine a theory he has devoted a lifetime to developing and promoting, while we, in turn, view him as a theoretical dinosaur who refuses to accept the reality of the falsification of critical parts of his theory" (Blanton 1990:3).

Blanton quotes from Imre Lakatos's (1970) "Falsification and the Methodology of Scientific Research Programmes" to draw a distinction between the Kuhnian "normal" science—characterized by dogmatic spirit and indoctrination—and Popperian "honesty"— "specifying precisely the conditions under which one is willing to give up one's position" (Lakatos 1970:92). Much of Lakatos's work centered on resolving what he saw as a conflict between Kuhn's revolutionary nature of science and Popper's doctrine of falsification. If Kuhn were right, Lakatos reasoned, then why would scientists so willingly give up their favored hypotheses when confronted with evidence that refuted them? They wouldn't. Blanton (1990:6) suggests that Sanders's paradigm is, to borrow a term Lakatos applied to Marxism and Freudism, "intellectually dishonest": "In paradigmatic science, criticism is anathema, and anything goes when it comes to protecting the integrity of the paradigm and its ideas.... Sanders and his followers have shown they are willing to go to extreme lengths to defend their theory." But isn't this pretty much the way science progresses, irrespective of Lakatos's disparaging remarks? Lakatos, after all, was a student of Popper's, so by tradition he would be expected to take a more rational approach to science than Kuhn's discontinuous sociological model affords.

Scientists, at least some of them, claim they work in an arena of falsifiability, but more often than not it is their colleagues who do the falsifying, not the scientist with the original hypothesis. We don't know any scientists who maintain a Mary Poppins-like "wonderfully self-critical attitude" (Popper 1983:190), in opposition to the Kuhnian "normal" scientist— "a person one ought to feel sorry for.... [one who] has been taught badly...a victim of indoctrination" (Popper 1970:52–53). But Popper is wrong: the "normal" scientist doesn't need our sympathy, nor has he or she been taught badly.

Science, as we have stressed repeatedly, is conducted by people who have ideas as well as strong opinions about those ideas. They might go through the falsification process early in the idea stage, but after they put it in print, they're not about to surrender it easily. In most cases their colleagues will do that for them, as the idea fails to be reproduced. Lakatos (1970) understood this, dividing research programs into two parts: the hard-core, unassailable foundations (first principles), which he referred to as the "negative heuristic"; and a "protective belt" around the core, which he referred to as the "positive heuristic." The protective belt consists of statements that are open to falsification. If and when they are falsified, they are replaced by other falsifiable statements, which also act to protect the core. Scientists thus do not have to try continually to falsify the core principles that underlie their research, only the "protective" hypotheses that emanate from the core.

Science, as we have also stressed repeatedly, is a marketplace where contextual, selective conditions determine the success and failure of products. Purveyors can extol the virtue of their wares to their hearts' content, just as they can run down the wares of their competitors, but in the long run consumers will make up their own minds. In opposition to the picture Blanton painted, the Michigan group was not setting forth falsifiable statements in print, ready to give them up if necessary because of any "wonderfully self-critical attitude." The group was as justifiably committed to its position as the Penn State group was to its position, so the members came out fighting. This happens in science when someone starts poking around in someone else's backyard. We do not see this as a bad thing. Although we understand what Robert Kelly meant when he said that archaeology rewards "polemic, bombast, and showmanship rather than the serious testing of ideas" (Kelly 2000:78), we don't think the dichotomy necessarily exists. The history of American archaeology demonstrates that the serious testing of ideas can take place in an arena of polemic, bombast, and showmanship.

Few disagreements last forever, and the one between the Michigan and Penn State groups was no exception. Our take is that the Michigan group came to realize that Bill Sanders was

not the strict environmental determinist seemed, and Sanders and his group be emphasize settlement variables other than those connected to the physical environment. This was Joyce Marcus's opinion of Bill Sanders in 1995: "From elite to blue collar and from art and aesthetics to science and ecology, Sanders—the man and his career—with his interest in regions, science, quantitative geography, ecology, and social evolution is a microcosm of archaeology and the evolution of settlement pattern studies" (Nichols 1996:93). That pretty well summarizes our view of Sanders as well.

ANALOGICAL ISSUES

We leave the Michigan–Penn State feud to examine other issues that came to the fore in the 1970s and '80s. We lump them under the broad heading of "analogical issues" and pick up our discussion from where we left it in Chapter 5. Here we focus almost exclusively on the work of archaeologists who were confronting the complex issues surrounding analogy head on, but this hides the fact that analogical reasoning is, and always has been, pervasive in archaeology. Not everyone identifies it by name, nor are they necessarily even aware of how they are using it, but it is inconceivable that there could be an archaeology that did not include analogy. For example, no one in the Michigan or Penn State groups ever said much about analogy, but analogical reasoning is clearly evident in the work of both, especially that by the Penn State group. Indeed, some of the calculations used in settlement-pattern analysis—the annual amount of maize required per family, the amount of various kinds of land required for maize production, and so forth—are based both on modern data and on data from the early Hispanic period. The same can be said of many propositions about sociopolitical organization made by both groups. Sanders (1974:109) was clear about this in his discussion of the transition from chiefdom to state at the Prehispanic center of Kaminaljuyú, Guatemala: "In a seminar at Pennsylvania State University, which I conducted over the past three years, we have attempted to relate material culture to levels of political organization, based upon an ethnographic sample of at least 100 contemporary or recent societies."

As we saw in Chapter 5, many archaeologists by the late 1970s had turned to ethnoarchaeology and experimental archaeology in an effort to build a solid foundation for inferring human behaviors. Nicholas David and Carol Kramer (2001) compiled data on the frequency of publications in ethnoarchaeology that appeared in various venues between 1956 and 1998. They found an average of 1.4 publications per year for 1956–1967, 13.4 per year for 1968–1981, 35.5 per year for 1982–1989, and 37.1 per year for 1990–1998. This demonstrates the marked increase in ethnoarchaeological research over that span. Although conducting studies to improve archaeological inference remained an important focus, many practitioners began to feel strongly that ethnoarchaeology was a legitimate subdiscipline of anthropology in its own right, capable of contributing to the larger field (David and Kramer 2001).

As the volume of ethnoarchaeological research increased, so too did discussions of how the resultant knowledge was to be used to generate valid processual conclusions. This became an epistemological and ontological issue, though it was seldom labeled as such. Many archaeologists again turned to the philosophy of science for guidance on how to build strong analogical arguments, whereas others, unconcerned with these issues, continued their ethnoarchaeological research. Still others took a different path, reasoning that the problems inherent in ethnographic analogy simply could not be fixed. Apparently, something else was called for—something called middle-range theory.

Ethnoarchaeology and Ethnographic Analogy

As noted in Chapter 5, one of the early leaders in modern ethnoarchaeology was Richard Gould (Figure 7.16). As he saw it in the 1970s, the goal of ethnoarchaeology—what he variously referred to as "living archaeology" and "the anthropology of human residues"—is to produce hypothetical lawlike propositions that can be tested against other present and past cases. By the late '70s, however, Gould was beginning to doubt the validity of conclusions based on ethnographic analogy. He became convinced that analogical arguments were not going to tell us much about behaviors unique to prehistory. Gould (1980) noted that although archaeologists generally assume that the processes that structure the ethnographic record have also structured the archaeological record, (1) this notion is self-limiting because we assume the very things we are trying to find out; (2) the notion is subject to the fallacy of affirming the consequent; (3) we have no good analogues for many adaptational forms of culture; and (4) uniformitarianism, which he did not define, is a "seductive notion" that presupposes that the modern world and the past are similar (Gould 1980:29–32). Gould argued that some processes may be subject to the principle of uniformitarianism, but others may not be. Therefore, analogical reasoning should be used solely to look for contrasts or anomalies between the modern world and the past. In Gould's view, this "contrastive approach" is "analogy's last hurrah"; "analogues are better at informing archaeologists about what they do know or can expect to know" (Gould 1980:37). The characteristics Gould attributed to uniformitarianist arguments were not those of methodological uniformitarianism but instead involved configurational properties (Chapter 5).

Gould (1980:37) outlined an alternative approach, beginning with the statement that "all scientific laws have irreducible properties of stating [causal] relations that are invariable in time and space. These laws are derived from observing regularities in time and space." In Gould's view, this applied equally to laws of human behavior. Gould was explicit about two requisite steps and implied a third for explaining the archaeological record: First, observe and model adaptive behavior in contemporary societies. Second, establish linkages between particular kinds of adaptive behavior (causes) and distinctive archaeological signatures in human residues (effects) that identify these particular behaviors. Third, compare attributes, the formation of which has been observed ethnoarchaeologically, to modern static phenomena created in the past and, when similar, infer on the basis of the causal linkage between behaviors and residues that similar processes created both. Gould correctly characterized ethnographic analogy as an analytic procedure for matching the forms of humanly created materials and inferring similar causes. His suggested procedure for explaining the archaeological record is an accurate rendition of the actualistic method, methodological uniformitarianism, and the role of immanent properties (Wylie 1982a).

Gould and Pat Watson participated in a "dialogue" in which each presented his or her views on the value of ethnoarchaeological research and on the utility of ethnographic analogy for archaeology. Gould argued that "uniformitarianism is a bridge between past and present" and that ethnoarchaeological observations permit us to posit linkages between certain kinds of behavior and the unique characteristics of the material residues produced by that behavior (Gould and Watson 1982:369). However, he again worried that the use of ethnographic analogies as signature criteria of particular behaviors would preclude discovery of past behaviors that have no known historic or ethnographic counterparts (Gould and Watson 1982:372).

Watson, on the other hand, was concerned that archaeologists could not translate the archaeological record into human behaviors and cultural processes because the discipline lacked "a well worked out theory of cultural dynamics" based on a "principle of generic uniformity of present and past cultural systems" (Gould

FIGURE 7.16. Richard Gould at the scene of the 2003 West Warwick, Rhode Island, nightclub fire that killed 100 people and injured more than 200 others. Gould, team leader for the Rhode Island Forensic Archaeology Recovery unit, tells the grisly yet fascinating story of the recovery of evidence from the fire in "Disaster Archaeology" (Gould 2004). (Courtesy Richard Gould.)

and Watson 1982:358). The critical part for her was to test the validity of linkages between material residues and culture processes in both ethnoarchaeological and archaeological contexts, and eventually to produce such a theory. Perhaps this is the kind of theory that Binford had in mind when he introduced the notion of middle-range theory five years before the Gould and Watson dialogue (see below).

Most of those who commented on analogy seemed to ignore ontological issues and to focus instead on epistemological ones. Thus, the concern for signature criteria of various causal processes permeated many discussions of archaeological reasoning through the 1970s and into the early '80s. John Fritz (1972), for example, implied that diagnostic criteria (static effects) indicate the presence of particular past phenomena (dynamic causes), but they might be difficult to establish. He noted that although the actualistic method is requisite to explaining the archaeological record, there was a lack of explicit arguments attempting to demonstrate that a particular cluster of criteria is diagnostic of a particular past dynamic. Drawing on philosophers, he labeled these "arguments of relevance," the requirements of which involved either undertaking actualistic research and establishing diagnostic criteria, or establishing the necessary (not just sufficient) causal linkage between a particular process and its archaeological signature. Bruce Smith's (1977) "plausibility considerations" narrowed the range of possible causes. If necessary, the final selection of one of several competing causes is accomplished by examining concomitant variation of different variables in the archaeological and actualistic records.

Like Gould, Ian Hodder believed that if we interpret the past by analogy to the present, we can never discover forms of society and culture that do not exist today. He argued that because similarities in some aspects do not certainly or even logically imply similarities in others, we can never prove analogically based interpretations. Importantly, Hodder (1982c:16) distinguished between what he called "formal analogies" and "relational analogies." He noted that the former produce conclusions based on simple form-related similarities between two objects, one of which is better or more fully known or understood than the other. Here, the conclusion takes the form that because the two objects share some properties visible or known for both, they also share other properties known or visible only for one.

Formal analogies are weak, Hodder argued, because the observed association of shared characteristics of the objects or situations can be fortuitous or accidental. He suggested that archaeologists use relational analogies, wherein associated attributes are causally related. For example, to determine the function of a stone tool, archaeologists once simply examined its shape. But because shape is not always directly related to tool function (a screwdriver shape denotes a screwdriver function until that screwdriver is used to pry open a can of paint), archaeologists turned to formal attributes of artifacts causally related to tool function, such as use wear (e.g., Salmon 1981). Relational analogies are strong precisely because they explicitly involve "some necessary relation between the various aspects of the analogy"; the associated attributes are thought to be causally related to the inferred properties (Hodder 1982c:19–20). To improve such analogies, Hodder (1982c: 20–21) suggested that archaeologists consider not only the "relevant causal links between the different parts of the analogy" but also the cultural and archaeological context of the phenomena of interest as potentially causally related to the observed and inferred properties (see also Salmon 1981).

Alison Wylie, a philosopher of archaeology, explored the structure of analogical arguments, noting that they are inductive and ampliative: they result in conclusions that contain more information than the initial data and premises. This sometimes leads to skepticism that any reliable knowledge of the past can be derived, but in Wylie's (1982b) view such skepticism is misplaced and reflects a misconception of science. She characterized a realist view of science as one that acknowledges and emphasizes the ampliative aspect of knowledge and seeks to improve the basis for that knowledge. Analogical arguments are not inherently faulty, but they can be categorized as involving either weakly or strongly argued formal or relational analogies, as noted by Hodder (1982c). This actually is quite similar to what Binford (1967) recommended with respect to the covariation of multiple variables.

Weakly argued analogies are those that fail to "specify the (usually limited) points on which an analogy holds (i.e., to specify the positive, negative and neutral aspects of an analogical comparison of items or contexts) and an indiscriminate carrying over of all features of the [actualistic] source to the [prehistoric] subject" (Wylie 1982b:43). Formal analogies are those that specify only points of similarity (and less often points of dissimilarity) between the modern source and the prehistoric subject phenomena, and conclude that similar processes created both phenomena without considering the possible causal and/or structural linkages between the observed phenomena and the processes (Hodder 1982c; Wylie 1982a, 1988). As Wylie (1988:136) put it, "[A]nalogical argument is formally valid; the difficulty is just that the relevant major premises are insecure." In constructing analogies one must not only consider formal similarities between the ethnographic source and the archaeological subject but also establish that the observed properties are somehow nonaccidentally related to, or more than simply correlated with, the inferred properties of interest.

Relational properties (causal linkages) warrant the analogical conclusion and guide inquiry toward strengthening a conclusion (Wylie 1988). Detailed work on the modern (source) side of the analogical equation "can serve not just to widen the range of analogues on which interpretation can draw, but also to sharply limit them, providing an important basis for critical assessment of their credibility" (Wylie 1989a:13). One manner of working on the subject (prehistoric) side of the equation involves calling on multiple independent lines of evidence (Wylie 1989a). Simply put, working back and forth (horizontally) between subject and source sides of the equation and up and down (vertically) within each side of the equation by studying multiple attributes should produce strong analogically based inferences. To use Wylie's (1989a) metaphor, such "tacking back and forth," and "building suspension cables," respectively, will simultaneously reinforce and constrain inferences. Building strong relational analogies, then, involves specifying the "number and extent of similarities between source and subject, the number and diversity of sources cited in the premises in which known and inferred similarities co-occur as postulated for the subject, and the expansiveness of the conclusions relative to the premises" (Wylie 1985b:98).

Middle-Range Theory

The discussions by Gould, Hodder, Wylie, and a host of others (e.g., Murray and Walker 1988; Wobst 1978) reflect a general, if not discipline-wide, unease with ethnographic analogy in general and the uniformitarianist assumptions that underpinned its use in particular. Some archaeologists opted for the easy way out and continued to do culture history, which did not always require explicit use of ethnographic analogues or ethnoarchaeological data. Others chose another option: because ethnographic analogy seemingly was the only method available for writing ethnographies of the past, they followed Wylie's advice and strengthened the source side of the analogy by using multiple lines of evidence. Lew Binford (1981a) proposed a third, terminologically unique option, which fully anticipated Hodder's discussion of relational analogies. He argued that to use ethnoarchaeological observations properly, a *nec-*

essary causal relation between a particular process and its result(s) must be established: "[I]f we can isolate causal relations between things, and if we can understand such relations in terms of more general principles of necessity, such as the theories of mechanics, then we have a strong warrant for the inference of the cause from the observed effect" (Binford 1981a:26).

For Binford, a necessary causal relation is one that is "constant and unique," and the establishment of such relations will allow us to specify archaeologically visible "signature patterns" that allow discrimination of one causal agent or process from all others. According to Binford, establishing these kinds of relations faced two challenges: (1) the relation must be shown in fact to be causal and not just correlational, and (2) the process must be characteristic of the past. The latter clearly involves immanent properties and processes in the sense that paleontologist George Gaylord Simpson (1963, 1970) used the terms (see Chapter 5). Binford (1977b) termed the search for immanent properties, or temporally invariant natural laws, "middle-range research."

Middle-range research was supposed to produce what Binford termed "middle-range theory," which he characterized as a method of converting "the observationally static facts of the archaeological record to statements of dynamics.... In approaching this problem, we must develop ideas and theories (middle-range theory) regarding the formation processes of the archaeological record" (Binford 1977b:6–7). Once the static archaeological record was converted to a dynamic cultural system, then one gained an "understanding of the processes responsible for change and diversification in the organizational properties of living systems" by turning to what Binford (1977b:7) called "general theory." This was a means of explaining the variation perceived in the archaeological record and thus involved the typical meaning of the term "theory" in virtually all sciences and in philosophy as well (Raab and Goodyear 1984). Middle-range theory was, in the hands of Binford, merely a different term for doing actualistic research (Arnold 2003).

FIGURE 7.17. James O'Connell in northern Tanzania with his young Hadza friend Hamisi, carrying a zebra pelvis back to camp, 1986. (Photograph by Kristen Hawkes, courtesy James O'Connell.)

The two kinds of theory—general explanatory and middle range—were to be developed hand in hand, Binford (1977b) said, but his own efforts over the next decade or so emphasized the production of middle-range theory (e.g., Binford 1978, 1981a, 1984, 1985, 1987b). By this time the need for parallel development of these two kinds of principles had been pointed out by behavioral archaeologists (e.g., Reid, Schiffer, and Rathje 1975; Schiffer 1975b, 1976), as we will see below.

James O'Connell (Figure 7.17), an archaeologist with extensive experience in ethnoarchaeology both in Australia and Africa (e.g., Binford and O'Connell 1984; Hawkes, O'Connell, and Rogers 1997; Lupo and O'Connell 2002; O'Connell 1987; O'Connell and Hawkes 1984; O'Connell, Hawkes, and Blurton Jones 1990), argued for general explanatory theory in an article titled "Ethnoar-

chaeology Needs a General Theory of Human Behavior" (O'Connell 1995). He preferred Darwinian-based human behavioral ecology as his explanatory theory of choice. This theory holds, in part, that natural selection has built wise humans who are aware of the immediate, but perhaps not the long-term, reproductive consequences of their actions. As a result, they are likely to choose those behaviors that enhance their reproductive success (Chapter 8).

Some later commentators who argued that ethnoarchaeology could be a subdiscipline of anthropology in its own right apparently agreed with O'Connell on the need for general explanatory theory. But they also noted that his preferred theory did not account for such things as "certain kinds of behavior driven by a fundamental human cognitive process of personal and social identification" (David and Kramer 2001:42). Their point was that behavioral ecology concerns the biological survival of the human organism and ignores the social interactions between organisms and groups of organisms. O'Connell obviously would disagree. Whatever the case, what concerns us more here is the fact that ethnoarchaeological research led to a major debate over the topic of formation of the archaeological record. To understand that debate, we first need to backtrack a bit.

BEHAVIORAL ARCHAEOLOGY, FORMATION-PROCESS THEORY, AND THE POMPEII PREMISE

Although it had much earlier roots, the systematic study of the processes that produce the archaeological record grew out of processual archaeology. This should not be surprising, given both an increased awareness of these processes brought about by ethnoarchaeological observations and an increased interest in relationships between human behavior and artifacts—what were referred to in much of the pertinent literature as "material culture." This interest was fostered by several of Binford's early statements, one of the more important being that "the loss, breakage, and abandonment of implements and facilities at different locations, where groups of variable structure performed different tasks, leaves a 'fossil' record of the actual operation of an extinct society" (Binford 1964a:425). Similar statements appear in some of his earlier and later publications. In "Archaeology as Anthropology," for example, he noted that "the formal structure of artifact assemblages together with the between element contextual relationships should and do present a systematic and understandable picture of *the total extinct* cultural system" (Binford 1962a:219). In his chapter in *Man the Hunter* (Lee and DeVore 1968), which was based on the work he and Sally had done with the Mousterian data (Binford and Binford 1966a), he assumed "that the size, composition, and spatial structure of an assemblage are jointly determined by: first, the size and composition of the social unit responsible; and second, the form of differential task performance carried out by individuals and segments of the occupying social unit" (Binford 1968b:272).

If these and similar assumptions were in fact correct, then the archaeological record was a remarkably clean, crisp, and direct reflection of past human behavior. In particular, the relationship between human behaviors and artifacts—their forms, frequencies, spatial distributions, and associations—was direct and positive; the correlation coefficient between the two was one. This assumption of a perfect correlation—termed by behavioralists an "equivalence assumption" or "equivalence transformation" (e.g., Reid 1985; Schiffer 1976)—led to a consideration of two questions. First, how could the correlation be exploited to its fullest? Second, was the correlation really perfect? The manner in which each of these questions was addressed rested largely on Binford's (1968a:23) statement that the "practical limitations on our knowledge of the past are not inherent in the nature of the archeological record; the limitations lie in our methodological naiveté, in our lack of development for principles determining the relevance of archeological remains to propositions regarding processes and events of the past."

What would follow, then, was more of a methodological revolution than an ontological one (Meltzer 1979, 1981b). For the revolution to occur, how the archaeological record was being viewed had to change. One initial nudge was provided by Binford (1962a) when he suggested abandoning the traditional definition of culture as shared and transmitted ideas in favor of the Whitean definition of culture as humankind's extrasomatic means of adaptation. That definition, as we have seen, explicitly informed the rethinking of archaeology undertaken by the processualists, who obviously had a keen interest in artifacts as reflections of human behaviors.

Four Strategies: The Birth of Behavioral Archaeology

Formalizing the relationship between artifacts and human behavior became a focus of research at the University of Arizona through the efforts of Jeff Reid, Bill Rathje, and Mike Schiffer (1974; Reid, Schiffer, and Rathje 1975). In their view the marked diversification of archaeology into such entities as public, ethno-, contract, processual, historical, systems, and other kinds of archaeology was expectable given the population explosion of archaeologists. This diversification, however, made it difficult to identify commonalities that crosscut the different approaches. Reid and his two colleagues first identified what they took to be *the* thread that was common to all archaeology: regardless of particular research interests or contexts, archaeology is a discipline composed of a body of methods and theories for describing and explaining human behaviors through the study of material culture (Reid, Rathje, and Schiffer 1974).

They then structured this commonality into four strategies based on the age (past or present) of the human behaviors and the age of the artifacts (Reid, Schiffer, and Rathje 1975). First, prehistoric and historical archaeology (traditional *and* processual) involved the study of past human behavior on the basis of artifacts produced in the past. Second, ethnoarchaeology and experimental archaeology involved the study of modern human behaviors and their resultant artifacts for the purpose of constructing laws useful for studying past human behaviors. Third, one could investigate artifacts resulting from past human behaviors in order to acquire principles of long-term behavioral change, as useful for investigating human behavior of the past and present. This strategy foreshadowed recent studies of prehistoric anthropogenic influences on local and global ecology (e.g., Redman 1999). Fourth, one could examine modern behaviors and the artifacts produced by those behaviors, exemplified by Rathje's (1974) Tucson Garbage Project and Schiffer's Reuse Project (Schiffer, Downing, and McCarthy 1981).

Importantly, there was a potential for information flow between the four strategies. The idiographic strategies fed research questions into the nomothetic strategies, and the latter in turn furnished principles useful for inferring and explaining human behavior. Reid and his colleagues believed that behavioral archaeology's interdependent strategies not only reintegrated the discipline but also explicitly recognized the contributions of all archaeologists—an important political consideration in the wake of the controversies still roiling around processualism. The four strategies embraced and embellished processualism while acknowledging the value of traditional archaeology.

The focus of archaeological method and theory on human behavior prompted Schiffer to title his first book *Behavioral Archeology* (1976). In his view it represented a clean break from Binford, his former mentor, insofar as archaeological inference was concerned. The break was founded on the fact that the archaeological record is far from a perfect reflection of human behaviors. The correlation coefficient, to continue the statistical metaphor, was often much less than one because the record had been created not only by human behaviors of interest but also by various noncultural processes. Both sets of processes often, if not always, distort the behavioral patterns reflected in the archaeological record. This insight was not Schiffer's alone, but he brought it to the forefront of archaeological thinking

and helped to develop principles and methods, especially the use of life-history models in various guises, for taking formation processes into account in every inference (e.g., Schiffer 1972a, 1976, 1983, 1987).

Schiffer, like Binford and Flannery, also adopted strategies for acquiring intellectual progeny. Appreciating that controversies with Binford usually attracted considerable attention, he baited his former mentor by aggressively attacking the claim that the archaeological record is a fossilized cultural system. That statement, Schiffer (1976) insisted, was false. Binford took serious issue with Schiffer's comments, and so ensued a head-to-head confrontation that would last many years (more on that below).

Disorganization and Destruction of the Archaeological Record

In 1968 Robert Ascher presented a clever discussion of the formation of the archaeological record. He modeled a formational history composed of three phases. He characterized the first, "inhabited," phase as a time when "disorganization and organization proceed simultaneously at different rates, and at different rates at different times.... People and nature in combination act as agents of disorganization" (Ascher 1968:44). The implication was that human behaviors organize and create order in phenomena, and subsequently nature and other human behaviors disorganize and destroy the original order. During the second, or "ghost," phase, apparently only "natural agents are disorganizing matter that was once arranged in patterns by human effort" (Ascher 1968:46). The third, "archaeological," phase begins when an archaeologist alters the trajectory of the disorganization process, such as by stopping the corrosion of a metal artifact while at the same time removing it from its original depositional location.

Ascher (1968:47) emphasized that an archaeologist must learn to recognize "man's purposeful arrangements [and this] depends on distinguishing between the action of natural agents and the action of human agents.... The path of disorganization from 'inhabited,' through 'ghost,' and on to archaeological disturbance is irreversible, but it must be figuratively reversed when inferring past human behavior." To underscore these points, Ascher mentioned the town of Pompeii, which had been buried suddenly and catastrophically by volcanic ash from the A.D. 79 eruption of Mt. Vesuvius. Pompeii provided a unique disorganizational path because the catastrophic burial event "instantly terminated the 'inhabited' phase of its existence and sealed it off from agents of natural disorganization" (Ascher 1968:47). The disorganization and destruction of Pompeii was stopped at the transition between the inhabited and ghost phases. As we will see shortly, Ascher's remarks were not the last time that Pompeii would figure prominently in discussions of disorganization and destruction of the archaeological record, and how those processes did or did not affect our explanations of past cultural behavior.

While still a graduate student, Schiffer began to explore the nature of, and influences on, the correlation between human behaviors and artifacts. He first identified "elements" as the items making up a complete inventory of material culture, and then distinguished between what he termed the "systemic context" and the "archaeological context" (Schiffer 1972a). The former refers to the past behavioral system in which an element participated, and the latter concerns the geoarchaeological context of that element once it leaves the behavioral system. Schiffer's point was simple: The archaeological record consists of "stuff" (artifacts, ecofacts, features, and the like) and a structure (the spatial distributions and associations of the stuff). Stuff and structure in a geological deposit can be completely natural: the attributes of each have been created only by natural processes, the principles of which Schiffer (1976) termed "n-transforms." Once the archaeological record is formed—meaning things have left the behavioral system—it, too, can be affected, often dramatically, by natural processes. Additionally, human behaviors—cultural formation processes—modify both natural stuff and nat-

ural structure; Schiffer termed the principles that describe these human processes "c-transforms."

Once an item enters the archaeological context, its attributes do not cease to be added to, subtracted from, or modified. Items can be mechanically broken by trampling, chemically altered by diagenic processes, and moved by geological, human-induced, and other turbation processes (Lewarch and O'Brien 1981; Schiffer 1983, 1987; Wood and Johnson 1978). The task of someone interested in inferring human behaviors from the formal attributes of artifacts and attributes of their distribution (location, quantity, associations, and so on) must analytically partition the attributes (traces) into their various contexts of production—the behaviors of interest, cultural formation processes, and noncultural formation processes (Sullivan 1978). This is done in part by using c-transforms and n-transforms as well as "correlates" (Schiffer 1975b, 1976), which describe relationships between behaviors and artifacts, and "local expertise," consisting of empirical generalizations (Reid 1985).

It was becoming obvious to Schiffer that without n-transforms, c-transforms, and correlates, inference and explanation in archaeology would be impossible. Correlates "function in inference justification by allowing the derivation or identification of some aspects of an operating cultural system from knowledge of those aspects, spatial and material, which would be or are present in the archeological record" (Schiffer 1976:14). Once the distortions introduced by formation processes have been isolated and taken into account, correlates can be employed to infer specific behaviors such as artifact manufacture and use as well as more abstract behaviors, including religious rituals and aspects of social and political organization (LaMotta and Schiffer 2001; Walker 1995).

In reacting to the new archaeologists' assertion that spatial patterns of artifacts in archaeological context represent systemic spatial patterns—that is, artifact distributions reflect past activity areas—Schiffer (1972a, 1976) defined several types of refuse. Use of these refuse types, he believed, would enable archaeologists to formulate methods of activity analysis that were sensitive to variation in cultural formation processes. What he referred to as "de facto refuse" is produced when a place is abandoned and cultural materials, often still usable, are left behind. "Primary refuse" is trash—broken artifacts and the like—that is discarded at its location of use, whereas "secondary refuse" is discarded away from use locations. If one wants to infer human behaviors from the structure of the archaeological record, then one has to be able to distinguish the three kinds of refuse.

In a later article, Schiffer (1983) presented in detail the lines of evidence and methods that could be used to infer the formation processes of specific deposits, such as the three major refuse types. Detailed identifications of formation processes sometimes require "refitting studies," in which flakes from a single core, or sherds from a single pot, are reassembled to detect human (and sometimes noncultural) transport (e.g., Cahen and Moeyersons 1977; Hofman 1981, 1986). Refitting often is labor intensive, but it sometimes furnishes insights into formation processes unavailable through any other method (e.g., Skibo, Schiffer, and Kowalski 1989).

Schiffer was not alone in stressing the importance of formation processes. In addition to Ascher, whose ethnoarchaeologically based study strongly influenced Schiffer's early formulations, was George Cowgill (1970), who proposed a model in the context of sampling theory. Stressing possible discontinuities between artifacts in a past cultural system and those recovered and analyzed by archaeologists, he identified two artifact populations: the "physical consequences" population, including artifacts and features (pits, walls, and the like), which was the immediate consequence of past activities; and the "physical finds" population, which archaeologists collect using a particular sampling design and recovery procedure. David Clarke (1973) also proposed the constructs "predepositional theory" and "depositional theory," which were meant to relate human be-

haviors to the formation of the archaeological record. In many ways Clarke's brief discussion presaged middle-range theory and formation-process theory.

Leslie Wildesen (1973) made many of the same points that Schiffer had. For example, she used the terms NC for the natural component and CC for the cultural component, where a component was a "developmental" subsystem that included stuff and the formation processes that influenced it. Wildesen did not talk about correlates but instead borrowed a formula concerning pedogenic (soil forming) processes from soil science and modified it for what she called "site development":

$$m = f(cl, o, r, p, C, t\ldots),$$

where m is the midden; cl is the climate; o is the organisms (macroscopic and microscopic) that exist in the sediment; r is the relief (including aspect and topography); p is the parent material of the sediments (lithology, geology, mineralogy, chemistry); C stands for the cultural inputs to the deposit (both stuff and processes such as movement and breakage of items); t is time (the longer the time, the more effects midden-development processes are likely to have); and the ellipsis indicates that additional variables can be added as needed. The formula is read, "The development and condition of the midden deposit is a function of its climate, the organisms in the sediments, the relief of the deposit, the parent material comprising the deposit, the cultural/behavioral inputs to the deposit, and the time over which all variables operate."[1]

Wildesen's point was that the formational history, as well as the preservational condition of sites and artifacts when an archaeologist studies them, is a function of these and similar variables. During the 1970s, others, too, recognized, much as Ascher had in the 1960s, the lack of correspondence between human behaviors and the archaeological record. Many of them were ethnoarchaeologists who witnessed the operation of formation processes firsthand (e.g., Gould 1978a; Heider 1967; Kramer 1979a; Stanislawski 1969a, 1969b) and as a result were becoming increasingly aware that it would be no simple matter to translate or transform the static archaeological record into human behavioral dynamics.

The archaeological grapevine indicated that Binford was unhappy that Schiffer, in an apparent jibe at Binford, had pointed out that the archaeological record was not a perfectly fossilized reflection of human behaviors. The two met, at the invitation of Fred Plog, in January 1978 to discuss their views in the hopes of reconciliation, accommodation, compromise, and perhaps a new synthesis. "Neither moved a millimeter" from his preferred position (Schiffer 1995a:19). In a symposium at the 1979 meeting of the Society for American Archaeology in Vancouver, Binford claimed Schiffer had "retarded" the study of formation processes. Schiffer requested and received time to reply during the symposium and pointed out that Binford "had been leading astray a generation of New Archaeologists while [Schiffer] was still in junior high school" (Schiffer 1995a:20). In the rush to be anthropological, Schiffer continued, that generation had seemingly swallowed hook, line, and sinker Binford's reasoning that the archaeological record was a good, reliable, valid, and undistorted reflection of human behavior. Schiffer's point was that the quality of the reflection—and its importance for specific inferences—depended entirely on the formational history of the portion of the record under scrutiny and the behavioral questions being asked of that portion.

Binford would have none of what he saw as complete nonsense and a gross misreading of his original statements. In 1981 he published an article titled "Behavioral Archaeology and the 'Pompeii Premise'" (Binford 1981b), claiming that behavioral archaeology as advocated by Schiffer adopted an inductive approach and thus inferred cultural and behavioral dynamics from the archaeological record. According to Binford, Schiffer and others who agreed with him were surprised and perhaps dismayed to find that the archaeological record was not a set of miniature Pompeiis. Binford said that he had always held that the linkages between the dynamics of human behaviors and the statics of the archaeological record were not simple and direct, and that the solution to this conundrum was to develop robust methods for making the linkages. After the publication of Binford's (1977a) *For Theory Building in Archaeology*, those linkages were to be discerned by means of middle-range research and used as middle-range theory to reconstitute the static archaeological record into prehistoric dynamic human behaviors.

To belittle Schiffer's theoretical framework for studying formation processes, Binford (1981b) cited Ascher's (1961a:324) notation that archaeologists do not dig up "the remains of a once living community stopped...at a point in time"; this "erroneous notion, often implicit in archaeological literature, might be called the Pompeii premise." Binford stated that he had never subscribed to such a premise. Binford also named several individuals who in his view had misunderstood his early work and had sided with Schiffer (e.g., Coe 1978; Collins 1975; DeBoer and Lathrap 1979; Jochim 1979). It is puzzling that, for more than a decade, Binford had not called attention to the many people doing what he regarded as flawed research, often in ethnoarchaeological contexts. Of course, they were not former students who, as Binford saw it, had turned on him. But once Binford had struck back at Schiffer, he had to broaden his scope to include the others.

Schiffer responded to Binford's attack in two ways. First, in a review of Binford's (1983a) second collection of reprinted articles, Schiffer (1985a) pointed out that Binford's 1960s' subscription to the notion of a perfect correlation between human behaviors and the archaeological record had changed subsequent to Binford's doing some ethnoarchaeological research himself. Contradicting his earlier claim about the archaeological record being a fossilized society, Binford (1973:242) later claimed that "there is little correlation between what is done [at a site] and the artifacts remaining." Schiffer pointed out that this had been his (Schiffer's) point all along (e.g., Schiffer 1972a, 1975b, 1976). Binford was changing his emphasis, now saying that archaeologists needed to construct "middle-range theory," which included but did not clearly distinguish among Schiffer's n-transforms, c-transforms, and correlates. Schiffer (1985a:193) noted that to him the basic difference between his approach and Binford's was that he (Schiffer) favored "handling formation processes 'up front'" and explicitly.

In Schiffer's view, Binford's middle-range theory was primarily a catchy rubric for labeling the sum total of principles (correlates, c-transforms, and n-transforms) needed for inference—that is, for going from statics to dynamics. Thus, this move was mainly political, not scientific. Not only was this an effective recruiting tool but it permitted Binford and his followers to discuss formation processes and inference without having to cite the literature of behavioral archaeology or employ its jargon. Perhaps for similar purposes, Binford and his followers in later years appropriated the term "taphonomy" from paleontology and paleoecology. Writing about sherd and lithic scatters in taphonomic terms doesn't fit with the definition of the term—the transformation of living organisms from the biosphere to the lithosphere (Lyman 1994)—but it was a devastatingly effective strategy for increasing the fitness of Binford's ideas.

Schiffer's (1985b) second response to Binford was to outline at length how the Pompeii premise as originally characterized by Ascher (1961a) was in fact still a significant part of archaeology in the American Southwest. With a nod to his own distinction between archaeological and systemic contexts, Schiffer (1985b:24) emphasized that "analytical strategies predicated on the assumption—implicit or explicit—that archaeological variability directly mirrors systemic variability must be abandoned." Continuing, he noted that only after the effects of formation processes, including recovery and analytical processes, have been factored out or controlled for, is one justified in seeking human behavioral causes for the remaining variation. Today, the study of formation processes occupies a good part of the ar-

chaeological literature (e.g., Goldberg, Nash, and Petraglia 1993; Nash and Petraglia 1987; Schiffer 1987; Tani 1995). Similarly, many of the central tenets of behavioral archaeology continue to guide various research endeavors (LaMotta and Schiffer 2001; Skibo, Walker and Nielsen 1995; Walker 1998). And, among the adherents of behavioral archaeology one can count the many practitioners of experimental archaeology and ethnoarchaeology who have constructed useful lawlike generalizations.

Likewise, middle-range theory has continued to be popular well after Binford coined the term. To its proponents it provides a means of translating a static archaeological record into a dynamic cultural system—to discover "invariant linkages between the archaeological record and the behavior that produced it" (Thomas 1986a:245). Although there was some concern (e.g., Raab and Goodyear 1984) that the meaning of "middle-range theory" was not always clear, we agree with Robert Bettinger's (1991:64) statement that "just about everyone agrees that middle-range theory concerns itself with interpreting the archaeological record." This is essentially the point Philip Arnold (2003) recently made. He was explicit that the "middle-range program" involves actualistic research along with uniformitarian assumptions aimed at using established causal links between behavioral dynamics and the statics of the archaeological record. These links serve as "points of reference" that guide research on past behaviors, just as readings of elevation on a sheet of paper guide one in drawing a topographic map. As we noted earlier, Binford (1987b) came to refer to middle-range research as a method for providing "frames of reference."

During the 1990s, a number of commentators tried to synthesize what they saw as two distinct yet similar approaches to the archaeological record—the middle-range program and the formation-process program. Both clearly are concerned with translating the static archaeological record into human-behavioral dynamics. The process of translation involves stripping away the influences of cultural and noncultural formation processes. It became evident that aspects of middle-range theory are commensurate with theories of formation of the archaeological record (Schiffer 1985b, 1988; Shott 1998; Tschauner 1996) and with aspects of both processual and postprocessual archaeology (Kosso 1991; Saitta 1992; Trigger 1995; Tschauner 1996) as the precise nature of middle-range theory became clearer.

The approach, despite what it might be called, was not strictly method as alleged by a few (e.g., Kosso 1991), but instead was a combination of method and theory (Schiffer 1988; Wylie 1989b). By means of lawlike generalizations obtained through actualistic research (buttressing Wylie's source side of analogies), archaeologists could convert observations on the archaeological record (a collection of broken rocks, broken pots, and other items distributed across the landscape) into inferences (statements about past human behavior that an ethnographer would recognize). The ultimate meaning of that converted record—in terms of cultural dynamics, especially cultural change—became, in the 1990s, a subject of consuming interest to processualists, behavioralists, and others.

Debates about middle-range theory and about the best ways to theorize formation processes serve to highlight the role played by recruitment and reproduction in American archaeology. Binford has shown himself to be a shrewd and skillful recruiter. When behavioralists claimed that basic tenets of his early methodological program were inaccurate and misleading, which they said Binford had learned for himself in his ethnoarchaeological research, he co-opted the critics by reformulating their program and expressing it in new terms. Correlates, c-transforms, and n-transforms were converted en masse into the simpler and more euphonious "middle-range theory," and the latter came to be widely reproduced in the literature even though the substantive differences between Binford's middle-range research and the behavioral program are at best obscure. They are simply different brands of an archaeology much more sophisticated than early processualism. In some respects, Binford and Schiffer each became the other's most effective recruit.

The 1980s witnessed the emergence of new issues as well as new intellectual alignments and realignments. If Willey and Sabloff (1993:257) are correct, and we believe they are, then much of the credit for the shape and complexity of the archaeological landscape can be laid at the feet of the new archaeology because of the "profound attitudinal change" it produced in the discipline. One did not have to boldly proclaim himself or herself a processualist to be labeled as such, for these leanings were evident in how one formulated and solved research problems. And based on our survey of the decade, there were lots of interesting problems to solve. One set of problems involved the evolution and organization of complex societies. The scale of investigations ranged from cities and states down to what were often referred to as "tribal" units (e.g., Braun and Plog 1982). Although earlier we focused on work in the Near East and especially in Mesoamerica, we need to point out that considerable attention also was given to sociopolitical organization in the American Southwest (e.g., Fish and Reid 1996; Graves 1987; Gumerman 1994; Gumerman and Gell-Mann 1994; McGuire and Saitta 1996; Mills 1996; Upham 1990; Upham, Lightfoot, and Jewett 1989; Upham and Plog 1986; Wills and Leonard 1994).

Much of the early archaeological work, regardless of region, was inspired by ethnologists such as Morton Fried (1967), Marvin Harris (1959), Marshall Sahlins (1958), and Elman Service (1962, 1971, 1975), but by the 1970s archaeologists were moving from ethnological models of cultural evolution to ones built in large part from the archaeological record (e.g., Renfrew 1974). Thus they had begun to do what Marvin Harris (1968a:359–360) had urged in his remarks at the Binfords' 1965 symposium (the one that led to *New Perspectives*): "Archeologists, shrive yourselves of the notion that the units which you seek to reconstruct must match the units in social organization which contemporary ethnographers have attempted to tell you exist."

Arguments over such things as actualistic research, with a focus on ontological and epistemological issues, indicate that by 1980 or so the great debates in American archaeology no longer were over only culture process, ceramic sociology, and the structure of science. Rather, they had expanded to cover all kinds of anthropological and archaeological concerns, including the degree of correlation between human behavior and the archaeological record. We might have made it appear as if these were academic pursuits, played out only in universities, but this was not the case. As we saw in Chapter 6, a huge population of M.A.s and Ph.D.s, newly minted in the 1970s, found jobs as agency or contract archaeologists. Many of them had been trained as processualists. They understood probabilistic sampling and the concept of research designs; they knew about the potential interpretive value of ethnoarchaeology, even if they hadn't participated in such research personally; and they were aware that formation processes had to be taken into account if they were to obtain anthropological insights into humankind's prehistoric past. Those archaeologists may never have obtained academic positions, but they applied what they had learned to the agency requests for proposals they issued and the reports they wrote.

By the end of the '70s, mechanistic programs for archaeological research, some inspired by a superficial acquaintance with philosophers of science, had become passé. Nonetheless, during the '80s there were still a few discussions on the role of the philosophy of science and how philosophical models could or could not assist archaeologists in attaining their discipli-

nary goals (e.g., Renfrew, Rowlands, and Segraves 1982; Salmon 1982; Schiffer 1981). In addition, a few major works in the philosophy of archaeology appeared (e.g., Gibbon 1989; Kelley and Hanen 1988), but they did not stir passions and generate lengthy debates as had the programmatic statements of the early new archaeology. Similarly, Pat Watson, Steve LeBlanc, and Chuck Redman (1984) issued a revised and more sophisticated version of their 1971 treatise on science and its operation, but this edition went all but unnoticed.

By about 1980 it seemed most archaeologists had concluded that philosophical commitments impinged little on the actual practice of archaeology. Perhaps Kent Flannery had been right: good archaeology and bad archaeology were done by adherents of all philosophies. What mattered, then, was the rigorous and explicit application of methods and principles to the archaeological record, regardless of which philosophical model of science one chose to cite. As Albert Spaulding (1968:34) put it, philosophers of science do "not legislate on what [scientists] can and cannot do." Others recognized this as well (e.g., Cartmill 1980). Debates in archaeology became much more substantive and topically focused—much more about doing science and less about talking about it. But things would soon change, because looming on the horizon was a competitor that apparently eschewed science altogether. The processualists could no longer afford to split hairs over which kind of science was better than another; they would have to regroup and try desperately to hold on to as many recruits as possible. The upstart challenger to processualism arose not in the United States but in Great Britain, and the rapidity with which it gained converts was nothing short of remarkable. We examine this development in Chapter 8.

8

Fall from Grace

In their clamor to enhance the scientific tra-
dition, and hoard for science all credit for
the remarkable and unprecedented mate-
rial advances which studded the century and
a quarter preceding 1930, these historians
[of science] have been more enthusiastic than
accurate.... Science emerged [in the popu-
lar mind] as the most prominent force re-
sponsible for making this modern world so
startlingly different from all preceding ages.
Thus when, for many people, the modern
world, in spite of all its resources, began to
slip from its role of "best of all imaginable
worlds," science came in for a proportion-
ate share of blame. Had a more accurate pic-
ture of the part science has played been pre-
sented, science would not now be the object
of so much suspicion and resentment.

—W. J. Lyons, "Science in an Unfriendly
World"

Lyons's statement, with minimal rewording,
could apply to the history of processual
archaeology from its inception to about 1980.
For almost two decades processualism, albeit
in various guises, dominated American archaeology, in the process maturing from an approach that was constantly trying to distance
itself from culture history to a complex, multi-
faceted research strategy that was becoming increasingly difficult to define. Despite changes
in processualism, it still exhibited some of the
core features that had characterized it in the
1960s. The most noticeable feature, and perhaps the most significant, was processualism's
theoretical and methodological ties to the physical sciences. To paraphrase Lyons, science was
regarded by processualists as the force that
would pull modern archaeology apart from its
predecessors.

In addition to its materialist theories of culture, processualism was built in large part on
the belief that it offered archaeologists two
things that culture history had not: a sound
epistemology and the methodological rigor provided by formal hypothesis testing. Processualists proclaimed that for the first time, archaeologists could be wrong and *know* they
were wrong. Knowing that one's conclusions
are wrong allows one to modify a hypothesis
and test it again. To the processualists this was
an exciting prospect, and it opened the doors
for American archaeology to set off in countless new directions. Sometimes those directions
led to substantive results, sometimes they led
to theoretical and methodological contributions, and sometimes they led only to fruitless
debates and dead ends, but regardless, processualism energized the discipline. Berthold
Laufer (1913:577), as cited in Chapter 1, might
have once remarked that chronology is "the
nerve electrifying the dead body of history," but
then he never had the opportunity to sit in on
one of Lew Binford's lectures.

We can appreciate the excitement that the early processualists felt as they contemplated the future of archaeology—a future that in the late 1960s and early '70s seemed destined to thrive on science and the scientific method. As Schiffer (1995a:3) put it, "By dismissing much of archaeology as traditionally practiced, Binford was wiping the slate clean, saying in effect that a young person entering archaeology could write on that slate something significant.... Binford inspired me to join his crusade to transform archaeology into a science." For a time, few if any processualists realized that hitching their wagon to the locomotive of physical science came with steep costs. One who did appreciate this Faustian bargain was David Clarke (1973), who in an article that in places is maddeningly incomprehensible, referred to the price as "the loss of innocence."

Clarke's point was that although the loss of disciplinary innocence is a continuous process, one nonetheless can recognize several significant thresholds. The first threshold, "consciousness," is crossed when the approach is named and the practitioners are linked within a common segment of reality, sharing intuitive procedures and tacit understandings while teaching by imitation and correction. This fairly characterizes the early years of the new archaeology, when Binford was laying out the basic guidelines, and graduate students at the University of Chicago were supplying the products.

The second threshold, "self-consciousness," is crossed when practitioners attempt self-knowledge—what Clarke (1973:6) referred to as "the contentious efforts to cope with the growing quantity of archaeological observations by explicit but debated procedures and the querulous definition of concepts and classifications." This creates a body of observations on particular classes of data, held together by a network of varying methods and implicit theory. With respect to teaching and learning, it becomes impossible either to teach or to learn the vast amount of data and complex procedures by rote. Instead, data and approaches are treated in terms of alternative models and rival paradigms. Here Clarke's depiction fits the middle stages of processualism perfectly:

> This process is also marked by the emergence of competitive individualism and authority, since the individual's living depends on the reputation he achieves as a focus in the media or by innovation and intensive work in a specialist field. The politics and sociology of the disciplinary environment increasingly develop this "authoritarian" state in which each expert has a specialist territory such that criticisms of territorial observations are treated as attacks upon personalities....
>
> So, the new sophisticates industriously sub-partition their discipline; each group deepens their specialist cells by concentrated research, thereby unconsciously raising barriers to communication.... The prevailing feeling is "look how much we know" and the general impression is that the discipline hardly exists as one subject at all. (Clarke 1973:6–7)

As on target as Clarke was in describing the first two thresholds vis-à-vis processualism, he improved his mark still more with the third threshold, "critical self-consciousness." Here attempts are made to control the direction and destiny of the system through an understanding of its internal structure and the effects of the external environment. Analytical focus shifts from "look at all the things these data tell us" to "look at all the things the data *don't* tell us and may *never* tell us, given the inappropriateness of our models and explanations." Further, he noted that

> A new environment develops as students and amateurs of an ever-widening background emerge in increasing numbers and archaeological units of all kinds multiply outside as well as inside the old Euro-American centres. From the Antipodes to Africa the old regionally self-centered "colonial" concepts are severely challenged and their weaknesses gravely exposed in the wider general debate.

Question leads to unrest, freedom to further self-consciousness and thought about thought, as the unformulated precepts of limited academic traditions give way to clearly formulated concepts whose very formulation leads to further criticism and more debate. (Clarke 1973:7–8)

In an unusually lucid sentence, Clarke (1973:8) elegantly summed up the result of the three-phase process: "The rate of change becomes as disconcerting as the uncertainty, insecurity and general unrest—no one can deny the high price of expanding consciousness."

Kent Flannery, in a report to the National Science Foundation on his Valley of Oaxaca Human Ecology Project (the exact reference is long out of our memory) made a similar point when he alluded to the age of innocence, without using the term, as "when we knew less and enjoyed it more." Flannery was right: doing archaeology as a processualist entailed responsibilities that perhaps archaeologists working before 1960 didn't have to face. Recall our earlier-used quote from Flannery (1976a), who remembered the good old days when you could roll out of your Jeep, plunk down a two-meter-square hole in a site, collect sherds by twenty-centimeter levels, and then race off to attack the next site. That's the exciting part of archaeology, and certainly the reason that many of us got into the field in the first place. We didn't get into archaeology to invent new paradigms or to write histories of the discipline, or to do "scientific" stuff (Wobst 1989). We got into it because at the time it looked like fun. And it *is* fun. As we mature, however, our sense of responsibility matures in step. The arrogance of youth fades, and we become self-conscious about what we're doing and begin to see all the holes in what we think we know about the archaeological record and the past. We try to plug the holes, but as Clarke pointed out, we begin to realize that our models and theories are inadequate for the job. This makes us uneasy.

The maturing process undoubtedly affected culture historians, but we suspect it was worse for processualist because of the equation of

archaeology with science. And doing science, they found out, is difficult. It might sound glamorous, but that's a siren song. We like what primatologist Matt Cartmill (1988:452) said about why he got into science: "As an adolescent I aspired to lasting fame, I craved factual certainty, and I thirsted for a meaningful vision of human life—so I became a scientist. This is like becoming an archbishop so you can meet girls."

Who among us old enough to remember archaeology in the '60s hasn't on occasion missed those simpler times, when no one talked much about hypothesis testing and research designs? Those topics were right around the corner, but there was still plenty of old-fashioned archaeology to talk about, even if Binford and his crowd wanted to talk about culture process or matrilineal social organization. Further, there was little or no governmental red tape to untangle, let alone much reason to deal with Native American tribal councils. Processualism didn't bring with it an increase in governmental bureaucracy, although it sometimes seemed like it, but it did usher in an increased awareness of just how destructive the archaeological enterprise is when we ask only, "Where do I put the next big test trench?"

This awareness at least made archaeologists think about the consequences of their actions. It was difficult to fool yourself that you were doing science when you had no stated reason for even being in the field other than to mine a site for its "goodies." This statement is not meant to imply that culture historians dug only to recover artifacts, but there is no denying that processual archaeology brought with it a complete overhaul of archaeologists' self-awareness.

What makes David Clarke's discussion so intriguing is not just his characterization of processualism's phases but his description of the second phase just as it was occurring and the last phase well before it began. Clarke never saw the final phase—he died in 1976 at the age of thirty-eight—but he was uncannily accurate about the course of processualism. Critics might well discount Clarke's seeming prescience, noting that he had access to other movements in other disciplines to use as models. This is true, but in reading his description of the phases, especially the third, one gets the feeling that Clarke was reading a script from a decade or more in the future—a script that called for a significant number of archaeologists to hold vastly different views of archaeology than his contemporaries. One could also view his third phase as a charter for a new generation of Cambridge-trained archaeologists to remove the last constraints on questioning received views, even that of physical science as the model for archaeology.

The general discontent with processualism (in all of its guises) began in Britain and quickly spread to America. The flaw in processualism, as the new voices saw it, lay in archaeology's attempt to be scientific—not in *how* it attempted to be scientific, but in its basic desire to *be* scientific. Science, the voices said, could never be "objective," and it was fraudulent to portray it as producing anything other than a modern, highly biased picture of the past. Science was, as Lyons (1971) put it, coming in for its share of the blame for society's ills, and archaeology was simply a miniature version of the larger stage.

Later in this chapter we examine some of the archaeological plays performed on that stage, many of which are still playing before packed houses. The plays go by different names, although there is a tendency to cram them under the term *postprocessualism*. British archaeologist Ian Hodder (1985) coined that term to refer specifically to the reaction against processualism that began in Britain during the late 1970s and early '80s, but it came to be used as an umbrella term for any number of diverse nonprocessual (antiprocessual is perhaps a better word) enterprises (Hegmon 2003; Hodder 1991b; Kohl 1985; Patterson 1990; Shennan 1986; VanPool and VanPool 1999; P. J. Watson 1991; Watson and Fotiadis 1990), including symbolic, structural, and interpretive archaeology, Marxist archaeology, Marxist-structuralist archaeology, gender studies, agency and practice studies, and postmodernism. These differ in conceptual structure and goals not only

from each other but also from Hodder's original definition of postprocessualism. Although we later use that term as a chapter subheading, we try to sort through some of the approaches it covers.

As the opening round of the antiscience backlash was ending, British archaeologist Stephen Shennan (1986:327) stated that the "center of gravity of theoretical archaeology [has shifted] from the United States to Europe—in fact, more specifically to Britain and Scandinavia." We don't particularly disagree with Shennan's assessment because it is difficult not to view Britain in particular as the hearth of the intense antiprocessual feeling. At the same time, his remark might give two impressions: (1) that *nothing* was happening theoretically in American archaeology during the 1980s, and (2) that everything antiprocessual going on in Europe was a theoretical contribution (not all rhetoric is theory). Certainly the term *postprocessualism* implies that processualism was dead or at least had been replaced. This was hardly the case, but processualists did have their hands full. While parrying attacks from the antiscience segment of the discipline, processualists were also responding to charges leveled by other archaeology-as-science advocates.

The roots of processualism's internal discontent ran deep. We highlighted in Chapter 4 the hostile reaction that Kent Flannery and others had to the staunch subscription by some processualists to Hempelian models of explanation, a deductivist scientific method, and the search for laws of human behavior (e.g., Fritz and Plog 1970; Watson, LeBlanc, and Redman 1971). These commitments had come under close scrutiny not only by other archaeologists (e.g., Hill 1972; Smith 1977) but also by philosophers (e.g., Salmon and Salmon 1979). It was increasingly recognized that applying the philosophical program of the early new archaeology too literally often led to rather sterile results. Two books written in the 1980s took this last point as their central focus (Courbin 1988; Gibbon 1989), but their message was already well recognized by the time they were published.

Another perceived problem with processualism was its tendency to showcase method at the expense of its anthropological roots. Where, it was asked, was the concern for furthering some anthropological objective—an activity that should have been commensurate with the development and perfection of method? James Moore and Arthur Keene (1983:4) referred to the processualist preoccupation with method as the law of the hammer, the metaphor being that given a hammer, "a young child will find that the world is poundable." Their point was that methods are tools typically developed for a specific analytical task that produces a specific kind of information. In the hands of children, however, the methods are used to pound away at any and every problem. Dave Thomas had made more or less the same point in "The Awful Truth about Statistics in Archaeology" (Thomas 1978), and George Cowgill echoed it in several places (e.g., Cowgill 1986, 1989, 1993).

Processualists were also embroiled over the nature of analogy, particularly ethnographic analogy. The role of ethnographic analogy in archaeology was an issue with which Binford (1967) had wrestled early on, culminating in his work on middle-range theory (e.g., Binford 1977a, 1978, 1981a). As we saw in Chapters 5 and 7, Richard Gould, among others, argued that the analogy-based explanations offered by many processualists were ontologically and epistemologically flawed by the fallacy of affirming the consequent. Gould's debates with Pat Watson (Gould and Watson 1982) and Binford (1985; Gould 1985) illustrated the sharp divisions that existed on the question of how ethnographic analogy can be used profitably to solve archaeological problems.

None of these issues, however, spun off its own program or distinct approach, if we can equate them with "isms." Ethnoarchaeology might have come the closest, but even here few people identified themselves primarily as ethnoarchaeologists; ethnoarchaeology was simply one major research interest or strategy among several. Most would have identified themselves as processualists who happened to do ethnoarchaeology. Two issues that did produce named approaches were human behavior and Darwinian evolution. Both issues can be traced to the early days of American archaeology, but it was only in the 1970s that they received sustained interest.

With respect to behavior, Jeff Reid, Mike Schiffer, and Bill Rathje challenged processualist thinking on the grounds that it failed to consider the formation processes that had created the archaeological record. How, it was asked, can we study relationships between human behaviors and material culture if we cannot distinguish the various processes that create and modify the archaeological record? Behavioral archaeology is a two-step approach: first, it addresses issues surrounding archaeological inference—formation processes and the linkages between behaviors and artifacts—and second, it seeks to explain variability and change in human behavior (Schiffer 1976). We covered the first step in Chapter 7 and focus on the second step in this chapter.

Archaeologists have long had at least a casual interest in evolution, and as discussed in Chapter 1, they have on occasion flirted with applying Darwin's brand of evolutionism to the archaeological record (e.g., Colton 1939; Colton and Hargrave 1937; Gladwin and Gladwin 1930, 1934; Kidder 1932). The results were mixed at best and became easy targets for critics (e.g., Brew 1946). In the late 1970s Robert Dunnell began to reconsider Darwinian evolutionary theory as a means of explaining archaeological change. Dunnell (1978b, 1980, 1982) claimed that despite considerable fanfare and rhetoric, processual archaeology had actually done little in the way of explaining culture change (a point also made by behavioralists). Further, given its reliance on ethnological theory for explanations and ethnographic analogy for insights into human behaviors, processualism had not yet matured into a self-contained, theory-driven discipline. These problems could be resolved, Dunnell argued, by adapting (not adopting) Darwinian evolutionary theory to the archaeological record. We examine some of these key arguments in a later section.

POSTPROCESSUALISM

Responsibility for sowing the seeds of discontent with processualism cannot be attributed to any single person. In fact, if David Clarke (1973) was correct, there were no seeds to sow. Rather, from the moment processualism was born, it was headed toward an inevitable collision with discontent. Some of the early discontent can be seen in the work of Bruce Trigger (e.g., 1968b, 1970, 1973) and its emphasis on history (Chapter 4). But at least with respect to the antifunctionalist perspectives that arose against processualism, it has long been fashionable to blame or praise, depending on one's viewpoint, Cambridge-trained archaeologist Ian Hodder (Figure 8.1). Hodder, to our knowledge, has never dodged the claim that he more than anyone else was responsible for at least bringing the reaction to the forefront. He began to argue in the late 1970s, initially rather softly but increasingly more stridently, that a change was necessary if archaeology was to become more than an esoteric discipline that blindly relied on science for direction.

As important as Hodder's voice was, he was not the first to explore nonecological, nonfunctionalist archaeological paths. In the 1970s, during the heyday of processualism, a few archaeologists were showing interest in where those paths might lead. Recall that Binford (1963, 1965) had rejected what he called the "normative theory" of traditional culture historians. He argued that were one to use that theory rigorously, one would be reduced to doing paleopsychology—an endeavor that in his view most archaeologists were "poorly trained" to undertake (Binford 1965:204). Of course, as noted in Chapter 3, that theory is precisely what Jim Deetz, Jim Hill, and Bill Longacre had used, perhaps without realizing it, when they did ceramic sociology (Stanislawski 1973). Despite Binford's res-

FIGURE 8.1. Ian Hodder, Cambridge, England, 1986. (Courtesy Ian Hodder.)

olute prohibition on probing dead minds, some archaeologists began to countenance the possibility of doing some paleopsychology. Ironically, John Fritz (1978), coauthor with Fred Plog of one of processualism's most hard-core philosophical tracts (Fritz and Plog 1970), was explicit about the potential of such investigations. He noted, for example, that studies of cosmology such as that by Kent Flannery and Joyce Marcus (1976) indicated how various aspects of cognition were integrated with the directly adaptive aspects of prehistoric cultures on which processualists had focused.

Mark Leone, also an early card-carrying processualist, had suggested (Leone 1972b, 1973) that aspects of prehistoric cognition might be accessible archaeologically. He offered the processually heretical notion that an archaeologist's view of time was culture specific and thus "the past is a cultural construction, no different from heaven" (Leone 1978:30). What he was getting at was that archaeologists need to be self-aware, constantly asking themselves how their concepts, explicit or implicit, influence what they believe they know about the past. This perspective represented Clarke's third stage of processualism: self-awareness.

Deetz (1960, 1965) had been one of the first archaeologists to use a form of normative theory when he analyzed Arikara pottery for evidence of social organization. He was also one of the first to interpret archaeological data in what many consider to be a postprocessual manner. With hindsight, one can almost see it coming in his writings of the 1960s. For example, Deetz (1968c) used a linguistic metaphor to equate attributes of artifacts identified by an archaeologist with allophones, and to equate the culturally meaningful attributes of artifacts—what might be termed emic attributes—with allomorphs. Deetz wanted to find a cultural grammar of a set of artifacts, just as a linguist looked for a grammar of a language. This clearly was a major step beyond traditional normative theory as Binford (1965, 1978) had characterized it. By the mid-1970s, Deetz (1977) posited what he termed "bilateral symmetry" as a subconscious template for New England artifacts that had been produced after 1680. It was, in a sense, a grammatical rule that influenced not only the form of architecture and other artifacts but also various aspects of contemporary life. As Robert Schuyler (1980:643) put it, Deetz's main theme was that "historical archaeologists can comprehend objects in their original cognitive context and not simply as products of behavior and environmental factors." Apparently, Hodder had predecessors as well as fellow travelers. The writings of Fritz, Leone, and Deetz, however, did not lead to a definable movement the same way that Hodder's did.

What was the catalyst for these new ideas? Various authors have invoked a multitude of candidate factors, any or all of which we are perfectly content to support, such as the highly centralized and hierarchical British archaeological community of the 1980s, the high levels of marginal employment in British archaeology, or even the remaking of British society during the Thatcher years (Patterson 1995). One catalyst undoubtedly was the large number of young, new professionals in the '70s and '80s who somehow had to make names for themselves in order to compete more effectively in an increasingly tight academic job market. What better way than to propose new and radical ideas about how to do archaeology?

Another view, championed by Hodder, is that processualism failed to deliver its promised goods. The fervor with which he defended this view caused one reviewer (Cullen 1984) to comment that "he writes as a crusader." Hodder had been a student of David Clarke's at Cambridge and thus was well versed in processualism. In fact, reading only Hodder's publications from the '70s (e.g., 1971, 1974, 1976, 1978; Hodder and Orton 1976), it would be difficult to see him as the same archaeologist who a few years later would become processualism's most strident critic. These works cover a variety of topics, including spatial analysis (one of Hodder's specialties), that interested many other processualists.

It was during field research in northern Kenya in the late 1970s that Hodder had his epiphany, although we agree with Matthew Johnson (1999) that one can see inklings of discontent in some of his earlier writings. As he studied material culture from an ethnoarchaeological standpoint, Hodder began to believe that processualism was ill-equipped to handle the structural context of, and symbolism in, material items. And yet it was these dimensions of artifacts that played such a large role in the daily lives of the people who made and used them. In an important yet often overlooked paper, "Economic and Social Stress and Material Culture Patterning," Hodder (1979) identified some weaknesses of processualism. Yes, it sought to complete what the traditional culture-historical approach had barely begun—showing that artifacts are configurations of culture traits that reflect social organization—but processualist "explanations" were ecological, functionalist, and mechanistic (see also Hodder 1981, 1982d, 1985); missing was any mention of the cognitive realm.

Hodder wanted archaeology to be an inclusive discipline; to seriously consider "internal structure and logic of cultural pattern"; and to study "internal generative process and the structure of cultural meaning" (Hodder 1981:7). Further, by "emphasizing the meaningful construction of social acts and the historical particularity of human culture I seek to dissolve the timeless past both in its role as the ultimate legitimation of the modern technocratic West and in its function as the prop of the professional theoretician" (Hodder 1985:22). These were strong words. Was Hodder really saying that processualists were creating an unreal past and then using it for their own ends? That's exactly what he was saying. His goal was to dissolve that past and replace it with a social theory that "seems to be as relevant for reconstructions of the past as it is for understanding the archaeologist at work in contemporary society" (Hodder 1985:22). To Hodder, the archaeologist is as much an actor in the story of "creating" the past as were the people being studied. Why replace processualism? Because it did not and could not emphasize the individual. In Hodder's eyes, processualism viewed individuals as basically nothing more than unthinking products of culture or nature—"faceless blobs," as Ruth Tringham (1991) put it.

Hodder's message was picked up quickly on both sides of the Atlantic, and in some quarters, especially among some of his students at Cambridge, it took on even more radical tones. The rallying cry was the same, but now it was even more shrill: Science not only dehumanizes, it is used by Western cultures for political purposes. As Hodder student Christopher Tilley (1989:110) put it, "[A]n apolitical archaeology is a dangerous academic myth." Thus, if archaeology is scientific, then it too both "[denies] people their freedom" (Hodder 1986:102) and serves Western political purposes. The only solution, from an ethical as well as an academic standpoint, was to throw processual (scientific) archaeology out and start over.

Remember that Clarke (1973:7) predicted precisely this "critical self-consciousness" when he said that "from the Antipodes to Africa the old regionally self-centred 'colonial' concepts are severely challenged and their weaknesses gravely exposed in the wider general debate." And there was a "wider general debate" going on in the 1980s with respect not only to science and archaeology but to archaeology's place in a society that science had tricked into thinking that it held the key to truth's door. As a historical note, the postprocessualists were not the first to raise the issue of the politicization of archaeology. Richard Ford (1973), for example, in his chapter in Chuck Redman's (1973a) *Research and Theory in Current Archeology,* had cautioned about mixing archaeology and politics. And almost every archaeologist knew that the Nazis had prostituted archaeology during the 1930s and '40s in order to promote their views on racial superiority.

Trigger's thoughts as he reported them in the mid-'80s form a benchmark in terms of how a fairly sizable segment of the discipline began to critically view archaeology's place in society at large (for a collection of his important writings on this subject, see Trigger 2003). Trigger (1984) related that after editing several collections of regional histories of archaeology, he began to see remarkable similarities and differences in the kinds of archaeologies undertaken in different countries. No one seriously doubts that archaeological research takes place within complex social milieus that have varied political and economic agendas—Hodder's (1999) brief discussion of the different agendas surrounding his work at Çatalhöyük in Turkey is enlightening—but Trigger went a step further and categorized archaeological research in terms of the agendas he found.

"Nationalistic archaeology" has as its goal the bolstering of pride and morale of nations or ethnic groups (e.g., Arnold 1990; Kohl and Fawcett 1995). "Colonialist archaeology" occurs in countries where the colonists doing the archaeology have no historical (cultural or genetic) ties to indigenous cultures. Here, archaeology tends to denigrate native peoples and cultures in order to justify colonial actions ranging from economic exploitation to genocide. Trigger's (1980) article "Archaeology and the Image of the American Indian" is well worth reading in this regard, as is Don Fowler's (1987) "Uses of the Past: Archaeology in the Service of the State." (Of course, archaeology can be used for just the opposite purpose—to illustrate the dehumanizing effects of colonialism, racism, and imperialism. Carmel Schrire's [1996] *Chronicles of an Archaeologist* examines this possibility in detail. And for several decades, beginning in 1946, dozens of American archaeologists furnished evidence on traditional territories that helped to bolster Native American land claims against the federal government [Zedeño 1997]. Conversely, some archaeologists testified against Indian claims.)

Finally, "imperialist archaeology" is that which exerts an influence over large areas of the world out of proportion to the size of the nation where it originates. Thus, for example, one might caricature American processual archaeology by asserting that it seeks laws of human behavior as reflected by artifacts rather than seeking the specific behaviors of the actual people who made and used those items at a specific time and in a specific place. One could further argue that national and regional traditions and histories are unimportant in processualism, serving merely as stepping stones to the larger goal of implementing a research program, typically sold as *the only method* for attaining the goal of generalizing about cultural processes.

Some would argue that colonialist and/or imperialist attitudes are still very much alive in how American archaeologists view Native Americans. The heat that can emanate from discussions of archaeologist-Indian interaction makes processualist-postprocessualist arguments look like high school debates. Beginning in the 1970s a low level in the relationship between archaeologists and Native Americans was reached, and the driving force was the often careless and insensitive manner in which museums had long treated human skeletons from archaeological sites. Some Native Americans didn't appreciate having the remains of their presumed ancestors shoved into cardboard boxes, being thin-sectioned for analysis, or being put on exhibit. These points had been raised early on by archaeologist Elden Johnson (1973), who argued that the Society for American Archaeology should recognize that it had responsibilities to Native Americans.

In the mid-1970s American Indians Against Desecration was formed to deal with the situation, which was summed up in 1985 by its director, Jan Hammil: "As we crossed the country and visited the universities, museums and laboratories, we found the bodies of our ancestors stored in cardboard boxes, plastic bags and paper sacks. We found our sacred burial places stripped and desecrated, the bodies and sacred objects buried with our dead on display for the curious and labeled 'collections,' 'specimens' and 'objects of antiquities.' A.I.D. estimates that between three and six hundred thousand Indian bodies have and continue to be so treated, most, as a result of federal proj-

ects, using federal monies and stored at federally supported institutions."[1] Hammil also noted that AID had "attempted to isolate the causes leading to Indian bodies being desecrated and [to] offer methods to avoid compounding the problem by additional bodies being added to the already intolerable situation." She noted that there was a need for federal policy aimed at avoiding "significant archaeological sites including sacred Indian burial sites," and emphasizing "consideration of traditional cultural values and the effect of federal projects on those values."

Hammil's comments were delivered in 1985, but by then the "reburial" issue, as it came to be known, was at least fifteen years old. It is impossible to pinpoint precisely the birth of the reburial controversy—in general it grew out of the civil rights movement of the 1960s (Trope and Echo-Hawk 1992)—but one event that marked the beginning of the movement was the discovery in Iowa in 1971, during highway construction, of the remains of a young Native American female and twenty-six Euroamericans (Anderson 1985). In typical fashion, the Euroamerican skeletons were reburied immediately, but the Indian skeleton was shipped to a lab for analysis. After a storm of protests from Native Americans, church organizations, and students, the state archaeologist declared the remains to be nonsignificant from a scientific standpoint and ordered them to be reburied. This was followed in 1975 by the excavation of an ossuary in Council Bluffs, Iowa, and the reburial of the skeletons after a nine-day examination period. Then, in 1976, the Iowa legislature passed a law requiring the reburial of *all* Native American skeletal remains. In addition, the law made it illegal for anyone, archaeologists or not, to disturb or remove burials. Archaeologists (at least those outside Iowa) were stunned by the passage of the Iowa law. Other states followed suit.

While states were passing local legislation to protect unmarked human burials, the federal government also was at work. In 1989 Sen. Daniel Inouye of Hawaii introduced a bill that would far surpass any law passed by individual states in terms of its effects on American archaeology. The bill, termed the Native American Repatriation of Cultural Patrimony Act, went through only minor changes before being signed into law by President George Bush on November 16, 1990. The law became known officially as the Native American Graves Protection and Repatriation Act, or NAGPRA. Proposed regulations for implementing provisions contained in NAGPRA were published in May 1993 (Morell 1994), and the final rule was published in December 1995.

Basically, NAGPRA did for human burials on federal lands what the state laws did for those on private lands—forbade unauthorized excavation. But the law was much more sweeping in that it also directed all federal agencies and museums and repositories that receive federal funding to conduct two inventories of their holdings. The first inventory, which was to have been completed by November 16, 1993, was to be a summary of all collections that contained unassociated funerary objects, sacred objects, or objects of cultural patrimony—objects that probably came from burial contexts but for which there existed no skeletal remains. The purpose of the summary was to provide information about the collections to lineal descendants and culturally affiliated Indian tribes that might want to request repatriation of the objects. The second inventory, to be completed by November 16, 1995 (a date that was amended several times, given that it fell before the final rules were published) was to be a listing of all human remains and associated funerary items in order to facilitate repatriation by groups having affiliation with the remains and objects.

Repatriation is not a new issue. Perhaps the most (in)famous case occurred in the late 1960s, when the New York State Museum was asked to return twenty-six Iroquois wampum belts that the museum had had for decades (Arnet 1970). But that event and others like it were only brush fires compared to the inferno set off by the passage of NAGPRA and the publication of its implementing language. Few museums were exempt from the legislation, because of the wording of the implementing rules

(43 CFR pt. 10, sec. 10.2): "Museum means any institution or State or local government agency (including any institution of higher learning) that has possession of, or control over, human remains, funerary objects, sacred objects, or objects of cultural patrimony and receives Federal funds."

One aspect of NAGPRA to which many archaeologists and physical anthropologists had a particularly negative reaction was the "lineal descent and cultural affiliation" clause. How, they asked, could anyone establish descent from groups of people who had died a millennium or more ago? For example, even though a historically documented group had been in an area during the nineteenth century, did that mean that a thousand-year-old skeleton from that same area was of an ancestor to that group? Could the modern group claim "lineal descent" and repatriate the remains? That issue came to a head with the discovery in 1996 of the remains of "Kennewick Man" washing out from along the Columbia River behind McNary Dam in Kennewick, Washington (Chatters 2001; Downey 2000; Thomas 2000). Radiocarbon dating showed the remains to be approximately 9,000 years old. Five Columbia River basin tribes claimed cultural affiliation with the remains, and the Walla Walla District of the U.S. Army Corps of Engineers, which controlled the land on which the remains were found, determined that Kennewick Man should be repatriated to the tribes under the provisions of NAGPRA. Suits were immediately filed to stop the repatriation.

Between 1998 and 2000, the Department of the Interior and the National Park Service, in cooperation with the Corps of Engineers, conducted numerous scientific examinations of the remains and prepared a series of background reports on the prehistory and linguistic history of the area. In September 2000, Secretary of the Interior Bruce Babbitt announced that the government had decided that Kennewick Man was culturally affiliated with the five tribes and should be repatriated to them. More legal wrangling took place, and in February 2004, a three-judge panel of the 9th U.S. Circuit

Court of Appeals ruled that the remains do not come under protection of NAGPRA. The next step could be the Supreme Court. One might have thought that with that ruling, the remains of Kennewick Man would be released for study, but that would be a naive view, given the government's stake in the case. As of November 2004, the National Park Service has not accepted any proposals for further study of the remains. The agency's chief archaeologist, Frank McManamon, stated that a forty-page plan submitted by a consortium of leading paleoanthropologists didn't "build on the substantial amount of scientific investigation that has already been done" (Holden 2004:591).

This attitude embodies the major complaint that archaeologists and physical anthropologists have against NAGPRA: it removes materials from the research arena (e.g., Buikstra 1982; Clark 1996; Meighan 1993). They argue that it is extremely shortsighted to think that we know everything there is to know about the demographic profile and health of prehistoric populations, and they cite example after example of current research in bioarchaeology that makes use of collections that have resided in museums for decades (Buikstra and Gordon 1981; Ubelaker and Grant 1989). There is no reason to suspect that similar analyses will not take place in the future, or that new and innovative analyses will not take place and quite possibly reveal undreamed of aspects of past humanity. Native American groups counter with the claim that the vast majority of the remains have sat on dusty shelves for years and have never been examined, and they see little prospect that the remains will ever be examined. Some also say that the fact that American scientists, most of whom are of Euroamerican descent, view the remains of the ancestors of Native Americans as "museum specimens" is an extension of the bias against Indians that has always existed in this country.

The debate rages, and we doubt the dialogue on this contentious issue will be over anytime soon. As a final note, we point out that although we have made it sound as if the division between competing interests is sharply drawn—archaeologists versus Native Americans—the line is much fuzzier. There are, in fact, Native American tribes, or segments thereof, that don't demand the return of human remains as long as it can be demonstrated that the remains are protected and are being treated respectfully. Similarly, there are archaeologists who have been at the forefront of the repatriation effort (e.g., Zimmerman 1992) or have at least strongly advocated working with Native Americans on the issue (e.g., Dongoske, Aldenderfer, and Doehner 2000; Swidler et al. 1997; various chapters in Bray 2001)—the official stance adopted by the Society for American Archaeology in its code of ethics (Lynott 1997; Lynott and Wylie 2000; see also Wylie 1996, 1999).

Sorting through the Flavors

Trying to sort through the various flavors of postprocessualist approaches is, as we noted earlier, no easy task. As more and more hands became involved, Hodder's postprocessualism became more or less what anyone wanted it to be. To Hodder (1991b:37–38) it was, by the start of the 1990s, "less a movement and more a phase in the development of the discipline.... It is simply 'post-,' without offering a new unity. Rather, it argues for diversity, a breaking down of barriers, closures, and dichotomies so that they can be argued across, and a critical evaluation of accepted dogmas." If one didn't know better, one might have mistaken Hodder's words for those Lew Binford had used to introduce the "New Perspectives" symposium at the 1965 American Anthropological Association meeting (Chapter 2). But Binford wasn't dealing with a multiplicity of approaches, or at least not many, and Hodder was.

In a telling comment, Hodder (1991b:37) pointed out that "there is as much or more variation within postprocessual archaeology as there is between it and processual archaeology." This sounds a lot like the situation with biological "races": so much internal variation is present that the units begin to lose meaning. To Hodder (1991b:38), this diversity was "the main defining (or undefining) feature of post-processualism." Being scientists, and thus committed to classification (or in deference to our postprocessualist friends, "enslaved by" classification), we are not fond of using "undefining" characters, but Hodder's point is well taken: postprocessualism as a whole is difficult to get one's arms around.

Opinions differ over how to subdivide post-processualism. Timothy Earle and Robert Preucel (1987), in their article titled "Processual Archaeology and the Radical Critique," identified two basic kinds of postprocessualism, which they referred to as "radical or critical archaeology." One approach was Hodder's; the other was Marxist, including dialectical Marxism (e.g., Friedman and Rowlands 1978; Gilman 1989; Leone 1984; McGuire 1992, 1993; McGuire and Saitta 1996; Spriggs 1984). Both approaches, to one degree or another, reject the positivism of processual archaeology. They seek to understand the archaeological record in terms of social and political constraints of both the present context in which the archaeologist operates and the prehistoric context of past human behaviors. To Earle and Preucel, scientific objectivity is a myth because *all* interpretation of the past is subjective. Structural Marxists, in particular, hold that the individual member of society can be a powerful agent of cultural change because such an agent can create internal conflict. Here, ideology and social structure, not economics, are the prime determinants of the past (see also Trigger 1991).

Tom Patterson (1989) argued that there are at least three kinds of postprocessual archaeology. The first is the approach advocated by Hodder (1985, 1986), which involves reading and decoding the archaeological record as if it were a text. The archaeologist is a cryptographer who is adept at deciphering and interpreting an imperfectly understood writing system. Chris Tilley (1990) furnished a set of readings that could guide archaeologists in this endeavor. The second kind of postprocessualism examines how our views of prehistory are influenced by the power and domination of one group of individuals or another. Major figures include Michael Shanks (another Cambridge-trained postprocessualist) and Tilley (Shanks and Tilley 1987a, 1987b). The third kind of postprocessualism focuses on communication and ideology, particularly on how archaeological constructs—implicit and explicit—influence what we think we know about the past. The work of Mark Leone (1986; Leone, Potter, and Shackel 1987) exemplifies this kind of post-processualism.

Leone (1986) also identified three kinds of postprocessual archaeology—symbolic, structural, and critical—and specified four properties that tend variously to crosscut them. First, culture is interactive and recursive; people are actors, and artifacts not only reflect culture, they create and order culture and its various meanings. Second, meaning—the social context of daily life—attempts to manipulate social relationships; ideology—the manner by which contradictory aspects of society are masked and thus conflict is averted—is a central focus of analysis and interpretation. Third, the present is shaped by the past, and our perceptions of the past are shaped by the present; thus science is neither objective nor perceptually and conceptually neutral. The fourth property is related to the third: the scientific method is a cultural creation and therefore ethnocentric and historically contingent, thus its results are at some level subjective interpretations.

Alternatively, Pat Watson (Watson and Fotiadis 1990) distinguished between two major postprocessual approaches, each with subgroups. Cognitive, structural, and symbolic archaeology make up one group, and critical and Marxist archaeologies make up the other. But recognize that even within subgroups there is tremendous variation: witness the divergence of views held by Colin Renfrew and his colleagues with respect to "cognitive archaeology" (Renfrew et al. 1993). We mostly follow Watson's division and discuss what we see as two not entirely mutually exclusive categories of postprocessual archaeology. One we term "symbolic, structural, and contextual archaeology," substituting Hodder's concept of "context" for Watson's "cognitive" subgroup. The other we term "critical archaeology," including under that heading two related issues: social dominance and power, and gender.

SYMBOLIC, STRUCTURAL, AND CONTEXTUAL ARCHAEOLOGY

Most authors who comment on the history and development of symbolic, structural, and contextual archaeology (e.g., Conkey 1989; Mithen 1988, 1995; Watson and Fotiadis 1990) refer to André Leroi-Gourhan's (e.g., 1967, 1968) and Annette Laming-Emperaire's (e.g., 1962) structuralist interpretations of Upper Paleolithic cave art as the seminal studies. Both Leroi-Gourhan and Laming-Emperaire were looking for the formal system, or cognitive structures and processes, that underlay the cave art. Later studies, such as those by Alexander Marshack (e.g., 1972) and Meg Conkey (e.g., 1978a, 1978b, 1982, 1989) were equally provocative but also more sophisticated. They showed how one might get inside the mind of prehistoric peoples, and thus their interpretations exceeded the boundaries of scientific inference set in the 1960s and early '70s by processual archaeologists. Their work has been joined by more-recent studies by, among others, Steven Mithen (e.g., 1988, 1994, 1996, 2001).

Getting inside people's minds was what Hodder became interested in after learning from his ethnoarchaeological research (Hodder 1979, 1982b, 1982c) that people didn't just participate in culture but also created it. He claimed to have discovered that human cognition and behavior were often only indirectly related to artifacts, and even then in complex ways. Where within the processual program, Hodder and his acolytes wondered, were the people behind the artifacts? Where were their ideas and individuality? Ironically, it was the early processualists who had high hopes of increasing their abilities to access just such cultural phenomena by fashioning appropriate laws—what Hodder (1982c) termed correlations between variables.

Given such laws, the inference, from archaeological evidence, of a variable with a particular value would furnish the basis for inferring the values of one or more other ethnological variables. To Hodder, this made archaeology mechanical and scientific, and certainly nonhumanistic. Hodder protested that in the process of building laws, processualists had fallen prey to the same inferential difficulties as their predecessors. This resulted, in Hodder's (1982c) view, from a too-strict adoption of the tenet that scientific endeavors had to be founded in empiricism, and a too-strict adherence to the narrow definition of culture as (solely) an extrasomatic means of adaptation. Thus we have the famous cartoon of Binford as a surgeon, trying to resuscitate a comatose patient (Hodder) by applying "general propositions" and several other (lethal?) medicines concocted by his attending nurses, Colin Renfrew and Mike Schiffer (Figure 8.2). The processualist position left considerable variation in the archaeological record unexplained, or if it was explained, it was in purely adaptive terms.

Echoing Jim Deetz, Hodder (1982c:7) stated that archaeologists should attempt to get at the "structure"—the "codes and rules"—that underpinned the human behaviors that had created the archaeological record. He enlisted the aid of philosopher Alison Wylie to deal with the alleged epistemological problem of ideologies not being directly visible. Wylie (1982b) did an excellent job of disarming empiricist criticisms of structural archaeology—an archaeology that looks for "grammars" of culture in the same sense that linguists look for grammars of languages. Structural archaeology is scientific in Wylie's view because all scientific observation is theory laden (Renfrew and Bahn 2000), and all explanation tends to be ampliative and enriched by theories that go beyond observables. She noted that "facts in any field are always and necessarily constituted within a theoretical context," and that "virtually any scientific knowledge (even descriptive knowledge of fact) involves some theoretical extension beyond the observable" (Wylie 1982b:42). She recommended (Wylie 1982a, 1985b, 1988, 1989a) that structural archaeologists use arguments with the form of analogies: "known

FIGURE 8.2. A cartoon that appeared in the front of Ian Hodder's (1982a) edited book *Symbolic and Structural Archaeology*, showing Lew Binford attempting to revive Hodder as the medical gallery looks on. As Binford applies the "middle-range thermometer," he is assisted by "nurses" Colin Renfrew (*left*) and Mike Schiffer. Binford and Schiffer had both lectured at Southampton University in the early 1980s at the invitation of Renfrew. (Courtesy Cambridge University Press.)

contexts may be expected to provide guidelines for the reconstruction of mechanisms or conditions that would have been capable of producing a given body of data" (Wylie 1982b:43). These would rest on the assumption that "cognitive factors" in the minds of prehistoric peoples were responsible at least in part for the structure (spatial distributions and associations) of the materials making up the archaeological record.

Hodder (1985, 1986) quickly became explicit about the kind of epistemology that he thought archaeology should employ. Individuals are agents of action, and their behaviors are not determined by a code embedded in their culture; rather, their behaviors *are* the culture. Thus, cultural processes are "inherent and continual in the mundane actions of daily life" (Hodder 1985:6). To Hodder (1985:13), "it is impossible to consider process without culture, social systems without individuals, adaptive change without history, science without the subjective." Archaeologists should, in Hodder's view, read the archaeological record like a text. Examine *all* (note the emphasis) aspects of the archaeological (etic) and ethnographic (emic) contexts and interassociations of all finds, and interpret what the finds meant to the humans who made, used, and discarded or lost them (Hodder 1986).

Hodder (1991a) used the concept of "hermeneutics" to illustrate how his version of interpretation worked. Hermeneutic approaches derive from philology and, in the words of one postprocessualist, "adopt a textual metaphor whereby understanding the meaning of a social practice is related to deciphering the meaning of a historical document" (Preucel 1991:21). To paraphrase Hodder (1991a), one evaluates interpretations or decipherments by assessing their goodness of fit in a particular context: Do they work well at making sense of some perception(s), or must they be adjusted or modified? As archaeologists we move, in Hodder's view, back and forth between the portion of the archaeological record under study and our understandings of formation processes (both natural and cultural), until

the two are aligned such that we think we know what created that record. The archaeological record is treated as a historical document and is interpreted much like a written text (Hodder 1987, 1988). What message did the author seek to convey in crafting a string of words? What is the social-behavioral meaning of a particular structure (inventory, distribution, association) of artifacts making up the archaeological record? Here Hodder was resurrecting a central tenet of R. G. Collingwood's (1946) philosophy of history—that the past does not exist entirely independent of the present, and thus to understand the past requires a reenactment of past experiences.

To Hodder, interpretive archaeology is about constructing narratives, or telling stories. He argued that all archaeologists tell stories about the past (see also Terrell 1990), but interpretive archaeology is unique in that its stories are "at the human scale, and [include] the viewpoints of the actors" (Hodder 1991a:13). Without using the terms, he advocated various nationalistic and ethnic archaeologies in the sense of Trigger (1984) so that these (previously suppressed) groups had "a voice." Hodder (1991b: 30) made clear why he advocated nationalistic and ethnic archaeology: "The aim of archaeology is not secure knowledge of the past for its own sake but secure knowledge of the past that is socially responsive in the present." The world is to be understood as "an object of human thought and action," and one must decipher the hidden meanings of objects to gain understanding of them (Hodder 1991b:33). This means that "we must understand any detail, such as an [artifact], in terms of the [cultural] whole, and the whole in terms of the detail. As an interpreter one plays back and forth between part and whole until one achieves the harmony of all the details with the whole. An understanding of the meanings of a situation is thereby achieved" (Hodder 1991b:34).

According to Hodder, the "hermeneutic circle" involves asking a question and seeking an answer, working back and forth in a dialectic between past and present, object and subject, in a nonrelativistic pattern that eventually "changes our experience and therefore changes our perspective" (Hodder 1991b:35). Hodder perceived this process as little different from the allegedly objective scientific practice of archaeology, although it is more explicit with respect to elucidating contexts of the observer (cultural, ethnocentric, and so on) as well as of the observed.

Critical Archaeology, Social Dominance and Power, and Gender

Some archaeologists (e.g., Leone 1986) have argued that if knowledge about another culture is constituted through categories and methods of the scholar's culture, then knowledge is always culture-centric and its validity is questionable. If knowledge has been created or generated for a politically or economically contingent purpose, then awareness of that purpose is significant so that abuses and misuses of that knowledge can be avoided. In short, the "ideological and class-centered nature of history is illuminated" (Leone 1986:429). Critical archaeology is a Marxist enterprise in the sense that knowledge and its production are grounded in the fundamental characteristic of humans as organisms whose behaviors are directed toward their survival (Wylie 1985a). Thus, there is no "value-free" behavior or, for that matter, knowledge. This makes perfect sense from the Darwinian standpoint of increasing one's fitness. If you can manipulate knowledge, perhaps you can boost your position while undermining someone else's.

Critical archaeology is "critical" in two senses. First, it involves reflection with respect to how knowledge is produced; the social context of knowledge production as well as the interests of the knowledge generator taint our knowledge. Second, knowing the first, one can understand and critique the social context and the self-serving interests, though as Wylie (1985a:140) noted, the latter "presupposes the possibility of securing relatively 'objective,' value-free knowledge of the past that supersedes all other (distorted, interest-relative) forms of historical understanding and provides a measure of their accuracy." This is a standard dilemma of radical critique (see also various comments in Leone, Potter, and Shackel 1987). Advocates of a critical archaeology such as Leone seek a self-aware discipline that brings underlying assumptions of archaeological analysis and interpretation to the surface so that they can be the subject of investigation (e.g., Leone 1981). This was no different from what processualists were trying to do with culture history—bring to light dubious assumptions about culture change that were simply taken for granted, such as the alleged inherent superiority of agriculture over hunting and gathering.

Shanks and Tilley (1987b:26) noted that archaeological interpretation is intertwined with "the historical, social and personal mediation of [archaeological] subject and object," thereby rendering interpretation subjective rather than objective, as the positivist processualists argued. In his review of Shanks and Tilley's (1987a) *Re-Constructing Archaeology*, Leone (1989:429) pointed out that the authors' major point was that plural interpretations of the past are desirable because each can be understood relative to all others, which militates against the empowerment of gross distortions of the past for repressive ends. Although beer cans (Figure 8.3) are artifacts that a processualist might interpret as signifying libations and aspects of nutrition, in Shanks and Tilley's (1987a, 1987b) view these artifacts signify a complex network of alcohol production, consumption, the history of labor, power relations, gender and family definitions, work discipline, health issues, alcohol abuse, government relations, and monopoly capital. David Meltzer (1990:187), in his review of Shanks and Tilley's (1987b) *Social Theory and Archaeology*, noted that the beer can example is strained; those artifacts *might* signify all the ideological and social things indicated, but then again, they might not.

Leone (1989:430) liked Shanks and Tilley's position because it makes archaeology "a part of daily life, makes daily life a philosophical pursuit, and stimulates us into an awareness of archaeology's real potential and relevance today." One suspects, then, that there is a "politically correct" archaeology (Flannery and

FIGURE 8.3. Some of the British beer and lager cans that formed the basis of Michael Shanks and Christopher Tilley's study of alcohol production and consumption. (From Shanks and Tilley 1987b, courtesy Cambridge University Press.)

Marcus 1994; Schiffer 1988). When asked to state their views on the future of archaeology, Shanks and Tilley (1989:4) remarked that "studying the past must be regarded as an act requiring self-reflexive discourse. The meaning of the past does not belong to the past but to the present." They, like most postprocessualists, found processual archaeology to be ecologically deterministic, essentialistic, reductionistic, and insufficiently cognizant of "the other," in this case, the human past.

A companion to viewpoints such as Leone's and Shanks and Tilley's, which lead to a critical examination of power relationships between social classes in the past and present, is the archaeology of gender. The first major article on this topic was by Meg Conkey and Janet Spector (1984) (Figure 8.4). Not long afterward, a small working conference on the topic was held in South Carolina, and the papers were published under the editorship of Joan Gero and Conkey (1991). This set of articles was meant to serve as a series of pilot projects that demonstrated the potential for an archae-

FIGURE 8.4. Janet Spector, 1993. (Courtesy Minnesota Historical Society and Janet Spector.)

ology of gender. There also was a 1989 Chacmool Conference sponsored by the Archaeology Student Association of the University of Calgary that took as its focus the archaeology of gender (Walde and Willows 1991).

The most visible product along these lines was Spector's (1993) *What This Awl Means: Feminist Archaeology at a Wahpeton Dakota Village*. The title derives from an excavated awl handle (Figure 8.5) that becomes the focal point of the story. A notable outgrowth of gender studies was the recognition (e.g., Claassen and Joyce 1997; Fedigan 1986; Gilchrist 1999; Kent 1990; Wall 1994; Wright 1996) that women are often left out of ecological and evolutionary models of cultural development, despite the fact that, as with the emergence of agriculture, women are known to have played significant roles (Watson and Kennedy 1991). For an early bibliography of gender in archaeology, see Bacus et al. (1993). For an excellent thumbnail sketch of the history of engendering archaeology, see the notes for Chapter 14 in Alison Wylie's (2002) *Thinking from Things: Essays in the Philosophy of Archaeology*.

FIGURE 8.5. Two views of a bone awl from a Wahpeton Dakota village site in Minnesota. The awl is the focus of Janet Spector's book *What This Awl Means* (1993). (Courtesy Minnesota Historical Society and Janet Spector.)

Wylie argued there as elsewhere (e.g., Wylie 1992, 1997) that one's interpretive (analogical) models and explanatory theories must include provisions for gender if archaeological data are to be "engendered." Similar arguments were made by Ericka Engelstad (1991), Elizabeth Brumfiel (1992), and Erica Hill (1998). Wylie stated that this will provide a more objective and value-free interpretation of the past, and Brumfiel (1992) pointed out that an explicitly engendered archaeology will reveal and help explain many aspects of the archaeological record that a processualist's functional and ecological models cannot. In her view these models presume adaptation is by way of culture-based behavior systems, and that humans play a limited role in determining the course of cultural development. The models thus divert attention from, and in fact render analytically and inferentially invisible, what Brumfiel (1992: 552) referred to as the "social actor." To the

processualist, individual or subgroup behaviors are abstract and not involved in social change, and catalysts of change are external to the cultural adaptive system.

Explicit acknowledgment of the particular social, behavioral, and adaptive roles played by groups of distinct gender, socioeconomic class, political faction, and/or ethnicity will not only put people back at the center of explanations but perhaps reveal nuances of social change not otherwise apparent (e.g., Aldenderfer 1993; Hodder and Cessford 2004; McGuire and Paynter 1991; Meskell 2001; Moore and Scott 1997; Nelson 1997; Nelson and Rosen-Ayalon 2002; Van Dyke 2004). For example, although Flannery (1968a) early on noted that a sexual division of labor could result in scheduling conflicts in subsistence activities, only an explicitly engendered archaeology has pursued this insight (Watson and Kennedy 1991).

As an aside, if what Americans read is any gauge, archaeology will see more, not less, work devoted to engendering the past. As we write this (November 2004), the fifth best-selling book on Amazon.com, out of the more than two million titles listed, is Dan Brown's (2003) *The Da Vinci Code*, which revolves around fictional efforts to cover up that Mary Magdalene was the wife of Christ. The book's wide appeal—it was the best-selling book on Amazon for almost a year—transcends its value as a first-rate mystery in that it highlights the underreporting of women's roles in religious history. The point is not whether Mary Magdalene was or was not the wife of Christ: the point is that through the centuries she, along with countless other women in the New Testament (not that there are too many to begin with), have been airbrushed out or highly modified by a male-dominated church. Mary Magdalene in all probability was a wealthy and powerful woman who had a lot to say in how the early Christian church was run, but her role was diminished by church historians to that of a prostitute on whom Christ took pity. American society has become fascinated with her rehabilitation at the hands of modern, mostly female historians (e.g., King 2003; Schaberg 2002), who have gone back to little-explored texts for evidence of her true role. Archaeologists and ethnohistorians undoubtedly will ride this wave of popular support for engendering the past.

Ideology always plays a part in influencing one's perceptions of the past, regardless of whether one is a church historian or an archaeologist. Ian Hodder made this an important plank of his postprocessualism, as did Mark Leone, who argued that "structuralism is the theoretical foundation of the most important innovation in archaeology since the new [processual] archaeology was introduced in the 1960s" (Leone 1982:742). The basic assumption of structuralism, according to Leone, is that the human mind operates in orderly ways that are not self-evident; it works on the basis of a cultural grammar (like language) and creates contrasts and oppositions and distinctions. The human mind orders and creates culture, including artifacts, and because the collective mind of a society similarly stamps all artifacts produced by its members, the mind is archaeologically recoverable. An early example of the use of structuralism cited by Leone was Jim Deetz's (1977) study of historical-period artifacts from New England.

Karl Marx developed the concept of ideology in order to understand why individuals do not perceive their true economic, social, and political condition. An ideology is what taints our perception of reality; it is a historically contingent, culturally and socially specific screen to perceptions that "reproduces society intact" by making acceptable or rationalizing or hiding social inequalities, frustrations, frictions, and the like (Leone, Potter, and Shackel 1987: 284). One's knowledge depends on ideological context. Importantly, if one recognizes this, then one can explore that dependence and perhaps be emancipated from it. Given such a view, critical self-reflection and personal awareness become important parts of archaeological research. How, for example, does an archaeologist's culture shape his or her reconstructions of a prehistoric culture?

Reactions to Postprocessual Archaeology

As one might suspect, advocates of processualism did not stand idly by while the postprocessualists voiced their criticisms. Those with the largest professional investments in processualism were some of the most vocal respondents. Binford (1988:875), for example, in reviewing Hodder's *Reading the Past: Current Approaches to Interpretation in Archaeology,* called it "a little book with a little message being blown through a large horn with a loud noise." Although he essentially agreed that data were generated through a theoretical filter, Binford (1987a, 1989c) repeated the processualists' argument that the discipline needed more than the half-century-old standard of evaluating archaeological conclusions on the basis of the polemicist's credentials. He reiterated much of his argument (Binford 1965) against the utility of normative theory in archaeology, though he used different wording: "Archaeologists have no informants. We cannot see the past from the ancients' cultural perspective because they cannot tell us what that might have been" (Binford 1987a:398). Not surprisingly, in his view the scientific method was the only procedure that allowed one to access the past in its own terms.

Colin Renfrew (in Shanks and Tilley 1989: 37) remarked that one must have a means of evaluating knowledge claims, else those of someone such as Eric von Däniken (that cultural evolution owes much of its direction and outcome to visitors from other worlds) are as valid as those of Shanks, Tilley, Hodder, Binford, or Flannery. Other critics made the not-insignificant point that reading or interpreting the archaeological record as if it were a text is a poor metaphor. A text generally has one or two authors, whereas the archaeological record has many "authors" (Preucel 1991), including noncultural agents. Further, a text is constructed in a linear direction and occupies two-dimensional space, whereas the archaeological record has no inherent direction and occupies three-dimensional space (Trigger

1991). Certainly Hodder, and perhaps Shanks and Tilley, would respond that it is for these reasons that an interpretation is never final but always situational, egocentric, and contextual.

Some of the most pointed comments about postprocessualism came from Bruce Trigger (1989b) and from philosopher Richard Watson, who published an extensive review of Shanks and Tilley's two major books (Shanks and Tilley 1987a, 1987b). In arguing that Shanks and Tilley mischaracterized science as a way of knowing, Watson (1990:674) highlighted the fact that "scientific statements are always open to doubt" and that what he called "mitigated skepticism"—a willingness to always doubt, test, revise, and replace hypotheses and theories that fail to work—is what causes scientific knowledge to advance and accumulate. What Shanks and Tilley advocated, in Watson's view, was "absolute skepticism," meaning that there is no absolute or valid knowledge but rather only contextual knowledge in the varied sense that knowledge depends on who creates it. This is because Shanks and Tilley take the theory-laden character of observation to mean "theory corrupted" (Watson 1990:677), and thus in Watson's view they hold that "there is no neutral [objective] way of talking about anything." In no small irony, Watson pointed out that the famous beer can study described by Shanks and Tilley was good, basic science.

Two aspects of Shanks and Tilley's argument were noteworthy, according to Watson. First, they never mentioned that science, however flawed it might be, helps us understand how the world works and why it works the way that it seems to. Elsewhere he put it this way: Modern science "has been judged to be successful on the basis of its practical results" (R. A. Watson 1991:275). The second noteworthy aspect of Shanks and Tilley's argument was that they seemed to have no solid position of their own, perhaps because "their own principles undercut their own position" (Watson 1990:678). For this reason, their argument seemed to be that "anything goes"—what Schiffer (1988)

in his brief critique had referred to as "extreme relativism."

Watson suggested that perhaps Shanks and Tilley's two books were "a put-on," though he doubted this. They chose to reprint one of them in a "second edition" but with minimal modification because, in their words, "we consider that the book can still contribute to the ongoing debate about the character of archaeology and the forms its practices take, to what extent it is humanity or science, indeed the very meaning of these terms" (Shanks and Tilley 1992:xvii). This suggests that the two volumes were not a "put-on" but instead were serious attempts to sell a particular approach to archaeology.

Some commentators have indicated that processual archaeology changed dramatically as a result of the postprocessualist critique. For example, processualists of the 1990s accepted that the archaeological record contains considerably more variation than was recognized in the 1960s. The term *normative*, once reserved for a kind of theory allegedly held by traditional, "preprocessual" culture historians, now came to mean any category of similar archaeological phenomena noted by one archaeologist that contains variation in which another archaeologist is interested (e.g., Claassen 1991; Cordell and Plog 1979, 1981). Many processualists now would agree with postprocessualists that observation is theory laden, meaning that data are observations we choose to make on the archaeological record. In choosing certain observations over others, we have a theory of measurement that includes concepts we call dimensions and units of measurement (Lyman and O'Brien 2002; O'Brien and Lyman 2002a). Further, archaeologists of virtually all philosophical persuasions are constantly discarding their ideas about what the past was like and constructing replacement ideas in the light of new evidence (Schiffer 1988; Trigger 1991; R. A. Watson 1991).

Processual archaeologists have been incorporating (perhaps co-opting) many postprocessual research questions. Questions about gender and social class, the construction of ethnicity, symbols and meaning, social power, social memory, agency, and so forth have augmented the earlier processual agenda and, most would acknowledge, immeasurably enriched the discipline and our reconstructions and explanations of the past. Indeed, postprocessualists have taken archaeology into social and ideological realms far deeper than Binford foresaw by showing that such factors do influence archaeological variability. In addition, processualists now engage more fully with living groups such as Native Americans and employ archaeology for (politically correct) social purposes. No one who peruses recent volumes of, for example, *American Antiquity, Journal of Anthropological Archaeology, Journal of Archaeological Research,* and *Journal of Archaeological Method and Theory* can fail to discern the many ways in which a moderated postprocessualism, shorn of its anti-science stance, has influenced the conduct and findings of American archaeology.

DARWINIAN ARCHAEOLOGY

Robert Dunnell (Figure 8.6) was a student of Irving Rouse's at Yale in the 1960s and thus was trained in the methods of traditional American archaeology. Dunnell (1996:viii) reported that when he began teaching at the University of Washington in the early '70s, he was also a committed processualist, but one who was having difficulty with processualism's approach to explaining culture change. In his opinion it really did not explain change; it only described it. Dunnell further reported that the essays of Stephen Jay Gould in *Natural History* began to convince him that it might be possible to adapt Darwinian evolutionary theory for use in archaeology. Inspiration also came from papers by Richard Alexander, a University of Michigan entomologist known for his work on animal behavior, including that of humans (e.g., Alexander 1974, 1975, 1979a, 1979b). A later inspiration, and the support of a kindred spirit, came from David Rindos's work on the evolution of plant domestication and agriculture, first in his *Current Anthro-*

pology article, "Symbiosis, Instability, and the Origins and Spread of Agriculture: A New Model" (Rindos 1980) and then in his book, *The Origins of Agriculture: An Evolutionary Perspective* (Rindos 1984).

To Dunnell, Darwin's theory of descent with modification provided a theoretical explanation for the unimodal frequency distributions displayed by historical types of artifacts when arrayed in a frequency seriation (Dunnell 2001)—something that had long been explained by the common-sense notion of types first gaining and subsequently losing popularity among their makers (Dunnell 2000; Lyman, O'Brien, and Dunnell 1997). Oddly, beyond a very early technical article (Dunnell 1970), Dunnell did not immediately publish his observations on seriation, perhaps because few processualists had bothered to learn about the method, given its association with culture history and the ready availability of radiocarbon dating and other chronometric tools.

As we have seen so often throughout this book, an effective way of calling favorable attention to an approach is to contrast its merits with its competitor's perceived weaknesses. In

FIGURE 8.6. Robert Dunnell, Castile Landing site, northeastern Arkansas, 1996. (Photograph by Carl Lipo.)

a span of just a few years Dunnell pointed out in at least three places (Dunnell 1978b, 1980, 1982) how Darwin's version of evolution was not only different than but, in his view, superior to the cultural evolutionism of Leslie White and the cultural-ecological evolutionism of Julian Steward. Although these forms of evolutionism had originated as *anthropological* theories, in the 1960s they had achieved the status of necessities in the processualists' theoretical tool kit. Archaeologists didn't always like having to choose between White's and Steward's brands of evolutionism, and neither did anthropologists. This was one reason why two of White's and Steward's students, Marshall Sahlins and Elman Service, tried to unite the two versions into a workable metatheory (Sahlins and Service 1960). Their book, *Evolution and Culture,* was important enough in archaeological circles to merit a review in *American Antiquity* (Willey 1961), an honor rarely bestowed on works on ethnological theory.

Despite the differences between the evolutionism of White and Steward, both variants were regarded as *cultural* evolutionism. Although a few anthropologists and archaeologists saw no significant differences between cultural evolutionism, regardless of kind, and Darwinism (e.g., Yoffee 1979), many in the disciplines *did* see differences, and major ones at that (e.g., Alland 1974; Blute 1979; Carneiro 1973; Freeman 1974). Further, most archaeologists and anthropologists (e.g., Harris 1979) held to the century-old belief that Darwin's version of evolutionary theory was inappropriate for cultural phenomena (Lyman and O'Brien 1997). After Dunnell proposed that cultural evolutionism did not provide scientific explanations of culture change, he turned to adapting Darwinism to cultural phenomena.

The adaptation process involved several steps. First, Dunnell had to invent Darwinian evolutionary concepts that were applicable to the archaeological record. This included identifying the phenomena on which natural selection works and doesn't work. This led to the crucial style-function dichotomy (Dunnell 1978a, 1978b), a source of considerable contention and confusion (for recent discussions, see Hurt and Rakita 2001). Dunnell's basic definition was that functional traits are subject to selection, whereas stylistic ones are not. Confusion arose because these terms already had many meanings in archaeology. This was an issue that Binford (1963, 1972f) had earlier raised but had not pursued. It would have been less confusing if Dunnell had used the biological term *neutral* instead of *stylistic*—a point Dunnell (2001) himself later made. Second, theoretically informed classification procedures were needed so that relevant variation in artifacts could be measured and recorded (Dunnell 1986). The main issue that had to be addressed was a fundamental one: biologists talk about evolution in terms of organisms, but archaeologists study materials in the archaeological record. How can the different subject matters be reconciled?

One answer lies in the fact that evolution works on organisms, but it shapes features, or characteristics. Take, for example, John Endler's (1986:5) definition of evolution: "any net directional change or any cumulative change in the characteristics of organisms or populations over many generations—in other words, descent with modification. It explicitly includes the *origin* as well as the *spread* of alleles, variants, trait values, or character states. Evolution may occur as a result of natural selection, genetic drift, or both." Changes in the composition of a population over time comprise evolution, and in evolutionary archaeology the population is artifacts, which are viewed as phenotypic features (Dunnell 1989; Leonard and Jones 1987; O'Brien and Holland 1990). Extension of the human phenotype to include ceramic vessels, projectile points, and the like is based on the notion that artifacts are material expressions of behavior, which is undeniably phenotypic (O'Brien and Lyman 2000a). Put another way, all activities (behaviors) involve artifacts, and so artifacts don't just express behavior, they are part of it. This extension of the phenotype has been viewed by some (Larson 2000; Maschner 1998; Preucel 1999) as problematic, but this skeptical view is not held widely outside anthropology. Biologists routinely view things such as spiders' webs and beavers' dams as phenotypic characters (Dawkins 1982; Turner 2000; von Frisch and von Frisch 1974).

As a dominant personality and department head at the University of Washington, Dunnell was ideally placed to effectively reproduce his ideas. For example, for many years he alone taught the first-year graduate core course in archaeological method and theory, which after 1978 included his ideas on a Darwinian archaeology. Dunnell, much more than most processualists or postprocessualists, succeeded

FIGURE 8.7. Robert Leonard, Chihuahua, Mexico, 1995. (Photograph by Anne Ogle, courtesy Robert Leonard.)

in reproducing his ideas with great fidelity, if one can judge by the reactions of nonevolutionary archaeologists. The derisive term "Dunnell-vision" came to describe the uniformity of basic ideas and arguments in this program. Indeed, University of Washington students could with ease recite the basic mantra and dismiss the theoretical contributions of other archaeological programs. Nonetheless, those same students exhibited an originality in finding new archaeological applications for their framework and in extending basic ideas. David Meltzer (1981a) provided the seminal study on how to analytically detect and differentiate between stylistic and functional variation. Bob Leonard (Figure 8.7) and Tom Jones showed the conceptual importance of "replicative success" to the program (Leonard and Jones 1987), and Leonard (1989) proposed that natural selection had served as the mechanism that produced change in the cultural record over time in the American Southwest.

Many of the early discussions of evolutionary archaeology (and some of the later ones) were highly polemical (e.g., Dunnell 1980, 1982, 1992a, 1992b; O'Brien and Holland 1990). Statements along the lines of "Archaeology

should adopt Darwinian theory and discard ill-conceived processualism and its attendant baggage" tend to capture both the essence and the confrontational tone of the evolutionary-archaeology literature. This is not surprising given that an allegedly new way of approaching the archaeological record was being propounded. Arguments had to be loud and confrontational in order to get people to listen and to recruit new disciples. By the mid-1990s the rhetoric had more or less died down, as more archaeologists became interested in evolutionary studies. Initially, only a few students who had taken Dunnell's classes in archaeological method and theory at Washington wrote about the topic (e.g., Leonard and Jones 1987; Meltzer 1981a), but that number expanded throughout the '90s as more of his students became involved (e.g., Allen 1996, 2004; Hunt, Lipo, and Sterling 2001; Kornbacher and Madsen 1999; Lipo 2001; Lipo et al. 1997; Pfeffer 2001; Teltser 1995).

Seattle was not the only center of evolutionary archaeology. By the late '80s and early '90s centers had developed at the University of Missouri (e.g., Lyman 2001; Lyman and O'Brien 1997, 1998, 2000; Neff 1992, 2000, 2001; Neff and Larson 1997; O'Brien 1987, 1996; O'Brien, Darwent, and Lyman 2001; O'Brien and Holland 1990, 1992, 1995a, 1995b; O'Brien and Lyman 2000a, 2000b, 2000c, 2002b, 2003a, 2003b, 2003d; O'Brien et al. 1994; O'Brien et al. 2002), the University of New Mexico (e.g., Hurt and Rakita 2001; Leonard 2001; Leonard and Reed 1993, 1996; Maxwell 1995, 2001; Ramenofsky 1990, 1995, 1998; Ramenofsky and Steffen 1998; VanPool 2001; VanPool and Leonard 2002; T. L. VanPool and C. S. VanPool 2003a; Vaughan 2001), and the University of Hawai'i (e.g., Cochrane 2001; Graves and Ladefoged 1995; Hunt, Lipo, and Sterling 2001; Ladefoged and Graves 2000). From the beginning the ties between the Missouri and New Mexico programs have been especially close, with students and faculty from both universities collaborating on problems of mutual interest (e.g., O'Brien, Lyman, and Leonard 1998, 2003; O'Brien and Leonard 2001).

One ingredient missing from early evolutionistic formulations was how to deal with information and its transmission, especially with respect to the units of analysis. During the first half of the twentieth century, *cultural trait* and the synonymous *cultural element* were commonly used to label units of transmission, but at the time neither the process of transmission nor the "thing" being transmitted was discussed within the context of a theory of cultural transmission. Most anthropologists provided commonsensical remarks about the unit and used it to determine something about the "development of American Indian cultures and tribal groups" (Bennett 1944:162). Considerable work on cultural transmission has taken place over the past several decades outside archaeology (e.g., Boyd and Richerson 1985; Cavalli-Sforza and Feldman 1981; Cloak 1975; Durham 1982; 1991; Lumsden and Wilson 1981; Richerson and Boyd 1992), including an attempt to answer the question of what constitutes a unit of cultural transmission (Aunger 2002). Modern researchers have proposed names for units of cultural transmission—"meme" (Aunger 1999, 2000, 2002; Blackmore 1999, 2000; Dawkins 1976) and "culturgen" (Lumsden and Wilson 1981) being two of the better-known terms—but there is little consensus as to what the units entail (Benzon 2002; Williams 2002).

Despite the considerable work done on cultural transmission, it was slow to enter archaeology. A few sporadic studies were undertaken—for example, Ben Cullen's (1993) modeling of cultural transmission as a kind of viral transmission, and Fraser Neiman's (1995) important study of ceramic decorative diversity in the Midwest—but for the most part evolutionists focused on other issues. This began to

change in the late nineties as evolutionists made transmission a central focus of their efforts. One influential study was Robert Bettinger and Jelmer Eerkens's (1997, 1999) analysis of projectile points from the Great Basin. Meanwhile, O'Brien and Lyman (2000a, 2003c; Lyman and O'Brien 2003a) began to explore what is entailed by adopting the concepts "vehicle," "interactor," and "replicator" (Dawkins 1982; Hull 1980, 1981, 1982, 1988a).

Interest in transmission spilled over into the construction of cultural phylogenetic hypotheses based on linguistic methods (e.g., Bellwood 1996; Kirch 1986; Kirch and Green 1987, 2001; Renfrew 1987b, 1999; Renfrew, McMahon, and Trask 2000); archaeological methods such as seriation (O'Brien and Lyman 1999a, 2000a); and biological methods such as genetic analysis (e.g., Renfrew 1992; Renfrew and Boyle 2000) and cladistics (e.g., Foley 1987; Foley and Lahr 1997, 2003; Harmon et al. 2000; Jordan and Shennan 2003; Leonard 2001; O'Brien, Darwent and Lyman 2001; O'Brien and Lyman 2000a, 2002b, 2003a, 2003b; O'Brien et al. 2002; Tehrani and Collard 2002). (Cladistics is a method for creating taxonomic trees that can be inferred to have phylogenetic implications. As opposed to other methods, cladistics excludes all traits except those that are shared only by two or more taxa and their immediate and common ancestor.) Some of the most fascinating, as well as controversial, work entails modeling the spread of prehistoric populations by comparing the fit between cladistically derived language trees (e.g., Gray and Atkinson 2003; Gray and Jordan 2000) and the archaeological record.

Many archaeologists have no problem seeing the applicability of genetic techniques to archaeology, but some (e.g., Moore 1994a, 1994b; Terrell 1988, 2001; Terrell, Hunt, and Gosden 1987) have questioned the use of cladistics and related methods to create hypotheses of cultural phylogeny. Evolutionists respond that the logical basis for extending cladistics into archaeology is the same as it is in biology: artifacts are complex systems, containing any number of replicators. The kinds

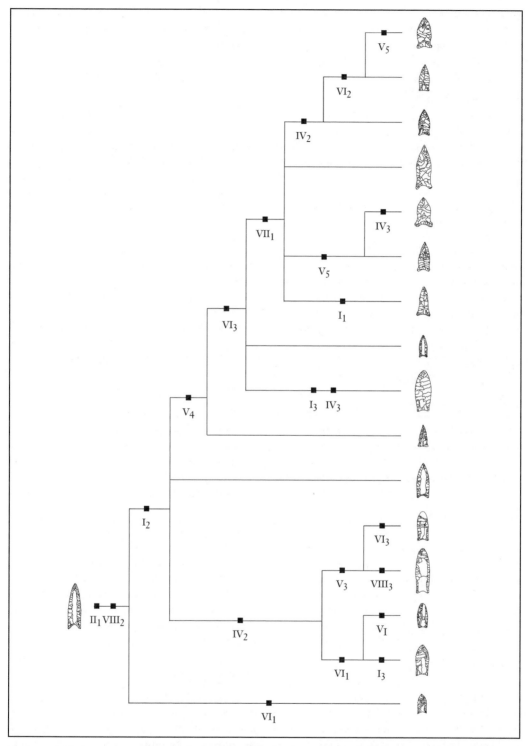

FIGURE 8.8. Phylogenetic tree showing the hypothesized relatedness of projectile-point taxa from the southeastern United States. The boxes refer to character-state changes—for example, a change in character (trait) V from state 4 to state 5. Some kinds of changes are helpful in ordering taxa, whereas other kinds confuse the situation. (After O'Brien, Darwent, and Lyman 2001.)

of changes that occur over generations of tool production are constrained: new structures and functions almost always arise through modification of existing structures and functions as opposed to arising de novo (O'Brien and Lyman 2003a). The history of these changes (additions, losses, and transformations) is recorded in the similarities and differences in the complex characteristics of related objects—that is, in objects that have common ancestors (Figure 8.8).

Reactions to Darwinian Archaeology

As might have been predicted, it didn't take long for the processualists to begin pointing out what they perceived to be fallacies in evolutionary archaeology. Pat Watson (1986) argued that Dunnell was a dogmatic empiricist because he allegedly did not condone any form of analogical argument. This left his program punctured by the "artifact physics" horn of the so-called "archaeologist's dilemma" (DeBoer and Lathrap 1979). Further, Watson, LeBlanc, and Redman (1984:254) suggested that cultural change may in fact be sufficiently different from biological change/evolution that the former cannot be explained by a "theory derived from [the latter]," thereby effectively missing Dunnell's admittedly telegraphed point that the theory would require some modification before it was applicable to cultural phenomena.

Schiffer (1996) pointed out that despite some of their rhetoric, what evolutionary archaeologists were trying to do was in many respects not all that different from what behavioral archaeologists were doing. This is true, although there are important differences. On the one hand, both approaches have as a focus the behaviors of artifact manufacture and use (e.g., Allen 1996; Bronitsky 1986; Bronitsky and Hamer 1986; Mabry et al. 1988; O'Brien et al. 1994; Pfeffer 2001; Schiffer and Skibo 1987, 1989; Skibo, Schiffer, and Reid 1989; VanPool 2001; VanPool and Leonard 2002; Vaz Pinto et al. 1987), and both are grounded in science. On the other hand, evolutionists ignore many aspects of human behavior seen as critical by behavioralists (Schiffer 1996). They do this not out of lack of interest but because they see these aspects as unknowable from the archaeological record. The fundamental difference between the behavioralists and the evolutionists involves inference. Although both programs employ inference, behavioral archaeology makes no distinction between configurational properties (those that are time- and space-specific) and immanent properties (those that are timeless and spaceless). Evolutionary archaeology does make the distinction (Lyman and O'Brien 1998; O'Brien and Lyman 2002b; O'Brien, Lyman, and Leonard 1998; Wolverton and Lyman 2000).

Other archaeologists have examined evolutionary archaeology and found it problematic. Charles Spencer (1997), for example, considered it too narrow and empirical, and expressed a preference for processual archaeology and the cultural evolutionism of White and Steward. Doug Bamforth (2002) found it to be strictly metaphorical and lacking in substance. Evolutionists responded to many of these critiques (e.g., Lyman and O'Brien 1998; O'Brien, Lyman, and Leonard 2003), noting that modern Darwinian evolutionary theory concerns descent with modification irrespective of the means of transmission.

One particularly important critique was provided by James Boone and Eric Smith (1998), who contrasted evolutionary archaeology and human behavioral ecology—an analytical framework that has seen considerable success in anthropological circles since its introduction in the mid-1970s (see Winterhalder and Smith 2000 for an excellent historical review). As with evolutionary archaeology and behavioral archaeology, there are numerous points of complementarity (Broughton and O'Connell 1999; O'Brien and Lyman 2002b). Both approaches view behaviors as phenotypic characters (as does behavioral archaeology), just as they view pots, projectile points, and the like as phenotypic characters. But there is a lack of consensus on how best to examine past behavior, just as there is between evolutionary and behavioral archaeology. Evolutionary archaeology is more a macroevolutionary approach, whereas behavioral ecology is geared more toward examination of microevolutionary processes (Lyman and O'Brien 2001b).

Behavioral-ecology models make two basic assumptions: first, that many human behaviors, including the artifacts that various behaviors produce, were built by natural selection and thus are relatively efficient if not optimal in some absolute sense; and second, that the considerable variation in human behavior inferable from the archaeological record is a reflection of adaptive plasticity rather than evolutionary change produced by natural selection (Boone and Smith 1998). Darwinian archaeologists agree with the first point but would expand it to include adaptively neutral traits (Lyman and O'Brien 1998; O'Brien and Lyman 2000a)— what Dunnell (1978) referred to as "style." Some Darwinian archaeologists (e.g., Neff 2001) agree with the second point, preferring to focus primarily on the "replicative success," or fitness, of artifacts (e.g., Leonard and Jones 1987). Others suspect that the fitness of artifacts often influences the fitness of the people who make and use them (e.g., Leonard 2001; Lyman and O'Brien 1998; O'Brien and Lyman 2000a).

One interest that human behavioral ecology brings to the table is foraging theory, which in archaeology has been used for studying such things as changes in human population size (e.g., Butler 2000) and how prehistoric human predators responded to changes in available prey (e.g., Broughton 1994, 1999; Broughton and Grayson 1993; Cannon 2000; Grayson and Cannon 1999; Grayson and Delpech 1998; Madsen 1993; O'Connell and Hawkes 1984). This kind of work was not unknown to processualists (e.g., Jochim 1976, 1979, 1981), who, like the human behavioral ecologists, were reading the work of economists, entomologists, and zoologists and applying optimization models.

It should be emphasized that the term *optimization* is misunderstood by critics of human behavioral ecology. Part of the problem resides in confusing human behavioral ecology with "optimal foraging theory" (Charnov 1976;

Emlen 1966; MacArthur and Pianca 1966). Although the charge has been leveled (e.g., Keene 1983), no behavioral ecologist we know would argue that humans always act rationally and in strict accordance with a list of resources ranked in terms of net rate of energy gain. Humans are not programmed to always act rationally, as if they were automatons. Human behavioral ecology makes use of foraging theory and models generated from it to create a *yardstick* of objective economic rationality that is used as a basis for the comparative study of behavior (Bettinger 1987, 1991). Behavioral ecology has been successful because, as Robert Kelly (2000:65) put it, the approach "has proceeded by constructing and testing models that have a substantial empirical content (and thus are falsifiable)."

The models derived from the behavioral-ecology perspective are valuable for underscoring the functional and adaptational aspects of an archaeological approach that seeks to adopt various Darwinian tenets. Because foraging theory derives from observations of living organisms, hypotheses are written in the equivalent of ethnographic terms and at the scale of ecological time. Human behavioral ecologists are not unaware of the disparity between ecological and evolutionary time, nor are they unaware that behavior evolves. Their response is that foraging theory and diet-breadth models are simply starting points for behavioral analysis. Excellent summaries of the theory and models used by human behavioral ecologists in archaeological contexts are Robert Bettinger's (1991) *Hunter-Gatherers: Archaeological and Evolutionary Theory* and Kelly's (1995) *The Foraging Spectrum: Diversity in Hunter-Gatherer Lifeways.*

The publication of a collection of essays in the mid-1990s helped clarify the diversity of evolutionary theory's underpinning assumptions and versions within the human sciences (Maschner 1996). Further, the publication of another collection of essays by the American Anthropological Association in its *Archeological Papers* (Barton and Clark 1997) signified disciplinary approval of the use of Darwinian theory in archaeology, if not total agreement in principle. Given the variation in ideas (e.g., Hart and Terrell 2002; Maschner 1996) and the increasing number of individuals interested in evolutionary theory, the approach has gained considerable breadth and stability (e.g., Leonard 2001; Shennan 2002). This is precisely what we would expect. Evolution of the discipline itself depends on such variation.

BEHAVIORAL ARCHAEOLOGY

In building bridges with evolutionary archaeology, Schiffer (1996) was moving behavioral archaeology in a direction that had become noticeable around the mid- to late 1980s. Behavioral archaeology had always been concerned with studying the relationships between material culture and human behavior, the programmatic basis of which had been outlined in the '70s (Reid, Rathje, and Schiffer 1974; Reid, Schiffer, and Rathje 1975; Schiffer 1975b, 1976, 1978a, 1979a). Yet, much of the program's early work involved the study of formation processes. As originally conceived, behavioral archaeology was built around three major tenets (see Reid 1985; Schiffer 1975b; Walker, Skibo, and Nielsen 1995). The first tenet holds that knowledge of the past is inferential and is based on modern material residues that owe their existence and structure (forms, quantities, distributions, and associations) to human behaviors such as subsistence and ritual; to cultural formation processes such as discard and abandonment; and to noncultural formation processes such as earthquakes and earthworms. Thus, only after the variability introduced by formation processes is factored out or otherwise taken into account can the past behaviors of interest be inferred from the archaeological record. The second tenet is that archaeologists can study any and all sociocultural phenomena, so long as such phenomena can be framed as people-artifact interactions at several scales (LaMotta and Schiffer 2001). The third tenet is that defining archaeology as the "study of people through artifacts and people-artifact interaction" (Reid 1995:16) not only furnishes an integrative focus for the discipline

but also establishes a foundation for building a new behavioral science, one emphasizing the many roles that artifacts play in human societies (Schiffer and Miller 1999a, 1999b).

In addition to laws of noncultural formation processes, inference rests on experimental laws (and empirical generalizations) regarding people-artifact interactions (correlates) and cultural formation processes (c-transforms). The emphasis on behavior renders the concept of culture superfluous in proximate explanations of archaeological variability. Behavioral archaeology, like its parent, processual archaeology, has a fundamental nomothetic component, and thus its adherents seek to formulate laws in ethnoarchaeological, experimental, and archaeological research contexts. However, like the evolutionists, behavioralists have always acknowledged that historical questions—seeking to understand contingent changes in specific societies—are also fundamental (Reid, Schiffer, and Rathje 1975; Schiffer 1975b). Behavioral archaeology's ultimate goal is to explain variability and change in human behavior in all times and all places using appropriate general principles (theories and experimental laws) and contingent factors.

In his review of Schiffer's (1976) *Behavioral Archaeology*, Albert Goodyear (1977:670) suggested that the approach was not a "special kind of archaeology" but instead a set of "methods of archaeological inference." The problem reduced, in Goodyear's eyes, to a lack of "theoretical direction" in the important sense that, for example, a study of the "laws" of recycling behavior comparing twentieth-century farming machinery and eighth-millennium B.C. Dalton points "would be trivial at best and at worst inane" (Goodyear 1977:671). Goodyear noted that in his view, and apparently in Schiffer's, one first has to produce laws and then has to specify an analytical problem to which a subset of available laws is relevant. Schiffer and his students spent considerable time beginning in the 1980s building such laws and generalizations (e.g., Schiffer 1987, 1988; Schiffer and Skibo 1987, 1989). At the same time, other archaeologists who did not necessarily identify themselves as behavioralists were conducting research in experimental archaeology and ethnoarchaeology, furnishing precisely the kinds of laws that behavioralists had called for. Yet, these studies, essential though they were for improving behavioral inference, skirted the issue raised by Goodyear: Would all these low-level principles ever add up to high-level theories of human behavior?

Schiffer also ignored this purported problem until the 1980s, when behavioralism had vigorous competitors, especially Darwinian and postprocessualist archaeologies. Concerned that the behavioral program was not taken seriously as a source of principles for explaining variability and change in human behavior, he and other behavioralists began to move their research agendas toward the creation of higher-level theory (Binford's "general theory"). But such theories would not necessarily resemble the social theories of postprocessualists or the evolutionary theories of Darwinians because they had to be written in behavioral terms. Thus, a long-dormant claim was revived that new explanatory theory could arise from the behavioralists' core interest in people-artifact interactions; investigators merely had to ask the right questions.

In the mid-1990s several University of Arizona graduate students put together a volume of case studies and assessments of behavioral archaeology, *Expanding Archaeology* (Skibo, Walker, and Nielsen 1995). Not surprisingly, one of the contributors was Jeff Reid, who was not only one of the original architects of behavioral archaeology but someone who thought it necessary to examine misperceptions of the approach that, in his view, had impeded its adoption by a large portion of the discipline. Reid (1995:15) claimed that the four strategies of behavioral archaeology widely presented and published between 1972 and 1976, "predicted fairly accurately the future course of American archaeology." He argued that behavioral archaeology consists of three research domains: understanding the formation of the archaeological record; reconstructing (inferring) the human behavior that created the record; and

explaining that behavior. To operate in the second and third domains, one must control the first. Curiously, and somewhat incongruously, Reid (1995:21) suggested that behavioral archaeology is "not a theory per se, nor is it a paradigm for explaining human behavior," despite the latter being one of its domains. One reviewer of the volume in which Reid's chapter appears noted that behavioral archaeology lacks "a theoretical basis of equal maturity to its methodological approaches" (Last 1997:384).

Also contributing to *Expanding Archaeology* was Schiffer (1995b:23), who in defense of behavioral archaeology's potential to create explanatory theory—and reacting to the stereotype that the program was limited to studies of middle-range theory—offered the following argument: "Just as Galileo's telescope revealed, literally, a new universe of phenomena for astronomers to explain, so too would an emphasis on people-artifact interactions change the phenomenological world of behavioral scientists. By privileging the study of human activities, the nexus of such interactions, archaeologists would show that behavioral science could not be behavioral or scientific unless it also attended to artifacts. Creative descriptions of this previously unperceived reality would supply the key to constructing new social theory." Following this agenda himself, Schiffer constructed a behavioral theory of communication (Schiffer and Miller 1999a), and from it drew implications for handling symbolic phenomena (Schiffer and Miller 1999b). Schiffer and his collaborators also constructed a general theory of artifact design (Schiffer and Skibo 1997; Skibo and Schiffer 2001) and built models for studying long-term competitions between aggregate technologies (Schiffer 2001) and technological differentiation (Schiffer 2002). Moreover, in case studies of technological change, they demonstrated that the behavioral framework could contribute to the construction of what Schiffer often referred to as "deeply contextualized and reader-friendly historical narratives" (Schiffer 1991; Schiffer, Butts, and Grimm 1994; Schiffer, Hollenback, and Bell 2003).

Recently, Vincent LaMotta and Schiffer (2001) provided a synopsis of behavioral archaeology. They emphasized that it was a myth that the program had as its sole concern the reconstruction of human behavior; explanation of such behavior was equally if not more important. The approach seeks "behaviorally defined units of analysis and explanation [because such units] can be designed to transcend or cross-cut the temporal and spatial boundaries that circumscribe the 'cultural systems' studied by processualists" (LaMotta and Schiffer 2001:15). Behavioral laws include boundary conditions—material, behavioral, social, and ecological—that indicate the particularistic contingencies of when a general principle of behavior is applicable. In LaMotta and Schiffer's view this gives behavioral archaeology its complementary nomothetic and idiographic strategies. Explanation involves subsuming particularistic empirical phenomena under nomothetic statements such as are found in sociobehavioral theory. The unit of analysis is *a behavior* at any scale, ranging from discrete person-object interactions, to an activity made up of a patterned behavior, to a behavioral system made up of multiple activities that link a human group to the physical world and other behavioral systems.

Behaviors and artifacts are seen as interacting and mutually influential in a systemlike or structural-functional kind of model. There are two points to this multivariate model. First, the derivation of behavioral laws (principles) rests on testing *experimental laws* (hypothetical low-level principles) in relevant contexts in experimental archaeology and ethnoarchaeology to ensure their validity and generality, and to identify their boundary conditions. Second, a change in the value of one variable—say, a particular artifact's performance characteristics in particular functional contexts—can have far-reaching influences on behaviors or artifacts in other contexts. The last is not an implicit endorsement of the cybernetic or adaptationist view of human behavior that processualism endorses, but it does incorporate the kind of sys-tems thinking that was perhaps processualism's greatest legacy.

THE MODERN LANDSCAPE

The wranglings between behavioralists and evolutionists, just as with those between processualists and postprocessualists, exemplify the broadening of interests that occurred during a dynamic period in American archaeology. If we need a beginning date for this period, 1982 stands out, for that year Ian Hodder published his trilogy of postprocessualist manuals: *Symbolic and Structural Archaeology, Symbols in Action,* and *The Present Past.* The next ten years or so would be a whirlwind in terms of the myriad directions that archaeology would take. Postprocessualism would provide shelter for those tired of science. Finding shelter, many of the new postprocessualists would ignore entirely what was occurring on the scientific side of the house among the processualists, behavioralists, and evolutionists. Those on the scientific side in turn ignored the postprocessualists, or "posties" for short—more a term of endearment that emphasized the "softness" of their humanistic approach than a derogatory term. The posties, however, were not soft when it came to attacking processualism, as Lew Binford found out during a lecture trip to Great Britain in the early '80s (Figure 8.2). British archaeologists are every bit as capable of a verbal dustup as their American colleagues are.

Maybe after trying to navigate one's way through the confusion of the 1980s and early '90s it is worth pausing to take stock of where, exactly, the discipline ended up. What kind of landscape did these tumultuous changes create? For help, we turn to George Cowgill, who presented his distinguished lecture in archaeology at the annual meeting of the American Anthropological Association in 1992. Cowgill (1993) summarized some of the shortcomings he saw in the three great "approaches" that characterized twentieth-century archaeology: culture history, processualism, and (broadly inclusive) postprocessualism.

Culture historians, according to Cowgill, lacked theory and offered commonsense interpretations of history and did not venture much beyond the archaeologically obvious, thereby largely ignoring the sociocultural aspects of humankind's prehistory. As a result, archaeologists did not contribute to general anthropological theory. They were, in Julian Steward's (1942:341) famous words, but "the tail on an ethnological kite"—providing needed stability but always being pulled along. But processual archaeologists wanted to be much more than an appendage. They wanted to contribute to and help build anthropological theory, and they not only identified problems with the traditional approach but offered an alternative. As we've seen, that alternative was not without its own problems. Cowgill identified four of them: an overemphasis on methods such as statistics and computer-assisted analytical techniques; adoption of a problematic model of scientific protocol from philosophers of science; weak linkages between archaeological data and theoretical concepts; and adoption of an unsatisfactory (ecological-functional) sociocultural theory.

Resolution of the first problem required, in Cowgill's view, greater knowledge of and sophistication with analytical tools rather than the blind faith that applying some seemingly powerful analytical technique would yield a significant aspect of past cultures or human behaviors. Importantly, Cowgill (1993:553) found that when postprocessualists employed such formal analytical tools as statistics, "their practice can be remarkably similar, defects and all, to that of the processualists." This shouldn't be surprising because, after all, the postprocessualists were the intellectual progeny of processualists. With respect to the model of scientific protocol, Cowgill agreed with the postprocessualists that all observation is theory laden and thus there can be no such thing as true objectivity. He also pointed out that there is a real past and that some of our stories about it are more accurate and true than others, though it is unlikely that any story or small set of stories can capture all of the past's complexities.

Strong links between archaeological materials and our impressions of them have been built by middle-range theory, formation-process studies, and the like. We need to expand and strengthen the links.

Cowgill's final point—inadequate theory—is perhaps the most critical. Explanatory models or theories may be simple and readily comprehended, but if they do not account for archaeological observations, then they are deficient or underconceptualized. Further, some aspects of the past, ideology for example, will be more difficult to link directly to archaeological materials than others—say, subsistence. But, as virtually everyone, regardless of preferred approach, would agree, we can perhaps eventually attain even those hard-to-reach aspects if we "acknowledge the unavoidable difficulties, roll up our sleeves, as it were, and try to deal with them" (Cowgill 1993:560).

If individual solutions to each of Cowgill's four problems were put in a blender in order to produce a broad-spectrum remedy, the concoction that resulted would be a "blended" processualism, or what Michelle Hegmon (2003) referred to as "processual-plus"—a term she applied to products from archaeologists who "would probably say that they are 'generally processual' but also interested in other perspectives," including those who combine processual and postprocessual insights (Hegmon 2003:216–217). Hodder (2002) used the term *hybridity* to refer to the products of combined approaches, although we doubt that any of them are 50/50 blends of the two parents. Despite dissatisfaction emanating from some quarters during the 1980s, processualism did not fold up its tent and disappear. Instead, it evolved in light of both the criticism and the new theoretical interests of young people entering the field. Both contributed to a more refined and sophisticated approach. It is difficult to specify the precise characteristics of that new processualism, given the diversity of its practices and its continuous evolution, but we think that few practitioners would disagree with our use of the term *anthropological archaeology* as a label for this developed form (see Chapter 4).

Many processual-plus products share a common heritage. From the beginning processualists borrowed heavily from ethnologists, especially Leslie White and Julian Steward and scholars influenced by them (e.g., Sahlins 1958, 1968; Service 1962, 1971, 1975). New anthropological models became available at the same time that processualism was hitting its stride (e.g., Carneiro 1970; Fried 1967), and these too were used by archaeologists attempting to answer some of the big questions, such as why sociopolitical organization seemed to develop from egalitarian bands to complex, stratified, state-level systems (e.g., Flannery 1972). But by the 1990s processualism, in its new guise as a more fully rounded anthropological archaeology, had begun to consider a wider range of issues (Feinman and Manzanilla 2000; Feinman and Price 2001; Spencer 1997). In some respects this program, as Liz Brumfiel (1992) and Michelle Hegmon (2003) pointed out, displays no theoretical allegiance to a particular issue or to a unified theory (e.g., Duke 1995).

In addition to Hegmon, other archaeologists have tried to show how various approaches might be linked to create a better product. These include Schiffer, whose volume *Social Theory in Archaeology* (2000a) resulted from a conference designed to build bridges between various theoretical approaches, and Todd and Christine VanPool, whose volume *Essential Tensions in Archaeological Method and Theory* (2003b) was the product of a symposium designed to showcase various approaches as they existed at the dawn of the new millennium. Some authors see a need for bridge building, lest archaeology become so full of insular units that it becomes a caricature of itself, like modern cultural anthropology, whereas others see no reason to develop any integrated theories or other conceptual integuments.

One of the more intriguing examples of integration is the VanPools' chapter in their book, "Agency and Evolution: The Role of Intended and Unintended Consequences of Action" (T. L. VanPool and C. S. VanPool 2003a). Their argument is that agency theory and Darwinian

evolutionism are not incompatible and that it is worth exploring possible linkages. We agree, pointing out that for that matter we see nothing inherently incompatible between behavioralism and agency theory. Agency, at least in the form usually applied in archaeology, derives from the work of sociologist Anthony Giddens (e.g., 1979, 1984), especially his eclectic theory of "structuration," the notion that social life is both more than a series of random individual acts while at the same time not merely a result of social forces. Viewed another way, social life is more than a mass of microlevel activity, but at the same time it cannot be studied by looking for macrolevel explanations.

In Giddens' view, humans are agents, and their agency and social structure are directly related in a recursive fashion. The acts of individual agents, taken in the aggregate, reproduce the social structure—institutions, moral codes, traditions, and the like—but those acts also change the structure when people begin to ignore or replace the institutions, codes, and traditions (Gauntlett 2002). To Giddens, structure and agency are a duality; one cannot exist without the other. One of the key elements of Giddens's theory is "practical consciousness," which refers to the actions that agents take for granted—actions that they cannot necessarily explain in words.

Agency often is conflated with "practice," which stems from the work of Pierre Bourdieu (e.g., 1977), a French sociologist/anthropologist who studied under Claude Lévi-Strauss but later began to view French structuralism as too limiting for understanding the actions of individuals. Bourdieu was interested in what humans actually did (their practices) as opposed to what they had the capacity to do (their agency). To Bourdieu, any attempt to dichotomize between individual and society was misguided. He argued that various kinds of structures not only constrain the interactions between individuals and society but help shape the underlying representations that guide those interactions. He used the term *practice* to connote the outcome of this interface between individual and society.

Agency and practice are becoming common topics of concern in archaeology (e.g., Barrett 1994, 2001; Bell 1992; Blanton et al. 1996; Brumfiel 1983; Dobres 1995, 1999, 2000; Dobres and Hoffman 1994; Dobres and Robb 2000; Dorman 2002; Drennan 2000; Joyce and Winter 1996; Spencer 1993; Tilley 1994). Part of the reason for this resides in the interest in the individual aroused by postprocessualists, although the argument has been made (e.g., Blanton et al. 1996) that the postprocessual view of agency and practice is too limited and fanciful, bordering on biography. Here we are not concerned with whether one prefers to refer to agency and practice as Marxist, structural, or post-structural issues; our point is that the reaction to processualism and its emphasis on culture as a system (as opposed to a collective of individuals) was behind the adoption of agency and practice theories in American archaeology. To some, this adoption was not a complete abandonment of processualism. Timothy Pauketat (Figure 8.9), for example, recently coined the term "historical processualism" (Pauketat 2000, 2001, 2003a, 2003b) for what he sees as an "emerging paradigm" that produces "historical explanations, in the process altering the questions that archaeologists ask and the data that they must gather to address those questions" (Pauketat 2001:73). Historical processualism represents a "theoretical ground-swell in archaeology [that] is moving the study of demographic displacements and migrations to the fore of explanations of causation" (Pauketat 2003b:39).

To a historical processualist, "history matters" (Pauketat 2001:74). This is not history in the sense that event A preceded and caused event B. Rather, by "history" is meant "what people did and how they negotiated their views of others and of their own pasts" (Pauketat 2001:73). Writing processual history involves chronicling what was going through people's minds as they made their way through life. The approach "relocates the processes that we seek to explain and revises how we understand cause and effect" (Pauketat 2001:75). Explanations involve identifying "the proximate causes of *how* a certain social feature...developed in a particular time or place" (Pauketat 2001: 74). One's analytical ability to account for near-term causes is assured, given that "people's actions and representations—'practices'—are generative.... Practices *are* the processes, not just consequences of processes. Thus, they generate change. That is, practices are always novel and creative, in some ways unlike those in other times or places. This means that practices are historical processes to the extent that they are shaped by what came before them and they give shape to what follows" (Pauketat 2001:74).

We agree (O'Brien and Lyman 2004). Practices are generative (including those of archaeologists [Preucel 1995]), meaning they generate new practices. And it is likely that all practices are in some ways unique, even if only in when and where they occur. If practices are the actual processes of cultural change, then we can always explain change in terms of what humans do—a formulation that also resonates in behavioral archaeology (LaMotta and Schiffer 2000; Walker, Skibo, and Nielsen 1995). All we need to do is "focus attention on the creative moments in time and space where change was actually generated" (Pauketat 2001:87). As long as we can correctly identify the kind of practice—accommodation, coercion, collaboration, revitalization, and the like (Pauketat 2001:80)—then we have an explanation composed of a proximate cause. If that is the kind

FIGURE 8.9. Timothy Pauketat at the Grossmann site, western Illinois, 2001. (Courtesy Timothy Pauketat.)

of explanation an archaeologist wants, then historical processualism is a way to attain it. Nothing prevents the archaeologist, however, from taking the next step and employing evolutionary theory to derive explanations that refer to ultimate causes. In this sense, historical processualism and evolutionism are not competing frames of reference.

Michael Shott, in reviewing *Expanding Archaeology* (Skibo, Walker, and Nielsen 1995), characterized its varied and sometimes contradictory contributions in this way: "Ardent banner waving that alienates like-minded archaeologists elides major similarities between the [processualist and behavioralist] approaches and obscures the promise that both hold" (Shott 1996:611). The same could be said about evolutionary archaeology and postprocessualism. Is there an archaeological approach out there that *doesn't* include ardent banner waving? Yes, and it is what we've referred to variously as processual-plus or anthropological archaeology. There may be a good reason why archaeologists engaged in this approach have not spent a lot of time flag waving. As with the culture historians of the 1940s and '50s, the new "old" guard is firmly established and doesn't need to be shrill to gain attention or to recruit disciples. It hasn't had to do these things for a long time, whereas some of its more youthful competitors have needed to toot horns and derogate the competition in an effort to gain market share.

Speaking of competition, if one wants to learn about the multitude of approaches available in the modern archaeological marketplace, be wary of the secondary literature, especially if it has been authored by someone who is a strong advocate of a competing approach. Critiques written by advocates of other approaches are valuable, of course, for highlighting an approach's perceived weaknesses, or at least inconsistencies, but one shouldn't rely solely on the critical literature to gain insights into the tenets and workings of an approach. All approaches in archaeology have been misrepresented, caricatured, and pilloried in the critical literature; students should peruse the primary sources and form their own judgments about the promise and pitfalls of each program. We think we have a pretty good handle on various approaches, but don't rely solely on us either.

As a final note about the modern archaeological landscape, we point out that 2001 was the inaugural year of a new archaeological journal, the *Journal of Social Archaeology*, published by Sage Publishing and edited by Lynn Meskell of Columbia University and Chris Gosden of Oxford University. The description of the journal that appears on its Web site is revealing:

> The *Journal of Social Archaeology* promotes interdisciplinary research focused on social approaches in archaeology, opening up new debates and areas of exploration. It engages with and contributes to theoretical developments from other related disciplines such as feminism, queer theory, postcolonialism, social geography, literary theory, politics, anthropology, cognitive studies and behavioural science. It is explicitly global in outlook with temporal parameters from prehistory to recent periods. As well as promoting innovative social interpretations of the past, it also encourages an exploration of contemporary politics and heritage issues.

Openly engaging with such things as feminism and queer theory? *JSA* is certainly not your father's archaeology journal. Who among the processualists coming out of the University of Chicago in the mid- to late 1960s could have guessed that American archaeology would ever engage with such diverse interpretive frameworks? How the evolutionary process will select from among this amazing variation is contingent on factors of the social environment that no one can predict. But we are confident that the processes of change that operate in scientific disciplines will produce in the decades ahead a different configuration of archaeological theory and practice than what we see today.

9

Tribal Encounters

The most fruitful attempts to achieve a better understanding of the anthropological enterprise have come not from single-purpose approaches, but rather from the pluralism of approaches and theoretical positions that have traditionally given anthropology its strength. What good will it do for archaeologists to develop deductive multiple hypotheses from general anthropological theory if the enterprise is dominated by a ruling theoretical structure? How does this differ, practically speaking, from the domination of a ruling hypothesis? In the long run, how does it really differ from the domination of a ruling ideology?

—R. H. THOMPSON, "Interpretive Trends and Linear Models in American Archaeology"

As noted in Chapter 8, several archaeologists have taken as one of their tasks the reconciliation and synthesis of disparate approaches in the hopes that an archaeology that is somehow better and more comprehensive will emerge (e.g., Hegmon 2003; T. L. VanPool and C. S. VanPool 2003b). Perhaps some of these authors hope to attain a "consilience," to borrow the title of a popular book by biologist E. O. Wilson (1998)—a true synthesis of current knowledge that allows construction of explanations that crosscut all levels of organization. We applaud efforts to find com-mon ground between competing programs and to increase the civility of theoretical disputes. Nonetheless, we believe that the disparity of viewpoints in archaeology is not only refreshing but mandatory for the continued development and improvement of the discipline. Consilience, in a Wilsonian sense, is but one of several strategies for producing answers to archaeological questions.

With respect to our personal interests and goals, Schiffer builds models and theories of human behavior that will yield insights into how and why people behave the way they do in particular contexts. O'Brien and Lyman want to understand the development and evolutionary history of artifact traditions in particular spatial and temporal contexts. Although numerous aspects of Schiffer's vision of archaeology and those of O'Brien and Lyman's are similar to the point of overlap, their perspectives are not completely reconcilable for the simple reason that in some instances they ask different questions of the archaeological record (O'Brien, Lyman, and Leonard 1998; Schiffer 1996, 1999). And these differences are important. Some archaeologists think the evolutionary program is completely without grounds, merit, or utility, and other archaeologists (or sometimes the same ones) think the behavioral program is too limited in scope, too materialist, and too positivist. Although we believe that most such labels are unhelpful and such judgments are misinformed, the critics' (mis)perceptions of our work (and ours of theirs) are not a disease of the discipline; rather, they are its lifeblood. How else can we gain ever more detailed insights into the past than through competition between distinct approaches?

The history of research in virtually every field of science indicates that competition between different approaches, paradigms, methods, theories, and so forth is exactly what causes a discipline to advance. As philosopher James Woodward and physicist David Goodstein (1996:485) put it, "[R]apid progress will be more likely if different [researchers] have quite different attitudes toward appropriate methodology." The maintenance of what Thomas Kuhn (1977) referred to as the "essential tension" between competing concepts, methods, and theories ensures that errors and incorrect assumptions have relatively brief shelf lives. The competition among approaches can sometimes be rigorous and harsh. Chris and Todd VanPool (2003) liken the scenario to gladiators fighting in a colosseum. (Or maybe, as our colleague Steve Nash suggested, a better analogy is a World Wrestling Federation match, with its pageantry, strutting, and blustering.)

Not all archaeologists choose to enter the arena. Some express an interest in theory but do not espouse a single program. An archaeologist without such a commitment has the luxury of kibitzing on the sideline, "tut-tutting" those who endorse a particular approach for their competitive (some might say childish and overly shrill) behavior. Although we appreciate her insights (Chapters 7 and 8), Alison Wylie has done this on occasion (e.g., Wylie 1989a, 1995, 2000, 2002), commenting that a particular approach is "empiricist" or "scientistic" because it rejects certain "inferences" and does not recognize that other kinds of insight to the past are also inferences. Wylie finds some of the rhetoric and polemic of the last decade to be "repugnant" and "hostile," and to read like "fundamentalist religion" (Denning and Wylie 2000). We're not sure that the work to which she alludes is "repugnant"—we hope not, given that O'Brien and Lyman wrote much of it—but

we admit that in several instances it could be mistaken for something that Elmer Gantry would preach. (Wylie is certainly not the only archaeologist to comment on the manner in which archaeologists sometimes communicate among themselves. Richard Pailes's [1981] "On the Archaeology of the Absurd and Green Slimy Frogs: A Plea for Civility and Mutual Respect" was an earlier statement.) The question one should ask, however, is not whether the rhetoric is repugnant or hostile, but whether it has noticeably moved the field in one direction or another. Have other archaeologists cited the work—positively or negatively—or have they ignored it? Reactions to what one writes are what matter. Silence is the kiss of death.

BLIND AMBITION OR ADVANCING THE DISCIPLINE?

One possible, though certainly unintended, consequence of the manner in which we have chronicled the four-plus decades of American archaeology from 1960 on is that in contrast, the preceding sixty years appear pale and uninteresting. Someone without much knowledge of pre-1960 archaeology could surmise from this book that archaeologists working and writing prior to that date had little in common with those who came after. One might think that instead of exhibiting the ambitious nature of the processualists and their progeny, the men and women of earlier generations were honest, hardworking people who with an altruistic spirit consistently placed professional goals ahead of personal ones. Even Walter Taylor, who upset more than a handful of fellow archaeologists with his strident criticism of the state of method and theory in the 1940s, might be viewed as a kind of John the Baptist—an altruistic individual who sacrificed his own career for the greater good of the discipline.

As nice a picture as this paints of pre-1960 American archaeology, we don't buy it for a second. Neither would anyone else who has even a passing familiarity with the earlier archaeology. Archaeologists of that period were hardworking, though hardly pious and altruistic, and some weren't even particularly honest. Take, for example, Aleš? Hrdlička, William Henry Holmes, and W J McGee, who through their positions with the Bureau of American Ethnology and the U.S. National Museum worked diligently during the late nineteenth and early twentieth centuries to refute any evidence served up in support of an American Paleolithic (Meltzer 1983, 1985). The ambitious processualists of the 1960s, who were interested in drawing sharp contrasts between what they were doing and what those before them had done, had nothing on Hrdlička and company and the lengths to which they would go in order to maintain the official party line that had been passed down intact from the founding of the BAE in 1879.

FIGURE 9.1. W J McGee and friends on an outing to the soapstone quarry in west Washington, D.C., ca. 1900. *Far left*, W J McGee and Anita McGee; *bottom, seated*, Otis T. Mason; *far right*, Rollin D. Salisbury. (From Hinsley 1994, courtesy National Museum of American Art.)

Some of the exchanges between opponents and supporters of an American Paleolithic were cordial, but often they became vitriolic, especially if McGee (Figure 9.1) was involved. For example, in commenting on geologist G. Frederick Wright's (1892) book *Man and the Glacial Period,* McGee (1893: 94, 95) labeled Wright's evidence of human occupation of the North American continent during the glacial period as a "tissue of error and misinterpretation," and Wright himself as a "betinseled charlatan whose potions are poison." McGee would have argued that he was simply defending archaeology, although his actions suggest otherwise (Meltzer 1983). McGee was not alone in terms of personal ambition, nor was he the only prehistorian ever to use his position—he was the first president of the American Anthropological Association—as a

FIGURE 9.2. David Hull, Chicago, 1988. (Courtesy David Hull.)

bully pulpit from which to attack his opponents.

David Hull (Figure 9.2) offered the following insights about personal ambition and disciplinary goals in science: "Scientists compete in a quite literal sense as they race to solve an easily identifiable, conspicuous problem. One danger in science is for career interests of the crassest sort to supersede the desire to produce work that other scientists can use. The two need not go together. However, in a sufficiently high percentage of cases, the best way for scientists to further their careers is to fulfill the loftier goals of their profession. Conflicts between these two goals are sufficiently rare that scientists are usually able to avoid admitting to themselves that they even have career interests" (Hull 1988b:514).

It is difficult to believe that archaeologists have ever consistently placed the "loftier goals of their profession" ahead of personal goals and ambitions. This holds true regardless of whether archaeology is viewed as a science, a humanity, or something else entirely. We say this because we don't think that a humanist is any kinder or gentler than a scientist—that the humanities train individuals to place professional goals ahead of personal ones, whereas science trains them to do just the opposite. Of course, maybe we're wrong. Maybe some archaeologists—scientists, humanists, or both—sacrifice self-interest for the greater good of the profession, but as Hull points out, conflicts between the two sets of goals are infrequent enough that for all practical purposes the issue is moot.

Our objective in the remainder of this chapter is to use our history of post-1960 archaeology to examine the effects of self-interest on the function and evolution of conceptual groups. How an individual perceives what is or is not of personal benefit affects not only the intellectual fitness of that individual but also the fitness of the group of which he or she is a member. Selection is the final arbiter of intellectual fitness and thus determines the group's success or failure. In our view selection occurs in the sciences and humanities just as it does in the rest of the organic world, and its sorting effects are no less dramatic. Nor are the adaptations, or strategies for survival, that scientists and humanists develop any less dramatic than those of other organisms. In fact, given the dizzying array of variation that humans are able to scare up, their adaptations are even more striking.

In deference to readers who abhor thinking about humans in terms familiar to an evolutionist, we later bring in two heuristic devices that we find helpful in thinking about not only the formation and evolution of conceptual groups but also the roles played by individuals in those groups. We also find them helpful

in thinking about how conceptual groups are recognized. One heuristic device is to model conceptual approaches as analogues of artistic movements, and the other, which uses a familiar sociocultural unit, is to model them as analogues of "tribes." The various conceptual approaches—"isms"—that have entered the mainstream of American archaeology over the past forty-plus years have much in common with both.

SELECTION AND INTELLECTUAL FITNESS

Selection is a process centered on the competition between conspecifics (organisms in the same "species") as they go about their daily business. There are, as we saw in Chapter 7, different kinds of competition, and each can have a different effect on both the composition and evolution of the groups in which organisms live and work. Competition can be either zero sum or not zero sum. Tennis is a zero-sum game, meaning that a player who scores a point takes that point away from the other player. Alternatively, golf is not a zero-sum game. Although we say that golfers compete against one another, they actually compete against themselves. What one player does has no bearing on what another player does (holding constant the mental part of the game).

Much of the selection that takes place in nature is of the zero-sum kind—involving, for example, access to finite resources such as food, shelter, parental attention, and mates. A morsel of food that one organism gets is a morsel denied to another. A check of homework that one child receives from a tired parent may be a check that a sibling does not receive. That resources are finite may or may not have dire consequences for an organism. As long as the "carrying capacity" remains high enough (or the number of organisms remains low enough), competition does not lead to an organism's removal from the game. Change the parameters, however, and it *could* lead to removal.

We do not see it as a stretch to model archaeology as a species and archaeologists as members of that species. In fact, doing so brings considerable clarity to how and why archaeologists behave as they do. Archaeologists compete among themselves for resources, but that competition is not necessarily a zero-sum game. Academic tenure, for example, doesn't have to be zero sum; at some (probably most) colleges and universities there are no quotas on how many faculty members can receive tenure in the same year. At many large research institutions, if, for example, fifty people come up for tenure, conceivably all of them can be successful, even if on occasion several of them are from the same department. The awarding of tenure is based strictly on the merits of a person's dossier. But some institutions *do* have tenure quotas, and there a candidate *is* competing in a zero-sum game. Most insidious are those institutions that do not advertise the fact that they have quotas, leaving it up to young faculty members to learn later that they were actually competing against other untenured faculty for a preset number of slots.

Even in situations where the granting of tenure is not a zero-sum game, tenure candidates have already participated in those kinds of games well before they come up for review. Academic positions are scarce, and although new positions are occasionally created, the increase is slow enough so that we can call the hiring process a zero-sum game. Because there are many more qualified persons than there are available jobs, a position given to one person is a position not given to someone else. As we saw in Chapter 7, another zero-sum game involves publication, the basis upon which most tenure decisions rest. How many articles, monographs, and books has someone published? In which journals do the articles appear? How often are the articles cited? What is the reputation of the press that published a particular book?

Publication normally is a zero-sum game because there are only so many journal pages available, and space in the most prestigious journals—*American Antiquity,* for example—is especially limited. Thus, every article published means that others were rejected. As long as the number of archaeologists remains below carrying capacity, then competition is not problematic. But once the number of available manuscripts outstrips the resource base—the number of pages available—the situation changes. At that point, various options are available: increase the number of pages by ginning up new journals or by adding signatures to existing journals; decrease the number of archaeologists; create new faculty positions; and/or lower tenure standards. Or, alternatively, leave things exactly as they are and let selection do its job.

We should be clear about exactly what is at stake in any discipline—reputation and prestige, career advancement, grants, and so on. In short, one's intellectual fitness is at stake. We could even claim that other aspects of one's fitness are at stake. For example, if the discipline as a whole thinks highly of one's archaeology, this conceivably could lead to awards, more publicity, more invitations to speak and associated honoraria, and so on. This in turn could lead a subset of one's peers—those in the National Academy of Sciences—to conclude that the person has demonstrated the necessary qualities for membership. Thus the members start the nomination process. If the person is eventually elected to the academy, his home institution might increase his salary by a substantial margin to preempt his jumping ship to join another institution. We could spin all kinds of other fitness-affecting scenarios, many or most of which undoubtedly have occurred at one time or another.

Archaeologists tend to be good ethnographers of the systems in which they participate. They understand which factors affect their intellectual fitness and how the game must be played. Thus, it is inconceivable to us that archaeologists fail to consider their fitness and work to maximize it. Maybe they don't think about it every day, or necessarily even think in terms of "fitness," but the subject cannot be buried too deeply in their subconscious. It seems to us that someone who has invested a decade or more in a Ph.D.—an investment not only of time but also money—and who maybe has sacrificed other aspects of his or her life, is not going to behave altruistically. We don't, for example, see many archaeologists who are coming up for tenure say, "Gee, I think Sally Jones is a much better archaeologist, so I'm going to turn down tenure so that the university can hire her." Neither do we believe that most archaeologists running for, say, the presidency of the Society for American Archaeology are doing it in order "to give back to the organization that has given so much to me over the years."

We know that there are those who will strongly criticize us for these views, in the process branding us as technofunctional evolutionary behavioralists who see humans as little more than selfish, fitness-maximizing creatures. We'll have to accept such criticism because we cannot envision a strongly competing alternative scenario. Does this make the story of American archaeology sterile and depressing? Not in the least. In our opinion it enriches it. Does it make the story any less enjoyable? Only if one prefers fairy tales. If archaeologists are as open to the effects of selection as all other organisms, then their aggregate actions should be as predictable as those of other organisms—not their specific actions (those are in large part contingency based) but the *kinds* of actions they generally exhibit.

Cognitive archaeologists should have no quarrel with this view, nor should agency-based theorists. Indeed, our view explicitly recognizes that individual archaeologists exercise specific kinds of agency in various institutional contexts that confer rewards. The alternative, if we may dignify it by that term, assumes that archaeologists are passive participants unconcerned with furthering their own interests—a view we regard as terminally naive. Again, we are not claiming that archaeologists, nor any humans for that matter, run around the landscape thinking up new and clever ways to maximize their fitness. What we *are* suggesting is that the intellects humans possess, taken in conjunction with their cultural environments, present them with many broad opportunities for personal advancement. And to no one's surprise, humans tend to jump at those opportunities. Sometimes—and here is where the picture becomes confused—those opportunities, as Hull (1988b)

pointed out, coincide with what is "good" for the profession. This has numerous implications for fitness enhancement, not the least of which is that humans can work to increase their personal fitness while operating just under selection's radar.

There are various kinds of selection, and each has a distinct effect on both the tempo and mode of evolution. One is "stabilizing" selection—the culling of variants that depart in either direction from a central value. Stabilizing selection plays a major role in keeping biological species in balance, and it plays a similar role in the evolution of human groups. As long as one individual looks and acts pretty much like the next one—hence the old saying, "go along to get along"—he or she usually can proceed unmolested. This is what we referred to above as flying under selection's radar. Species evolution under conditions of stabilizing selection is a slow process characterized by incremental movement in one direction, then back toward the norm, then slowly in another direction, and so on. In a sense, it is mere random fluctuation of a population's mean value around a grand mean value over some multiple-population span of time.

At some point one path might have such favorable effects on overall fitness that "directional" selection takes over, nudging the group out of the grasp of stabilizing selection and slowly drawing it away from the norm. Stabilizing selection may or may not take over again. Paleobiologists Steve Gould and Niles Eldredge (1977:117) point out that "the norm for a species during the heyday of its existence as a large population is morphological stasis, minor non-directional fluctuation in form, or minor directional change bearing no relationship to pathways of alteration in subsequent daughter species."

Once in a while the "nudge" provided by directional selection is more like a hard kick that propels a species along a trajectory at a much faster tempo than normal. We can borrow the term coined by Eldredge and Gould (1972)—"punctuated equilibria"—to describe this evolutionary mode. It is an appropriate term because it conveys the point that the "equilibrium" associated with evolutionary stasis is "punctuated" by a rapid spurt of change, seemingly overnight creating a new "species." With respect to a biological species, it might spend 99 percent of its life in stasis and only 1 percent going through a punctuational event (Gould 1982b, 1982c). What comes out of this event are two (or perhaps more) species—the "parent" and its offspring. The term we use for this kind of event is *cladogenesis*, or diversification through branching, as opposed to *anagenesis*, or straight-line evolution where one species turns into another.

What does this have to do with the history of archaeology? Are we saying that archaeology evolves? Yes, and we think it does so through cladogenesis. Viewing archaeology as a species, however, obscures a key point—one that is also obscured in biology when we place an analytical premium on species. What really matters in biological evolution is not species but *demes*—usually localized, not necessarily genetically isolated breeding populations. Demes are where intraspecific change often occurs, and what goes on within and between demes controls the fate of species. Conceptual groups, like biological demes, hold properties in common, one of which involves cooperation among members. In his examination of the social and conceptual development of science in *Science as a Process,* Hull commented on the cooperation that occurs between scientists:

> Because scientists must use the work of other scientists, they are forced to "cooperate" in a metaphorical sense with even their closest competitors, i.e., use their work. Science can proceed and on occasion does proceed in the absence of cooperation of the more literal sort. However, many problems require an array of cognitive resources that no single scientist is liable to possess. As a result, scientists frequently join together for periods in their careers to develop a particular area of science or to investigate a particular set of problems. These research groups serve to enhance a scientist's conceptual inclusive fitness. Conceptual demes and larger invisible colleges are responsible for the "tribal" behavior of scientists. Scientists continue to cooperate and compete with each other but as members of particular research groups and conceptual demes. One would expect the presence of research groups and conceptual demes to have the same effects on conceptual evolution that population biologists have shown that kinship groups and biological demes have on biological evolution. (Hull 1988b:514)

Here Hull is using *deme* to refer to a population in which intellectual transmission and replication take place. *Inclusive fitness* is a term introduced into evolutionary biology by William Hamilton (1964) to refer to an individual's own fitness plus the effect she or he has on the fitness of any relative. Here "relative" refers to intellectual relative. Hamilton's notion of inclusive fitness helps us explain not only why some female birds hang around the nest and help raise their siblings, in the process "sacrificing" precious reproductive time of their own, but also why archaeologists train graduate students. Unless we want to invoke some simplistic, nonexplanatory principles such as "It's what they're supposed to do" or "It's what they get paid to do," we might look to inclusive fitness as an ultimate explanation for the many hours that graduate advisers invest in correcting yet another dissertation draft, or the large effort they devote to commenting on articles and book manuscripts that friends send them to review. In doing all of these tasks, archaeologists are hoping to increase the replicative success of their own ideas about archaeology.

With respect to cooperation among individuals, it takes place at numerous levels simultaneously. The least amount of cooperation occurs at the highest level—Hull's conceptual deme—which is really a collection of individual research "families." The closest cooperation occurs among members of the same research group (akin to a family), each of whom has a vested interest in the success of the group.

Why? Because this helps ensure individual success—others working for you while you work for them. Members work as an entire group or as a subset of the group, with members sharing more or less equally in rewards—publications, grants, royalties, and so on. Conceptual demes rarely remain static for very long, changing as members leave individual research groups and either join other groups or start their own groups. Thus a conceptual deme is defined on the basis of the individuals within it at any given moment; its membership and structure are historically contingent, or what paleontologist George Gaylord Simpson (1963, 1970) would term "configurational."

This creates a major problem when one tries to define the boundaries of a conceptual deme. What, for example, are the boundaries of post-processualism? This problem is no different than the one facing a biologist interested in defining a species. The biological definition of (sexual) species is based on reproduction: Organisms that can mate and create viable offspring are members of the same species. That's a good definition in theory, but it has its practical limitations. Using it to determine which individuals belong in which species, a biologist would have to survey literally the entire animal kingdom and examine each individual's reproductive compatibility relative to every other individual. Using similar reasoning to create conceptual groups, we would have to survey all archaeologists and ask them in which group they belong—similar to what Dave Thomas (1976) and Melinda Zeder (1997) did. Clearly, identifying conceptual groups is not particularly easy. They, like species and demes, might be difficult to delineate, but this makes them no less real than a group more easily specified.

By "real" we mean that conceptual groups, species, and demes are not simply creations of our minds—entities that look as if they are real but that fade away as we approach them. Importantly, and it is difficult to overemphasize this point, that reality does not mean that conceptual groups, species, or demes are "natural kinds" that can be identified on the basis of some inherent "essence." Indeed, the only way something with an essence can change (evolve) is somehow to transform itself (or be transformed) into something else. It must become a member of another kind by dropping one essence and taking on another, much like Midas could turn any other material into gold.

Instead of essences, what we are looking for when we attempt to delineate a species, deme, or conceptual group is properties held in common by a collective of individuals—the group's "defining characters."

In any conceptual group, ideas are what matter in the long run. Further, individuals in the group are vehicles for those ideas. In this respect scientists and humanists are no different than any other individuals. What, for example, is the difference between an archaeologist's vision of a new disciplinary direction and a Zapotec lord's personal vision for his reign over the Valley of Oaxaca? Both visions revolve around ideas, and both individuals need followers—vehicles for their ideas. They need to attract new followers as well as to keep the ones they have. The archaeologist produces a collection of ideas materialized on paper, the Zapotec lord chisels his ideas in stone (Figure 9.3).

Ideas, regardless of medium, compete in marketplaces, and it serves an idea well to have a well-oiled vehicle that can move it efficiently around the intellectual landscape as it seeks to replicate itself in other vehicles. An archaeolo-

FIGURE 9.3. Stela 1 from Monte Albán, Oaxaca, Mexico, showing a Zapotec lord on his throne. (From Marcus 1983; drawing by Mark Orsen, courtesy Academic Press and Joyce Marcus.)

gist serves in the same capacity as a Zapotec lord—as a vehicle. Ideas cannot interact; it is the interaction between vehicles that contributes to replication. Whether interaction leads to idea transmission is a complicated issue, the outcome of which depends on many factors, including the salience of a particular signal and the receptivity of the audience. These in turn are conditioned by the social and conceptual contexts in which the vehicles find themselves. As we have seen throughout this book, archaeology has had its share of highly successful vehicles.

One useful characteristic for defining a conceptual group is the presence of a shared terminology. Philosopher Phillip Kitcher (1982) finds the common use of terms to be a defining characteristic of a linguistic community, even though members of the community may have vastly different beliefs. But community members agree on term usage and also on the term's etymology. Hull (1988b) points out that linguistic communities do not coincide with scientific research groups, for the latter are based more on cooperation than on common terminology. Although we won't debate which is more important—common terminology or cooperation—it appears that without a consensus on terms and the concepts that underlie them, it is questionable whether a particular "approach" even exists.

We cannot, for example, imagine an evolutionary archaeology in which there was little agreement over terms such as "cultural transmission" (e.g., Cavalli-Sforza and Feldman 1981). We can, however, imagine an evolutionary archaeology where there is considerable debate over the role played by cultural transmission in determining the fitness of culture-bearing organisms. We can imagine it because it exists (e.g., Leonard 2001; Lyman and O'Brien 2001b; Neff 2000). Terminology is important because it signals how well someone understands the basic language of a conceptual group. Incorrect usage of the term *nomothetic* by a budding processualist in the 1970s, for example, could have immediately labeled the person as a wannabe.

ARTISTIC MOVEMENTS

Commonly recognized movements in both music and painting exhibit properties that can illustrate some of the preceding points. For example, like disciplinary approaches, artistic movements (traditions) do not contain essences—there is no essential property that a movement possesses that makes it that particular movement as opposed to another. Artistic movements are defined by properties that at any moment their members have in common and that are reflected in their work. Members of a musical movement hold in common such things as basic instruments and how much adherence there will be to the musical structure. In jazz the basic instruments are a string bass, piano, drums, and maybe a guitar. With respect to structure, jazz thrives on an ability to improvise new melodies that fit a chord progression. These characteristics help define jazz, but they are not essences.

Importantly, jazz players know they hold those properties in common; they don't have to wonder about it. Louis Armstrong put it best when he was asked to define jazz: "Man, if you gotta ask, you ain't never gonna know." Armstrong knew he was a jazz musician the same as Jim Hill knew he was a processual archaeologist. Because processual archaeology and jazz do not have essences, the properties held in common shift as members come and go. If the properties didn't change, movements would never evolve, but we know they *do* evolve—or go extinct.

Likewise, we would be hard pressed to identify an essence within the painting movement known as Impressionism. Why? Because no essence ever existed. We can, however, define Impressionism based on common properties that its members exhibited at a particular point in time, such as the use of a bright palette and flickering brush strokes, a spontaneous recording of color and light (Stokstad 2004), and an absence of biblical allegories and ruined buildings—characteristics that set the Impressionists apart from traditional painters in the French Academy of Fine Arts. Helping us in our delineation of Impressionism is the fact that the

Impressionists identified themselves as such after art critic Louis Leroy coined the term in a disparaging reference to one of Claude Monet's works. Likewise, the Post-Impressionists— and they, too, identified themselves as such after English art critic Roger Fry created the term in 1910—exhibited certain shared properties such as a sense of structure and order. Where did those characteristics come from? They evolved out of Impressionism. Post-Impressionists began life as Impressionists but later began to react to what they saw as the strictures of Impressionist canon.

In terms we introduced earlier, the evolution of Post-Impressionism out of Impressionism was a cladogenetic event as opposed to an anagenetic one. This means that the genesis of Post-Impressionism was a branching event in contrast to one in which Post-Impressionism replaced Impressionism in a straight-line kind of evolution. The birth of Post-Impressionism did not signal the death of Impressionism. Rather, the two movements coexisted for a while. Was the evolution of Post-Impressionism a gradual or a punctuated process? We strongly believe that it was the latter, just as we believe the evolution of Impressionism out of traditional French Academy painting was a punctuational event. This does not mean that the Impressionists discarded all the tenets of traditional painting, any more than the Post-Impressionists discarded the tenets of Impressionism. Neither movement arose de novo, just as species don't generate themselves spontaneously. Rather, conceptual groups and species evolve out of precursors as the characteristics of their members change. When those characteristics have changed to the point that we as onlookers can detect a group of offspring that differ (usually) markedly from the parent population, we say that speciation has taken place. Art critics did not have trouble pinpointing the evolution of a new species (Impressionism) in Paris in 1874 or one (Post-Impressionism) in New York in 1913 (see below), just as archaeology critics did not have difficulty in the 1960s and '70s identifying processualism.

Early in an artistic movement's existence it needs an outward sign not only of where it is headed, but of what it has accomplished in a very short time. Take, for example, the impact that the first Impressionist exhibition had when it opened in Paris in 1874. Rejected by the traditionalist Salon juries, fifty-five painters— Renoir, Monet, and Pissarro among them— formed the "Limited Company" and exhibited 165 pieces in a former photography studio. Some critics liked what they saw, but most of them trashed the exhibition, and it made headlines across Europe. It was the shot in the arm that the Impressionists needed in their movement away from the tradition of the French Academy.

Thirty-nine years later, the New York Armory Show of 1913 introduced Post-Impressionist art to the United States. Like the earlier Paris show organized by the Impressionists, the Armory Show was viewed in most traditional quarters as an affront to society and a threat to values—the triumph of anarchy over tradition. Others heralded the fresh flow of ideas from young artists tired of the status quo. Regardless, the show had the impact that its planners wanted: a huge disturbance that cast the spotlight on the supposedly radical ideas springing up in European painting and sculpture. American newspapers loved the conflict, warning in headlines for traditionalists to take heed: Your enemy approacheth. Four decades earlier, Impressionism was the radical child; now it had become the conservative parent. Sounds a lot like processualism and its enfant terrible, post-processualism.

TRIBAL UNITS

Notice in an earlier quote above what Hull (1988b:514) said about cooperation among scientists: "Conceptual demes and larger invisible colleges are responsible for the 'tribal' behavior of scientists." What *are* the "tribal behaviors" of scientists? The first order of business would seem to be defining the key term. Tribes—using characteristics supplied by Marshall Sahlins (1968), Elman Service (1971), and others—are "social networks integrated by cross-cutting panresidential institutions, but lacking class structure or full-time segmental specialization. Such systems also may be termed 'nonhierarchical,' in the sense that decision-making occurs primarily through consensus rather than through the full-time exercise of power by formally sanctified authorities" (Braun and Plog 1982:504).

What better definition could we possibly devise for conceptual groups and the manner in which they function? Conceptual groups are nothing if not social networks. True, we normally think of think of them in methodological and theoretical terms, but where do the methods and theories reside? They reside in people's minds and in activities and material forms—from books to computer screens. Conceptual approaches are collections of people strung together—sometimes loosely, sometimes more securely—by replicators (ideas). Those replicators are moved through social networks. Conceptual approaches crosscut residential units. Processualism, for example, might have started life as a small residential unit at the University of Chicago, but it quickly diffused to other institutions. Likewise, postprocessualism started life in Great Britain but quickly spread to America. Conceptual groups do lack class structure in the sense of rigid socio-economic strata, but they do not lack status differentiation.

Just because decision making occurs primarily through consensus rather than through the full-time exercise of power does not mean that tribes are egalitarian. There are any number of status positions available, and they are ranked. There might be enough valued prestige positions for all qualified persons to have one, or if necessary the number of recognized prestige positions can be expanded. And certainly there are opportunities for movement from one status position to another—downward as well as upward. Tribal leaders do not get where they are by chance. Positions of tribal leadership can be based on numerous criteria, but probably the two most important ones are hard work and charisma. We would also place signaling

(advertising) near the top of the list. Signaling includes such things as the people with whom one is seen at meetings, the names that are casually dropped in conversation, and the number of times one's name appears in a meeting program and in top-rated journals. It also includes such phenotypic traits as clothing (think "dress for success") and business-related gear (a leather briefcase or ornately engraved business cards).

Tribal leaders might be elected, but usually the outcome is a foregone conclusion because everyone knows who the leader will be on the basis of his or her past activities. The "anointing" is a mere formality. No one, for example, elected Kent Flannery as the leader of the Michigan school of anthropological archaeology, yet few would question his place at the head of the table (Feinman and Manzanilla 2000). Likewise, few could fail to recognize Ian Hodder as the chief figure in the postprocessual movement. Once in a recognized position, successful tribal leaders usually do not have to resort to the naked use of power to maintain their positions or to achieve party discipline. A successful leader melds his or her desires with those of others, creating what at one level appears to be a seamless product but at a closer one is actually a complex amalgam of views, needs, and desires. But make no mistake: A leader can also attempt to squelch anyone or any idea that he or she deems to be too far removed from canon, creating what Michael Shanks and Christopher Tilley (1989:9) refer to as "structures of oligarchic orthodoxy," where prestige is distributed unevenly, with one or a few archaeologists deciding who receives grant money and who is allowed to publish in which journals (Hutson 1998).

Liz Brumfiel, in commenting on an article by Rich Blanton and his colleagues (Blanton et al. 1996) on the evolution of Mesoamerican civilization, makes an excellent point with respect to coalition building: "Because humans wield power only as groups, coalition building is indispensable for constructing social inequality. Any explanation of the origins of social inequality must indicate how some individuals were able to put together power-wielding coalitions while others were not" (Brumfiel 1996:48). It appears to us that this holds true regardless of whether one is talking about Prehispanic Mesoamerica or modern American archaeology.

Tribes, like other, more complex sociocultural entities, promote themselves, signaling by word and accomplishment their superiority over other tribes. This would appear to be important in situations where members are being recruited. Nothing keeps a tribe, or any other kind of group, from exaggerating its claims of importance and superiority, either through "bluffing" or outright misrepresentation. Joyce Marcus (2003) made an important discovery vis-à-vis the timing in numerous prehistoric cultures of construction of large prehistoric public monuments (pyramids and the like). Such monuments presumably were erected to show the power and prestige of a political entity relative to that of its rivals. Contrary to what we might think, quite often the most impressive monuments—for example, Khufu's pyramid at Giza in Egypt, and the Pyramid of the Sun at Teotihuacán in the Valley of Mexico—were built early in the life of the entity, prior to its emergence as a recognizable power. Such monuments, Marcus proposes, were built for propaganda purposes, precisely to conceal the entity's lack of real clout. As Jared Diamond (2003:891) put it, "[T]he Great Pyramid is a bluff, a proclamation of power as empty as that by Shelley's Ozymandias." Later dynasties were much more powerful than Khufu's, but they put time and energy into other activities, such as conquest, trading expeditions, and building fortresses. Khufu wasn't anywhere near being able to do these things, but he could run a good bluff.

Conceptual groups need big splashes, too, and as we saw with both the Impressionists and the Post-Impressionists, this is what they made with their early shows. Parallels exist in archaeology. A good example is Sally and Lew Binford's 1965 symposium that produced *New Perspectives in Archeology* (1968). The Binfords needed a solid product in order to show the viability of their processualist program, and they got it in spades. Lew followed that up in 1972 with his first collection of papers, *An Archaeological Perspective.* That was an important book from a number of perspectives, not the least of which was that it gave Lew the opportunity to write history as he saw it.

Binford was the consummate pitchman for processualism, and in the autobiographical sections of *An Archaeological Perspective* he gave an accounting of how he assumed that position. In writing his own history, he took pains to show how he had distanced himself from two legendary figures in the field, Jimmy Griffin and Robert Braidwood, and how both had tried to get even with him for striking off in different theoretical and methodological directions. On top of that, Lew reported that he had been proclaimed an intellectual heavyweight by another heavyweight, François Bordes. By 1972 Binford not only had created a big splash in American archaeology but also had assembled a good-sized conceptual group around him and penned its mythic origins.

We see much the same thing in 1982 with the publication of Ian Hodder's *Symbolic and Structural Archaeology,* which grew out of a conference held in Cambridge in 1980. It is worthwhile quoting at length from Hodder's preface to the volume because of the seeming candor with which he chronicled the beginnings of postprocessualism:

During the early period of exploration and development of ideas, premature conference presentations and individual seminars were given by various members of the Cambridge group in other archaeology departments in England and abroad. Individual scholars who were invited to talk to us in Cambridge in that period often felt, understandably, obliged to maintain a distinct opposition. While it is certainly the case that these presentations had occurred before our views had even begun to settle down, and that they were excessively aggressive, they played an important role in the process of enquiry and reformulation. In particular, the contrasts which were set up by us and by outside scholars allowed the views of the seminar group, and the differences of viewpoint within the group, to be clarified. The opposition highlighted our own opinions but also threw the spotlight on the blind alleys down which there was a danger of straying. (Hodder 1982a:vii)

This was a useful strategy for the early postprocessualists to employ: invite into your village members of the tribal group from which you're planning to distance yourself while simultaneously visiting their villages, all done in order to check on the strength of your position relative to theirs.

Like the early processualists, the budding postprocessualists were not shy in staking out their position, putting other tribes on notice that there was a competitor afoot:

Our aggression resulted from the conviction that we were doing something new. This, too, was important. In the initial period there was a clear idea of what was wrong with existing approaches and there was a faith that something else could be done. But there may have been no clear idea of how the vague hopes could be converted into rigorous analyses. There was a phase in which there was more faith than evidence that the approach would succeed. Advances in the human sciences must often go through similar phases and I find it difficult to see how progress can be made in archaeology at the moment without the willingness of individuals to make a "jump" and be criticised for it. It is the sense and excitement of newness which provide the energy to continue through this early stage. (Hodder 1982a:vii)

We agree completely with Hodder's assessment: Progress *cannot* be made in archaeology or any other discipline without individuals being willing not only to make a "jump" but to be criticized for it. Those jumps—punctuations—are, in the biological sense, speciational events.

Members of tribes, as we saw with members of conceptual groups, cooperate with each other while at the same time ensuring their own individual success. The closest cooperation occurs among members of the same family. The analogous unit within a conceptual group—let's refer to it here as a conceptual deme to avoid ambiguity—is the research group, composed of members working in close proximity, say, in the same laboratory. Each member of a research group has a vested interest in the success of the entire group. Members work as a unit—on occasion as a subset of the larger unit—with members sharing more or less equally in rewards such as publications, grants, and so on. A lesser degree of cooperation occurs at the level of what are often ephemeral interconnected research groups—megagroups created for cooperative research purposes but which are much more fluid than the individual "families" within the groups. Finally, the least amount of cooperation, although it still serves an important role, is at the level of the tribe, or conceptual deme. It is here where fragmentation occurs.

Fragmentation might or might not lead to further divergence and eventually to the creation of a new conceptual group. Think in terms of biological speciation. A gene pool, for any of several reasons, may start to divide. If it continues, the end result may be the production of a new species that coexists alongside the parent species. Or, the initial separation may reverse course. The same thing happens with conceptual groups (Figure 9.4). Take, for example, the schism between the Penn State and Michigan research groups that we discussed in Chapter 7. Actually, the schism developed between two megaresearch groups, given that the players were not confined to the tribal capitals of State College and Ann Arbor. Prior to the schism, there was a more or less unified vision of archaeology as anthropology—a view, not surprisingly, that had its roots in both the cultural evolutionism of Leslie White and Julian Steward, and the long-standing emphasis on human-land relationships on the part of the

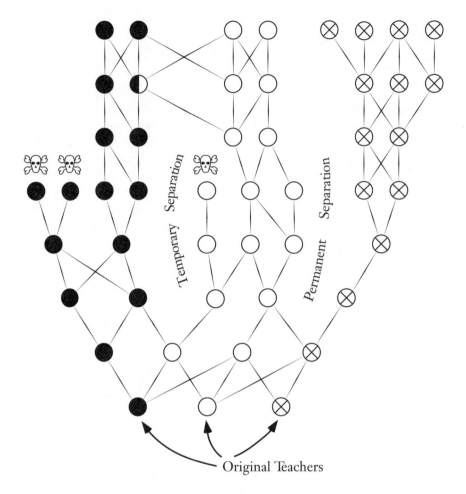

FIGURE 9.4. The evolution of conceptual groups, or intellectual lineages, showing the splitting of some groups and the intermixing of others.

University of Chicago's Oriental Institute, which produced Kent Flannery, and Harvard University, which produced Bill Sanders.

For years it would have been difficult to distinguish between graduate students from Michigan or Penn State solely on the basis of their archaeological perspectives. Titles of dissertations produced at the two schools during the 1970s show considerable overlap in terms of both project conception and approach. The archaeology faculty at both schools emphasized cultural ecology and never strayed from the view that archaeology is a subdiscipline of anthropology. Somewhere along the line the Michigan group began to see too much em-

phasis being placed on the physical environment by Sanders and his Penn State group, and not enough on other variables. The Michigan group—in particular, Flannery and Joyce Marcus, but certainly including others such as Rich Blanton—while not ignoring the effects of the physical environment on human activities, placed considerable emphasis on the cognitive aspects. This emphasis is seen in numerous publications (e.g., Blanton et al. 1996; Flannery 1986a, 1999; Flannery and Marcus 1983, 1993, 1994). By the late 1980s the Penn State group saw the Michigan group as placing too little emphasis on physical-environmental factors and too much on other factors.

A few years after the appearance of *Debating Oaxaca Archaeology* (Marcus 1990a), the book in which the Michigan group presented its case against environmental determinism, things changed dramatically, with a movement of the two groups back to a more or less unified anthropological approach. In symbolic terms, the two little glyph guys who were last seen yelling at each other (Figure 7.15) when they graced the cover of *Debating Oaxaca Archaeology* had within a few years made up and were buddies again (Figure 9.5). ("Glyphs," by the way, don't always have to be carved in stone [Figure 9.6]). The significance of the Michigan–Penn State realignment goes well beyond the symbolic, however. What emerged from the reunification is a strengthened approach to the archaeological study of complex societies. Here was a case of "almost speciation" (Figure 9.4)—a split in a conceptual deme that sent segments on their own trajectories but which after a time came back together.

The history of archaeology has become something of a hot topic since about 1980, as witnessed by the number of books that have appeared both in the United States and abroad. We have tried to produce a history that includes not only an examination of some of the basic theoretical and methodological work that has gone on in American archaeology but also a detailed look at some of the people who have done the work. To our way of thinking, the doers are a big part of the story. When he examined how science is done, physicist Gerald Holton (1986: 238) remarked that "amazingly enough, the process of science works so well even in the hands of mere humans." We would argue the same is true of archaeology, regardless of whether one views it as a science, a humanity, or both.

FIGURE 9.5. Revised "glyph" (see Figure 7.15) that adorned the cover of *Debating Oaxaca Archaeology* (Marcus 1990a). (Original courtesy the Museum of Anthropology, University of Michigan, and Joyce Marcus.)

As a final note, we invite our colleagues who have more programming capability than we have to use SWARM (e.g., Kohler et al. 2000) or some other simulation program capable of modeling the social interactions of agents to examine what archaeologists do. We think the result would pretty much parallel what we have laid out in our history of American archaeology over the past forty years—in particular the

FIGURE 9.6. *Left,* Ian Hodder and *right,* Lewis Binford, Chile, 1998. (Courtesy Lewis Binford.)

fissioning and fusing of groups of individuals to form conceptual demes, and the behaviors of the highly visible individuals in those demes. We would vary the scale (inclusiveness) of the agent from a single individual to a group of, say, fewer than ten individuals, to a group of several tens of individuals. We also would vary the kind and complexity of transmission networks, as well as the spatial distribution of the agents and networks. Such models might tell us much about what to expect regarding the future of archaeology—not necessarily what new approaches will look like, but how they will be structured and how they will operate as social units that compete for such things as recruits, grant dollars, and air time at national meetings. In short, the models might tell us more about how humans will be, well, human.

Notes

Chapter 2

1. Four other archaeologists who received their Ph.D. degrees at Chicago between 1963 and 1967 also were later elected to the National Academy of Sciences: Robert McCormick Adams, Richard Klein, Craig Morris, and Henry Wright.

2. For a partial transcript of Mario Savio's speech, see the Free Speech Movement Archives Web site (www.fsm-a.org).

3. Binford (1972b) lists the year incorrectly as 1966.

Chapter 3

1. Just to finish the story of Longacre and ethnoarchaeology, it's worth noting that his commitment to the approach extended throughout his career. After a stint as director of the University of Arizona's field school at Grasshopper, in 1973 he began ethnoarchaeological research in the Philippines, focused on the Kalinga of northern Luzon, a group that still made domestic pottery. Longacre and several generations of his students demonstrated the fruitfulness of a long-term commitment to ethnoarchaeological research (e.g., Graves 1985, 1991; Longacre 1981b, 1985, 1991; Longacre and Skibo 1994; Longacre, Xia, and Yang 2000; Neupert 2000; Skibo 1992, 1999; Stark 1991, 1992, 1999; Stark, Bishop, and Miksa 2000; Stark and Longacre 1993).

Chapter 4

1. This was not the first time that Flannery had used the term *Mickey Mouse*. As Schiffer recalls, after receiving his Ph.D. from Arizona in 1968, Mark Leone, then a senior staff member at Paul Martin's field camp at Vernon, sent Flannery a copy of his dissertation (Leone 1968a). Apparently unimpressed—even Arizona processualists saw it as creative but deeply flawed (Schiffer 1995a)—Flannery wrote back, "this is Mickey Mouse." Mickey Mouse or not, Leone (1968b) published his results in *Science* the same year he completed his dissertation.

Chapter 7

1. Not to belabor the point, but Wildesen never published her ideas, whereas Schiffer did. O'Brien and Lyman point out that Schiffer was a household name in the 1970s and 1980s because of his publication record. Further, Schiffer had students, whereas Wildesen didn't. It was no contest as to whose ideas would last longer.

Chapter 8

1. Statement read by Jan Hammil before the Interior and Insular Affairs Committee's Subcommittee on Public Lands, U.S. House of Representatives, July 30, 1985, Washington, D.C.

References

Aberle, D. F.
1987   Distinguished Lecture: What Kind of
        Science Is Anthropology? *American
        Anthropologist* 89:551–566.
Adams, R. McC.
1956   Review of *Theory of Culture
        Change: The Methodology of Multi-
        linear Evolution*, by J. H. Steward.
        American Antiquity 22:195–196.
1960   Some Hypotheses on the Develop-
        ment of Early Civilizations. *American
        Antiquity* 21:227–232.
1962   Agriculture and Urban Life in Early
        Southwestern Iran. *Science*
        136:109–122.
1965   *Land behind Baghdad: A History of
        Settlement on the Diyala Plains*. Uni-
        versity of Chicago Press, Chicago.
1966   *The Evolution of Urban Society:
        Early Mesopotamia and Prehispanic
        Mexico*. Aldine, Chicago.
1968   Archeological Research Strategies:
        Past and Present. *Science*
        160:1187–1192.
1971   Illicit International Traffic in Antiqui-
        ties. *American Antiquity* 36:ii–iii.
Adams, R. McC., and H. J. Nissen
1972   *The Uruk Countryside: The Natural
        Setting of Urban Societies*. University
        of Chicago Press, Chicago.
Adovasio, J. M.
1977   *Basketry Technology: A Guide to
        Identification and Analysis*. Tarax-
        acum, Washington, D.C.

Albarella, U. (editor)
2001   *Environmental Archaeology: Mean-
        ing and Purpose*. Kluwer, New York.
Aldenderfer, M. S. (editor)
1993   *Domestic Architecture, Ethnicity,
        and Complementarity in the South-
        Central Andes*. University of Iowa
        Press, Iowa City.
Aldenderfer, M. S., and R. K. Blashfield
1978   Cluster Analysis and Archaeological
        Classification. *American Antiquity*
        43:502–505.
Aldenderfer, M. S., and C. A. Hale-Pierce
1984   The Small-Scale Archaeological Sur-
        vey Revisited. *American Archeology*
        4(1):4–5.
Alenen, A. R., and R. Z. Melnick (editors)
2000   *Preserving Cultural Landscapes in
        America*. Johns Hopkins University
        Press, Baltimore.
Alexander, D. A.
1983   The Limitations of Traditional Sur-
        veying Techniques in a Forested Envi-
        ronment. *Journal of Field Archae-
        ology* 10:177–186.
Alexander, R. D.
1974   The Evolution of Social Behavior.
        *Annual Review of Ecology and Sys-
        tematics* 5:325–383.
1975   The Search for a General Theory of
        Behavior. *Behavioral Science*
        20:77–100.
1979a   Evolution and Culture. In *Evolution-
        ary Theory and Human Social Orga-*

nization, edited by N. A. Chagnon and W. G. Irons, pp. 59–78. Duxbury Press, Scituate, Mass.

1979b *Darwinism and Human Affairs*. University of Washington Press, Seattle.

Alland, A., Jr.

1974 Why Not Spencer? *Journal of Anthropological Research* 30:271–280.

Allen, M. S.

1996 Style and Function in East Polynesian Fish-Hooks. *Antiquity* 70:97–116.

2004 Bet-Hedging Strategies, Agricultural Change, and Unpredictable Environments: Historical Development of Dryland Agriculture in Kona, Hawaii. *Journal of Anthropological Archaeology* 23:196–224.

Allen, W. L., and J. B. Richardson III

1971 The Reconstruction of Kinship from Archaeological Data: The Concepts, the Methods, and the Feasibility. *American Antiquity* 36:41–53.

Ammerman, A. J.

1981 Surveys and Archaeological Research. *Annual Review of Anthropology* 10:63–88.

Anderson, D. C.

1985 Reburial: Is It Reasonable? *Archaeology* 35(5):48–51.

Anderson, K. M.

1969 Ethnographic Analogy and Archeological Interpretation. *Science* 163:133–138.

Andrefsky, W., Jr.

1998 *Lithics: Macroscopic Approaches to Analysis*. Cambridge University Press, New York.

Arnet, C.

1970 The Constitution and the Custody Law. *The Indian Historian* 3(2):11–12.

Arnold, B.

1990 The Past as Propaganda: Totalitarian Archaeology in Nazi Germany. *American Antiquity* 64:464–478.

Arnold, P. J., III

2003 Back to Basics: The Middle-Range Program as Pragmatic Archaeology. In *Essential Tensions in Archaeologi-cal Method and Theory*, edited by T. L. VanPool and C. S. VanPool, pp. 55–66. University of Utah Press, Salt Lake City.

Ascher, R.

1961a Analogy in Archaeological Interpretation. *Southwestern Journal of Anthropology* 17:317–325.

1961b Experimental Archeology. *American Anthropologist* 63:793–816.

1962 Ethnography for Archeology: A Case from the Seri Indians. *Ethnology* 1:360–369.

1968 Time's Arrow and the Archaeology of a Contemporary Community. In *Settlement Archaeology*, edited by K. C. Chang, pp. 43–52. National Press, Palo Alto, Calif.

Ashby, W. R.

1956 *Introduction to Cybernetics*. Wiley, New York.

Aten, L. E.

1974 Comments. In *Proceedings of the 1974 Cultural Resource Management Conference*, edited by W. D. Lipe and A. J. Lindsay, Jr., pp. 93–97. Technical Series No. 14. Museum of Northern Arizona, Flagstaff.

Athens, J. S.

1977 Theory Building and the Study of Evolutionary Process in Complex Societies. In *For Theory Building in Archaeology: Essays on Faunal Remains, Aquatic Resources, Spatial Analysis, and Systemic Modeling*, edited by L. R. Binford, pp. 353–384. Academic Press, New York.

Aunger, R.

1999 Culture Vultures. *The Sciences* 39(5):36–42.

2000 (Editor) *Darwinizing Culture: The Status of Memetics as a Science*. Oxford University Press, Oxford.

2002 *The Electric Meme: A New Theory of How We Think*. Free Press, New York.

Bacus, E. A., A. W. Barker, J. D. Bonevich, S. L. Dunavan, J. B. Fitzhugh, D. L. Gold, N. S. Goldman-Finn, W. Griffin, and K. Mudar (editors)

1993   *A Gendered Past: A Critical Bibliography of Gender in Archaeology.* Technical Report No. 25. Museum of Anthropology, University of Michigan, Ann Arbor.

Bamforth, D. B.
2002   Evidence and Metaphor in Evolutionary Archaeology. *American Antiquity* 67:435–452.

Banning, E. B.
2000   *The Archaeologist's Laboratory: The Analysis of Archaeological Data.* Kluwer Academic/Plenum, New York.
2002   *Archaeological Survey.* Kluwer Academic/Plenum, New York.

Barber, B.
1961   Resistance by Scientists to Scientific Discovery. *Science* 134:596–602.

Bareis, C. J., and J. W. Porter (editors)
1984   *American Bottom Archaeology: A Summary of the FAI-270 Project Contribution to the Culture History of the Mississippi River Valley.* University of Illinois Press, Urbana.

Barnes, M. R., A. K. Briggs, and J. J. Neilsen
1980   A Response to Raab and Klinger on Archeological Site Significance. *American Antiquity* 45:551–553.

Barrett, J. C.
1994   *Fragments from Antiquity: An Archaeology of Social Life in Britain, 2900–1200 B.C.* Blackwell, London.
2001   Agency, the Duality of Structure, and the Problem of the Archaeological Record. In *Archaeological Theory Today,* edited by I. Hodder, pp. 141–164. Polity Press, Cambridge.

Barrett, R. A.
1989   The Paradoxical Anthropology of Leslie White. *American Anthropologist* 91:986–999.

Barton, C. E.
2001   *Sites of Memory: Perspectives on Architecture and Race.* Princeton Architectural Press, New York.

Barton, C. M., and G. A. Clark (editors)
1997   *Rediscovering Darwin: Evolutionary Theory and Archeological Explanation.* Archeological Papers No. 7.

American Anthropological Association, Arlington, Va.

Bartovics, A. F.
1974   The Experiment in Archaeology: A Comparison of Two Studies. *Journal of Field Archaeology* 1:197–205.

Bass, W. M.
1995   *Human Osteology: A Laboratory and Field Manual,* 4th ed. Missouri Archaeological Society, Columbia.

Bayard, D. T.
1969   Science, Theory, and Reality in the "New Archaeology." *American Antiquity* 34:376–384.
1978   Comment on "Descriptive Statements, Covering Laws, and Theories in Archaeology," by D. W. Read and S. A. LeBlanc. *Current Anthropology* 19:318.

Beals, R. L., G. W. Brainerd, and W. Smith
1945   Archaeological Studies in Northeast Arizona: A Report on the Archaeological Work of the Rainbow Bridge–Monument Valley Expedition. *Publications in American Archaeology and Ethnology* 44:1–236. University of California, Berkeley.

Beck, C., and G. T. Jones
1994   On-Site Artifact Analysis as an Alternative to Collection. *American Antiquity* 59:304–315.

Behrensmeyer, A. K., and A. P. Hill (editors)
1980   *Fossils in the Making: Vertebrate Taphonomy and Paleoecology.* University of Chicago Press, Chicago.

Bell, J.
1992   On Capturing Agency in Theories about Prehistory. In *Representations in Archaeology,* edited by J.-C. Gardin and C. S. Peebles, pp. 30–55. Indiana University Press, Bloomington.

Bellwood, P.
1996   Phylogeny vs Reticulation in Prehistory. *Antiquity* 70:881–890.

Benfer, R. A.
1967   A Design for the Study of Archeological Characteristics. *American Anthropologist* 69:719–730.

Bennett, J. W.
1943 Recent Developments in the Functional Interpretation of Archaeological Data. *American Antiquity* 9:208–219.
1944 The Development of Ethnological Theory as Illustrated by Studies of the Plains Sun Dance. *American Anthropologist* 46:162–181.
1946 Empiricist and Experimental Trends in Eastern Archaeology. *American Antiquity* 11:198–200.

Bennett, M. A.
1974 *Basic Ceramic Analysis.* Eastern New Mexico University Contributions in Anthropology 6(1). Portales.

Benzon, W. L.
2002 Colorless Green Homunculi. *Human Nature Review* 2:454–462.

Berr, H., and L. Febvre
1932 History. *Encyclopedia of the Social Sciences* 7:357–368.

Berry, B. J. L., and D. F. Marble (editors)
1968 *Spatial Analysis.* Prentice-Hall, Englewood Cliffs, N.J.

Bettinger, R. L.
1987 Archaeological Approaches to Hunter-Gatherers. *Annual Review of Anthropology* 16:121–142.
1991 *Hunter-Gatherers: Archaeological and Evolutionary Theory.* Plenum, New York.

Bettinger, R. L., and J. Eerkens
1997 Evolutionary Implications of Metrical Variation in Great Basin Projectile Points. In *Rediscovering Darwin: Evolutionary Theory in Archaeological Explanation,* edited by C. M. Barton and G. A. Clark, pp. 177–191. Archeological Papers No. 7. American Anthropological Association, Arlington, Va.
1999 Point Typologies, Cultural Transmission, and the Spread of Bow-and-Arrow Technology in the Prehistoric Great Basin. *American Antiquity* 64:231–242.

Binford, L. R.
1962a Archaeology as Anthropology. *American Antiquity* 28:217–225.
1962b A New Method of Calculating Dates from Kaolin Pipe Stem Samples. *Southeastern Archaeological Conference Newsletter* 9(1):19–21.
1963 "Red Ochre" Caches from the Michigan Area: A Possible Case of Cultural Drift. *Southwestern Journal of Anthropology* 19:89–107.
1964a A Consideration of Archaeological Research Design. *American Antiquity* 29:425–441.
1964b *Archaeological Investigations in the Carlyle Reservoir, Clinton County, Illinois, 1962.* Archaeological Salvage Report No. 17. Southern Illinois University Museum, Carbondale.
1965 Archaeological Systematics and the Study of Cultural Process. *American Antiquity* 31:203–210.
1967 Smudge Pits and Hide Smoking: The Use of Analogy in Archaeological Reasoning. *American Antiquity* 32:1–12.
1968a Archeological Perspectives. In *New Perspectives in Archeology,* edited by S. R. Binford and L. R. Binford, pp. 5–32. Aldine, Chicago.
1968b Methodological Considerations of the Archaeological Use of Ethnographic Data. In *Man the Hunter,* edited by R. B. Lee and I. DeVore, pp. 268–273. Aldine, Chicago.
1968c Post-Pleistocene Adaptations. In *New Perspectives in Archeology,* edited by S. R. Binford and L. R. Binford, pp. 313–341. Aldine, Chicago.
1968d Some Comments on Historical versus Processual Archaeology. *Southwestern Journal of Anthropology* 24:267–275.
1971 Archeological Inquiry into Social Organization: Review of *Reconstructing Prehistoric Pueblo Societies,* edited by W. A. Longacre. *Science* 172:1225–1226.
1972a *An Archaeological Perspective.* Seminar Press, New York.
1972b Introduction to *An Archaeological Perspective,* by L. R. Binford, pp. 1–14. Seminar Press, New York.

1972c Model Building—Paradigms, and the Current State of Paleolithic Research. In *An Archaeological Perspective*, by L. R. Binford, pp. 244–294. Seminar Press, New York.

1972d Introduction (untitled) to Part IV: Analysis. In *An Archaeological Perspective*, by L. R. Binford, pp. 329–342. Seminar Press, New York.

1972e The "Binford" Pipestem Formula: A Return from the Grave. *Conference on Historic Site Archaeology Papers* 6:230–253.

1972f Introduction (untitled) to Part III: Theory and Assumptions. In *An Archaeological Perspective*, by L. R. Binford, pp. 187–194. Seminar Press, New York.

1972g Archaeological Reasoning and Smudge Pits—Revisited. In *An Archaeological Perspective*, by L. R. Binford, pp. 52–58. Seminar Press, New York.

1973 Interassemblage Variability—The Mousterian and the "Functional" Argument. In *The Explanation of Culture Change: Models in Prehistory*, edited by C. Renfrew, pp. 227–254. Duckworth, London.

1977a (Editor) *For Theory Building in Archaeology: Essays on Faunal Remains, Aquatic Resources, Spatial Analysis, and Systemic Modeling.* Academic Press, New York.

1977b General Introduction to *For Theory Building in Archaeology: Essays on Faunal Remains, Aquatic Resources, Spatial Analysis, and Systemic Modeling,* edited by L. R. Binford, pp. 1–10. Academic Press, New York.

1978 *Nunamiut Ethnoarchaeology.* Academic Press, New York.

1980 Willow Smoke and Dogs' Tails: Hunter-Gatherer Settlement Systems and Archaeological Site Formation. *American Antiquity* 45:4–20.

1981a *Bones: Ancient Men and Modern Myths.* Academic Press, New York.

1981b Behavioral Archaeology and the "Pompeii Premise." *Journal of Anthropological Research* 37:195–208.

1983a *Working at Archaeology.* Academic Press, New York.

1983b Working at Archaeology: The Late 1960s and the Early 1970s. In *Working at Archaeology,* by L. R. Binford, pp. 3–20. Academic Press, New York.

1983c Working at Archaeology: The Mousterian Problem—Learning How to Learn. In *Working at Archaeology,* by L. R. Binford, pp. 65–69. Academic Press, New York.

1983d *In Pursuit of the Past: Decoding the Archaeological Record.* Thames and Hudson, New York.

1984 *Faunal Remains from Klasies River Mouth.* Academic Press, Orlando.

1985 "Brand X" versus the Recommended Product. *American Antiquity* 50:580–590.

1987a Data, Relativism, and Archaeological Science. *Man* 22:391–404.

1987b Research Ambiguity: Frames of Reference and Site Structure. In *Method and Theory for Activity Area Research: An Ethnoarchaeological Approach,* edited by S. Kent, pp. 449–512. Columbia University Press, New York.

1988 Review of *Reading the Past: Current Approaches to Interpretation in Archaeology,* by I. Hodder. *American Antiquity* 53:875–876.

1989a *Debating Archaeology.* Academic Press, San Diego.

1989b Multidimensional Analysis of Sheep and Goats: Baa-ck and Forth. In *Debating Archaeology,* by L. R. Binford, pp. 267–281. Academic Press, San Diego.

1989c Science to Seance, or Processual to "Post-Processual" Archaeology. In *Debating Archaeology,* by L. R. Binford, pp. 27–40. Academic Press, San Diego.

2001 *Constructing Frames of Reference: An Analytical Method for Archaeological Theory Building Using Ethno-*

graphic and Environmental Data Sets. University of California Press, Berkeley.

Binford, L. R., and S. R. Binford

1966a A Preliminary Analysis of Functional Variability in the Mousterian of the Levallois Facies. *American Anthropologist* 68:238–295.

1966b The Predatory Revolution: A Consideration of the Evidence for a New Subsistence Level. *American Anthropologist* 68:508–512.

Binford, L. R., S. R. Binford, R. Whallon, and M. A. Hardin

1970 *Archaeology at Hatchery West, Carlyle, Illinois.* Memoirs No. 24. Society for American Archaeology, Washington, D.C.

Binford, L. R., and J. F. O'Connell

1984 An Alyawara Day: The Stone Quarry. *Journal of Anthropological Research* 40:406–432.

Binford, S. R.

1968 Variability and Change in the Near Eastern Mousterian of Levallois Facies. In *New Perspectives in Archeology*, edited by S. R. Binford and L. R. Binford, pp. 49–60. Aldine, Chicago.

Binford, S. R., and L. R. Binford

1968a (Editors) *New Perspectives in Archeology.* Aldine, Chicago.

1968b Preface to *New Perspectives in Archeology*, edited by S. R. Binford and L. R. Binford, pp. vii–viii. Aldine, Chicago.

1969 Stone Tools and Human Behavior. *Scientific American* 220(4):70–84.

Blackmore, S.

1999 *The Meme Machine.* Oxford University Press, Oxford.

2000 The Power of Memes. *Scientific American* 283(4):64–73.

Blanton, R. E.

1972 *Prehispanic Settlement Patterns of the Ixtapalapa Peninsula Region, Mexico.* Occasional Papers in Anthropology No. 6. Department of Anthropology, Pennsylvania State University, University Park.

1976a Anthropological Studies of Cities. *Annual Review of Anthropology* 5:249–264.

1976b The Origins of Monte Albán. In *Cultural Change and Continuity: Essays in Honor of James Bennett Griffin*, edited by C. E. Cleland, pp. 223–232. Academic Press, New York.

1978 *Monte Albán: Settlement Patterns at the Ancient Zapotec Capital.* Academic Press, New York.

1988 Comment on "Ecological Theory and Cultural Evolution in the Valley of Oaxaca," by W. T. Sanders and D. L. Nichols. *Current Anthropology* 29:52–54.

1990 Theory and Practice in Mesoamerican Archaeology: A Comparison of Two Modes of Scientific Inquiry. In *Debating Oaxaca Archaeology,* edited by J. Marcus, pp. 1–16. Anthropological Papers No. 84. Museum of Anthropology, University of Michigan, Ann Arbor.

Blanton, R. E., G. M. Feinman, S. A. Kowalewski, and L. M. Nicholas

1999 *Ancient Oaxaca.* Cambridge University Press, Cambridge.

Blanton, R. E., G. M. Feinman, S. A. Kowalewski, and P. N. Peregrine

1996 A Dual-Processual Theory for the Evolution of Mesoamerican Civilization. *Current Anthropology* 37:1–14.

Blanton, R. E., S. A. Kowalewski, G. M. Feinman, and J. Appel

1982 *The Prehispanic Settlement Patterns of the Central and Southern Parts of the Valley of Oaxaca, Mexico.* Part 1 of *Monte Albán's Hinterland.* Memoirs No. 15. Museum of Anthropology, University of Michigan, Ann Arbor.

Blanton, R. E., S. A. Kowalewski, G. M. Feinman, and L. Finsten

1993 *Ancient Mesoamerica: A Comparison of Change in Three Regions.* 2nd ed. Cambridge University Press, Cambridge.

Bloom, F. E.
1999 The Importance of Reviewers. *Science* 283:789.

Blute, M.
1979 Sociocultural Evolutionism: An Untried Theory. *Behavioral Science* 24:46–59.

Boas, F.
1896 The Limitations of the Comparative Method of Anthropology. *Science* 4:901–908.

1902 Some Problems in North American Archaeology. *American Journal of Archaeology* 6:1–6.

1904 The History of Anthropology. *Science* 20:513–524.

1913 Archaeological Investigations in the Valley of Mexico by the International School, 1911–12. *Proceedings of the Eighteenth International Congress of Americanists,* pp. 176–179.

Bobrowsky, P. T.
1982 Introduction to "Approaches to the Evaluation of Cultural Resources: Canadian Perspectives." In *Directions in Archaeology: A Question of Goals,* edited by P. D. Francis and E. C. Poplin, p. 245. *Proceedings of the Fourteenth Annual Chacmool Conference.* Archaeological Association of the University of Calgary, Calgary.

Bohannan, P., and M. Glazer
1988 *High Points in Anthropology.* 2nd ed. McGraw-Hill, New York.

Boone, J. L., and E. A. Smith
1998 Is It Evolution Yet? A Critique of Evolutionary Archaeology. *Current Anthropology* 39:S141–S173.

Bordes, F.
1961 Mousterian Cultures in France. *Science* 134:803–810.

Borillo, M.
1974 A Few Remarks on Whallon's "A New Approach to Pottery Typology." *American Antiquity* 39:371–373.

Boulding, K. W.
1956a General Systems Theory—the Skeleton of Science. *General Systems* 1:11–17.

1956b Toward a General Theory of Growth. *General Systems* 1:66–75.

Bourdieu, P.
1977 *Outline of a Theory of Practice.* Cambridge University Press, Cambridge.

Boyd, R., and P. J. Richerson
1985 *Culture and the Evolutionary Process.* University of Chicago Press, Chicago.

Braidwood, R. J.
1951 From Cave to Village in Prehistoric Iraq. *American School of Oriental Research Bulletin* 124:12–18.

1958 Near Eastern Prehistory. *Science* 127:1419–1430.

1959 Archeology and the Evolutionary Theory. In *Evolution and Anthropology: A Centennial Appraisal,* edited by B. J. Meggers, pp. 76–89. Anthropological Society of Washington, Washington, D.C.

1960 The Agricultural Revolution. *Scientific American* 203(3):130–148.

1963 *Prehistoric Men.* 6th ed. Popular Series: Anthropology No. 37. Natural History Museum, Chicago.

Braidwood, R. J., and L. S. Braidwood
1950 Jarmo: A Village of Early Farmers in Iraq. *Antiquity* 24:189–195.

1953 The Earliest Village Communities of Southwest Asia. *Journal of World History* 1:282–310.

Braidwood, R. J., and C. A. Reed
1957 The Achievement and Early Consequences of Food Production. *Cold Spring Harbor Symposia on Quantitative Biology* 22:19–31.

Braidwood, R. J., and G. R. Willey
1962 Conclusions and Afterthoughts. In *Courses toward Urban Life: Archaeological Considerations of Some Cultural Alternates,* edited by R. J. Braidwood and G. R. Willey, pp. 330–359. Aldine, Chicago.

Brain, C. K.
1967 The Contribution of Namib Desert Hottentots to an Understanding of Australopithecine Bone Accumula-

tions. *Namib Desert Research Station Scientific Papers* 39:13–22.

Brainerd, G. W.

1951a The Place of Chronological Ordering in Archaeological Analysis. *American Antiquity* 16:301–313.

1951b The Use of Mathematical Formulations in Archaeological Analysis. In *Essays on Archaeological Methods,* edited by J. B. Griffin, pp. 117–127. Anthropological Papers No. 8. Museum of Anthropology, University of Michigan, Ann Arbor.

Braun, D. P.

1985 Ceramic Decorative Diversity and Illinois Woodland Regional Integration. In *Decoding Prehistoric Ceramics,* edited by B. A. Nelson, pp. 128–153. Southern Illinois University Press, Carbondale.

1987 Coevolution of Sedentism, Pottery Technology, and Horticulture in the Central Midwest, 200 B.C.–A.D. 600. In *Emergent Horticultural Economies in the Eastern Woodlands,* edited by W. F. Keegan, pp. 153–181. Occasional Paper No. 7. Center for Archaeological Investigations, Southern Illinois University at Carbondale.

Braun, D. P., and S. Plog

1982 Evolution of "Tribal" Social Networks: Theory and Prehistoric North American Evidence. *American Antiquity* 47:504–525.

Bray, T. L. (editor)

2001 *The Future of the Past: Archaeologists, Native Americans, and Repatriation.* Garland, New York.

Breternitz, D. A., C. K. Robinson, and G. T. Gross (compilers)

1986 *Dolores Archaeological Program: Final Synthetic Report.* Report submitted to the Bureau of Reclamation, Denver.

Brew, J. O.

1946 *The Archaeology of Alkali Ridge, Southeastern Utah.* Papers Vol. 21. Peabody Museum of Archaeology and Ethnology, Harvard University, Cambridge, Mass.

1961 Emergency Archaeology: Salvage in Advance of Technological Progress. *Proceedings of the American Philosophical Society* 105:1–9.

1971 Review of *Archaeology as Anthropology: A Case Study,* by W. A. Longacre. *American Anthropologist* 73:1391–1394.

Bronitsky, G.

1986 The Use of Materials Science Techniques in the Study of Pottery Construction and Use. *Advances in Archaeological Method and Theory* 9:209–276.

Bronitsky, G., and R. Hamer

1986 Experiments in Ceramic Technology: The Effects of Various Tempering Materials on Impact and Thermal-Shock Resistance. *American Antiquity* 51:89–101.

Bronson, B.

2003 Berthold Laufer. In *Curators, Collections, and Contexts: Anthropology at the Field Museum, 1893–2002,* edited by S. E. Nash and G. M. Feinman, pp. 117–126. Fieldiana: Anthropology 36. Field Museum of Natural History, Chicago.

Brose, D. S.

1985 Good Enough for Government Work? A Study in "Grey Archeology." *American Anthropologist* 87:370–377.

Broughton, J. M.

1994 Declines in Mammalian Foraging Efficiency during the Late Holocene, San Francisco Bay, California. *Journal of Anthropological Archaeology* 13:371–401.

1999 *Resource Depression and Intensification during the Late Holocene, San Francisco Bay: Evidence from the Emeryville Shellmound Vertebrate Fauna.* Anthropological Records Vol. 32. University of California, Berkeley.

Broughton, J. M, and D. K. Grayson

1993 Diet Breadth, Adaptive Change, and the White Mountains Faunas. *Journal of Archaeological Science* 20:331–336.

Broughton, J. M., and J. F. O'Connell
1999 On Evolutionary Ecology, Selectionist Archaeology, and Behavioral Archaeology. *American Antiquity* 64:153–165.

Browman, D. L.
2002 Origins of Stratigraphic Excavation in North America: The Peabody Museum Method and the Chicago Method. In *New Perspectives on the Origins of Americanist Archaeology*, edited by D. L. Browman and S. Williams, pp. 242–264. University of Alabama Press, Tuscaloosa.

Browman, D. L., and D. R. Givens
1996 Stratigraphic Excavation: The First "New Archaeology." *American Anthropologist* 98:80–95.

Brown, D.
2003 *The Da Vinci Code.* Doubleday, New York.

Brown, J. A., and L. G. Freeman, Jr.
1964 A Univac Analysis of Sherd Frequencies from the Carter Ranch Pueblo, Eastern Arizona. *American Antiquity* 30:162–167.

Brown, J. A., and S. Struever
1973 The Organization of Archeological Research: An Illinois Example. In *Research and Theory in Current Archeology*, edited by C. L. Redman, pp. 261–280. Wiley, New York.

Brumfiel, E. M.
1976 Review of *Guide to Ethnohistorical Sources: Handbook of Middle American Indians*, Vols. 12–15, edited by H. F. Cline. *American Antiquity* 41:398–403.
1983 Aztec State Making: Ecology, Structure, and the Origin of the State. *American Anthropologist* 85:261–284.
1992 Distinguished Lecture in Archeology: Breaking and Entering the Ecosystem—Gender, Class, and Faction Steal the Show. *American Anthropologist* 94:551–567.
1996 Comment on "A Dual-Processual Theory for the Evolution of Mesoamerican Civilization," by R. E. Blanton, G. M. Feinman, S. A. Kowalewski, and P. N. Peregrine. *Current Anthropology* 37:48–50.

Bruner, E. M.
1956 Cultural Transmission and Cultural Change. *Southwestern Journal of Anthropology* 12:191–199.

Brush, S.
1974 Should the History of Science Be Rated X? *Science* 183:1164–1172.

Buikstra, J. E.
1982 Reburial: How We All Lose. *Society for California Archaeology Newsletter* 1:1–4.

Buikstra, J. E., and C. C. Gordon
1981 The Study and Restudy of Human Skeletal Series: The Importance of Long-Term Curation. *Annals of the New York Academy of Sciences* 376:449–466.

Bunzel, R.
1929 *The Pueblo Potter: A Study of Creative Imagination in Primitive Art.* Columbia University Press, New York.

Burgh, R. F.
1950 Comment on Taylor's "A Study of Archeology." *American Anthropologist* 52:114–117.

Butler, B. R.
1974 Review of *An Archaeological Perspective,* by L. R. Binford. *American Antiquity* 39:646–647.

Butler, V. L.
2000 Resource Depression on the Northwest Coast of North America. *Antiquity* 74:649–661.

Butler, W. B.
1979 The No-Collection Strategy in Archaeology. *American Antiquity* 44:795–799.
1987 Significance and Other Frustrations in the CRM Process. *American Antiquity* 52:820–829.

Butzer, K. W.
1971 *Environment and Archaeology: An Ecological Approach to Prehistory.* 2nd ed. Aldine, Chicago.
1982 *Archaeology as Human Ecology: Method and Theory for a Contextual*

Archaeology. Cambridge University Press, Cambridge.

Cahen, D., and J. Moeyersons

1977 Subsurface Movements of Stone Artefacts and Their Implications for the Prehistory of Central Africa. *Nature* 266:812–815.

Caldwell, J. R.

1958 *Trend and Tradition in the Prehistory of the Eastern United States*. Memoirs No. 88. American Anthropological Association, Washington, D.C.

1959 The New American Archeology. *Science* 129:303–307.

1962 Eastern North America. In *Courses toward Urban Life: Archaeological Considerations of Some Cultural Alternates*, edited by R. J. Braidwood and G. R. Willey, pp. 288–308. Aldine, Chicago.

1971 Review of *New Perspectives in Archeology*, edited by S. R. Binford and L. R. Binford. *American Anthropologist* 73:411–414.

Campbell, S. (editor)

1985 *Summary of Results, Chief Joseph Dam Cultural Resources Project, Washington*. Report submitted to the U.S. Army Corps of Engineers, Seattle District.

Cannon, M. D.

2000 Large Mammal Relative Abundance in Pithouse and Pueblo Period Archaeofaunas from Southwestern New Mexico: Resource Depression among the Mimbres–Mogollon. *Journal of Anthropological Archaeology* 19:317–347.

Canouts, V. (assembler)

1972 *An Archaeological Survey of the Santa Rosa Wash Project*. Arizona State Museum, Tucson.

Carneiro, R. L.

1960 The Culture Process. In *Essays in the Science of Culture in Honor of Leslie A. White*, edited by G. E. Dole and R. L. Carneiro, pp. 145–161. Crowell, New York.

1970 A Theory of the Origin of the State. *Science* 169:733–738.

1973 Structure, Function, and Equilibrium in the Evolutionism of Herbert Spencer. *Journal of Anthropological Research* 29:77–95.

1981 Leslie A. White. In *Totems and Teachers: Perspectives on the History of Anthropology*, edited by S. Silverman, pp. 208–252. Columbia University Press, New York.

2000 *The Muse of History and the Science of Culture*. Kluwer Academic/Plenum, New York.

2003 *Evolutionism in Cultural Anthropology: A Critical History*. Westview, Cambridge, Mass.

Carson, R.

1962 *Silent Spring*. Houghton Mifflin, Boston.

Cartmill, M.

1980 John Jones's Pregnancy: Some Comments on the Statistical-Relevance Model of Scientific Explanation. *American Antiquity* 82:382–385.

1988 Why I Became a Scientist. *American Scientist* 76:452.

Casteel, R. W.

1980 National Science Foundation Funding of Domestic Archaeology in the United States: Where the Money Ain't. *American Antiquity* 45:170–180.

Cavalli-Sforza, L. L., and M. W. Feldman

1981 *Cultural Transmission and Evolution: A Quantitative Approach*. Monographs in Population Biology 16. Princeton University Press, Princeton, N.J.

Chakrabarti, D.

1999 *India: An Archaeological History*. Oxford University Press, Oxford.

Chaney, R. P.

1972 Scientific Inquiry and Models of Socio-Cultural Data Patterning: An Epilogue. In *Models in Archaeology*, edited by D. L. Clarke, pp. 991–1031. Methuen, London.

Chang, K. C.

1958 Study of the Neolithic Social Grouping: Examples from the New World.

American Anthropologist
50:298–334.

1962 A Typology of Settlement and Community Patterns in Some Circumpolar Societies. *Arctic Anthropology* 1:28–41.

1967a *Rethinking Archaeology*. Random House, New York.

1967b Major Aspects of the Interrelationship of Archaeology and Ethnology. *Current Anthropology* 8:227–234.

Charnov, E. L.

1976 Optimal Foraging: The Marginal Value Theorem. *Theoretical Population Biology* 9:129–136.

Chatters, J. C.

2001 *Ancient Encounters: Kennewick Man and the First Americans*. Simon and Schuster, New York.

Chazan, M.

1995 Conceptions of Time and the Development of Paleolithic Chronology. *American Anthropologist* 97:457–467.

Chenhall, R. G.

1971 Positivism and the Collection of Data. *American Antiquity* 36:372–373.

Childe, V. G.

1934 *New Light on the Most Ancient East: The Oriental Prelude to European Prehistory*. Kegan Paul, Trench, Trubner, London.

1936 *Man Makes Himself*. Watts, London.

1944 Archaeological Ages as Technological Stages. *Royal Anthropological Institute Journal* 74:1–19.

Christenson, A. L.

1979a On the Virtues of Simplicity: Some Comments on Statistical Analysis in Anthropology. *Plains Anthropologist* 24:35–38.

1979b The Role of Museums in Cultural Resource Management. *American Antiquity* 44:161–163.

Christenson, A. L., and D. W. Read

1977 Numerical Taxonomy, R-Mode Factor Analysis, and Archaeological Classification. *American Antiquity* 42:163–179.

Claassen, C.

1991 Normative Thinking and Shell-Bearing Sites. *Archaeological Method and Theory* 3:249–298.

1994 (Editor) *Women in Archaeology*. University of Pennsylvania Press, Philadelphia.

Claassen, C., and R. A. Joyce (editors)

1997 *Women in Prehistory: North America and Mesoamerica*. University of Pennsylvania Press, Philadelphia.

Clark, G. A.

1996 NAGPRA and the Demon-Haunted World. *Society for American Archaeology Bulletin* 16(5):22, 24–25.

Clark, J. D.

1968 Studies of Hunter-Gatherers as an Aid to the Interpretation of Prehistoric Societies. In *Man the Hunter*, edited by R. B. Lee and I. DeVore, pp. 276–280. Aldine, Chicago.

Clark, J. G. D.

1954 *Excavations at Star Carr*. Cambridge University Press, Cambridge.

Clarke, D. L.

1968 *Analytical Archaeology*. Methuen, London.

1972a Review of *Explanation in Archeology: An Explicitly Scientific Approach*, by P. J. Watson, S. A. LeBlanc, and C. Redman. *Antiquity* 46:237–239.

1972b *Models in Archaeology*. Methuen, London.

1973 Archaeology: The Loss of Innocence. *Antiquity* 47:6–18.

Cleland, C. E.

2002 Methodological and Epistemic Differences between Historical Science and Experimental Science. *Philosophy of Science* 69:474–496.

Clements, F. E., S. M. Schenck, and T. K. Brown

1926 A New Objective Method for Showing Special Relationships. *American Anthropologist* 28:585–604.

Clemmer, R. O.

1999 Steward's Gap: Why Steward Did Not Use His Theory of Culture Change to Explain Shoshoni Culture

Change. In *Julian Steward and the Great Basin: The Making of an Anthropologist,* edited by R. O. Clemmer, L. D. Myers, and M. E. Rudden, pp. 144–163. University of Utah Press, Salt Lake City.

Clemmer, R. O., and L. D. Myers

1999   Introduction to *Julian Steward and the Great Basin: The Making of an Anthropologist,* edited by R. O. Clemmer, L. D. Myers, and M. E. Rudden, pp. ix-xxii. University of Utah Press, Salt Lake City.

Cloak, F. T., Jr.

1975   Is a Cultural Ethology Possible? *Human Ecology* 3:161–182.

Cochrane, E. E.

2001   Style, Function, and Systematic Empiricism: The Conflation of Process and Pattern. In *Style and Function: Conceptual Issues in Evolutionary Archaeology,* edited by T. D. Hurt and G. F. M. Rakita, pp. 183–202. Bergin and Garvey, Westport, Conn.

Coe, M. D.

1978   The Churches on the Green: A Cautionary Tale. In *Archaeological Essays in Honor of Irving B. Rouse,* edited by R. C. Dunnell and E. S. Hall, pp. 75–85. Mouton, The Hague.

Coe, M. D., and K. V. Flannery

1964a Microenvironments and Mesoamerican Prehistory. *Science* 143:650–654.

1964b The Pre-Columbian Obsidian Industry of El Chayal, Guatemala. *American Antiquity* 30:43–49.

1967   *Early Cultures and Human Ecology in South Coastal Guatemala.* Smithsonian Contributions to Anthropology Vol. 3. Smithsonian Institution, Washington, D.C.

Cohen, M. N.

1975   Archaeological Evidence for Population Pressure in Pre-Agricultural Societies. *American Antiquity* 40:471–475.

1977   *The Food Crisis in Prehistory: Overpopulation and the Origins of Agri-*

culture. Yale University Press, New Haven, Conn.

Collingwood, R. G.

1946   *The Idea of History.* Clarendon, Oxford.

Collins, H. B., Jr.

1927   Potsherds from Choctaw Village Sites in Mississippi. *Washington Academy of Sciences Journal* 17: 259–263.

Collins, M. B.

1975   Sources of Bias in Processual Data: An Appraisal. In *Sampling in Archaeology,* edited by J. W. Mueller, pp. 26–32. University of Arizona Press, Tucson.

Colton, H. S.

1939   *Prehistoric Culture Units and Their Relationships in Northern Arizona.* Bulletin No. 17. Museum of Northern Arizona, Flagstaff.

Colton, H. S., and L. L. Hargrave

1937   *Handbook of Northern Arizona Pottery Wares.* Bulletin No. 11. Museum of Northern Arizona, Flagstaff.

Conant, J. B.

1960   History in the Education of Scientists. *American Scientist* 48:528–543.

Conkey, M. W.

1978a Style and Information in Cultural Evolution: Toward a Predictive Model for the Paleolithic. In *Social Archeology: Beyond Subsistence and Dating,* edited by C. L. Redman, M. J. Berman, D. V. Curtin, W. T. Langhorne, Jr., N. M. Versaggi, and J. C. Wanser, pp. 61–85. Academic Press, New York.

1978b *An Analysis of Design Structure: Variability among Magdalenian Engraved Bones from Northcoastal Spain.* Ph.D. dissertation, Department of Anthropology, University of Chicago.

1982   Boundaries in Art and Society. In *Symbolic and Structural Archaeology,* edited by I. Hodder, pp. 115–128. Cambridge University Press, Cambridge.

1989   The Structural Analysis of Paleolithic Art. In *Archaeological Thought in*

America, edited by C. C. Lamberg-Karlovsky, pp. 135–154. Cambridge University Press, New York.

Conkey, M. W., and J. M. Gero
1997   Programme to Practice: Gender and Feminism in Archaeology. *Annual Review of Anthropology* 26:411–437.

Conkey, M. W., and J. D. Spector
1984   Archaeology and the Study of Gender. *Advances in Archaeological Method and Theory* 7:1–38.

Connolly, T. J., and P. W. Baxter
1983   The Problem with Probability: Alternative Methods for Forest Survey. *Tebiwa* 20:22–34.

Cordell, L. S.
1993   Women Archaeologists in the Southwest. In *Hidden Scholars: Women Anthropologists and the Native American Southwest,* edited by N. Parezo, pp. 202–220. University of New Mexico Press, Albuquerque.

Cordell, L. S., and F. Plog
1979   Escaping the Confines of Normative Thought: A Reevaluation of Puebloan Prehistory. *American Antiquity* 44:405–429.
1981   Building Theory from the Bottom Up? *American Antiquity* 46:198–199.

Courbin, P.
1988   *What Is Archaeology? An Essay on the Nature of Archaeological Research*. University of Chicago Press, Chicago.

Cowgill, G. L.
1964   The Selection of Samples from Large Sherd Collections. *American Antiquity* 29:467–473.
1968   Archaeological Applications of Factor, Cluster, and Proximity Analysis. *American Antiquity* 33:367–375.
1970   Some Sampling and Reliability Problems in Archaeology. In *Archéologie et Calculateurs: Problemes Sémiologiques et Mathématiques,* pp. 161–175. Editions du Centre National de la Recherche Scientifique, Paris.
1986   Archaeological Applications of Mathematical and Formal Methods.

In *American Archaeology Past and Future: A Celebration of the Society for American Archaeology, 1935–1985,* edited by D. J. Meltzer, D. D. Fowler, and J. A. Sabloff, pp. 369–393. Smithsonian Institution Press, Washington, D.C.
1989   Formal Approaches in Archaeology. In *Archaeological Thought in America*, edited by C. C. Lamberg-Karlovsky, pp. 74–88. Cambridge University Press, New York.
1993   Distinguished Lecture in Archeology: Beyond Criticizing New Archeology. *American Anthropologist* 95:551–573.

Crabtree, D. E.
1972   *An Introduction to the Technology of Stone Tools*. Part 1 of *An Introduction to Flintworking*. Occasional Papers No. 28. Idaho State University Museum, Pocatello.

Cribb, R. L. D.
1980   A Comment on Eugene L. Sterud's "Changing Aims of Americanist Archaeology: A Citations Analysis of *American Antiquity*—1946–1975." *American Antiquity* 45:352–354.

Cronin, C.
1962   An Analysis of Pottery Design Elements, Indicating Possible Relationships between Three Decorated Types. *Fieldiana: Anthropology* 53:105–114. Field Museum of Natural History, Chicago.

Crown, P. L., and W. J. Judge (editors)
1991   *Chaco and Hohokam: Prehistoric Regional Systems in the American Southwest*. School of American Research, Santa Fe, N.M.

Crumley, C.
1979   Three Locational Models: An Epistemological Assessment for Anthropology and Archaeology. *Advances in Archaeological Method and Theory* 2:142–173.

Cullen, B. R. S.
1993   The Darwinian Resurgence and the Cultural Virus Critique. *Cambridge Archaeological Journal* 3:179–202.

Cullen, T.
1984   Review of *The Present Past: An Introduction to Anthropology for Archaeologists,* by I. Hodder. *American Journal of Archaeology* 88:266–267.

Custer, J. F.
1981   Comments on David Meltzer's "Paradigms and the Nature of Change in American Archaeology." *American Antiquity* 46:660–661.

Dacey, M. F.
1973   Statistical Tests of Spatial Association in the Locations of Tool Types. *American Antiquity* 38:320–328.

Dancey, W. S.
1981   *Archaeological Field Methods: An Introduction.* Burgess, Minneapolis.

Daniel, G.
1976   *A Hundred and Fifty Years of Archaeology.* Harvard University Press, Cambridge, Mass.
1981a   *A Short History of Archaeology.* Thames and Hudson, London.
1981b   (Editor) *Towards a History of Archaeology.* Thames and Hudson, London.

Darwin, C.
1859   *On the Origin of Species by Means of Natural Selection; or the Preservation of Favoured Races in the Struggle for Life.* Murray, London.

Darwin, F.
1914   Francis Galton, 1822–1911. *Eugenics Review* 6:1–17.

David, N., and C. Kramer
2001   *Ethnoarchaeology in Action.* Cambridge University Press, Cambridge.

Davis, E. L.
1975   The "Exposed Archaeology" of China Lake, California. *American Antiquity* 40:39–53.

Davis, H. A.
1971   Is There a Future for the Past? *Archaeology* 24:300–306.
1972   The Crisis in American Archeology. *Science* 175:267–272.

Dawkins, R.
1976   *The Selfish Gene.* Oxford University Press, Oxford.
1982   *The Extended Phenotype: The Gene as the Unit of Selection.* Freeman, San Francisco.

DeBoer, W. R., and D. W. Lathrap
1979   The Making and Breaking of Shipibo-Conibo Ceramics. In *Ethnoarchaeology: Implications of Ethnography for Archaeology,* edited by C. Kramer, pp. 102–138. Columbia University Press, New York.

Deetz, J.
1960   *An Archaeological Approach to Kinship Change in Eighteenth Century Arikara Culture.* Ph.D. dissertation, Department of Anthropology, Harvard University, Cambridge, Mass.
1965   *The Dynamics of Stylistic Change in Arikara Ceramics.* Illinois Studies in Anthropology No. 4. Urbana.
1967   *Invitation to Archaeology.* Natural History Press, Garden City, N.Y.
1968a   The Inference of Residence and Descent Rules from Archeological Data. In *New Perspectives in Archeology,* edited by S. R. Binford and L. R. Binford, pp. 41–48. Aldine, Chicago.
1968b   Late Man in North America: Archeology of European Americans. In *Anthropological Archeology in the Americas,* edited by B. J. Meggers, pp. 121–130. Anthropological Society of Washington, Washington, D.C.
1968c   Cultural Patterning of Behavior as Reflected by Archaeological Materials. In *Settlement Archaeology,* edited by K. C. Chang, pp. 31–42. National Press Books, Palo Alto, Calif.
1970   Archeology as a Social Science. *American Anthropological Association Bulletin* 3(3)(2):115–125.
1977   *In Small Things Forgotten: The Archeology of Early American Life.* Anchor Press/Doubleday, Garden City, N.Y.

Deetz, J., and E. Dethlefsen
1965   The Doppler Effect and Archaeology: A Consideration of the Spatial Aspects of Seriation. *Southwestern*

Journal of Anthropology 21:196–206.

1967 Death's Head, Cherub, Urn and Willow. *Natural History* 76(3):29–37.

1971 Some Social Aspects of New England Colonial Mortuary Art. In *Approaches to the Social Dimensions of Mortuary Practices,* edited by J. A. Brown, pp. 30–38. Memoirs No. 25. Society for American Archaeology, Washington, D.C.

Denning, K., and A. Wylie

2000 Philosophy from the Ground Up: An Interview with Alison Wylie. *Assemblage: University of Sheffield Graduate Student Journal of Archaeology* 5. (http://www.shef.ac.uk/assem/5/wylie.html)

Dethlefsen, E., and J. Deetz

1966 Death's Heads, Cherubs, and Willow Trees: Experimental Archaeology in Colonial Cemeteries. *American Antiquity* 31:502–510.

DeVore, I.

1968 Comments. In *New Perspectives in Archeology,* edited by S. R. Binford and L. R. Binford, pp. 346–349. Aldine, Chicago.

Diamond, J.

1992 *The Third Chimpanzee: The Evolution and Future of the Human Animal.* HarperCollins: New York.

2003 Archaeology: Propaganda of the Pyramids. *Nature* 424:891–893.

Dibble, H. L., and M. J. Shott

2004 *Lithic Analysis: The Study of Stone Tools and Assemblages.* Oxford University Press, New York.

Dincauze, D. F.

1981 Editor's Corner. *American Antiquity* 46:467.

2000 *Environmental Archaeology: Principles and Practice.* Cambridge University Press, Cambridge.

Dixon, K. A.

1977 Applications of Archaeological Resources: Broadening the Basis of Significance. In *Conservation Archaeology: A Guide for Cultural Resource Management Studies,* edited by M. B. Schiffer and G. J. Gumerman, pp. 277–290. Academic Press, New York.

Dixon, R. B.

1913 Some Aspects of North American Archeology. *American Anthropologist* 15:549–566.

Dobres, M.-A.

1995 Gender and Prehistoric Technology: On Social Agency of Technological Strategies. *World Archaeology* 27:25–49.

1999 Technologies, Links and Chains: The Processual Unfolding of Technique and Technician. In *Making Culture: Essays on Technological Practice, Politics, and World Views,* edited by M.-A. Dobres and C. R. Hoffman, pp. 124–146. Smithsonian Institution Press, Washington, D.C.

2000 *Technology and Social Agency: Outlining a Practice Framework for Archaeology.* Blackwell, Oxford.

Dobres, M.-A., and C. R. Hoffman

1994 Social Agency and the Dynamics of Prehistoric Technology. *Journal of Archaeological Method and Theory* 1:211–258.

Dobres, M.-A., and J. Robb (editors)

2000 *Agency in Archaeology.* Routledge, New York.

Dongoske, K. E., M. Aldenderfer, and K. Doehner (editors)

2000 *Working Together: Native Americans and Archaeologists.* Society for American Archaeology, Washington, D.C.

Donnan, C. B., Jr., and C. W. Clewlow (editors)

1974 *Ethnoarchaeology.* Monograph No. 4. Institute of Archaeology, University of California, Los Angeles.

Doran, J. E.

1970 Systems Theory, Computer Simulations, and Archaeology. *World Archaeology* 1:289–298.

Doran, J. E., and F. R. Hodson

1966 A Digital Computer Analysis of Palaeolithic Flint Assemblages. *Nature* 210:688–689.

Dorman, J. L.

2002 Agency and Archaeology: Past, Present, and Future Directions. *Journal of Archaeological Method and Theory* 9:303–329.

Downey, R.

2000 *The Riddle of the Bones: Politics, Science, Race, and the Story of Kennewick Man.* Copernicus, New York.

Dragoo, D. W.

1975 Archaeological Theory and Practice. *Archaeology of Eastern North America* 3:9–24.

Drennan, R. D.

1996 *Statistics for Archaeologists: A Commonsense Approach.* Plenum, New York.

2000 Games, Players, Rules, and Circumstances: Looking for Understandings of Social Change at Different Levels. In *Cultural Evolution: Contemporary Viewpoints,* edited by G. M. Feinman and L. Manzanilla, pp. 177–196. Kluwer Academic/Plenum, New York.

Driver, H. E.

1938 Culture Element Distributions: VIII, the Reliability of Culture Element Data. *Anthropological Records* 1:205–220.

1953 Statistics in Anthropology. *American Anthropologist* 55:42–59.

1965 Survey of Numerical Classification in Anthropology. In *The Use of Computers in Anthropology,* edited by D. Hymes, pp. 302–344. Mouton, The Hague.

Driver, H. E., and A. L. Kroeber

1932 Quantitative Expression of Cultural Relationships. *University of California Publications in American Archaeology and Ethnology* 31:211–256.

Duke, P.

1995 Working through Theoretical Tensions in Contemporary Archaeology: A Practical Attempt from Southwestern Colorado. *Journal of Archaeological Method and Theory* 2:201–229.

Dumond, D. E.

1965 Population Growth and Cultural Change. *Southwestern Journal of Anthropology* 21:302–324.

1974 Some Uses of R-Mode Analysis in Archaeology. *American Antiquity* 39:253–270.

1977 Science in Archaeology: The Saints Go Marching In. *American Antiquity* 42:330–349.

Dumont, E. M.

1975 The Old vs. the New in Archaeology: A Philosophical Overview. *Archaeology of Eastern North America* 3:1–9.

Dunnell, R. C.

1970 Seriation Method and Its Evaluation. *American Antiquity* 35:305–319.

1971 *Systematics in Prehistory.* Free Press, New York.

1973a Fire, Air, Earth, and Water: A Rational Classificatory Scheme. *Mankind* 9:127–131.

1973b Reply to Bayard. *Mankind* 9:135–137.

1978a Archaeological Potential of Anthropological and Scientific Models of Function. In *Archaeological Essays in Honor of Irving B. Rouse,* edited by R. C. Dunnell and E. S. Hall Jr., pp. 41–73. Mouton, The Hague.

1978b Style and Function: A Fundamental Dichotomy. *American Antiquity* 43:192–202.

1980 Evolutionary Theory and Archaeology. *Advances in Archaeological Method and Theory* 3:35–99.

1982 Science, Social Science, and Common Sense: The Agonizing Dilemma of Modern Archaeology. *Journal of Anthropological Research* 38:1–25.

1986 Methodological Issues in Americanist Artifact Classification. *Advances in Archaeological Method and Theory* 9:149–207.

1989 Aspects of the Application of Evolutionary Theory in Archaeology. In *Archaeological Thought in America,* edited by C. C. Lamberg-Karlovsky, pp. 35–49. Cambridge University Press, New York.

1992a Archaeology and Evolutionary Science. In *Quandaries and Quests: Visions of Archaeology's Future*, edited by L. Wandsnider, pp. 209–224. Occasional Paper No. 20. Center for Archaeological Investigations, Southern Illinois University at Carbondale.

1992b Is a Scientific Archaeology Possible? In *Metaarchaeology*, edited by L. Embree, pp. 75–97. Kluwer Academic, Dordrecht, Netherlands.

1992c The Notion Site. In *Space, Time, and Archaeological Landscapes*, edited by J. Rossignol and L. Wandsnider, pp. 21–41. Plenum, New York.

1996 Foreword to *Evolutionary Archaeology: Theory and Application*, edited by M. J. O'Brien, pp. vii–xii. University of Utah Press, Salt Lake City.

2000 Seriation. In *Archaeological Method and Theory: An Encyclopedia*, edited by L. Ellis, pp. 548–551. Garland, New York.

2001 Foreword to *Style and Function: Conceptual Issues in Evolutionary Archaeology*, edited by T. D. Hurt and G. F. M. Rakita, pp. xiii–xxiv. Bergin and Garvey, Westport, Conn.

Dunnell, R. C., and W. S. Dancey

1978 Assessments of Significance and Cultural Resource Management Plans. *ASCA Newsletter* 5(5):2–7.

1983 The Siteless Survey: A Regional Scale Data Collection Strategy. *Advances in Archaeological Method and Theory* 6:267–287.

Durham, W. H.

1982 Interactions of Genetic and Cultural Evolution: Models and Examples. *Human Ecology* 10:289–323.

1991 *Coevolution: Genes, Culture, and Human Diversity*. Stanford University Press, Stanford, Calif.

Earle, T. K., and R. W. Preucel

1987 Processual Archaeology and the Radical Critique. *Current Anthropology* 28:501–538.

Ehrich, R. W.

1961 Archaeology and Cultural Anthropology: Theory and Methodology among American Archaeologists. *Památky Archeologické* 52:623–630.

1963 Further Reflections on Archeological Interpretation. *American Anthropologist* 65:16–31.

Ehrlich, P. R.

1968 *The Population Bomb*. Ballantine, New York.

Eldredge, N., and S. J. Gould

1972 Punctuated Equilibria: An Alternative to Phyletic Gradualism. In *Models in Paleobiology*, edited by T. J. M. Schopf, pp. 82–115. Freeman, Cooper, San Francisco.

Ellis, F. H.

1972 Review of *Reconstructing Prehistoric Pueblo Societies*, edited by W. A. Longacre. *American Anthropologist* 74:133–134.

Emlen, J. M.

1966 The Role of Time and Energy in Food Preference. *American Naturalist* 100:611–617.

Endler, J. A.

1986 *Natural Selection in the Wild*. Princeton University Press, Princeton, N.J.

Engelstad, E.

1991 Images of Power and Contradiction: Feminist Theory and Post-Processual Archaeology. *Antiquity* 65:502–514.

Ereshefsky, M.

1992 The Historical Nature of Evolutionary Theory. In *History and Evolution*, edited by M. H. Nitecki and D. V. Nitecki, pp. 81–99. State University of New York Press, Albany.

Euler, R. C.

1997 Walter Willard Taylor, Jr., 1913–1997. *SAA Bulletin* 15(4):23.

Evans, J.

1850 On the Date of British Coins. *The Numismatic Chronicle and Journal*

of the Numismatic Society
12(4):127–137.

Fedigan, L. M.
1986   The Changing Role of Women in
Models of Human Evolution. *Annual
Review of Anthropology* 15:25–66.

Feinman, G. M.
2000a Cultural Evolutionary Approaches
and Archaeology: Past, Present, and
Future. In *Cultural Evolution: Con-
temporary Viewpoints,* edited by G.
M. Feinman and L. Manzanilla, pp.
3–14. Kluwer Academic/Plenum,
New York.
2000b A Concluding Perspective on the
Theoretical Contributions of Kent V.
Flannery: Tenets for the Next Cen-
tury of U.S. Archaeology. In *Cultural
Evolution: Contemporary View-
points,* edited by G. M. Feinman and
L. Manzanilla, pp. 235–241. Kluwer
Academic/Plenum, New York.

Feinman, G. M., and L. Manzanilla (editors)
2000   *Cultural Evolution: Contemporary
Viewpoints.* Kluwer
Academic/Plenum, New York.

Feinman, G. M., and L. M. Nicholas
1988   Comment on "Ecological Theory and
Cultural Evolution in the Valley of
Oaxaca," by W. T. Sanders and D. L.
Nichols. *Current Anthropology*
29:55–57.

Feinman, G. M., and T. D. Price
2001   *Archaeology at the Millennium: A
Sourcebook.* Kluwer
Academic/Plenum, New York.

Ferguson, L. G.
1977   Review of *The Cache River Archeo-
logical Project: An Experiment in
Contract Archeology,* assembled by
M. B. Schiffer and J. H. House.
American Antiquity 42:289–291.

Ferrie, H.
1995   A Conversation with K. C. Chang.
Current Anthropology 36:307–325.

Fewkes, J. W.
1900   Tusayan Migration Traditions.
*Annual Report of the Bureau of
American Ethnology* 19:577–633.

Figgins, J. D.
1927   The Antiquity of Man in America.
Natural History 27:229–239.

Fish, P. R., and J. J. Reid (editors)
1996   *Interpreting Southwestern Diversity:
Underlying Principles and Overarch-
ing Patterns.* Anthropological
Research Papers No. 48. Arizona
State University, Tempe.

Fitting, J. E. (editor)
1973   *The Development of North American
Archaeology: Essays in the History of
Regional Traditions.* Anchor, Garden
City, N.Y.

Fitzgerald, F. S.
1936   The Crack-Up. *Esquire* 5(2):41, 164.

Flannery, K. V.
1964   *The Middle Formative in the Tehuacan Valley: Its Pattern and Place in
Mesoamerican Prehistory.* Ph.D. dissertation, Department of Anthropology, University of Chicago.
1965   The Ecology of Early Food Production in Mesopotamia. *Science*
147:1247–1255.
1966   The Postglacial "Readaptation" as
Viewed from Mesoamerica. *American Antiquity* 31:800–805.
1967   Culture History v. Cultural Process:
A Debate in American Archaeology.
Scientific American 217(2):119–122.
1968a Archeological Systems Theory and
Early Mesoamerica. In *Anthropological Archeology in the Americas,*
edited by B. J. Meggers, pp. 67–87.
Anthropological Society of Washington, Washington, D.C.
1968b The Olmec and the Valley of Oaxaca: A Model for Inter-Regional
Interaction in Formative Mesoamerica. In *Dumbarton Oaks Conference
on the Olmec,* edited by E. P. Benson,
pp. 79–110. Dumbarton Oaks, Washington, D.C.
1969   Origins and Ecological Effects of
Early Domestication in Iran and the
Near East. In *The Domestication and
Exploitation of Plants and Animals,*
edited by P. J. Ucko and G. W. Dimbleby, pp. 73–100. Aldine, Chicago.

1972   The Cultural Evolution of Civilizations. *Annual Review of Ecology and Systematics* 3:399–426.

1973a Archeology with a Capital S. In *Research and Theory in Current Archeology*, edited by C. L. Redman, pp. 47–53. Wiley, New York.

1973b Origins of Agriculture. *Annual Review of Anthropology* 2:271–310.

1976a A Prayer for an Endangered Species. In *The Early Mesoamerican Village*, edited by K. V. Flannery, pp. 369–373. Academic Press, New York.

1976b Sampling on the Regional Level. In *The Early Mesoamerican Village*, edited by K. V. Flannery, pp. 131–136. Academic Press, New York.

1976c (Editor) *The Early Mesoamerican Village*. Academic Press, New York.

1977   Review of *Mesoamerican Archaeology: New Approaches,* edited by N. Hammond. *American Antiquity* 42:659–661.

1982a Early Pig Domestication in the Fertile Crescent: A Retrospective Look. In *The Hilly Flanks and Beyond: Essays on the Prehistory of Southwestern Iran, Presented to Robert J. Braidwood*, edited by T. C. Young Jr., P. E. L. Smith, and P. Mortensen, pp. 163–188. Studies in Ancient Oriental Civilization No. 36. Oriental Institute, University of Chicago.

1982b The Golden Marshalltown: A Parable for the Archeology of the 1980s. *American Anthropologist* 84:265–278.

1986a A Visit to the Master. In *Guilá Naquitz: Archaic Foraging and Early Agriculture in Oaxaca, Mexico,* edited by K. V. Flannery, pp. 511–519. Academic Press, Orlando.

1986b Ecosystem Models and Information Flow in the Tehuacán–Oaxaca Region. In *Guilá Naquitz: Archaic Foraging and Early Agriculture in Oaxaca, Mexico,* edited by K. V. Flannery, pp. 19–28. Academic Press, Orlando.

1986c (Editor) *Guilá Naquitz: Archaic Foraging and Early Agriculture in Oaxaca, Mexico*. Academic Press, Orlando.

1988   Comment on "Ecological Theory and Cultural Evolution in the Valley of Oaxaca," by W. T. Sanders and D. L. Nichols. *Current Anthropology* 29:57–58.

1994   Childe the Evolutionist: A Perspective from Nuclear America. In *The Archaeology of V. Gordon Childe: Contemporary Perspectives,* edited by D. R. Harris, pp. 101–119. University College London Press, London.

1997   In Defense of the Tehuacán Project. *Current Anthropology* 38:660–662.

1999   Process and Agency in Early State Formation. *Cambridge Archaeological Journal* 9:3–21.

Flannery, K. V., and M. D. Coe

1968   Social and Economic Systems in Formative Mesoamerica. In *New Perspectives in Archeology,* edited by S. R. Binford and L. R. Binford, pp. 267–283. Aldine, Chicago.

Flannery, K. V., A. V. Kirkby, M. J. Kirkby, and A. W. Williams.

1967   Farming Systems and Political Growth in Ancient Oaxaca, Mexico. *Science* 158:445–454.

Flannery, K. V., and J. Marcus

1976   Formative Oaxaca and the Zapotec Cosmos. *American Scientist* 64:374–383.

1983   (Editors) *The Cloud People: Divergent Evolution of the Zapotec and Mixtec Civilizations*. Academic Press, New York.

1990   Borrón, y Cuenta Nueva: Setting Oaxaca's Archaeological Record Straight. In *Debating Oaxaca Archaeology,* edited by J. Marcus, pp. 17–69. Anthropological Papers No. 84. Museum of Anthropology, University of Michigan, Ann Arbor.

1993   Cognitive Archaeology. *Cambridge Archaeological Journal* 3:260–270.

1994   On the Perils of "Politically Correct" Archaeology. *Current Anthropology* 35:441–445.

2001   Richard Stockton MacNeish, 1918–2001. *National Academy of Sciences Biographical Memoirs* 80:1–27.

Flannery, K. V., C. L. Moser, and S. Maranca

1986   The Excavation of Guilá Naquitz. In *Guilá Naquitz: Archaic Foraging and Early Agriculture in Oaxaca, Mexico,* edited by K. V. Flannery, pp. 65–95. Academic Press, Orlando.

Foley, R.

1981   *Off-Site Archaeology and Human Adaptation in Eastern Africa: An Analysis of Regional Artefact Density in the Amboseli, Southern Kenya.* International Series Vol. 97. British Archaeological Reports, Oxford.

1987   Hominid Species and Stone-Tool Assemblages: How Are They Related? *Antiquity* 61:380–392.

Foley, R., and M. M. Lahr

1997   Mode 3 Technologies and the Evolution of Modern Humans. *Cambridge Archaeological Journal* 7:3–36.

2003   On Stony Ground: Lithic Technology, Human Evolution, and the Emergence of Culture. *Evolutionary Anthropology* 12:109–122.

Ford, J. A.

1936   *Analysis of Village Site Collections from Louisiana and Mississippi.* Anthropological Study No. 2. Department of Conservation, Louisiana State Geological Survey, Baton Rouge.

1938   A Chronological Method Applicable to the Southeast. *American Antiquity* 3:260–264.

1949   Cultural Dating of Prehistoric Sites in Virú Valley, Peru. *American Museum of Natural History Anthropological Papers* 43(1):29–89.

1952   Measurements of Some Prehistoric Design Developments in the Southeastern States. *American Museum of Natural History Anthropological Papers* 43(3):313–384.

1954a   Comment on A. C. Spaulding's "Statistical Techniques for the Discovery of Artifact Types." *American Antiquity* 19:390–391.

1954b   Spaulding's Review of Ford. *American Anthropologist* 56:109–112.

1954c   The Type Concept Revisited. *American Anthropologist* 56:42–53.

1962   *A Quantitative Method for Deriving Cultural Chronology.* Technical Bulletin No. 1. Pan American Union, Washington, D.C.

Ford, J. A., and J. B. Griffin

1938   Report of the Conference on Southeastern Pottery Typology. Mimeographed. Reprinted in *Newsletter of the Southeastern Archaeological Conference* 7(1):10–22.

Ford, J. L., M. A. Rolingson, and L. D. Medford

1972   *Site Destruction Due to Agricultural Practices.* Research Series No. 3. Arkansas Archeological Survey, Fayetteville.

Ford, R. I.

1973   Archeology Serving Humanity. In *Research and Theory in Current Archeology,* edited by C. L. Redman, pp. 83–93. Wiley, New York.

Forde, C. D.

1934   *Habitat, Economy, and Society.* Methuen, London.

Fowler, D. D.

1982   Cultural Resources Management. *Advances in Archaeological Method and Theory* 5:1–50.

1987   Uses of the Past: Archaeology in the Service of the State. *American Antiquity* 52:229–248.

1999   Review of *The Land of Prehistory,* by A. B. Kehoe. *Journal of Anthropological Research* 55:599–602.

Freeman, D.

1974   The Evolutionary Theories of Charles Darwin and Herbert Spencer. *Current Anthropology* 15:211–237.

Freeman, L. G., Jr.

1966   The Nature of Mousterian Facies in Cantabrian Spain. *American Anthropologist* 68:230–237.

1968   A Theoretical Framework for Inter-
        preting Archaeological Materials. In
        Man the Hunter, edited by R. B. Lee
        and I. DeVore, pp. 262–267. Aldine,
        Chicago.

Freeman, L. G., Jr., and J. A. Brown
1964   Statistical Analysis of Carter Ranch
        Pottery. *Fieldiana: Anthropology*
        55:126–154. Field Museum of Nat-
        ural History, Chicago.

Fried, M. H.
1967   *The Evolution of Political Society.*
        Random House, New York.

Friedman, J., and M. Rowlands
1978   *The Evolution of Social Systems.*
        Duckworth, London.

Friedrich, M. H.
1970   Design Structure and Social Interac-
        tion: Archaeological Implications of
        an Ethnographic Analysis. *American
        Antiquity* 35:332–343.

Frison, G. C.
1968   A Functional Analysis of Certain
        Chipped Stone Tools. *American
        Antiquity* 33:149–155.

Fritz, J. M.
1972   Archaeological Systems for Indirect
        Observation of the Past. In *Contem-
        porary Archaeology*, edited by M. P.
        Leone, pp. 135–157. Southern Illinois
        University Press, Carbondale.

1973   Relevance, Archeology, and Subsis-
        tence Theory. In *Research and The-
        ory in Current Archeology*, edited by
        C. L. Redman, pp. 59–82. Wiley,
        New York.

1978   Paleopsychology Today: Ideational
        Systems and Human Adaptation in
        Prehistory. In *Social Archeology:
        Beyond Subsistence and Dating*,
        edited by C. L. Redman, M. J.
        Berman, D. V. Curtin, W. T. Lang-
        horne Jr., N. M. Versaggi, and J. C.
        Wanser, pp. 37–59. Academic Press,
        New York.

Fritz, J. M., and F. T. Plog
1970   The Nature of Archaeological Expla-
        nation. *American Antiquity*
        35:405–412.

Frodeman, R.
1995   Geological Reasoning: Geology as an
        Interpretive and Historical Science.
        *Geological Society of America Bul-
        letin* 107:960–968.

Gamio, M.
1913   Arqueología de Atzcapotzalco, D.F.,
        Mexico. *Proceedings of the Eigh-
        teenth International Congress of
        Americanists*, pp. 180–187.

Gauntlett, D.
2002   *Media, Gender, and Identity: An
        Introduction.* Routledge, London.

Gero, J. M.
1991   Genderlithics: Women's Roles in
        Stone Tool Production. In *Engender-
        ing Archaeology: Women and Prehis-
        tory*, edited by J. M. Gero and M. W.
        Conkey, pp. 163–193. Blackwell,
        Oxford.

Gero, J. M., and M. W. Conkey (editors)
1991   *Engendering Archaeology: Women
        and Prehistory.* Blackwell, Oxford.

Gibbon, G.
1989   *Explanation in Archaeology.* Black-
        well, Oxford.

Giddens, A.
1979   *Central Problems in Social Theory:
        Action, Structure, and Contradiction
        in Social Analysis.* University of Cali-
        fornia Press, Berkeley.

1984   *The Constitution of Society: Outline
        of the Theory of Structuration.* Uni-
        versity of California Press, Berkeley.

Gifford, J. C.
1960   The Type–Variety Method of
        Ceramic Classification as an Indica-
        tor of Cultural Phenomena. *Ameri-
        can Antiquity* 25:341–347.

Gilbert, B. M.
1990   *Mammalian Osteology.* Missouri
        Archaeological Society, Columbia.

Gilbert, B. M., L. D. Martin, and H. G. Savage.
1981   *Avian Osteology.* Missouri Archaeo-
        logical Society, Columbia.

Gilchrist, R.
1999   *Gender and Archaeology: Contesting
        the Past.* Routledge, London.

Gilman, A.

1989   Marxism in American Archaeology.
       In *Archaeological Thought in Amer-*
       ica, edited by C. C. Lamberg-
       Karlovsky, pp. 89–102. Cambridge
       University Press, New York.

Gilsen, L.

2001   Archaeological Gray Literature. *The*
       SAA Archaeological Record
       1(5):30–31.

Gladwin, H. S.

1936   Editorials: Methodology in the
       Southwest. *American Antiquity*
       1:256–259.

Gladwin, W., and H. S. Gladwin

1930   *A Method for the Designation of*
       Southwestern Pottery Types. Medal-
       lion Papers No. 7. Gila Bend Pueblo,
       Globe, Ariz.

1934   *A Method for the Designation of*
       Cultures and Their Variations.
       Medallion Papers No. 15. Gila Bend
       Pueblo, Globe, Ariz.

Glassow, M. A.

1977   Issues in Evaluating Significance of
       Archaeological Resources. *American*
       Antiquity 42:413–420.

1978   The Concept of Carrying Capacity in
       the Study of Culture Process.
       Advances in Archaeological Method
       and Theory 1:31–48.

Goldberg, P., D. T. Nash, and M. D. Petraglia

1993   *Formation Processes in Archaeologi-*
       cal Context. Monographs in World
       Archaeology No. 17. Prehistory
       Press, Madison, Wis.

Goldenweiser, A.

1916   Diffusion vs. Independent Invention:
       A Rejoinder to Professor G. Elliot
       Smith. *Science* 44:531–533.

1925   Diffusion and the American School
       of Historical Ethnology. *American*
       Journal of Sociology 31:19–38.

Goodyear, A. C.

1975   *Hecla II and III: An Interpretive*
       Study of Archeological Remains from
       the Lakeshore Project, Papago Reser-
       voir, South-Central Arizona. Anthro-
       pological Research Papers No. 9. Ari-
       zona State University, Department of
       Anthropology, Tempe.

1977   Review of *Behavioral Archeology,* by
       M. B. Schiffer. *American Antiquity*
       42:668–671.

Goodyear, A. C., L. M. Raab, and T. C. Klinger

1978   The Status of Archaeological
       Research Design in Cultural
       Resource Management. *American*
       Antiquity 43:159–173.

Gould, R. A.

1966   *Archaeology of the Point St. George*
       Site, and Tolowa Prehistory. Publica-
       tions in Anthropology Vol. 4. Univer-
       sity of California, Berkeley.

1968a Chipping Stones in the Outback.
       Natural History 77(2):42–49.

1968b Living Archaeology: The Ngatatjara
       of Western Australia. *Southwestern*
       Journal of Anthropology
       24:101–122.

1971   The Archaeologist as Ethnographer:
       A Case from the Western Desert of
       Australia. *World Archaeology*
       3:143–177.

1974   Some Current Problems in Ethnoar-
       chaeology. In *Ethnoarchaeology,*
       edited by C. B. Donnan and C. W.
       Clewlow, Jr., pp. 27–48. Monograph
       No. 4. Institute of Archaeology, Uni-
       versity of California, Los Angeles.

1978a (Editor) *Explorations in Ethnoar-*
       chaeology. University of New Mexico
       Press, Albuquerque.

1978b The Anthropology of Human
       Residues. *American Anthropologist*
       80:815–835.

1978c Beyond Analogy in Ethnoarchaeol-
       ogy. In *Explorations in Ethnoarchae-*
       ology, edited by R. A. Gould, pp.
       249–293. University of New Mexico
       Press, Albuquerque.

1980   *Living Archaeology.* Cambridge Uni-
       versity Press, Cambridge.

1985   The Empiricist Strikes Back. *Ameri-*
       can Antiquity 50:639–644.

2004   Disaster Archaeology at the West
       Warwick, Rhode Island Nightclub
       Fire Scene. *SAA Archaeological*
       Record 4(1):6–11.

Gould, R. A., D. A. Koster, and A. H. L. Sontz
1971   The Lithic Assemblage of the Western Desert Aborigines of Australia. *American Antiquity* 36:149–169.

Gould, R. A., and P. J. Watson
1982   A Dialogue on the Meaning and Use of Analogy in Ethnoarchaeological Reasoning. *Journal of Anthropological Archaeology* 1:355–381.

Gould, S. J.
1965   Is Uniformitarianism Necessary? *American Journal of Science* 263:223–228.

1979   Agassiz's Marginalia in Lyell's *Principles*, or the Perils of Uniformity and the Ambiguity of Heroes. *Studies in the History of Biology* 3:119–138.

1981   *The Mismeasure of Man.* Norton, New York.

1982a Hutton's Purposeful View. *Natural History* 91(5):6–12.

1982b The Meaning of Punctuated Equilibrium and Its Role in Validating a Hierarchical Approach to Macroevolution. In *Perspectives in Evolution*, edited by R. Milkman, pp. 83–104. Sinauer, Sunderland, Mass.

1982c Punctuated Equilibrium—A Different Way of Seeing. *New Scientist* 94:137–141.

1986   Evolution and the Triumph of Homology, or Why History Matters. *American Scientist* 74:60–69.

Gould, S. J., and N. Eldredge
1977   Punctuated Equilibria: The Tempo and Mode of Evolution Reconsidered. *Paleobiology* 3:115–151.

Grace, R.
1996   Use-Wear Analysis: The State of the Art. *Archaeometry* 38:209–229.

Grady, M. A.
1977   Significance Evaluation and the Orme Reservoir Project. *In Conservation Archaeology: A Guide for Cultural Resource Management Studies*, edited by M. B. Schiffer and G. J. Gumerman, pp. 259–267. Academic Press, New York.

Grady, M. A., and W. D. Lipe
1976   The Role of Preservation in Conservation Archaeology. *Proceedings of the American Society for Conservation Archaeology, 1976*, pp. 1–11.

Graves, M. W.
1985   Ceramic Design Variation within a Kalinga Village: Temporal and Spatial Processes. In *Decoding Prehistoric Ceramics,* edited by B. A. Nelson, pp. 5–34. Southern Illinois University Press, Carbondale.

1987   Rending Reality in Archaeological Analysis: A Reply to Upham and Plog. *Journal of Field Archaeology* 14:243–249.

1991   Pottery Production and Distribution among the Kalinga: A Study of Household and Regional Organization and Differentiation. In *Ceramic Ethnoarchaeology*, edited by W. A. Longacre, pp. 112–143. University of Arizona Press, Tucson.

1998   The History of Method and Theory in the Study of Prehistoric Puebloan Pottery in the American Southwest. *Journal of Archaeological Method and Theory* 5:309–343.

Graves, M. W., and T. N. Ladefoged
1995   The Evolutionary Significance of Ceremonial Architecture in Polynesia. In *Evolutionary Archaeology: Methodological Issues,* edited by P. A. Teltser, pp. 149–174. University of Arizona Press, Tucson.

Gray, R. D., and Q. D. Atkinson
2003   Language-Tree Divergence Times Support the Anatolian Theory of Indo-European Origin. *Nature* 426:435–439.

Gray, R. D., and F. M. Jordan
2000   Language Trees Support the Express-Train Sequence of Austronesian Expansion. *Nature* 405:1052–1055.

Grayson, D. K.
1983   *The Establishment of Human Antiquity.* Academic Press, New York.

1986   Eoliths, Archaeological Ambiguity, and the Generation of "Middle-Range" Research. In *American*

Archaeology Past and Future: A Celebration of the Society for American Archaeology, 1935–1985, edited by D. J. Meltzer, D. D. Fowler, and J. A. Sabloff, pp. 77–133. Smithsonian Institution Press, Washington, D.C.

Grayson, D. K., and M. D. Cannon

1999   Human Paleoecology and Foraging Theory in the Great Basin. In *Models for the Millennium: Great Basin Anthropology Today,* edited by C. Beck, pp. 141–151. University of Utah Press, Salt Lake City.

Grayson, D. K., and F. Delpech

1998   Changing Diet Breadth in the Early Upper Palaeolithic of Southwestern France. *Journal of Archaeological Science* 25:1119–1129.

Griffin, J. B.

1952   (Editor) *Archeology of Eastern United States.* University of Chicago Press, Chicago.

1976   Some Suggested Alterations of Certain Portions of *An Archaeological Perspective. American Antiquity* 41:114–119.

1985   The Formation of the Society for American Archaeology. *American Antiquity* 50:261–271.

Gruhn, R.

1972   Archaeological Looting and Site Destruction. *Science* 176:353–354.

Gumerman, G. J.

1973   The Reconciliation of Theory and Method in Archeology. In *Research and Theory in Current Archeology,* edited by C. L. Redman, pp. 287–299. Wiley, New York.

1994   (Editor) *Themes in Southwest Prehistory.* School of American Research Press, Santa Fe, N.M.

Gumerman, G. J., and M. Gell-Mann (editors)

1994   *Understanding Complexity in the Prehistoric Southwest.* Addison-Wesley, Reading, Mass.

Haag, W. G.

1959   The Status of Evolutionary Theory in American History. In *Evolution and Anthropology: A Centennial Appraisal,* edited by B. J. Meggers,

pp. 90–105. Anthropological Society of Washington, Washington, D.C.

1961   Review of *The Evolution of Man: Man, Culture and Society,* edited by S. Tax. *American Antiquity* 26:439–441.

1985   Federal Aid to Archaeology in the Southeast, 1933–1942. *American Antiquity* 50:272–280.

Haggett, P.

1965   *Locational Analysis in Human Geography.* Arnold, London.

Hamilton, W. D.

1964   The Genetical Evolution of Social Behaviour. *Journal of Theoretical Biology* 7:1–52.

Hammond, A. L.

1971   The New Archeology: Toward a Social Science. *Science* 172:1119–1120.

Hammond, N.

1984   On Anonymity. *American Antiquity* 49:161–163.

Haneberg, W. C.

1983   A Paradigmatic Analysis of Darwin's Use of Uniformitarianism in *The Origin of Species. Sigma Gamma Epsilon, Compass* 60:89–94.

Hanson, J. A., and M. B. Schiffer

1975   The Joint Site—A Preliminary Report. In *Chapters in the Prehistory of Eastern Arizona, IV.* Fieldiana: Anthropology 65:47–91. Field Museum of Natural History, Chicago.

Hanson, L. H., Jr.

1971   Kaolin Pipe Stems—Boring in on a Fallacy. *Conference on Historic Site Archaeology Papers* 4:2–15.

Hardesty, D. L.

1977   *Ecological Anthropology.* Wiley, New York.

1980   The Use of General Ecological Principles in Archaeology. *Advances in Archaeological Method and Theory* 3:157–187.

Hardesty, D. L., and B. J. Little

2000   *Assessing Site Significance: A Guide for Archaeologists and Historians.* AltaMira, Walnut Creek, Calif.

Hardy, B. L., and G. T. Garufi
  1998 Identification of Woodworking on Stone Tools through Residue and Use-Wear Analysis. *Journal of Archaeological Science* 25:177–184.

Harmon, M. J., R. D. Leonard, C. S. VanPool, and T. L. VanPool
  2000 Cultural Transmission: Shared Intellectual Traditions in Ceramics of the Prehistoric American Southwest and Northern Mexico. Paper presented at the 65th annual meeting of the Society for American Archaeology, Philadelphia.

Harrington, J. C.
  1954 Dating Stem Fragments of Seventeenth and Eighteenth Century Clay Tobacco Pipes. *Archaeological Society of Virginia Quarterly Bulletin* 9(1).

Harris, M.
  1959 The Economy Has No Surplus? *American Anthropologist* 61:185–199.
  1968a Comments. In *New Perspectives in Archeology,* edited by S. R. Binford and L. R. Binford, pp. 359–361. Aldine, Chicago.
  1968b *The Rise of Anthropological Theory: A History of Theories of Culture.* Crowell, New York.
  1979 *Cultural Materialism: The Struggle for a Science of Culture.* Random House, New York.

Hart, J. P., and J. E. Terrell (editors)
  2002 *Darwin and Archaeology: A Handbook of Key Concepts.* Bergin and Garvey, Westport, Conn.

Hawkes, C.
  1954 Archeological Theory and Method: Some Suggestions from the Old World. *American Anthropologist* 56:155–168.

Hawkes, J.
  1968 The Proper Study of Mankind. *Antiquity* 42:255–262.

Hawkes, K., J. F. O'Connell, and L. Rogers
  1997 The Behavioral Ecology of Modern Hunter-Gatherers and Human Evolution. *Trends in Ecology and Evolution* 12:29–32.

Hayden, B. (editor)
  1979 *Lithic Use-Wear Analysis.* Academic Press, New York.

Hayden, D.
  1997 *The Power of Place: Urban Landscapes as Public History.* MIT Press, Cambridge, Mass.

Haynes, H. W.
  1893 Paleolithic Man in North America. *American Antiquarian and Oriental Journal* 15:37–42.

Hays-Gilpin, K., and D. S. Whitley
  1998 *Reader in Gender Archaeology.* Routledge, London.

Headland, T. N.
  1997 Revisionism in Ecological Anthropology. *Current Anthropology* 38:605–630.

Hegmon, M.
  2003 Setting Theoretical Egos Aside: Issues and Theory in North American Archaeology. *American Antiquity* 68:213–243.

Heider, K.
  1967 Archaeological Assumptions and Ethnographic Facts: A Cautionary Tale from New Guinea. *Southwestern Journal of Anthropology* 23:52–64.

Heizer, R. F.
  1966 Salvage and Other Archaeology. *Masterkey* 40:54–60.

Heizer, R. F., and S. F. Cook (editors)
  1960 *The Application of Quantitative Methods in Archaeology.* Publications in Anthropology No. 28. Viking Fund, Wenner-Gren Foundation for Anthropological Research, New York.

Hempel, C. G.
  1962 Deductive-Nomological vs. Statistical Explanation. In *Scientific Explanation, Space, and Time,* vol. 3 of *Minnesota Studies in the Philosophy of Science,* edited by H. Feigl and G. Maxwell, pp. 98–169. University of Minnesota Press, Minneapolis.

1965a   Aspects of Scientific Explanation. In *Aspects of Scientific Explanation and Other Essays in the Philosophy of Science,* by C. G. Hempel, pp. 331–496. Free Press, New York.

1965b   *Aspects of Scientific Explanation and Other Essays in the Philosophy of Science.* Free Press, New York.

1966   *Philosophy of Natural Science.* Prentice-Hall, Englewood Cliffs, N.J.

Hempel, C. G., and P. Oppenheim

1948   Studies in the Logic of Explanation. *Philosophy of Science* 15:135–175.

Herold, E. B.

2003   Recollections of the Department of Anthropology in the Mid-twentieth Century. In *Curators, Collections, and Contexts: Anthropology at the Field Museum, 1893–2002,* edited by S. E. Nash and G. M. Feinman, pp. 179–187. Fieldiana: Anthropology 36. Field Museum of Natural History, Chicago.

Hester, T. R.

1981   CRM Publication: Dealing with Reality. *Journal of Field Archaeology* 8:493–496.

Hester, T. R., D. Gilbow, and A. D. Albee

1973   A Functional Analysis of "Clear Fork" Artifacts from the Rio Grande Plain, Texas. *American Antiquity* 38:90–96.

Hill, E.

1998   Gender-Informed Archaeology: The Priority of Definition, the Use of Analogy, and the Multivariate Approach. *Journal of Archaeological Method and Theory* 5:99–128.

Hill, J. N.

1965   *Broken K: A Prehistoric Society in Eastern Arizona.* Ph.D. dissertation, Department of Anthropology, University of Chicago.

1966   A Prehistoric Community in Eastern Arizona. *Southwestern Journal of Anthropology* 22:9–30.

1968   Broken K Pueblo: Patterns of Form and Function. In *New Perspectives in Archeology,* edited by S. R. Binford and L. R. Binford, pp. 103–142. Aldine, Chicago.

1970a   *Broken K Pueblo: Prehistoric Social Organization in the American Southwest.* Anthropological Papers No. 18. University of Arizona, Tucson.

1970b   Prehistoric Social Organization in the American Southwest: Theory and Method. In *Reconstructing Prehistoric Pueblo Societies,* edited by W. A. Longacre, pp. 11–58. University of New Mexico Press, Albuquerque.

1970c   Review of *Anthropological Archeology in the Americas,* edited by B. J. Meggers. *American Antiquity* 35:392.

1972   The Methodological Debate in Contemporary Archaeology: A Model. In *Models in Archaeology,* edited by D. L. Clarke, pp. 61–107. Methuen, London.

1977a   (Editor) *Explanation of Prehistoric Change.* University of New Mexico Press, Albuquerque.

1977b   Preface to *Explanation of Prehistoric Change,* edited by J. N. Hill, pp. ix–xi. University of New Mexico Press, Albuquerque.

1977c   Systems Theory and the Explanation of Change. In *Explanation of Prehistoric Change,* edited by J. N. Hill, pp. 59–104. University of New Mexico Press, Albuquerque.

Hill, J. N., and R. K. Evans

1972   A Model for Classification and Typology. In *Models in Archaeology,* edited by D. L. Clarke, pp. 231–273. Methuen, London.

Hinsley, C. M., Jr.

1994   *The Smithsonian and the American Indian: Making of a Moral Anthropology in Victorian America.* Smithsonian Institution Press, Washington, D.C.

Hirth, K. G.

1980   *Eastern Morelos and Teotihuacan: A Settlement Survey.* Publications in Anthropology No. 25. Vanderbilt University, Nashville, Tenn.

Hodder, I.

1971 The Use of Nearest Neighbour Analysis. *Cornish Archaeology* 10:35–36.

1974 A Regression Analysis of Some Trade and Marketing Patterns. *World Archaeology* 6:172–189.

1976 A Model for the Distribution of Coins in the Western Roman Empire. *Journal of Archaeological Science* 2:1–23.

1978 (Editor) *Simulation Studies in Archaeology*. Cambridge University Press, Cambridge.

1979 Economic and Social Stress and Material Culture Patterning. *American Antiquity* 44:446–454.

1981 Towards a Mature Archaeology. In *Pattern of the Past: Studies in Honour of David Clarke*, edited by I. Hodder, G. Isaac, and N. Hammond, pp. 1–13. Cambridge University Press, Cambridge.

1982a Preface to *Symbolic and Structural Archaeology*, edited by I. Hodder, pp. vii–viii. Cambridge University Press, Cambridge.

1982b (Editor) *Symbols in Action: Ethnoarchaeological Studies of Material Culture*. Cambridge University Press, Cambridge.

1982c *The Present Past: An Introduction to Anthropology for Archaeologists*. Batsford, London.

1982d Theoretical Archaeology: A Reactionary View. In *Symbolic and Structural Archaeology*, edited by I. Hodder, pp. 1–16. Cambridge University Press, Cambridge.

1985 Postprocessual Archaeology. *Advances in Archaeological Method and Theory* 8:1–26.

1986 *Reading the Past: Current Approaches to Interpretation in Archaeology*. Cambridge University Press, Cambridge.

1987 (Editor) *The Archaeology of Contextual Meanings*. Cambridge University Press, Cambridge.

1988 Material Culture Texts and Social Change: A Theoretical Discussion and Some Archaeological Examples. *Proceedings of the Prehistoric Society* 54:67–75.

1991a Interpretive Archaeology and Its Role. *American Antiquity* 56:7–18.

1991b Postprocessual Archaeology and the Current Debate. In *Processual and Postprocessual Archaeologies: Multiple Ways of Knowing the Past*, edited by R. W. Preucel, pp. 30–41. Occasional Paper No. 10. Center for Archaeological Investigations, Southern Illinois University at Carbondale.

1999 *The Archaeological Process: An Introduction*. Blackwell, London.

2002 Two Approaches to an Archaeology of the Social. *American Anthropologist* 104:320–324.

Hodder, I., and C. Cessford

2004 Daily Practice and Social Memory at Çatalhöyük. *American Antiquity* 69:17–40.

Hodder, I., and C. Orton

1976 *Spatial Analysis in Archaeology*. Cambridge University Press, Cambridge.

Hodson, F. R., P. H. A. Sneath, and J. E. Doran

1966 Some Experiments in the Numerical Analysis of Archaeological Data. *Biometrika* 53:311–324.

Hofman, J. L.

1981 The Refitting of Chipped-Stone Artifacts as an Analytical and Interpretive Tool. *Current Anthropology* 22:691–693.

1986 Vertical Movement of Artifacts in Alluvial and Stratified Deposits. *Current Anthropology* 27:163–171.

Hogarth, A. C.

1972 Common Sense in Archaeology. *Antiquity* 46:301–304.

Holden, C.

2004 Court Battle Ends, Bones Still Off-Limits. *Science* 305:591.

Hole, B. L.

1980 Sampling in Archaeology: A Critique. *Annual Review of Anthropology* 9:217–234.

Hole, F.
　1974　Editorial Comment. *American Antiquity* 39:405.
　1979　Review of *Advances in Archaeological Method and Theory,* vol. 1, edited by M. B. Schiffer. *American Scientist* 67:618–619.

Hole, F., K. V. Flannery, and J. A. Neely
　1969　*Prehistory and Human Ecology of the Deh Luran Plain: An Early Village Sequence from Khuzistan, Iran.* Memoirs No. 1. Museum of Anthropology, University of Michigan, Ann Arbor.

Hole, F., and R. F. Heizer
　1973　*An Introduction to Prehistoric Archeology.* 3rd ed. Holt, Rinehart, and Winston, New York.

Holliday, V. T.
　1993　*Soils in Archaeology: Landscape Evolution and Human Occupation.* Smithsonian Institution Press, Washington, D.C.

Holmes, W. H.
　1892　Modern Quarry Refuse and the Paleolithic Theory. *Science* 20:295–297.
　1893　Are There Traces of Man in the Trenton Gravels? *Journal of Geology* 1:15–37.
　1897　Stone Implements of the Potomac–Chesapeake Tidewater Province. *Bureau of American Ethnology Annual Report* 15:13–152.

Holton, G.
　1986　Niels Bohr and the Integrity of Science. *American Scientist* 74:237–243.

Hooykaas, R.
　1970　*Catastrophism in Geology: Its Scientific Character in Relation to Actualism and Uniformitarianism.* North Holland, Amsterdam.

House, J. H., and M. B. Schiffer
　1975a　Archeological Survey in the Cache River Basin. In *The Cache River Archeological Project: An Experiment in Contract Archeology,* assembled by M. B. Schiffer and J. H. House, pp. 37–53. Research Series No. 8. Arkansas Archeological Survey, Fayetteville.

　1975b　Significance of the Archeological Resources of the Cache River Basin. In *The Cache River Archeological Project: An Experiment in Contract Archeology,* assembled by M. B. Schiffer and J. H. House, pp. 163–186. Research Series No. 8. Arkansas Archeological Survey, Fayetteville.

Hull, D.
　1970　Contemporary Systematic Philosophies. *Annual Review of Ecology and Systematics* 1:19–54.
　1974　*Philosophy of Biological Science.* Prentice-Hall, Englewood Cliffs, N.J.
　1980　Individuality and Selection. *Annual Review of Ecology and Systematics* 11:311–332.
　1981　Units of Evolution: A Metaphysical Essay. In *The Philosophy of Evolution,* edited by U. J. Jenson and R. Harré, pp. 23–44. St. Martin's Press, New York.
　1982　The Naked Meme. In *Learning, Development, and Culture,* edited by H. C. Plotkin, pp. 273–327. Wiley, New York.
　1988a　Interactors versus Vehicles. In *The Role of Behavior in Evolution,* edited by H. C. Plotkin, pp. 19–50. MIT Press, Cambridge, Mass.
　1988b　*Science as a Process: An Evolutionary Account of the Social and Conceptual Development of Science.* University of Chicago Press, Chicago.

Hunt, T. L., C. P. Lipo, and S. L. Sterling (editors)
　2001　*Posing Questions for a Scientific Archaeology.* Bergin and Garvey, Westport, Conn.

Huntington, E.
　1915　*Civilization and Climate.* Yale University Press, New Haven, Conn.
　1919　*World-Power and Evolution.* Yale University Press, New Haven, Conn.

Hurley, W. M.
　1979　*Prehistoric Cordage: A Guide to Identification of Impressions on Pottery.* Taraxacum, Washington, D.C.

Hurt, T. D., and G. F. M. Rakita (editors)

2001   *Style and Function: Conceptual Issues in Evolutionary Archaeology.* Bergin and Garvey, Westport, Conn.

Hurt, W. R.

1966   Review of *The Dynamics of Stylistic Change in Arikara Ceramics,* by J. Deetz. *American Antiquity* 31:587–588.

Hutson, S.

1998   Strategies for the Reproduction of Prestige in Archaeological Discourse. *Assemblage: University of Sheffield Graduate Student Journal of Archaeology* 4. (http://www.shef.ac.uk/assem/4/4hutson.html)

Huxley, J. S.

1942   *Evolution, the Modern Synthesis.* Allen and Unwin, London.

Ingersoll, D., and W. MacDonald

1977   Introduction to *Experimental Archeology,* edited by D. Ingersoll, J. E. Yellen, and W. MacDonald, pp. xi–xvii. Columbia University Press, New York.

Ingersoll, D., J. E. Yellen, and W. MacDonald (editors)

1977   *Experimental Archeology.* Columbia University Press, New York.

Institute of Medicine

1985   *Personnel Needs and Training for Biomedical and Behavioral Research.* National Academy Press, Washington, D.C.

Isaac, G. L.

1967   Towards the Interpretation of Occupation Debris: Some Experiments and Observations. *Kroeber Anthropological Society Papers* 37:31–57.

Jaroslav, M., and Z. Vasicek

1990   *Archaeology Yesterday and Today: The Development of Archaeology in the Sciences and Humanities.* Translated by M. Zvelebil. Cambridge University Press, Cambridge.

Jennings, J. D.

1985   River Basin Surveys: Origins, Operations, and Results, 1945–1969. *American Antiquity* 50:281–296.

1986   American Archaeology, 1930–1985. In *American Archaeology Past and Future: A Celebration of the Society for American Archaeology, 1935–1985,* edited by D. J. Meltzer, D. D. Fowler, and J. A. Sabloff, pp. 53–62. Smithsonian Institution Press, Washington D.C.

Jepsen, G. L., E. Mayr, and G. G. Simpson (editors)

1949   *Genetics, Paleontology and Evolution.* Princeton University Press, Princeton, N.J.

Jochim, M. A.

1976   *Hunter-Gatherer Subsistence and Settlement: A Predictive Model.* Academic Press, New York.

1979   Breaking Down the System: Recent Ecological Approaches in Archaeology. *Advances in Archaeological Method and Theory* 2:77–117.

1981   *Strategies for Survival: Cultural Behavior in an Ecological Context.* Academic Press, New York.

Johnson, E.

1973   Professional Responsibilities and the American Indian. *American Antiquity* 38:129–130.

Johnson, F.

1966   Archeology in an Emergency. *Science* 152:1592–1597.

1967   Radiocarbon Dating and Archeology in North America. *Science* 155:165–169.

Johnson, L., Jr.

1972   Problems in "Avant-Garde" Archaeology. *American Anthropologist* 74:366–377.

Johnson, M.

1999   *Archaeological Theory: An Introduction.* Blackwell, Oxford.

Jordan, P., and S. Shennan

2003   Cultural Transmission, Language, and Basketry Traditions amongst the California Indians. *Journal of Anthropological Archaeology* 22:42–74.

Joyce, A. A., and M. Winter
  1996 Ideology, Power, and Urban Society in Pre-Hispanic Oaxaca. *Current Anthropology* 37:33–47.

Judge, J. W.
  1978 Review of *Explanation of Prehistoric Change*, edited by J. N. Hill. *Journal of Anthropological Research* 34:291–294.

Kamminga, J.
  1980 Review of *Experimental Determination of Stone Tool Uses: A Microwear Analysis*, by L. H. Keeley. *Science* 210:58–59.

Katzenstein, P. J.
  2001 Area and Regional Studies in the United States. *Political Science and Politics* 34:789–791.

Keeley, L. H.
  1974a The Methodology of Microwear Analysis: A Comment on Nance. *American Antiquity* 39:126–128.
  1974b Technique and Methodology in Microwear Studies: A Critical Review. *World Archaeology* 5:323–336.
  1977 The Functions of Paleolithic Flint Tools. *Scientific American* 237(5):108–126.
  1980 *Experimental Determination of Stone Tool Uses: A Microwear Analysis*. University of Chicago Press, Chicago.

Keeley, L. H., and M. H. Newcomer
  1977 Microwear Analysis of Experimental Flint Tools: A Test Case. *Journal of Archaeological Science* 4:29–62.

Keene, A. S.
  1983 Biology, Behavior, and Borrowing: A Critical Examination of Optimal Foraging Theory in Archaeology. In *Archaeological Hammers and Theories*, edited by J. A. Moore and A. S. Keene, pp. 137–155. Academic Press, New York.

Kehoe, A. B.
  1998 *The Land of Prehistory: A Critical History of American Archaeology*. Routledge, New York.

Kehoe, A. B., and M. B. Emmerichs (editors)
  1999 *Assembling the Past: Studies in the Professionalization of Archaeology*. University of New Mexico Press, Albuquerque.

Kelley, J. H., and M. P. Hanen
  1988 *Archaeology and the Methodology of Science*. University of New Mexico Press, Albuquerque.

Kelly, R. L.
  1995 *The Foraging Spectrum: Diversity in Hunter-Gatherer Lifeways*. Smithsonian Institution Press, Washington, D.C.
  2000 Elements of a Behavioral Ecological Paradigm for the Study of Prehistoric Hunter-Gatherers. In *Social Theory in Archaeology*, edited by M. B. Schiffer, pp. 63–78. University of Utah Press, Salt Lake City.

Kent, S. (editor)
  1990 *Gender in African Prehistory*. AltaMira, Walnut Creek, Calif.

Kerns, V.
  1999 Learning the Land. In *Julian Steward and the Great Basin: The Making of an Anthropologist*, edited by R. O. Clemmer, L. D. Myers, and M. E. Rudden, pp. 1–18. University of Utah Press, Salt Lake City.
  2003 *Scenes from the High Desert: Julian Steward's Life and Theory*. University of Illinois Press, Urbana.

Kidder, A. V.
  1915 Pottery of the Pajarito Plateau and Some Adjacent Regions in New Mexico. *American Anthropological Association Memoirs* 2:407–462.
  1916 Archeological Explorations at Pecos, New Mexico. *Proceedings of the National Academy of Sciences* 2:119–123.
  1917 A Design-Sequence from New Mexico. *Proceedings of the National Academy of Sciences* 3:369–370.
  1924 *An Introduction to the Study of Southwestern Archaeology, with a Preliminary Account of the Excavations at Pecos*. Papers of the South-

western Expedition No. 1. Yale University Press, New Haven, Conn.

1927   Southwestern Archaeological Conference. *Science* 66:489–491.

1932   *The Artifacts of Pecos.* Papers of the Southwestern Expedition No. 6. Yale University Press, New Haven, Conn.

1936   Speculations on New World Prehistory. In *Essays in Anthropology,* edited by R. Lowie, pp. 143–152. University of California Press, Berkeley.

Kidder, M. A., and A. V. Kidder

1917   Notes on the Pottery of Pecos. *American Anthropologist* 19:325–360.

King, K.

2003   *The Gospel of Mary of Magdala: Jesus and the First Woman Apostle.* Polebridge, Santa Rosa, Calif.

King, T. F.

1971   A Conflict of Values in American Archaeology. *American Antiquity* 36:255–262.

1977a   Preservation and Rescue: Challenges and Controversies in the Protection of Archaeological Resources. *Journal of Field Archaeology* 4:473–474.

1977b   Resolving a Conflict of Values in American Archaeology. In *Conservation Archaeology: A Guide for Cultural Resource Management Studies,* edited by M. B. Schiffer and G. J. Gumerman, pp. 87–95. Academic Press, New York.

1978   Allegories of Eligibility: The Determination of Eligibility Process and the Capacity for Thought among Archeologists. In *Cultural Resources: Planning and Management,* edited by R. S. Dickens, Jr., and C. E. Hill, pp. 43–54. Westview Press, Boulder, Colo.

1983   Professional Responsibility in Public Archaeology. *Annual Review of Anthropology* 12:143–164.

1985   If an Orange Falls in the Forest, Is It Eligible? A Comment on Tainter and Lucas. *American Antiquity* 50:170–172.

1998   *Cultural Resource Laws and Practice: An Introductory Guide.* AltaMira, Walnut Creek, Calif.

2000   *Federal Planning and Historical Places: The Section 106 Process.* AltaMira, Walnut Creek, Calif.

King, T. F., and M. M. Lyneis

1978   Preservation: A Developing Focus of American Archaeology. *American Anthropologist* 80:873–893.

Kintigh, K. W.

1988   The Effectiveness of Subsurface Testing: A Simulation Approach. *American Antiquity* 53:686–707.

Kirch, P. V.

1980   The Archaeological Study of Adaptation: Theoretical and Methodological Issues. *Advances in Archaeological Method and Theory* 3:101–156.

1986   Rethinking East Polynesian Prehistory. *Journal of the Polynesian Society* 95:9–40.

Kirch, P. V., and R. C. Green

1987   History, Phylogeny, and Evolution in Polynesia. *Current Anthropology* 28:431–456.

2001   *Hawaiki, Ancestral Polynesia: An Essay in Historical Anthropology.* Cambridge University Press, Cambridge.

Kitcher, P.

1982   Genes. *British Journal for the Philosophy of Science* 33:337–359.

Kitts, D. B.

1963a   Historical Explanation in Geology. *Journal of Geology* 71:297–313.

1963b   The Theory of Geology. In *The Fabric of Geology,* edited by C. C. Albritton, Jr., pp. 49–68. Addison-Wesley, Reading, Mass.

Kleindienst, M., and P. J. Watson

1956   Action Archaeology: The Archaeological Inventory of a Living Community. *Anthropology Tomorrow* 5:75–78.

Klejn, L. S.

1973   On Major Aspects of the Interrelationship of Archeology and Ethnology. *Current Anthropology* 14:311–320.

Klimek, S.

1935   Culture Element Distributions: I, The Structure of California Indian Culture. *University of California Publications in American Archaeology and Ethnology* 37:1–70.

Klinger, T. C., and L. M. Raab

1980   Archaeological Significance and the National Register: A Response to Barnes, Briggs, and Neilsen. *American Antiquity* 45:554–557.

Kluckhohn, C.

1939   The Place of Theory in Anthropological Studies. *Philosophy of Science* 6:328–344.

1940   The Conceptual Structure in Middle American Studies. In *The Maya and Their Neighbors,* edited by C. L. Hay, S. K. Lothrop, R. L. Linton, H. L. Shapiro, and G. C. Vaillant, pp. 41–51. Appleton–Century, New York.

1959   The Role of Evolutionary Thought in Anthropology. In *Evolution and Anthropology: A Centennial Appraisal,* edited by B. J. Meggers, pp. 144–157. Anthropological Society of Washington, Washington, D.C.

1960   The Use of Typology in Anthropological Theory. In *Selected Papers of the Fifth International Congress of Anthropological and Ethnological Sciences,* edited by A. F. C. Wallace, pp. 134–140. University of Pennsylvania Press, Philadelphia.

Kohl, P. L.

1985   Symbolic Cognitive Archaeology: A New Loss of Innocence. *Dialectical Anthropology* 9:105–118.

Kohl, P. L., and C. Fawcett

1995   *Nationalism, Politics, and the Practice of Archaeology.* Cambridge University Press, Cambridge.

Kohler, T. A., J. Kresl, C. Van West, E. Carr, and R. H. Wilshusen

2000   Be There Then: A Modeling Approach to Settlement Determinants and Spatial Efficiency among Late Ancestral Pueblo Populations of the Mesa Verde Region, U.S. Southwest. In *Dynamics in Human and Primate Societies: Agent-Based Modeling of Social and Spatial Processes,* edited by T. A. Kohler and G. J. Gumerman, pp. 145–178. Oxford University Press, New York.

Kornbacher, K., and M. Madsen

1999   Explaining the Evolution of Cultural Elaboration. *Journal of Anthropological Archaeology* 18:241–242.

Kosso, P.

1991   Method in Archaeology: Middle-Range Theory as Hermeneutics. *American Antiquity* 56:621–627.

2001   *Knowing the Past: Philosophical Issues of History and Archaeology.* Humanity Books, Amherst, N.Y.

Kowalewski, S. A.

1990   The Evolution of Complexity in the Valley of Oaxaca. *Annual Review of Anthropology* 19:39–58.

2003   Scale and the Explanation of Demographic Change: 3,500 Years in the Valley of Oaxaca. *American Anthropologist* 105:313–325.

Kowalewski, S. A., G. M. Feinman, L. Finsten, R. E. Blanton, and L. M. Nicholas

1989   *Prehispanic Settlement Patterns in Tlacolula, Etla, and Ocotlán, the Valley of Oaxaca, Mexico.* Part II of *Monte Albán's Hinterland.* Memoirs No. 23. Museum of Anthropology, University of Michigan, Ann Arbor.

Kowalewski, S. A., and L. Finsten

1988   Comment on "Ecological Theory and Cultural Evolution in the Valley of Oaxaca," by W. T. Sanders and D. L. Nichols. *Current Anthropology* 29:59–60.

Krakker, J. J., M. J. Shott, and P. D. Welch

1983   Design and Evaluation of Shovel-Test Sampling in Regional Archaeological Survey. *Journal of Field Archaeology* 10:469–480.

Kramer, C.

1979a   (Editor) *Ethnoarchaeology: Implications of Ethnography for Archaeology.* Columbia University Press, New York.

1979b Introduction to *Ethnoarchaeology: Implications of Ethnography for Archaeology,* edited by C. Kramer, pp. 1–20. Columbia University Press, New York.

Krantz, D. L., and L. Wiggins
1973 Personal and Impersonal Channels of Recruitment in the Growth of Theory. *Human Development* 16:133–156.

Krech, S., III
2000 *The Ecological Indian: Myth and History.* Norton, New York.

Krieger, A. D.
1944 The Typological Concept. *American Antiquity* 9:271–288.
1953 Basic Stages of Cultural Evolution. In *An Appraisal of Anthropology Today,* edited by S. Tax, pp. 247–250. University of Chicago Press, Chicago.
1960 Archaeological Typology in Theory and Practice. In *Men and Culture: Selected Papers of the Fifth International Congress of Anthropological and Ethnological Sciences*, edited by A. F. C. Wallace, pp. 141–151. University of Pennsylvania Press, Philadelphia.

Kroeber, A. L.
1909 The Archaeology of California. In *Putnam Anniversary Volume,* edited by F. Boas, pp. 1–42. Stechert, New York.
1916 Zuni Potsherds. *Anthropological Papers of the American Museum of Natural History* 18(1):1–37.
1923 The History of Native Culture in California. *University of California Publications in American Archaeology and Ethnology* 20:123–142.
1931 Historical Reconstruction of Culture Growths and Organic Evolution. *American Anthropologist* 33:149–156.
1936 Culture Element Distributions: III, Area and Climax. *University of California Publications in American Archaeology and Ethnology* 37:101–116.

1939 Cultural and Natural Areas of Native North America. *University of California Publications in American Archaeology and Ethnology* 38:1–242.
1958 Gray's Epicyclical Evolution. *American Anthropologist* 60:31–39.

Kroeber, A. L., and C. Kluckhohn
1952 *Culture: A Critical Review of Concepts and Definitions.* Papers Vol. 47. Peabody Museum of Archaeology and Ethnology, Harvard University, Cambridge, Mass.

Kuhn, T. S.
1962a Historical Structure of Scientific Discovery. *Science* 136:760–764.
1962b *The Structure of Scientific Revolutions.* University of Chicago Press, Chicago.
1977 *The Essential Tension: Selected Studies in Scientific Tradition and Change.* University of Chicago Press, Chicago.

Kushner, G.
1970 A Consideration of Some Processual Designs for Archaeology as Anthropology. *American Antiquity* 35:125–132.
1973 Review of *Contemporary Archaeology,* edited by M. P. Leone. *Science* 180:616–618.

Ladefoged, T. N., and M. W. Graves
2000 Evolutionary Theory and the Historical Development of Dry-Land Agriculture in North Kohala, Hawai'i. *American Antiquity* 65:423–448.

Lakatos, I.
1970 Falsification and the Methodology of Scientific Research Programmes. In *Criticism and the Growth of Knowledge,* edited by I. Lakatos and A. Musgrave, pp. 91–196. University of Illinois Press, Urbana.

Laming-Emperaire, A.
1962 *La Signification de l'Art Rupestre Paleolithique.* Picard, Paris.

LaMotta, V. M., and M. B. Schiffer
2001 Behavioral Archaeology: Toward a New Synthesis. In *Archaeological*

Theory Today, edited by I. Hodder, pp. 14–64. Polity Press, Cambridge.

Larson, D.
2000 On the Extrapolationist Bias of Evolutionary Archaeology. *Current Anthropology* 41:840–841.

Last, J.
1997 Review of *Behavioral Archaeology: First Principles,* by M. B. Schiffer, and *Expanding Archaeology,* edited by J. M. Skibo, W. H. Walker, and A. E. Nielsen. *Journal of Archaeological Science* 24:381–384.

Laufer, B.
1913 The Relation of Archeology to Ethnology: Remarks. *American Anthropologist* 15:573–577.

Layton, R.
1997 *An Introduction to Theory in Anthropology*. Cambridge University Press, Cambridge.

Lee, R. B.
1968 Comments. In *New Perspectives in Archeology,* edited by S. R. Binford and L. R. Binford, pp. 343–346. Aldine, Chicago.

Lee, R. B., and I. DeVore (editors)
1968 *Man the Hunter*. Aldine, Chicago.

Leeds, A., and A. P. Vayda (editors)
1965 *Man, Culture, and Animals: The Role of Animals in Human Ecological Adjustments*. American Association for the Advancement of Science, Washington, D.C.

Lehmer, D. J.
1951 Robinson's Coefficient of Agreement—A Critique. *American Antiquity* 17:151.

Lekson, S. H.
2001 The Legacy of Lewis Binford: Review of *Constructing Frames of Reference. American Scientist* 89:558–559.

Leonard, R. D.
1989 Resource Specialization, Population Growth, and Agricultural Production in the American Southwest. *American Antiquity* 54:491–503.
2001 Evolutionary Archaeology. In *Archaeological Theory Today,* edited

by I. Hodder, pp. 65–97. Polity Press, Cambridge.

Leonard, R. D., T. D. Maxwell, T. L. VanPool, C. S. VanPool, G. Rakita, and M. J. Harmon
2002 The Connection between Casas Grandes and West-Mexico. Paper presented at the Southwest Symposium 2002: Society and Politics in the Greater Southwest, Tucson, Ariz.

Leonard, R. D., and G. T. Jones
1987 Elements of an Inclusive Evolutionary Model for Archaeology. *Journal of Anthropological Archaeology* 6:199–219.

Leonard, R. D., and H. E. Reed
1993 Population Aggregation in the Prehistoric American Southwest: A Selectionist Model. *American Antiquity* 58:648–661.
1996 Theory, Models, Explanation, and the Record: Response to Kohler and Sebastian. *American Antiquity* 61:603–608.

Leone, M. P.
1968a *Economic Autonomy and Social Distance*. Ph.D. dissertation, Department of Anthropology, University of Arizona, Tucson.
1968b Neolithic Economic Autonomy and Social Distance. *Science* 162:1150–1151.
1971 Review of *New Perspectives in Archeology,* edited by S. R. Binford and L. R. Binford. *American Antiquity* 36:220–222.
1972a (Editor) *Contemporary Archaeology: A Guide to Theory and Contributions*. Southern Illinois University Press, Carbondale.
1972b Issues in Anthropological Archaeology. In *Contemporary Archaeology: A Guide to Theory and Contributions,* edited by M. P. Leone, pp. 14–27. Southern Illinois University Press, Carbondale.
1973 Archeology as the Science of Technology: Mormon Town Plans and Fences. In *Research and Theory in Current Archeology,* edited by C. L.

Redman, pp. 125–150. Wiley, New York.

1978 Time in American Archeology. In *Social Archeology: Beyond Subsistence and Dating,* edited by C. L. Redman, M. J. Berman, D. V. Curtin, W. T. Langhorne, Jr., N. M. Versaggi, and J. C. Wanser, pp. 25–36. Academic Press, New York.

1981 Archaeology's Relationship to the Present and the Past. In *Modern Material Culture: The Archaeology of Us,* edited by R. A. Gould and M. B. Schiffer, pp. 5–14. Academic Press, New York.

1982 Some Opinions about Recovering Mind. *American Antiquity* 47:742–760.

1984 Interpreting Ideology in Historical Archaeology: The William Paca Garden in Annapolis, Maryland. In *Ideology, Power, and Prehistory,* edited by D. Miller and C. Tilley, pp. 25–35. Cambridge University Press, Cambridge.

1986 Symbolic, Structural, and Critical Archaeology. In *American Archaeology, Past and Future: A Celebration of the Society for American Archaeology, 1935–1985,* edited by D. J. Meltzer, D. D. Fowler, and J. A. Sabloff, pp. 415–438. Smithsonian Institution Press, Washington, D.C.

1989 Review of *Re-Constructing Archaeology: Theory and Practice,* by M. Shanks and C. Tilley. *American Antiquity* 54:429–430.

Leone, M. P., P. B. Potter, Jr., and P. A. Shackel
1987 Toward a Critical Archaeology. *Current Anthropology* 28:283–302.

Leroi-Gourhan, A.
1967 *Treasures of Prehistoric Art.* Abrams, New York.

1968 The Evolution of Paleolithic Art. *Scientific American* 218(2):58–70.

Levin, M. E.
1973 On Explanation in Archaeology: A Rebuttal to Fritz and Plog. *American Antiquity* 38:387–395.

Lewarch, D. E., and M. J. O'Brien
1981 The Expanding Role of Surface Assemblages in Archaeological Analysis. *Advances in Archaeological Method and Theory* 4:297–342.

Lightfoot, K. G.
1986 Regional Surveys in the Eastern United States: The Strengths and Weaknesses of Implementing Subsurface Testing Programs. *American Antiquity* 51:484–504.

1989 A Defense of Shovel Test Sampling: A Reply to Shott. *American Antiquity* 54:413–416.

Lipe, W. D.
1974 A Conservation Model for American Archaeology. *The Kiva* 39:213–245.

Lipe, W. D., and V. Steponaitis
1998 SAA to Promote Professional Standards through ROPA Membership. *Society for American Archaeology Bulletin* 16(2):15–17.

Lipo, C. P.
2001 *Science, Style, and the Study of Community Structure: An Example from the Central Mississippi River Valley.* International Series No. 918. British Archaeological Reports, Oxford.

Lipo, C., M. Madsen, R. C. Dunnell, and T. Hunt
1997 Population Structure, Cultural Transmission, and Frequency Seriation. *Journal of Anthropological Archaeology* 16:301–333.

Lischka, J. J.
1975 Broken K Revisited: A Short Discussion of Factor Analysis. *American Antiquity* 40:220–227.

Little, B. J. (editor)
2002 *Public Benefits of Archaeology.* University Press of Florida, Gainesville.

Longacre, W. A.
1963 *Archaeology as Anthropology: A Case Study.* Ph.D. dissertation, Department of Anthropology, University of Chicago. Chicago.

1964 Archaeology as Anthropology: A Case Study. *Science* 144:1454–1455.

1966 Changing Patterns of Social Integration: A Prehistoric Example from the

American Southwest. *American Anthropologist* 68:94–102.

1968   Some Aspects of Prehistoric Society in East-Central Arizona. In *New Perspectives in Archeology*, edited by S. R. Binford and L. R. Binford, pp. 89–102. Aldine, Chicago.

1970a   A Historical Review. In *Reconstructing Prehistoric Pueblo Societies*, edited by W. A. Longacre, pp. 1–10. University of New Mexico Press, Albuquerque.

1970b   Current Thinking in American Archaeology. *American Anthropological Association Bulletin* 3(3):126–138.

1970c   *Archaeology as Anthropology: A Case Study.* Anthropological Papers No. 17. University of Arizona, Tucson.

1970d   (Editor) *Reconstructing Prehistoric Pueblo Societies.* University of New Mexico Press, Albuquerque.

1973   Comment. In *Research and Theory in Current Archeology*, edited by C. L. Redman, pp. 329–335. Wiley, New York.

1974   Kalinga Pottery-Making: The Evolution of a Research Design. In *Frontiers in Anthropology*, edited by M. J. Leaf, pp. 51–67. Van Nostrand, New York.

1981a   CRM Publication: A Review Essay. *Journal of Field Archaeology* 8:487–493.

1981b   Kalinga Pottery Making: An Ethnoarchaeological Study. In *Pattern of the Past: Studies in Honour of David Clarke,* edited by I. Hodder, G. Isaac, and N. Hammond, pp. 49–66. Cambridge University Press, Cambridge.

1985   Pottery Use-Life among the Kalinga, Northern Luzon, the Philippines. In *Decoding Prehistoric Ceramics,* edited by B. A. Nelson, pp. 334–346. Southern Illinois University Press, Carbondale.

1991   Sources of Ceramic Variability among the Kalinga of Northern Luzon. In *Ceramic Ethnoarchaeol-*

ogy, edited by W. A. Longacre, pp. 95–111. University of Arizona Press, Tucson.

1998   Review of *Conversations with Lew Binford: Drafting the New Archaeology,* by P. L. W. Sabloff. *American Antiquity* 63:703.

2000   Exploring Prehistoric Social and Political Organization in the American Southwest. *Journal of Anthropological Research* 56:287–300.

Longacre, W. A., and J. E. Ayres

1968   Archeological Lessons from an Apache Wickiup. In *New Perspectives in Archeology*, edited by S. R. Binford and L. R. Binford, pp. 151–159. Aldine, Chicago.

Longacre, W. A., and J. M. Skibo (editors)

1994   *Kalinga Ethnoarchaeology.* Smithsonian Institution Press, Washington D.C.

Longacre, W. A., and R. G. Vivian

1972   Salvage Archeology. *Science* 178:811–812.

Longacre, W. A., J. Xia, and T. Yang

2000   I Want to Buy a Black Pot. *Journal of Archaeological Method and Theory* 7:273–293.

Lovis, W. A., Jr.

1976   Quarter Sections and Forests: An Example of Probability Sampling in the Northeastern Woodlands. *American Antiquity* 41:364–372.

Lowie, R. H.

1912   On the Principle of Convergence in Ethnology. *Journal of American Folk-Lore* 25:24–42.

1918   Survivals and the Historical Method. *American Journal of Sociology* 23:529–535.

Lumsden, C. J., and E. O. Wilson

1981   *Genes, Mind, and Culture: The Coevolutionary Process.* Harvard University Press, Cambridge, Mass.

Lupo, K., and J. F. O'Connell

2002   Cut and Tooth Marks on Large Animal Bones: Ethnoarchaeological Data from the Hadza and Their Implications about Early Human Carnivory.

Journal of Archaeological Science 29:85–109.

Lyell, C.
1830 *Principles of Geology*. Vol. I. Murray, London.

Lyman, R. L.
1985 Cultural Resource Management and Archaeological Research in the Interior Pacific Northwest: A Note to NARN Readers on the Translucency of Northwest Archaeology. *Northwest Anthropological Research Notes* 19:161–169.

1994 *Vertebrate Taphonomy*. Cambridge University Press, New York.

1997 Impediments to Archaeology: Publishing and the (Growing) Translucency of Archaeological Research. *Northwest Anthropological Research Notes* 31:5–22.

2000 Building Cultural Chronology in Eastern Washington: The Influence of Geochronology, Index Fossils, and Radiocarbon Dating. *Geoarchaeology* 15:609–648.

2001 Culture Historical and Biological Approaches to Identifying Homologous Traits. In *Style and Function: Conceptual Issues in Evolutionary Archaeology*, edited by T. D. Hurt and G. F. M. Rakita, pp. 69–89. Bergin and Garvey, Westport, Conn.

Lyman, R. L., and J. L. Harpole
2002 A. L. Kroeber and the Measurement of Time's Arrow and Time's Cycle. *Journal of Anthropological Research* 58:313–338.

Lyman, R. L., and M. J. O'Brien
1997 The Concept of Evolution in Early Twentieth-Century Americanist Archaeology. In *Rediscovering Darwin: Evolutionary Theory in Archeological Explanation*, edited by C. M. Barton and G. A. Clark, pp. 21–48. Archeological Papers No. 7. American Anthropological Association, Washington, D.C.

1998 The Goals of Evolutionary Archaeology: History and Explanation. *Current Anthropology* 39:615–652.

1999 Americanist Stratigraphic Excavation and the Measurement of Culture Change. *Journal of Archaeological Method and Theory* 6:55–108.

2000 Measuring and Explaining Change in Artifact Variation with Clade-Diversity Diagrams. *Journal of Anthropological Archaeology* 19:39–74.

2001a Introduction to *Method and Theory in American Archaeology*, by G. R. Willey and P. Phillips, 11–178. University of Alabama Press, Tuscaloosa.

2001b On Misconceptions of Evolutionary Archaeology: Confusing Macroevolution and Microevolution. *Current Anthropology* 42:408–409.

2001c The Direct Historical Approach: Analogical Reasoning and Theory in Americanist Archaeology. *Journal of Archaeological Method and Theory* 8:303–342.

2002 Classification. In *A Handbook of Concepts in Modern Evolutionary Archaeology*, edited by J. P. Hart and J. E. Terrell, pp. 69–88. Greenwood Press, Westport, Conn.

2003a Cultural Traits: Units of Analysis in Early Twentieth-Century Anthropology. *Journal of Anthropological Research* 59:225–250.

2003b *W. C. McKern and the Midwestern Taxonomic Method*. University of Alabama Press, Tuscaloosa.

2004a Nomothetic Science and Idiographic History in Twentieth-Century Americanist Anthropology. *Journal of the History of the Behavioral Sciences* 40:77–96.

2004b A History of Normative Theory in Americanist Archaeology. *Journal of Archaeological Method and Theory* 11:369–396.

Lyman, R. L., M. J. O'Brien, and R. C. Dunnell
1997 *The Rise and Fall of Culture History*. Plenum, New York.

Lyman, R. L., S. Wolverton, and M. J. O'Brien
1998 Seriation, Superposition, and Interdigitation: A History of Americanist Graphic Depictions of Culture

Change. *American Antiquity* 63:239–261.

Lynch, M.
1980   Site Artifact Density and the Effectiveness of Shovel Probes. *Current Anthropology* 21:516–517.

Lynott, M. J.
1980   The Dynamics of Significance: An Example from Central Texas. *American Antiquity* 45:117–120.

1997   Ethical Principles and Archaeological Practice: Development of an Ethics Policy. *American Antiquity* 64:589–599.

Lynott, M. J., and A. Wylie (editors)
2000   *Ethics in American Archaeology.* Society for American Archaeology, Washington, D.C.

Lyon, E. A.
1996   *A New Deal for Southeastern Archaeology.* University of Alabama Press, Tuscaloosa.

Lyons, W. J.
1971   Science in an Unfriendly World. In *Science in America*, edited by J. C. Burnham, pp. 377–384. Holt, Rinehart and Winston, New York.

Mabry, J., J. M. Skibo, M. B. Schiffer, and K. Kvamme
1988   Use of a Falling-Weight Impact Tester for Assessing Ceramic Impact Strength. *American Antiquity* 53:829–839.

MacArthur, R. H., and E. R. Pianka
1966   On Optimal Use of a Patchy Environment. *American Naturalist* 100:603–609.

MacDonald, G. F., and D. Sanger
1968   Some Aspects of Microscope Analysis and Photomicrography of Lithic Artifacts. *American Antiquity* 33:237–240.

MacDonald, W. K. (editor)
1976   *Digging for Gold: Papers on Archaeology for Profit.* Technical Reports No. 5. Museum of Anthropology, University of Michigan, Ann Arbor.

MacNeish, R. S.
1958   *Preliminary Archaeological Investigations in the Sierra de Tamaulipas,*

Mexico. Transactions of the American Philosophical Society 48(6). Philadelphia.

1964   Ancient Mesoamerican Civilization. *Science* 143:531–537.

1992   *The Origins of Agriculture and Settled Life.* University of Oklahoma Press, Norman.

MacNeish, R. S., M. L. Fowler, A. García Cook, F. A. Peterson, and J. A. Neely
1972   *Excavations and Reconnaissance.* Vol. 5 of *The Prehistory of the Tehuacan Valley.* University of Texas Press, Austin.

MacWhite, E.
1956   On the Interpretation of Archeological Evidence in Historical and Sociological Terms. *American Anthropologist* 58:3–25.

Madden, L.
1983   On Significance for Cultural Resource Management: Dealing with Common Historical Sites. In *Forgotten Places and Things: Archaeological Perspectives on American History*, edited by A. E. Ward, pp. 55–61. Contributions to Anthropological Studies No. 3. Center for Anthropological Studies, Albuquerque, N.M.

Maddox, J.
1989   Where Next with Peer-Review? *Nature* 339:11.

Madrigal, L.
1998   *Statistics for Anthropology.* Cambridge University Press, Cambridge.

Madsen, D. B.
1993   Testing Diet Breadth Models: Examining Adaptive Change in the Late Prehistoric Great Basin. *Journal of Archaeological Science* 20:321–329.

Manners, R. A.
1973   Julian Haynes Steward, 1902–1972. *American Anthropologist* 75:886–903.

Marcus, J.
1976   *Emblem and State in the Classic Maya Lowlands: An Epigraphic Approach to Territorial Organiza-*

tion. Dumbarton Oaks, Washington, D.C.

1983   Topic 42: Stone Monuments and Tomb Murals of Monte Albán IIIa. In *The Cloud People: Divergent Evolution of the Zapotec and Mixtec Civilizations,* edited by K. V. Flannery and J. Marcus, pp. 137–143. Academic Press, New York.

1990a   (Editor) *Debating Oaxaca Archaeology.* Anthropological Papers No. 84. Museum of Anthropology, University of Michigan, Ann Arbor.

1990b   Preface to *Debating Oaxaca Archaeology,* edited by J. Marcus, pp. ix–x. Anthropological Papers No. 84. Museum of Anthropology, University of Michigan, Ann Arbor.

1993   *Mesoamerican Writing Systems: Propaganda, Myth, and History in Four Ancient Civilizations.* Princeton University Press, Princeton, N.J.

2003   Monumentality in Archaic States: Lessons Learned from Large-Scale Excavations of the Past. In *Theory and Practice in Mediterranean Archaeology: Old World and New World Perspectives,* edited by J. K. Papadopoulos and R. M. Leventhal, pp. 115–134. Cotsen Institute of Archaeology, University of California, Los Angeles.

Marquardt, W. H., A. Montet-White, and S. C. Scholtz

1982   Resolving the Crisis in Archaeological Collections Curation. *American Antiquity* 47:409–418.

Marshack, A.

1972   Upper Paleolithic Notation and Symbol. *Science* 178:817–828.

Martin, P. S[chultz], and H. E. Wright Jr. (editors)

1967   *Pleistocene Extinctions: The Search for a Cause.* Yale University Press, New Haven, Conn.

Martin, P. S[idney]

1971   The Revolution in Archaeology. *American Antiquity* 36:1–8.

Martin, P. S., and F. Plog

1973   *The Archaeology of Arizona: A Study of the Southwest Region.* Doubleday/Natural History Press, Garden City, N.Y.

Martin, P. S., G. I. Quimby, and D. Collier

1947   *Indians before Columbus: Twenty Thousand Years of North American History Revealed by Archeology.* University of Chicago Press, Chicago.

Martin, P. S., and J. B. Rinaldo

1950   Sites of the Reserve Phase, Pine Lawn Valley, Western New Mexico. *Fieldiana: Anthropology* 38:397–577. Field Museum of Natural History, Chicago.

Maruyama, M.

1963   The Second Cybernetics: Deviation-Amplifying Mutual Causal Processes. *American Scientist* 51:164–179.

Maschner, H. D. G.

1996   (Editor) *Darwinian Archaeologies.* Plenum, New York.

1998   Review of *Evolutionary Archaeology: Theory and Application,* edited by M. J. O'Brien. *Journal of the Royal Anthropological Institute* 4:354–355.

Mason, O. T.

1896   Influence of Environment upon Human Industries or Arts. *Annual Report of the Smithsonian Institution,* 1894, pp. 639–665. Washington, D.C.

Matson, R. G.

1980   The Proper Place of Multivariate Techniques in Archaeology. *American Antiquity* 45:340–344.

Maxwell, T.

1995   The Use of Comparative and Engineering Analyses in the Study of Prehistoric Agriculture. In *Evolutionary Archaeology: Methodological Issues,* edited by P. A. Teltser, pp. 113–128. University of Arizona Press, Tucson.

2001   Directionality, Function, and Adaptation in the Archaeological Record. In *Style and Function: Conceptual Issues in Evolutionary Archaeology,* edited by T. D. Hurt and G. F. M.

Rakita, pp. 41–50. Bergin and Garvey, Westport, Conn.

Mayr, E.
1982 *The Growth of Biological Thought: Diversity, Evolution, and Inheritance.* Harvard University Press, Cambridge, Mass.

McGee, W J
1893 Man and the Glacial Period. *American Anthropologist* 6:85–95.

McGimsey, C. R., III
1972 *Public Archeology.* Seminar Press, New York.
1976 The Past, the Present, the Future: Public Policy as a Dynamic Interface. In *Anthropology and the Public Interest: Fieldwork and Theory,* edited by P. R. Sanday, pp. 25–28. Academic Press, New York.
1985 "This, Too, Will Pass": Moss-Bennett in Perspective. *American Antiquity* 50:326–331.
1989 Perceptions of the Past: Public Archaeology and Moss-Bennett. *Southeastern Archaeology* 8:72–75.
2003 The Four Fields of Archaeology. *American Antiquity* 68:611–618.

McGimsey, C. R., III, and H. A. Davis (editors)
1977 *The Management of Archeological Resources: The Airlie House Report.* Society for American Archaeology, Washington, D.C.

McGuire, R. H.
1992 *A Marxist Archaeology.* Academic Press, New York.
1993 Archaeology and Marxism. *Archaeological Method and Theory* 5:101–158.

McGuire, R. H., and R. Paynter (editors)
1991 *The Archaeology of Inequality.* Blackwell, London.

McGuire, R. H., and D. Saitta
1996 Although They Have Petty Captains, They Obey Them Badly: The Dialectics of Prehispanic Western Pueblo Social Organization. *American Antiquity* 61:197–216.

McKern, W. C.
1937 Certain Culture Classification Problems in Middle Western Archaeology.

In *The Indianapolis Archaeological Conference,* pp. 70–82. Circular No. 17. National Research Council, Committee on State Archaeological Surveys, Washington, D.C.
1939 The Midwestern Taxonomic Method as an Aid to Archaeological Culture Study. *American Antiquity* 4:301–313.

McManamon, F. P.
1984 Discovering Sites Unseen. *Advances in Archaeological Method and Theory* 7:223–292.

Meggers, B. J.
1946 Recent Trends in American Ethnology. *American Anthropologist* 48:176–214.
1954 Environmental Limitation on the Development of Culture. *American Anthropologist* 56:801–824.
1955 The Coming of Age of American Archeology. In *New Interpretations of Aboriginal American Culture History,* edited by B. J. Meggers and C. Evans, pp. 116–129. Anthropological Society of Washington, Washington, D.C.
1959 (Editor) *Evolution and Anthropology: A Centennial Appraisal.* Anthropological Society of Washington, Washington, D.C.
1960 The Law of Cultural Evolution as a Practical Research Tool. In *Essays in the Science of Culture in Honor of Leslie A. White,* edited by G. E. Dole and R. L. Carneiro, pp. 302–316. Crowell, New York.
1961 Field Testing of Cultural Law: A Reply to Morris Opler. *Southwestern Journal of Anthropology* 17:352–354.
1968 (Editor) *Anthropological Archeology in the Americas.* Anthropological Society of Washington, Washington, D.C.

Meggers, B. J., and C. Evans
1955 (Editors) *New Interpretations of Aboriginal American Culture History.* Anthropological Society of Washington, Washington, D.C.

1962   The Machalilla Culture: An Early Formative Complex on the Ecuadorian Coast. *American Antiquity* 28:186–192.

Meggers, B. J., C. Evans, and E. Estrada

1965   *Early Formative Period of Coastal Ecuador: The Valdivia and Machalilla Phases.* Smithsonian Contributions to Anthropology No. 1. Washington, D.C.

Meighan, C. W.

1993   The Burial of American Archaeology. *California Scholar* 4:11–19.

Meighan, C. W., D. M. Pendergast, B. K. Swartz, Jr., and M. D. Wissler

1958a   Ecological Interpretation in Archaeology: Part I. *American Antiquity* 24:1–23.

1958b   Ecological Interpretation in Archaeology: Part II. *American Antiquity* 24:131–150.

Meltzer, D. J.

1979   Paradigms and the Nature of Change in American Archaeology. *American Antiquity* 44:644–657.

1981a   A Study of Style and Function in a Class of Tools. *Journal of Field Archaeology* 8:313–326.

1981b   Paradigms Lost, Paradigms Found? *American Antiquity* 46:662–665.

1983   The Antiquity of Man and the Development of American Archaeology. *Advances in Archaeological Method and Theory* 6:1–51.

1985   North American Archaeology and Archaeologists, 1879–1934. *American Antiquity* 50:249–260.

1990   Review of *Social Theory and Archaeology,* by M. Shanks and C. Tilley. *American Antiquity* 55:186–187.

Meltzer, D. J., D. D. Fowler, and J. A. Sabloff (editors)

1986   *American Archaeology, Past and Future: A Celebration of the Society for American Archaeology, 1935–1985.* Smithsonian Institution Press, Washington, D.C.

Merton, R. K.

1969   Behavior Patterns of Scientists. *American Scientist* 57:1–23.

Meskell, L.

2001   Archaeologies of Identity. In *Archaeological Theory Today,* edited by I. Hodder, pp. 187–213. Polity Press, Cambridge.

Miller, J. G.

1965a   Living Systems: Basic Concepts. *Behavioral Science* 10:193–237.

1965b   Living Systems: Structure and Process. *Behavioral Science* 10:337–379.

Miller, P. S.

1984   The Big Business of Small-Scale Surveys. *American Archeology* 4(1):11–14.

Mills, B. J. (editor)

1996   *Alternative Leadership Strategies in the Prehispanic Southwest.* University of Arizona Press, Tucson.

Mithen, S.

1988   Looking and Learning: Upper Palaeolithic Art and Information Gathering. *World Archaeology* 19:297–327.

1994   Technology and Society during the Middle Pleistocene. *Cambridge Archaeological Journal* 4:3–33.

1995   Paleolithic Archaeology and the Evolution of the Mind. *Journal of Archaeological Research* 3:305–322.

1996   *The Prehistory of the Mind: A Search for the Origins of Art, Science, and Religion.* Thames and Hudson, London.

2001   Archaeological Theory and Theories of Cognitive Evolution. In *Archaeological Theory Today,* edited by I. Hodder, pp. 98–121. Polity Press, Cambridge.

Moore, J., and E. Scott (editors)

1997   *Invisible People and Processes: Writing Gender and Childhood into European Archaeology.* Leicester University Press, London.

Moore, J. A., and A. S. Keene

1983   Archaeology and the Law of the Hammer. In *Archaeological Hammers and Theories,* edited by J. A. Moore and A. S. Keene, pp. 3–13. Academic Press, New York.

Moore, J. H.

1994a Ethnogenetic Theories of Human Evolution. *Research and Exploration* 10:10–23.

1994b Putting Anthropology Back Together Again: The Ethnogenetic Critique of Cladistic Theory. *American Anthropologist* 96:925–948.

Moratto, M. J., and R. E. Kelly

1977 Significance in Archaeology. *The Kiva* 42:193–202.

1978 Optimizing Strategies for Evaluating Archaeological Significance. *Advances in Archaeological Method and Theory* 1:1–30.

Morell, V.

1994 An Anthropological Culture Shift. *Science* 264:20–22.

Morgan, C. G.

1973 Archaeology and Explanation. *World Archaeology* 4:259–276.

1974 Explanation and Scientific Archaeology. *World Archaeology* 6:133–137.

Morgan, L. H.

1877 *Ancient Society.* Holt, New York.

Morse, D. F.

1975 Reply to Schiffer. In *The Cache River Archeological Project: An Experiment in Contract Archeology*, assembled by M. B. Schiffer and J. H. House, pp. 113–119. Research Series No. 8. Arkansas Archeological Survey, Fayetteville.

Morse, D. F., and A. C. Goodyear

1973 The Significance of the Dalton Adze in Northeast Arkansas. *Plains Anthropologist* 18:316–322.

Morton, S. G.

1839 *Crania Americana; or a Comparative View of the Skulls of Various Aboriginal Nations of North and South America.* Dobson, Philadelphia.

Mueller, J. W.

1974 *The Use of Sampling in Archaeological Survey.* Memoirs No. 28. Society for American Archaeology, Washington, D.C.

1975 (Editor) *Sampling in Archaeology.* University of Arizona Press, Tucson.

Munson, P. J.

1969 Comments on Binford's "Smudge Pits and Hide Smoking: The Use of Analogy in Archaeological Reasoning." *American Antiquity* 34:83–85.

Murdock, G. P.

1940 The Cross-Cultural Survey. *American Sociological Review* 5:361–370.

1956 How Culture Changes. In *Man, Culture, and Society*, edited by H. L. Shapiro, pp. 247–260. Oxford University Press, New York.

Murphy, R. F.

1970 Basin Ethnography and Ecological Theory. In *Language and Culture of Western North America: Essays in Honor of Sven S. Liljeblad*, edited by E. H. Swanson, Jr., pp. 152–171. Idaho State University Press, Pocatello.

1977 Introduction: The Anthropological Theories of Julian H. Steward. In *Evolution and Ecology: Essays on Social Transformation*, edited by J. C. Steward and R. F. Murphy, pp. 1–40. University of Illinois Press, Urbana.

Murray, T., and M. J. Walker

1988 Like WHAT? A Practical Question of Analogical Inference and Archaeological Meaningfulness. *Journal of Anthropological Archaeology* 7:248–287.

Nader, L.

1997 The Phantom Factor: Impact of the Cold War on Anthropology. In *The Cold War and the University: Toward an Intellectual History of the Postwar Years*, by N. Chomsky et al., pp. 107–146. Free Press, New York.

Nagel, E.

1961 *The Structure of Science.* Harcourt, Brace and World, New York.

Nance, J. D.

1971 Functional Interpretations from Microscopic Analysis. *American Antiquity* 36:361–366.

1979 Regional Subsampling and Statistical Inference in Forested Habitats. *American Antiquity* 44:172–176.

1983 Regional Sampling in Archaeological Survey: The Statistical Perspective. *Advances in Archaeological Method and Theory* 6:289–356.

Nance, J. D., and B. F. Ball

1986 No Surprises? The Reliability and Validity of Test Pit Sampling. *American Antiquity* 51:457–483.

Nash, D. T., and M. D. Petraglia (editors)

1987 *Natural Formation Processes and the Archaeological Record.* International Series No. 352. British Archaeological Reports, Oxford.

Nash, S. E.

1999 *Time, Trees, and Prehistory: Tree-Ring Dating and the Development of North American Archaeology, 1914 to 1950.* University of Utah Press, Salt Lake City.

2001 A Gentleman Scholar. *Archaeology* 54(3):60–63.

2003 Paul Sidney Martin. In *Curators, Collections, and Contexts: Anthropology at the Field Museum, 1893–2002,* edited by S. E. Nash and G. M. Feinman, pp. 165–177. *Fieldiana: Anthropology* 36. Field Museum of Natural History, Chicago.

Neff, H.

1992 Ceramics and Evolution. *Archaeological Method and Theory* 4:141–193.

2000 On Evolutionary Ecology and Evolutionary Archaeology: Some Common Ground? *Current Anthropology* 41:427–429.

2001 Differential Persistence of What? The Scale of Selection Issue in Evolutionary Archaeology. In *Style and Function: Conceptual Issues in Evolutionary Archaeology,* edited by T. D. Hurt and G. F. M. Rakita, pp. 25–40. Bergin and Garvey, Westport, Conn.

Neff, H., and D. O. Larson

1997 Methodology of Comparison in Evolutionary Archaeology. In *Rediscovering Darwin: Evolutionary Theory and Archeological Explanation,* edited by C. M. Barton and G. A. Clark, pp. 75–94. Archeological

Papers No. 7. American Anthropological Association, Washington, D.C.

Neiman, F. D.

1995 Stylistic Variation in Evolutionary Perspective: Inferences from Decorative Diversity and Interassemblage Distance in Illinois Woodland Ceramic Assemblages. *American Antiquity* 60:7–36.

Nelson, M. C., S. M. Nelson, and A. Wylie (editors)

1994 *Equity Issues for Women in Archaeology.* Archeological Papers No. 5. American Anthropological Association, Washington, D.C.

Nelson, N. C.

1906 [1996] Excavation of the Emeryville Shellmound, Being a Partial Report of Exploration for the Dep't. of Anthrop. during the Year 1906. In *Excavation of the Emeryville Shellmound, 1906: Nels C. Nelson's Final Report,* edited by J. M. Broughton, pp. 1–47. Contributions No. 54. Archaeological Research Facility, University of California, Berkeley.

1910 The Ellis Landing Shellmound. *University of California Publications in American Archaeology and Ethnology* 7:357–426.

1913 Ruins of Prehistoric New Mexico. *American Museum Journal* 13:62–81.

1916 Chronology of the Tano Ruins, New Mexico. *American Anthropologist* 18:159–180.

1932 The Origin and Development of Material Culture. *Sigma Xi Quarterly* 20:102–123.

Nelson, S. M.

1997 *Gender in Archaeology: Analyzing Power and Prestige.* AltaMira, Walnut Creek, Calif.

Nelson, S. M., and M. Rosen-Ayalon (editors)

2002 *In Pursuit of Gender: Worldwide Archaeological Approaches.* AltaMira, Walnut Creek, Calif.

Neupert, M. A.

2000 Clays of Contention: An Ethnoarchaeological Study of Factionalism and Clay Composition. *Journal of Archaeological Method and Theory* 7:249–272.

Nichols, D. L.

1996 An Overview of Regional Settlement Pattern Studies in Mesoamerica: 1960–1995. In *Arqueología Mesoamericana: Homenaje a William T. Sanders,* vol. 1, edited by A. G. Mastache, J. R. Parsons, R. S. Santley, and M. C. Serra Puche, pp. 59–95. Instituto Nacional de Antropología e Historia, Mexico City.

2004 The Rural and Urban Landscapes of the Aztec State. In *Mesoamerican Archaeology,* edited by J. A. Herndon and R. A. Joyce, pp. 265–295. Blackwell, London.

Nickerson, G. S.

1962 Professional, Amateur, and Pot-Hunter: The Archaeological Hierarchy in the United States. *Washington Archaeologist* 6(3):8–12.

1963 The Provenience, Reinterpretation, and Persistence of an American Archaeological Derogation. *American Antiquity* 28:555–557.

O'Brien, M. J.

1984 *Grassland, Forest, and Historical Settlement: An Analysis of Dynamics in Northeast Missouri.* University of Nebraska Press, Lincoln.

1987 Sedentism, Population Growth, and Resource Selection in the Woodland Midwest: A Review of Coevolutionary Developments. *Current Anthropology* 28:177–197.

1996 (Editor) *Evolutionary Archaeology: Theory and Application.* University of Utah Press, Salt Lake City.

2003 Nels Nelson and the Measure of Time. In *Picking the Lock of Time,* edited by J. Truncer, pp. 64–87. University Press of Florida, Gainesville.

O'Brien, M. J., J. Darwent, and R. L. Lyman

2001 Cladistics Is Useful for Reconstructing Archaeological Phylogenies: Palaeoindian Points from the Southeastern United States. *Journal of Archaeological Science* 28:1115–1136.

O'Brien, M. J., and T. D. Holland

1990 Variation, Selection, and the Archaeological Record. *Archaeological Method and Theory* 2:31–79.

1992 The Role of Adaptation in Archaeological Explanation. *American Antiquity* 57:3–59.

1995a Behavioral Archaeology and the Extended Phenotype. In *Expanding Archaeology,* edited by J. M. Skibo, W. H. Walker, and A. E. Nielsen, pp. 143–161. University of Utah Press, Salt Lake City.

1995b The Nature and Premise of a Selection-Based Archaeology. In *Evolutionary Archaeology: Methodological Issues,* edited by P. A. Teltser, pp. 175–200. University of Arizona Press, Tucson.

O'Brien, M. J., T. D. Holland, R. J. Hoard, and G. L. Fox

1994 Evolutionary Implications of Design and Performance Characteristics of Prehistoric Pottery. *Journal of Archaeological Method and Theory* 1:259–304.

O'Brien, M. J., and R. D. Leonard

2001 Style and Function: An Introduction to *Style and Function: Conceptual Issues in Evolutionary Archaeology,* edited by T. D. Hurt and G. F. M. Rakita, pp. 1–23. Bergin and Garvey, Westport, Conn.

O'Brien, M. J., and D. E. Lewarch (editors)

1981 *Plowzone Archeology: Contributions to Theory and Technique.* Publications in Anthropology No. 27. Vanderbilt University, Nashville, Tenn.

O'Brien, M. J., and R. L. Lyman

1998 *James A. Ford and the Growth of Americanist Archaeology.* University of Missouri Press, Columbia.

1999a *Seriation, Stratigraphy, and Index Fossils: The Backbone of Archaeological Dating.* Kluwer Academic/Plenum, New York.

1999b The Bureau of American Archaeology and Its Legacy to Southeastern

Archaeology. *Journal of the Southwest* 41:407–440.

2000a *Applying Evolutionary Archaeology: A Systematic Approach*. Kluwer Academic/Plenum, New York.

2000b Darwinian Evolutionism Is Applicable to Historical Archaeology. *International Journal of Historical Archaeology* 4:71–112.

2000c Evolutionary Archaeology: Reconstructing and Explaining Historical Lineages. In *Social Theory in Archaeology*, edited by M. B. Schiffer, pp. 126–142. University of Utah Press, Salt Lake City.

2002a The Epistemological Nature of Archaeological Units. *Anthropological Theory* 2:37–57.

2002b Evolutionary Archeology: Current Status and Future Prospects. *Evolutionary Anthropology* 11:26–36.

2003a *Cladistics and Archaeology*. University of Utah Press, Salt Lake City.

2003b Resolving Phylogeny: Evolutionary Archaeology's Fundamental Issue. In *Essential Tensions in Archaeological Method and Theory*, edited by T. L. VanPool and C. S. VanPool, pp. 115–135. University of Utah Press, Salt Lake City.

2003c Style, Function, Transmission: An Introduction to *Style, Function, Transmission: Evolutionary Archaeological Perspectives*, edited by M. J. O'Brien and R. L. Lyman, pp. 1–52. University of Utah Press, Salt Lake City.

2003d (Editors) *Style, Function, Transmission: Evolutionary Archaeological Perspectives*. University of Utah Press, Salt Lake City.

2004 History and Explanation in Archaeology. *Anthropological Theory* 4:173–197.

O'Brien, M. J., R. L. Lyman, and R. D. Leonard

1998 Basic Incompatibilities between Evolutionary and Behavioral Archaeology. *American Antiquity* 63:485–498.

2003 What Is Evolution? A Reply to Bamforth. *American Antiquity* 68:573–580.

O'Brien, M. J., R. L. Lyman, Y. Saab, E. Saab, J. Darwent, and D. S. Glover

2002 Two Issues in Archaeological Phylogenetics: Taxon Construction and Outgroup Selection. *Journal of Theoretical Biology* 215:133–150.

O'Brien, M. J., R. E. Warren, and D. E. Lewarch (editors)

1982 *The Cannon Reservoir Human Ecology Project: An Archaeological Study of Cultural Adaptations in the Southern Prairie Peninsula*. Academic Press, New York.

O'Connell, J. F.

1987 Alyawara Site Structure and Its Archaeological Implications. *American Antiquity* 52:74–108.

1995 Ethnoarchaeology Needs a General Theory of Human Behavior. *Journal of Archaeological Research* 3:205–255.

O'Connell, J. F., and K. Hawkes

1984 Food Choice and Foraging Sites among the Alyawara. *Journal of Anthropological Research* 40:504–535.

O'Connell, J. F., K. Hawkes, and N. G. Blurton Jones

1990 Reanalysis of Large Mammal Body Part Transport among the Hadza. *Journal of Archaeological Science* 17:301–316.

Odell, G. H.

1975 Micro-Wear in Perspective: A Sympathetic Response to Lawrence H. Keeley. *World Archaeology* 7:226–240.

2001 Stone Tool Research at the End of the Millennium: Classification, Function, and Behavior. *Journal of Archaeological Research* 9:45–100.

Odell, G. H., and F. Odell-Vereecken

1980 Verifying the Reliability of Lithic Use-Wear Assessments by "Blind Tests": The Low-Power Approach. *Journal of Field Archaeology* 7:87–120.

O'Hara, R. J.
  1988 Homage to Clio, or, Toward an His-
       torical Philosophy for Evolutionary
       Biology. *Systematic Zoology*
       37:142–155.
Olausson, D. S.
  1980 Starting from Scratch: The History of
       Edge-Wear Research from 1838 to
       1978. *Lithic Technology* 9:48–60.
Opler, M. E.
  1946 A Recent Trend in the Misrepresenta-
       tion of the Work of American Eth-
       nologists. *American Anthropologist*
       48:669–671.
  1961 Cultural Evolution, Southern Atha-
       paskans, and Chronology in Theory.
       *Southwestern Journal of Anthropol-
       ogy* 17:1–20.
  1962 Two Converging Lines of Influence in
       Cultural Evolutionary Theory. *Amer-
       ican Anthropologist* 64:524–547.
  1963 Cultural Anthropology: An Adden-
       dum to a "Working Paper." *Ameri-
       can Anthropologist* 65:897–902.
Orme, B.
  1973 Archaeology and Ethnography. In
       The Explanation of Culture Change,
       edited by C. Renfrew, pp. 481–492.
       Duckworth, London.
  1974 Twentieth-Century Prehistorians and
       the Idea of Ethnographic Parallels.
       Man 9:199–212.
Orton, C.
  2000 *Sampling in Archaeology.* Cambridge
       University Press, Cambridge.
Packard, V. O.
  1960 *The Waste Makers.* New York,
       McKay.
Pailes, R.
  1981 On the Archaeology of the Absurd
       and Green Slimy Frogs: A Plea for
       Civility and Mutual Respect. *Ameri-
       can Antiquity* 46:468.
Park, R. E., E. W. Burgess, and R. D. McKenzie
  1925 *The City.* University of Chicago
       Press, Chicago.
Parrini, P., W. C. Salmon, and M. H. Salmon
       (editors)

  2003 *Logical Empiricism: Historical &
       Contemporary Perspectives.* Univer-
       sity of Pittsburgh Press, Pittsburgh.
Parsons, J. R.
  1971 *Prehistoric Settlement Patterns in the
       Texcoco Region, Mexico.* Memoirs
       No. 3. Museum of Anthropology,
       University of Michigan, Ann Arbor.
  1972 Archaeological Settlement Patterns.
       Annual Review of Anthropology
       1:127–150.
Parsons, J. R., E. Brumfiel, M. Parsons, and D.
       Wilson
  1982 *Prehispanic Settlement Patterns in
       the Southern Valley of Mexico: The
       Chalco-Xochimilco Region.* Memoirs
       No. 14. Museum of Anthropology,
       University of Michigan, Ann Arbor.
Patterson, T. C.
  1986 The Last Sixty Years: Toward a
       Social History of Americanist Arche-
       ology in the United States. *American
       Anthropologist* 88:7–26.
  1989 History and the Post-Processual
       Archaeologies. *Man* 24:555–566.
  1990 Some Theoretical Tensions within
       and between the Processual and Post-
       processual Archaeologies. *Journal of
       Anthropological Archaeology*
       9:189–200.
  1995 *Toward a Social History of Archae-
       ology in the United States.* Harcourt
       Brace, Fort Worth, Tex.
Pauketat, T. R.
  2000 The Tragedy of the Commoners. In
       Agency in Archaeology, edited by
       M.-A. Dobres and J. Robb, pp.
       130–147. Routledge, New York.
  2001 Practice and History in Archaeology:
       An Emerging Paradigm. *Anthropo-
       logical Theory* 1:73–98.
  2003a Materiality and the Immaterial in
       Historical–Processual Archaeology. In
       *Essential Tensions in Archaeological
       Method and Theory*, edited by T. L.
       VanPool and C. S. VanPool, pp.
       41–53. University of Utah Press, Salt
       Lake City.

2003b Resettled Farmers and the Making of a Mississippian Polity. *American Antiquity* 68:39–66.

Peace, W. J.
1993 Leslie White and Evolutionary Theory. *Dialectical Anthropology* 18:123–151.

Peace, W. J., and D. H. Price
2001 The Cold War Context of the FBI's Investigation of Leslie A. White. *American Anthropologist* 103:164–167.

2003 Un-American Anthropological Thought: The Opler / Meggers Exchange. *Journal of Anthropological Research* 59:183–203.

Pearsall, D. M.
2001 *Paleoethnobotany: A Handbook of Procedures*. Academic Press, San Diego.

Perlman, J. L.
1977 Comments on Explanation, and on Stability and Change. In *Explanation of Prehistoric Change*, edited by J. N. Hill, pp. 319–333. University of New Mexico Press, Albuquerque.

Petersen, K. L., V. L. Clay, M. H. Matthews, and S. W. Neusius (compilers)
1985 *Studies in Environmental Archaeology*. Dolores Archaeological Program. Report submitted to the Bureau of Reclamation, Denver.

Petersen, K. L., and J. D. Orcutt (compilers)
1987 *Supporting Studies: Settlement and Environment*. Dolores Archaeological Program. Report submitted to the Bureau of Reclamation, Denver.

Petrie, W. M. F.
1899 Sequences in Prehistoric Remains. *Journal of the Royal Anthropological Institute of Great Britain and Ireland* 29:295–301.

1901 *Diospolis Parva*. Memoir No. 20. Egypt Exploration Fund, London.

Pfeffer, M. T.
2001 Implications of New Studies of Hawaiian Fishhook Variability for Our Understanding of Polynesian Settlement History. In *Style and Function: Conceptual Issues in Evolutionary Archaeology*, edited by T. D. Hurt and G. F. M. Rakita, pp. 165–181. Bergin and Garvey, Westport, Conn.

Phillips, P.
1955 American Archaeology and General Anthropological Theory. *Southwestern Journal of Anthropology* 11:246–250.

1958 Application of the Wheat–Gifford–Wasley Taxonomy to Eastern Ceramics. *American Antiquity* 24:117–125.

Phillips, P., J. A. Ford, and J. B. Griffin
1951 *Archaeological Survey in the Lower Mississippi Valley, 1940-1947*. Papers Vol. 25. Peabody Museum of Archaeology and Ethnology, Harvard University, Cambridge, Mass.

Phillips, P., and G. R. Willey
1953 Method and Theory in American Archaeology: An Operational Basis for Culture-Historical Integration. *American Anthropologist* 55:615–633.

Piperno, D. R., and D. M. Pearsall
1998 *The Silica Bodies of Tropical American Grasses: Morphology, Taxonomy, and Implications for Grass Systematics and Fossil Phytolith Identification*. Smithsonian Institution Press, Washington, D.C.

Plog, F. T.
1968 *Archaeological Survey—A New Perspective*. M.A. thesis, Department of Anthropology, University of Chicago.

1973a Diachronic Anthropology. In *Research and Theory in Current Archeology*, edited by C. L. Redman, pp. 181–198. Wiley, New York.

1973b Laws, Systems of Laws, and the Explanation of Observed Variation. In *The Explanation of Culture Change: Models in Prehistory*, edited by C. Renfrew, pp. 649–661. Duckworth, London.

1974 *The Study of Prehistoric Change*. New York, Academic Press.

1975 Systems Theory in Archeological Research. *Annual Review of Anthropology* 4:207–224.

1982 Is a Little Philosophy (Science?) a Dangerous Thing? In *Theory and Explanation in Archaeology: The Southampton Conference,* edited by C. Renfrew, M. J. Rowlands, and B. A. Segraves, pp. 25–33. Academic Press, New York.

Plog, S.

1976a Measurement of Prehistoric Interaction between Communities. In *The Early Mesoamerican Village,* edited by K. V. Flannery, pp. 255–272. Academic Press, New York.

1976b The Inference of Prehistoric Social Organization from Ceramic Design Variability. *Michigan Discussions in Anthropology* 1:1–47.

1976c Relative Efficiencies of Sampling Techniques for Archeological Surveys. In *The Early Mesoamerican Village,* edited by K. V. Flannery, pp. 136–160. Academic Press, New York.

1978 Social Interaction and Stylistic Similarity: A Reanalysis. *Advances in Archaeological Method and Theory* 1:143–182.

1980 *Stylistic Variation in Prehistoric Ceramics.* Cambridge University Press, New York.

1983 Analysis of Style in Artifacts. *Annual Review of Anthropology* 12:125–142.

Plog, S., F. Plog, and W. Wait

1978 Decision Making in Modern Surveys. *Advances in Archaeological Method and Theory* 1:384–421.

Pond, A. W.

1930 *Primitive Methods of Working Stone: Based on Experiments of Halvor L. Skavlen.* Logan Museum, Beloit College, Beloit, Wis.

Popper, K.

1959 *The Logic of Scientific Discovery.* English translation. Basic Books, New York.

1968 *Conjectures and Refutations: The Growth of Scientific Knowledge.* Harper and Row, New York.

1970 Normal Science and Its Dangers. In *Criticism and the Growth of Knowledge,* edited by I. Lakatos and A.

Musgrave, pp. 51–58. Cambridge University Press, Cambridge.

1983 *Realism and the Aim of Science.* Rowman and Littlefield, Totowa, N.J.

Preucel, R. W.

1991 The Philosophy of Archaeology. In *Processual and Postprocessual Archaeologies: Multiple Ways of Knowing the Past,* edited by R. W. Preucel, pp. 17–29. Occasional Paper No. 10. Center for Archaeological Investigations, Southern Illinois University at Carbondale.

1995 The Postprocessual Condition. *Journal of Archaeological Research* 3:147–175.

1999 Review of *Evolutionary Archaeology: Theory and Application,* by M. J. O'Brien. *Journal of Field Archaeology* 26:93–99.

Preucel, R. W., and I. Hodder

1996 Communicating Present Pasts. In *Contemporary Archaeology in Theory,* edited by R. W. Preucel and I. Hodder, pp. 3–20. Blackwell, Oxford.

Price, D. H.

1997 Anthropologists on Trial: The Lessons of McCarthyism. Paper presented at the 96th annual meeting of the American Anthropological Association, Washington, D.C.

Putnam, F. W.

1897 Early Man of the Delaware Valley. *Proceedings of the American Association for the Advancement of Science* 46:344–348.

Raab, L. M.

1976a *The Structure of Prehistoric Community Organization at Santa Rosa Wash, Southern Arizona.* Ph.D. dissertation, Department of Anthropology, Arizona State University. Tempe.

1976b (Compiler) *Pine Mountain: A Study of Prehistoric Human Ecology in the Arkansas Ozarks.* Research Report No. 7. Arkansas Archeological Survey, Fayetteville.

1982 Cultural Resource Management in the University: Getting What We Deserve. *Journal of Field Archaeology* 9:126–128.

1984 Toward an Understanding of the Ethics and Values of Research Design in Archaeology. In *Ethics and Values in Archaeology*, edited by E. L. Green, pp. 75–88. Free Press, New York.

Raab, L. M., and A. C. Goodyear

1984 Middle-Range Theory in Archaeology: A Critical Review of Its Origins and Applications. *American Antiquity* 49:255–268.

Raab, L. M., and T. C. Klinger

1977 A Critical Appraisal of "Significance" in Contract Archaeology. *American Antiquity* 42:629–634.

1979 A Reply to Sharrock and Grayson on Archaeological Significance. *American Antiquity* 44:328–329.

Raab, L. M., T. C. Klinger, M. B. Schiffer, and A. C. Goodyear

1980 Clients, Contracts, and Profits: Conflicts in Public Archaeology. *American Anthropologist* 82:539–551.

Radin, P.

1933 *The Method and Theory of Ethnology: An Essay in Criticism.* McGraw-Hill, New York.

Ramenofsky, A. F.

1990 Historical Science and Contact Period Studies. In *Columbian Consequences: Archaeological and Historical Perspectives on the Spanish Borderlands East,* vol. 2, edited by D. H. Thomas, pp. 31–48. Smithsonian Institution Press, Washington, D.C.

1995 Evolutionary Theory and Native American Artifact Change in the Postcontact Period. In *Evolutionary Archaeology: Methodological Issues,* edited by P. A. Teltser, pp. 129–147. University of Arizona Press, Tucson.

1998 Evolutionary Theory and the Native American Record of Artifact Replacement. In *Studies in Culture Contact,* edited by J. G. Cusick, pp. 77–101. Occasional Paper No. 25.

Center for Archaeological Investigations, Southern Illinois University at Carbondale.

Ramenofsky, A. F., and A. Steffen

1998 Units as Tools of Measurement. In *Unit Issues in Archaeology: Measuring Time, Space, and Material,* edited by A. F. Ramenofsky and A. Steffen, pp. 3–17. University of Utah Press, Salt Lake City.

Rappaport, R. A.

1967 Ritual Regulation of Environmental Relations among a New Guinea People. *Ethnology* 6:17–30.

1968 *Pigs for the Ancestors: Ritual in the Ecology of a New Guinea People.* Yale University Press, New Haven, Conn.

2000 *Pigs for the Ancestors: Ritual in the Ecology of a New Guinea People.* 2nd ed. Waveland, Prospect Heights, Ill.

Rathje, W. L.

1974 The Garbage Project: A New Way of Looking at the Problems of Archaeology. *Archaeology* 27:236–241.

Rathje, W. L., and C. Murphy

1992 *Rubbish! The Archaeology of Garbage.* HarperCollins, New York.

Rathje, W. L., and M. B. Schiffer

1982 *Archaeology.* Harcourt Brace Jovanovich, New York.

Read, D. W.

1974 Some Comments on the Use of Mathematical Models in Anthropology. *American Antiquity* 39:3–15.

Read, D. W., and A. L. Christenson

1978 Comments on "Cluster Analysis and Archaeological Classification." *American Antiquity* 43:505–506.

Read, D. W., and S. A. LeBlanc

1978 Descriptive Statements, Covering Laws, and Theories in Archaeology. *Current Anthropology* 19:307–335.

Reaves, R. W., III

1976 Historic Preservation Laws and Policies: Background and History. In *Symposium on Dynamics of Cultural Resource Management*, edited by R. T. Matheny and D. L. Berge, pp.

24–32. Archeological Report No. 10. USDA Forest Service, Southwestern Region. Albuquerque, N.M.

Redfield, R.
1947 The Folk Society. *American Journal of Sociology* 52:293–308.

Redman, C. L.
1973a (Editor) *Research and Theory in Current Archeology*. Wiley, New York.
1973b Multistage Fieldwork and Analytical Techniques. *American Antiquity* 38:61–79.
1991 Distinguished Lecture in Archeology: In Defense of the Seventies—The Adolescence of New Archeology. *American Anthropologist* 93:295–307.
1999 *Human Impact on Ancient Environments*. University of Arizona Press, Tucson.

Redman, C. L., and P. J. Watson
1970 Systematic, Intensive Surface Collection. *American Antiquity* 35:279–291.

Reid, J. J.
1985 Formation Processes for the Practical Prehistorian. In *Structure and Process in Southeastern Archaeology,* edited by R. S. Dickens, Jr. and H. T. Ward, pp. 11–13. University of Alabama Press, Tuscaloosa.
1990 Peer Review at *American Antiquity*. *American Antiquity* 55:665–666.
1995 Four Strategies after Twenty Years: A Return to Basics. In *Expanding Archaeology*, edited by J. M. Skibo, W. H. Walker, and A. E. Nielsen, pp. 15–21. University of Utah Press, Salt Lake City.

Reid, J. J., W. L. Rathje, and M. B. Schiffer
1974 Expanding Archaeology. *American Antiquity* 39:125–126.

Reid, J. J., M. B. Schiffer, and W. L. Rathje
1975 Behavioral Archaeology: Four Strategies. *American Anthropologist* 77:864–869.

Reid, J. J., and S. M. Whittlesey
2005 *Thirty Years into Yesterday: A History of Archaeology at Grasshopper Pueblo*. University of Arizona Press, Tucson.

Reif, F.
1961 The Competitive World of the Pure Scientist. *Science* 134:1957–1962.

Reitz, E. J., and E. S. Wing
1999 *Zooarchaeology*. Cambridge University Press, New York.

Renfrew, C.
1973a *Before Civilization: The Radiocarbon Revolution and Prehistoric Europe*. Cape, London.
1973b Review of *Explanation in Archeology: An Explicitly Scientific Approach,* by P. J. Watson, S. A. LeBlanc, and C. L. Redman. *American Anthropologist* 75:1928–1930.
1973c (Editor) *The Explanation of Culture Change: Models in Prehistory*. Duckworth, London.
1974 Beyond a Subsistence Economy: The Evolution of Social Organization in Prehistoric Europe. In *Reconstructing Complex Societies: An Archaeological Colloquium*, edited by C. B. Moore, pp. 69–95. Supplement No. 20. Bulletin of the American Schools of Oriental Research, Boston.
1983 Divided We Stand: Aspects of Archaeology and Information. *American Antiquity* 48:3–16.
1987a An Interview with Lewis Binford. *Current Anthropology* 28:683–694.
1987b *Archaeology and Language: The Puzzle of Indo-European Origins*. Cape, London.
1992 Archaeology, Genetics and Linguistic Diversity. *Man* 27:445–478.
1999 Time Depth, Convergence Theory and Innovation in Proto-Indo-European: "Old Europe" as a PIE Linguistic Area. *Journal of Indo-European Studies* 27:257–293.

Renfrew, C., and P. Bahn
2000 *Archaeology: Theories, Methods, and Practice*. 3rd ed. Thames and Hudson, London.

Renfrew, C., and K. Boyle (editors)
2000 *Archaeogenetics: DNA and the Population Prehistory of Europe.*

McDonald Institute for Archaeological Research, Cambridge.

Renfrew, C., A. McMahon, and L. Trask (editors)

2000 *Time Depth in Historical Linguistics.* McDonald Institute for Archaeological Research, Cambridge.

Renfrew, C., C. S. Peebles, I. Hodder, B. Bender, K. V. Flannery, and J. Marcus

1993 What Is Cognitive Archaeology? *Cambridge Archaeological Journal* 3:247–270.

Renfrew, C., M. J. Rowlands, and B. A. Segraves (editors)

1982 *Theory and Explanation in Archaeology: The Southampton Conference.* Academic Press, New York.

Rhode, D.

1999 The Role of Paleoecology in the Development of Great Basin Archaeology, and Vice-Versa. In *Models for the Millennium: Great Basin Anthropology Today,* edited by C. Beck, pp. 29–49. University of Utah Press, Salt Lake City.

Rice, P. M.

1987 *Pottery Analysis: A Sourcebook.* University of Chicago Press, Chicago.

Richerson, P. J., and R. Boyd

1992 Cultural Inheritance and Evolutionary Ecology. In *Evolutionary Ecology and Human Behavior,* edited by E. A. Smith and B. Winterhalder, pp. 61–92. Aldine, Hawthorne, N.Y.

Riley, T. J.

1974 Constraints on Dimensions of Variance. *American Antiquity* 39:489–490.

Rindos, D.

1980 Symbiosis, Instability, and the Origins and Spread of Agriculture: A New Model. *Current Anthropology* 21:751–772.

1984 *The Origins of Agriculture: An Evolutionary Perspective.* Academic Press, Orlando.

Robinson, W. S.

1951 A Method for Chronologically Ordering Archaeological Deposits. *American Antiquity* 16:293–301.

Robinson, W. S., and G. W. Brainerd

1952 Robinson's Coefficient of Agreement—A Rejoinder. *American Antiquity* 18:60–61.

Rootenberg, S.

1964 Archaeological Field Sampling. *American Antiquity* 30:181–188.

Roper, D. C.

1976 Lateral Displacement of Artifacts due to Plowing. *American Antiquity* 41:372–374.

Rouse, I. B.

1939 *Prehistory of Haiti: A Study in Method.* Publications in Anthropology No. 21. Yale University, New Haven, Conn.

1954 On the Use of the Concept of Area Co-Tradition. *American Antiquity* 19:221–225.

1955 On the Correlation of Phases of Culture. *American Anthropologist* 57:713–722.

1960 The Classification of Artifacts in Archaeology. *American Antiquity* 25:313–323.

1972 Settlement Patterns in Archaeology. In *Man, Settlement, and Urbanism,* edited by P. J. Ucko, R. Tringham, and G. W. Dimbleby, pp. 95–107. Duckworth, London.

Rowe, J. H.

1975 The Spelling of "Archaeology." *American Anthropological Association Newsletter* 16 (June):11–12.

Rudner, R. S.

1966 *Philosophy of Social Science.* Prentice-Hall, Englewood Cliffs, N.J.

Sabloff, J. A., and W. Ashmore

2001 An Aspect of Archaeology's Recent Past and Its Relevance in the New Millennium. In *Archaeology at the Millennium: A Sourcebook,* edited by G. M. Feinman and T. D. Price, pp. 11–32. Kluwer Academic/Plenum, New York.

Sabloff, J. A., T. W. Beale, and A. M. Kurland, Jr.

1973 Recent Developments in Archaeology. *Annals of the American*

Academy of Political and Social Science 408:103–118.

Sabloff, J. A., and G. R. Willey

1967   The Collapse of Maya Civilization in the Southern Lowlands: A Consideration of History and Process. *Southwestern Journal of Anthropology* 23:311–336.

Sabloff, P. L. W.

1998   *Conversations with Lew Binford: Drafting the New Archaeology.* University of Oklahoma Press, Norman.

Sackett, J. R.

1966   Quantitative Analysis of Upper Paleolithic Stone Tools. *American Anthropologist* 68:356–394.

1968   Method and Theory of Upper Paleolithic Archaeology in Southwestern France. In *New Perspectives in Archeology,* edited by S. R. Binford and L. R. Binford, pp. 61–83. Aldine, Chicago.

1969   Factor Analysis and Artifact Typology. *American Anthropologist* 71:1125–1130.

1981   From de Mortillet to Bordes: A Century of French Palaeolithic Research. In *Toward a History of Archaeology,* edited by G. Daniel, pp. 85–99. Thames and Hudson, London.

Sahlins, M. D.

1958   *Social Stratification in Polynesia.* University of Washington Press, Seattle.

1968   *Tribesmen.* Prentice-Hall, Englewood Cliffs, N.J.

Sahlins, M. D., and E. R. Service (editors)

1960   *Evolution and Culture.* University of Michigan Press, Ann Arbor.

Saitta, D. J.

1992   Radical Archaeology and Middle-Range Theory. *Antiquity* 66:886–897.

Salmon, M. H.

1975   Confirmation and Explanation in Archaeology. *American Antiquity* 40:459–464.

1976   "Deductive" versus "Inductive" Archaeology. *American Antiquity* 41:376–381.

1978   What Can Systems Theory Do for Archaeology? *American Antiquity* 43:174–183.

1981   Ascribing Functions to Archaeological Objects. *Philosophy of the Social Sciences* 11:19–26.

1982   *Philosophy and Archaeology.* Academic Press, New York.

Salmon, M. H., and W. C. Salmon

1979   Alternative Models of Scientific Explanation. *American Anthropologist* 81:61–74.

Salmon, W. C.

1953   The Uniformity of Nature. *Philosophy and Phenomenological Research* 14:39–48.

1967   *The Foundations of Scientific Inference.* University of Pittsburgh Press, Pittsburgh.

1971   *Statistical Explanation and Statistical Relevance.* University of Pittsburgh Press, Pittsburgh.

Sanders, W. T.

1956   The Central Mexican Symbiotic Region. In *Prehistoric Settlement Patterns in the New World,* edited by G. R. Willey, pp. 115–127. Publications in Anthropology No. 23. Viking Fund, Wenner-Gren Foundation for Anthropological Research, New York.

1965   *The Cultural Ecology of the Teotihuacan Valley.* Department of Sociology and Anthropology, Pennsylvania State University, University Park.

1967   Settlement Patterns. In *Social Anthropology,* edited by M. Nash, vol. 6 of *Handbook of Middle American Indians,* pp. 53–86. University of Texas Press, Austin.

1971   Settlement Patterns in Central Mexico. In *Archaeology of Northern Mesoamerica,* part I, edited by G. Ekholm and I. Bernal, vol. 10 of *Handbook of Middle American Indians,* pp. 3–44. University of Texas Press, Austin.

1974   Chiefdom to State: Political Evolution at Kaminaljuyu, Guatemala. In *Reconstructing Complex Societies:*

An Archaeological Colloquium, edited by C. B. Moore, pp. 97–116. Supplement No. 20. Bulletin of the American Schools of Oriental Research, Boston.

Sanders, W. T., and D. L. Nichols

1988 Ecological Theory and Cultural Evolution in the Valley of Oaxaca. *Current Anthropology* 29:33–80.

Sanders, W. T., J. R. Parsons, and R. Santley

1979 *The Basin of Mexico: The Cultural Ecology of a Civilization.* Academic Press, New York.

Sanders, W. T., and B. Price

1968 *Mesoamerica: The Evolution of a Civilization.* Random House, New York.

Santley, R. S., and P. J. Arnold III

1984 Obscured by the Clouds. *Journal of Anthropological Research* 40:211–230.

Saraydar, S., and I. Shimada

1971 A Quantitative Comparison of Efficiency between a Stone Axe and a Steel Axe. *American Antiquity* 36:216–217.

1973 Experimental Archaeology: A New Outlook. *American Antiquity* 38:344–350.

Schaberg, J.

2002 *The Resurrection of Mary Magdalene: Legends, Apocrypha, and the Christian Testament.* Continuum, New York.

Scharnberger, C. K., J. R. Bushman, and J. H. Shea

1983 Comments and Reply on "Twelve Fallacies of Uniformitarianism." *Geology* 11:312–313.

Scheps, S.

1982 Statistical Blight. *American Antiquity* 47:836–851.

Schiffer, M. B.

1972a Archaeological Context and Systemic Context. *American Antiquity* 37:156–165.

1972b Cultural Laws and the Reconstruction of Past Lifeways. *Kiva* 37:148–157.

1974 On Whallon's Use of Dimensional Analysis of Variance at Guila Naquitz. *American Antiquity* 39:490–492.

1975a Archeological Research and Contract Archeology. In *The Cache River Archeological Project: An Experiment in Contract Archeology,* assembled by M. B. Schiffer and J. H. House, pp. 1–7. Research Series No. 8. Arkansas Archeological Survey, Fayetteville.

1975b Archaeology as Behavioral Science. *American Anthropologist* 77:836–848.

1975c Review of *Contemporary Archaeology,* edited by M. P. Leone. *American Antiquity* 40:508–510.

1976 *Behavioral Archeology.* Academic Press, New York.

1978a Methodological Issues in Ethnoarchaeology. In *Explorations in Ethnoarchaeology,* edited by R. A. Gould, pp. 229–247. University of New Mexico Press, Albuquerque.

1978b Preface to *Advances in Archaeological Method and Theory* 1:xiii–xv.

1979a A Preliminary Consideration of Behavioral Change. In *Transformations: Mathematical Approaches to Culture Change,* edited by C. Renfrew and K. Cooke, pp. 353–368. Academic Press, New York.

1979b Some Impacts of Cultural Resource Management on American Archaeology. In *Archaeological Resource Management in Australia and Oceania,* edited by J. R. McKinlay and K. L. Jones, pp. 1–11. New Zealand Historic Places Trust, Wellington.

1981 Some Issues in the Philosophy of Archaeology. *American Antiquity* 46:899–908.

1983 Toward the Identification of Formation Processes. *American Antiquity* 48:675–706.

1985a Review of *Working at Archaeology,* by L. R. Binford. *American Antiquity* 50:191–193.

1985b Is There a "Pompeii Premise" in Archaeology? *Journal of Anthropological Research* 41:18–41.

1987 *Formation Processes of the Archaeological Record.* University of New Mexico Press, Albuquerque.

1988 The Structure of Archaeological Theory. *American Antiquity* 53:461–485.

1989 Formation Processes of Broken K Pueblo: Some Hypotheses. In *Quantifying Diversity in Archaeology,* edited by R. D. Leonard and G. T. Jones, pp. 37–58. Cambridge University Press, Cambridge.

1991 *The Portable Radio in American Life.* University of Arizona Press, Tucson.

1995a A Personal History of Behavioral Archaeology. In *Behavioral Archaeology: First Principles,* by M. B. Schiffer, pp. 1–24. University of Utah Press, Salt Lake City.

1995b Social Theory and History in Behavioral Archaeology. In *Expanding Archaeology,* edited by J. M. Skibo, W. H. Walker, and A. E. Nielsen, pp. 22–35. University of Utah Press, Salt Lake City.

1996 Some Relationships between Behavioral and Evolutionary Archaeologies. *American Antiquity* 61:643–662.

1999 Behavioral Archaeology: Some Clarifications. *American Antiquity* 64:166–168.

2000a (Editor) *Social Theory in Archaeology.* University of Utah Press, Salt Lake City.

2000b Social Theory in Archaeology: Building Bridges. In *Social Theory in Archaeology,* edited by M. B. Schiffer, pp. 1–13. University of Utah Press, Salt Lake City.

2001 The Explanation of Long-Term Technological Change. In *Anthropological Perspectives on Technology,* edited by M. B. Schiffer, pp. 215–235. University of New Mexico Press, Albuquerque.

2002 Studying Technological Differentiation: The Case of 18th-Century Electrical Technology. *American Anthropologist* 104:1148–1161.

Schiffer, M. B., T. C. Butts, and K. K. Grimm

1994 *Taking Charge: The Electric Automobile in America.* Smithsonian Institution Press, Washington, D.C.

Schiffer, M. B., T. E. Downing, and M. McCarthy

1981 Waste Not, Want Not: An Ethnoarchaeological Study of Reuse in Tucson, Arizona. In *Modern Material Culture: The Archaeology of Us,* edited by R. A. Gould and M. B. Schiffer, pp. 67–86. Academic Press, New York.

Schiffer, M. B., and G. J. Gumerman

1977a (Editors) *Conservation Archaeology: A Guide for Cultural Resource Management Studies.* Academic Press, New York.

1977b Cultural Resource Management. Part I of *Conservation Archaeology: A Guide for Cultural Resource Management Studies,* edited by M. B. Schiffer and G. J. Gumerman, pp. 1–17. Academic Press, New York.

Schiffer, M. B., K. L. Hollenback, and C. L. Bell

2003 *Draw the Lightning Down: Benjamin Franklin and Electrical Technology in the Age of Enlightenment.* University of California Press, Berkeley.

Schiffer, M. B., and J. H. House

1975 (Assemblers) *The Cache River Archeological Project: An Experiment in Contract Archeology.* Research Series No. 8. Arkansas Archeological Survey, Fayetteville.

1977a Cultural Resource Management and Archaeological Research: The Cache Project. *Current Anthropology* 18:43–68.

1977b An Approach to Assessing Scientific Significance. In *Conservation Archaeology: A Guide for Cultural Resource Management Studies,* edited by M. B. Schiffer and G. J. Gumerman, pp. 249–257. Academic Press, New York.

Schiffer, M. B., and A. R. Miller
  1999a A Behavioral Theory of Meaning. In
        *Pottery and People: A Dynamic
        Interaction,* edited by J. M. Skibo
        and G. M. Feinman, pp. 199–217.
        University of Utah Press, Salt Lake
        City.
  1999b *The Material Life of Human Beings:
        Artifacts, Behavior, and Communica-
        tion.* Routledge, London.
Schiffer, M. B., and J. M. Skibo
  1987 Theory and Experiment in the Study
        of Technological Change. *Current
        Anthropology* 28:595–622.
  1989 A Provisional Theory of Ceramic
        Abrasion. *American Anthropologist*
        91:101–115.
  1997 The Explanation of Artifact Variabil-
        ity. *American Antiquity* 62:27–50.
Schiffer, M. B., A. P. Sullivan, and T. C. Klinger
  1978 The Design of Archaeological Sur-
        veys. *World Archaeology* 10:1–28.
Schiffer, M. B., and S. Wells
  1982 Archaeological Surveys: Past and
        Future. In *Hohokam and Patayan:
        Prehistory of Southwestern Arizona,*
        edited by R. H. McGuire and M. B.
        Schiffer, pp. 345–383. Academic
        Press, New York.
Schmidt, N. J.
  1984 NTIS Reports on Contract Archeol-
        ogy: Their Bibliographic Characteris-
        tics and Place in an Academic
        Library Collection. *American Antiq-
        uity* 49:586–598.
Schrire, C.
  1996 *Chronicles of an Archaeologist.* Uni-
        versity Press of Virginia, Char-
        lottesville.
Schuyler, R. L.
  1973 Review of *Explanation in Arche-
        ology: An Explicitly Scientific
        Approach,* by P. J. Watson, S. A.
        LeBlanc, and C. L. Redman. *Ameri-
        can Antiquity* 38:372–374.
  1980 Review of *In Small Things Forgotten,*
        by J. Deetz. *American Antiquity*
        45:643–644.
Scovill, D. H., G. J. Gordon, and K. M. Ander-
        son
  1972 *Guidelines for the Preparation of
        Statements of Environmental Impact
        on Archeological Resources.*
        National Park Service, Arizona
        Archeological Center, Tucson.
Sears, W. H.
  1954 The Sociopolitical Organization of
        Pre-Columbian Cultures on the Gulf
        Coastal Plain. *American Anthropolo-
        gist* 56:339–346.
  1958 Burial Mounds on the Gulf Coastal
        Plain. *American Antiquity*
        23:274–284.
  1960 Ceramic Systems and Eastern
        Archaeology. *American Antiquity*
        25:324–329.
  1961 The Study of Social and Religious
        Systems in North American Arche-
        ology. *Current Anthropology*
        2:223–246.
Semenov, S. A.
  1964 *Prehistoric Technology: An Experi-
        mental Study of the Oldest Tools and
        Artefacts from Traces of Manufac-
        ture and Wear.* Cory, Adams and
        Mackay, London.
Service, E. R.
  1962 *Primitive Social Organization.* Ran-
        dom House, New York.
  1971 *Cultural Evolutionism: Theory in
        Practice.* Holt, Rinehart, and Win-
        ston, New York.
  1975 *Origins of the State and Civilization.*
        Norton, New York.
Shankman, P. A., and A. T. Dino
  2001 The FBI File of Leslie A. White.
        American Anthropologist
        103:161–164.
Shanks, M., and C. Tilley
  1987a *Re-Constructing Archaeology: The-
        ory and Practice.* Cambridge Univer-
        sity Press, Cambridge.
  1987b *Social Theory and Archaeology.*
        Cambridge University Press, Cam-
        bridge.
  1989 Archaeology into the 1990s. *Norwe-
        gian Archaeological Review* 22:1–54.
  1992 *Re-Constructing Archaeology: The-
        ory and Practice,* 2nd ed. Routledge,
        London.

Shannon, C. E.
  1948 A Mathematical Theory of Communication. *Bell System Technical Journal* 27:379–423, 623–656.

Shannon, C. E., and W. Weaver
  1949 *The Mathematical Theory of Communication*. University of Illinois Press, Urbana.

Sharrock, F. W., and D. K. Grayson
  1979 "Significance" in Contract Archaeology. *American Antiquity* 44:327–328.

Shea, J. J.
  1992 Lithic Microwear Analysis in Archaeology. *Evolutionary Anthropology* 1:143–150.

Sheets, P. D.
  1972 The Pillage of Prehistory. *American Antiquity* 38:317–320.
  1973 Edge Abrasion during Biface Manufacture. *American Antiquity* 38:215–218.

Shennan, S.
  1986 Towards a Critical Archaeology? *Proceedings of the Prehistoric Society* 52:327–338.
  1988 *Quantifying Archaeology*. Edinburgh University Press, Edinburgh.
  2002 *Genes, Memes and Human History*. Thames and Hudson, London.
  2004 Forty Years On: Review of *Constructing Frames of Reference*, by L. R. Binford. *Journal of Human Evolution* 46:507–515.

Shepard, A. O.
  1956 *Ceramics for the Archaeologist*. Publication No. 609. Carnegie Institution of Washington, Washington, D.C.

Shott, M. J.
  1985 Shovel-Test Sampling as a Site Discovery Technique: A Case Study from Michigan. *Journal of Field Archaeology* 12:458–469.
  1989 Shovel Test Sampling in Archaeological Survey: Comments on Nance and Ball, and Lightfoot. *American Antiquity* 54:396–404.

  1996 Review of *Expanding Archaeology*, edited by J. M. Skibo, W. H. Walker, and A. E. Neilsen. *American Antiquity* 61:610–611.
  1998 Status and Role of Formation Theory in Contemporary Archaeological Practice. *Journal of Archaeological Research* 6:299–329.
  2004 Guilt by Affiliation: Merit and Standing in Academic Archaeology. *SAA Archaeological Record* 4(2):30–37.

Siegel, B. J.
  1957 Review of *Seminars in Archaeology: 1955*, edited by R. Wauchope. *American Anthropologist* 59:924–926.

Simpson, G. G.
  1961 *Principles of Animal Taxonomy*. Columbia University Press, New York.
  1963 Historical Science. In *The Fabric of Geology*, edited by C. C. Albritton, Jr., pp. 24–48. Freeman, Cooper, Stanford, Calif.
  1970 Uniformitarianism: An Inquiry into Principle, Theory, and Method in Geohistory and Biohistory. In *Essays in Evolution and Genetics in Honor of Theodosius Dobzhansky*, edited by M. K. Hecht and W. C. Steere, pp. 43–96. Appleton, New York.

Skibo, J. M.
  1992 *Pottery Function: A Use-Alteration Perspective*. Plenum, New York.
  1999 *Ants for Breakfast: Archaeological Adventures among the Kalinga*. University of Utah Press, Salt Lake City.

Skibo, J. M., and M. B. Schiffer
  2001 Understanding Artifact Variability and Change: A Behavioral Framework. In *Anthropological Perspectives on Technology*, edited by M. B. Schiffer, pp. 139–149. University of New Mexico Press, Albuquerque.

Skibo, J. M., M. B. Schiffer, and N. Kowalski
  1989 Ceramic Style Analysis in Archaeology and Ethnoarchaeology: Bridging the Analytical Gap. *Journal of Anthropological Archaeology* 8:388–409.

Skibo, J. M., M. B. Schiffer, and K. C. Reid
  1989 Organic-Tempered Pottery: An
        Experimental Study. *American Antiq-
        uity* 54:122–146.
Skibo, J. M., W. H. Walker, and A. E. Nielsen
        (editors)
  1995 *Expanding Archaeology.* University
        of Utah Press, Salt Lake City.
Smith, B. D.
  1977 Archaeological Inference and Induc-
        tive Confirmation. *American Anthro-
        pologist* 79:598–617.
Smith, W.
  1962 Schools, Pots, and Potters. *American
        Anthropologist* 64:1165–1178.
Sonnenfeld, J.
  1962 Interpreting the Function of Primitive
        Implements. *American Antiquity*
        28:56–65.
Sørensen, M. L. S.
  2000 *Gender Archaeology.* Polity Press,
        Cambridge.
South, S.
  1977a *Method and Theory in Historical
        Archaeology.* Academic Press, New
        York.
  1977b (Editor) *Research Strategies in His-
        torical Archaeology.* Academic Press,
        New York.
  1978 Pattern Recognition in Historical
        Archaeology. *American Antiquity*
        43:223–230.
Spaulding, A. C.
  1952 The Origin of the Adena Culture of
        the Ohio Valley. *Southwestern Jour-
        nal of Anthropology* 8:260–268.
  1953a Review of "Measurements of Some
        Prehistoric Design Developments in
        the Southeastern States," by J. A.
        Ford. *American Anthropologist*
        55:588–591.
  1953b Statistical Techniques for the Discov-
        ery of Artifact Types. *American
        Antiquity* 18:305–313.
  1954a Reply [to Ford]. *American Anthro-
        pologist* 56:112–114.
  1954b Reply to Ford. *American Antiquity*
        19:391–393.
  1960a Statistical Description and Compari-
        son of Artifact Assemblages. In *The

Application of Quantitative Methods
in Archaeology,* edited by R. F.
Heizer and S. F. Cook, pp. 60–83.
Publications in Anthropology No.
28. Viking Fund, Wenner-Gren Foundation for Anthropological Research,
New York.
  1960b The Dimensions of Archaeology. In
        *Essays in the Science of Culture in
        Honor of Leslie A. White,* edited by
        G. E. Dole and R. L. Carneiro, pp.
        437–456. Crowell, New York.
  1966 Review of *The Dynamics of Stylistic
        Change in Arikara Ceramics,* by J.
        Deetz. *American Anthropologist*
        68:1064–1065.
  1968 Explanation in Archeology. In *New
        Perspectives in Archeology,* edited by
        S. R. Binford and L. R. Binford, pp.
        33–39. Aldine, Chicago.
  1973 Archeology in the Active Voice: The
        New Anthropology. In *Research and
        Theory in Current Archeology,* edited
        by C. L. Redman, pp. 337–354.
        Wiley, New York.
  1977 On Growth and Form in Archae-
        ology: Multivariate Analysis. *Journal
        of Anthropological Research*
        33:1–15.
Spector, J. D.
  1993 *What This Awl Means: Feminist
        Archaeology at a Wahpeton Dakota
        Village.* Minnesota Historical Society
        Press, St. Paul.
Spencer, C. S.
  1993 Human Agency, Biased Transmission,
        and the Cultural Evolution of Chiefly
        Authority. *Journal of Anthropologi-
        cal Archaeology* 12:41–74.
  1997 Evolutionary Approaches in Archae-
        ology. *Journal of Archaeological
        Research* 5:209–264.
Spencer, H.
  1851 *Social Statics.* Chapman, London.
  1876 *Principles of Sociology.* Williams and
        Norgate, London.
Speth, J. D., and G. A. Johnson
  1976 Problems in the Use of Correlation
        for the Investigation of Tool Kits and
        Activity Areas. In *Cultural Change

and Continuity: Essays in Honor of James Bennett Griffin, edited by C. E. Cleland, pp. 35–57. Academic Press, New York.

Spicer, E. H.
1957   Review of Seminars in Archaeology: 1955, edited by R. Wauchope. American Antiquity 23:186–188.

Spier, L.
1916   New Data on the Trenton Argillite Culture. American Anthropologist 18:181–189.
1917   An Outline for a Chronology of Zuñi Ruins. Anthropological Papers of the American Museum of Natural History 18(3):207–331.
1931   N. C. Nelson's Stratigraphic Technique in the Reconstruction of Prehistoric Sequences in Southwestern America. In Methods in Social Science, edited by S. A. Rice, pp. 275–283. University of Chicago Press, Chicago.

Spindler, L. S., and G. D. Spindler
1959   Culture Change. In Biennial Review of Anthropology 1959, edited by B. J. Siegel, pp. 37–66. Stanford University Press, Stanford, Calif.

Spooner, B. (editor)
1972   Population Growth: Anthropological Implications. MIT Press, Cambridge, Mass.

Spriggs, M. (editor)
1977   Archaeology and Anthropology: Areas of Mutual Interest. Supplementary Series No. 19. British Archaeological Reports, Oxford.
1984   Marxist Perspectives in Archaeology. Cambridge University Press, Cambridge.

Stadler, F. (editor)
2003   The Vienna Circle and Logical Empiricism: Re-evaluation and Future Perspectives. Kluwer, Dordrecht, Netherlands.

Stanislawski, M. B.
1969a What Good Is a Broken Pot? An Experiment in Hopi-Tewa Ethno-Archaeology. Southwestern Lore 35:11–18.

1969b The Ethno-Archaeology of Hopi Pottery Making. Plateau 421:27–33.
1973   Review of Archaeology as Anthropology: A Case Study, by W. A. Longacre. American Antiquity 38:117–122.

Stark, M. T.
1991   Ceramic Production and Community Specialization: A Kalinga Ethnoarchaeological Study. World Archaeology 23:64–78.
1992   From Sibling to Suki: Social and Spatial Relations in Kalinga Pottery Exchange. Journal of Anthropological Archaeology 11:137–151.
1999   Social Dimensions of Technical Choice in Kalinga Ceramic Traditions. In Material Meanings: Critical Approaches to Interpreting Material Culture, edited by E. Chilton, pp. 24–43. University of Utah Press, Salt Lake City.

Stark, M. T., R. L. Bishop, and E. Miksa
2000   Ceramic Technology and Social Boundaries: Cultural Practices in Kalinga Clay Selection and Use. Journal of Archaeological Method and Theory 7:295–331.

Stark, M. T., and W. A. Longacre
1993   Kalinga Ceramics and New Technologies: An Ethnoarchaeological Perspective. In The Social and Cultural Contexts of New Ceramic Technologies, edited by W. D. Kingery, pp. 1–32. American Ceramic Society, Waterville, Ohio.

Stein, J. K., and W. R. Farrand
2001   Sediments in Archaeological Context. University of Utah Press, Salt Lake City.

Sterud, E. L.
1978   Changing Aims of Americanist Archaeology: A Citations Analysis of American Antiquity—1946–1975. American Antiquity 43:294–302.

Steward, J. H.
1929   Diffusion and Independent Invention: A Critique of Logic. American Anthropologist 31:491–495.

1937   Ecological Aspects of Southwestern Society. *Anthropos* 32:87–104.

1938   *Basin-Plateau Aboriginal Sociopolitical Groups.* Bulletin No. 120. Bureau of American Ethnology, Washington, D.C.

1942   The Direct Historical Approach to Archaeology. *American Antiquity* 7:337–343.

1948   A Functional-Developmental Classification of American High Cultures. In *A Reappraisal of Peruvian Archaeology,* edited by W. C. Bennett, pp. 103–104. Memoirs No. 4. Society for American Archaeology, Menasha, Wis.

1949   Cultural Causality and Law: A Trial Formulation of the Development of Early Civilizations. *American Anthropologist* 51:1–27.

1953   Evolution and Process. In *Anthropology Today,* edited by A. L. Kroeber, pp. 313–326. University of Chicago Press, Chicago.

1954   Types of Types. *American Anthropologist* 56:54–57.

1955   *Theory of Cultural Change: The Methodology of Multilinear Evolution.* University of Illinois Press, Urbana.

1960   Review of *The Evolution of Culture: The Development of Civilization to the Fall of Rome,* by L. A. White. *American Anthropologist* 62:144–148.

1968   Cultural Ecology. In *International Encyclopedia of the Social Sciences,* vol. 4, edited by D. L. Sills, pp. 337–344. Macmillan, New York.

Steward, J. H., and F. M. Setzler
1938   Function and Configuration in Archaeology. *American Antiquity* 4:4–10.

Stiles, D.
1977   Ethnoarchaeology: A Discussion of Methods and Applications. *Man* 12:87–103.

Stokstad, M.
2004   *Art: A Brief History.* 2nd ed. Pearson Education, Upper Saddle River, N.J.

Stoltman, J. B.
1984   Review of *Working at Archaeology,* by L. R. Binford. *American Journal of Archaeology* 88:599–600.

Strong, W. D.
1935   *An Introduction to Nebraska Archaeology.* Smithsonian Miscellaneous Collections 93(10). Washington, D.C.

1952   The Value of Archeology in the Training of Professional Anthropologists. *American Anthropologist* 54:318–321.

Struever, S.
1965   Middle Woodland Culture History in the Great Lakes Riverine Area. *American Antiquity* 31:211–223.

1968a   Problems, Methods, and Organization: A Disparity in the Growth of Archeology. In *Anthropological Archeology in the Americas,* edited by B. J. Meggers, pp. 131–151. Anthropological Society of Washington, Washington, D.C.

1968b   Woodland Subsistence–Settlement Systems in the Lower Illinois Valley. In *New Perspectives in Archeology,* edited by S. R. Binford and L. R. Binford, pp. 285–312. Aldine, Chicago.

1971   Comments on Archaeological Data Requirements and Research Strategy. *American Antiquity* 36:9–19.

Sullivan, A. P.
1978   Inference and Evidence in Archaeology: A Discussion of the Conceptual Problems. *Advances in Archaeological Method and Theory* 1:183–222.

Swanson, E. (editor)
1975   *Lithic Technology: Making and Using Stone Tools.* Mouton, The Hague.

Swartz, B. K., Jr.
1967   A Logical Sequence of Archaeological Objectives. *American Antiquity* 32:487–497.

Swidler, N., K. E. Dongoske, R. Anyon, and A. S. Downer (editors)

1997 *Native Americans and Archaeologists: Stepping Stones to Common Ground.* AltaMira, Walnut Creek, Calif.

Tainter, J. A., and G. J. Lucas

1983 Epistemology of the Significance Concept. *American Antiquity* 48:707–719.

Talmage, V., and O. Chesler

1977 *The Importance of Small, Surface, and Disturbed Sites as Sources of Significant Archaeological Data.* Interagency Archeological Service, National Park Service, Washington, D.C.

Tani, M.

1995 Beyond the Identification of Formation Processes: Behavioral Inference Based on Traces Left by Cultural Formation Processes. *Journal of Archaeological Method and Theory* 2:231–252.

Tax, S. (editor)

1960 *Evolution After Darwin.* 3 vols. University of Chicago Press, Chicago.

Taylor, R. E.

1985 The Beginnings of Radiocarbon Dating in *American Antiquity*: A Historical Perspective. *American Antiquity* 50:309–325.

2000 The Introduction of Radiocarbon Dating. In *It's About Time: A History of Archaeological Dating in North America*, edited by S. E. Nash, pp. 84–104. University of Utah Press, Salt Lake City.

Taylor, W. W.

1948 *A Study of Archeology.* Memoirs No. 69. American Anthropological Association, Washington, D.C.

1957 (Editor) *The Identification of Non-artifactual Archaeological Materials; Report of a Conference Held in Chicago, March 11–13, 1956, by the Committee on Archaeological Identification, Division of Anthropology and Psychology, National Academy of Sciences, National Research Council.* Publication No. 565. National Research Council, Washington, D.C.

1968 Foreword to the 1968 Printing. In *A Study of Archeology*, by W. W. Taylor, pp. 1–2. Southern Illinois University Press, Carbondale.

1969 Review of *New Perspectives in Archeology*, edited by S. R. Binford and L. R. Binford. *Science* 165:382–384.

1972 Old Wine and New Skins: A Contemporary Parable. In *Contemporary Archaeology*, edited by M. Leone, pp. 28-33. Southern Illinois University Press, Carbondale.

Tehrani, J. J., and M. Collard

2002 Investigating Cultural Evolution through Biological Phylogenetic Analyses of Turkmen Textiles. *Journal of Anthropological Archaeology* 21:443–463.

Teltser, P. A. (editor)

1995 *Evolutionary Archaeology: Methodological Issues.* University of Arizona Press, Tucson.

Terrell, J. E.

1988 History as a Family Tree, History as an Entangled Bank: Constructing Images and Interpretations of Prehistory in the South Pacific. *Antiquity* 62:642–657.

1990 Storytelling and Prehistory. *Archaeological Method and Theory* 2:1–29.

2001 (Editor) *Archaeology, Language, and History: Essays on Culture and Ethnicity.* Bergin and Garvey, Westport, Conn.

Terrell, J. E., T. L. Hunt, and C. Gosden

1997 The Dimensions of Social Life in the Pacific: Human Diversity and the Myth of the Primitive Isolate. *Current Anthropology* 38:155–195.

Thomas, C.

1884 Who Were the Mound Builders? *The American Antiquarian* 6:90–99.

1891 *Catalogue of Prehistoric Works East of the Rocky Mountains.* Bulletin No. 12. Bureau of Ethnology, Washington, D.C.

1894 Report on the Mound Explorations of the Bureau of Ethnology. *Bureau*

of Ethnology Annual Report
12:3–742.

Thomas, D. H.

1969 Regional Sampling in Archaeology: A Pilot Great Basin Research Design. *University of California Archaeological Survey, Annual Report* 11:87–100.

1972a The Use and Abuse of Numerical Taxonomy in Archaeology. *Archaeology and Physical Anthropology in Oceania* 7:31–49.

1972b A Computer Simulation Model of Great Basin Shoshonean Subsistence and Settlement Patterns. In *Models in Archaeology*, edited by D. L. Clarke, pp. 671–704. Methuen, London.

1973 An Empirical Test for Steward's Model of Great Basin Settlement Patterns. *American Antiquity* 38:155–176.

1974 An Archeological Perspective on Shoshonean Bands. *American Anthropologist* 76:11–25.

1975 Nonsite Sampling in Archaeology: Up the Creek without a Site? In *Sampling in Archaeology*, edited by J. W. Mueller, pp. 61–81. University of Arizona Press, Tucson.

1976 *Figuring Anthropology: First Principles of Probability and Statistics.* Holt, Rinehart, and Winston, New York.

1978 The Awful Truth about Statistics in Archaeology. *American Antiquity* 43:231–244.

1979 *Archaeology.* Holt, Rinehart and Winston, New York.

1980 The Gruesome Truth about Statistics in Archaeology. *American Antiquity* 45:340–345.

1983 On Steward's Model of Shoshonean Sociopolitical Organization: A Great Bias in the Basin? In *The Development of Political Organization in Native North America*, edited by E. Tooker and M. H. Fried, pp. 59–67. American Ethnological Society, Washington, D.C.

1986a Contemporary Hunter-Gatherer Archaeology in America. In *American Archaeology Past and Future: A Celebration of the Society for American Archaeology, 1935–1985*, edited by D. J. Meltzer, D. D. Fowler, and J. A. Sabloff, pp. 237–276. Smithsonian Institution Press, Washington, D.C.

1986b *Refiguring Anthropology: First Principles of Probability and Statistics.* Waveland Press, Prospect Heights, Ill.

1989 *Archaeology.* 2nd ed. Holt, Rinehart, and Winston, Ft. Worth, Tex.

2000 *Skull Wars: Kennewick Man, Archaeology, and the Battle for Native American Identity.* Basic Books, New York.

Thompson, R. H.

1956 An Archaeological Approach to the Study of Cultural Stability. In *Seminars in Archaeology: 1955*, edited by R. Wauchope, pp. 31–57. Memoirs No. 11. Society for American Archaeology, Salt Lake City.

1958 *Modern Yucatecan Maya Pottery Making.* Memoirs No. 15. Society for American Archaeology, Salt Lake City.

1972 Interpretive Trends and Linear Models in American Archaeology. In *Contemporary Archaeology: A Guide to Theory and Contributions*, edited by M. P. Leone, pp. 34–38. Southern Illinois University Press, Carbondale.

2000 An Old and Reliable Authority: An Act for the Preservation of American Antiquities. *Journal of the Southwest* 42:191–381.

Tilley, C.

1989 Archaeology as Socio-Political Action in the Present. In *Critical Traditions in Contemporary Archaeology: Essays in the Philosophy, History, and Socio-Politics of Archaeology*, edited by V. Pinsky and A. Wylie, pp. 104–116. Cambridge University Press, Cambridge.

1990 *Reading Material Culture: Structuralism, Hermeneutics, and Post-Structuralism.* Blackwell, Oxford.

1994   *A Phenomenology of Landscape: Places, Paths and Monuments.* Berg, Oxford.

Tolstoy, P., and S. K. Fish

1975   Surface and Subsurface Evidence for Community Size at Coapexco, Mexico. *Journal of Field Archaeology* 2:97–104.

Tozzer, A. M.

1926   Chronological Aspects of American Archaeology. *Proceedings of the Massachusetts Historical Society* 59:283–292.

Transeau, E. N.

1935   The Prairie Peninsula. *Ecology* 16:423–437.

Trigger, B. G.

1965   *History and Settlement in Lower Nubia.* Publications in Anthropology No. 69. Yale University, New Haven, Conn.

1967   Settlement Archaeology: Its Goals and Promise. *American Antiquity* 32:149–160.

1968a   The Determinants of Settlement Patterns. In *Settlement Archaeology,* edited by K. C. Chang, pp. 53–78. National Press, Palo Alto, Calif.

1968b   Major Concepts of Archaeology in Historical Perspective. *Man* 3:527–541.

1970   Aims in Prehistoric Archaeology. *Antiquity* 44:26–37.

1973   The Future of Archeology Is the Past. In *Research and Theory in Current Archeology,* edited by C. L. Redman, pp. 95–111. Wiley, New York.

1980   Archaeology and the Image of the American Indian. *American Antiquity* 45:662–676.

1984   Alternative Archaeologies: Nationalistic, Colonialist, Imperialist. *Man* 19:355–370.

1989a   *A History of Archaeological Thought.* Cambridge University Press, Cambridge.

1989b   Hyperrelativism, Responsibility, and the Social Sciences. *The Canadian Review of Sociology and Anthropology* 26:776–797.

1991   Post-Processual Developments in Anglo-American Archaeology. *Norwegian Archaeological Review* 24:65–76.

1995   Expanding Middle-Range Theory. *Antiquity* 69:449–458.

2000   Review of *The Land of Prehistory,* by A. B. Kehoe. *American Antiquity* 65:776–777.

2003   *Artifacts & Ideas: Essays in Archaeology.* Transaction, New Brunswick, N.J.

Tringham, R.

1978   Experimentation, Ethnoarchaeology, and the Leapfrogs in Archaeological Methodology. In *Explorations in Ethnoarchaeology,* edited by R. A. Gould, pp. 169–199. University of New Mexico Press, Albuquerque.

1991   Households with Faces: The Challenge of Gender in Prehistoric Architectural Remains. In *Engendering Archaeology: Women and Prehistory,* edited by J. M. Gero and M. W. Conkey, pp. 93–131. Blackwell, Oxford.

Tringham, R., G. Cooper, G. Odell, B. Voytek, and A. Whitman

1974   Experimentation in the Formation of Edge Damage: A New Approach to Lithic Analysis. *Journal of Field Archaeology* 1:171–196.

Trope, J. F., and W. R. Echo-Hawk

1992   The Native American Graves Protection and Repatriation Act: Background and Legislative History. *Arizona State Law Journal* 24:35–78.

Tschauner, H.

1996   Middle-Range Theory, Behavioral Archaeology, and Postempiricist Philosophy of Science in Archaeology. *Journal of Archaeological Method and Theory* 3:1–30.

Tugby, D. J.

1965   Archaeological Objectives and Statistical Methods: A Frontier in Archaeology. *American Antiquity* 31:1–16.

Tuggle, H. D.

1972   Review of *Explanation in Archeology: An Explicitly Scientific*

Approach, by P. J. Watson, S. A. LeBlanc, and C. L. Redman. *Philosophy of Science* 39: 564–566.

Tuggle, H. D., A. H. Townsend, and T. J. Riley
1972 Laws, Systems, and Research Designs: A Discussion of Explanation in Archaeology. *American Antiquity* 37:3–12.

Turner, J. S.
2000 *The Extended Organism: The Physiology of Animal-Built Structures.* Harvard University Press, Cambridge, Mass.

Tyler, N.
1999 *Historic Preservation: An Introduction to Its History, Principles, and Practice.* Norton, New York.

Tylor, E. B.
1881 *Anthropology: An Introduction to the Study of Man and Civilization.* Appleton, New York.

Ubelaker, D. H., and L. G. Grant
1989 Human Skeletal Remains: Preservation or Reburial. *Yearbook of Physical Anthropology* 32:249–287.

Ucko, P. J. (editor)
1995 *Theory in Archaeology: A World Perspective.* Routledge, London.

Uhle, M.
1907 The Emeryville Shellmound. *University of California Publications in American Archaeology and Ethnology* 7:1–107.

Upham, S. (editor)
1990 *The Evolution of Political Systems.* Cambridge University Press, Cambridge.

Upham, S., K. Lightfoot, and R. Jewett (editors)
1989 *The Sociopolitical Structure of Southwestern Societies.* Westview Press, Boulder, Colo.

Upham, S., and F. Plog
1986 The Interpretation of Prehistoric Political Complexity in the Central and Northern Southwest: Toward a Mending of the Models. *Journal of Field Archaeology* 13:223–238.

Vaillant, G. C.
1935 Early Cultures of the Valley of Mexico: Results of the Stratigraphical

Project of the American Museum of Natural History in the Valley of Mexico, 1928–1933. *Anthropological Papers of the American Museum of Natural History* 35(3):281–328.
1937 History and Stratigraphy in the Valley of Mexico. *Scientific Monthly* 44:307–324.

Van Dyke, R. M.
2004 Memory, Meaning, and Masonry: The Late Bonito Chacoan Landscape. *American Antiquity* 69:413–431.

VanPool, C. S., and T. L. VanPool
1999 The Scientific Nature of Postprocessualism. *American Antiquity* 64:33–54.
2003 Introduction: Method, Theory, and the Essential Tension. In *Essential Tensions in Archaeological Method and Theory*, edited by T. L. VanPool and C. S. VanPool, pp. 1–4. University of Utah Press, Salt Lake City.

VanPool, T. L.
2001 Style, Function, and Variation: Identifying the Evolutionary Importance of Traits in the Archaeological Record. In *Style and Function: Conceptual Issues in Evolutionary Archaeology,* edited by T. D. Hurt and G. F. M. Rakita, pp. 119–140. Bergin and Garvey, Westport, Conn.

VanPool, T. L., and R. D. Leonard
2002 Specialized Ground Stone Production in the Casas Grandes Region of Northern Chihuahua, Mexico. *American Antiquity* 67:710–730.

VanPool, T. L., and C. S. VanPool
2003a Agency and Evolution: The Role of Intended and Unintended Consequences of Action. In *Essential Tensions in Archaeological Method and Theory*, edited by T. L. VanPool and C. S. VanPool, pp. 89–113. University of Utah Press, Salt Lake City.
2003b (Editors) *Essential Tensions in Archaeological Method and Theory.* University of Utah Press, Salt Lake City.

van Riper, A. B.

   1993   *Men among the Mammoths: Victorian Science and the Discovery of Human Prehistory.* University of Chicago Press, Chicago.

Vaughan, C. D.

   2001   A Million Years of Style and Function: Regional and Temporal Variation in Acheulean Handaxes. In *Style and Function: Conceptual Issues in Evolutionary Archaeology,* edited by T. D. Hurt and G. F. M. Rakita, pp. 141–163. Bergin and Garvey, Westport, Conn.

Vayda, A. P. (editor)

   1969   *Environment and Cultural Behavior: Ecological Studies in Cultural Anthropology.* Natural History Press, Garden City, N.Y.

Vayda, A. P., and R. A. Rappaport

   1968   Ecology: Cultural and Non-Cultural. In *Introduction to Cultural Anthropology,* edited by J. Clifton, pp. 477–497. Houghton Mifflin, Boston.

Vaz Pinto, I., M. B. Schiffer, S. Smith, and J. M. Skibo

   1987   Effects of Temper on Ceramic Abrasion Resistance: A Preliminary Investigation. *Archeomaterials* 1:119–134.

Vescelius, G.

   1960   Archeological Sampling: A Problem of Statistical Inference. In *Essays in the Science of Culture in Honor of Leslie A. White,* edited by G. A. Dole and R. L. Carneiro, pp. 457–470. Crowell, New York.

Vogt, E. Z., and R. Leventhal (editors)

   1983   *Prehistoric Settlement Patterns: Essays in Honor of Gordon R. Willey.* University of New Mexico Press, Albuquerque.

von Bertalanffy, L.

   1950a   The Theory of Open Systems in Physics and Biology. *Science* 111:23–29.

   1950b   An Outline of General Systems Theory. *British Journal for the Philosophy of Science* 1:139–164.

von Foerster, H.

   1949   (Editor) *Cybernetics: Transactions of the Sixth Conference.* Josiah Macy, Jr. Foundation, New York.

   1981   *Observing Systems: Selected Papers of Heinz von Foerster.* Intersystems Publications, Seaside, Calif.

von Frisch, K., and O. von Frisch

   1974   *Animal Architecture.* Harcourt Brace Jovanovich, New York.

Walde, D., and N. Willows (editors)

   1991   *The Archaeology of Gender.* Archaeological Association, University of Calgary.

Walker, I. C.

   1972   Binford, Science, and History: The Probabilistic Variability of Explicated Epistemology and Nomothetic Paradigms in Historical Archaeology. *Conference on Historic Site Archaeology Papers* 7:159–201.

Walker, W. H.

   1995   Ceremonial Trash. In *Expanding Archaeology,* edited by J. M. Skibo, W. H. Walker, and A. E. Nielsen, pp. 67–79. University of Utah Press, Salt Lake City.

   1998   Where Are the Witches of Prehistory? *Journal of Archaeological Method and Theory* 5:245–308.

Walker, W. H., J. M. Skibo, and A. E. Nielsen

   1995   Introduction to *Expanding Archaeology,* edited by J. M. Skibo, W. H. Walker, and A. E. Nielsen, pp. 1–12. University of Utah Press, Salt Lake City.

Wall, D. diZ.

   1994   *The Archaeology of Gender: Separating the Spheres of Urban America.* Plenum, New York.

Wandsnider, L., and E. L. Camilli

   1992   The Character of Surface Archaeological Deposits and Its Influence on Survey Accuracy. *Journal of Field Archaeology* 19:169–188.

Warren, R. E., and M. J. O'Brien

   1981   Regional Sample Stratification: The Drainage Class Technique. *Plains Anthropologist* 26:213–227.

Waters, M. R.

1997   *Principles of Geoarchaeology: A North American Perspective*. University of Arizona Press, Tucson.

Watson, P. J.

1973a   Explanation and Models: The Prehistorian as Philosopher of Science and the Prehistorian as Excavator of the Past. In *The Explanation of Culture Change*, edited by C. Renfrew, pp. 47–52. Duckworth, London.

1973b   The Future of Archeology in Anthropology: Culture History and Social Science. In *Research and Theory in Current Archeology*, edited by C. L. Redman, pp. 113–124. Wiley, New York.

1977   Design Analysis of Painted Pottery. *American Antiquity* 42:381–393.

1979a   The Idea of Ethnoarchaeology. In *Ethnoarchaeology: Implications of Ethnography for Archaeology*, edited by C. Kramer, pp. 277–287. Columbia University Press, New York.

1979b   *Archaeological Ethnography in Western Iran*. Publications in Anthropology No. 57. Viking Fund, Wenner-Gren Foundation for Anthropological Research, New York.

1983   Foreword to *A Study of Archeology*, by W. W. Taylor. Center for Archaeological Investigations, Southern Illinois University, Carbondale.

1986   Archaeological Interpretation, 1985. In *American Archaeology, Past and Future: A Celebration of the Society for American Archaeology, 1935–1985*, edited by D. J. Meltzer, D. D. Fowler, and J. A. Sabloff, pp. 439–457. Smithsonian Institution Press, Washington, D.C.

1991   A Parochial Primer: The New Dissonance as Seen from the Midcontinental United States. In *Processual and Postprocessual Archaeologies: Multiple Ways of Knowing the Past*, edited by R. W. Preucel, pp. 265–274. Occasional Paper No. 10. Center for Archaeological Investigations, Southern Illinois University at Carbondale.

Watson, P. J., and M. Fotiadis

1990   The Razor's Edge: Symbolic-Structuralist Archeology and the Expansion of Archeological Inference. *American Anthropologist* 92:613–629.

Watson, P. J., and M. C. Kennedy

1991   The Development of Horticulture in the Eastern Woodlands of North America: Women's Role. In *Engendering Archaeology: Women and Prehistory*, edited by J. M. Gero and M. W. Conkey, pp. 255–275. Blackwell, Oxford.

Watson, P. J., S. A. LeBlanc, and C. Redman

1971   *Explanation in Archeology: An Explicitly Scientific Approach*. Columbia University Press, New York.

1974   The Covering Law Model in Archaeology: Practical Uses and Formal Interpretations. *World Archaeology* 6:125–132.

1984   *Archeological Explanation: The Scientific Method in Archeology*. Columbia University Press, New York.

Watson, R. A.

1966   Is Geology Different? *Philosophy of Science* 33:172–185.

1969a   Explanation and Prediction in Geology. *Journal of Geology* 77:488–494.

1969b   Review of *Uniformity and Simplicity: A Symposium on the Principle of the Uniformity of Nature*, edited by C. C. Albritton, Jr. *Philosophy of Science* 36:219–221.

1970   Review of *The Principle of Uniformity in Geology, Biology, and Theology: Natural Law and Divine Miracle*, by R. Hooykaas. *Philosophy of Science* 37:316–317.

1972   The "New Archeology" of the 1960s. *Antiquity* 46:210–215.

1976   Inference in Archaeology. *American Antiquity* 41:58–66.

1990   Ozymandias, King of Kings: Postprocessual Radical Archaeology as

Critique. *American Antiquity* 55:673–689.

1991 What the New Archaeology Has Accomplished. *Current Anthropology* 32:275–291.

Watson, R. A., and P. J. Watson

1969 *Man and Nature: An Anthropological Essay in Human Ecology.* Harcourt, Brace and World, New York.

Watson, R. A., and H. E. Wright, Jr.

1980 The End of the Pleistocene: A General Critique of Chronostratigraphic Classification. *Boreas* 9:153–163.

Wauchope, R.

1956 Preface to *Seminars in Archaeology: 1955,* edited by R. Wauchope, pp. v–vii. Memoirs No. 11. Society for American Archaeology, Salt Lake City.

1977 Review of *The Early Mesoamerican Village,* edited by K. V. Flannery. *American Antiquity* 42:656–659.

Wedel, W. R.

1938 *The Direct-Historical Approach in Pawnee Archaeology.* Smithsonian Miscellaneous Collections 97(7). Washington, D.C.

Wesler, K. W.

1997 Review of *A New Deal for Southeastern Archaeology,* by E. A. Lyon. *American Antiquity* 62:154–155.

Whallon, R., Jr.

1968 Investigations of Late Prehistoric Social Organization in New York State. In *New Perspectives in Archeology,* edited by S. R. Binford and L. R. Binford, pp. 223–244. Aldine, Chicago.

1972 A New Approach to Pottery Typology. *American Antiquity* 37:13–33.

1973 Spatial Analysis of Occupation Floors, part I: Application of Dimensional Analysis of Variance. *American Antiquity* 38:266–278.

1974a Spatial Analysis of Occupation Floors, part II: The Application of Nearest Neighbor Analysis. *American Antiquity* 39:16–34.

1974b Reply to Riley and Schiffer. *American Antiquity* 39:492–494.

1974c Working with the "New Paradigm." *Reviews in Anthropology* 1:25–33.

1982 Editorial Introduction. *Journal of Anthropological Archaeology* 1:1–4.

Whallon, R., Jr., and J. A. Brown (editors)

1982 *Essays on Archaeological Typology.* Center for American Archeology Press, Evanston, Ill.

Wheat, J. B., J. C. Gifford, and W. W. Wasley

1958 Ceramic Variety, Type Cluster, and Ceramic System in Southwestern Pottery Analysis. *American Antiquity* 24:34–47.

White, J. P.

1967 Ethno-Archaeology in New Guinea: Two Examples. *Mankind* 6:409–414.

White, J. P., and D. H. Thomas

1972 What Mean These Stones? Ethno-Taxonomic Models and Archaeological Interpretations in the New Guinea Highlands. In *Models in Archaeology,* edited by D. L. Clarke, pp. 275–308. Methuen, London.

White, L. A.

1943 Energy and the Evolution of Culture. *American Anthropologist* 45:335–356.

1945 "Diffusion vs. Evolution": An Anti-evolutionist Fallacy. *American Anthropologist* 47:339–356.

1947 The Expansion of the Scope of Science. *Washington Academy of Sciences Journal* 37:181–210.

1949 *The Science of Culture: A Study of Man and Civilization.* Grove Press, New York.

1950 The Individual and the Culture Process. *Centennial, American Association for the Advancement of Science,* pp. 74–81. Washington, D.C.

1959 *The Evolution of Culture: The Development of Civilization to the Fall of Rome.* McGraw–Hill, New York.

White, N. M., L. P. Sullivan, and R. A. Marrinan (editors)

1999 *Grit-Tempered: Early Women Archaeologists in the Southeastern United States.* University Press of Florida, Gainesville.

Whiteley, P. M.
2003 Leslie White's Hopi Ethnography: Of Practice and Theory. *Journal of Anthropological Research* 59:151–181.

Whittaker, J. C.
1994 *Flintknapping: Making and Understanding Stone Tools.* University of Texas Press, Austin.

Wiener, N.
1948 *Cybernetics; or, Control and Communication in the Animal and the Machine.* Wiley, New York.
1950 *The Human Use of Human Beings: Cybernetics and Society.* Houghton Mifflin, Boston.

Wildesen, L. E.
1973 *A Quantitative Model of Archaeological Site Development.* Ph.D. dissertation, Department of Anthropology, Washington State University, Pullman.

Wilkinson, T. J.
2000 Regional Approaches to Mesopotamian Archaeology: The Contribution of Archaeological Surveys. *Journal of Archaeological Research* 8:219–267.

Willer, D., and J. Willer
1973 *Systematic Empiricism: Critique of a Pseudoscience.* Prentice-Hall, Englewood Cliffs, N.J.

Willey, G. R.
1945 Horizon Styles and Pottery Traditions in Peruvian Archaeology. *American Antiquity* 10:49–56.
1953a Archaeological Theories and Interpretation: New World. In *Anthropology Today,* edited by A. L. Kroeber, pp. 361–385. University of Chicago Press, Chicago.
1953b *Prehistoric Settlement Patterns in the Virú Valley, Peru.* Bulletin No. 155. Bureau of American Ethnology, Washington, D.C.
1956 (Editor) *Prehistoric Settlement Patterns in the New World.* Publications in Anthropology No. 23. Viking Fund, Wenner-Gren Foundation for Anthropological Research, New York.
1960 New World Prehistory. *Science* 131:73–86.
1961 Review of *Evolution and Culture,* edited by M. D. Sahlins and E. R. Service. *American Antiquity* 26:441–443.
1966 *North and Middle America.* Vol. 1 of *An Introduction to American Archaeology.* Prentice-Hall, Englewood Cliffs, N.J.
1988 *Portraits in American Archaeology: Remembrances of Some Distinguished Americanists.* University of New Mexico Press, Albuquerque.

Willey, G. R., and P. Phillips
1958 *Method and Theory in American Archaeology.* University of Chicago Press, Chicago.

Willey, G. R., and J. A. Sabloff
1974 *A History of American Archaeology.* Freeman, New York.
1993 *A History of American Archaeology,* 3rd ed. Freeman, New York.

Willey, G. R., and R. B. Woodbury
1942 A Chronological Outline for the Northwest Florida Coast. *American Antiquity* 7:232–254.

Williams, B. J.
1968 Establishing Cultural Heterogeneities in Settlement Patterns. In *New Perspectives in Archeology,* edited by S. R. Binford and L. R. Binford, pp. 161–170. Aldine, Chicago.

Williams, J. R.
1967 *Land Leveling Salvage Archaeological Work in Southeast Missouri: 1966.* Report submitted to the National Park Service. Midwest Archeological Center, Lincoln, Neb.

Williams, P. A.
2002 Of Replicators and Selectors. *Quarterly Review of Biology* 77:302–306.

Wills, W. H, and R. D. Leonard (editors)
1994 *The Ancient Southwestern Community: Models and Methods for the Study of Prehistoric Social Organization.* University of New Mexico Press, Albuquerque.

Wilmsen, E. N.

1968a Functional Analysis of Flaked Stone
Artifacts. *American Antiquity*
33:156–161.

1968b Paleo-Indian Site Utilization. In
*Anthropological Archeology in the
Americas*, edited by B. J. Meggers,
pp. 22–40. Anthropological Society
of Washington, Washington, D.C.

Wilson, E. O.

1998 *Consilience: The Unity of
Knowledge*. Knopf, New York.

Wilson, L. G.

1972 *Charles Lyell, the Years to 1841: The
Revolution in Geology*. Yale University Press, New Haven, Conn.

Winterhalder, B., and E. A. Smith

2000 Analyzing Adaptive Strategies:
Human Behavioral Ecology at
Twenty-Five. *Evolutionary Anthro-
pology* 9:51–72.

Winters, H. D.

1963 *An Archaeological Survey of the
Wabash Valley in Illinois*. Reports of
Investigations No. 10. Illinois State
Museum, Springfield.

1969 *The Riverton Culture: A Second Millennium Occupation in the Central
Wabash Valley*. Reports of Investigations No. 13. Illinois State Museum,
Springfield.

Wiseman, J.

1974 Editorial Comment. *Journal of Field
Archaeology* 1:1–2.

Wissler, C.

1915 Explorations in the Southwest by the
American Museum. *American
Museum Journal* 15:395–398.

1917 The New Archaeology. *American
Museum Journal* 17:100–101.

1926 *The Relation of Nature to Man in
Aboriginal America*. Oxford University Press, New York.

Witthoft, J.

1955 Worn Stone Tools from Southeastern
Pennsylvania. *Pennsylvania Archaeologist* 25:16–31.

Wobst, H. M.

1978 The Archaeo-Ethnology of Hunter-
Gatherers or the Tyranny of the
Ethnographic Record in Archaeology.
American Antiquity 43:303–309.

1983 We Can't See the Forest for the Trees:
Sampling and the Shapes of Archaeological Distributions. In *Archaeological Hammers and Theories*, edited by
J. A. Moore and A. S. Keene, pp.
32–80. Academic Press, New York.

1989 Commentary: A Socio-Politics of
Socio-Politics in Archaeology. In *Crit-
ical Traditions in Contemporary
Archaeology: Essays in the Philoso-
phy, History, and Socio-Politics of
Archaeology*, edited by V. Pinsky and
A. Wylie, pp. 136–140. Cambridge
University Press, Cambridge.

Wolf, E.

1960 Review of *The Science of Culture: A
Study of Man and Civilization*, by L.
A. White. *American Anthropologist*
62:148–151.

Wolverton, S., and R. L. Lyman

2000 Immanence and Configuration in
Analogical Reasoning. *North American Archaeologist* 21:233–247.

Wood, W. R., and D. L. Johnson

1978 A Survey of Disturbance Processes in
Archaeological Site Formation.
*Advances in Archaeological Method
and Theory* 1:315–381.

Woodall, J. N., and P. J. Perricone

1981 The Archeologist as Cowboy: The
Consequence of Professional Stereotype. *Journal of Field Archaeology*
8:506–509.

Woodbury, R. B.

1954 An Appraisal of *A Study of Archeology*, by W. W. Taylor. *American
Antiquity* 19:292–296.

Woods, C. M.

1975 *Culture Change*. Brown, Dubuque,
Iowa.

Woodward, J., and D. Goodstein

1996 Conduct, Misconduct, and the Structure of Science. *American Scientist*
84:479–490.

Wright, G. F.

1892 *Man and the Glacial Period*. Appleton, New York.

Wright, H. E., Jr.

1968 Natural Environment of Early Food Production North of Mesopotamia. *Science* 161:334–339.

Wright, H. T.

1977 Recent Research on the Origin of the State. *Annual Review of Anthropology* 6:379–397.

1981 (Editor) *An Early Town on the Deh Luran Plain: Excavations at Tepe Farukhabad.* Memoirs No. 15. Museum of Anthropology, University of Michigan, Ann Arbor.

1986 The Evolution of Civilizations. In *American Archaeology Past and Future: A Celebration of the Society for American Archaeology, 1935–1985,* edited by D. J. Meltzer, D. D. Fowler, and J. A. Sabloff, pp. 323–365. Smithsonian Institution Press, Washington, D.C.

1998 Uruk States in Southwestern Iran. In *Archaic States,* edited by G. M. Feinman and J. Marcus, pp 171–197. School of American Research Press, Santa Fe, N.M.

Wright, H. T., and G. A. Johnson

1975 Population, Exchange, and Early State Formation in Southwestern Iran. *American Anthropologist* 77:267–289.

Wright, R. P.

1996 *Gender and Archaeology.* University of Pennsylvania Press, Philadelphia.

Wylie, A.

1982a An Analogy by Any Other Name Is Just as Analogical: A Commentary on the Gould–Watson Dialogue. *Journal of Anthropological Archaeology* 1:382–401.

1982b Epistemological Issues Raised by a Structuralist Archaeology. In *Symbolic and Structural Archaeology,* edited by I. Hodder, pp. 39–46. Cambridge University Press, Cambridge.

1983 Comments on the Socio-Politics of Archaeology: The Demystification of the Profession. In *The Socio-Politics of Archaeology,* edited by J. M. Gero, D. M. Lacy, and M. L. Blakey, pp.

119–130. Research Report No. 23. Department of Anthropology, University of Massachusetts, Amherst.

1985a Putting Shakertown Back Together: Critical Theory in Archaeology. *Journal of Anthropological Archaeology* 4:133–147.

1985b The Reaction against Analogy. *Advances in Archaeological Method and Theory* 8:63–111.

1988 "Simple" Analogy and the Role of Relevance Assumptions: Implications for Archaeological Practice. *International Studies in the Philosophy of Science* 2:134–150.

1989a Archaeological Cables and Tacking: The Implications of Practice for Bernstein's "Options beyond Objectivism and Relativism." *Philosophy of the Social Sciences* 19:1–18.

1989b Matters of Fact and Matters of Interest. In *Archaeological Approaches to Cultural Identity*, edited by S. Shennan, pp. 94–109. Unwin Hyman, London.

1992 The Interplay of Evidential Constraints and Political Interests: Recent Archaeological Research on Gender. *American Antiquity* 57:15–35.

1995 An Expanded Behavioral Archaeology: Transformation and Redefinition. In *Expanding Archaeology,* edited by J. M. Skibo, W. H. Walker, and A. E. Nielsen, pp. 198–209. University of Utah Press, Salt Lake City.

1996 Ethical Dilemmas in Archaeological Practice: Looting, Repatriation, Stewardship, and the (Trans)formation of Disciplinary Identity. *Perspectives on Science* 4:154–194.

1997 The Engendering of Archaeology: Refiguring Feminist Science Studies. *Osiris* 12:80–99.

1999 Science, Conservation, and Stewardship: Evolving Codes of Conduct in Archaeology. *Science and Engineering Ethics* 5:319–336.

2000 Questions of Evidence, Legitimacy, and the (Dis)Unity of Science. *American Antiquity* 65:227–238.

2002   *Thinking from Things: Essays in the Philosophy of Archaeology.* University of California Press, Berkeley.

Yellen, J. E.

1977   *Archaeological Approaches to the Present: Models for Reconstructing the Past.* Academic Press, New York.

Yellen, J. E., and M. W. Greene

1985   Archaeology and the National Science Foundation. *American Antiquity* 50:332–341.

Yellen, J. E., M. W. Greene, and R. T. Louttit

1980   A Response to "National Science Foundation Funding of Domestic Archaeology in the United States: Where the Money Ain't," by R. W. Casteel. *American Antiquity* 45:180–181.

Yoffee, N.

1979   The Decline and Rise of Mesopotamian Civilization: An Ethnoarchaeological Perspective on the Evolution of Social Complexity. *American Antiquity* 44:3–35.

Zedeño, M. N.

1997   Landscapes, Land Use, and the History of Territory Formation: An Example from the Puebloan South-west. *Journal of Archaeological Method and Theory* 4:67–103.

Zeder, M. A.

1997   *The American Archaeologist: A Profile.* AltaMira, Walnut Creek, Calif.

Zimmerman, L. J.

1992   Archaeology, Reburial, and the Tactics of a Discipline's Self-Delusion. *American Indian Culture and Research Journal* 16:37–56.

Zubrow, E. B. W.

1971   Carrying Capacity and Dynamic Equilibrium in the Prehistoric Southwest. *American Antiquity* 36:127–138.

1972   Environment, Subsistence, and Society: The Changing Archaeological Perspective. *Annual Review of Anthropology* 1:179–206.

1975   *Prehistoric Carrying Capacity: A Model.* Cummings, Menlo Park, Calif.

1980   International Trends in Theoretical Archaeology. *Norwegian Archaeological Review* 13:14–23.

1981   The Centralization and Cost of Archaeological Information. *American Antiquity* 46:443–446.

Index